William Dugdale, John Stevens, James Wright, Roger Dodsworth

Monasticon Anglicanum

The history of the ancient abbies, and other monasteries, hospitals, cathedral and collegiate churches in England and Wales.

William Dugdale, John Stevens, James Wright, Roger Dodsworth

Monasticon Anglicanum
The history of the ancient abbies, and other monasteries, hospitals, cathedral and collegiate churches in England and Wales.

ISBN/EAN: 9783744737753

Printed in Europe, USA, Canada, Australia, Japan

Cover: Foto ©ninafisch / pixelio.de

More available books at **www.hansebooks.com**

MONASTICON ANGLICANUM,
OR, THE
HISTORY

Of the Ancient
Abbies, *and other* Monasteries,
Hospitals, Cathedral *and* Collegiate Churches
IN
ENGLAND and *WALES*.
WITH DIVERS
French, Irish, *and* Scotch *Monasteries*
Formerly relating to
ENGLAND.

Collected, and Published in *Latin*, by Sir *William Dugdale*, Knt.
late Garter King of Arms.

In Three Volums.
And now Epitomized in *English*, Page by Page.

With Sculptures of the several Religious Habits.

—— *Forsan & hæc olim meminisse juvabit.*
Virg. Æn. 1.

LICENSED,
May the 25th, 1692.   R. MIDGLEY.

LONDON:
Printed, for **Sam. Keble** at the *Turks-Head* in *Fleet-street*; **Hen. Rhodes**
at the *Star* the Corner of *Bride-lane* in *Fleetstreet*, MDCXCIII.

MONASTICON ANGLICANUM

HISTORY

of the

Abbies, and other Monasteries,
Hospitals, Cathedral and Collegiate Churches

in ENGLAND and WALES.

With divers French, Irish, and Scotch Monasteries formerly relating to ENGLAND.

In Three Volumes.

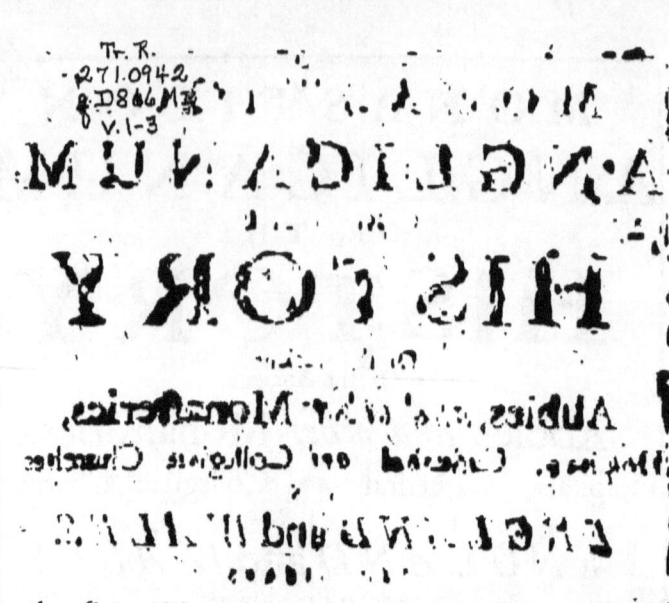

To the much Honoured

WILLIAM BROMLEY, Esq;

One of the Knights of the Shire for the County of WARWICK.

SIR,

THAT which I here present you is Originally the Product of your own Country, since the Great Artist from whose elaborate and curious hand I Coppy this Peice in little, owed his Birth and Habitation to *Warwickshire*. I know not therefore to whom (in the number of my Friends) more properly to dedicate these Collections than to your self: for thus it is an act of Justice to restore to the proper County (in your Person who represent it) what came from thence at first.

Nothing deterr'd my Presumption in this more than to think I should expose the Imperfections of my Pen to so accurate and excellent a Judgment. A Judgment that has taught you the true use of Foreign Travails, by which you have brought home from the politest Nations of *Europe*, all their Virtues and Accomplishments, and left behind their Fopperies and Vice. It is this Judgment that has so signalized your Merit in the Eye of your Country, that she has justly fixt her choice on you for one of her Representatives in our Great Senate; and it is the same Judgment that you have since most worthily employ'd in that High and Honourable Assembly, by assisting, and complying with the best Methods and Endeavours for the Publick Good: Or, to use the words of *Horace*,

——*Quid expediat, communiter, aut melior pars,*
Malis carere quæritis laboribus.

Yours are the Publick Cares; that's your noble Province. While I, and those in my inferiour and unactive Station, can only wish Success to the Proceedings of such Good Patriots as your self; Our thoughts are best imploy'd with our own private Business, and inoffensive Studies.

The Epistle Dedicatory.

Concerning this Book, Sir, it is a Subject that gives Posterity such a View of the decays of Time, and the Inconstancy of Fortune, as the like cannot, perhaps, be produced in the History of any other Nation. Since of all that stupendious number of Monastick Foundations in *England* and *Wales*, the continued Work of many Ages, by which the greatest Kings, Princes, and Noblemen of this Island were once thought to have eternized their names, and in those magnificent and costly Structures to have built themselves so many Monuments as lasting as the Earth they stood on, not one remains at this day; nay the very Ruines of many are become invisible. To this purpose (tho' on a different occasion) a modern *French* Poet hath well exprest himself in these Lines,

Aussi le temps a fait sur ces Masses hautaines
D'iluftres chaftimens des Vanitez humaines.
Ces Tombaux font tombez, and ces superbes Rois
Sous leur chute font morts une seconde fois.

And yet their Memory still lives in our History and Records; so much more durable and lasting is Paper than Brass and Marble. For this we are beholding to the Labours of your Sir *William Dugdale*, a Person so highly meritorious in the study, and discovery, of our *English* Antiquities, that his Reputation can never die among the learned.

Warwickshire has certainly produced two of the most famous and deserving Writers, in their several ways, that *England* can boast of; a *Dugdale*, and a *Shakespear*, both *Williams*; a name that has been of eminent Grace to this County in many Instances; nor will it ever cease to be so while you are living.

I might here enlarge in your just Encomium, but I fear to displease you even with truth, when it must be so very much to your Commendation. I know your Modesty as well as Merits, and I have ever observed that Praise is most uneasie to those who best deserve it. I will therefore only add that I am,

SIR,

Your very Humble and most Affectionate Servant,

J. W.

MONASTICON ANGLICANUM,
ABRIDGED.

VOL. I.

OF THE
Benedictine Monks,
CLUNIACS,
CISTERSIANS, *and*
CARTHUSIANS.

MONASTICON ANGLICANUM,
ABRIDGED.

VOL. I.

OF THE
Benedictine Monks,
Cluniacs,
Cistercians, and
Carthusians.

Of the first Institution of Monks.

Those who have writ of this Subject have produced for Examples of the Monastick Life, out of the Old Testament, *Samuel, Elias,* and the Sons of the Prophets; and out of the New, St. *John* the *Baptist,* and our Saviour *Christ* himself, who exhorted his Disciples to leave all Secular concerns and follow him. After his Ascention the Apostles and Disciples lived in common; But after the Apostles were martyr'd, some Christians retain'd Property; others still endeavour'd to continue the Apostolick Life, and live in Common: such were the Monks in *Egypt; Anthony, Hilarion, Macarius,* &c. After them St. *Jerome,* St. *Augustin,* till at last St. *Benedict* in the year 516. at *Mount-Cassin,* writ his Rule, which was approved by the whole Church. *In the Proem.*

Of the Rules of Monks, and other Religious Persons there have been several Authors, some of the Principle were, St. *Basil,* who writ his Rule for Monks, *Anno Dom.* 350. St. *Augustin* Bishop of *Hippo* made a Rule for Canons Regular, *Anno Dom.* 400. St. *Benedict,* before-mention'd, about *Anno* 516. St. *Bruno,* for *Carthusians, An.* 1083. *Robert* an Abbot in *Burgundy* instituted the *Cistercians, An.* 1098. *Norbert,* the *Premonstratenses An.* 1120. In the same year began also the *Hospitallers* and *Templers.* St. *Gilbert* of *Sempringham* founded his Order, *An.* 1148. St. *Dominick, An.* 1198. St. *Francis* 1260. The *Carmelites* were settled and establisht by Pope *Martin, An. Dom.* 1279.

Kings of this Land who have become Monks.

Petroc, King of *Wales; Constantine,* King of *Cornwall; Sebby, Offa,* and *Sigebert,* Kings of the *East-Saxons; Ethelred,* and *Kynred,* Kings of *Mercia; Coelwulph,* and *Edbricht,* Kings of *Northumberland.*

The Old Form of admitting a Brother into a Convent.

His first Petition, in the Colloquium.

Syr I besyche you and alle the Covent for the luffe of God, our Lady sanct Marye, sanct John of Baptiste, and all the hoyle Cowrte of Hevyne, that ʒe wolde resave me, to lyve and dye here among yow in the state of a Monke, as prebendarye and servant unto alle, to the honour of God, solace to the Company, profflet to the place, and helth unto my Sawle.

His Answer unto the Examinacyon.

Syr I tryste thrugh the helpe of God and your good prayers to keep all thes things which ʒe have now heyr reherfede.

His Petition before the Profession.

Syr I have beyn heyr now this twell month nere hand, and lovyde be God, me lyks right well, both the order and the company; wherapon I besyche yow and all the company for the luffe of God, our Lady sanct Marye, sanct John of Baptiste and all the hoyle company of hevyne that ʒe will resave me unto my profession at my twell month day according to my petycion whyche I made when I was fyrst resaved heyr amongs you, &c.

Of the *Benedictine* Order have been four Emperors, twelve Empresses, six and forty Kings, one and fifty Queens, not to mention those of lesser Quality.

ERRATA.

Page 6. l. 24. r. *Lindisfarn.* p. 37. l. r. ult. or an Oxe. p. 39. l. 30. r. *for the.* p. 69. l. 4. r. *Infpeximus.* p. 78. l. 12. r. *or any.* l. 20. r. *be put in.* p. 84. l. antepenul. r. *Dapifer.* p. 168. l. antepenul. r. *of the same.* p. 196. l. 14. r. HETHE *in Kent.* p. 210. l. 32. r. *Earl.* p. 220 l. 35. r. *special.* p. 231. l. 30. r. *East-Angles.* p. 232. l. 3. r. *Derham* p. 252. l. 7. r. *Marches.* p. 267. l. 4. r. *Patron of the.* p. 294. l. 19. r. *colours.* p. 328. l. 25. r. *Wyndesore.*

Some other literal Mistakes, and false Pointings, have happen'd, which the Reader may easily perceive and correct.

TO THE
READER.

Something may be said here, by way of Preface, of the Work it self, and of this Abridgment or Epitome of that Work. First for the Work it self, it will perhaps be thought by some that the Monasticon Anglicanum, or History of the Foundations and Endowments of the antient Abbies, Priories, &c. once flourishing in England, and long since utterly supprest, is in these our days (in which their very Memory seems to some People, odious and ungrateful) more useless and insignificant than an Old Almanack. 'Tis true, the matter appears very obsolete and neglected, yet is the Monasticon Anglicanum so far from being useless, that it is in effect the most useful Evidenciary, and Repertory of Titles that is in print. Considering, 1. The vast Quantity of Lands which formerly belong'd to Religious Houses in this Kingdome. 2. The divers sorts of Liberties and Immunities which most of those Houses and their Possessions were endow'd with, as Courts of Pleas, Markets, Fairs, Commons, Free Pastures, Estovers, Exemptions from Tithes, Tolls, Taxes and Contributions, with other Franchises of various sorts and not easily reckon'd up. 3. That by the Statutes 27 H. 8. ch. 28. §. 1. &. 31 H. 8. ch. 13. §. 2. 3. it is expresly provided that the King and his Patentees shall have and hold the said Lands in as large and ample manner as the said Houses enjoy'd them, and §. 21. of the last mention'd Statute, that such Lands as were before discharged of the Payment of Tithes shall so continue. By which Provisions such Persons as enjoy any

of

To the Reader.

of those *Lands* are intituled to many of the same *Liberties* and *Franchises* as were at first given with the said *Lands* to those *Houses* respectively, such *Franchises* being real and annext to the *Estate*. 4. All the Monasticon is a *Transcript* of antient *Manuscripts* coppyed by that laborious *Antiquary* Mr. Roger Dodsworth, and that eminently learn'd *Historian* Sr. William Dugdale *Knt.* late *Garter King of Armes*, out of the very *Original Grants*, or *Leiger Books*, or *Publick Records*, or other *Muniments* formerly kept by the respective *Monasteries*, and (when they perused them) choicely preserved either in some of our most famous *Libraries*, or in the *Possession* of those *Gentlemen* and *Persons* of honour, who since the *Suppression* enjoy the *Lands* to which those *Deeds* relate, or some part of them; whose names are cited in the *Margin* of the said *Book*. And such credit hath it received from the integrity of the *Authors* or *Collectors* thereof, that (as I am credibly inform'd) it hath been admitted as a good *Circumstantial Evidence* in the *Courts* of Westminster when the *Records* therein transcribed could not upon diligent *Search* be otherwise recovered. Further, this *Book* is of use to enlighten and assist the young *Student* of our *Common Laws*, it shewing in divers parts of it, the *Commencements* of *Tenures*, the *Nature* and manner of *Corrodies*, *Appropriations*, *Endowment* of *Vicarages*, *Reservation* of *Services* upon *Grants* in Frankalmoine, or upon *Tenures* by *Divine Service*, the old *Ways* of *tithing*, *Conveyancing*, and something of *Pleading*. It is also useful in *History*, giving us a lively *Idea* of the manner of our *Forefathers* way of *Living*, their *Zeal* for *Gods Publick Worship*, as then profest, and the *Simplicity* of their *Devotions*; and of the great *Charity* to the *Poor*, and *Hospitality* and *Beneficence* to all *Comers*, maintain'd and exercised in the *Monasteries*. But these things have been thought faults, and therefore I will mention no more of that; but observe in the last place, that this *Book* is of great use in matters of *Heraldry* and *Genealogies*; there being few or none among the *Great Families*, and old *Nobility*, of England, who have not been *Founders* or *Principal Benefactors* to some *Monastery* or *Religious House*, and the *Monks* and *Canons* have for the most part taken special *Care* to record in the *Leiger Book* of their respective *Houses*

the

To the Reader.

the History of their Founder's and Patron's Family, setting down their several Matches, and Issue, and often-times the day of their Births and Deaths, with the most remarkable Circumstances of their Lives, and where buried; which seems also to be done at the time when every thing happen'd or soon after, and is therefore of greater Credit. In this Work we must note that the Author saies nothing of the four Orders of Fryers, viz. The Franciscans or Gray-Friers, the Dominicans or Black-Friers, the Carmelites or White-Friers, and the Augustine Friers; the Reason was, I suppose, because their Houses, generally speaking, were not endow'd with Lands and Revenues, but they subsisted for the most part by daily and accidental Charities.

Thus much of the Book at large, now as to this Abridgment or Epitome, I have only this to say; It gives you a short view in English of the Principal, and (as I thought,) most material Passages of what is contain'd in Latin, and sometimes old French, in the three great and copious Tomes of the Monasticon Anglicanum: The Names of Persons and Places, being variously written according to the different Orthography of several Ages, and Writers, I have not thought convenient to alter the ancient way of spelling, but have transcribed them here in the same variety as I found 'em there: In the Margin I have exactly observed and markt out the Pages successively in order, that so the Reader may have a ready recourse to the Book at large for a fuller and more particular Information. And in my opinion this is the best use that can be made of any Abridgment; namely to serve as a larger and better sort of Table, which not only represents the substance of a voluminous Author in little, but refers and directs the Reader to the place where the Subjects is more expresly handled. On the whole, you have here a short Historical Account of the Foundation of all the Principal Churches and Religious Structures in England and Wales, as well those that were demolisht at the Suppression of the Monasteries, as those that are still in being (except Parish Churches.) And here we must note that of all those Cathedral Churches and Episcopal Seats, whose venerable Fabricks we behold at this day, some were formerly Abbies, where the Prior and Convent of Monks were the Bishops Chapter;

To the Reader.

ter; *such were* Canterbury, Rochester, Winchester, Ely, Norwich, Worcester, Durham, Carlile; (*and in such Churches where there was a Bishop, the Superior of the Monks was always call'd a Prior, the Bishop being in effect the Abbot*) *others never were Abbies, but the Chapter did always consist of a Dean and Secular Canons (or Prebendaries) as at present; such were* York, London, Lincoln, Salisbury, Exeter, Wells, Litchfield, Hereford, Chichester, *and in* Wales, St. Davids, Landaff, Bangor, *and* St. Asaph. *Besides these, there were five new Bishopricks erected by King* Henry VIII. *in certain Abbies, after their dissolution,* viz. Peterborough, Oxford, Chester, Glocester, *and* Bristol, *whose Churches were left standing, with some of their old Buildings for the Habitation of the Bishop, Dean and Chapter,* &c. (*for which see the Statutes,* 31 H. 8. ch. 9. 34 H. 8. ch. 17.) Westminster-Abby *was also made an Episcopal Seat, but that continued so but a while. Some other Monastick Churches were made Parochial, and are still in being, as St.* Albans, St. Mary Overies, Royston, &c. *To conclude, I think I may, not unfitly, apply to my present undertaking the words used on the like occasion, in the Second Book of* Maccabees, *ch.* 2. *v.* 23. All these things (*I say*) being declared by *Jason of Cyrene* in five Books, we will essay to abridge in one Volum. For considering the infinite number, and the difficulty which they find that desire to look into the Narrations of the Story, for the variety of the Matter, we have been careful that they that will read might have delight, and they that are desirous to commit to memory might have ease, and that all into whose hands it comes might have profit.——To stand upon every point, and to go over things at large, and to be curious in particulars, belongeth to the first Author of the Story. But to use Brevity, and avoid much labouring of the Work, is to be granted to him that will make an Abridgment. Here then will we begin the Story: only adding thus much to that which hath been said, that it is a foolish thing to make a long Prologue and to be short in the Story it self.

A BENEDICTINE MONK
Place this & ye following plates according to ye pages in ye margin.

MONASTICON ANGLICANUM,
Abridg'd in English.

Vol. I.

Of the BENEDICTINE Order.

The Monastery at GLASTONBURY, *in* Somersetshire.

IN the 31th. year after our Saviour's Passion, twelve Disciples of St. *Philip* the Apostle, among whom *Joseph* of *Arimathea* was one, came to this place, and preacht the Christian Religion to King *Arviragus*. They obtained of that King the Ground where the Monastery afterwards stood, and twelve Hides of Land, and built there the first Church of the Kingdom, in a poor and homely manner. They lived here in a kind of heremitical life, and converted many Pagans to the Faith of Christ. After they were all dead, and here buried, the holy men *Phaganus* and *Diruvianus*, having baptized King *Lucius*, obtained this place of that King, and for a great while they and their Successors remained here in a kind of Society consisting of twelve only, till the arrival of St. *Patrick*, who taught them the monastical Life, and became himself their first Abbot. Afterwards St. *David* Archbishop of *Menevia* (now called St. *David's*) added to the *East* end of the Old Church a lesser Chappel in manner of a Chancel, and consecrated it in honour of the Virgin *Mary*.

This Church for its Antiquity was by the old *English* call'd *Ealdechirche*, and the Men of those days had no Oath more sacred and formidable than to swear by this *Old Church*. And it was reverenced like *Rome* it self, for as that became Famous for its multitude of Martyrs, so did this for its multitude of Confessors here buried.

The Isle in which this Church stood was by the *Britions* call'd *Ynswyrtryn*, i. e. the Isle of *Glass*, from the clear and cristaline stream of Water which runs into the Marsh here. It has been also called *Avallonia*. By the *Saxons* it was named *Glastynbury*. This Isle with several other places adjoyning, were call'd the twelve Hides, and did enjoy from the beginning very great Priviledges. The Bounds of which twelve Hides may be seen in the *Monasticon* at large, *p.* 2, 3. These places there mentioned enjoyed all sorts of Immunities from the first beginning of Christianty in this Land, confirm'd to the Church of *Glastonbury*, by the *British*, *English*, and *Norman* Kings.

In this Church did rest and lie buried the twelve Disciples of the Apostle *Philip*, above mentioned, whose chief was *Joseph* of *Arimathea*, with

B *his*

his Son *Josephus*. Here also lies St. *Patrick* the Apostle of *Ireland*, and two of his Disciples, St. *Gildas* the *British Historaographer*, St. *David* Archbishop of
4. *Menevia*, St. *Dunstan* Archbishop, St. *Indractus* with his seven Companions all Martyrs, St. *Urbanus*, the Bones of Venerable *Bede*, with the Relicks of a great number of other Saints, and holy Martyrs, and Confessors.

5. To recite all the Reliques that were in this Church would be too large for any Abridgement, I only mention those of most note. Several things relating to the Old Testament, as *Moses*'s Rod, *Manna*, &c. things relating to our Lord *Jesus Christ*, two small pieces of his Cradle, some of the Gold which the Wise-men of the *East* offer'd, some pieces of Bread of those five Loaves with which *Jesus* fed five thousand men, some of our Lord's Hair, some pieces of his Cross, and of his Sepulchre, one Thorn of his Crown of Thorns, &c. Things relating to the Virgin *Mary*, some of her Milk, one thread of her Garment, and some of her Hair, &c. Besides these a multitude of Reliques relating to St. *John Baptist*, the Apostles, Martyrs, Confessors and Virgins. On this account the Church of *Glastonbury* was highly re-
6. verenced by Kings, Queens, Archbishops, Bishops, Dukes, and the Nobility of both Sexes, and of all Orders and Degrees; and happy did he think himself who could give any thing to the increase of its Possessions, or could here obtain a place of Sepulture. In this Isle, which was call'd
7. the *Tomb of Saints*, was interr'd *Coel* King of the *Britons*, Father of St. *Helena*, Mother of *Constantine* the Great; *Caraducus* Duke of *Cornwall*, the renowned King *Arthur* and *Guenevera* his Queen, which King died at *Glastonbury* about *Whitsontide* in the Year of our Lord 542. King *Kentwynus*, King *Edmund* Son of *Edward* the Elder, King *Edgar*, King *Edmund Ironside*, with several Bishops and Dukes who were great Benefactors to this House, and many other Great men. In so great Reverence was the Church and Church-yard where these were interr'd, that our forefathers did not dare to use any idle discourse or to spit therein, without great necessity, enemies and naughty men were not suffer'd to be buried therein, neither did any bring any Hawk, Dog, or Horse upon the Ground,
9. for if they did, it was observed that they immediately died thereupon.

Bishops and famous Prelates that have gone from this House to govern other Churches, are as follows, viz. *Birthwaldus*, Abbot here, was made Archbishop of *Canterbury*; *Athelmus* Monk here, Bishop of *Wells*, and after that Archbishop of *Canterbury*; St. *Dunstan*, Monk and Abbot here, Bishop of *Worcester*, then of *London*, and lastly of *Canterbury*; *Egelganus* Monk here, Bishop of *Chichester* and Archbishop of *Canterbury*; *Sigericus* Monk here, Bishop of *Wells* and Archbishop of *Canterbury*; St. *Elphegus* a Martyr, Bishop of *Winchester*, and after that Archbishop of *Canterbury*; *Elnothus*, Monk here and Archbishop of *Canterbury*, in the time of King *Knute*.

To these may be added *Gaufridus* a Bishop, and Monk here, *ob. Anno Dom.* 782. *Ethelwinus*, a Bishop, who died the same year; *Wibertus*, a Bishop, *ob. Anno Dom.* 800. *Wigthagu* Bishop, *ob. Anno Dom.* 836. *Alstanus*, Bishop, *ob. Anno Dom.* 842. *Tumbertus*, Bishop, *ob.* 866. *Daniel*,
10. Bishop, *ob.* 956. *Elfricus*, Bishop, *ob.* 988. Also in the time of King *Edgar*, *Sigegarus* Bishop of *Wells*, *Britelmus* Bishop of *Wells*, *Alfwoldus*, *Sigefridus*, St. *Ethilwoldus*, *Wilfinus*, *Aelfstanus*, *Egelricus*, *Kenwaldus*, *Elmerus*, *Livingus*, *Brithwius*, *Britwaldus*, who died *Anno Dom.* 1045. All these, of Monks in this House became Bishops of divers places in *England*.

The Benefactors to this House were, first, *Arviragus* King of the *Britains*, who, though a Pagan, gave to St. *Joseph* and his Companions the
Isle

Isle in which the Monastery was built, call'd by the Inhabitants *Ynswyrtryn*, which, King *Lucius* did afterwards confirm to *Phaganus* and *Diruvianus*, and their Disciples. King *Arthur* gave many other adjoyning Lands. King *Kenwalli*, King *Kentwinus*, King *Baldredus*, Bishop *Hedda*, King *Kedwala*, King *Ina*, gave other Lands. So did St. *Wilfridus* Archbishop of *York*, and abundance of others of both Sexes, among the Principal of which were King *Sigebert*, King *Offa*, King *Alfred* or *Alured*, King *Athelstan*, King *Edmund*, King *Edwin*, King *Edgar*, King *Edmund Ironside*, with several Queens. These and many other names, with the Lands by the several Benefactors given, may be read of in the *Monasticon* at large, p. 9, 10, 14, 15, &c.

St. *Patrick*, who was born in the year of our Lord 361. after his Conversion of *Ireland* to Christianity, became Abbot of this Place, and obtained of Pope *Celestine*, twelve years Indulgence to all those who should with pious Devotion visit the Church of the Blessed Virgin *Mary* here erected, and honour her with any part of their Goods.

About the year of our Lord 505. *Augustine* the Monk was sent into *England* by the holy Pope *Gregory* to preach the Faith to the *English Saxons*. He converted *Ethelbert* the King of *Kent* and his People. Afterwards being made Archbishop, he established his Metropolitan Seat at *Canterbury*, and there placed certain Monks living according to the Rule of St. *Benedict*; after this several Monasteries in *England* were erected under the same Rule, which obtained so great reputation that there were no Monks to be found in *England*, but what were of this Order; and in those times the Rule of St. *Benedict* began to be first observed in the Monastery of *Glastonbury*, they living here before that, after the manner of the Monks of *Egypt*.

King *Ina* began his Reign over the *West Saxons* Anno 689. and gave much Land to this Monastery, he also built the greater Church at *Glastonbury*, in honour of our Saviour, and of the holy Apostles *Peter* and *Paul*. And by his Charter bearing date *Anno Dom.* 725. Granted to this Monastery many and great Priviledges and Immunities. King *Ina* dying in a Pilgrimage to *Rome*, his Successor, *Ethelardus*, became also a bountiful Benefactor, as were several other succeeding Kings of the *West Saxons*, &c.

King *Edmund* granted to the Church of the holy Mother of God at *Glastonbury*, and to the venerable *Dunstan* Abbot there, the Liberty and Power, Rights and Customs, and all Forfeitures in all their Lands, *i. e. Burgbrice Hundred, Socna, Athas, Ordelas, Infangenetheofas, Homsecna, Frithbrice, Foresteall, Toll* and *Team*, through the Kingdom of *England*, and that they should enjoy their Lands as free from all Claims as he enjoy'd his own, especially to the Town of *Glastonbury* it self, with many other Liberties, &c. and this was by his Charter dated *Anno Dom.* 944.

King *Edgar*, by his Charter dated at *London Anno Dom.* 971. granted to the said Monastery the same and greater Liberties, among other things, that the said Monastery and some Parishes there mentioned subject and belonging to it, should be exempt from the ordinary Jurisdiction of the Bishop, except in some things, with a Salvo to the holy Church of *Rome*, and that of *Canterbury*: And gave and confirmed to this Church two hundred and fifteen Hides of Land given by several Benefactors.

William the Conqueror at his first coming to the Crown, did very much mutilate the Possessions of this Church. He made one *Turstinus* a *Norman* Abbot here, in the year 1081. And in order to make some amends to the Monks, he confirm'd to them several Lands which they complained to have been unjustly taken from them.

Herlewin,

18. *Herlewin*, and *Henry* Brother of *Theobald* Earl of *Blois*, and Nephew of King *Henry* the I. were two Abbots of this Monastery, who through their industrious endeavours obtained much good to this House, and the Restoration of many Lands which had been taken from it.

Vid. Vol. 2. *p.* 837.

[This Abby was valued before the Suppression at 3311 *l.* 7 *s.* 4 *d.* ob. *per Annum.*]

The Cathedral Church of Canterbury.

IN the time of the blessed *Gregory*'s Papacy, St. *Augustine* with several other Monks were sent to convert the *English* People, who in the year of Grace 600. (or according to others 596.) coming into *England*, converted King *Ethelbert* and some thousands of his People, which King gave them a Mansion in his Capital City of *Canterbury*, then called *Dorobernia*, there to Preach and Baptize. Hereupon the blessed *Augustine* having received a Pall from Pope *Gregory*, built a Church there, and dedicated it to the honour of our Saviour Jesus Christ, he also did here institute the Metropolitan Seat of himself and Successors. And having rais'd here a Monastery of Monks, the People flow'd in to him from all parts, some for Baptism, and some to become Monks, devoting themselves and all they had to God's service.

The Principal Benefactors were King *Ethelbert*, who gave them his Palace in *Canterbury*, which Pope *Gregory* decreed to be the Metropolitan
19. Seat, and made it the first in Dignity, it having first received the Faith, *Ethelbaldus* Son of *Ethelbert*. King *Cedwalla*, King *Offa*, *Edmundus* King of *Kent*. *Cenulphus* King of *Kent*, *Beornulphus* King of *Mercia*, King *Athelstan*,
20. King *Edmund*, St. *Edward* the Confessor, *William* the Conqueror, King
21. *Henry* the I. *Henry* the II. *Richard* the I. *Edward* the III. *Edward* Prince
22. of *Wales*, his Son; *Henry* the IV. These and abundance of others of inferiour condition gave and confirmed to this Church many Lands, Priviledges, and Immunities, the particulars of all which Lands, &c. may be seen in the *Monasticon* at large.

The Monastery of St. AUGUSTINES in Canterbury.

23. SAint *Augustine* being sent by Pope *Gregory* as aforesaid, arrived at the Isle of *Thanet* in *Kent*, in the year 596. with several Monks and Ministers of God's Word about forty in number; they were kindly received by King *Ethelbert*, who received holy Baptism on *Whitsonday Anno Dom*: 597. After this *Augustine* went over to the Bishop of *Arles* in *France*, and being by him ordain'd a Bishop, he returned into *England*. At *Canterbury* he fixt his Metropolitan Seat as above-mentioned. A little without this City on the *East*-side had been an Idol Temple formerly made use of by King *Ethelbert*, before his Conversion, this *Augustine* chang'd into a Church; and dedicated in the name of St. *Pancrace* the Martyr. Afterwards in the year 605. *Augustine* obtain'd this Church, and the adjacent Ground of King *Ethelbert*, upon which place a new Church was built and dedicated to the honour of St. *Peter* and St. *Paul*; which Church was stored with Monks, endow'd with Revenues by that King, and appointed for the

burial

burial place, of himself and Successors, as also chosen for the burial of *Augustine* and his Successors, Archbishops of *Canterbury*.

King *Ethelbert* having built and endow'd this Monastery he placed there, by the Council of Archbishop *Augustine*, one *Peter* a Monk to be Abbot of it.   24.

The Archbishop *Augustine* granted several Priviledges to this Monastery, and denounced heavy Censures against any who should violate the same in future times.   25.

This Monastery was used for a burial place of the Archbishops, the Monks, and others of *Canterbury*, for many years; it being in those times not usual to bury within a City, till the Venerable *Cuthbert* came to be Archbishop, being the 11*th*. after *Augustine*, who being at *Rome*, obtain'd of the Pope the liberty of having burial places in *England*, within Cities.

On the *East*-side of *Canterbury* without the City and near this Monastery stood the Church of St. *Martin*, which Church was the Seat of a Bishop, who always remain'd at home, or in the County, and in the absence of the Archbishop used to act for him. The last Bishop of this Church was one *Godwyn*, who dying in the time of *William* the Conqueror, when *Lanfrank* was Archbishop of *Canterbury*, he refused to subrogate any other Bishop in his place, but instead of a Bishop constituted an Archdeacon there.   26.

[Valued before the Suppression at 1413 *l*. 4 *s*. 11 *d*. ob. q. *per Annum*.]

ROCHESTER, in Kent.

Anno Dom. 600. King *Ethelbert* founded the Church of St. *Andrew* the Apostle at *Rochester*, and gave to it several Lands, as did also *Eadbert* King of *Kent*, *Offa* King of *Mercia*, and divers others; denouncing to the Violators of their pious Donations, heavy Curses and Imprecations. All which Lands and Liberties King *Henry* the I. did confirm to the said Church, to *Gundulf* the Bishop there, and the Monks serving God in it. Other principal Benefactors to this Church, and the Monks here, were King *William* the Conqueror, King *William Rufus*, *Rodbert* Son of King *Henry*, *Robert Fitz Hamon*, and *William de Albeiney* the King's Butler. *Vid. Vol.* 2. *p.* 844. *Vol.* 3. *p.* 1.   27.   29.

[Valued before the Suppression at 486 *l*. 11 *s*. 5 *d. per Annum*.]

WINCHESTER Cathedral Church.

Anno Dom. 608. *Kinegilsus* Son of *Celric*, King of the *West Saxons*, after his Baptism and his peoples conversion to Christianty, designed to build this Church, and to it give all the Land lying about *Winchester* for the space of seven *Leucas* or Miles. But himself being prevented by death from perfecting what he intended, his Son and Successor *Kinwalcus* perform'd the Work, and confirm'd the Lands above-mentioned to the said Church.   31.

Other principal Benefactors to this Church were King *Ina*; *Ethelardus*, King of the *West Saxons*; *Egbert*, King of all *England*, who lies buried here; King *Alured*, who built a new Monastery within the Coemitery of the Episcopal   32.

33. copal Church, endow'd it with Possessions, and gave the Government of it to *St. Grimbaldus*. (This King first instituted Hundreds and Tithings); *Edward* his Son and Successor, King *Ethelstan* his Son, King *Edred* his Brother; King *Edgar*; Queen *Emma* Mother of *Hardecanute*, and *Edward* surnamed the Confessor; which Queen having perform'd her purgation of supposed incontinency with *Elwin* Bishop of *Winchester*, according to the

34. Law *Ordel*, by going over nine red hot Plowshares, unhurt, gave to the

35. Church of St. *Swithin*, here, nine Manors; so also did the said Bishop *Elwin*; all which gifts were confirm'd by King *Edward* the Confessor.

36. *Anno Dom.* 1079. Bishop *Walkelinus* began to new build the Church from the Foundation, towards which Work the King gave so much Wood, as could be cut down and carried away from his adjoyning Wood called *Hanepinges*, in three days and nights; upon which, such an innumerable Company of Carpenters assembled, that in the time limited, they conveyed away the whole Wood.

37. *Anno Dom.* 963. In the time of Bishop *Ethelwold*, the secular Clergy of this Church, living licentiously, were displaced, and Monks put in their room. *Vide infra*, p. 979.

[Valued at 1507 *l*. 17 *s*. 2 *d*. per Annum.]

DURHAM *Monastery*.

38. *Anno Dom.* 635. Eighty eight years from the first coming of the *English* into *Britain*, and thirty nine years from the coming of St. *Augustine*, pious King *Oswald* erected a Bishops Seat in the Island of *Landisfarn*, of which *Agdanus* became Bishop, and placed there the Monks that came along with him.

39. Of this See, *Cuthbert* was Consecrated Bishop, at *York*, on *Easter-day Anno Dom.* 685. To him *Egfrid* King of *Northumberland* gave *Creec*, with the Lands three Miles about it, and also *Lugubalia*, now called *Carlile*, with the Lands fifteen Miles about it. *Ob. Cuthbert* 687.

Anno Dom. 729. *Coelwolf* King of *Northumberland* began his Reign; he was a great Benefactor to this Church, and became himself a Monk here.

40. All the Land lying between the two Rivers of *Tyne* and *Tese*, was formerly given to St. *Cuthbert*, and was subject to the Government of the Bishop of St. *Cuthbert*'s Church, till the *Danes* took away a great part of the Lands, which were however restored again by King *Ethelstan*.

41. In the year 1074. *Aldwinus* a Monk and two of his Companions led a Monastick Life at a place then called *Girecum* or *Girne* in *Northumberland*, from which three Monks, three Monasteries proceeded, namely one at *Durham*, in honour of the blessed Virgin *Mary*, and of St. *Cuthbert*, one at *Lestingham*, and one at a place then called *Streneshalgh*, all three within the Kingdom of the *Northumbers*.

43. *William de Karilepho* by his Deed dated *Anno Dom* 1082. declared the many and great Liberties granted by Pope *Gregory* the VII. and adds others to the Church of St. *Cuthbert*, with an *Anathema* to the Impugnors.

44. King *William* the Conqueror upon the precept of Pope *Gregory* the VII. and at the Petition of *William* Bishop of *Durham*, removed the Secular Canons out of the Church of *Durham*, and placed Monks in their room, and confirmed all the Liberties and Priviledges granted to the said Church, and this by his Charter dated in the 18*th*. year of his Reign. *Thomas*

Thomas Archbishop of *York* set forth and declared the Diocess of the Bishop of *Durham* to be all the Land betwixt *Tyne* and *Tese*, *Northumberland*, *Tevydale*, *Tyndal*, *Carleol*, *Weredale*, with the Church of *Herteskam*, and *Lindisfarn*.

Principal Benefactors to this Church were, King *William* the Conqueror, who gave great Posessions to the Bishop and his Succeïlors, to hold all as free and quiet as he himself held them in his own hands.   45.

Edgar Son of *Malcolm* King of the *Scots*, he gave to the Church of *Durham*, the Mansion of *Berwic*, and *Coldynghamschyr*.

King *Richard* the I. he granted and confirm'd to the Bishop of *Durham* and his Succeïlors many great Priviledges, with the Dominion and Liberty of a Count *Palatin*, for ever, &c. *Vid. Vol.* 2. *p.* 845.   46. 47.

[Valued at 1366 *l*. 10 *s*. 9 *d*. per *Annum*.]

MALMESBURY, in Wiltshire.

*M*Ayldulphus, by Nation a *Scotchman*, a Philosopher by Erudition, and a Monk by Profession, was the first Founder of the Monastery here.   49.

Anno Dom. 635. King *Berthwald*, with the Consent and Confirmation of King *Æthelred*, gave to this Monastery for ever *Summerford*, lying upon the River *Thames*.   50.

Other Benefactors to this Monastery were *Lutherius* Bishop of *Winchester*, who by his deed dated *Anno Dom.* 680. gave to it for ever the Town of *Malmesbury*, King *Athelred* in the year 681. gave other Lands; so did King *Chedwalla Anno* 682. in the year 1065. King *Edward* the Confessor confirm'd all former Donations, and himself granted to this House great Liberties and Priviledges; the like did King *William* the Conqueror in the year 1081. the same year *Mauld* his Queen became also a Benefactrice.   51. 52. 53.

Pope *Innocent* in the year 1248. granted to the Abbot and Monks of *Malmesbury* in the Diocess of *Salisbury*, a Confirmation of all their Lands and Revenues, which see in the *Monasticon* at large, together with several great Immunities; and ordain'd that the Rule of St. *Benedict* should be for ever observed in this Monastery.   54.

[Valued at 803 *l*. 17 *s*. 7 *d*. *ob*. *q*. per *Annum*.]

WESTMINSTER-ABBY, in Middlesex.

IN the days of King *Lucius* the first Christian King of *Britain*, who was baptized *Anno Dom.* 184. this place was first consecrated to God's honour, and especially appointed for the Royal Sepulture and a Repository of the Regalia. Thus it remained till, under *Dioclesian's* persecution, Christianity was expelled from hence, and the place turned to a profane Temple of *Apollo*. Afterwards when the *Saxons* had conquered this Kingdom and were in possession of it, the blessed *Gregory* in the year of Grace 604. sent *Augustine* the Monk together with *Mellitus*, *Justus*, *Laurentius*, and others, to teach the Christian Religion in *Britain*. He arrived in *Kent*, as hath been already noted, and having converted and baptized *Ethelbert*, King of that province, he afterward did the same to *Sebert*, King of the *East-Saxons*, King *Ethelbert's* Sister's Son; who upon his Conversion   55.

to

to Christianity, cast down the foresaid Temple of *Apollo*, and in the same place (then called *Thorney* Isle) built a Church in honour of St. *Peter* Prince of the Apostles.

56. In the same year the blessed *Augustine*, ordained two Bishops *Mellitus*
57. Bishop of *London*, and *Justus* Bishop of *Rochester*. The History of this
58. Church says, that *Mellitus* going to consecrate it, he found the Work already performed by St. *Peter* himself.

59. This Church being afterwards new built by St. *Edward* the King and Confessor, Pope *Nicholas* granted to it large immunities, appointing it to be for ever a Seat of Benedictine Monks, the place of Consecration of our Kings, and Repository of the *Regalia*, and exempted it from the Bishops Jurisdiction, placing it under the sole and immediate Government of the King and his Successors.

60. The said King *Edward* the Confessor, by his Charter dated in the year 1066. reciting that at the Dedication of this new Church he had placed here certain Relicks, *viz*. Two pieces of our Lord's Cross, a piece of his Seamless Coat, with other Relicks of the blessed Virgin, and of the Apostles, *&c*. he renew'd and confirm'd the Lands and Priviledges formerly granted
61. to this Church by his Ancestors, granting others of his own; and giving to the praise of Almighty God, and for a perpetual Endowment to this Church, several Lands and Hereditaments, among others *Roteland* after the death of Queen *Edgith*, &c. With blessings denounced to those who shall in the future increase or improve these Gifts, but heavy Curses and Anathemas against those of what degree or quality soever who shall infringe or diminish the same. *Vid. Vol. 22. p. 847.*

[Valued at 3471 *l*. 0 *s*. 2 *d*. q. *per Annum*.]

SHERBURN, in Dorsetshire.

62. Founders and Benefactors to this Monastery were *Kenewale, Edgar, Offa, Egbert, Sigebert, Ina,* and several other *Saxon* Kings. In the year of our Lord 1122. *Sherburn* and *Horton* made both but one Abby; but afterwards about the year 1139. *Roger* Bishop of *Salisbury* changed the Priory of *Sherburn* into an Abby, that of *Horton* being destroy'd and annext to this. See more of this Abby *infra, p*. 423.

[Valued at 682 *l*. 14 *s*. 7 *d*. ob. *per Annum*.]

LESTINGHAM, in Yorkshire.

63. Anno Dom. 648. *Edilwald* Son of *Oswald* King of the *Northumbers*, gave to *Cedde* Bishop of the *East Saxons* (or Bishop of *London*) a piece of Ground on a high Mountain, called *Lestingay*, for the building of a Monastery. For the erecting of which *Cedde* prepared himself by fasting a whole Lent (except Sundays) eating nothing till the Evening, and then only a little Bread, one Hen-Egg, and a little Milk mingled with Water. After this he built the Monastery, and instituted there the same Discipline as was used in that of *Lindisfarn*, where he himself had been educated. He govern'd his Diocess for many years after, but died in this Monastery, and was here buried.

PETERBOROUGH Abby, in Northamptonshire.

THIS Monastery was begun by *Peada* the first Christian King of *Mercia*, by and with the assistance of a great and eminent man called *Saxulphus* the first Abbot here. The place where it was built was in those old Times called *Medeshamstede*, but the Church being dedicated to St. *Peter*, it was afterwards called *Peterborough*. The Foundation was perfected and the Endowment compleared by *Wulfer* King of *Mercia*, and younger Brother of King *Peada*, who after his conversion to Christianity by his Deed *An. Do.* 664. not only confirmed what had been already given by his Predecessors, but gave to this Monastery a very great quantity of Lands lying in the Country round about. King *Edgar* by his Charter dated *A. D.* 972. granted other Lands and many Privileges. Pope *Agatha* granted many Priviledges to this Monastery, which were confirmed in a Council of twenty five Bishops, assembled in a place called *Estfeild A. D.* 680. These Grants, Liberties and Priviledges, were in succeeding times confirm'd by King *Edward* the Elder, King *Ethelred*, King *Cnut*, *Edward* the Confessor, and *William* the Conqueror.

64.
65.
66.
67.
68.

The Monastery of St. *Peter* at *Medeshamstede*, being built *A. D.* 654. remained in Peace till the year 870. at which time the *Pagan Danes* coming down out of *Torkshire* into *Lincolnshire*, Earl *Algar*, *Morcar*, a Lay-Brother of *Crowland-Abby*, call'd *Tolius* (who had been a famous Souldier before he entered into Religion) *Hardingus* of *Reihalle*, and under his Command all the men of *Stamford*, made head against them, and at first conquered the *Pagans*; but they being soon after reinforced with greater power, they in a second Battel over-threw the Christians with grievous slaughter; burnt down the Abby and Church of *Croyland*, and from thence marcht to *Medeshamsted* where they slew the Abbot and all the Monks to the number of eighty four, and utterly destroyed the Church and all other Buildings. From hence they march'd to *Cambridge* destroying all the Country as they went.

69.

70.

In the year of Christ 970. St. *Adelwold* Bishop of *Winchester* began to re-edifie the Monastery of *Medeshamstede*, and call'd it the Borough of St. *Peter*, one hundred year after it was destroyed by the *Danes*.

The foregoing Particulars of this History have been curiously painted in the Windows of the Cloysters belonging to this Abby, with *English* Verses under each Picture explaining the Story: Which see in the *Monasticon* at large.

[Valued at 1721 *l*. 14 *s*. 0 *d*. ob. q. *per Annum*.]

WHITBY, (of Old call'd STRENSHALE,) in Yorkshire.

ANno Dom. 655. *Penda* the Pagan King of *Mercia* making War upon *Oswy* King of *Northumberland*, *Oswy* made a Vow to Almighty God that if he overcame his Enemies, he would dedicate his Daughter to perpetual Virginity, and give twelve of his Manour-houses to be converted into Monasteries. Hereupon he fought, and tho' much inferiour in number obtain'd a Signal Victory, and *Penda* was slain in the Battle. In performance of his Vow, he gave his Daughter named *Etkelfleda*, then scarce one year old to be a Nun, and the Ground then called *Streneshal* for the building of a

71.

C Monastery

72. Monastery. It was begun by *Hilda*, a Woman of great Religion; and was at first a Nunnery, but afterwards a House of Monks.

In the year 1067. *William de Percy*, who came into *England* with the Conquerour, and had obtained to himself and Heirs the Town of *Whitby* and all its Members, made a new Foundation of the Abby of *Whitby*, and gave all the said Town and Members to God, St. *Peter*, and St. *Hilda* of *Whitby*, and to the Monks there serving God, in perpetual Alms, with
73. divers other Lands; and made *Reinfridus* a Monk of *Evesham*, Prior of the
74. Monastery. This was after this place had been destroyed by the *Danes* above two hundred years.

Many were the Benefactors to this Abby, besides the Founder *William de Percy*, a particular of the Lands, Possessions, Forests, Churches, Tithes, and Liberties by them given, may be seen in the *Monasticon* at large, *p.* 74, 75. *Vid. inf. p.* 988.

[Valued at 437 *l*. 2 *s*. 9 *d*. *per Annum*.]

CHERTSEY, in Surrey.

75. THE Abby of *Chertsey* was founded in the Reign of King *Egbert*, in the year of our Lord 666. by *Frithwaldus* a petty King or Gover-
76. nor of the Province of *Surrey*, under *Wulfar* King of *Mercia*, and endow'd with large Possessions; all which were confirm'd by the said *Wulfar* King of *Mercia*.

The Limits of the Lands belonging to *Chertsey-Abby* may be seen in the *Monasticon* at large, *p.* 77.

78. Pope *Alexander* granted to this Abby many Priviledges; among other, that they should pay no Tithes of their Lands in their own hands, nor of the Beasts which they themselves kept.

[Valued at 659 *l*. 15 *s*. 8 *d*. ob. *per Annum*.]

BERKING, in the County of Essex.

79. THE Nunnery at *Berking*, eight miles from *London*, was founded by *Erkenwaldus* Bishop of that City, for his Sister *Ethelburge*, who was the first Abbess of this Nunnery.

Hodelredus a Kinsman of *Sebby* King of the *East Saxons* gave to this
80. House fair Revenues, which Guift was confirm'd by the said King *Sebby*.

The Ancient Profits and Expences of this Nunnery, as they were charg'd to the Account of the Celerefs, may be seen in the *Monasticon* at large, *p.* 80, 81, 82, 83.

[Valued at 862 *l*. 12 *s*. 5 *d*. ob. *per Annum*.]

The Monastery of St. Mildred, in the Isle of Thanet, in Kent.

84. MIldred the Virgin, was the Daughter of *Merwaldus* Son of *Penda* King of *Mercia*, and *Domneva* of the Family of the Kings of *Kent*. Which *Domneva* with her Husband's assistance built this Monastery for Nuns, and placed here seventy Virgins, of whom their Daughter *Mildred* was consecrated Abbess. This House was destroy'd by the *Pagan Danes*

A BENEDICTINE NUN.

Vol.1. P.99

the year 1011. Afterwards in the time of King *Cnut*, it was annext by that King's Grant to St. *Augustines* Monastery, and the Body of St. *Mildred* translated from hence to St. *Augustines* at *Canterbury*, A. D. 1033. The Lands belonging hereunto in the Isle of *Thanet*, were confirm'd to the said Monastery of St. *Augustines* by King *Edward* the Confessor.

85.

FALKSTONE, in Kent.

EAnswida Daughter of *Eadbaldus* Son of *Ethelbert* King of *Kent*, built this Monastery in a remote Part from Commerce, situated seven Acers breadth from the Sea, which in process of time quite wore away the Land, and destroyed this House; but the Reliques of the holy Virgin the Foundress, who lived and died here, were removed to the Neighbouring Church of St. *Peter*.

See more of this House, *infra, p.* 560.

[Valued at 41 *l.* 15 *s.* 10 *d. per Annum.*]

LIMING, in Kent.

THE Monastery here was built by *Ethelburge* Daughter of King *Ethelbert*, and Wife of *Edwin* King of *Northumberland*, after whose death she return'd into *Kent*, and founded this Nunnery, and lies here buried.

RACULFE, in Kent.

BIrthwald Archbishop of *Canterbury* was before his election to that See, in the year 692. Abbot of *Raculfe*.

86.

In the year 949. King *Eadred* King of all *England*, gave the Monastery of *Raculfe* and all the Lands belonging thereunto, to the Church of *Canterbury, Odo* being then Archbishop and Metropolitan there. The Lands belonging to this House did amount to twenty five Carucates, and one Carucate assigned only to the Repairs of the Church.

87.

ELY Abby, in Cambridgeshire.

ANno Dom. 627. The blessed *Augustine*, built a Church at *Ely* in a place called *Cradindene*, a mile distant from the present City, it was consecrated to the honour of the blessed Virgin, and stored with Ministers for God's service, but these were all expell'd by *Penda* King of *Mercia*, and the place turn'd into a Desert.

Afterwards in the year 673. *Ethelreda* the Virgin, built a Monastery in a more eminent place in *Ely*, for both Sexes, of which she her self became the first Abbess. In the year 870. the Church of *Ely* was again destroy'd and burnt by the *Pagans*.

87.
90.

In the year 970. *Ethelwaldus* Bishop of *Winchester* bought this Isle of King *Edgar*, rebuilt the Church and placed *Monks* in it, under the Rule of an Abbot; and in this state it remained till the year 1108. (9 *H.* 1.) at which time Pope *Paschal* at the request of that King, changed the Abby into a Bishoprick. C 2 The

87.
9.2
95.
88.

The foresaid *Ethelred* was Daughter of *Anna* King of the *East-Angels*, and was buried in *Ely* together with several other holy Women of her Relations and Blood.

90. The History of this Church says, that an Apparition appear'd to one of the Monks, and foretold to him the destruction of the Monastery, because not one of both Sexes in this House, but himself, did use to pass the night in religious Exercises, but in Vanity and Sin. After which the
91. *Danes* destroyed it to the Ground, *An. Dom.* 870.
92. Benefactors to this House were the abovesaid *Ethelwald* Bishop of *Winchester*, who bought the whole Isle of *Ely*, and gave it and other Lands and
93. rich Moveables to this Church; King *Edgar* and King *Edward* the Elder, granted and confirmed to it many Lands and Priviledges, approved and ratified by Pope *Victor*.

[Valued at 1084 *l.* 6 *s.* 9 *d.* ob. *per Annum*.]

WIRMOUTH, and GYRWY, now called YARROW, in the Bishoprick of Durham.

96. IN the year 674. *Egfrid* King of the *Northumbers* gave a quantity of Ground lying at the mouth of the River *Wyra*, to the holy Abbot *Benedict* an *Englishman*, who had been five times at *Rome*, for the building a Monastery to St. *Peter*; and other Lands in a place then called *Gyrwy*, not far distant for another Monastery to the honour of St. *Paul*. Both which he indow'd, and filled with Monks.

Gyrwy, is four miles distant from *New-Castle*, of this House Venerable
97. *Bede*, was heretofore a Monk, and educated under the above-mentioned *Benedict*.

[Valued at 25 *l.* 8 *s.* 4 *d. per Annum*.]

ABBINGTON, in Barkshire.

AT such time as the wicked *Hengist* destroyed 460 of the Barons and Great men of this Land, by fraud and treachery, one of the Noblemen's Sons named *Aben*, made a shift to escape the slaughter, and concealed himself in a Wood on the *South-side* of *Oxfordshire* for a great while; but being at last taken notice of for his great sanctity, people built there for him a House and Chappel, which was afterwards from his name called *Abendun*. In the year 675. one *Heane*, a man of great Riches begun to build in the same place a Monastery (though after removed to some distance) and gave to it a part of his Inheritance. Sister of this *Heane* was *Cissa*, who built at a place called *Helneston* near the *Thames* a Monastery for Nuns, of which she became her self the Abbess. This Lady had obtained a small piece of one of the Nails of our Lord's passion, to which she caused some other Iron to be added, and made of that, a Cross, which she caused to be placed upon her breast after her death, and so buried. This Cross was in the time of *Adelwold* Abbot here (and afterwards Bishop of *Winchester*) found accidentally, in digging to make an Aqueduct, it was translated into the Monastery of Monks, and there preserved with great reverence; and call'd the black Cross.

The

The Monks here at their first Institution were but twelve and the Abbot; they never went abroad without great necessity and with the Abbot's leave; they did eat no flesh, unless sick, &c.   98.

The Town of *Abbington* was in old time called *Seuekesham*. It was a Regal Seat, and a place of great concourse for religious Worship, as well before the times of Christianity, as since, (*tam tempore Religionis fanaticæ, quam tempore religionis Christianæ*, are the Words of the old Historian).   99.

Benefactors to this House were *Cedwalla* King of the *West-Saxons*; King *Ina* his Son *An. Dom.* 699. *Kenulfus* King of *Mercia*, *An. Dom.* 821. *Edred* King of all *England*, *An. Dom.* 955. *Edgar* King of all *England*, *An. Dom.* 958. in the Reign of this King, the above-mentioned *Adelwold* was Abbot here, who built the Church in honour of the holy Mother of God, and sent one of his Monks beyond the Seas for the rule of St. *Benedict*, he settled here several good Orders, and gave great Riches and Ornaments to this Church; after this, he was by King *Edgar* chosen to be Bishop of *Winchester*, *An. Dom.* 963. King *Hen.* I. was also a great Benefactor. And Pope *Eugenius* III. granted to this Abby great Priviledges by his Bull dated, *An. Dom.* 1146.   100. 101. 102. 104. 105. 107.

[Valued at 1876 *l.* 10 *s.* 9 *d.* per Annum.]

GLOUCESTER *Abby*.

Anno Dom. 680 or 681. In the Reign of King *Æthelred*, one *Osrich* a petty King, or *Subregulus*, first founded the Church of St. *Peters* in *Gloucester*, and placed his Sister *Kineburga* Abbess of the Monastery there. This Monastery was built at the Expences of King *Ethelred* and his Wife *Elfleda*. Which being afterwards destroyed by the *Danes*, was in the year 1058. restored and consecrated by *Aldredus* then Bishop of *Worcester*, and afterward Archbishop of *York*.   108.

The foresaid King *Ethelred*, in the the 30*th*. year of his Reign became a Monk at *Bardeney*, and after that Abbot; and departed this life in the year 716.   109.

The fore-mentioned *Osrich*, became King of the *Northumbers* after the death of *Kenred*, and died, *An. Dom.* 729.

The Nuns of this House were dispersed after the year 767. and *Benedictine* Monks were placed here, *An. Dom.* 1022. by *Wolstan* then Bishop of *Worcester*.

This Church was again new built from the Foundation by *Serlo* the first Abbot after the Conquest, and consecrated in the year 1100. by *Sampson* Bishop of *Worcester*. Two years after which this Church together with the whole City of *Gloucester* was burnt down.   110. 111.

Many were the Benefactors to this Church of all sorts and qualities, whose Names together with the Lands given, amounting in all to a great Revenue, may be seen at large in the *Monasticon*, from *p.* 111, to *p.* 120.

See more of this Church *infra p*, 993, and *Vol.* 3. *p.* 7.

[Valued at 1946 *l.* 5 *s.* 9 *d.* per Annum.]

WOR-

WORCESTER Abby.

120. Anno Dom. 680. In the Reign of King *Athelred* in the Kingdom of *Mercia*, *Worcester* was first made a Bishops seat; and *Boselus* the first Bishop.

St. *Oswald* who was Bishop here in the year 871. or according to others 959. introduced the first Monks, into this Church, in the room of the Clerks.

King *Offa*, King *Edgar*, and many others of the *Saxons*; were great Benefactors to this Church, as may be seen in the *Monasticon*, from *p.* 121, to *p.* 136. and from thence to *p.* 140. a Recapitulation of their Lands and Endowments.

[Valued at the Suppression at 1229 *l*. 12 *s*. 8 *d*. ob. per *Annum*.]

BARDENEY Abby, in Lincolnshire.

142. WHEN the Body of St. *Oswald* was first buried at *Bardeney*, there were three hundred Monks in this Abby. It was first built by King *Ethelred*, and destroyed to the Ground by the *Danes*, and re-edified again by *Gilbert de Gaunt* Uncle to *William* the Conqueror; whose Son and Heir *Walter de Gaunt* did, in the year 1115, confirm to the Church and Monastery of St. *Peter* and St. *Paul*, and St. *Oswald*, at *Bardeney*, all those Lands and Possessions which his Father had given in pure and perpetual Alms to the same: And did also inlarge their Possessions of his own Charity. All which was afterwards confirm'd by King *Henry* the first.

143. Vid. Vol. 2. p. 847.

[Valued at 366 *l*. 6 *s*. 1 *d*. per *Annum*.]

EUESHAM Abby, in Worcestershire.

144.
145. Saint *Egwin*, who was the third Bishop of *Worcester* founded this Monastery. *Kenredus* King of *Mercia*, and *Offa* Governour of the *East Angles* in the year 709, being both then at *Rome*, endow'd it with large Possessions. The Towns which St. *Egwin* obtain'd to his Monastery of

146. the said Kings were in all twenty two. There were belonging to this House sixty seven Monks, five Nuns, three poor People, three Clerks, who had all the same allowance as the Monks had; and besides these, sixty five Servants. The under Officers of this House as Prior, Sub-Prior, third

147. Prior, Precentor, Sacristan, Celarer, &c. were created by the Abbot with the advice and consent of the major part of the Covent, in Chapter. All which Officers had their several Rents arising from distinct and several

148. places appropriated to their several Offices.
149. In the year 1174. *Waldemarus* King of *Danemark* gave and confirm'd the Priory of *Othenesia* in that Kingdom as a Cell to this Abby of *Euesham*.

This Abby was first founded, as aforesaid, by St. *Egwin* in the year of grace 692. and dedicated to the honour of the glorious Virgin *Mary*. The Founder himself leaving his Bishoprick, became the first Abbot here. After whose death succeeded eighteen Abbots until the year 941. at which time the Monks here were dispersed, and secular Chanons substituted in

their

their room. In the time of King *Edgar, Anno Dom.* 660, the Monks were again restored; but after his death expell'd again, in the year 977. This House and Estate was afterwards given to a potent man called *Godwin,* and successively it came into several hands, till at last in the year 1014. King *Ethelred* made *Ailfwardus* a Monk of *Ramsey,* Abbot of *Euesham;* he was also Bishop of *London* at the same time. From his time the Abby of *Euesham* flourisht under divers Abbots, whose names from the *Norman* Conquest till the year 1379. are as follows, *Egelwinus, Walterus, Robertus, Mauricius, Reginaldus, Willielmus de Andivilla, Rogerus, Adam, Rogerus Norreys, Radulphus, Thomas de Marleberg, Ricaadus le Cras, Thomas de Glovernia, Henricus, Willielmus de Wytechurch, Johannes de Brokehampton, Willielmus de Chyriton, Willielmus de Boys, Johannes de Ombresleje, Rogerus Zatten* 1379. *Vid Vol.* 2. *p.* 851.

152.

[Valued at 1183 *l.* 12 *s.* 9 *d. per Annum.*]

SHEPEY Monastery of Nuns, in Kent.

Founded by Queen *Sexburga,* about the year of our Lord 710. *William* Archbishop of *Canterbury,* after the Conquest restored this Monastery, it having lain a long time burnt down and destroyed by the *Danes.* King *Henry* the II. King *Richard* the I. King *Henry* the III. and others, were Benefactors to this Church of St. *Sexburg,* here, and to the Nuns serving God in the same; all whose Donations of Lands and Liberties were confirm'd in the 1*st.* year of King *Henry* the IV.

153.

[Valued at 129 *l.* 7 *s.* 10 *d.* ob. *per Annum.*]

SELSEY, in Sussex.

IN the year of our Lord 711. *Wilfred* Bishop of *Hagulstad* remaining five years in the Isle of *Selsey* to avoid persecution, built there a Monastery in honour of the blessed *Mary,* to which *Ethelwold* King of the *South Saxons,* gave Lands.

TUKESBURY, in Gloucestershire.

THIS Monastery was founded in the year 715. by two Dukes of great account in the Kingdom of *Mercia* named *Oddo* and *Doddo,* to the honour of the glorious Virgin *Mary.*

154.

Robert Fiz-Hamon in the year. 1102. new built this Church and Monastery, making it an Abby, and subjecting to it the Priory of *Cranburne.* His Daughter *Mabilla* was afterwards married to *Robert* base Son of King *Henry* I. who was created Earl of *Gloucester*; he built the Priory of St. *James* at *Bristol,* and annext it also to this House. From him descended *Gilbert de Clare* Earl of *Gloucester* and *Hertford,* who was a great Benefactor to this House, and buried here; as were the rest of his descendants, Earls of *Gloucester,* and the *Dispencers* who descended from one of the Heirs General. All these and more of their Blood, among whom *Henry de Beauchamp* Duke of *Warwick,* were Benefactors to this Abby, their pious gifts being all confirm'd and ratified by the King, 1462.

155.

156.

157.

159.
160.

The

163. The several parcels of Lands and Hereditaments given and confirm'd to this House by former Kings may be seen, p. 161, 162.

[Valued at 1598 l. 1 s. 3 d. per Annum.]

WINBURNE, in Dorsetshire.

Saint *Quinburga*, and St. *Cuthburga*, Sisters of *Ina* King of the *West Saxons*, built here a Monastery for Nuns, Anno Dom. 718.

CROYLAND, in Lincolnshire.

Croyland is one of those small Islands which lie in the *East Fens*. Here St. *Guthlac*, at the age of twenty five years, became a Hermite, and in his life time delivered the Island from Devils and evil Spirits, and dying, was here buried.

164. *Ethelbald* King of *Mercia*, by his Charter dated in the year 716. gave to God, the blessed *Mary*, and St. *Batholomew*, the whole Isle of *Croyland*, containing four *Leucas*, or miles in length, and three in breadth, for the erecting of a Monastery under the Rule of St. *Benedict*: and endow'd the said Monastery with large Possessions lying about the Place.

165.   All which was confirm'd to them by *Offa* King of *Mercia*, in the year
166.   793. and by *Withlaf* King of *Mercia*, in the year 833.
167.   This Abby being afterwards burnt down and destroyed by the Pagan *Danes*, was re-edified and restored to its former Possessions and Liberties, by King *Eadred*, who stiled himself King of Great *Britain*, in the year 948. *Vid. Vol.* 2. *p.* 853.

[Valued at 1863 l. 15 s. 10 d. ob. per Annum.]

BEVERLEY, in Yorkshire.

169. Saint *John* Archbishop of *York* was the first Dr. of Theology in *Oxford*.
170. He converted the Parish-Church of St. *John* in the Town of *Beverly* into a Monastery, building to it a new Quire; and made his Deacon *Bithunus* the first Abbot here. Both which lie buried in this Church. One hundred years after this the Monastery of *Beverley* was destroyed by the *Danes*, and lay in Ruines three years, before it was repair'd. King *Athelstan* built here a Colledge of secular Chanons. And granted and confirm'd to this Church of St. *John* of *Beverley* many great Priviledges and Liberties An. Dom. 938. King *Edward* the Confessor was a great Benefactor to this Church, and augmented the number of the Prebendaries.
171. *William* the Conqueror was also a Benefactor. *Thomas* the first Archbishop of *York*, erected a new Dignity in the Collegiate Church of *Beverley*, viz. a *Prepositus* or Provost, who has neither voice in the Chapter nor Stall in the Quire; of these, there is a List of thirty eight, *Thomas Becket* being the fifth in number. *Vid. Vol.* 3. *part.* 2 *p.* 3.

[Valued at 109 l. 8 s. 8 d. ob. per Annum.]

R I P.

RIPPON, in Yorkshire.

Wilfrid Archbishop of York founded a Monastery at *Rippon*, which was afterwards burnt down, in the Devastation which King *Adred* made upon the *Northumbers*. But being in after-times re-edified, King *Athalstan* granted to this Church the Priviledge of Sanctuary, with the same Liberties which he had given before to the Church of *Beverly*; and that the men of *Rippon* should be believed by their *yea*, and by their *na*.

St. FRIDISWADE, at Oxford.

Fridiswade the holy Virgin was Daughter of *Didanus* a petty King (*Sub-regulus*) of *Oxford*; her Father built a Church there in honour of St. *Mary*, and *all Saints*, and gave it for his Daughters Habitation, who with twelve other Nuns led there a religious Life. St. *Fridiswade* died on the 14th. of the *Calends* of *November* 735. and was buried in the said Church. This Monastery and Church was afterwards burnt down, with the *Danes* in it, who had fled thither for Refuge; but King *Etkelred* did soon after rebuild it with additions, as appears by his Charter dated in the year 1004. In the year 1111. *Roger* Bishop of *Salisbury*, in lieu of Nuns, instituted in this Monastery a Prior and Cannons, to whom King *Henry* I. gave a fair Estate in Lands and Tyths, which was confirm'd to them by Pope *Adrian*.

Benefactors to this Church of St. *Fridiswade* in *Oxford*, were *Maud* the Empress, Earl *Simon*, *Ralph Foliot*, and others.

See more of this Monastery, *infra*, p. 983.

DEREHAM, in Norfolk.

Withburga Daughter of *Anna* King of the *East Angles*, built a Monastery for Nuns in this Town and was buried here. After the Incursion of the Pagan *Danes*, the Nuns were all dispers'd, and the Church was made parochial. In the year 798, the Body of St. *Withburga* was found here, uncorrupted, near fifty five years after her death. *Vid. Vol.* 2. p. 853.

St. ALBANS-ABBY, in Hertfordshire.

Saint *Alban* was martyr'd in this place, then called *Verolamium*, in the time of *Dioclesian*'s persecution. Ten years after that persecution ceas'd, the Christians built here a Church to his memory; which being destroy'd by the incursion of the barbarous People, *Offa* King of *Mercia*, about the year 793. repair'd the Church, built here a Monastery, stored it with Monks, translated the Reliques of the Martyr into a rich Shrine, and obtain'd of Pope *Adrian* to have him canonized. And by his Charter dated in the above-mentioned year granted to the said Monastery several Lands and great Priviledges. In the year 1154. *Nicholas* Bishop of *Alba* (an English-born man near this Monastery) being chosen Pope by the name of *Adrian* IV.

D   granted

granted to the Abbot of this Abby, that as St. *Alban* was the first Martyr of *England*, so this Abbot should be the first of all the Abbots of *England* in order and dignity.

178. King *John* by his Charter dated the 11*th.* of *June* in the first year of his Reign, granted to God, and the Church of St. *Alban*, and the Monks there, divers Lands and great Liberties.

179. Pope *Honorius*, by his Bull dated in the year 1218. confirm'd to this Church all Lands and Liberties granted to it by former Popes, Kings, and
180. others, granting also to the Abbot and his Successors Episcopal Rights, and the Episcopal Habit, and that he and his Monks should be exempt
181. from the Jurisdiction of the Bishop; with other exemptions, &c. reserving as a Rent to the Apostolick See yearly, for these Liberties, the payment of one ounce of Gold.

In the Windows of the Cloysters of this Abby, were formerly painted abundance of Historical Passages out of the Bible, with *Latin* Verses underneath each Story, explaining the same. In like manner were the Windows of the Library, and Presbytery painted, with the Pictures of famous men, with explanatory Verses, which Verses may be seen in the *Monasticon* at large, p. 182, 183, 184.

[Valued at 2102 *l.* 7 *s.* 1 *d.* ob. q. *per Annum*.]

BATH, in Somersetshire.

184. KING *Osric* was the first Founder of this Monastery for Nuns, *Anno. Dom.* 676. *Offa* King of *Mercia*, placed here secular Cannons; and King *Edgar* introduced Monks instead of Cannons.

185. King *William* the Conqueror gave the City of *Bath* to God, St. *Peter*, and *John* Bishop of *Wells*, for the augmentation of his Episcopal Seat King *Henry* the I. confirm'd the same, and constituted and confirm'd the
186. Episcopal Seat of *Somersetshire*, which was formerly at *Wells*, to be at *Bath*, by Charter dated in the year 1111. and in the twelfth year of his Reign. The said *John* the Bishop, by his Deed dated 1106. appointed the Church of St. *Peter* here, to be the Head and Mother-Church of the whole Diocess, and restored the Lands which the King had given him in *Bath*, to the Monastery there, to which they did formerly belong; with an *Anathema* against the Violators of his said Gift and Restoration.

Oliver King Bishop of *Bath*, and *Gibbs* the last Prior here, built the present Church, *p.* 185.

[Valued at 617 *l.* 2 *s.* 3 *d. per Annum*.]

WELLS, in Somersetshire.

Cynewulf King of the *West Saxons*, in the year 766. gave to the Monastery at *Wells* dedicated to St. *Andrew* the Apostle, several parcels of Land adjoyning.

187. King *Edward* the Confessor *Anno* 1065. gave and confirm'd to the Church and Bishop of *Wells*, the Lands and Liberties formerly to the said Church given, with additions.

WINCHCUMB, in Gloucestershire.

ANno Dom. 787. *Offa* King of *Mercia*, built here a Monastery for Nuns. Or as others say, it was built by *Kenulphus* King of *Mercia* A.D. 798. and the Church dedicated by *Wilfridus* Archbishop of *Canterbury*, and twelve other Bishops; at which dedication that King released at the Altar, the King of *Kent*, his Prisoner of War. This Monastery being almost utterly decay'd, in the time of King *Edgar*, was repaired by St. *Oswald* Archbishop of *York*, and *Germanus* made Abbot here. King *Kenulfus* is said to have placed here at the first Foundation no less then three hundred Monks. Of these three hundred Monks there might possibly be not above forty who were Priests or Clerks, the rest might be Hermits, or as meer Lay-men get their living by Working, as in ancient Times Monks did use to do. The Mannors and Lands formerly belonging to this Monastery were eleven Towns with their Members, the names of which may be seen, *p.* 190. *Vid. Vol.* 2. *p.* 854.

188.
189.
190.

[Valued at 759 *l.* 11 *s.* 9 *d. per Annum.*]

WILTON, in Wiltshire.

WUlstan Earl of *Wiltshire* repaired an ancient Church here dedicated to St. *Mary*, and placed therein a Colledge of Priests. After whose death, his Widow *Alburga*, converted the Foundation to a Nunnery of Virgins, *Anno Dom* 800. Afterwards King *Alfred* built at *Wilton* a new Monastery, and dedicated the Church to St. *Mary* and St. *Bartholomew*; here he placed twelve Nuns and an Abbess, and translated the other Nuns hither from St. *Mary's*, which made the number in all twenty six. Subsequent Benefactors were King *Edward* the Elder, King *Athelstan*, King *Edgar*, *William* the Conqueror, &c. *Vid. Vol.* 2. *p.* 857.

191.

[Valued at 601 *l.* 1 *s.* 1 *d.* q. *per Annum.*]

AMBRESBURY, in Wiltshire.

THE Nunnery at *Ambresbury* was built by Queen *Elfrida* by way of expiation for the murder of King *Edward* the Younger, called St. *Edward* of which she had been guilty. In the Reign of *Henry* the II. *Anno Dom.* 1177. the Nuns here were expell'd from this House and shut up in other religious Houses under stricter Custody, for their incontinency and notorious scandal. And other Nuns of *Font-Everard* introduced here, by the Authority of Pope *Alexander*, King *Henry* the II. and *Richard* Archbishop of *Canterbury*. Which King *Henry* the II. gave to the said Nunnery of *Font-Everard* this Church as a Cell, with many other Lands and great Liberties, all which were confirm'd by King *John* in the first year of his Reign; with a Gift of 50 *s. per Annum* out of the *Exchequer* for ever, in the fifth year of his Reign. *Vid.* 2. *Vol p.* 868.

192.
193.

[Valued at 495 *l.* 15 *s.* 2 *d. per Annum.*]

MIDLETON, in Dorsetshire.

194. KING *Athelstan*, having upon false accusations unjustly banisht his youngest Brother *Edwyn*, and put him to Sea in an old Vessel without either Sails or Oars, where he was drown'd; and being afterwards extream penitent, he built and endowed here a Church and Monastery
195. in honour of St. *Mary* and St. *Sampson* the Archbishop; and stored it with Black Monks, for the Soul of his said Brother *Edwyn*.

He also purchased from *Rome* and other places beyond the Seas several holy Reliques; and gave them to this Monastery as a piece of our Saviour's Cross; a Great Cross composed of Gold, Silver, and precious Stones;
196. the Arm and several Bones of St. *Sampson* the Archbishop, &c. King *Athelstan*'s Charter of Endowment bears date in the year 843. and was exemplified and confirm'd by King *Henry* the II.

197. The same Founder built another Monastery on the same occasion, at a place called *Michel*, in *Dorsetshire*.

[Valued at 578 *l*. 13 *s*. 11 *d*. ob. per Annum.]

POLESWORTH, in Warwickshire.

Egbert King of the *West Saxons* built here a Nunnery, and made his Daughter *Edith* the first Abbess there. King *William* the Conquer-
198. or gave this Estate to a Favourite of his called Sir *Robert Marmion*, whose chief Seat was at the Neighbouring Castle of *Tamworth*, he expell'd the Nuns for a while, but not long after restored them again to their old Estate, and was reputed their Founder. The Nuns of *Polesworth* had a Cell at *Olbury*, which was given to their Monastery by *Walter de Hastings*, and
199. confirm'd to them by *Roger* Bishop of *Chester* (then the same Diocess with *Coventry* and *Litchfield*) and others.

[Valued at 87 *l*. 16 *s*. 3 *d*. per Annum.]

St. WERBURGS, at Chester.

THE holy Virgin *Werburg* was Daughter of *Wulfer* King of *Mercia*, and *Ermenilda* his Wife. She lived and died in a Monastery at
200. *Chester*, which had been built of old time for the Habitation of Nuns; but after the Conquest *Hugh* Earl of *Chester* placed Monks there.

The Monastery was built by King *Edgar* in the year 858. *Hugh* Earl of *Chester* having establisht Monks here, endow'd the Foundation with great Revenues, his Barons also giving very liberally to the same, whose Charter bears date Anno Dom. 1093. The Particulars given may be seen in the *Monasticon* at large, *p*. 201. 202.

See more of this House, *p*. 985.

[Valued at 1003 *l*. 5 *s*. 11 *d*. per Annum.]

ATHE-

ATHELING, in Somersetshire.

KING *Elfred* being driven out of his Kingdom by the *Danes*, conceal'd himself for some time in this place, then compast about with Marishes and Water, that it was inaccessable but with a Boat. Upon his restoration he built here a Church and Monastery. His Charter of Endowment bears date *Anno Dom.* 878.

About the same time that King *Elfred* founded this Monastery for Monks, he founded another for Nuns at *Shaftesbury*.

[Valued at 209 *l.* 0 *s.* 3 *d.* q. *per Annum.*]

PERSHORE, in Worcestershire.

THE Monastery here was built in the time of King *Edgar* by Duke *Egelwardus*; but the greatest part of its Estate was in aftertime transferred by King *Edward* and King *William* to *Westminster*. Others say, it was founded about the year 604. by *Oswald* Nephew of King *Athelred*. *Oswald* did at first place here secular Canons, which were after changed to Monks, then Canons restored, and then Monks once again introduced by King *Edgar. Anno Dom.* 1223. there happened a grievous fire here, and the Monks for some time having left the place, their Estate was usurpt by the Monks of *Westminster*. The Deeds and Charters of Priviledges of this House being burnt, Witnesses were examined and made several Depositions of the ancient Liberties and Customs used, and of right belonging to this Monastery, which may be seen in the *Monasticon* at large.

[Valued at 643 *l.* 4 *s.* 5 *d. per Annum.*]

HIDE, in Hampshire.

THIS is otherwise called the new Monastery at *Winchester*, and was designed by King *Elfred*, but built after his death by his Son King *Edward*, who placed therein secular Canons under the Rule of a holy man call'd *Grimbaldus*. This new Monastery being at first built within the City, close to the Cathedral Church, was on the account of several inconveniencies in the Scituation, removed in the year 1121. to the place called *Hide*. Great was the Revenue given to this Monastery, and many the Benefactors besides the Founder, as King *Athelstan*, King *Edmund*, King *Edred*, King *Edgar* (who expell'd the Canons and placed Monks here) King *Edmund Ironside*, *Edward* the Confessor, *William* the Conqueror, *Henry* I. and *Maud* his Queen, &c.

But this House was not without its misfortunes, *William* the Conqueror at his first coming finding the Abbot and twelve of his Monks in arms against him, seiz'd upon their Estate and held it from them almost two years. And in the Reign of King *Stephen*, *Henry* then Bishop of *Winchester* committed such extortions upon the Monks here, that he got from them almost all their Church Plate, and was so oppressive that of forty Monks, there remain'd but ten in the House.

211. King *Edgars* Diploma to this House was written in Letters of Gold, and dated *Anno Dom.* 966.
The Priviledges of this House were agreed and settled between *William* Bishop of *Winchester* and *Gaufridus* Abbot here, *An. Dom.* 1110.

[Valued at 865 *l.* 18 *s.* 0 *d.* ob. q. *per Annum.*]

212. WINCHESTER *Monastery of Nuns.*

About the year 903. *Alswitha* Wife of King *Alfred*, began the Foundation of a Nunnery at *Winchester*, which was after her death compleated by her Son King *Edward* the Elder.

[Valued at 179 *l.* 7 *s.* 2 *d. per Annum.*]

213. St. PETROCUS, *at* Bodmin, *in* Cornwall.

KING *Athelstan* was the first Founder of this Monastery for Monks; which after the Conquest, came into the Crown, but was purchased by *Alganus*, and stored with Canons regular.

St. GERMAINS, *in* Cornwall.

KING *Athelstan* founded a Monastery here, which at that time was the Seat of a Bishop, but was afterwards removed by King *Edward* the Confessor from hence to *Exeter*. *Bartholomew* Bishop of *Exeter* introduced into this Church by the King's Authority, Canons Regular, eight in number, and a Prior.

[Valued at 243 *l.* 8 *s. per Annum.*]

SHAFTESBURY, *in* Dorsetshire.

KING *Elfred* built this Town in the year 880. *Elgiva* Wife of *Edmund*, great Grand-child of the said *Elfred*, built here a Monastery for Nuns. King *Edward* the younger, commonly called St. *Edward* the Martyr, murder'd by his Mother-in-Laws procurement; was here interr'd, on which account this Church was afterwards call'd by his name.

214. Benefactors to this House were King *Edmund*, King *Edred*, A. D. 948.
215. and King *Etheldred*, 1001.
216. See more of this Monastery, *p.* 983.

[Valued at 1166 *l.* 8 *s.* 9 *d: per Annum.*]

217. TAVESTOCK, *in* Devonshire.

ORdgarus an Earl in these Parts, and Father of *Elfrid* Wife of King *Edgar*, built this Monastery in the year 961, for Monks. It was afterwards burnt down by the *Danes*. King *Edelred*, in the year 981. en-
218. dow'd it with Lands and Liberties; the like did King *Henry* the I. all which

which was exemplified and confirm'd by King Edward the III. in the twenty second Year of his Reign.

See more of this Monastery, p. 995.

[Valued at 902 l. 5 s. 7 d. per Annum.]

RUMSEY, in Hampshire.

KING *Edward* the Elder, built here a Monastery, in which his Grandson King *Edgar* placed religious Nuns, under the Government of *Merwina* their Abbess, *Anno Dom.* 907.

King *Edgar*, King *Henry* III. and King *Edward* I. were Benefactors to this House, and confirm'd the Lands and Liberties to them given.

[Valued at 393 l. 10 s. 10 d. ob. per Annum.]

HORTON, in Dorsetshire.

ORgarus Earl of *Devonshire* (formerly mention'd) was the first Founder of this Monastery, who after his decease, which happen'd in the year 971. was here buried.

Roger Bishop of *Shirburn*, obtain'd of King *Henry* the I. that this House and the Possessions thereunto belonging should be transfer'd and annext to the Monastery of *Shirburn*, so that in after-times it was accounted only as a Cell of that House, tho' it had been before that reckon'd as an Abby of it self.

EXETER, in Devonshire.

THE Kingdom of the *West Saxons* having been destitute of a Bishop for full seven years before, Pope *Formosus* threatn'd to curse King *Edward* the Elder, in the year 905. unless he would restore Bishops according to the ancient Tradition. Hereupon that King calling a Synod, in which presided *Plegmundus* Archbishop of *Canterbury*, did, by their advice constitute several Bishops Seats, and set out their several Dioceses; and the Archbishop ordain'd seven Bishops in one day to seven Churches, among which *Athelstan* was made Bishop of *Cornwall*, and *Eadulf* of *Cridington*. In the year 1046. King *Edward* the Confessor united these two Bishopricks, and soon after at the request of Pope *Leo* fixt the Seat of the Bishop in the Monastery of St. *Mary* and St. *Peter* at *Exeter*, the then Bishop *Leofric* being introduced into the Cathedral Church betwixt the King and Queen. Which Bishop finding the said Church much decay'd and impoverisht in its Goods and Revenues became a great Benefactor, giving to it not only several Books and Church Ornaments, but divers Lands; and recover'd for the Monastery other Lands which had been formerly given, and since lost and taken from them.

King *Athelstan*, soon after his coming to the Crown of this Kingdom, erected the Monastery here to St. *Mary* and St *Peter*, and endow'd it with twenty six Towns and Villages, and gave to it the third part of those many Relicks which he had caused to be collected beyond the Seas, *viz.* some pieces of our Lord's Cross, Sepulcher, Garment, Cradle, &c. with many others,

227. others, which may be seen at large, *p.* 225, 226. After him King *Athelred*,
228. King *Canut*, King *Edward* the Confessor, King *John*, and King *Henry* the III.
229. became Benefactors: so also King *Henry* the I. who restored to this Mona-
230. stery several Churches which had been taken from it.

231.   R A M S E Y, *in* Huntingdonshire.

IN the year 969. *Ailwinus* Duke of the *East Angels*, at the instigation of *Oswald* Archbishop of *York*, founded the Monastery of *Ramsey*, which was consecrated by St. *Dunstan* Archbishop of *Canterbury*, and the said *Oswald*, in the year 974. and the Church dedicated to the blessed *Mary* and all holy Virgins, and to St. *Benedict*.

232. *Ramsey* is a small Island, situated among Fens and Marishes, in the East corner of *Huntingdonshire*, about two miles long, and near as broad. It was formerly very much abounding with Alders and other Trees that delight in moist Ground, from whence it might take its name *Ramsey à ramis, quasi Insula Ramorum*.

233. At the Foundation of this Church King *Edgar* gave to it five Hides of Land. St. *Oswald* also gave several Ornaments and Lands, and procured to it others.

234. Duke *Ailwinus* the Founder gave to this Abby the whole Isle in which it stood with the adjacent Marishes and Meers, and divers other Lands.
235. All which, with other Lands from other Benefactors, King *Edgar* confirm'd to this Abby, granting also divers great Priviledges as a Sanctuary,
236. &c. The like was done by King *Edward* the Confessor, with the addition
237. of several other Liberties and Priviledges. King *Henry* the I. King *Henry*
238. the II. King *Richard*, King *John*, and King *Edward* the I. were also Royal Benefactors.

239. *Ailwinus* the Founder gave many precious Ornaments besides two hundred Hides of Land, and departed this Life on the 8*th*. of the Calends of *May*. His Epitaph was as follows,

240.   *Hic requiescit* Ailwinus, *inclyti regis* Edgari
       cognatus, totius Angliæ Aldermannus, *& hujus*
       sacri cænobii, miraculosè, fundator.

ABBOTS of *RAMSEY*.

1 *Ædnothus*, A. D.	970.	12 *Willielmus*	1161.
2 *Wufilus*	1008.	13 *Robertus Trianel*	1180.
3 *Withmannus*	1016.	14 *Eudo*	1200.
4 *Ethelstanus*	1020.	15 *Robertus de Redinges*	1202.
5 *Alfwinus*	1043.	16 *Richardus*	1214.
6 *Aielsinus*	1080.	17 *Hugo Foliot*	1216.
7 *Herbertus* made Bishop of *Norwich*	1087.	18 *Ranulfus*	1231.
		19 *Willielmus Acolt*	1253.
8 *Aldwinus*	1091.	20 *Hugo de Sulgrave*	1254.
9 *Bernardus* was Abbot for five years in the life of *Aldwinus*.		21 *Willielmus*	1267.
		22 *Johannes*	1285.
10 *Reginaldus*	1114.	23 *Simon*	1316.
11 *Walterus*	1133.	24 *Robertus*	1342.
		25 *Ricardus*	

25 Ricardus	1349.	28 Johannes Tychemarsh	1419.
26 Edmundus	1382.	29 Johannes Crowland	1434.
27 Thomas Botterwick	1400.	30 Johannes Stowe	1436.

The memorable Occurrances in the times of these several Abbots may be seen in the *Monasticon*, p. 241, 242. *Vid.* 2. *Vol.* p. 869.

[Valued at 1716 l. 12 s. 4 d. per Annum.]

THORNEY, in Cambridgeshire.

THIS Monastery was founded in the year 972. by St. *Adelwold* Bishop of *Winchester*, in the Reign of King *Edgar*. In the year 1085. the Church was new built by *Gunterius* the then Abbot here, and dedicated by *Hervey* the first Bishop of *Ely*. In the year 973. King *Edgar* granted to this Abby several Lands and Priviledges.   243.

Principal Benefactors to this House were *Nigellus* Bishop of *Ely*, *William Peverel*, several of the *Beauchamps*, *Henry de Merch*, *William de Albeneis*, *Brito*, *Thurstan de Montfort*, and *John de Stutavill*, &c. The Lands and Benefactions of whom, were recited and confirm'd to this Abby by the Bull of Pope *Alexander* dated A. D. 1162.   245. 247. 249. 250.

ABBOTS of THORNEY.   251.

A. D.		A. D.	
1085.	Gunterius.	1244.	Thomas Castre.
1113.	Robertus I.	1261.	Willielmus Yakesley.
1151.	Gilbertus.	1293.	Odo de Whitlesey.
1154.	Galterus.	1305.	Willielmus Clopton.
1158.	Herbertus.	1322.	Reginoldus de Water Newton.
1163.	Walterus.	1347.	Willielmus Haddon.
1176.	Solamon.	1365.	Johannes Depying.
1193.	Robertus II.	1396.	Nicholaus Islep.
1198.	Radulphus.	1402.	Thomas Charw.
1216.	Robertus III.	1425.	Alanus Kirketon.
1231.	Wido Wake.	1437.	Johannes Kirketon.
1237.	Ricardus.	1450.	Johannes Ramsey.
1238.	David.		

[Valued at 411 l. 12 s. 11 d. per Annum.]

CHATERIZ, in Cambridgeshire.

THE Mannor of *Chateriz* was given by King *Edgar*, to the Abbot of *Ramsey*. *Ednodus* Abbot of *Ramsey* built a Church and Monastery for Nuns at *Chateriz*, and endow'd it with necessaries; which *Ednodus* or *Ednothus* being Bishop of *Dorchester* was murdered by the *Danes*, 1016.

King *Henry* the I. gave and annext this Abby to the Church of *Ely*, and *Herveus* the first Bishop there. Pope *Innocent* the IV. confirm'd the Estate and Priviledges of this Abby to the Abbess and Sisters here, about the year 1242. *Vid.* 2. *Vol.* p. 869.   252.

[Valued at 97 l. 3 s. 4 d. q. per Annum.]

CERNE,

CERNE, in Dorsetshire.

253. Saint *Augustine* the Monk after he had converted *Kent*, travelled with his Companions over the rest of King *Ethelbert's* Dominions, which extended as far as the *Northumbers*, preaching the Gospel of Christ. And being in *Dorsetshire*; a great Company of people offer'd themselves to Baptism in a place where water was wanting, whereupon by miracle a

254. Fountain of Water burst out of the Ground, which was in the succeeding times call'd St. *Augustin's* Fountain. Here *Edwaldus* Brother of St. *Edmund* the King and Martyr, led a Hermits life, and died with the reputation of great Sanctity; which occasion'd that *Egelwaldus* or *Ethelwerdus* built here a Monastery to the honour of St. *Peter*, which his Son *Ethelmer* Earl of *Cornwall* A. D. 987. endow'd with divers Lands.

[Valued at 515 *l*. 17 *s*. 10 *d*. q. per Annum.]

St. IVES, in Huntingtonshire.

255. IN the year 1001. the Body of St. *Ivo* being found in this Town then called *Slepe*, and translated from his Grave to a Shrine, the Town ever after took name from the Saint, and *Ednothus* Abbot of *Ramsey*, built here a Church. Pope *Urban* confirm'd the Estate of this Monastery to the Prior and Monks of the same and to their Successors, granting them many great Priviledges, among others, that they should pay no Tithes of their Lands and Cattle which they should hold in their own proper hands.

256. It was found by Inquisition in the 36 *H*. 3. that the Parish Church of St. *Ives* dedicated to the honour of all Saints, is a Vicarage of the Presentation of the Abbot of *Ramsey*, that the Prior of St. *Ives* as Parson receives all Corn-Tithes, and of the Vicar for his portion 4 *l*. 13 *s*. 4 *d*. That the Vicar receives all small Tithes, obventions, Mortuaries (*Testamenta*) Plowalms, Rates and other Customs, which see in the Book at large.

WARWELL, in Hampshire.

KING *Edgar* hearing extraordinary Commendations of the beauty of *Elfrida* Daughter of *Odgar* Duke of *Devonshire*, sent Earl *Ethelwold*, to discover if the young Lady's beauty was equal to report, the Earl finding it so, disparaged her to the King, and secretly married her himself. After a while the King perceiving himself to have been treacherously deceived, took occasion one day to take the Earl aside as they were hunting in *Warewell-wood*, and there slew him. In expiation of which Deed *Elfrida*, who was after her first Husband's death married to King *Edgar*, built here a

258. Monastery for Nuns, in honour of the holy Cross. This Monastery was afterwards endowed with Lands by King *Ethelred* Son of the said *Edgar* and *Elfrid* in the year 1002. as appears by *Inspectimus* 44. *H*. 3. *Vid*. 3. *Vol*. p. 9.

[Valued at 339 *l*. 8 *s*. 7 *d*. per Annum.]

EYNESHAM, in Oxfordshire.

THIS Monastery was situated near the River *Thames,* founded and 259.
endowed by one *Ethelmarus,* a man of Quality under King *Ethelred,* who confirmed the Lands given to it, and granted divers Liberties
and Priviledges to the same; in the year of our Lord 1005.

To this House a Monastery at *Stow* near *Lincoln,* built and endow'd by 262.
Godiva Wife of *Leofrick* Earl of *Chester,* was formerly annext as a Cell. 263.

In the year 1109. King *Henry* the I. repair'd this Monastery, at that 264.
time decay'd, and confirm'd to it all its Lands and Liberties. 265.

[Valued at 44 *l.* 12 *s.* 2 *d.* ob. q. *per Annum.*]

BURTON, in Staffordshire.

WUlfricus Spot, an Officer in the Court of King *Ethelred* built this
Abby and endow'd it with all his paternal Inheritance, amounting 266.
to 700 *l.* and gave to that King three hundred *Mancas* of Gold to purchase
his Confirmation of what he had done. The Names of the several Lands
and Mannors given to this Abby may be seen, *p.* 268, 269.

King *Ethelred* granted to this Abby great Liberties in all their Lands, by 270.
his Charter dated in the year 1006. And Pope *Lucius* the III. in the 271.
year 1185. confirm'd to them all their Lands, granting also many great
Priviledges to the said Abby, as that they should pay no Tithes of what
they held in their own hands, &c.

The afore-mention'd *Wulfricus Spot,* the Founder of this Abby, was
Earl of *Mercia,* and one of the Blood Royal. Upon the Foundation, (which
was in the year 1004.) certain Monks were removed to this House from
Winchester. Wulfricus was slain in a Battle against the *Danes, A. D.* 1010.
and was buried in the Cloyster of this House.

A List of the Abbots of *Burton* upon *Trent* from the first Foundation to 272.
the Dissolution. 273.
274.
275.

1 *Wulfgetus.* ob. 1026.
2 *Britericus.* ob. 1050.
3 *Leuricus.* ob. 1085.
4 *Galfridus Malaterra* expell'd 1094.
5 *Nigellus.* ob. 1114.
6 *Galfridus* resigned 1150. to
7 *Robertus* deposed and expell'd 1159.
8 *Barnardus* ob. 1175.
9 *Robert* chosen again ob. 1177.
10 *Rogerus Malebraunch* ob. 1182.
11 *Ricardus* ob. 1188.
12 *Nicholaus.* ob. 1197.
13 *Willielmus Melburne* ob. 1210.
14 *Rogerus Normannus* ob. 1218.
15 *Nicholas de Wallingford* ob. 1222.
16 *Richardus de Insula,* removed to be Abbot of St. *Edmunds* 1229.
17 *Laurentius* ob. 1240.
18 *Johannes Stafford* ob. 1280.
19 *Thomas Pakington* ob. 1305.
20 *Johannes Pisoator* alias *Stapunhull.* ob. 1316.
21 *Willielmus de Bromley.* ob. 1329.
22 *Robertus Longdone.* ob. 1340.
23 *Robertus Brickhull.* ob. 1348.
24 *Johannes Ipstoke.* ob. 1366.
25 *Thomas Southam.* ob. 1400.
26 *Johannes Sudburie* resign'd 1424.
27 *Willielmus Mathew.* ob. 1430.
28 *Robertus Ousby* resign'd 1432.
29 *Radulphus Henley* resign'd 1454.
30 *Willielmus Bronston.* ob. 1472.
31 *Thomas Feylde.* ob. 1493.
32 *Willielmus Heigh.* ob. 1502.
33 *Willielmus Beyne* ob. 1525.
34 *Johannes Boston.*
35 *Ricardus Edes,* the last Abbot of *Burton.*

The remarkable Occurrences during the times of the said several Abbots may be seen in the Book at large. *Vid Vol. 2. p.* 869.

[Valued at 267 *l.* 14 *s.* 3 *d. per Annum.*]

ABBOTSBURY, in Dorsetshire.

276.

About the year 1026. one *Orcus* a Great man in the Court of K. *Canutus*, together with his Wife *Tola*, being both without hope or possibility of issue, built and endow'd the Monastery at *Abbotsbury*, and dedicated it to St. *Peter* the Apostle. The said *Orcus* did also give a hall to a *Guild* or Fraternity in this Town, and by agreement between him and the Brethren, certain Orders were settled for the Rule and Governance of the said Fraternity, to the glory of God, and honour of St. *Peter.* King *Edward* the Confessor, and King *William* the Conqueror ratified *Orcus* and his Wives Benefactions to the Monks here, and granted them certain Franchises. By inquisition taken before the Escheator and Sheriff of this County, in the 53 *Hen.* 3. The several Lands, Rents, and Liberties of this Abby were found and set forth; the Jury also found that the Abbot here held his Estate of the King *in Capite* by the service of one Knight's Fee only, and not, *in Baronia*, by the service of a Barony.

278.

279.

280.

In the year 1505. *Thomas Strangeways* Esq; founded a perpetual Chantry in the Chappel of the Blessed *Mary* in the Church of this Abby, and endow'd it with Rents, for the maintenance of one Mass to be said in the said Chappel daily for ever, for the Souls of his Ancestors and Friends, and for all the Faithful, subjecting it to the Visitation of the Bishop; and the Abbot did oblige himself to find a Monk (in case he should have above eight Monks, Priests, in the Monastery) to perform the Office: and this under the penalty of 3 *s.* 4 *d.* to the Bishop of the Diocess, and 3 *s.* 4 *d.* to the Heirs of the said *Strangeways*, for every omission.

281.

282.

[Valued at 390 *l.* 19 *s:* 2 *d.* ob. q. *per Annum.*]

HULME, in Suffolk.

283.

Canutus the *Danish* King of *England*, returning from *Rome*, built two Monasteries to the honour of St. *Benedict*, one in *Norwey*, and the other this in *England*. Which last he founded in a fenny place then call'd *Couholm*, where, in former-times, before the *Danes* came into *England*, one *Suneman* a Hermite did inhabit, spending his time in devotion there for above fifty years. To the Abby here built, the said King *Canutus* gave many Lands and Priviledges. All which King *Edward* the Confessor confirm'd, and granted others, *Sacne*, and *Sokne*, *Toll*, and *Theam*, &c. and all other Liberties and free Customs which he himself enjoy'd in his own Demeans, and Lands belonging to the Crown.

284.

St.

St. EDMUNDS-BURY, in Suffolk.

Saint *Edmund* the last King of the *East Angles*, being overcome by *Inguar*, and *Hubba* Pagan Danes, was cruelly bound to a Tree, whipt, and then shot to death, suffering martyrdom for the Christian Religion, in the year of our Lord 870. and the 29th. of his Age. His Head and Body were thrown into a thick Wood by the Pagans, but being afterwards found out by miracle, he was buried at a Neighbouring place call'd by the *Saxons Beodrichesworth* (now *St. Edmunsbury*) where the Christians built a small Church. But afterwards King *Canutus* (who had erected at *Rome* an English School, and assign'd for its maintenance a Sum of Money which was yearly sent from *England*, and call'd *Romescot*) by advice of his Bishops and Barons, changed the secular Clergy, belonging to this Church, to Monks, in the year 1020 and brought hither from the Abby of *Hulme* thirteen religious Benedictines, whose first Abbot here was one *Wius*. He also caused half the Books, Vestments, and Utinsils of that Abby to be removed hither. King *Edmund* the Elder in the year 942. gave Lands to this Church, and after him the foresaid King *Canutus* gave many Lands to this Monastery, and rebuilt it in a magnificent manner.

285.

286.

287.

Controversies arising in the Reign of King *William* the Conqueror, between the Abbot and the Bishop of the Diocess, the Abbot went to *Rome*, and found such favour with Pope *Alexander* the II. that he granted to him and his Successors Episcopal Jurisdiction, and this special priviledge, viz. That so long as they kept a porphery Altar, which he then gave him, tho' the whole Kingdom should fall under Excommunication, yet the Divine Office should not cease in this Abby unless specially interdicted by name. His Bull bears date *An. Dom.* 1071. In the year 1081. the Contest between the Bishop and Abbot was examined before King *William* the Conqueror, and upon hearing both sides, that King did declare the Church of St. *Edmund*, and the Town in which it stands, to be exempt from the Bishops Jurisdiction.

288.

289.

The Steward or Seneschall's Office for the Liberty of St. *Edmund*, was a place of great honour, and the Family of *Hastings* held it in Fee. They enjoy'd several great Fees and Advantages by Custom, in case they executed the Office in their own Person, but if by Deputy or Lieutenant, then the said Deputy received half. All which particulars were found by inquisition in the 30th. year of *Edward* the I.

In the year 1010. the Body of St. *Edmund* was translated to *London*, this Country being infested by the *Danes*; but after three years it was brought back again. In the year 1021. soon after King *Canutus* had introduced Monks here, *Aldwinus* Bishop of the *East Angles*, began to build a stately new Church, to which work and for the maintenance of the Fabrick, the Inhabitants of *Norfolk* and *Suffolk* did freely give yearly 4 d. out of every Carucate of Land in the Country. This Church was in the year 1032. dedicated in honour of Christ, the Blessed *Mary*, and St. *Edmund*.

291.

King *Edward* the Confessor, King *William* the I. King *Henry* the I. King *Steven*, and King *Richard*, with many Bishops, and other Persons of Quality of both Sexes gave Lands and great Revenues to this Abby.

292.
293.
294.

The Body of St. *Edmund* remain'd intire and uncorrupted, and was so seen by many witnesses.

A. B.

ABBOTS of St. EDMUNSBURY.

295.
296.

1 *Wius*, Monk of *Hulme*, ob. 1044.
2 *Leoffranus*, ob. 1065.
3 *Baldwinus*, ob. 1097.
4 *Robert*, Son of *Hugh* Earl of *Chester* depos'd 1102.
5 *Robert*, Prior of *Westminster*, ob. 1107.
6 *Alboldus*, ob. 1119.
7 *Anselmus*, Nephew of *Anselm* Archbishop of *Cant* was 1138. chosen Bishop of *London*, but not received there, ob. 1148.
8 *Ordingus*, ob. 1156.
9 *Hugh*, Prior of *Westminster*, ob. 1180.
10 *Sampson*, ob. 1211.
11 *Hugo*, chosen Abbot 1213. consecrated Bishop of *Ely* 1229. ob. 1254.
12 *Richard*, Abbot of *Burton*, ob. 1233.
13 *Henry*, ob. 1248.
14 *Edmund de Walpool*, Doctor in the Decretals, ob. 1256.
15 *Simon*, elected, 1257.
16 *John de Norwold*, ob. 1301.
17 *Thomas de Tottington*, ob. 1312.
18 *Richard de Draugton*, ob. 1337.
19 *William de Bernham*, ob. 1361.
20 *Henry de Hunstanston* died before Confirmation.
21 *Johannes de Brinkele* ob. 1379.
22 *Johannes Tynmouth*, created, 7 R.2.
33 *Willielmus de Cratfeild*, created 13 R. 2.
24 *Willielmus Exeter*. 5 H. 6.
25 *Willielmus Curteys*, 7 H. 6.
26 *Johannes Boon*, created Abbot 1457.
27 *Richardus Hengham* 1475.
28 *Thomas Raclesden*. 1478.
29 *John Reeve*, alias *Melford*, the last Abbot of *Bury* created 5 *Hen*.8.

297.

By Covenant made between the above-mentioned *John Norwood* Abbot here on the one part, and the Prior and Convent of this Monastery on the other, the Mannors, Lands, and Revenues belonging to this Abby were divided and appropriated to the several Offices of the House, as such and such Lands and Revenues to the Abbot, such to the *Celerarius*, for

298. the diffraying of his Office, such to the *Sacristan* for the Charges incumbant on him, such to the *Camerarius*, such to the *Almoner*, such to the

299. *Pitanciarius*, such to the *Infirmarius*, such to the *Hostillarius*, and such to the *Præcentor*. But all Law-Suits concerning any the Lands or Estate of the Abby the Abbot was to manage at his own proper Charges. Also the Abbot was to entertain all secular Guests as well Horse-men as Footmen, in case he was resident with his Family in Town, but the Convent was to entertain religious Persons, and in case the Abbot be absent, then the Convent to entertain also secular persons, if under thirteen Horse. This agreement between the Abbot and Convent was made in the year 1281. And exemplified by King *Edward* the I. in the same year, being the 9*th*. of his Reign.

300.
301.

The Names of the *Sacristans* of BURY:

1 *Thurstan*. ⎫ In the time of Abbot
2 *Tolimus*. ⎬ Baldwin.
3 *Godefridus*.
4 *Radulphus*.
5 *Haruēus*.
6 *Helias Widewell*.
7 *Frodo*.
8 *Willielmus Schuch*.
9 *Willielmns Wardel*.
10 *Hugo*.
11 *Walterus de Banham*.
12 *Willielmus de Disce*.

13 *Robertus*

BENEDICTINES.

13 *Robertus de Granele*, chosen Abbot of *Thorney*.
14 *Richardus de Insula*, chosen Abbot of *Burton*, and at last Abbot here 1233.
15 *Dominus de Newport*.
16 *Georgius*, first Precentor, then Sacristan, than Prior here, reputed a Saint.
17 *Nicholaus*.
18 *Simon de Luyton*, chosen Prior, and then Abbot here 1257.
19 *Richardus de Horninshe*.
20 *Richardus de Colecester*.
21 *Simon de Kingston*, first Celarer, and then Chamberlain.
22 *Willielmus de Luyton*.
23 *Richardus le Brun*.

Of the Buildings about the Church and Abby, perform'd, in the times of the Sacristans abovemention'd, see the Book at large.

To the Cellarer of this House (whose Office was to make provision for the diet of the whole Covent) did belong many Rights and Priviledges by ancient Custom. He kept the Court of the Lordship in the Town, from which he received divers annual Profits. His Officers were to be first served in the Market in buying provisions, if the Abbot were not in Town. Also the Cellarar and Abbots Officers were to have Herrings a half-penny in the hundred cheaper than any other people.

[Valued at 1659 *l*. 13 *s*. 11 *d*. ob. *per Annum*.]

COVENTRY, in 𝔚𝔞𝔯𝔴𝔦𝔠𝔨𝔰𝔥𝔦𝔯𝔢.

THIS Monastery was built by *Leofricus* Earl of *Chester*, and *Godiva* his Wife (a most pious Lady) and plentifully endow'd with Lands and Revenues. The Church was so richly adorn'd with Gold and Silver, and precious Stones, that the Walls seem'd too narrow to contain all the Treasure.

The Founder Earl. *Leofrick* died in the year 1057. and was buried at *Coventry*, as was also his Wife *Godiva*, in the Church-Porch of their own Foundation. In which Church was formerly kept an Arm of the Great St. *Augustine*, inclosed in Silver.

Robert de Limesey (who was made Bishop of *Chester*, A.D. 1088. and died 1116.) obtain'd of King *Henry* the I. The Monastery of *Coventry*, and constituted it the Capital Cathedral of that Diocess. Whose Successor in that See, *Hugh* Bishop of *Coventry*, A.D. 1191. expell'd the Monks out of the Cathedral Church here, and placed in their room, secular Canons. But in the year 1198. *Hubert* Archbishop of *Canterbury*, by order of Pope *Celestine*, restored the Monks to the possession of their Church again.

It appears by Earl *Leofrick*'s Charter of Foundation that he built this Church and Monastery to the honour of God and St. *Mary* his Mother, St. *Peter* the Apostle, St. *Osburga* the Virgin, and all Saints. And gave to the Maintenance of the Monks here serving God, twenty four Villages, with the Moiety of the Town of *Coventry* in which it stands, with all Liberties and Customs which he himself enjoy'd in the said Estate, and that the Abbot of the said House should be subject to none but the King. All which grants King *Edward* the Confessor did confirm to *Leofwinus* the first Abbot there and his Successors. Also Pope *Alexander* by his Bull directed to the said King *Edward* bearing date 1043. confirm'd all their Liberties and Exemptions, granting them full power to chose their own

own Abbots or Deans, without any Lett or Hindrance from the Apostolick Authority.

305. *Leofwinus*, the first Abbot of *Coventry*, being created Bishop of *Chester*, ordain'd with the Consent of the Monks, that his Successors, Superiors of that Monastery should be call'd Priors and not Abbots.

PEYKIRK, in Northamptonshire.

IN the year 1048. one *Wulgatus* then Abbot of a Monastery in this Town, lost his Abby and the Lands thereunto belonging, to the Abbot of *Peterborough*, who claim'd the same as parcel of his Estate. And this was by Judgment given in the Court of King *Hardi Canute*.

SPALDING, in Lincolnshire, a Cell of Croyland, &c.

ANno Dom. 1052. *Thoroldus de Bukenhale* Brother to *Godiva* Countess of *Leicester*, having obtain'd six Monks from *Wulgate* Abbot of *Croyland*, began the Priory of *Spalding*, assigning to it divers Lands, and annext it as a Cell to *Croyland*.

In the year 1074. *Iuo Taylboys* Earl of *Anjou* (*Andegavia*) having married *Lucia* Great Grand-daughter of the foresaid *Godiva* became Lord of *Spalding* and all *Holland*; and gave the Cell of *Spalding* to a Monk of St. *Nicholas* of *Anjou*. He also confirm'd the Estate which his Great Uncle *Thorold* had given to this House, and procured the like Confirmation from the 2 *Williams* and *Hen.* 1*st.* Kings of *England*. In the year
307. 1085. *Iuo Taylboys*, by License of King *William* the Conqueror, gave this Cell to the Abby of St. *Nicholas* of *Anjou*, with the Lands and Estate thereunto belonging. All which, with divers Liberties, was confirm'd to the
308. said Abby of St. *Nicholas* by King *William* the I. *William* the II. and *Henry*
309. the I. And also by King *John* in the first year of his Reign.

See more, *Vol.* 2. *p.* 871.

[Valued at 767 l. 8 s. 11 d. per Annum.]

BATTEL Abby, in Sussex.

310. IN the year 1067. King *William* the Conqueror built this Abby in the same place where he fought and overcame *Harold* and his Army, that herein perpetual praise and thanks might be given to God for the said Victory and Prayers made for the Souls of those who were here slain. It was dedicated to St. *Martin*, and largely endow'd with Lands and Priviledges.
312. In this Battle, it is said, that above ten thousand men lost their lives, on the conquering side; but what number of the conquered may be guest with astonishment.
314. King *William* design'd to have endow'd this Abby with Lands sufficient for the constant maintenance of sevenscore Monks, but death prevented. However he granted to it, to be free from the Bishops Jurisdiction, to have Sanctuary, to have Treasure troue, with many other Royal Liberties and Exemptions. He translated from an Abby in *Normandy* called *Major-Monasterium*, several Monks, among whom one *Gausbertus*, who he appointed the first
Abbot

Abbot of *Battail*. And gave to this Abby the Mannor of *Wi* in *Kent*, with other Mannors in *Suffex*, *Surry*, *Effex*, *Barkfhire*, *Oxfordfhire*, and *Devonfhire*, with free Warren in all their Lands. 315. 317.

Yet King *William* gave this caution or reftriction to the Abbot, that he fhould not waft the Alms belonging to this Abby upon his fecular kindred or others, but take care to beftow them upon poor People and Travellers, &c. 318.

King *William Rufus*, and King *Henry* the I. were alfo Benefactors to this Houfe.

[Valued at 880 *l*. 14 *s*. 7 *d*. ob. q. *per Annum*.]

BRECKNOCK, *in* Wales, *a Cell to* Battel *Abby*. 319.

BErnard de Newmarch was a Noble *Norman* in the Reign of King *Henry* the I. and was the firft Conqueror of the Lands about *Brecknock*. He gave to *Battel* Abby his Church of St. *John* the Evangelift in his Caftle of *Brecknock*. *Roger* Earl of *Hereford*, Grandfon of the forefaid *Bernard* gave divers Lands and Tithes to the Monks in the Church of St. *John* of *Brecknock*, together with divers Liberties and Exemptions. All which was afterwards confirm'd by *Maikel de Hereford*, and *William de Brainfe*. Other Benefactors were *Herbert Fitz Peter*, *John Fitz Reginald*, &c. 320. 321. 322. 323.

[Valued at 1,12 *l*. 14 *s*. 2 *d*. *per Annum*.]

ARMETHWAYT, *in* Cumberland. 324.

KING *William* the Conqueror founded here a Monaftery for black Nuns; and endow'd it with divers Lands, and fuch Priviledges as were granted to the Church of *Weftminfter*. This he granted in pure and perpetual Alms as freely as here may it think or may it fe.

This Nunnery being feated fo very near the Borders of *Scotland*, was fo impoverifht by the *Scots* frequent Spoils and Inroads, that it was in a manner reduced to nothing; whereupon King *Edward* the IV. did in the thirteenth year of his Reign, new grant, ratifie, and confirm their Lands and Eftate unto the then Priorefs and Nuns here. 325.

[Valued at 18 *l*. 18 *s*. 8 *d*. *per Annum*.]

BEAULEIU (*Bellus Locus*) *in* Bedfordfhire, *a Cell of* St. Albans.

THE Church of St. *Mary* in this place, of old call'd *Moddry*, was at firft a Hermitage and built by a Hermite called *Radulfus*. It was afterwards given by *Robert de Albeneio*, with the confent of his Mother *Secilia*, to the Abby of St. *Albans*, and became a Cell of that Houfe. Which *Robert* endow'd it with divers Lands, all which he gave to God, and St. *Alban*, and to the Monks of *Beauleiu*, in Fee, to hold in free Alms. 326.

F WAL-

WALLINGFORD, in Barkshire, a Cell of St. Albans.

327. THE Church here, dedicated to the holy Trinity, was made a Cell of St. *Albans*, in the time of *Paul* Abbot there. King *Henry* the VI. was a Benefactor to the Priory of *Wallingford*. *Vid. Vol.* 3. *p.* 11.

BELVOIR or Beaver, in Lincolnshire, a Cell of St. Albans.

Robertus de Toteneio Lord of the Castle of *Belvoir*, gave the Church of St. *Mary*, adjoyning to his said Castle, to the Abby of St. *Albans* to be a Cell of that House, endowing it with divers Lands and Tithes; appointing it for the Burial-place of himself and Wife, in case they died in

328. *England*, and such it afterwards proved to be for his descendents.
329. The Lands hereunto given were confirm'd successively by the Heirs and Progeny of the said *Robert*, and lastly by *Thomas* Lord *Ros*, in the 8. *Hen.* 6.

[Valued at 104 *l.* 19 *s.* 10 *d. per Annum.*]

330. HATFEILD-PEVERELL, in Hertfordshire, a Cell of St. Albans

William Peverell gave the Church of St. *Mary* at *Hatfeild* with his own Mansion-House there, for a Habitation of Monks, and endow'd the same with Lands; all which was afterwards annext to St. *Albans*, and became a Cell of that House.

[Valued at 60 *l.* 14 *s.* 11 *d.* ob. *per Annum.*]

331. HERTFORD, a Cell of St. Albans.

Radulfus de Limesey, having erected a Church at *Hertford*, he gave the same for a Cell to the Abby of St. *Albans*, and with it divers Lands in *Hertford* and elsewhere. The Abbot of St. *Albans* obliging himself to send thither six Monks of his House to serve God at *Hertford*, and in case the Revenue should be augmented then to send a greater number.

332. *Hadwisa*, Wife of the said *Radulfus*, *Alan de Limesey* their Son, *Gerard* his Son, and *John de Limesey* his Son, were all Benefactors to this Church of St. *Mary*'s at *Hertford*, and to the Monks of St. *Albans* serving God herein.

[Valued at 72 *l.* 14 *s.* 2 *d.* ob. *per Annum.*]

333. TINEMOUTH, in Northumberland, a Cell of St. Albans.

334. *Robert de Mulbray* a *Norman* of noble extraction, to whom King *William* the Conqueror gave the Earldom of *Northumberland*, endow'd the Church of St. *Mary*, adjoyning to his Castle of *Tinemouth*, and in which the Body of St. *Oswin* King and Martyr rested, with fair Revenues,
335. and gave it for a Cell to the Monks of St. *Albans*. *David* King of *Scotland* was

was a Benefactor to this House; so were King *Henry* the I. of *England*, King *Henry* the II. and King *John*, who granted to God and the Church of St. *Oswin* in *Tinmouth*, and the Monks of St. *Albans* serving God here, many Lands, and great Liberties, which Liberties tho' seiz'd by King *Edward* the III. yet were by him in the second year of his Reign regranted to them in as large a manner as ever, out of the special Devotion which he bore to the two glorious Martyrs St. *Alban* and St. *Oswin*. 336.

[Valued at 397 *l*. 10 *s*. 5 *d*. ob. per *Annum*.]

WYMUNDHAM, in Norfolk, a Cell of St. Albans. 337.

*A*Nno Dom. 1139. *William de Albaneio* Butler to King *Henry* the I. built the Church of St. *Mary* and Priory of Monks at this Town, endow'd the same with Revenues, and annext it as a Cell to St. *Albans*; yet so as they might chuse a Prior among themselves and present him to their Founder, whom he was not to refuse without good Cause. And the Monks here paid only a Mark of Silver yearly to the Abbot of St. *Albans* as an acknowledgment of subjection. 338.

King *Henry* the I. confirm'd the Estate given to this House with the grant of many great Liberties. The like did also *William* Earl of *Sussex*, Grandson of the foresaid *William* the Founder. 339.

Afterwards in the 27*th*. of King *Henry* the VI. by Authority of Pope *Nicholas* the V. and at the Petition of Sir *Andrew Ogard* Kt. then Patron of this Monastery, it was discharged from any dependency on the Abby of St. *Albans*, and from paying the Mark per *Annum*, and made an Abby of it self, and *Steven London* then Prior, the first Abbot. All which was allow'd and confirm'd by the said King *Henry* the VI. who at the same time pardon'd all penalties incurr'd by the Parties concern'd in procuring the Popes Bull, by reason of the Statute of *Provisors*, or any other Statute. 340. 341. 342.

[Valued at 211 *l*. 16 *s*. 6 *d*. q. per *Annum*.]

BINHAM, in Norfolk, a Cell of St. Albans. 343.

*P*Eter de *Valoniis* and *Albreda* his Wife gave the Church of St. *Mary* at *Binham* to the Abby of St. *Albans*, but to be subject only in such manner as St. *Pancrace* at *Lewis* is subject to St. *Peter* of *Clugni*, paying yearly to the Church of St. *Alban* a Mark of Silver and no more. *Roger de Valoniis* confirm'd to God, and St. *Mary*, and the Monks of St. *Albans* serving God at *Binham*, all the Lands which his Father *Peter* had given them, and gave to them besides several other Lands and Tithes. The like was done by others of that Family, and *John* Bishop of *Norwich*. 344. 345. 346.

St. MARY de PRATO, near St. Albans. 347.

*T*HIS was a small Nunnery given, with certain Lands, by *Garinus* Abbot of St. *Albans*, for the maintenance of Leprous Nuns. Confirm'd by King *John*, in the fifth year of his Reign.

F 2 SOPE.

SOPEWELL, in Hertfordshire, a Cell of St. Albans.

About the year 1140. two religious Women led a solitary life in a small Habitation made of Boughs of Trees, near a Wood called *Eiwoda*, who being taken notice of for their austerities and pious Lives, *Gaufridus* the sixteenth Abbot of St. *Albans*, built there for them a Cell, gave them the Vail of Nuns, and constituted their way of living according to the Rule of St. *Benedict*. He also endow'd the House with Possessions and Rents, and assigned them a Coemitery, in which none were to be buried but the Virgins of the House, whose number was not to exceed thirteen.

348. *Henry de Albaneio* and *Cecilia* his Wife, and several of their Descendants, were great Benefactors to this Cell of St. *Mary* of *Sopewell*; and so was *Richard de Tany*.

349. *Michael* Abbot of St. *Albans*, made and publisht here in his Visitation, Anno Dom. 1338. certain good Rules and Orders to be observed by the Nuns of this House: among others, that the Door that goes into the Garden, and that of the Parlour, should not be open'd till the Bell sounds to the *ninth hour*, and that all the year they should be shut up at night when the Abby-Bell sounds the *Coverfeu*, &c.

[Valued at 40 l. 7 s. 10 d. per Annum.]

350. MERGATE, in Bedfordshire, a Cell of St. Albans.

In the time of *Gaufridus* Abbot of St. *Albans*, one *Roger* a Monk of that Abby, became a Hermite in a Hermitage between St. *Albans* and *Dunstable*, where he lived in a most austere manner, with the reputation of great Sanctity; at the same time *Christina* a Virgin renouncing the World became an Anchoress at the same place, yet the said *Roger* never 351. saw her face, tho' they lived together four years. *Roger* died and was buried in the Abby-Church of St. *Albans*; but *Christina* surviving, became of so great note for her Sanctity, that the abovesaid *Gaufridus*, built here from the Foundation a Monastery for Nuns, and endow'd the same with Revenues, of which House *Christina* became the first Prioress. Vid. Vol. 2. p. 872.

352. St. NICHOLAS, Priory, at Exeter, a Cell of Battel-Abby.

This Church formerly dedicated to St. *Olive* King and Martyr, was by King *William Rufus* given to the Monks of *Battel-Abby*, for a Cell; and by them new dedicated to St. *Nicholas*. King *William Rufus*, King *Henry* the I. and King *John*, conferr'd many Lands and Liberties upon this House.

[Valued at 147 l. 12 s. per Annum.]

MAL-

MALLINGE, in Kent.

KING *Edmund* gave certain *Lands* in *Mallinges* to the Monaftery of St. *Andrew* the Apoftle, which afterwards was by *Gundulfus* Bifhop of *Rocheſter*, converted to an Abby of Nuns here, dedicated to St. *Mary*; to which King *Henry* the I. and King *John*, and *Anſelme* Archbifhop of *Canterbury*, were alfo Benefactors.

353.

[Valued at 218*l*. 4*s*. 2*d*. ob. *per Annum*.]

TUTBURY, in Staffordſhire.

354.

Henry *de Ferariis* built the Church and Monaftery, to the honour of the bleſſed Virgin, at his Caftle of *Tutbury*, which by the Grant and Licenſe of King *William Rufus*, he endow'd with divers Lands and Tithes. Earl *Robert de Ferariis* the younger, Grandſon of the Founder, was a great Benefactor, and ſo were many others whoſe names, with the parcells by them given, may be ſeen in the *Monaſticon* at large.

355.

John Duke of *Lancaſter*, being Lord of the Honour and Caftle of *Tutbury*, granted his Letters Pattents to the King of the Minſtalls in *Tutbury*, impowring him and his Succeſſors, to arreft all Minſtralls within the ſaid Honour and Franchiſe who refuſe to do their ſervice of minſtralſie on the Feaſt of the aſſumption of our Lady yearly, and conftrain them to it, according to Cuſtom. Dated in the 4 *Rich*. 2.

There is alfo another Cuſtom of the Place, that the Stage-players who come to Matins on the Feaſt of the Aſſumption, ſhould have from the Prior of *Tutbury* a Bull in caſe they can catch him before he gets over the River there, or elſe the Prior is to give them 40 *d*. in mony. *Vid. Vol*. 2. p. 873.

EYE, in Suffolk.

356.

Robert *Malet*, to whom King *William* the Conqueror had given the honour of *Eye*, with the aſſent of that King, built a Monaftery there, and to it gave the Church dedicated to St. *Peter*, in *Eye*, with a great quanity of Lands and Churches, with Liberties and Franchiſes, to hold as freely as King *William* gave them to him. In the year 1138. King *Stèven* confirm'd to the Monks here, all their Lands and Liberties, with a formal Curſe to the Violators. The like Confirmation from *William* Earl of *Boloign* that King's eldeſt Son. This Houſe was a Cell to the Abby of *Bernay* in *Normandy*, ſo that neither the Prior nor any Monk could be placed here without the aſſent of the Abbot of *Bernay*; neither upon the death of the Prior here, could the Founder, or his Heirs or Succeſſors, Patrons of this Priory, meddle with, or receive any profit from the Goods and Poſſeſſions of this Houſe during the vacancy; but only, in ſign of Dominion, he uſed to place a Porter at the Gate of the Priory, who during the Vacation was maintain'd out of the Revenues of the Houſe, and at the Inſtalment of the next Prior uſed to receive for his Fee the Sum of 5 *s*. for an Ox.

357.

358.

359. In the 8*th*. year of King *Richard* the II. the Estate of this Priory being then seiz'd into the King's hands because of his Wars with *France*, the Prior and Covent complain'd that they were extreamly impoverished by Foreign Exactions, so that the Revenues of this House could hardly maintain the Prior and three or four Monks; that King therefore by his Letters Patents, at their Petition and Request, discharged them for ever of their Foreign Subjection to the Abby of *Bernay*, and made them a Prior and Covent of themselves independent, like other *English* Priories.

[Valued at 161 *l*. 2 *s*. 3 *d*. q. *per Annum*.]

HELENSTOW, *in* Berkshire.

360. *Judith* Countess of *Huntington*, Wife of Earl *Waltheof*, built a Church and Monastery here for Nuns; and dedicated it to the holy Trinity, St. *Mary*, and St. *Helen*. She and others endow'd it with divers Lands; all which were afterwards confirm'd to the Nuns here by King *Henry* the II. together with large Priviledges and Exemptions.

PENWORTHAM, *in* Lancashire, *a Cell of* Evesham.

361. *Warinus Bussell*, and *Richard Bussell* his Son, gave the Church at *Penwortham*; and with it divers Lands, to the Abby of *Evesham*, for a Cell of that Abby. All which was confirm'd to God, and St. *Mary*, and to the Monks serving God in *Penvercham*, by *Hugh Buissell*, Grandson of the foresaid *Warinus*, in pure and perpetual Alms. This was in the Reign of King *William* the Conqueror.

[Valued at 29 *l*. 18 *s*. 7 *d*. *per Annum*.]

KILBURN, *in* Middlesex, *a Cell of* Westm.

362. IN the Reign of King *Henry* the I. *Herebertus* Abbot of *Westminster*, *Osbert de Clara*, Prior, and the whole Convent of *Westminster*, gave a Hermitage at *Kilburn* to three Maids *Emma*, *Gunilda*, and *Christina*, for a Nunnery; and endow'd the same with Lands and Rents. *Gilbert* Bishop of *London* gave the Jurisdiction of this Cell of *Kilburn* to the said Abbot and his Successors, exempting it from the Jurisdiction of the Bishop of *London* for ever. But new Contests arising about this House between the Bishop of *London* and Abbot of *Westminster*, they came to an Agreement in the year 1231. That the Bishop might visit the Nunnery to preach to them, and to hear their Confessions, but without exacting any Procurations; and that the Government of the House placing, and displacing

363. the Abbess and Nuns, should belong to the Abbot, as a Cell of his House, &c.

[Valued at 74 *l*. 7 *s*. 11 *d*. *per Annum*.]

HURLEY, in Barkshire, a Cell of Westminster.

GOdefridus de Magnavilla gave to God, and St. Peter, and to the Church of Westminster, and St. Mary of Hurley, the Town of Hurley, with divers other Lands and Tithes, for the Maintenance of a Convent of Monks to serve God in the said Church for ever. All which was confirm'd to the Priors and Monks of Hurley by William Bishop of London. In the year 1258. Godefridus Prior of Hurley and his Covent made an exchange, with Absolon Abbot of Walden, of some of their Revenues.

364.
365.

[Valued at 121 l. 18 s. 5 d. per Annum.]

MALVERNE, in Worcestershire, a Cell of Westminster.

IN the eighteenth year of William the Conqueror, one Aldwine a Hermit and his Brethren began the Monastery here.
King William the Conqueror and others gave Lands and Revenues to this House, but more especially King Henry the first who by his Charter dated in the year 1127. granted and confirm'd to them many Lands and great Liberties and Immunities. Vid. Vol. 2. p. 876.

366.
367.

[Valued at 98 l. 10 s. 9 d. ob. per Annum.]

AUCOT, in Warwickshire, a Cell of Malverne-magna.

WIlliam Burdet gave all his Land in Aucot to God and St. Mary of Malverne and to the Monks there, in the year 1159. From among which Monks he was to have, by agreement betwixt him and Roger, Prior of that House, a certain number for the Institution of a Monastery here. The Prior of which House was to be constituted by the Prior of Malverne, by and with the advice of the Abbot of Westminster.

[Valued at 28 l. 6 s. 2 d. per Annum.]

SUDBURY, in Suffolk, a Cell of Westminster.

KING Edward the III. in the thirty fifth year of his Reign, granted his License to Richard Roke of Westminster, to settle certain Land in Sudbury and Holgate upon the Abbot and Convent of Westminster, or the relief of their poor Cell of St. Bartholomew near Sudbury.

368.

St. NEOTS, in Huntingtonshire.

SAint Neot was Son of King Adulphus, and Brother of King Aluted, who founded the University of Oxford. He was a Monk at Neotestoke, in Cornwall, and from thence his Body was translated to Anulphesbury, in Huntingtonshire, where Earl Elfrid converted his Palace into a Monastery of black Monks. Which being afterwards spoild and burnt down by the
Danes,

369. Danes, was in the Reign of King *Henry* the I. *An. Dom.* 1113. re-edified by *Rohesia* Wife of *Richard* Son of Earl *Giflibert*; about which time it was given as a Cell to the Abby of *Bec* in *Normandy*. The forefaid Lady and divers others gave Lands and Revenues to the Monks of *Bec* ferving God at St. *Neots*. It appears by the Bull of Pope *Celestine*, directed to the Bifhop of *Lincoln*, that the Prior and Convent of St. *Neots*, being their House was fituated on a famous and great Road, did ufe to beftow meat

370. and drink on all Travellers who defired it, and to this only ufe they did appropriate certain Rents and Penfions which they received yearly from the Churches of *Eynesbury* and *Torney*.

In the Reigns of *Henry* the IV. and *Henry* the V. This Monaftery was discharg'd of its Foreign Subjection to the Abby of *Bec*, and made an *English* Priory. *Vid. Vol. 2. p. 876.*

[Valued at 241 *l*. 11 *s*. 4 *d*. q. per *Annum*.]

SELBY, in **Yorkshire**.

371. **K**ING *William* the Conqueror founded the Abby here for *Benedictine* Monks, in honour of our Lord *Jesus Christ*, and his bleffed Mother the Virgin *Mary*, and St. *Germain* the Bifhop. Which King, and feveral other perfons, did endow it with large Poffeffions, in particular *Guido de Raincourt* gave to this Church of St. *Germain* in *Selby* his Town of *Stamford* in *Northamptonfhire*. *Thomas* Archbifhop of *York*, *Gilbert*

372. *Tifon* chief Standard-bearer of *England*, *Gaulerannus* Earl of *Mellent*, *Henry*
373. *de Lacy* Earl of *Lincoln* and Conftable of *Chefter*, &c. gave other Lands
374. and great Liberties. All which King *Richard* the I. in the firft year of his Reign, confirm'd to the Monks here. Alfo King *Edward* the III. did in the fecond year of his Reign, confirm to them all their Liberties and Exemptions, whereupon in the twenty fecond of that King, they were

375. excufed from paying to the King, in any of their Lands purchafed before the abovefaid fecond year, any aid for knighting his eldeft Son, &c.

[Vaued at 729 *l*. 12 *s*. 10 *d*. q. per *Annum*.]

SHREWSBURY, in **Shropshire**.

376. **I**N the year 1083. *Roger* Earl of *Montgomery* built here a Monaftery in honour of St. *Peter*. To this Houfe he gave great Poffeffions, and after his Example other Barons and Knights of that County did the like.

377. After the death of the faid *Roger*, *Hugh* his Son and Heir gave other Lands and great Liberties and Immunities, with a heavy Curfe to the Violaters. The like did King *Henry* the I. and King *Steven*, confirming

378. their faid Liberties in fo large a manner that nothing could be added to them. Other principal Benefactors were *Matilda de Lungefpe* Daughter and

380. Heir of *Walter de Clifford*, *Walchelinus Maminot*, *Willielmus Peverell*, and
381. *Richard Fitz-Allen* Earl of *Arundel*, &c. All whofe Guifts and Benefacti-
382. ons were confirm'd to the Abbot and Monks of this Houfe by King *Henry* the III. in the eleventh year of his Reign.

[Valued at 132 *l*. 4 *s*. 10 *d*. per *Annum*.]

St.

St. MARY's, at York.

THE History of the Foundation of this Abby was writ by *Stephen* who had been Abbot of *Whitby*, and was after that made the first Abbot of this House. In which the most observable matters are as follows,

Alan Son of *Eudo* Earl of *Brittain*, having built a Church adjoyning to the City of *York* in honour of St. *Olave*, gave it to the foresaid *Stephen* and his Companions, with four Acres of Land, thereon to erect a Monastery. This was about the year 1088. in the Reign of King *William* the Conqueror. Who dying, his Son and Successor King *William Rufus*, gave them Land whereon to build a larger Church, and gave to the Monastery, divers Lands, Liberties, and Exemptions. Also Earl *Alan* their first Founder gave them the adjoynig Suburbs lying without the City of *York*, to hold freely for ever. And gave the Advowson of this Abby to the King, that so he might be the Defendor and Patron of it for the future. *Thomas* Archbishop of *York* claim'd the four Acres of Land on which this Abby was built as belonging to him, and was a continual vexation to the Monks, till King *William Rufus* gave him the Church of St. *Steven's* in *York*, in exchange and full satisfaction.

When King *William Rufus*, seeing the Old Church to be too strait, laid the Foundation of a new one, he changed the name of St. *Olave*, and gave it the name of St. *Mary*.

King *Henry* the II. granted to this Abby very great Liberties and Franchises, the same as are enjoy'd by St. *Peters* of *York*, and St. *John* of *Beverley*. And confirmed to them all their Lands and Revenues given them by their several Benefactors amounting to a very great number, some of the principal of whom were King *William* the I. and II. King *Henry* the I. *Alan* Earl of *Britaign*, *Odo* Earl of *Campania*, *Berengerius de Todenei*, *Willielmus Peverel*, *Petrus de Ros*, *Robertus de Brus*, *Ivo Tallebois*, *Walterus de Daincourt*, and *Conan* Earl of *Britaigne*, &c.

In the year 1343. *William* Archbishop of *York* in his Visitation, questioning by what Right and Title the Abbot and Covent here, did claim and receive the Tithes, Portions, and Pensions, from several places there mention'd (amounting to a very great number) they produced the Bulls of several Popes, and Grants of his Predecessors, Archbishops of *York*, whereupon they were by the said Archbishop allow'd, and their Title declared good and sufficient.

A List of some of the ABBOTS of St. *Mary's* at *York*.

1088	*Stephanus Wittebiensis.*	1239	*Willielmus Rondele.*
1112	*Richardus.*	1244	*Thomas de Warterhill.*
1131	*Godfridus.*	1258	*Simon de Warwick.*
1132	*Sauaricus.*	1296	*Benedictus de Malton.*
1161	*Clemens.*	1303	*Johannes de Gillyngs.*
1184	*Robertus de Harpham.*	1313	*Alanus de Nesse.*
1189	*Robertus de Longo-Campo.*		

Vid. Vol. 3. *p.* 9.

[Valued at 1550 *l*. 7 *s*. 0 *d*. q. *per Annum*]

395. *St.* BEES, *or St.* Beges, *in* **Cumberland**, *a Cell of St.* Mary's, *at* **York**.

Saint *Bega* was a vailed Nun, born in *Ireland*, she built a small Monastery in *Caupland* in the furthermost parts of *England*, not far from *Carlile*. This Monastery, together with several Lands and Tithes, was afterwards in the Reign of King *Henry* the I. given to the Abby of St. *Mary*'s at *York*, by *William Meschines*, Son of *Ranulph*, Lord of *Caupland*, for a Cell to that Abby; which was to send hither a Prior, and at least six Monks to be constantly here resident. To this House, also *William*

396. *Forz* Earl of *Albemarl* was a Benefactor.

[Valued at 143 *l.* 17 *s.* 2 *d.* ob. *per Annum.*]

397. WETHERHAL, *in* **Cumberland**; *a Cell to St.* Mary's *at* **York**.

At the time of the Foundation of St. *Mary*'s at *York*, *Radulph Meschines* Earl of *Cumberland*, gave the Cell of St. *Constantine* at *Wedderhal*, to the said Abby of St. *Mary*'s; which guift was confirm'd by King *William* the Conqueror in the last year of his Reign: (Or rather by King *William*

398. *Rufus* in the first of his.)

Benefactors to this House were *David* King of *Scotland* and Earl of *Huntington*, and his Son *Henry* Prince of *Scotland*, with divers o-

399. thers.

Adelwald, (or *Athelwulph*, who was the first) Bishop of *Carlile*, confirm'd to the Monks of St. *Mary*'s at *York* the Churches, and Tithes to them given, in his Diocess. Providing however that the said Monks shall allot a sufficient proportion out of the same for the Priests in the several Churches, and that they should also pay the Synodals.

400. King *William* the Conqueror, upon his Conquest of this Kingdom, gave to *Ralph de Meschines* the County of *Cumberland*, to his Brother *Hugh de Meschines*, the County of *Chester*, and to a third Brother *William de Meschines* (who founded this House at *Wetherhal*) all the Land of *Copland*, lying between *Duden* and *Darwent*. Which Great men soon after subdivided, and parcell'd out their respective Territories so given, to certain Barons and Knights their Dependents, *viz. Ralph de Meschines* enfeoft *Hubert de Vaux* of the Barony of *Gillesland*, &c. *William de Meschines* Lord of *Copland*, enfeofft *Waldeuus* Son of *Cospatrick* of all his Land between *Cocar* and *Derwent*, &c. These chief Lords reserving from their Feoffees certain services, in like manner as they themselves held their Estates by some services of the King. (Yet were Lands often granted to the Monasteries, to hold free from all services whatsoever, except the Divine Service of Prayers for their Founders, &c.)

And note, *That after this manner were Lands and Liberties first derived from the Crown, and Tenures raised in relation to them, since the* Norman *Conquest.*

[Valued at 117 *l.* 11 *s.* 10 *d.* ob. q. *per Annum:*

St. MARTINS, at Richmund, a Cell to St. Mary's at York.

WYmar, Sewer to the Earl of *Richmund*, gave the Chappel of St. Martins at *Richmund*, and with several Lands, to God and the blessed *Mary* at *York*.

Roaldus Grandson of *Alan* Constable of *Richmund*, and divers others were Benefactors, and gave Lands and Tithes to God, the Church of St. *Mary* at *York*, and Priory of St. *Martins* near *Richmund*, and to the Monks there.

In the year 1146. Pope *Eugenius* the III. confirmed the Cell of St. *Martins*.

Peter Capell, Rector of the Church of *Richmund* granted a Pension of 5 l. per Annum to the Monks of St. *Mary*'s at *York*, and 20 l. of *Wax* to their Cell of St. *Martins* of *Richmund*, yearly.

The several Rents and Revenues of this House; where, and from whom they arise, may be seen in the Book at large, *p.* 402, 403.

[Valued at 43 *l*. 16 *s*. 8 *d*. per Annum.]

ROMBURGH, in Cambridgeshire, a Cell to St. Mary's at York.

A *Lan* (otherwise, as I suppose, called *Steven*) Earl of *Britany* and *Richmond*, gave the Cell of *Romburgh* to God, St. *Mary*, and the Monks of the Abby at *York*; which Gift was confirm'd to them by *Everard* Bishop of *Norwich*, and that the Abbot and Convent of St. *Mary*'s at *York*, might place and displace the Prior and Monks at their pleasure. The like Confirmations were granted by *Theobald* Archbishop of *Canterbury*, and *Gaufridus* Bishop of *Ely*.

SANTOFT and HENES, in Lincolnshire, Cells of St. Mary's at York.

Roger *Moubray* gave the Isle called *Santoft*, and large Possessions with it, for a Cell to the Church of St. *Mary*'s at *York*, and to the Monks there. And *William* Earl of *Waren* gave *Henes* to the said Church.

HEREFORD Priory, a Cell of St. Peter's at Gloucester.

IN the year 1101. *Hugo de Lacy* gave the Church of St. *Peters* at *Hereford*, which his Father *Walter* had built from the Foundation, to the Monks of St. *Peters* at *Gloucester*, with all the Estate belonging to it, given by his said Father *Walter de Lacy*, and Confirm'd by King *William* the Conqueror.

In the Reign of King *Edward* the II. great Contests arising in this House between *William de Irby* who claim'd to be Prior, under the Kings Patronage, and *Thomas de Burghull* who claim'd under another Title: the Estate of the Priory was so wasted and impoverisht betwixt them that there did not remain sufficient to discharge the Works of Piety, for which it was at first built, and the House running to utter ruin; that King therefore,

fore, to prevent its final destruction, in the fifteenth year of his Reign, directed his Writ to the Sheriff of *Hereford*, commanding him to seize the said Priory with all its Possessions as well moveable as immoveable into his hand, and them safely to keep until further Order.

NORWICH, in Norfolk.

407.

THE Church of the holy Trinity in *Norwich* was founded in the Reign of King *William Rufus*, *An. Dom.* 1096. by *Herbert Losenge*, who had been Prior of *Fischampe* in *Normandy*, then Abbot of *Ramsey*, and then Bishop of the *East-Angles*, of which Diocess he fixt the Seat at *Norwich*, and built this Church for his Cathedral; erecting on the *North*-side of it his own Palace, and on the *South*-side a Monastery for Monks.

408. Certain Limits were appointed about this Church and Monastery, within which, Bishop *Herbert* obtain'd great Priviledges and Franchise from both Regal and Papal Authority. Notwithstanding which, great Contests arose between the Citizens and the Monks about their Liberties, which continued for many years, and were never perfectly compos'd till the sixth

409. year of King *John*. The said Bishop *Herbert* endow'd this Monastery,
410. so founded by him, with large Revenues, as appears by his Deed dated
411. *An. Dom.* 1101. King *Henry* the I. confirm'd his Gift, and also gave them
412. other Lands in the same year. King *Henry* the II. also made a large Confirmation of all their Lands and Liberties.

Vid. infra p. 1003. and *Vol.* 3. *p.* 5.

EWYAS Priory, in Herefordshire.

413.

THIS Priory was founded and endow'd by *Harald* Lord of *Ewyas*, *An. Dom.* 1100. whose Gift was afterwards confirm'd by *Robert* his Son, who also gave other Lands; all which was also confirm'd by *Theobald* Archbishop of *Canterbury*, and *John* Bishop of *Salsbury*.

MIDLESBURG, in Yorkshire, a Cell to Whitby.

ROBERT *de Brus* and *Agnes* his Wife, and *Adam de Brus* their Son gave the Church of St. *Hylda* in *Midlesburg*, and with it divers Lands, in perpetual Alms to the Monks of St. *Peter* and St. *Hilda* at *Whitby*, for a Cell of that House, and that certain of those Monks might live and reside here for God's service in the Church of *Midlesburg*. *William Malebiss* was also a Benefactor to the Church of St. *Hylda* at *Midlesburg* and the Monks there.

MAKENES,

HAKENES, in Yorkshire.

IN the Reign of King *William Rufus*, the Monastery of *Whitby* being much infested not only by robbers from the Woods on the Land, but also by Pirates from the Sea, who carried from them almost all they had, *Serlo de Percy* then Prior of that House, and his Monks, applied themselves to *William de Percy*, Brother of *Serlo*, and desired of him a place of Refuge at *Hakenes*; who readily granted them the Church of St. *Mary* in that Town, which had been built by St. *Hilda* the Abbess, with License to erect a Monastery there, and in it to remain till they could return in peace to *Whitby*; which accordingly they did, and remain'd here for some time.

HORSHAM, in Norfolk.

Robert *Fitz-Walter* and *Sibill* his Wife, returning through *France* from *Rome*, where they had been in Pilgrimage, were set upon by Thieves, robb'd, and kept in Prison, till by their Prayers to Almighty God, and to the holy Virgin St. *Faith*, they were miraculously deliver'd out of their Confinement. After which they visited in Devotion the Shrine of St. *Faith* at the Abby of *Couchei* in *France*, where for the space of twelve days they remain'd, being kindly entertain'd by the Abbot and Convent there. Vowing at their return into *England* to their own Mannor, to built there a Monastery in the Worship of God and St. *Faith*. Which accordingly they did; endowing the same with Lands, and placing therein two Monks of the Abby of *Couches*, to which Abby they annext this House as a Cell. Their Deed of Foundation and Endowment, was made in the time of *Henry* the I. and *Herbert* Bishop of *Norwich*, who died 19. *H.* 1.

Pope *Alexander*, by his Bull dated in the year 1163. confirm'd to the Monks here all their Lands and Liberties.

In the 14. *Rich.* 2. this Priory was discharged of its Foreign Subjection to the Abby of *Couches*, and made an *English* Priory of it self.

[Valued at 162 *l.* 16 *s.* 11 *d.* ob. per Annum.]

RADINGFEILD, in Suffolk.

THIS was a Priory of Nuns founded to the honour of God and St. *Andrew*, by *Manasses* Earl of *Gisnensis*, and *Emme* his Wifes Daughter and Heir of *William de Arras*, and endow'd by them with the Mannor of *Radingseild*, &c. late held by the said *William de Arras*; their Deed bears date 1120.

[Valued at 67 *l.* 0 *s.* 1 *d.* ob. per Annum.]

READING, in Barkshire.

HERE was formerly a Monastery of Nuns. But that having been for many years destroyed, King *Henry* the I. *An. Dom.* 1126. built

46 BENEDICTINES. Vol. I.

418. built here a most noble Abby for Monks, and dedicated it in honour of the Virgin *Mary* and St. *John Baptist*, and endow'd it with great Possessions and Franchises as may be seen in his Charter dated 1125. all which was confirm'd by King *Hen.* 2.

419. *Hugh* Abbot of *Reading* and his Covent, reciting by their Deed, that King *Henry* the 1. had erected that Abby for the maintenance of Monks there devoutely and religiously serving God, for the receit of Strangers and Travellers, but chiefly Christ's poor People, they therefore did erect an Hospital without the Gate of the Abby there, to maintain twenty six poor People; and to the maintenance of Strangers passing that way they gave the profits of their Mill at *Leominstre*. Also *Auckerius* Abbot of *Reading*, built near this Abby a House for Lepers, which was call'd St. *Mary Magdalens*, alloting for their sustenance sufficient of all things, as well for Diet, as other matters.

420. If any Brother of this House were guilty of Adultery, or of striking his Brother in Pride, Anger, or Hatred, he was to be expell'd the House; none were to go abroad without a Companion; what Charity happens to be given to any one, to be common to all; these and several others were the Rules observed in the Lepers House of St. *Mary Magdalen*.

[Valued at 1938 *l*. 14 *s*. 3 *d*. ob. q. *per Annum*.]

LEOMINSTER, in Herefordshire, a Cell to Reading.

421. HERE was formerly a Nunnery built by *Merwald* one of the Kings of *Mercia*; but that having been long destroy'd by the *Danes*, King *Henry* the I. when he built the Abby of *Reading*, gave them also *Leominster*, with all the Estate belonging to it, and those Monks made it a Cell of their Abby. It was confirm'd to them by *Richard* and *Hugh* Bishops of *Hereford*.

RINDELGROS, in Scotland, a Cell to Reading.

422. DAvid King of *Scotland* gave this Town to the Abbot and Covent of *Reading*, to have and enjoy as freely and quiety as any Abby in his Kingdom enjoy their Estates. With a Provision that if he or his Successors shall add to this Donation sufficient wherewith to maintain a Covent here, that then the said Abbot of *Reading* should send a Covent hither.

MAY, in Scotland, a Cell to Reading.

THIS Priory was founded by *David* King of *Scotland*, and endow'd with several Lands in *Scotland*, by the said *David*, and *Malcolm* and *William* successively Kings of *Scotland*.

SHIRBURN, in Dorsetshire.

THE Bishops Seat which is now at *Salisbury*, did of old time, for many years, remain at *Shirburn*; but since that time Monks were placed here instead of secular Canons. The Abby-Church here, dedicated to our Lady, was in the time of Abbot *Bradeford*, set on fire, and a great part burnt, in a Dissention which happened between the Townesmen and the Monks; but the Townesmen were made to contribute to the Reparation. King *Hen.* 2. granted and confirm'd certain Lands to this Abby.

[Valued at 682 *l.* 14 *s.* 7 *d.* ob. *per Annum.*]

CADWELLI, in the Diocess of St. David's, in Wales, a Cell to Shirburn.

THIS Priory of *Cadwelli* was given to the Church of St. *Mary*'s of *Shirburn,* and to *Thurstan* Prior there and his Successors, by *Roger* Bishop of *Salsbury*. *Maurice* of *London* and others were Benefactors. Pope *Alexander*, by his Bull dated 1163. confirm'd to the Abby of *Shirburn* all its Lands and Revenues, among others the Parish Church of St. *Mary* of *Shirburn,* which the Abbot of that Abby held as a Prebend of the Church of *Salisbury*, also the Church of St. *Mary* of *Cadwelli* with all the Chappels, and Tithes thereunto belonging, &c. all which Grants and Deeds were ratified, approved, and confirm'd, and also exemplified by *David* Bishop of St. *David's*, *Anno Dom.* 1303.

[Valued at 29 *l.* 10 *s. per Annum.*]

CARHOW, in Norfolk.

THIS was a Nunnery founded and endow'd by King *Steven* near the City of *Norwich*. King *John* in the first year of his Reign granted to the Nuns here a Fair, to be held yearly at the Nativity of our Lady, with the like Liberties as the Monks enjoy in their Fair at *Norwich*. King *Henry* the III. in the thirteenth year of his Reign confirmed their Estate.

[Valued at 64 *l.* 16 *s.* 6 *d.* q. *per Annum.*]

GRENDALE, in Yorkshire.

A Vicia Prioress of the Covent of Nuns in the Church of St. *Mary* of *Grendale,* granted in fee-farm to *Ralf* Prior, and to the Convent of *Gisburn,* certain Lands which had been to the said Nuns given by *Eugeramus de Bovington*; to hold at the yearly Rent of four Quarters of Wheat yearly, to be paid half at the Feast of St. *Martins* in *Winter*, and half at *Whitsontide*. *Richard de Percy*, then Patron of this Priory, granted the Advowson thereof to *Richard Malebisse* and his Heirs for ever, yeilding, in lieu of all Service, one pound of Incense yearly at the Feast of Pentecost; which by the same Deed he assigned to be paid to the said Priory.

CLERK-

CLERKEN,WELL, in Middlesex.

JOrdanus, Son of *Radulfus*, Son of *Brian*, gave to God, St. *Mary*, and all Saints, and to *Robert* the Chaplain, in Alms, fourteen Acres of Land lying near the Clerks-well (*fons clericorum*) freed and discharged from all Claims of the Hospitallers of St. *John* of *Jerusalem*; this he gave to the said *Robert*, to the end that he might there build a religious House, such as he thought fit for God's service. Which being built and made a Nunnery, *Matilda de Ros*, Daughter of *Richard Canvill*, *Girard de Canvill*, *Henry de Essex*, and others were Benefactors; whose Gifts were confirm'd by *Richard* Bishop of *London*, An. Dom. 1194. and by the Heirs General of the Founder, who also granted other Lands and Possessions lying round the Nunnery. All which Lands and Possessions were confirm'd to the Church of St. *Mary de Fonte Clericorum* adjoyning to *London*, and the Nuns there by King *Henry* the II.

[Valued at 262 l. 19 s. per Annum.]

429.
430.
431.
432.
433.

WROXHALL, in Warwickshire.

HUgh Lord of *Wroxhall* and *Hatton*, being taken Prisoner at the holy War (in *Palestine*) and detain'd in Chains there, was by miracle removed from thence and set down in his own Estate at *Wroxhall*; whereupon he built a Nunnery here for *Benedictine* Nuns, in honour of God and St. *Leonard*, to whom he had made his Prayers when in distress; and made his two Daughters Nuns here.

434.

The Names of the Prioresses;

1 *Ernborow*.   5 *Mawd*.   9 *Ide*.
2 *Helin*.   6 *Emme*.   10 *Amis Abtot*.
3 *Sabina*.   7 *Mawd*.   11 *Annis*.
4 *Helin*.   8 *Cecelie*.   12 *Sibill Abtot*. 1284.

King *Henry* the II. and several others were Benefactors, all whose Gifts were confirm'd to this House in the first of King *Edward* the III.

[Valued at 72 l. 15 s. 6 d. per Annum.]

435.

COLNE, in Essex, a Cell to Abington.

ALbericus de *Veer*, the Kings *Chamberlain*, gave and confirm'd to God and St. *Mary*, and to the Monks of *Abington* at *Coln*, serving God in the Church of St. *Andrew* there, divers Land and Revenues. King *Henry* the I. in the year 1111. authorized and confirm'd the Subjection of this Church to that of *Abington*, and all the Estate given unto it by the said *Albericus de Veer* and others of his Family. Which *Albericus*, before his death, became a Monk in this House, and dying, was here buried; as were also his Sons. In the year 1311. a Composition and Agreement was made between *Richard* Abbot of *Abington*, and *John de Campeden* Prior of *Colun*, and their several Convents, containing that the Prior and Covent of *Coln* might choose and admit their own Monks

436.
437.
438.

from

from what parts they please, and that no Monks should be sent thither from the Convent of *Abyndon*; that the Convent of *Coln* might choose their own Prior, who was to be presented to, and allow'd by the Abbot of *Abyndon*; saving to the Abbot the right of visiting the said Priory of *Coln*. In consideration of which Liberty the Monks of *Coln*, did with the Consent of *Robert de Veer* Earl of *Oxford* their Patron, grant to the Abbot of *Abyndon* their Lordship of *Kensington*. *Vid. Vol.* 2. *p.* 877.

[Valued at 156 *l*. 12 *s*. 4 *d*. ob. *per Annum*.]

439.

CANEWELL, in Staffordshire.

G Eva Daughter of *Hugh* Earl of *Chester*, and Wife of *Jeoffrey Ridell*, founded the Church in honour of St. *Mary*, and St. *Giles*, and All Saints in *Canewell*, for Monks; and, with the grant and allowance of her Heirs *Jeoffrey Ridell*, and *Ralph Basset*, endow'd it with divers Lands. The said *Ralph Basset* was a Benefactor to this House, and so was *Waleran* Earl of *Warwick*.

440.
441.

FARWELL, in Staffordshire.

R Oger Bishop of *Chester* (whose Seat was since translated to *Lichfield*) gave the Church of St. *Mary* at *Faurwelle* to Nuns and devout Women; this he did at the request of three Hermits inhabiting at *Faurwelle*; and endow'd the same with Lands, to hold as freely as he himself did from God and the King; all which King *Henry* the II. confirm'd to the said Nuns, and also gave them of his own Charity divers other Lands and Liberties.

442.

PINLEY, in Warwickshire.

R *de Pilardinton*, gave this place to be a Nunnery, which was confirm'd to the Nuns here by *Alured* Bishop of *Worcester*, and by *Simon* and *John* his Predecessors. *John* Son of *Jeoffrey de Langele* gave to God and St. *Mary* of *Pinley* and the Nuns there, his Brother *Robert de Langely*, his Homage, and Service, and Rent of 6 *d*. for the maintenance of our Ladies Lamp at *Pinley* (ad Lumen beatæ Mariæ de Pineleia.)

[Valued at 23 *l*. 5 *s*. 11 *d*. *per Annum*]

STRATFORD Priory.

T HE Nunnery here dedicated to St. *Leonard*, was founded and endowed by *Christiana de Sumeri*, and her Son; as seems by the Confirmation of King *Steven*. King *Richard* the I. did confirm other Lands to it, given by *Galiena* and her Son *Bartholmew de Daumartin*, Patrons of the House.

443.

H FRE-

FRESTONE in Lincolnshire, a Cell of Croyland.

444.

ALan de Creun, with Muriel his Wife, and Maurice his Son gave the Church of St. James of Frestone, with several Lands and Tithes, to be a Cell to the Abby of Croyland. From which Creun, or Croune, descended the Family of Pedwardyn; who became Heirs of the Founder, the Male Line ceasing.

St. DOGMELS, in Pembrokshire, (Cella Cœnobii Tyronensis.)

445.

These Monks were Benedictines of the same Order with those of St. Martins at Tours. The Priory here was founded by Martin de Turribus, a Norman who first Conquered the Country hereabouts call'd Kames, or Kemish. Robert the Son of this Martin, endow'd it with Lands, confirm'd to it by King Henry the I.

[Valued at 87 l. 8 s. 6 d. per Annum.]

WALDEN Abby, in Essex.

446.

THE Abby at Walden was founded in the year 1136. by Gaufridus de Mandevilla Earl of Essex. He was Grandson of Jeoffrey who came into England with the Norman Conqueror, and was of most signal

447. note in his Army for his great Performances. From the noble Founder of this Abby (who died in the year 1144.) descended the illustrious Family of the Bohuns Earls of Hereford, Essex, and Northampton.

448. This Abby was dedicated to the honour of the blessed Mary, and St. James the Apostle.

The Family of Bohuns were great Benefactors to this Abby, and most of them buried here.

449. This Abby was built on the West-side of the Town and adjoyning to the High-way, which place was chosen as more proper for the relief of Travellers, and for Hospitality.

451. After the death of the Founder, Rohesia his Widow built a Nunnery at Chinkfand, to which she did all good Offices, and for the sake of that House, became very unkind to this of her Husbands Foundation.

452. William de Mandevilla second Son of the Founder, while Jeoffrey his elder Brother lived, led a military life in Flanders with Philip Earl of that Country, but upon his Brother's death without issue, he return'd into England, and inherited his Estate. Soon after which he made a Pilgrimage to Jerusalem and visited the holy Places, from whence being return'd into England he visited this House, and was here received with great Ceremony, where he presented at the Altar several Relicks which be had purchased in the holy Land, and became a great Benefactor to this House, giving them

453. by his Testament the Moiety of his Lordship of Walden, &c. and died in Normandy without issue. After whose decease this Barony came by his

454. Heirs General to one Jeffrey Fitz-Peter, who disseiz'd the Monks of what
456. Earl William had given them, and kept the Estate from them a great while,
458. till after King John's Coronation, being made Earl of Essex, he restored part of their Lands again, and confirm'd them to the Monks here. This

Jeoffery

Jeffrey Filius Petri was very vexatious to this Abby, the manner and particulars may be seen in the Book at large. Yet did, *Gaufridus de Mandavilla*, the first Founders Deed of Foundation contain a heavy Curse to any of his Successors or Tenants who should vex or disturb these Monks in any of their Possessions, or alienate or diminish the same. The Founders Endowment was confirm'd by several of his Descendents; also by King *Steven*, and King *Henry* the II. And King *Edward* the III. in the seventeenth year of his Reign Licensed *William de Bohun* Earl of *Northampton* to give and annext the Priory of *Bereden* in *Essex* as a Cell to this Abby. 459. 460. 461. 462. 463.

[Valued at 372 *l.* 18 *s.* 1 *d.* per Annum.]

BROMFEILD, in Shropshire. 464.

Anno Dom. 1155. The Canons of *Bromfeild*, by the Authority of *Theobald* Archbishop of *Canterbury*, gave their Church of *Bromfeild* to the Abby of St. *Peters* at *Gloucester*.

King *Henry* the II. confirm'd all the Estate belonging to the Church of St. *Mary* of *Bromfeild*, to the Prior and Monks there serving God, to hold of him and his Heirs in perpetual Alms. The like did King *Henry* the III.

BRETFORD, in Warwickshire.

Gaufridus Camerarius de Clintona gave certain Lands in this Lordship to one *Noemi* a Nun, for the erecting a Cell of Nuns here.

Afterwards, at the request of the said *Gaufridus de Clinton*, the Nuns here, being only two, *viz. Sehure* and *Naumi*, gave their House and Estate here to the Canons of *Killingworth*. 465.

TALLACH, in the Diocess of St. David's in Wales.

THE Abby here, dedicated to God, St. *Mary* and St. *John Baptist*, was founded by *Resus* the younger Son of *Resus* the younger, of the Family of the Princes of *South-wales*, and by him, and others endow'd with many Lands, the particulars may be seen in the *Monasticon* at large, fol. 466, 467. all which was confirm'd to this House by King *Edward* the II. in the seventeenth year of his Reign, and by King *Edward* the III. in the fifth year of his Reign. 467.

[Valued at 136 *l.* 9 *s.* 11 *d.* per Annum.]

BLITHBURY Priory, in Staffordshire. 468.

Hugh Malvisin gave *Blytheburgh* to Monks and Nuns there dwelling, for the service of God and St. *Giles*, to hold in pure and perpetual Alms. Which Estate tho' for a while taken away by *William Malvisin*, Son of the Founder *Hugh*, yet it was soon restored again.

EDWARDSTON, in Suffolk, a Cell to Abbington.

469. **H**Ubertus *de Monte Canesi* Lord of the Town of *Edwardston* in *Suffolk*, gave the Church there, to the Monks of *Abbendon*, to be a Cell of that House, and confirm'd his Gift in the fifteenth year of *Henry* the I. Which was also ratified by that King, *An. Dom.* 1115.

DEPING, in Lincolnshire, a Cell to Thorney.

470. **B**Aldewinus *Wac* gave the Church of St. *James* in *Deping* with divers Lands belonging to it, to God, St. *Mary*, and the Church of *Thorney*, which was confirm'd by his Son and Grandson: and also by Pope *Innocent* the III. in the first year of his Pontificate. (1198)

ALCESTER, in Warwickshire.

471. **I**N the year 1140. *Radulfus Pincerna* (or *Boteler*) founded this Monastery (then called from its Situation St. *Mary's of the Isle*) and made *Robert* a Monk of *Worcester* the first Abbot here. At which time it was agreed between the two Houses, viz. The Abby of *Worcester*, and this, that there should be a constant Love and Brotherhood betwixt them, and that upon the death of the Abbot here, another should be chosen indifferently out of either House; the said Founder endow'd this Monastery with divers Lands ordaining that the Abbot should not spend any of the Revenues to enrich his secular kindred, but upon the Poor and Travellers. *Robert* Earl of *Leicester* (of whom this Estate was holden by the foresaid Founder) confirm'd the same to the Monks here, and granted to them divers Liberties.

472. The like did King *Steven*. King *Henry* the II. confirm'd to them

473. all their Lands by their several Benefactors given, and also granted them full power to choose their own Abbot from among themselves, in their Convent. King *Edward* the IV. in the fifth year of his Reign, seeing

474. the Estate of this Monastery to run to decay, it being so far wasted that it was not sufficient to maintain any Monks, but the Abbot only, granted this House and what Estate it had left, to the Abby of *Evesham*, to which he annext it for ever; so that from that time it became a Cell of that Abby.

[Valued at 65 *l*. 7 *s*. 11 *d*. per Annum.]

LINGEBROOK Priory, in Herefordshire.

IT seems by an Inquisition taken 24. *Edw.* 3. that *Adam Esgar* Clerk, was a Benefactor to the Monastery of Nuns here, and founded an Anniversary for *William de Power*.

[Valued at 22 *l*. 17 *s*. 8 *d*. per Annum.]

NUNKELLING, in Yorkshire.

Agnes *de Archis* gave the Church here and divers Lands to God, St. *Mary*, and St. *Helen*, and to the Nuns of *Killing*, in pure and free Alms. The Nuns Estate here was afterwards confirm'd by *Richard de Sancto Quintino*, and *William de Fortibus* Earl of *Albemarle*, and by *Aeliz de Sancto Quintino* Daughter of the foresaid *Agnes*, who also gave other Lands; and lastly by the Archbishops of *York*.

475.

[Valued at 35 *l*. 15 *s*. 5 *d*. per Annum.]

SANDWELL, in Staffordshire.

William Son of *Guido de Offney* founded a Hermitage in *Bromwich*, near the Well call'd *Sandwell* for a Habitation of Monks, and endow'd the same with divers Lands lying about the same. Which was confirm'd to the said Monks by *Gervais Paganellus*, Lord of the honour of *Dudley*, of which Barony the Lands were holden.

MONKETON, in Yorkshire.

William *de Arches* and *Juetta* his Wife founded a Nunnery here, of which their Daughter *Matilda* was a Nun, endowing the same with divers Lands. All which was confirm'd to the said Nunnery by *Henry Murdac* Archbishop of *York*. (He died 1153.)

476.

[Valued at 75 *l*. 12 *s*. 4 *d*. ob. per Annum.]

HÁLISTANE, in Northumberland.

Richard Bishop of *Durham*, in the year 1311. united the Churches of *Crossanet*, and *Harbottell*, to the Church of *Halistan* and the Nunnery there, and gave the Patronage of the same to *Richard de Umframvill* Patron of the said Nunnery. King *Henry* the III. in the thirty ninth year of his Reign, confirm'd to the Prioress and Nuns of *Halystan*, the Lands given to them by *Alice de Alneto*, and *Roger Bertram*.

[Valued at 11 *l*. 5 *s*. 7 *d*. per Annum.]

DUNSTER, in Somersetshire.

THE Monastery of Monks here, dedicated to the honour of St. *George*, was founded and endow'd with sundry Lands and Revenues by the Ancestors of *John de Moouu* Lord of *Dunsterre*, which *John* did, in the fifteenth year of King *Edward* the III. ratifie and confirm to the Monks here all his Ancestors Donations.

477.

[Valued at 37 *l*. 4 *s*. 8 *d*. per Annum.]

MAR-

MARGAN Abby, in Wales.

478.

THIS Abby was founded by *Robert* Earl of *Gloucester* in the year 1147. King *John* in the sixth year of his Reign confirm'd to the Church of St. *Mary's* of *Margan*, and the Monks there, all the Lands and Estate given to them by the said *Robert* and several others.

[Valued at 181 *l*. 7 *s*. 4 *d*. per Annum.]

BLACKBURGH, in Norfolk.

ROger *de Scales* and *Muriell* his Wife gave to God, St. *Mary*, and St. *Catherine*, and to the Brethren serving them in this place, called *Shiplade*, otherwise *Blackbergh*, divers Lands and Possessions. The same *Roger* by an other Deed gave the same Lands and others to the Sisters here serving God. *Vid. Vol.* 2. *p.* 879.

[Valued at 42 *l*. 6 *s*. 7 *d*. ob. per Annum.]

HENWOOD, in Warwickshire.

479.

KEtelbernus *de Langedona*, gave to God, and St. *Margaret* the Virgin, and to the Nuns at *Eastwell* (so was this Monastery then called by reason of its situation) part of his Demeans of *Langedon* in which Lordship this Nunnery stood; with divers other Lands and Liberties, to hold as freely as he himself held them of his chief Lord *Hugh* of *Arden*. Pope *Innocent* in the first year of his Pontificate incorporated, annext, and united to this Nunnery of *Henwood* divers Churches given to the same by King *Rich.* II. and King *Henry* the IV.

[Valued at 21 *l*. 2 *s*. 0 *d*. ob. per Annum]

St. RADEGUNDS, adjoyning to Cambridge.

480.

481.

KING *Steven* confirm'd to the Church and Nuns of St. *Mary* of *Cambridge* certain Lands which *William* a Monk and Goldsmith gave them; and also other Lands given them by Countess *Constance* Wife of his Son *Eustace*. It was found by Inquisition taken at *Cambridge*, 3. *Edw.* I. that the Prioress and Nuns of St. *Radegund* at *Cambridge* hold a certain piece of Ground called *Greencroft*, containing ten Acres on which their Church and House is founded, which was given for that purpose by *Malcolme* King of *Scotland*: and that *Nigellus* and *Eustachius* Bishops of *Ely* had been Benefactors to this Nunnery.

LANGLEY, in Leicestershire.

THE Nunnery of St. *Mary's* of *Langly* was founded by *William Pantulphe* and *Burgia* his Wife, from whom descended *Robert de Tatesale* Patron of this Priory 5. *H.* 3. The Nuns here upon the death of their
Prioress

Prioress, had power to choose another without asking leave of their Patron, who did use during the time of such Vacation to appoint a Boy (*unum Garcionem*) with a white Wand to keep the Gate of the Nunnery, for which he was to have his Diet there.

[Valued at 29 *l.* 7 *s.* 4 *d.* ob. *per Annum*.]

SANDFORD, in Barkshire.

KING *Edward* the I. in the 21st. year of his Reign granted to the Prior and Convent of *Sandelford*, free Warren in their Demeans. *Saiverus de Sancto Andrea* granted to God, and the Church of St. *Nicholas* of *Sandford*, and to the Nuns there, a Rent of Five Shillings *per Annum* in his Town of *Littlemore*. *Vid. Vol.* 3. *p.* 13.

482.

SETON, in Cumberland.

HEnry Duke of *Lancaster*, Earl of *Derby*, *Lincoln* and *Leicester*, being inform'd that the Revenues of this Priory were so small that they could not maintain the Prioress and Nuns, gave and annext to this House, the Hospital of St. *Leonard's* in *Lancaster*, to hold in pure and perpetual Alms. Which Hospital was first founded by King *John* for a Master, a Chaplain, and nine poor People, three of which to be Lepers, and the rest found.

[Valued at 12 *l.* 12 *s.* ob. *per Annum*.]

ANKERWIK, in Buckinghamshire.

GIlbert and *Richard Muntschet*, Knights, founded a Nunnery here, and endow'd it with Lands. King *Henry* the III. in the one and fortieth year of his Reign, confirm'd their Estate given by many Benefactors, whose Names, and Parcels given are exprest in his Charter.

483.

[Valued at 32 *l.* 0 *s.* 2 *d.* *per Annum*.]

WINTENEY, in Hampshire.

RIchard, Son of *Richard de Hereard* endow'd the Nunnery here built to God, the blessed *Mary*, St. *Mary Magdalen*, and All Saints, with divers Lands, which King *Edward* the I. confirm'd.

[Valued at 43 *l.* 3 *s.* *per Annum*.]

SNELLESHALL, in Buckinghamshire.

RAlph Martell, and others, gave to the Prior and Monks here serving God in the Church of St. *Leonard*, at *Snelleshall*, divers Lands, which were confirm'd to them by King *Henry* the III.

[Valued at 18 *l.* 1 *s.* 11 *d.* *per Annum*.]

BIRKENED,

484.

BIRKENED, in Chelshire.

HAmo de Massie endow'd the Church of St. Mary and St. James here with Lands, and granted and confirm'd to the Prior and Monks, and their Successors, power and liberty to choose their own Prior upon any vacancy, from among themselves, according as Pope *Alexander* had granted to them.

[Valued at 90 l. 13 s. per Annum.]

MARRIGG, in Yorkshire.

TO the Nuns here serving God, *Roger de Asco, Conan de Asch,* and many others, among the rest *Conan* Duke of *Britanny* and *Richmond* were great Benefactors; giving divers Lands and Liberties, all which were recited and confirm'd by the Charter of King *Edward* the III. in the twenty second year of his Reign.

485.

[Valued at 48 l. 18 s. 3 d. per Annum.]

STYKESWOULD, in Lincolnshire.

486.

IT appear'd by Inquisition taken in the Reign of King *Edward* the I. that the Master and Nuns of *Stikeswold* held several Lands of the Gift of *Lucy* Mother of *Ranulf* Earl of *Chester*, and others. And that they had been so held for the space of one hundred years.

[Valued at 114 l. 5 s. 2 d. ob. per Annum.]

STODELY, in Oxfordshire.

BErnard de Sancto Walerico, and *Thomas de Sancto Walerico* his Son endow'd a Nunnery here, and gave power to the Nuns upon the vacancy of the Prioress to choose another with the assent of the Patron or his Steward. *Thomas de S. Walerico* lived in the time of King *John* 1207. *Richard* King of the *Romans*, and *Edmund* Earl of *Cornwall*, and *Godfrey de Craucumbe* were Benefactors. *Vid. Vol.* 3. *p.* 13.

487.

[Valued at 82 l. 4 s. 4 d. q. per Annum.]

KIRKLEY, in Yorkshire.

REinerus Flandrensis, gave divers Lands to the Nuns here, which were confirm'd to them by *William* Earl of *Warren* in pure and perpetual Alms. They had also other Lands from other Benefactors, all which were confirm'd by King *Henry* the III. in the twentieth year of his Reign.

488.

[Valued at 19 l. 8 s. per Annum.]

STAN-

STANFORD, in Lincolnshire.

William Abbot of *Peterborough*, in the Reign of King *Henry* the II. founded at *Stanford* a Priory of Nuns in honour of God and St. *Michael*, he built their Church, and placed there forty Nuns. Saving to himself and Successors, Abbots of *Peterburgh*, the placing of the Prioress, &c. reserving also a Rent of half a Mark yearly to be paid to the Church of *Peterburgh*.

William de *Humet* gave a Rent of ten Marks *per Annum* to the *Cistercian* Monks in *Stanford*, which was confirm'd to them by King *John* in the sixteenth year of his Reign. *Lucy* Wife of the said *William* gave certain Rents to the Nuns of St. *Michaels* at *Stanford*.

The Prioress and Nuns here did by their Act and Deed acknowledge and promise fidelity and obedience to the Abbot and Convent of *Peterborough*; that the Prior or Curator of their Monastery might be placed and displaced by the said Abbot and Convent; that upon the death of the Prioress, no Election of another should be made without the Abbots License; and that the admitting of the Nuns into the said House should be wholly in the power of the said Abbot; also that the said Nunnery should pay a yearly Pention of a Mark of Silver to the said Abby of *Peterburgh* for the buying of Books. *Vid. Vol.* 2. p. 880.

489.

[Valued at 65 *l*. 19 *s*. 9 *d*. per Annum.]

WYRTHORP, in Northamptonshire.

IN the 28th. of *Edw.* 3. *Thomas de Holland* and *Joan* his Wife (the Kings Kinswoman) were Patrons of a Nunnery at *Wyrthorp*, at which time this House was so impoverished and decayed, by reason of the Pestilence, and other reasons, that there was here but one Nun remaining, whereupon, by the King's License the said House and Church of *Wyrthorp*, with all its Possessions, were by the Bishop for ever united and annext to the Nunnery of St. *Michaels* by *Stanford*, and the Nun here remaining, was removed thither.

IVINGHO, in Buckinghamshire.

490.

KING *Edward* the I. in the eighth year of his Reign, gave divers Lands, to the Prioress and Nuns of St. *Margaret* of *Ivingho*, and their Successors, to hold of the King in free, pure, and perpetual Alms.

WABURN, in Norfolk.

THE Priory of *Waburn* was founded by Sir *Ralph Meyngaryn* Knight, from whom descended by the Mothers side *John de Veer* Earl of *Oxford*.

[Valued at 24 *l*. 19 *s*. 6 *d*. ob. per Annum.]

I   CAMPESS,

GAMPESS, or Campsey, in 𝕾𝖚𝖋𝖋𝖔𝖑𝖐.

491.
492.

TEobandus de Valoines gave his Land in *Campess* to his two Sisters *Joan* and *Agnes*, for the Foundation of a Nunnery there to the honour of God and the glorious Virgin *Mary*. Which was confirm'd by King *John*. *Matilda de Lancaster*, Countess of *Ulster*, did in the Reign of King *Edw*. III. by License of that King, found a Chantry of five Priests to officiate in this Church, which Chantry, was removed afterwards to a Town call'd *Brusseyard* in the Mannor of *Rokhall*; the Revenues and Scite whereof was afterwards, in the said King's Reign given to a Prioress and Nuns of St. *Clares* Order, which Nunnery was there erected (at *Brusseyard*) in place of the said Chantry Priests or Chaplains.

[Valued at 182 *l*. 9 *s*. 5 *d*. per Annum.]

DENNEY Abby, in 𝕮𝖆𝖒𝖇𝖗𝖎𝖉𝖌𝖊𝖘𝖍𝖎𝖗𝖊.

493.
494.
495.

IN the last year of *Nigellus* Bishop of *Ely*, who died 1169. one *Robert*, Chamberlain to the Earl of *Britony* and *Richmond*, founded the Monaittery here as a Cell to *Ely*, becoming a Monk himself. In the year 1341. *Maria de Sancto Paulo*, Countess of *Pembroke*, gave this Mannor of *Denney* to Sister *Katherine de Bolwyk* Abbess, and to the Nuns of St. *Clare*, or Minoresses, there serving God, in free, pure, and perpetual Alms. She also annext and united the Advowson of the Abby of Minoresses at *Waterbeche* to this at *Denney*, and translated the Nuns of *Waterbeche* hither. All which she did by License of King *Edward* the III. Vid. Vol. 2. p. 883.

[Valued at 172 *l*. 8 *s*. 3 *d*. ob. per Annum.]

SEWARDSLEY, in 𝕹𝖔𝖗𝖙𝖍𝖆𝖒𝖕𝖔𝖓𝖘𝖍𝖎𝖗𝖊.

496.

Robert *de Pinkeny*, and *Simon de Pinkeny*, gave certain Lands to the Nuns here, and *William de Sancto Johanne*, was also a Benefactor.

[Valued at 12 *l*. 6 *s*. 7 *d*: q. per Annum.]

LITTLEMAREIS, near Yedingham, in 𝖄𝖔𝖗𝖐𝖘𝖍𝖎𝖗𝖊.

497.
498.

ROger *de Clere*, endow'd the Nunnery here with divers Lands. The Church of *Teddingham* was dedicated in honour of the most blessed Virgin in the year 1241. on the seventeenth of the *Kalends* of *September*, at which time divers indulgences were granted. *Richard de Breuse* became Patron of this House in right of *Alice* his Wife who was descended from the Founders. King *Henry* the III. in the 30*th*. year of his Reign confirm'd to the Nuns of *Teddingham* all the Lands given by their several Benefactors.

There was delivered in this House, to the Prioress and Convent sixty and two Loaves daily; to nine Brethren twelve Loaves a piece, weekly; to Brother *James* fourteen Loaves, to three Priests, to four Chaplains, and

other

other Officers accordingly, &c. among the rest of the Deliveries is set down.—*Canibus in singulis Maneriis triginta novem panes de pane duriori.*— To the Dogs in each Manor thirty nine Loaves of the courfest fort of Bread.

[Valued at 21 *l*. 16 *s*. 6 *d*. ob. *per Annum*.]

NUNBURNHAM, in Yorkshire.

THE Anceftors of *Roger de Merlay* Lord of the Barony of *Morpath* were founders of the Nunnery of *Brunham*. And it was found by Inquifition 38. *Hen*. 3. that thefe Nuns held Lands here of the Fee of *Thomas de Grayftoc*.

[Valued at 8 *l*. 1 *s*. 11 *d*. per *Annum*.]

LYTHOM, in Lancashire, a Cell to Durham. 499.

Richardus filius Rogeri, or *Richard Fitz-Rogers*, gave his Land at *Lythum* with the Church there, to the Prior and Monks of *Durham* for the erecting and eftablifhing at *Lytham* a Cell of their Order, which he endow'd with divers Lands. This was confirm'd by King *John* in the fecond year of his Reign.

CHIRBURY, in Shropshire. 500.

THE Monks here having formerly inhabited at *Snede*, and removed from thence; King *Edward* the I. in the ninth year of his Reign, underftanding this place not to be convenient for them removed them back again to *Snede*.

ARDEN, in Yorkshire.

PEter de Hotona founded and endowed an Abby of Nuns at *Arden*, and dedicated it to St. *Andrew*; which was confirm'd by *Roger de Mowbray* Lord of the Fee: and by *Elizabeth* Heir of the faid *Peter* in the tenth year of *Edward* the I. In the 6*th*. of *Henry* the IV. *Jeoffrey Pigot*, as Heir of *Peter* the firft Founder, and *Elizabeth* abovefaid, was admitted by the Nuns here as Founder or Patron.

[Valued at 12 *l*. *per Annum*.]

DAVINTON, in Kent. 501.

KING *Henry* the III. in the thirty ninth year of his Reign, confirm'd to the Priorefs of the Church of St. *Mary Magdalene* of *Davyntone*, and to the Nuns there ferving God, divers Lands and Rents, given by feveral Benefactors.

FOSS,

FOSS, in Lincolnshire.

KING *Henry* the III. in the 21*st*. year of his Reign gave to the Prioress and Nuns of *Foss* without *Torkesey*, sixscore Acres of Land and seven Tofts in *Torkesey* to hold for ever at the yearly Rent of forty six Shillings.

[Valued at 7 *l*. 3 *s*. 6 *d*. per *Annum*.]

WALLINGWELLS, in Nottinghamshire.

RAlph *de Cheurolcurt*, gave to God and St. *Mary* a place in his Park of *Carletuna*, for the building a place of Religion; and to it gave other Lands and Liberties, in pure and perpetual Alms.

From this Founder, is descended by a Daughter, the Family of *Furneux*; the Male Line of which Family is now in Being in *Darbyshire* under the name of *Rooper*.

[Valued at 58 *l*. 9 *s*. 10 *d*. per *Annum*.]

St. CATHERINES Nunnery, without Exeter, in Devonshire.

KING *John* in the second year of his Reign, confirm'd to the Church of St. *Catherine* without *Exeter*, and the Nuns there, the Lands given to them by *William de Trascy*, and *Henry de Pomerya*, with the grant of many Liberties.

FLAMSTED Priory, in Hartfordshire.

AGatha, Widow of *William de Gatesden*, endowed the Church of St. *Giles* of *Flamsted* with certain Lands, which Gift was confirm'd by King *Henry* the III. in the twelfth year of his Reign.

[Valued at 30 *l*. 19 *s*. 8 *d*. ob. per *Annum*.]

CRESSEWELL, in Herefordshire.

WAlter *de Lascy* gave to the Church of St. *Mary* at *Cressewell*, and to the Monks there of the Order call'd *Grandimontenses*, divers Lands and Revenues; confirm'd by King *Henry* the III. who also granted to them divers Liberties. Other Benefactors gave them other Lands, all which was confirm'd to them by King *Edward* the III. in the first year of his Reign. *Vid*. Vol. 3. *p*. 17.

DARBY

DARBY *Priory, in* Darbyshire.

KING *Henry* the III. granted to the Prioress and Nuns *de Pratis* at *Derby,* an Augmentation of one hundred Shillings *per Annum,* out of the Fee-farm of the Town of *Nottingham.* It was found upon an Extent in the 15. *E.* 1. that the Scite of the Abby at *Derby* with a Garden and Curtilage, was worth yearly 20 *s.* And that the said Abby held there, in Demean, four Carucates of Land, each Carucate containing sixty Acres of Land, (*i. e. Arable* Land,) &c.

LAMBLEY *Nunnery, in* Northumberland.

KING *John* in the second year of his Reign, confirm'd to God, and St. *Mary,* and St. *Patrick,* and to the Nuns at *Lamleleya,* the Scite of the Abby of *Lambeleya Super Tinam,* and the Lands which *Adam de Tindale* and *Helewisa* his Wife gave to the said House.

STEINFEILD *Priory, in* Lincolnshire.

THIS was a Priory of Benedictine Nuns, founded by *Henry* Son of *Henry de Percy.* The Patronage of this House came to *Jocelin de Lovein* by *Agnes* his Wife, one of the Daughters and Co-heirs of *William de Percy.* King *Edward* the I. in the one and twentieth year of his Reign, granted the Prioress and Nuns here, free Warren in their Demean Lands, the same not being within the bounds of his Forests.

[Valued at 98 *l.* 8 *s. per Annum.*]

MODBURY, *in* Devonshire.

THE Mannor of *Modbury,* and right of Patronage of the Priory there, being in *Ida* Widow of Sr. *James Exton,* Knight, by Virtue of a Fine in the 9. *Edw.* 2. the said *Ida* through the mediation of Friends, released all her title to *Richard de Campo-Arnulphi.*

CHESTER *Nunnery.*

THE Monastery of St. *Mary* here, was founded for Nuns, and endow'd by *Ranulph* Earl of *Chester* with Lands and Liberties.
[Valued at 66 *l.* 18 *s.* 4 *d. per Annum.*]

ROSSE.

ROSSEDALE, in Yorkshire.

Robert de Stutevill founded and endow'd the Nunnery at *Rossedale* to God and St. *Laurence*, which was confirm'd by King *John*. *Sibilla de Valoniis*, *Adam de Neuton*, &c. gave other Lands to the Prioress and Nuns here, all which was confirm'd by King *Edward* the III. in the second year of his Reign.

[Valued at 37 *l*. 12 *s*. 5 *d*. per Annum.]

PEMBROK Priory.

Walter *Marescallus*, and *William Marescallus* both Earls of *Pembrok*, gave divers Lands and Endowments to the Priory of St. *Nicholas* at *Pembroke*.

St. CLEMENTS, adjoyning to York.

Thurstan Archbishop of *York* gave to God and St. *Clement*, and the Nuns there, divers Lands to hold in pure and perpetual Alms; whose Letters of Endowment were confirm'd by the Dean and Chapter of *York*. Other Benefactors gave other Lands, all which was confirm'd by King *Edward* the III. in the first year of his Reign. *Anno. Dom.* 1192. *Gaufridus* Archbishop of *York* gave the Priory of St. *Clements* to the Abby of *Godestave*, but the Nuns here refused to submit to such Donation, and appeal'd to the Pope.

[Valued at 55 *l*. 11 *s*. 11 *d*. per Annum.]

CHESTHUNT, in Hertfordshire.

King *Henry* the III. gave to the Prioress and Nuns here all the Lands and Tenements belonging to the Canons of *Cathale*, whom he caused to be removed.

[Valued at 14 *l*. 10 *s*. per Annum.]

FINCHALE, in the Bishoprick of Durham.

Finchale is a solitary place not far from the City of *Durham*, where a certain Hermit named *Godricus de Finchale*, who in his youth had visited the holy Sepulcher, spent his old Age in Devotion, and here died with the reputation of great Sanctity. After the death of this *Godficus*, *Ranulphus* Bishop of *Durham* granted this Hermitage, and the Lands adjoyning, to *Algarus* the Prior, and the Monks of *Durham*. *Hugh* Bishop of *Durham* founded and endow'd the Priory of *Finchale* for such Monks of *Durham* as the Prior of *Durham* should from time to time send thither in the service of God and St. *John*.

[Valued at 122 *l*. 15 *s*. 3 *d*. per Annum.]

The Priory of St. James at Bristol, a Cell of **Tewkesbury**.

WIlliam Earl of *Gloucester* gave to this House divers Lands and Tithes, and the Profits of the Fair at *Bristol*, in *Whitsun-week*, which with other Lands given by other Benefactors was confirm'd by King *Henry* the II. The same King gave the Monks here certain Liberties in his Forrest. *Robert* Earl of *Gloucester* was buried in this Church of St. *James*, at *Bristol*.

BUNGEY, in **Suffolk**.

Roger *de Glanvill* and *Gundreda* the Countess, his Wife, founded a Nunnery in the Church of the Holy Cross at *Bungey*. The Endowments whereof as well by the said *Roger* and his Wife as by a great number of other Benefactors, were all confirm'd to the said Nuns and their Successors to hold in pure and perpetual Alms, by King *Henry* the II. in the nineteenth year of his Reign.

514.
515.

[Valued at 62 *l*. 0 *s*. 1 *d*. ob. per *Annum*.]

SYLLEY *Isle*, near **Cornwall**.

516.

THIS Isle was given of old by the Kings of *England* to the Abbot and Monks of *Tavestock*, who used to send two of their Monks hither to perform the Divine Offices, till the Wars with *France* in the Reign of King *Edward* the III. And then that King gave License to the Abbot of *Tavestock*, in the nineteenth year of his Reign, to place here two secular Chaplains instead of Monks.

ROWNEY Priory, in **Hertfordshire**.

IN the 36. *H*. 6. *Agnes Selby* Prioress of this House and the Covent of Nuns here, in respect of the poverty of the place, did by their Deed seal'd with their Common-Seal, resign up their Church, House, and Lands, into the hands of their Patron *John Fray* who designed to convert the same in a better manner. Which *John Fray* was chief Baron of the *Exchequer*, and being thus possest of this Priory, he would not convert it to any other use but to the service of God, and therefore obtain'd the King's License in the 37. *H*. 6. to found and endow here a Chantry for one Priest.

517.

The first Founder of the Priory was *Conan* Duke of *Britony* and *Richmond*, who, with others, endow'd it with Possessions of the value of ten Marks per *Annum*.

[Valued at 13 *l*. 10 *s*. 9 *d*. per *Annum*.]

NUNEATON, in Warwickshire.

THIS House was founded and endow'd by *Robert* Earl of *Leicester*, Son of *Robert de Mellento*, in the Reign of King *Henry* the II. for Nuns of the same Order with those at *Font-Ebraud*.

Whose Gifts were confirm'd by his Son *Robert*, and by King *Henry* the II.

The Prioress and Covent of *Font-Ebrald* granted to this House the immunity to receive and retain to their own proper use all such gifts as should be made unto them, without any exaction of the said Abbess and Covent of *Font-Ebrald*. Which immunity and several others were confirm'd to them by Pope *Alexander* the III.

[Valued at 253 *l*. 14 *s*. 5 *d*. ob. *per Annum*.]

LUFFELD, in Northamptonshire, a Cell to Westminster.

THE Priory of *Luffeild* was founded by *Robert* Earl of *Leicester*, for the Souls of King *William* the I. and Queen *Matilda*, &c.

King *Henry* the I. his Daughter *Maud* the Empress, and King *Edward* the I. were Benefactors, and Pope *Alexander* the III. granted to *Ralph* Prior of St. *Mary*'s at *Luffeild*, his Brethren, and their Successors, divers Priviledges by his Bull dated 1174.

Radulfus de Cahienes, *Hugo de Sancto Martino*, and others gave them divers Churches and Tithes.

King *Henry* the III. in the fifty sixth year of his Reign, reciting the Priory of *Luffeild* to have been founded by his Predecessors Kings of *England*, granted to the Prior and Monks there free Chiminage in his Forrest of *Whitlewood*, for five years next ensuing.

WILBERFOSS, in Yorkshire.

THIS was a House of Nuns dedicated to St. *Mary*, founded by *Helias de Cotton*, and endow'd by *Alan* his Son with divers Lands.

King *Henry* the II. in the fourth year of his Reign, and King *Henry* the III. in the twelfth year of his Reign, confirm'd their Lands and Estate. *Vid. Vol.* 3. *p.* 12.

[Valued at 21 *l*. 16 *s*. 10 *d*. per Annum.]

GODSTOW Priory of Nuns, in Oxfordshire.

THE Church here was built by their Prioress *Editha*, and in the year 1138. dedicated in honour of the blessed Virgin *Mary* and St. *John Baptist*, by *Alexander* then Bishop of *Lincoln*, in presence of King *Steven*, and *Maud* the Queen, with abundance of Bishops, Earls, and Barons, and others of prime quality, who all gave to the said Church at that time some Rents and Endowments: Whereupon *Albericus* Bishop of *Hostia* the Pope's Legate in *England* released to every of the said Benefactors

factors one year of injoyn'd Penance, and granted moreover a Remission of forty days in every year to all those who should in Devotion visit the said Church on the day of St. *Prisca* the Virgin, or on the Nativity of St. *John Baptist*.

Their Lands and Revenues were confirm'd by King *Steven*, and by King *Richard* the I. in the first year of his Reign.

In the year 1191. *Hugh* Bishop of *Lincoln* visiting in this part of his Diocess, and seeing in this Church a Tomb before the Altar with more than ordinary Ornaments, and being inform'd upon enquiry that it was the Tomb of *Rosamond* Concubine to King *Henry* the II. he caused her body to be removed out of the Church, and to be buried in the Church-yard to avoid the scandal of Religion, and to deter other Women from Whoredom.

About the time of the Suppression of this House, *Rosamonds* Tomb was open'd and her Bones found inclosed in Leather, and that in Lead. When it was opened a very sweet smell came out from it. The following Inscription was formerly read on a Cross near *Godstow*,

Qui meat hac cret, signum salutis adoret,
Utque sibi detur veniam Rosamunda precetur.

Vid. 2. Vol. p. 884.

[Valued at 274 *l*. 5 *s*. 10 *d*. ob. *per Annum*.]

526.

527.
528.

LILLECHIRCHE, *in the County of* ······

KING *John* gave to the Abby of St. *Mary* and St. *Sulpice* at *Lillechurch*, and the Prioress and Nuns there the Mannor of *Lillechurch* in pure and perpetual Alms, and granted them a Fair to be there held yearly on the Feast of St. *Michael*, and two days after; all which was confirm'd by King *Henry* the III. in the eleventh year of his Reign, who also in the fiftieth year of his Reign released and pardon'd their Suit-service to his Court at St. *Martins le Grand*, in *London*.

529.

TYKEHEAD *Priory, in* Yorkshire.

KING *John* in the fifth year of his Reign confirm'd to God and the Church of St. *Mary* of *Tykeheved*, and to the Nuns there serving God, the Lands and Possessions then given them by several Benefactors.

In the year 1264. the Prior and Canons of *Ellerton*; and the Nuns of *Tykehead*, exchanged certain Lands and Houses which had been the occasions of former Suits and Controversies.

Sir *Robert de Aske* Kt. the Founder, gave to this House the Rent of 7 *s* 4 *d*. *per Annum*, for the maintaining of a yearly Obit for himself and *Elizabeth* his Wife, conditionally that if the Obit were not diligently observ'd, then the said Sum or Rent to be restored to his Heirs. Dated 1522.

[Valued at 20 *l*. 18 *s*. 10 *d*. *per Annum*.]

530.

K HUNTING-

HUNTINGTON Priory of Nuns.

IN the time of *Richard de Gravesend* Bishop of *Lincoln*, *Elena Walensis* was elected Prioress of the Priory of St. *James extra Huntedon*. the Lady *Dervorgull de Galewidia*, being then Patroness of the said Priory, and *Richard de Foxton* her Seneschal, or Steward.

CLIVE, in Somersetshire.

531.

William de Romare, who married *Lucy* Countess of *Lincoln*, founded the Abby of the blessed Virgin and St. *Laurence*, at *Rewsby* in *Lincolnshire*, 8. *Steph*.

William his youngest Son by the said *Lucy*, who married *Phillip* Daughter of *Hubert de Burgh* Earl of *Kent*, founded the Abby of our blessed Lady of the *Cliff*, in *Somersetshire*, in the 9. *Rich*. 1. of which one *Ralph* was the first Abbot.

King *Henry* the III. confirm'd their Lands and Estate, and moreover, granted to the Abbot and Convent of *Clive*, the Mannor and Hundred of *Bramton*, in *Devonshire*, to be held of the King and his Heirs at the yearly Farm of 22 *l*. per Annum.

[Valued at 155 *l*. 9 *s*. 5 *d*. q. per Annum.]

HALIWEL Priory, in Middlesex.

532.

KING *Richard* the I. in the sixth year of his Reign confirm'd to the Nuns of *Haliwell* the several Lands given to them by *Galfredus Camerarius* and others.

The same King in the first year of his Reign confirm'd to the Church of St. *John Baptist* of *Haliwell*, and to the Nuns there serving God, the Ground on which the said Church stands *cum pertin*. viz. the Marish or Meadow in which the Fountain call'd *Haliwell* rises, with other Lands given by *Richard* late Bishop of *London*, *Walter* Precentor of *St. Pauls*, &c.

These Nuns held also certain Lands at *Camerwell* and *Pecham* given to them by several Benefactors.

KERSEY Priory, in Suffolk.

533.

Nesta de Cokefeld, Widow of *Thomas de Burgo*, gave to God, and to the Church of St. *Mary*, and St. *Anthony* of *Kersey*, and to the Canons there, divers Lands, of which she and her second Husband past a fine in the 24. *Hen*. 3.

KINGTON Priory, in Wiltshire.

Robert Burnell Bishop of *Bath*, and *Wells* founded this House to God and St. *Mary*, for Nuns, whose Deed of Foundation was exemplified by *Inspeximus* 19. *E*. 1.
Vid. Vol. 2. *p.* 887.

[Valued at 25 *l.* 9 *s.* 1 *d.* ob. *per Annum.*]

BURNHAM, in Buckinghamshire.

Anno. Dom. 1266. *Richard* King of the *Romans* founded a Monastery here for Nuns, which he dedicated to God and St. *Mary*, and endow'd it with his Mannor and Advowson of *Burnham* and other Lands. Witnesses to whose Deed or Charter of Foundation, were his Brother King *Henry* the III. and Prince *Edward* his eldest Son, with others.

[Valued at 51 *l.* 2 *s.* 4 *d.* q. *per Annum.*]

STOKE-CLARE Priory, in Suffolk.

THIS House was founded in the year 1248. by *Richard de Clare* Earl of *Gloucester*, from whom descended the *Mortimers* Earls of *March*, and the Royal House of *York*, as is set forth in a long Pedigree in *Latin* and *English* Verse, in Dialogue between a Fryer and a Secular at the Tomb of *Joan* of *Acres* Daughter of *Edward* the I. and Wife of *Gilbert de Clare* Earl of *Gloucester*. This House being an alien Priory and Cell to the Abby of *Beekeherlewyn*, in *Normandy*, King *Richard* the II. in the ninteenth year of his Reign, made it *Indigena*, and gave it as a Cell to St. *Peters* at *Westminster*.

Pope *John*, in the fifth year of his Pontificate, translated this House from a Priory of Monks into a Colledge of a Dean and Secular Canons. This was done at the Petition of *Edmund* Earl of *March*, Heir of the first Founders, who by his Deed dated 7. *Hen.* 5. granted and confirm'd to the Dean and Canons here all the Lands and Priviledges belonging to the Priory. *Vid. infra*, 1004. *Vol.* 3. part 2. *p.* 164.

[Valued at 324 *l.* 4 *s.* 1 *d.* ob. *per Annum.*]

GLOUCESTER-HALL, in the Suburbs of Oxford.

THIS was founded and endow'd *An.* 1283. (11. *E.* 1.) for the maintenance of thirteen *Benedictine* Monks of the Abby of *Gloucester*, by *John Giffard* Lord of *Brimesfeild*. 19. *E.* 1. That King granted his License of *Mortmain*.

It appears by the Founders Deed of Foundation, that the House was built upon certain Ground purchased of the Knights of St. *John* of *Jerusalem*, in a Lane commonly then called *Stockwell street*, that the Church here was dedicated to St. *John* the Apostle, and St. *Benedict* the Abbot and Confessor, and that the House was erected for Benedictine Monks *Causa studii*.

K 2 MIS-

MISSENDEN, in Buckinghamshire.

542.

IT was found by Inquisition taken at *Aylesbury*, 51. *E.* 3. that the Abby of *Muſſenden* was founded in the year 1293. by *William de Muſſenden*, who held the Mannor of *Muſſenden* of the Earl of *Gloucester* by Knights service. In the Chapter-House and Church belonging to this Abby did lie buried several of the *Miſſendens* descended from the Founder, whose names may be seen in the Book at large. *Vid. Vol.* 3. *p.* 18.
[Valued at 261 *l.* 14 *s.* 6 *d.* q. per *Annum.*]

The MINORESSES, at London.

KING *Edward* the I. in the one and twentieth year of his Reign granted his Licenſe of *Mortmain* to *Edmund* his Brother and his Wife, *Blanch* Queen of *Nauarre*, to build a Houſe in the Parish of St. *Botulphs* without *Algate*, for Nuns of the Order of *Minoreſſes*, there to remain in the service of God, the bleſſed *Mary*, and St. *Francis*.
[Vaued at 318 *l.* 8 *s.* 5 *d.* per *Annum.*]

543.

WATERBECHAM, in Cambridgeshire.

KING *Edward* the I. in the twenty second year of his Reign granted to *Dioniſia de Monte-Caniſu*, the Mannor of *Waterbeche*, to build a Religious House there for *Minoreſſes* of the Order of St. *Clare* to be brought over from beyond the Seas. All which was confirm'd by King *Edward* the III. in the eleventh year of his Reign.

HOLAND, in Lancashire.

544.

HERE being formerly a Collegiate Church or Chappel of St. *Thomas* the Martyr, served by Secular Chaplains, *Walter* Bishop of *Coventry* and *Litchfeild*, in the year 1319. by conſent of *Robert de Holland* the Patron, alter'd the Foundation into a Priory conſiſting of a Prior and twelve *Benedictine* Monks. Upon every Vacation or Death of the Prior, the Monks were to chooſe three of their Houſe, one of which being approved by the Patron, and preſented to the Biſhop, was to be by him conſtituted Prior. *Vid. Vol.* 2. *p.* 889.
[Valued at 53 *l.* 3 *s.* 4 *d.* per *Annum.*]

546.

Of certain Antient Monaſteries in Wales.

MOrcant a King in *Wales* having treacherouſly kill'd his Uncle *Frioc*, after he had in a most solemn manner ſworn an inviolable peace with him before the holy Altar, was by *Oudoceus* Biſhop of *Landaff*, in a Synod of his Clergy, which he had aſſembled for that purpoſe, enjoyn'd for the said perjury and homicide, to perform Faſtings, Prayers, and Alms Deeds; and being on his ſincere Repentance, received again in the Chriſtian Communion, he granted and quit claim'd to the Abbies of *Catoc*, *Ildut*, and *Docun*, and to the Cathedral Church of *Landaff*, divers Liberties and Immunities.

Alien

Alien Priories, of Benedictines.

Viz. Such Monasteries here in *England* as did belong to certain greater and elder Monasteries of the same Order beyond the Seas, and were subject to, and did depend on the same; and had the name of Cells.

547.

DEREHURST, in **Gloucestershire**, *a Cell to St.* Denis *in* France.

HERE was an old Abby destroy'd by the *Danes.* But after the *Norman* Conquest, in the year 1069. King *William* the Conqueror endow'd here a new Priory and made it a Cell to St. *Denis* in *France*: or rather confirm'd what King *Edward* the Confessor had done before. King *Henry* the VI. in the twenty first year of his Reign made this Priory *Indigena.*

548.

OTERY, *in* **Devonshire**, *a Cell to St.* Mary's *at* Roan.

549.

THIS Priory was given to the Church of St. *Mary* at *Roan* by King *Edward* the Confessor in the year 1060. In the 8. *Edw.* 3. the Dean and Chapter of St. *Mary's* at *Roan,* by the King's Licenfe, granted their Mannor of *Otery,* and Advowson of the Church there, to *John de Grandison* Bishop of *Exeter,* who in the eleventh year of that King founded here a Colledge of Secular Canons.

550.

LEVISHAM, *in* **Kent**, *a Cell to St.* Peter's *at* Gaunt, *in* Flanders.

KING *Henry* the I. in the thirteenth year of his Reign confirm'd to the Abbot and Monks of St. *Peters* of *Gant,* the Mannor of *Levesham* and *Greenwich,* &c. with divers Liberties, formerly granted by King *Edward* and King *William* his Father.
Vid. Vol. 2. *p.* 890.

St. MICHAELS *of the* MOUNT, *in* **Cornwall**, *a Cell to St.* Michael, *in* Normandy.

551.

Robert Earl of *Morton* gave St. *Michaels Mount,* in *Cornwall,* to God and the Monks of the Church of St. *Michael de Periculo Maris,* in *Normandy, Anno Dom.* 1085.
Vid. 2. *Vol. p.* 902.

MERSEY,

MERSEY, in Essex, a Cell to St. Owens at Roan.

552.

IT was found by Inquisition 4. E. 3. that the Mannors of *Mersey Fyngrinko* and *Peet*, and half the hundred of *Wenestr*, in the County of *Essex*, were given to the Abby of St. *Owens*, in *Normandy*, by St. *Edward* the Confessor, and confirm'd by King *William*, and King *Henry* the II.

ANDEVER, in Hampshire, a Cell to St. Florence at Saumurs.

553.

KING *William* the Conqueror (or as the Words of the Deed are, *Wilhelmus Rex qui armis Anglicam terram sibi subjugavit*) gave to Sr. *Florence*, the Church of *Andever*, with divers Lands and Revenues to the same Church belonging: Confirm'd by King *Edward* the II. in the eighth year of his Reign.

BLITH Priory, in Nottinghamshire, a Cell to St. Catherines at Rohan.

554.

ANno Dom. 1088. *Roger de Builly* and *Muriel* his Wife founded and endowed this House with Lands and great Liberties. All which was afterwards confirm'd to the Monks here by King *Henry* the II. and by *Idonea de Veteri ponte* Daughter and Heir of *John de Bullei*, by her Deed dated 1232. King *John* in the second year of his Reign gave the Chapelry of *Blyth*, and divers other Churches and Lands to St. *Mary's* at *Rohan*.

555. COVENHAM, in Lincolnshire, a Cell of St. Karileph, in le Maine in France.

556.

KING *William* the Conqueror *Anno* 1082. gave this Town situated in that part of *Lincolnshire*, called *Lyndsey* to God and St. *Karileph*. 31. *Edw*. 1. A Writ of *Quod Damnum* was executed at *Lincoln*, in order to an alienation of this Cell, from the Abbot and Covent of St. *Karileph* in the Diocess of *Mans*, to the Abbot and Covent of *Kirkestede* here in *England*.

ABERGAVENNY, in Monmouthshire a Cell of St. Vincents in Maine.

557.
558.

THIS Priory was founded by *Hamelinus* who came into *England* with the Conqueror, and died in the Reign of King *William Rufus*. *William de Brewosa*, and others of the founders Linage were Benefactors. Vid. 2. Vol. p. 904.

WOTTON-

WOTTON-WAVEN, in Warwickshire.

Robert de Toenio gave this Estate to the Monks of St. *Peter* at *Conchis*, in *Normandy*; on whom King *Henry* the I. conferred great Priviledges.   559.

FOLKESTON, in Kent, a Cell to the Abby of Lolley in Normandy.

Nigellus de Munevilla, An. 1095. gave this Church of *Folkston* to *Ranulph* then Abbot of the Church of St. *Mary de Lonleyo*, and to the Monks there, in pure and perpetual Alms. Which, with divers other Lands and Revenues, was confirm'd to them by *William de Abrincis* Lord of *Folkeston*, who descended from the said *Nigellus*.   560.

KIRKBY, in Warwickshire, a Cell of St. Nicholas in Anjou.   562.

Anno 1077. Gosfredus de Wirchia gave to God and the Monastery of St. *Nicholas* in *Anjou*, Lands in *Kirkby* with other Lands and Possessions elsewhere; from whom descended *Roger de Mulbraio*, who gave to the Church of St. *Nicholas* of *Kirkeby* the Church of *Newbold*. Afterwards *Thomas* Earl of *Nottingham* having founded a House of *Carthusians* at *Epworth* in the Isle of *Axholme*, the Abbot of St. *Nicholas* at *Anjou* was prevailed with to assign his Estate in *Monks-Kirkby*, *Newbold*, &c. to the said House of *Carthusians*, which was confirm'd by King *Henry* the V. in the third year of his Reign.   563.

The Priory of the Holy Trinity at York, a Cell to * Majus-Monasterium in France.

* *Marmonstier in Tourain.*

Radulphus Paganellus gave the Church of the holy Trinity at *York* to the Monks of St. *Martin* in the *Majus-Monastery*, with divers other Possessions. It was found by Inquisition taken at *York* 34. *Edw.* 1. That the Heirs of the Founder claim'd no right in the Temporals of this Priory upon the death of any Prior, but only to place a Porter to see that the Goods of the Priory be not stollen during the Vacation, and that upon the arrival of a new Prior from the Abbot of *Majus-monasterium*, he did use to enter upon the Possession of his Office, without fealty or other duty to the Patron.   564. 565.

HEDLAY, in Yorkshire, a Cell to the Holy Trinity at York.

Ypolitus de Bram gave to God and St. *Mary* of *Hedlay* and the Monks there certain Lands in *Midelton*. All which was confirm'd to the Prior and Convent of the *Trinity* at *York*, and to their Cell at *Hedlay*, by *Peter de Midleton*, in the year 1290.

LAN-

566.   LANCASTER, *a Cell to St. Martins at Sees in France.*

567. Roger Earl of *Poictiers* gave the Church of St. *Mary* at *Lancaster* with divers Lands and Revenues to the Monastery of St. *Martin*. All which was confirm'd by *John* Earl of *Morton*; and by King *Richard* the II.

568. *An.* 1246. *John Romanus* Archdeacon of *Richmond*, appropriated the Church of *Lancaster* and Chappels thereunto belonging to this Priory, reserving twenty Marks *per Annum* for a Vicar presentative.

569.   OTTERY, *in* Devonshire, *a Cell to the Abby of St.* Michael pericul. mar. *in* Normandy.

THIS Priory was founded by King *John* for four Monks and endow'd with Lands of 100 *l.* value *per Annum*. These Monks were to distribute to the Poor at their Gates, bread to the value of 16 *s.* every week.

570.   LODRES, *in* Dorsetshire, *a Cell to the Abby of St.* Mary de Mon-Bur.

Benedict *de Redueriis* gave this Mannor to the Monastery of St. *Mary de Monte Burgo*; confirm'd by King *Henry* the I.

571.   APLEDERCOMB, *in the Isle of* Wight, *a Cell to the Abby of* Mont-Burg, *in* Normandy.

THIS Priory consisted only of a Prior and two Monks, who were removed by Command of King *Edward* the III. to a more Inland Habitation, first to the Abby of *Hyde*, and after that in the 13. *E.* 3. to Salisbury.

    FRAMPTON, *in* Dorsetshire, *a Cell to* Caen, *in* Normandy.

THIS was given to St. *Stephens* at *Caen*, and the Monks there, by King *William* the Conqueror, and with divers other Lands and Liberties confirm'd to them by King *Richard* the II.

572.   SWANESEY, *in* Cambridgeshire. *a Cell to St.* Sergius, *in* Angiers.

573. THE Church of *Swanesey* with all manner of Tithes there, and in the Vills thereunto belonging, were given by *Alin* Earl of *Britain*, to the Abby of St. *Sergius* and St. *Bachus* at *Angiers*; who presented the Prior to this Priory, as often as the Office avoided.

BLAK-

BLAKENHAM, in Suffolk, a Cell to St. Mary at Bec.

THIS was given to the Abby abovesaid by *Walter Giffard*, and confirm'd by King *William Rufus*.

COGES, in Oxfordshire, a Cell of Fischamp.

Mauresses Arsc gave this Estate with other Tithes and Revenues to the Church of *Fiscampe*, Anno 1103.

WESTWOOD, in Worcestershire, a Cell to Font-Ebraud. 574.

Osbert Fitz-Hugh, and *Eustachia de Say* his Mother erected here a Convent of Nuns of *Font-Ebraud*.

WELLS, in Norfolk, a Cell of the Abby at Caen, in Normandy.

KING *Edward* the III. in the forty seventh year of his Reign (being 575. then in War with *France*) committed the Custody of the Priory of *Panusfeild* and *Wells* to *Hugh Fastolf*, to hold at the yearly Rent of 40 l. per Annum to the King, and 10 l. per Annum to each Monk there, for his support. This Priory being first given by *William de Estois* to the Abby of St. 576. Steven at *Caen*, and after seized into the King's hands by *Edward* the III. it continued in the Crown till 9. *Edw.* 4. at which time that King desirous to restore this Estate to its antient use, the Spiritualty, and out of the Devotion which he bore to St. *Stephen*, he conferr'd the whole Estate which did formerly belong to this Priory on the Dean and Canons of his free Chappel of St. *Steven* at *Westminster*.

PATRICKSBURN, in Kent, a Cell to Beau-Lieu, in Normandy.

IT was found by Inquisition taken at *Canterbury* the 6 *Edw.* 3. that this Mannor was given to the Priory of *Beau-Lieu*, in *Normandy*, by *Johannes de Pratellis*, and confirm'd by King *John*.

STOKE-CURCY, in Devonshire, a Cell to Lonley, in France. 577.

Hugh de Novilla gave to God and the Monks at *Stok-curcy*, the Church of St. *Andrew* of *Stoke-curcy*, with other Revenues. *William de Curcy*, and *John de Novilla* were also Benefactors.

SHIRBURN, in Hampshire, a Cell of St. Vigor Cerasius.

578.
579.

Henry de Portu, or Port gave the West part of Shirburn with the Church there, and divers other Revenues, to God and St. Vigor Cerasius, all which was confirm'd to the Monks at Shirburn by his Descendents. King Edward the III. gave the Custody of the Hospital of St. Julian, or Domus Dei, at Southampton to Queens Colledge in Oxford; to which Hospital King Edward the IV. in the first year of his Reign gave the alien Priory of Shireburn, in Hampshire.

BURWELL, in Lincolnshire, a Cell of St. Mary Silvæ Majoris.

580.

John de Hay gave to God and the Monastery of St. Mary Silvæ-Majoris; and to the Monks at Burwell, divers Possessions; from whom descended Gilbert de Umframvill Earl of Angos, who lived at Burwell.

LANKYWAN, in Wales, a Cell to the Abby of Lyra.

Edmund, Son of King Henry the III. discharged this House from all Exactions and Troubles from his Heirs or their Bayliffs, in the Vacation of a Prior.

SELE, in Sussex, a Cell of St. Florence at Saumurs.

581.

William de Braiosa, by his Deed dated 1075. gave the Church of St. Peter at Sele, with other Churches and Revenues both in England and Normandy to the Abbot and Monks of St. Florence. This Priory of Sele was made Indigena, or Denison 19. R. 2.

OKEBURN, in Wiltshire, a Cell to Bec, in Normandy.

582.
583.

Matilda de Wallengfort gave to the Church of St. Mary of Bec, both the Okeburns, viz. the greater and the less. Richard Earl of Cornwall by his Deed dated 1253. discharg'd the Abbot and Monks of Bec from all Exactions and Suit of Court in his honour of Walingford, except only that his Bayliff of Walingford should once a year keep a view of Frankpledge at Okeburn, and then be entertain'd for that day, with four Horses at most.

584.

WILLESFORD, in Lincolnshire, a Cell to Bec in Normandy.

By Inquisition taken at Stranford, it was found that the Prior of the Order of Bec held in Willesford and Ancaster, Lands of the value 16 l. per Annum of the Gift of Hugh de Evermewe.

WEDEN-

WEDEN-PINKNEY, in Northamptonshire, a Cell to St. Lucian near Beauvoys in France.

Giles, Ralph, Gilbert, Henry, and Robert de Pinkeni, succeffively gave Lands and Revenues to the Abby of St. Lucian and the Monks at St. Mary's of Weden. Anno Dom. 1392, The Abbot and Convent of St. Lucian convey'd their Priory of Weden, and all the Estate thereunto belonging to the Abbot and Convent of Bitlefden and their Succeffors, in confideration of a Sum of Gold received, and the yearly pension of ten Marks to be paid to the Abbot and Convent of St. Lucian and their Succeffors in the Church of St. Mary at Calais, on the Feast of St. John Baptist. 585.

TYWARDREIT, in Cornwall, a Cell to Angiers in France. 586.

Robert de Cardinan gave divers Lands and Revenues in Cornwall, to the Church of St. Sergius and St. Bachus at Angiers, and to the Church of St. Andrew of Tywardrait, and to the Monks there; all which was confirm'd by King Henry the III. 587.

BIRSTALL, in Yorkshire, a Cell of St. Martins at Albamarle.

This was given among other Lands and Revenues to the Church and Monks of St. Martin without the Castle of Albamarle in Normandy, by Steven Earl of Albamarle 1115. Walter Archbishop of York first fettled the Monks of Albamarle here at Birftal, and granted to them divers Immunities. Charles the VI. King of France by his Deed dated 1395. fetting forth that the Abbot and Convent of St. Martin had paft over to his beloved Coufin the Duke of Lancafter their Priory of Birftal in England for the Sum of one thousand Livers, granted them his Licenfe to purchafe Lands of the like value in France. The faid Abbot and Convent of St. Martin by their Deed dated 18. Rich. 2. granted all their Lands, Tithes and Penfions here in England to the Abbot and Convent of Kirkftal (in Yorkfhire.) 588. 589.

GOLDCLIVE, in Monmouthshire, a Cell to Bec in Normandy. 590.

Robert de Candos gave this Church of St. Mary Magdalen of Goldclive with divers other Lands, &c. to the Monks of St. Mary at Bec. All which was confirm'd by King John in the fecond year of his Reign. This Priory was afterwards united to the Abby of Teukesbury, which union, was ratified by Pope Eugenius, Anno Dom. 1402. 591.
Vid. 2. Vol. p. 904.

MINTING,

592.   MINTING, in **Lincolnshire**, a Cell of St. Benedict Super Leyre.

THIS was given to that Monastery, by *Ranulph* Earl of *Chester*.

BOXGRAVE, in **Sussex**, a Cell of l'Essay in Normandy.

593.
594.
595.
596.

THIS Priory was founded in the Reign of King *Henry* the I. *William* Earl of *Arundell* endow'd it with great Possessions, and gave and confirm'd it to the Monks of the Holy *Trinity* at *l'Essay*. The first Founder of this House, (dedicated to the blessed *Mary* and St. *Blase*) at *Boxgrave*, was *Robert de Haja*, who placed here three Monks of the Order of St. *Benedict*; *Roger de Sancto Johanne* who married *Cecily*, his Daughter, doubled the number of Monks, whose Sons *William* and *Robert de Sancto Johanne*, still encreas'd them to fifteen, conferring divers Revenues for their maintenance, out of which he reserved only an annual Pension of three Marks to the Abby of *l'Essay*. *Thomas* Abbot of the Holy *Trinity* at *l'Essay*, granted to the Prior of *Boxgrave* and his Successors, that they might constantly have fifteen Monks in their Priory, and that upon the decease of any, they might supply their number with whom they pleas'd to elect. King *Edward* the III. in the thirteenth year of his Reign discharged this Priory of all seizures as an alien Priory in time of War, and made it Denison.

LONG-BENINGTON, in **Lincolnshire**, a Cell to Savigny in Normandy.

567.

R*Adulfus Filgeriarum* gave *Belintone* to the Abby of *Savigny*. The Monks here held four Carucates of Land each Carucate worth 4 *l. per Annum*.

GROMOND, in **Yorkshire**, a Cell to the Abby of Gramont in France.

THIS was given to the said Abby by *Joan* late Wife of *Robert de Turneham*, and confirm'd by King *John* in the fifteenth year of his Reign. Vid. Vol. 3. p. 15.

MONKENLEN, in **Herefordshire**, a Cell to Conchis in Normandy.

598.

W*.Illiam* Bishop of *Hereford* did by his Episcopal Authority confirm and appropiate to the Abby of St. *Peter* at *Conchis* the Mannor and Church of *Monekeslen*, and other Revenues, given by *Ralph de Tony* Senior.

TOFT

A CISTERCIAN MONK Vol 1 P. 595

TOFT Priory in Norfolk, a Cell to Preaux.

THIS was given by *Robert* Earl of *Mellent*, and with divers other Lands confirm'd to the Abby of *St. Peter* at *Preaux* by King *Henry* the II. and by King *Edward* the I. with great Liberties.   599.

ALVERTON, in Yorkshire, a Cell to the Majus-Monasterium.

Richard *Mulleverer* gave the Church of *St. Martin* in *Alverton* to the Monks of *Majus Monasterium* in *Alverton*. Confirm'd by King *Henry* the II.   600.

MONMOUTH, a Cell to the Abby of St. Florence at Saumurs.

W*Ihenocus de Monemue* built in his Castle of *Monemue* a Church to the honour of God, St. *Mary*, and St. *Florence*, and gave it in perpetual Alms to the Monks of St. *Florence* at *Saumurs*. *John de Monemula* gave to the Church of St. *Mary* of *Monmouth*, and to the Abby of *Saumurs*, the Hospital of St. *John* at *Monmouth*.   601.

HAGH, in Lincolnshire, a Cell to the Abby de Voto near Cherburg.   602.

KING *Henry* the II. gave and confirm'd to the Abby and Cannons of *Cherburg* in *France*, the Mannor and Church of *Hagh* with large Liberties, as they were formerly confirm'd by King *Henry* his Grandfather.

The particulars and values of their Estate was found by Inquisition 22. *Edw.* 3. Among other things, that they had certain Rents in *Grantham*, &c.   603.

HINKLEY, Leicestershire, a Cell to Lyra in Normandy.

Robert Earl of *Leicester* gave to the Abby of *Lyra*, the Church of *Hinkelai* with divers Chappels and other Churches adjoyning, with their Tithes. All which was confirm'd by King *Henry* the II.   604.

HORSELEGH, in Essex, a Cell to St. Martin of Troarn.

THE Abby and Covent of St. *Martins* at *Troarn* in *Normandy*, granted the Churches of *Horselegh* and *Whitenhirst*, to the Prior and Convent of *Bruton*, in exchange for other Lands which the Priory of *Bruton* had in *Normandy*, from which time the Prior of *Bruton* placed a Prior in *Horselegh* from among his own Canons, and presented secular Vicars to the said two Churches. This was confirm'd by King *Edward* the III. in the forty fifth year of his Reign.   605.

A B.

ABBERBURY, in Shropshire, a Cell to the Abby of Gramount.

606.

Fulco Fitz-Warin founded and gave this Priory to the Monks of Gramount with divers Lands, &c. confirm'd by King Henry the II. in the seventeenth of his Reign. And by Thomas Corbeth in the year 1262.

LEVENESTRE, in Sussex, a Cell to Almenesches.

607.

THE Possessions of the Benedictine Nuns of St. Mary of Almenesches as well in France as England were confirm'd to them by Pope Alexander, and their Lands in their own hands exempted from Tithes, by his Bull dated 1178.

608.

BY the Stat. made at Carlile 35. E. 1. commonly called *De asportatis Religiosorum*, it is enacted that no Foreign Abby, &c. shall impose any Tallage, Payment, or Assessment whatsoever, oo any of their Houses subject to them in England, under the Penalty of forfeiting their Estate here. In the Parliament held at Westminster 13. R. 2. it was ordain'd that no alien of the French Nation should enjoy any Benefice in this Kingdom; notwithstanding several Frenchmen having purchased Letters of Denization, continued to enjoy Benifices, &c. whereby great Treasures were transported out of the Kingdom, the King's Council discovered to his Enemies in France, &c. It was therefore enacted 1 H. 5. ch. 7. that the foresaid Ordinance be but in due execution against all, but such Priors Alien as are conventual, and such as have Induction and Institution, provided that such be Catholicks, and that they give security not to discover, &c. It was finally enacted in the Parliament held at Leicester 2 H. 5. for the Inconveniencies above-mentioned, and also for that the English had their Possessions seiz'd in France, that all the Possessions of the Priors aliens (except Conventuals, &c.) be vested in the King's hands and his Heirs for ever, to the intent that Divine Services in the places aforesaid may for the time to come be more duly perform'd by English people, than they have been by French.

A CLVNIAC MONK

OF THE
Cluniacenses *or Monks of* Clugny.

The first Institutor of this Order, or rather Reformation of Monks, was Abbot *Beruo*, to whom *William* then Duke of *Aquitain*, gave the place call'd *Clugny* or *Cluny* in *Burgundy* for their first Habitation, in the year of our Lord 890. This was a Reform of St. *Bennet*'s Order.

WENLOCK, *in* Shropshire.

HERE was formerly a Nunnery in which *Milburg* Neice of *Wilphere* King of *Mercia*, lived, and died Abbess, with the Reputation of great Sanctity. Which House being totally decayed, *Roger* Earl of *Mongomery*, built here a Monastery for the Monks of *Cluny*. The Church here was dedicated to St. *Mildred*. *Isabel de Say* Wife of *William Fitz-Alan* was a Benefactress. And this Priory was made *Indigena* 18. R. 2. *Vid.* 2. *Vol. p.* 907.

[Vaued at 401 *l*. 0 *s*. 7 *d*. q. *per Annum*.]

DUDLEY, *in* Staffordshire, *a Cell to Wenlock*.

THE Church here was dedicated to St. *James*, which with other Churches and Lands, Pope *Lucius* did confer and appropriate to this Priory in the year 1190. granting in the same Deed divers great Priviledges and Immunities to the Monastery. *Vid.* 2. *Vol. p.* 907.

LEWES, *in* Sussex.

THIS House was founded by *William de Warren* Earl of *Surrey* in the time of King *William* the Conqueror. Which Earl obtain'd from the Abby of St. *Peter* in *Burgundy* four *Cluniac* Monks, to whom he gave the Church of St. *Pancrace* adjoyning to his Castle of *Lewis*, and endow'd them with divers Lands and Possessions, by the License, and Confirmation of King *William*; with a Curse to the Violators of his Gift, and a Blessing to the Defenders. Yet this Priory remain'd a Cell to the Abby of *Clugny* in *Burgundy* till the forty seventh year of King E. 3. at which time that King made it *indigena*, and independant; so also the Priories of *Castleacre*, *Prittlewell*, *Farleigh*, *Horton*, and *Stanesgate*, which were all Cells belonging to the Priory of *Lewis*. *Vid.* 2. *Vol. p.* 908.

[Valued at 920 *l*. 4 *s*. 6 *d*. *per Annum*.]

PRIT-

PRITTLEWELL, in Essex, a Cell to Lewes.

619.

Robert Fitz-Suene gave the Church of Prittlewell to the Priory of St. Pancrace at Lewes, to be a Cell of that House, and to be furnish'd with Monks of the Rule of St. Bennet, and Order of Clugny from Lewes; ordaining by his Deed of Foundation that the Prior of Prittlewel should pay yearly to the Prior of Lewes one mark for an acknowledgment.

[Valued at 155 l. 11 s. 2 d. ob. per Annum.]

WESTACRE, in Norfolk, a Cell to Lewes.

This House was granted and confirm'd by Rodulphus de Teneio Lord of the Soil, to Oliver, Priest of Acre, and Walter his Son, who became Canons regular here.

[Valued at 260 l. 13 s. 7 d. q. per Annum.]

FARLEY, in Wiltshire, a Cell to Lewes.

620.

This Priory was founded Anno Dom. 1125. and dedicated to God and St. Mary Magdalen. It was endow'd by Humphrey de Bohun the King's Sewer, and Margery his Wife, with the Mannor of Farley and the Park there, and with divers other Lands and Revenues. All which was confirm'd to them by King Henry the III. in the eleventh year of his Reign.

621.

[Valued at 153 l. 14 s. 2 d. ob. per Annum.]

HORTON, in Kent, a Cell to Lewes.

622.

This House was founded and endow'd by Robert de Ver Constable of England, and Adeliza his Wife, and subjected to the Priory of Lewes, to which they were to pay a Mark per Annum as an acknowledgment. In this House did inhabit thirteen, or at least eight Monks: who were to say three Masses dayly, viz. the High Mass, our Lady's Mass, and the third pro defunctis. Their Seal was kept by three Monks, viz. the Prior, Sub-prior, and another.

[Valued at 95 l. 12 s. 2 d. per Annum.]

STANESGATE, in Essex, a Cell to Lewes.

623.

Anno Dom 1177. Alexander Prior of this House, and the Covent of the same, with the assent of the Covent of Lewis, granted the Tithes of their Fee at Clerkenwell, with their Land there, to the Nuns of St. Mary at Clerkenwell, they paying to the Prior of Stanesgate, a yearly Pension of ten shillings for the said Tithes and Lands.

CLIFFORD, in Herefordshire, *a Cell to* Lewes.

IT appeared by Inquisition 20. *E.* 3. that this Priory was founded by *Simon Fitz-Richard Fitz-Ponce* formerly Lord of *Clifford* and Ancestor of the Countess of *Lincoln*, and that this House was not alien, or dependant on any other beyond Sea. It was subjected by the Founder to the Priory of *Lewes.*   624.

[Valued at 57 *l.* 7 *s.* 4 *d.* per *Annum.*]

CASTLE-ACRE, in Norfolk.

Founded *An. Dom.* 1090. *William de Warren* Earl of *Surrey*, the first of that name, and his Son Earl *William* the II. were great Benefactors, and gave to God, and St. *Mary*, and to the holy Apostles *Peter* and *Paul*, and to the Cluniac Monks of St. *Pancrace* (*i. e.* of the Priory of *Lewes*) serving God at *Achra*, divers Lands and Revenues. Besides whom many other Benefactors gave other Mannors and Lands, Tithes and Churches, as may be seen in particular in the Book at large. *p.* 626, 627, 628, 629.   625.

Herbert Bishop of *Norwich* constituted the Church and Monastery here, and placed therein Cluniac Monks, under the Rule of St. *Benedict.* Bishop *Ebrard* impropriated and confirm'd to them their several Churches, given to them by the Earls of *Surrey* and other Benefactors.   630.

It was certified to King *Edw.* the I. in the thirty fourth year of his Reign that the Prior and Convent of *Castle-acre* were English, and not Aliens of the Subjects of the King of *France*, or his Adherers; and that no Rent or Pension was paid by them to any of his Dominion or Adherents, nor did they owe obedience to any such, except only, that when the Abbot of *Clugny* comes sometimes into *England* he uses to visit in the said Priory. Hereupon this House was allow'd to be *Indigena* and not *Alienigena*, and to be priviledged accordingly, 18. *E.* 2.

[Valued at 306 *l.* 11 *s.* 4 *d.* ob. q. per *Annum.*]

MENDHAM, in Norfolk, *a Cell to* Castle-acre.   631.

William Son of *Roger de Huntingfeild* gave to God, and St. *Mary* of *Acre*, and to the Monks there, the Isle of St. *Mary* of *Mendham* to be in the same manner subject to *Castle-acre*, as that House is to St. *Pancrace*, and that to the Church of *Clugny*.

The Prior of *Castle-acre* and Convent there did grant to *Roger de Huntingfeild*, who was their great Benefactor, to maintain at least eight Monks at this Priory of *Mendham*, and not to depose the Prior here unless for one of these three causes, Disobedience, Incontinence, or Dilapidation of the House.   632.

M   BROM-

BROMHOLM, in Norfolk a Cell of Castle-acre.

THE Estate here, with divers other Lands, was given to the Monks of *Acre*, by *William de Glanville*, and confirm'd to them by *Bartholmew* his Son.

633. The Prior and Convent of *Bromholm*, held Lands in Fee-farm of the Prior and Convent of *Acre*, at the Annual Rent of fourteen Marks, five shillings and four pence payable at three terms by the year, *viz.* at the Feast of St. *Michael* 64 s. at the *Purification* 64 s. and at *Penticoft* 64 s.

634. Controversie arising between the Priors of *Lewes*, and *Acre*, and the Prior of *Bromholm*, about placing the Prior of this House. The whole matter was referr'd by Pope *Gregory* the IX. to be heard and determin'd by the Prior of *Osolveston* in *Leicestershire*, and the Dean of *Rutland*; who decreed among other things, that upon the death of the Prior of *Bromholm*, the Prior of *Acre* should nominate six Monks, three of *Acre* and three of *Bromholm*, out of which number, the Convent of *Bromholm* should choose one for their Prior, &c.

635. This Decree was made in the Church of St. *Mary* near the Bridge in *Stanford*, on *Wednesday* next before *Palm-Sunday* 1229.

Pope *Celestin* by his Bull dated in the fourth year of his Pontificate, granted that this Priory should be free from any subjection to that of *Acre*.

636. King *Henry* the III. in the thirteenth year of his Reign granted to the Prior and Monks of St. *Andrew* of *Bromholm* to have a Fair there yearly at the Feast of the Exhaltation of the holy Cross, and a Market weekly on the *Monday*. *Vid. Vol.* 2. *p.* 909.

[Valued at 100 *l.* 5 *s.* 3 *d.* q. *per Annum.*]

REINHAM, in Norfolk, a Cell to Castle-acre.

William de Lisewis founded here a House for three Monks at least in a place then called *Normannesberch*, and endow'd it with Lands, in honour of the blessed Virgin and St. *John* the *Evangelist*, all which *Jeoffrey* his Son gave and confirm'd to the Monks of *Acre*.

637. Roger Prior of *Reinham*, granted to *Lena*, a Nun and other Nuns there serving God, a certain Solitary Place or Hermitage near *Winghale*, parcel of the Possessions of this House, to be held by them at the yearly Rent of twelve pence. To which House of Nuns *Riginald Fitz-Hamon* gave other Lands with his Daughter whom he made a religious Woman there.

---

638. ### SLEVESHOLM, in Norfolk, a Cell of Castle-acre.

Founded by *William* Earl of *Warren*, and by him given to Monks of *Castle-acre*. *John* Earl of *Warren* confirm'd his Great Grand-fathers Foundation *Anno Dom.* 1309. (3. *E.* 2.) and granted, that as often as the Priory of this House should be void, the Prior of *Castle-acre* should have full power to confer the place on a Monk of that House, which new Prior being first presented to the said *John* Earl of *Warren* or his Heirs, and having done his Fealty, should be admitted with effect.

639.

BER-

BERMUNDSEY, in Surrey.

THIS Monastery of St. *Saviours* of *Burmundsey* was founded by *Alwinus Child* a Citizen of *London*, in the year 1082.
Many were the Benefactors to this House. King *Henry* the I. in the year 1127. gave to the Monks here the Mannors of *Bermundsey, Rederhith,* and *Delwich,* the hide of *Southwark,* and other Lands. *Walkelinus Mammynot* gave them a Moiety of all *Greenwich.*

King *Henry* the II. in the year 1159. confirm'd to them the Donation of divers Churches, as *Camberwell,* and others.

Anno 1213. the Prior of *Burmundsey* raised from the Foundation a new Building adjoyning to the Walls of his House, which was call'd the *Elemosinary,* or *Hospitale conversorum & puerorum,* in honour of St. *Thomas* the Martyr.

An. 1268. King *Henry* the III. granted to the Monks of *Burmundsey* a Market every *Monday* at their Mannor of *Charleton* in *Kent,* and a Fair to be held there at the Feast of the Holy *Trinity* yearly.

The Mannor of *Bermundsey* was ancient Demesn of the Crown, and all the Lands and Tenements in this Mannor *cum pertin.* are impleadable in the Court of this Mannor by the King's writ of Right according to the Custom of the said Mannor, and not at the Common Law.

Within the Mannor of *Burmundsey* were comprised the several Towns of *Bermondesey, Camberwell, Rederhith,* the Hide of *Southwark, Dilwich, Waddon,* and *Reyham,* with their Appurtenants.

[Valued at 474 *l.* 14 *s.* 4 *d.* ob. q. *per Annum.*]

640.

641.

642.

The Priory of St. James by Exeter, in Devonshire.

BAldwin Earl of *Devonshire* founded this Priory without the Walls at *Exeter* for Cluniac Monks, and endowed it with Revenues. Confirm'd by *Richard* Earl of *Devonshire,* Son of *Baldwin,* 1157. and by *Robert.* Bishop of *Exeter, Anno* 1146. Also by *Maud* the Empress. *Infra* p. 1025.

[Valued at 502 *l.* 12 *s.* 9 *d. per Annum.*]

643.

644.
645.

LENTON, in Nottinghamshire.

William Peverel built this House for Cluniac Monks, and gave to the Abby of *Clugny* great Revenues for the Maintenance of certain Monks of their Order in this Priory, providing however that this House should be free and discharged from all exactions of that Abby, paying only one Mark *per Annum* as an acknowledgment. To this Priory of the Holy *Trinity* at *Lenton* King *Henry* the II. was a Benefactor, so were also King *Steven,* and King *John,* which last granted them the Tithes of his hunting (*Decimam venationis nostræ*) in the Counties of *Nottingham* and *Derby.* All whose Grants were confirm'd by King *Edward* the II. in the tenth year of his Reign. *Vid. Vol.* 3. *p.* 30.

[Valued at 329 *l.* 15 *s.* 10 *d.* ob. *per Annum.*]

646.

647.

648.

PONTE-

PONTEFRACT, in Yorkshire.

649
650.
651.
652.
653.
655.

THE first Founder of this House was *Robert de Laceio*, who built it in a place then called *Kirkeby*, in honour of St. *John* the Apostle and Evangelist, subjecting it to the Church of *Clugny* from whence it was furnisht with Monks, and gave them several Lands and Revenues; confirm'd by *Hugo de la Val*. *Henry de Lascy* Son of the said *Robert*, gave to these Monks the Custody of the Hospital of St. *Nicholas* in *Pomfract*, in the year 1159. Pope *Celestin* confirm'd the Estate given to this Monastery, and granted them several Priviledges, among others, that in the time of a general Interdiction it may be lawful for the Monks here to celebrate the Divine Offices, with a low Voice, their Church-Doors shut, and without the sound of any Bells. *Adam Fitz-Swany* gave divers Lands to the Monks of *Pontfract*, he also gave them for a Cell, the Priory of St. *Mary Magdalen* of *Lunda*, or *Monk-Breton*, which he had founded on his paternal Estate. After many Controversies between the Monks of *Pontfract* and the Monks of *Breton*, it was at last agreed and determin'd by Deed dated in the year 1269. that the Monks of *Breton* should pay a Pitance of 20 s. per Annum to the Covent of *Pontfract*, that the Monks of *Breton* should freely choose their own Prior, but that he should be created or install'd by the Prior of *Pontfract*, &c. To this House were several Persons of great Quality, Benefactors; whose names and parcels by them given may be seen in the Book at large. *p.* 656, 657, 658, 659.

[Valued at 337 l. 14 s. 8 d. per Annum.]

MONK-BRETON, in Yorkshire, a Cell to Pontfract.

660.

663.

THIS Priory was founded to the glory of God and honour of St. *Mary Magdalen* of *Lunda*, by *Adam* the Son of *Suanus* who endow'd it with the Town of *Breton*, &c. The then Prior of the *Charity* (being the Capital House of this Order beyond Seas) granted that the Monks of this House, might choose their own Prior, the Prior of *Pontfract* (if required) being present at the Election. *Adam Fitz Swane* the Founder gave this House as a Cell to the Priory of St. *John* at *Pontfract*, and ordered this House to pay to that Priory a Recognition of one Mark of Silver per Annum. Pope *Urban* the III. confirm'd the Foundation 1186.

[Valued at 239 l. 3 s. 6 d. per Annum.]

THETFORD, in Norfolk.

664.
666.
668.

FOunded *Anno Dom.* 1103. by *Roger Bigot*, whose Gifts and Endowments to this House were all confirm'd and ratified by his Son *William Bigot Dapifer* to the King; and also by King *Henry* the I. and King *Henry* the II. This Priory was made Denison 50. *E.* 3.

[Valued at 312 l. 14 s. 4 d. ob. per Annum.

MONTACUTE, in Somerſetſhire.

FIRST founded by *William* Earl of *Moriton* in *Normandy*, who endowed this Priory with three fair Lordſhips, *viz. Montegue* and two others. King *Henry* the I. gave and confirm'd to God and the bleſſed Apoſtles St. *Peter* and St. *Paul* of *Montacute*, and the Cluniac Monks there, divers Lands, with great Liberties and Exemptions. The like did King *Henry* the II. and King *Henry* the III. in the four and thirtieth year of his Reign. King *Edward* the III. in the fourteenth year of Reign, granted the Advowſon, and Cuſtody of this Priory and four Cells thereunto belonging, to *William de Monte-acuto* Earl of *Salisbury*, and Marſhal of *England*, and to his Heirs. *Vid.* 2. *Vol. p.* 909.

[Valued at 456 *l.* 14 *s.* 7 *d.* q. *per Annum*.]

669.
670.
671.

DAVENTREY, in Northamptonſhire.

THIS Priory was firſt founded at *Preſton* by *Hugh de Leyceſtre* (call'd the *Vicount*) but that place being found inconvenient, they were by Licenſe of *Simon de Seynliz* the elder, Earl of *Northampton*, removed to *Daventre*, where he built a Monaſtery in honour of St. *Auguſtine* the Apoſtle of the *Engliſh*. King *Henry* the II. confirm'd their Liberties and Franchiſes granted by King *Henry* the I. to St. *Mary of Charity* (*i. e.* the Capital Houſe of this Order beyond Seas) and to St. *Auguſtine* of *Daventrey* and the Monks there. Many were the Benefactors to this Houſe, as *Matilda de Senliz*, *Richard de Foxton*, whoſe Daughter *Ann* was married to *Alan Baſſet* of *Luſphenam* (*com. Roteland*) *Steven de Welton*, *Henry de Braybrok* (whoſe Geneologies may be ſeen, Fo. 677. 678.)

672.

673.

674.
675.

St. ANDREWS, at Northampton.

THIS Priory was founded in the eighteenth year of King *William* the Conqueror, by *Simon de Seynliz*, who came into *England* in the Army of that King. He married *Maud* Daughter and Co-heir of *Waldelfus* Earl of *Huntington*, with whom he had the honour of *Huntington*; *Alice* the other Daughter was by him given to *Ralph de Tonny* with 100 *l. per Annum* in Land (*centum Librarum terræ*) out of the ſaid honour. In the Reign of King *Henry* the I. the ſaid *Simon* made a Voyage to the Holy Land, and died in his return at the Monaſtery of the bleſſed *Mary of Charity* (to which Monaſtery he had ſubjected this of St. *Andrew.*) After his death King *Henry*, having married *Maud* Siſter of *Alexander* King of *Scotland*, gave *Maud* Earl *Simons* Widow to *David* Brother of *Alexander*, and with her the Cuſtody of Earl *Simons* Son and Heir, *Simon de St. Lyz*, junior. *Hugh* Biſhop of *Lincoln* confirm'd the Churches and Tithes given to this Priory, among which were the Churches of *Ryal* and *Exton* in *Rutland*. King *Henry* the I. alſo confirm'd the Lands to them given, and granted them many Liberties and Franchiſes. This Priory was made Deniſon 6 *H.* 4.

To the Hoſpital of St. *David* at *Kingſthorp* built upon the Lands of this Priory, for the Relief of Travellers and poor People, *Walter* Prior of this Houſe with the aſſent of his Convent, gave two yard Land and a Meſſuage,

679.

681.

682.

683. age, &c. in *Thorp*, constituting several Orders for the Government of the said Hospital, among others that there should be three rows of Beds placed in length before the Chappel, so as the Poor, and especially the sick People, might most conveniently bear Mass, &c. subjecting the said Hospital to the Prior of St. *Andrews* at *Northampton*, and the Abbot of *Sullebi*. This Deed bears date 1200. being the second of King *John*.

(This Priory was valued at 263 *l*. 7 *s*. 1 *d*. q. per Annum.)

BARNESTAPLE, in Devonshire.

684.
685. THIS House was founded for Cluniac Monks, and dedicated to the honour of God, and our Lord Jesus Christ, and St. *Mary*, the holy Apostles St. *Peter* and St. *Paul*, and St. *Mary Magdalen*, by *Joel* Son of *Alured*, who endow'd it with large Possessions, subjecting it to the Church of St. *Martin de Campis*, in which he himself became a Monk. Confirm'd by King *Henry* the I. and by *Henry de Tracy*, who descended from the Founder, *An.* 1146. (11. *Steph.*)

[Valued at 123 *l*. 6 *s*. 7 *d*. per Annum]

TIKEFORD, in Buckinghamshire.

687. *F*ULCODIUS *Paganellus* was the first Founder of this Priory, who with other Benefactors, endowed it with divers Lands and Rents. All which together with a *Court-Leet*, King *Henry* the II. confirm'd to the Monks here. King *Edward* the II. in the fifth year of his Reign, granted further to *William de la Manerere* then Prior of this House, and his Successors, to have a Pillory and Tumbrel in their Lordship of *Tikeford*, for the punishment of Malefactors.

Vid. Vol. 2. *p.* 910.

FEVERSHAM, in Kent.

688.
689. *A*Nno 1148. King *Steven* founded the Abby here to the honour of our Saviour, and endow'd it with divers Mannors, Lands, Liberties, and free Customs to hold in perpetual Alms, discharged and quit of all secular Exactions. King *Steven* and *Maud* his Queen, and *Eustacius* their Son were buried here. King *Henry* the II. confirm'd to the Cluniac Monks of *Feversham*, all their Lands and Franchises, granting to them a Fair yearly for eight days beginning at the Feast of St. *Peter ad vincula*. The like confirmation was made by King *John* in the sixteenth year of his Reign; and by King *Henry* the III. in the eleventh year of his Reign. *Peter* Abbot of *Clugny* granted to King *Steven*, *Clarembaldus* then Prior of *Bermundesey* with twelve Monks of that House, for the Composing an Abby at *Feversham*, and at the same time absolved the said *Clarembaldus* and his Monks from all Obedience and Subjection to the Church of *Clugny*, and that of the *Charity*: The like Emancipation or discharge of subjection was also granted by the then Prior of the *Charity*.

[Valued at 286 *l*. 12 *s*. 6 *d*. ob. q. per Annum.]

A R-

ARTHINGTON, in Yorkshire.

THIS was a Priory of Nuns, built and endow'd by *Peers* of *Arthington*, and confirm'd by Pope *Alexander*; as is set forth in an award made in the twenty eighth year of the Reign of King *Henry* the VI. *Alicia de Romeli* was a Benefactress to this Nunnery whose Gift was confirm'd by her Son *William de Curcy* the Kings Sewer, and by *Warinus Fitz-Gerald* the King's Chamberlain.

[Valued at 11 *l.* 8 *s.* 4 *d.* ob. *per Annum.*]

OF

Of the Cistercian Order.

Anno Dom. 1098. *Robert* Abbot of *Molesme* by License of *Hugo* Archbishop of *Lyons* the Pope's Legate, first instituted this Order, in a Desert Place called *Cistercium* in the Dutchy of *Burgundy*, the Rule of St. *Bennet*, being not duly observed, in his old Monastery. In this Order therefore they betook themselves to the strict observance of St. *Bennet's* Rule, and obtain'd great Priviledges from the Pope. To avoid Pride and Superfluity, they were to retain no Crosses of Gold or Silver, but only of Wood; their Chalices were to be of Silver and not of Gold, *&c.* The second Abbot of this Order was one *Stephen* an *Englishman.*

WAVERLEY, in Surrey.

THIS Abby was founded in the year of Christ 1128. by *William Gifford* Bishop of *Winchester*. The first Monks of this Order, being twelve and an Abbot, came to this House from a Foreign Abby call'd *Elemosina.* The said *William* Bishop of *Winchester* endow'd this House with divers Lands, and with Common in *Farnham* Woods, all which was by consent of the King, and the Convent of *Winchester*, and confirm'd by his Successors. *Vid.* 2. *Vol. p.* 912.

[Valued at 174*l.* 8 *s.* 3 *d.* ob. *per Annum.*]

FURNES, in Lancashire.

Anno Dom. 1127. being twenty nine years from the first Institution of the *Cistercian* Order (26. H. 1.) This House was founded by *Steven* Earl of *Morton* and *Boloign*, afterwards King of *England.*

The Names of the Abbots of FURNES.

1. *Evanus de Albrincis.* 2. *Eudo de Sourdeval.* 3. *Michael de Lancastria.* 4. *Petrus de Eboraco.* 5. *Richardus de Bajocis.* 6. *Johannes de Cawnesfeild.* 7. *Walterus de Millum.* 8. *Jostenus de Pennington.* 9. *Conanus de Bardoule.* 10. *Willielmus Niger.* 11. *Giraldus Bristaldon.* 12. *Michael de Dalton.* 13. *Richardus de Sancto Quintino.* 14. *Radulfus de Fletcham.* 15. *Johannes de Newby.* 16. *Stephanus de Alverston.* 17. *Nicholaus de Meaux*, who was after Bishop of *Sodor.* 18. *Robertus de Denton.* 19. *Laurentius de Acclom.* 20. *Willielmus de Midleton.* 21. *Hugo de Bron.* 22. *Willielmus de Cockeram.* 23. *Hugo Skiller.* 24. *Johannes de Cockeram.* 25. *Alexander de Walton.* 26. *Johannes de Cockham.* 27. *Johannes de Bolton.* 28. *Willielmus de Dalton.*

King

CISTERCIANS.

King *Steven's* double Relation to *Maud* the Empress:

Steven Earl of Morton, &c. was Son of Steven E. of Bloys and Adela Daughter of K. William the Conqueror, and Sister of K. H. I. married ─────

Edgar Edling had two Sisters, Margaret, and Christiana; who had issue as follows,

- Christiana
  - Eustace E. of Bolon ── Mary
    - William Earl of Warren and Bolon. ──── Maud

- Margaret Wife of Malcolm K. of Scots.
  - Matilda Wife of Hen. I. K. of Eng.
    - Maud, first married to the Emperor, then to Jeoffery Earl of Anjou, by which last she had issue.
      - Hen. the II. K. of Eng.
      - Mary.

William de Lancaster, the third of that Name was a great Benefactor to this Abby, as appears by his Deeds dated 1240. &c. Which *William* married *Agnes de Brus* and had issue

706.
707.

- Halewisa ux. Petri de Brus
  - Petrus de Brus jun. ob. s. h.
  - Agnes ux. Walteri de Fawkunbergh.
- Alicia ux. Williel. de Lindesey.
  - Lucia ux. Marmaduci de Thweng.
  - Margareta ux. Dom. Rob. de Ros.
- Sorota ux. Alani de Multon
  - Laderina ux. Johannis de Belew.

Pope *Eugenius* granted to *John* Abbot of St. *Mary's* of *Furnes*, among other Priviledges that they should not pay any Tithes for their Lands or Cattel held in their own hands and occupation. And (*Anno Dcm* 1305.) it was agreed between the Abbot of *Furnes* and the Prior of St. *Mary* of *Lancaster* (which last was intituled to the Tithes of their Grange of *Bellomonte*) that in case the Abbot of *Furnes* let the said Lands, then the Prior of *Lancaster* should receive Tithes of the Lands so let, but in case the Abbot and Covent of *Furnes* should occupy the same in their own hands, then the said Prior to receive only a Pension of two Marks *per Annum*.

709.

[Valued at 805 *l*. 16 *s*. 5 *d*. per *Annum*.]

CISTERTIANS. VOL. I.

710.   RUSSIN, *in the Isle of Man, a Cell to* Furnes.

711.   THE Abby of *Ruffin* was founded in the year 1134. *Olauus* King of *Man*, a very devout Prince, gave the Land whereon this Abby stands to *Ivo* then Abbot of *Furnes*, for the erecting of this Monastery.
    Certain Antient Synodals, and Ecclesiastical Constitutions for the Isle of *Man*, made by *Simon* Bishop of *Sodor* 1229.

712.   Other Constitutions made in the Church of St. *Bradan* in *Man* 1291. under *Mark* Bishop of *Sodor*.

716.   Other Additional Constitutions made in the Church of St. *Michael* the Archangel, by *William Ruffel* Bishop of *Sodor*, and the whole Clergy of *Man* 1350. All which see at large in the *Monasticon*.

718.   *Thomas* Lord *Stanley*, Earl of *Darby*, and K. of the Isle of *Man*, by his Letters Patents dated at *Lathum*, 28. *Mar*. 1505. confirm'd to *Huan* then Bishop of *Sodor* and his Successors, all the Lands, Revenues, Rights and Priviledges belonging to the Church in the Isle and Kingdom of *Man*.

YNES, *in Ireland, a Cell to* Furnes.

THIS was first founded in the year 1126. by a King of *Ulster* named *Magnellus Makenlefe*, in a place call'd *Erynach*, but that being almost destroyed in the Wars, it was translated by *John de Curcy* Conqueror of *Ulster*, and new founded at *Ynes*, and at the same time he subjected this Abby to *Furnes*, An. 1180.

719.   NETHE, *in* Glamorganshire.

Richard de Grainvilla gave to God and the Church of the holy *Trinity* at *Savigny*, *Nethe* and other Lands and Possessions, to the Intention that the Abbot and Convent of *Savigny* should institute here a Convent of Monks under an Abbot. King *John* confirm'd the said Lands to the Church of the *Holy Trinity* at *Nethe* and the Monks there, in the ninth year of his Reign granting them also many Priviledges and Immunities.

[Valued at 132 *l*. 7 *s*. 7 *d*. ob. per *Annum*.]

720.   BASINGWERK *Abby, in* Flintshire.

Founded *Anno* 1131. by *Ranulph* Earl of *Chester*, confirm'd by King *Henry* the II. and by *Lewellin* Prince of *North-Wales*. The like Confirmation to this Monastery, and the Monks here was made by *David* Prince of *Northwales*, Son of the foresaid *Lewelin*, who also gave them certain Lands and Revenues, in the year 1240.

[Valued at 150 *l*. 7 *s*. 3 *d*. per *Annum*.]

TINTERN, in Wales.

Founded 1131. *William*, Mareschal of *England*, and Earl of *Pembroke*, in the seventh year of *Henry* the III. confirm'd to God, and the blessed *Mary* of *Tyntern*, and to the Abbot and Monks there, all the Lands and Revenues given to them by his Ancestors; granting also to the said Abby great Liberties and Immunities: prohibiting all Men to vex or disturb them or theirs, under the penalty of twenty Marks, besides the curse of God. Their Estate was also confirm'd by *Roger Bigod* Earl of *Norfolk* and Mareschal of *England*, Anno 1301. *Walter Fitz-Richard* appears to be the Founder of this House *Anno* 1131. Who dying without issue, his Brother *Gilbert Stronghowe* became his Heir, and was the first Earl of *Pembroke*, from whom descended *Isabel*; she became the Wife of *William Mareschall*, who died 1219. and lies buried in the Temple at *London*: he left five Sons all successively Earls of *Pembroke*, but they all died without issue. *Matilda* the eldest of their Sisters and Co-heirs, was married to *Hugh le Bigod* Earl of *Norfolk* and *Suffolk*, &c.

[Valued at 192 *l*. 1 *s*. 4 *d*. ob. per Annum.]

722.
723.
724.
725.

RIEVALL, in Yorkshire.

Anno 1132. *Gualterus Especk* a Great man in the Court of King *Henry* the I. founded this Monastery in a place called *Blachomour* near the River *Rie*, for the receipt of certain Monks of the *Cistercian* Order sent over by *Bernard* Abbot of *Clarevallis*, whose first Abbot was *William*.

This *Walter Especk*, having unhappily lost his Son and Heir who broke his Neck by a fall from a Horse, built and endow'd with part of his Estate three Monasteries, viz. *Kirkham*, *Rievall*, and *Wardon*. The rest of his Estate was divided between his three Sisters and Co-heirs, one of which married to *Peter* Lord *Roos*, the Descent of which Noble Family, the Reader may see set forth in the Book at large, with their several Matches and Issue, down to *George Manners*, Lord *Roos*, who died *An*. 1513.

Many were the Benefactors, and large the Possessions of this Monastery, exprest *Fol*. 729, 730, 731.

Pope *Alexander* the III. by his Bull dated 1140. granted to *Aelredo* Abbot of St. *Mary*'s of *Rievalle* and his Brethren, and their Successors in that Monastery, a Confirmation of all their Possessions, with divers Priviledges, in particular that they might celebrate the Divine Offices in the time of a general Interdict, &c.

[Valued at 278 *l*. 10 *s*. 2 *d*. per Annum.]

727.
728.
732.

FOUNTAINS, in Yorkshire, *a Cell of* Clarevallis. Founded 1132.

The Rule and Discipline of St. *Benedict* being relaxt in the Abby of St. *Mary*'s at *York*, and a great Dissention happening therein on that occasion between the Abbot and Prior, *Turstin* then Archbishop of *York* gave leave to thirteen of the Monks to retire from the said Abby. To these the said Archbishop appointed a Solitary, and then Desert place for

733.
739.

for their Habitation, at that time called *Skeldale*, since *Fountains*. Here for a time a great Elme was their only fence from the Weather, under which they slept, fed, and performed their Offices according to their Rule. *Richard*, who had been their Prior at *York*, being elected their first Abbot and confirm'd by the Archbishop *Turstin* aforesaid. They having past a Winter in this manner, sent to the holy *Bernard* Abbot of

741. *Claravellis* submitting themselves to his Rule and Direction. Abbot *Bernard* sends back with the Messengers one of his Monks named *Galfridus*, who taught them the *Cistercian* Discipline. Hitherto they were in great want, being forced to dress for their Food the Leaves of the Trees and

742. Herbs of the Fields. Yet in their distress having in their poor House but two Loaves and a half, they gave one of them to a Poor man who demanded an Alms for Christ his sake. Two years they labour'd under this grievous Poverty; after which God sent them many Benefactors; the first of which was *Hugh* Dean of *York*. Five years after the first Foundation of

743. the Monastery of *Fountains*, a certain Nobleman called *Ranulph de Merlay* built for them a new Monastery to which they sent some of their Monks under the Government of Abbot *Robert* formerly a Monk at *Witheby*. Be-

746. sides which, many Cells were founded and given to this House, as *Wo-*
747. *burne, Kirkstall, Bitham,* otherwise called *Vallis dei, Lisa* in *Norway*, &c.
252.   Benefactors to this House were *Alanus de Aldeburg; Roger de Mubrai*
754. *de Aldeburg, Swanus de Fornetun, de Bramkia, Roger de Laci* Constable of
757. *Chester, Nigellus de Mubrai, Alice de Gant*, &c. who gave to God and the
758. Church of St. *Mary de Fontibus* divers Mannors and Lands. All which were confirm'd to the Monks of the *Cistercian* Order here, and their Suc-
759. cessors for ever by King *Richard* the I.

[Valued at 998 *l*. 6 *s*. 8 *d*. ob. per Annum.]

---

760.   QUARRE (*Quarrera*) *in the Isle of* 𝔚𝔢𝔦𝔤𝔥𝔱, *a Cell to* Savigny. *Founded* 1132.

*R*ichard Earl of *Exeter*, Son of *Baldwin*, confirm'd to God, the holy Virgin, and *Gaufridus* Abbot of *Savigny*, this House and divers Lands and Revenues thereunto belonging, first given by his Father. Benefactors to this House were, *Henry Fitz-Empress*, who writ himself Son of

761. the Duke of *Normandy* and Earl of *Anjou, Engelgerius de Bohun; William de Vernun* Earl of *Devon*, &c.

762.   Controversie arising between the Abbot and Covent of *Lyra*, and this Church of *Quarre* about certain Tithes and Revenues in and about *Carisbrok*, and other Neighbouring Towns here in this Island, the Matter was agreed and settled by Deed dated in the year 1289.

[Valued at 134 *l*. 3 *s*. 11 *d*. per Annum]

---

764.   CUMBERMERE, *in* Cheshire. *Founded* 1133.

*H*ugo Malbanc founded this Abby in the Honour of the blessed Virgin, and St. *Michael*, and endow'd it with very large Lands and Posses-
765. sions; among others, with the fourth part of the Town of *Wiche*, and the Tithes of the Salt and Boylries there. Yet by the same Deed he granted that

that *Ralph* Earl of *Chester* his chief Lord, should be accounted the Principal Founder and Defender of the said Church and Monks there. King *Henry* the III. in the sixteenth year of his Reign, confirm'd all their Possessions; and again in the fiftieth year of his Reign. In the year 1230. *Ralph* Earl of *Chester* confirm'd their Estate given by *Hugo Malbanc*, and granted them several Liberties and Immunities. *Vid. 2. Vol. p.* 913.

[Valued at 225 *l.* 9 *s.* 7 *d. per Annum.*]

767.

GEROUDON, *in* Leicestershire.

768.

THIS was founded *Anno* 1133. as a Cell to *Waverle.* The Founder, *Robert* Earl of *Leicester,* endow'd this Monastery with all his Lands in *Disseley,* and with the Wood of *Shepehed.* Many were the Benefactors who gave to this Church of St. *Mary* of *Geroldon,* and the Monks here large Possessions, *viz. Margaret* Countess of *Wynton* Sister of the said *Robert, Margaret de Ferrariis* Countess of *Derby, Roger de Quincy, Gilbert de Coleville, William* Son of *Richard Wareyn, William Peverell,* &c. All whose Gifts were confirm'd to them by King *Edward* the III. in the fourteenth year of his Reign.

769.
770.
771.

[Valued at 1594 *l.* 19 *s.* 10 *d.* ob. *per Annum.*]

SWINESHEAD, *in* Lincolnshire. *Founded* An. Do. 1134.

773.

THIS was founded and endow'd by *Robert Greslei*; whose several Lands and Possessions were recited and confirm'd to God and the Church of St. *Mary* of *Swynesheved* and the Monks there, by King *Henry* the II.

[Valued at 167 *l.* 15 *s.* 3 *d. per Annum.*]

CALDER, *in* Cumberland, *Founded* An. Do. 1134.

774.

KING *Henry* the II. confirm'd to the Abbot and Monks here all the Lands and Possessions given by *Ralph de Meschin* their Founder, and other Benefactors.

[Valued at 50 *l.* 9 *s.* 3 *d.* ob. *per Annum.*]

BILAND, *in* Yorkshire. *Founded* An. Do. 1134.

775.

THIS House was at first founded for certain Monks of *Savigny,* by *Roger de Mulbray*; which *Roger* died in the *Holy Land. Walter de Sciflings* Parson of *Kildale, Hugo de Wake,* and others were Benefactors. In the ninth of *Richard* the II. *Thomas* Earl *Mareschall* and Earl of *Nottingham,* Lord *Mowbray* and *Segrave,* did by his Deed recite, ratifie, and confirm the Foundation of this Abby by his said Progenitor *Roger de Mulbray. Vid. infra, p.* 1027.

776.

778.

[Valued at 238 *l.* 9 *s.* 4 *d. per Annum.*]

BILD.

BILDWAS, in Shropshire. Founded An. 1135.

KING *Steven* in the third year of his Reign (*An. Dom.* 1139.) gave and confirm'd to God and the Church of St. *Ceadde*, and to the Abbot and Monks here, their Estate in like manner as *Roger* Bishop of *Chester* had given it, and further, granted them several Immunities. *Walter de Dunstanville, Robert Corbet,* and others were Benefactors. Their Estate was confirm'd to them by King *Richard* the I. in the first year of his Reign. *Vid. Vol.* 2. *p.* 914.

[Valued at 110 *l.* 19 *s.* 3 *d.* ob. *per Annum.*]

St. Mary's *near* Dublin, *in* Ireland, *a Cell to* Bildwas. *Founded* 1139.

KING *Henry* the II. confirm'd to the white Monks of St. *Mary's* near *Dublin,* all their Lands and Possessions; and by another Deed subjected the said Monks to the Abbot of *Bildewas.*

BITLESDEN, in Buckinghamshire. Founded An. 1147.

THE Lordship of *Bitlesden* escheating in the time of King *Steven,* from one *Robert de Meperteshall,* to the then Earl of *Leicester,* the said Earl granted it to his Steward *Ernaldus de Bosco,* who founded here an Abby, which the Earl also confirm'd; but after some time the abovesaid *Robert de Meperteshal* being about to commence a Suit in Law for this Estate, the Monks here in consideration of ten Marks obtain'd from the said *Robert* also a Charter of Confirmation. This House was first given by the abovesaid *Arnold de Bosco* for a Cell to the Abby of *Geroudon.*

[Valued at 125 *l.* 4 *s.* 3 *d.* q. *per Annum.*]

WARDON, in Bedfordshire. Founded An. 1136.

THE first Founder of this House was *Walter Espec,* who endow'd it for Monks from the Abby of *Rieval,* which was confirm'd by King *Steven Anno Dom.* 1135. and by King *Richard* the I. in the tenth year of his Reign.

[Valued at 389 *l.* 16 *s.* 6 *d.* q. *per Annum.*]

FORD, in Devonshire.

IN the year 1133. *Richard* Viscount or Sheriff of *Devonshire,* a near Kinsman of King *William* the Conqueror, and to whom that King had given the Castle of *Exeter,* and Honour and Barony of *Okehampton* in *Devonshire,* gave his Land of *Brightley,* within the said Honour of *Okehampton,* for the founding of an Abby, and obtained twelve Monks for the same from the Abby of *Waverly.* These Monks having remained at *Brightley* for five years, were at last forced through the great want and sterility

sterility of the place, to return back to *Waverly*: Which the Sister and Heiress of their Founder seeing, she gave them the Mannor of *Thorncomb* for their maintenance, and her house therein, then called *Ford*, for their more convenient habitation. From this Lady did descend *Hawisia* who was married to *Reginald de Courtnay*, who was the Grandson of *Lewis* the Gross of *France*, from whom descend the noble Family of *Courtnays*, Patrons of this Abby, and great Benefactors. Whose descent and lineage is set forth in the Book at large. One of which Family, namely the Lord *John Courtnay*, was, through the divine Mercy, his great Faith, and his Hope in the Prayers of these Monks, miraculously delivered from a terrible Storm at Sea in the Night time, when all the Seamen despair'd of life. *Hugh Courtnay* the second of that name, became Earl of *Devonshire*, and died 9 E. 3. *Josline de Pomerei*, and others, were Benefactors to this Monastery; all whose gifts are confirm'd by King *Richard* I. in the first year of his Reign.

786.
787.
789.
791.

[Valued at 374 *l*. 10 *s*. 6 *d*. ob. per Annum.]

BUCKFAST in Devonshire.

792:

Founded for Monks and endowed with Lands by *Richard Banzan*, to hold by the 30*th*. part of a Knight's Fee; and confirm'd by King *Hen*. II.

[Valued at 466 *l*. 11 *s*. 2 *d*. ob. per Annum.]

MEAUX, in Yorkshire. *Founded*, Anno 1136.

MEaux was so called by its Inhabitants, who came into *England* with the *Norman* Conqueror, and named their new Seat according to the name of the City of *Meaux* in *Normandy* from whence they came. The Founder of this Abby was *William le Gross* Earl of *Albemarl*, and Lord of *Holderness*, and in a manner of all *Yorkshire*; who having vow'd a Journey to *Jerusalem*, and being by reason of his age, and unweildyness of his Body, not well able to perform such a Voyage, built this Monastery by way of commutation of his Vow. This he gave to God and the Blessed Virgin *Mary*, introducing a Convent of Monks from the Monastery of *Fountains*, of whom one *Adam* was made the first Abbot; which Monks at first got their living by the work of their hands and sweat of their brows; but were not long after plentifully endow'd with Lands and Revenues by the said Earl. This *William le Gross* was Grandson of *Odo* to whom *William* the Conqueror gave his Sister in marriage, and the Isle of *Holderness*; the Archbishop of *Roan* gave him the County of *Albemarl* to hold of him by the Service of being his Standard Bearer in his Expeditions attended with ten Knights. The Line of this *William* being not long after extinct, the County of *Albemarl*, and Honour of *Holderness* escheated to the Crown for want of heirs. This Monastery was begun, and the Monks first entred there under their Abbot *Adam*, on the Calends of *January* 1150. *Richard de Otringham* Rector of the Church of *Schelford* in the Diocess of *Ely*, by his Deed dated, *An. Dom.* 1317. gave divers Lands to the Abbot and Convent here, for the maintenance of a perpetual Chantery of seven Monks of this House, at the Porch of their Abby Church. The number of the Monks in this Abby were 50. The Lands given to this Abby were confirm'd to it by King *John*, in the 6*th.* year of his Reign.

793.
794.
795.
796.
797.
799.
800.

[Valued at 299 *l*. 6 *s*. 4 *d*. q. per Annum.]   NEW-

NEW-MINSTER, *near* Morpeth, *in* Yorkshire.

801. THIS was founded and endow'd in the year 1138. by a certain Nobleman call'd *Ranulf de Merley*, it was furnisht with Monks from the Abby of *Fountains*. Their Lands were confirm'd to them by King *Henry* the III. in the thirty ninth year of his Reign. *Vid. Vol.* 2. *p.* 916.

802. TAME, *in* Oxfordshire. *Founded* 1138.

THIS House was founded and endow'd by Sir *Robert Gait* a Knt. and was furnisht with *Cistercian* Monks from *Waverley*. Their Estate was confirm'd to them by King *Henry* II. in the eleventh year of his Reign, and by King *Edward* the II. in the tenth year of his Reign.

[Valued at 256 *l.* 13 *s.* 7 *d.* ob. *per Annum.*]

803. BORDESLEY, *in* Worcestershire. *Founded*, An. 1138.

This Abby was founded by *Mawd* the Empress for *Cistercian* Monks, in honour of the most blessed Virgin *Mary* (*Regina Cælorum*) so are the words of her Charter.) Endowing it with divers Lands and Revenues to hold free and quit of all Secular Service. Besides whom, many 804. other Benefactors conferr'd upon this Abby great Possessions, all which were confirm'd by King *Richard* the I. in the first year of his Reign.

[Valued at 388 *l.* 9 *s.* 10 *d.* ob. q. *per Annum.*]

805. LOUTH-PARK *in* Lincolnshire. *Founded*, An. 1139.

THe Founder of this Monastery was *Alexander* Bishop of *Lincoln*, who procured Monks for it from the Abby of *Fountains*, but their first Settlement being at a place called *Haverholm*, which Seat not being convenient for their Habitation, he removed them from thence to this Place, Besides the said Bishop they had divers other Benefactors, all whose donations were confirm'd to God, and St. *Mary*, and the Monks *de Parcho Lude*, by King *Henry* the III. in the tenth year of his Reign.

[Valued at 147 *l.* 14 *s.* 6 *d. per Annum.*]

806. KIRKSTED, *in* Lincolnshire.

THIS House was founded in the year 1139. by *Hugh de Bretone* a Baron of those times, and by him endow'd with divers Lands. Other Benefactors were the *Furnivalls*, *D'Aencurts*, and *D'arci's*, &c. *Richard de* 807. *Luvetot* gave and annext to this House the Hermitage of St *John* in the 808. Parish of *Ecclesfeild*, with the Land thereunto belonging. *Conan* Duke of *Britain* and Earl of *Richmund* gave to this Abby the Church of *Gaiton* with two Carucates and a half of Land, &c.

[Valued at 286 *l.* 2 *s.* 7 *d. per Annum.*]

KINGSWOOD, in Gloucestershire. *Founded*, An. 1139.

This House was founded by *William de Berkeley* for *Cistercian* Monks, and the Foundation confirm'd by *Maud* the Empress: but afterwards for many years it became a Grange depending on the Abby of *Teitebiry*, and a long contest was had about this Matter, till at last it was from a Grange advanced to the name of the Abby of *Kingeswode*. The Lands and Endowments given to this Abby by the Founder, were confirm'd by several of the *Berkleys*, his noble Descendants.

[Valued at 244 *l*. 11 *s*. 2 *d*. per Annum.]

PIPWELL, in Northamptonshire.

This Monastry was first founded, *An. Dom.* 1143. (and then called *Sancta Maria de Divisis*,) among thick Woods, which were in after times destroyed. In the year 1323. the Monks here were dispersed thro' Poverty. Their first Founder was *William Boutevileyn* of *Cottesbrook*; from whom descended one *Robert Boutevileyn*, who did many unkindnesses to these Monks. This was before their dispersion. *Hugh Senlize* and *Emma* his Wife one of the Daughters and Heirs of the Lord of *Braybroke*, gave to the Monks of *Pipwell* divers Lands and Tenements in *Braybroke*, confirm'd by the Capital Lord of the Fee *Simon de Foxton*, and these seem to be the second Founders. King *Henry* III. granted to these Monks pasture on *Benifield* Laund for 250 Cattle.

[Valued at 286 *l*. 11 *s*. 8 *d*. q. per Annum.]

STONELEY, in Warwickshire.

Maud the Empress first founded the Priory of *Rademere* in the Forest *Kanoc*, confirmed by King *Steven*. This Priory was afterwards advanced to an Abby of *Cistercian* Monks by *Henry Fitz Empress* then Duke of *Normandy*. In the year 1154. which was thirteen years after the Monks had remained at *Rademore*, the foresaid *Henry Fitz Empress*, being now King of *England*, they changed their habitation of *Radmore* for *Stanley*, and the whole Lordship of the same, which was before that the Kings Demesn. The first stone of the Abby Church there was laid on the Ides of *April, An. Dom.* 1154. The said King *Henry* I. endow'd this House with divers other Lands and Revenues elsewhere.

[Valued at 151 *l*. 0 *s*. 3 *d*. ob. per Annum.]

COGESHAL, in Essex.

This Abby was founded by King *Steven* and *Maud* his Queen, in the year 1142. *William de Humberstane*, with the Kings License, gave the Mannor of *Tyllingham-Hall* for the finding of one Wax-light to burn before the High Altar at the Abby Church here in the time of high Mass, daily

daily. The Monks of this House were endowed with great Immunities.
[Valued at 25.1 l. 2 s. per Annum.]

REVESBY, in Lincolnshire. Founded An. 1142.

823.
The Founders of this House were *William de Romara*, Earl of *Lincoln*, and *William* his Son, who gave to the Abbot and Monks of *Rievalle*, *Revesby*, *Thoresby*, and other Lands in *Lincolnshire* for the building and endowment of this House. This Abby was dedicated to St. *Laurence*. The Lands and Revenues were confirm'd by *Ralph* Earl of *Chester*, and by King *Richard* I. in the tenth year of his Reign.
[Valued at 287 l. 2 s. 4 d. ob. per Annum.]

CUMHIRE, in Pembrokshire.

825.
826.
This House was founded by *Cadwathel ap Madok* in the year 1143, for Sixty White Monks. King *Henry* III, in the sixteenth year of his Reign confirm'd to these Monks all their Lands and Revenues.
[Valued at 24 l. 19 s. 4 d. per Annum.]

BOXLEY in Kent.

827.
William de *Ipre* a great Commander in King *Stevens* Army founded this Abby of *Boxley* for White Monks in the year 1144. King *Richard* the I. in the first year of his Reign confirm'd their Estate with *Sac & Soc*.
[Valued at 204 l. 4 s. 11 d. per Annum.]

SINNINGTHWAIT, in Yorkshire.

828.
This House was founded for Nuns, by *Bertram Haget*, and confirm'd by *Roger de Mubrai* his superiour Lord. *Jeffery* Archbishop of *York*, took these Nuns and their Possessions into his protection, and denounced a malediction against those who should dare to wrong them, and a blessing to their Benefactors. *Alice* Widow of *Adam de Stanelcy* gave, with her self, nine Bovates of Land in *Berewik* (*super Theseiam*) which was afterwards changed with *Ranulf Fitz Henry* for other Lands in *Lofthows*.
[Valued at 60 l. 9 s. 2 d. per Annum.]

ESSEHOLT, in Yorkshire, a Cell to Sinningthwait.

829.
Pope *Alexander* the third, by his Bull dated in the year 1172. confirm'd to *Christian* Prioress of *Sinningthwait*, and the Nuns there, and their Successors, their House and Estate both at *Sinningthayte*, and at *Esseholt*, with all Lands already given, or to be given to their said Houses. With Priviledge of Sanctuary.
[Valued at 13 l. 5 s. 4 d. per Annum.]

WOBURN, in Bedfordshire. Founded An. 1145.

THIS was founded and endowed by *Hugh de Bolebeck*, by advice of *Henry* Abbot of *Fountains*, from whence a Convent of Monks was sent to this place. King *John* in the second year of his Reign confirmed the Estate of this House, so did also King *Henry* the II.

[Valued at 391 *l*. 18 *s*. 2 *d*. ob. *per Annum*.]

MEREVAL, in Warwickshire. Founded An. 1148.

830.

THIS was founded by *Robert* Earl of *Ferrariis*, and by him endowed with all the Forest of *Arden*, with other Lands. All which was confirm'd By King *Henry* the II.

[Valued at 254 *l*. 1 *s*. 8 *d*. *per Annum*.]

HAMPOLE, in Yorkshire.

THIS House was founded for Nuns by *Avicia de Tanai*, and endowed by her with divers Lands of her Inheritance, all which were confirmed by *Ralph de Tilli* her Grandson, by *Roger* Archbishop of *York*, and by *William Fitz William*, An. 1331.

[Valued at 63 *l*. 5 *s*. 8 *d*. *per Annum*.]

VALLE-DEI, alias Vaudey, in Lincolnshire.

831.

THE Abby here was founded by *William* Earl of *Albemari* in the year 1147. It was at first called *Biham*, but afterwards *Vallis-dei*, and was planted with Monks from *Fountains*. The same Founder, erected also the Abby of *Meaux* of which *supra*, p. 792. Many were the Benefactors to this House, among whom *Gilbertus de Gant*, *Roger de Mulbray*, &c. all whose Gifts were recited and confirm'd by King *Richard* the I. in the first year of his Reign. See the Genealogy of *Gilbert de Gant* Nephew of *William* the Conqueror, and the Noble Families descended from him in the Book at large.

833.

834.

[Valued at 124 *l*. 5 *s*. 11 *d*. q. *per Annum*:

SWINE, in Yorkshire.

ERinburch de Burtona was the Foundress of this Abby, giving divers Lands of her Patrimony and Inheritance to God and the Church of St. *Mary* at *Swine*, and to the Brethren and Sisters there serving God. Pope *Alexander* exempted the Nuns here from paying Tithes for their Lands in their own Occupation. *Vide infra, fol.* 1026.

[Valued at 82 *l*. 3 *s*. 9 *d*. ob. *per Annum*]

BRUERE,

BRURE, in Oxfordshire. Founded An. 1147.

835. KING *Henry* the III. *Roger* Earl of *Warwick*, and others, were Benefactors to this Abby, all whose Gifts were confirm'd to the *Cistercian* Monks here, by King *John* in the sixth year of his Reign.

[Valued at 134 *l*. 10 *s*. 10 *d*. per Annum.]

RUPE, alias Roche, in Yorkshire. Founded An. 1147.

836.
837. *Richard de Bulli*, and *Richard Fitz-Turgis*, were joint Founders of this Abby. Besides those of the Family of *Bully*, the Monks here were endow'd with Lands and Revenues by other Benefactors, among whom
839. *Edmund de Lacy* Constable of *Chester*, and *William* Earl *Warren*, &c. Pope *Urban* the III. confirmed their Estate and Lands given, and to be given, and exempted them from Tithes for their Lands in their own Tenure, and this was by his Bull dated 1186. Their first Abbot was *Durandus*, who governed twelve years. 2. *Dionisius* 12. 3. *Rogerus de Tikehill* 8. 4. *Hugo de Waddeworth* 5. 5 *Osmundus* 39. 6 *Reginaldus* 15. 7 *Richardus* 16. 8. *Walter* 14. 9 *Alanus*. 10. *Jordanus*. 11 *Philippus*.

[Valued at 224 *l*. 2 *s*. 5 *d*. per Annum.]

HOTON, in Yorkshire.

840. THIS House was founded for Nuns, and endow'd by *Radulf de Nevil*. With the Licenses of *Adam de Brus*, and *Ernald de Percy*.

BASEDALE, in Yorkshire.

841. JOhn de Ever by his Deed dated *An.* 1304. released to *Joan* Prioress of *Basedale*, and to the Convent of the same, and their Successors, all homage and suit of Court for all their Lands holden of him in *Kirkeby*, *Cliveland*, and *Ingelby*. *William de Percy* and others were Benefactors to this Nunnery; all whose Gifts were recited and confirm'd by King *Henry* the III. in the twentieth year of his Reign. *Robert de Longo-Campo* Abbot of St. *Mary's* at *York* and the Convent there, granted to these Nuns a Coemitery for themselves, but their Servants and Tenants to be buried at the Parish Church.

Guido de Bouincurt was the Founder of this Priory of Nuns.

(Valued at 20 *l*. 1 *s*. 4 *d*. per Annum.)

SALLEY, in Yorkshire.

842.
843. THIS Abby was founded by *William de Percy An. Dom.* 1147. *Matilda de Percy* Countess of *Warwick*, Daughter of the said *William*, was a great Benefactress to this Abby, and gave them the Church of *Tadcaster*, and was accounted a second Founder; *Agnes de Percy* her Sister

and

and Heiress, did add to her bounty. *William Vavasor* gave and confirm'd all the Lands which his Father *Malgarus Vavasor* had given to this House, placing his Confirmation (*una cum Corpore meo*) together with his own body on the Altar of the blessed *Mary de Saltay*; providing thereby that in case he happens to die within the Kingdom of *England*, that his Body be buried in this Abby. *John de Lacy* Constable of *Chester* was among others a Benefactor to these Monks, *An.* 1223. *William de Percy* who founded this Abby, was Grandson to *William de Percy* who came into *England* with the Conqueror. His Estate came to his two Daughters *Matilda* who was married to *William* Earl of *Warwick*, but died without issue, and *Agnes* married to *Goseline Lovain*, Brother to the Duke of *Brabant*, the issue of this Match kept the name of their Mothers Family, and are the Progenitors of the Earls of *Northumberland*. This Abby was wasted and part of it burnt down by the Scots in their Wars.

845.
846.
847.

[Valued at 147 *l.* 3 *s.* 10 *d.* per Annum.]

RUFFORD, in Nottinghamshire. Founded 1148.

THIS Abby was founded and endowed by *Gilbert de Gaunt* Earl of *Lincoln*. Many were the Benefactors, whose Gifts were confirm'd to the Abbot and Monks here, with the Grant of divers Priviledges in the Forest of *Shirewood*, by King *Henry* the III. in the thirty sixth year of his Reign.

848.
849.

[Valued at 176 *l.* 11 *s.* 6 *d.* per Annum.]

SALTRE, in Huntingtonshire. Founded, An. 1147.

SImon Earl of *Northampton* founded and endowed this Abby with all his Land at *Saltre*, and with all the Marish Ground between that and *Witlemare*, and in *Witlemare*, &c. With very large Immunities and Franchises, such as his Ancestor *Judith* Countess of *Huntington* (Neice of the Conqueror) had formerly obtain'd of her said Unkle for this Town and Lordship of *Saltre*, as (*inter alia*) to be exempt from the County and Hundred Courts, to find neither Man nor Arms for the War, &c. The abovesaid Countess *Judith* had a special Love for this place, and did very much frequent it, and on that account did obtain from her said Unkle as great and large Priviledges as could then be granted for this Lordship. Which Priviledges, and also the Limits and Bounds of the Estate of this Abby, are particularly and at large set forth in the *Monasticon*. Controversie arising between the Abbot of *Ramsey* and the Abbot of *Saltre*, about their Rights in *Withlesmare* and *Ulbemare*, the matter was determin'd by a final Concord before the Kings Justices at *Huntedon*, Anno 3: *Rich.* the I.

850.
851.
853.
854.

[Valued at 141 *l.* 3 *s.* 8 *d.* per Annum.]

KIRKSTALL, in Yorkshire.

THIS Abby was first founded by *Henry de Laceio* in the year 1147. and first instituted with a Convent of Monks under their Abbot *Alexander,*

855. *Alexander*, from the Abby of *Fountains*. Their firſt Habitation was at a Town call'd *Bernolſwick*, but this place proving to theſe Monks very inconvenient on divers accounts, after they had been here ſomewhat above ſix years, they removed to a place called *Kirkeſtall*, in a Vally called *Aierdale*, which place was then only inhabited by ſome Hermits: This
856. laſt Seat they obtain'd of *William Pictavenſis* who own'd the Soil, at the yearly Rent of five Marks. Their firſt Abbot *Alexander* govern'd the Monks here thirty five years, and after his death was ſucceeded by *Radulfus Hageth*, and after him Abbot *Lambert*, to whom ſucceed Abbot
857. *Helias*, who at firſt was refuſed by the then Patron *Roger de Lacy*, but became afterwards much in his favour. King *John* did ſome ill Offices to this Abby in taking from them ſome of their Lands. *Robert de Lacy*, who died *Anno* 1194. was accounted a ſecond Founder of this Abby.

859. King *William* the Conqueror gave to *Ilbertus de Lacy*, who came into *England* in his Army, all *Blackburnſhire* (in the County of *York*) with the Lordſhip and Honour of *Pontfract*, and other Lands. This *Ilbertus* built the Caſtle at *Pontefract*, and in it a Chappel for a Dean and Canons. Son of this *Ilbertus* was *Robert Lacy* who built the Monaſtery of *Pontefract*, who was the Father of *Henry Lacy* the Founder of this Abby of *Kirkſtall*, this *Henry* married the Siſter of *William Veſci* Rector of *Berwick*. Of
860. this Family was *Roger Conſtable* of *Cheſter*, who hearing that his Lord *Ranulphus* Earl of *Cheſter* was diſtreſt in *Wales*, raiſed on the ſudden a great Force among the Shoo-makers and Stage-players of *Cheſter*, and with them went and relieved his Lord from the Power of the *Welch*; whereupon the ſaid Earl *Ranulph* granted to him and his Heirs the Dominion and Patronage of the Shoo-makers and Players at *Cheſter* for ever. His
861. Son and Heir *John de Lacy* became the firſt Earl of *Lincoln* of this name, *Anno Dom.* 1221 and died 1240. From the Heirs General of this Family did deſcend Our Kings of the Houſe of *Lancaſter*.

[Valued at 329 *l.* 2 *s.* 11 *d.* per Annum.]

DORE, in Herefordſhire.

862. Robert Earl of *Ferrars* founded this Monaſtery, and endowed it with Lands, to hold free and quit of all ſecular Service, by the Rent of three ſhillings yearly to be paid at the Feaſt of St. *Peter ad vincula*: and this was expreſt to be given not only for the Health of the Souls of his
863. Anceſtors and Heirs, but alſo (*pro pace & ſtabilitate totius Angliæ & Walliæ*) for the Peace and Stability of all *England* and *Wales*. King *John* by his Deed dated in the ſeventeenth year of his Reign gave divers Lands to the Church of the bleſſed *Mary* at *Dore* and the *Ciſtercian* Monks there. *Walter*
864. *de Clifford* and others were Benefactors. All whoſe Gifts were confirm'd to
865. this Houſe by King *Henry* the III. in the ſeventeenth year of his Reign. *Vid. Vol.* 2. *p.* 918.

[Valued at 101 *l.* 5 *s.* 2 *d.* per Annum.]

SIBETON, in Norfolk. Founded An. 1150.

866. THIS Abby was founded and endowed by *William* Son of *Robert Fitz Walter*. The Lands given to the Monks here were confirm'd by

Vol. I.   CISTERCIANS.   103

by King *Steven* and King *Henry* the II. The said *Robert Fitz-Walter* was 867.
the Founder of the House of St. *Faith*'s at *Horsham*, and married *Sibill*
Daughter of *Radulfus de Cayneto*, who came into *England* with the Con-
queror; from whom descended the Families of *Cressi* and *Ufford*.
Vid. Vol. 3. p. 32.
[Valued at 250 *l.* 15 *s.* 7 *d.* ob. *per Annum.*]

STANLEIGH, in Wiltshire.

THIS Abby was first founded by *Maud* the Empress at *Lokeswell* in the
year 1151. and three years afterwards translated to *Stanlegh*, by
her Son King *Henry* the II. The Monks of this House came from *Quarre* 868.
in the Isle of *Wight*. King *Richard* the II. confirm'd to them all their
Lands, and took them into his protection.
[Valued at 177 *l.* 0 *s.* 8 *d. per Annum.*]

JERVAL, in Yorkshire.   869.

A*Karius Fitz-Bardolf* (a potent man in *Yorkshire*, in the time of King
Steven) gave to *Peter de Quinciaco*, and certain other Monks of
Savigny, a parcel of Land in *Wandesleydale*, for the erection of an Abby
of their Order, which Abby was at first call'd *Fors*, and afterwards *Jorvalle*. 870.
This Foundation was confirm'd by *Alan* Earl of *Britan* and *Richmond*,
which Earl *Alan*, being present at the beginning of the Erection of
the first Buildings, prevailed with several of his Knights to be assistant
to the Work, and this was in the year 1145. *Roger de Molbray* gave
also divers Lands to this House before his first Voyage to *Jerusalem*. The 871.
abovesaid *Peter* inhabited this House at first with only two Companions
labouring with their hands for their sustentation, but in a while they had
of the said Earl of *Richmond*'s Gift, five Plows, forty Cows, sixteen
Horses, three hundred Sheep, &c. After this *Serlo* Abbot of *Savigny*
(having a property in this House of *Jorevalls* by reason that the first Monks
came from thence) granted the same to the Abby of *Biland*. Whereupon the foresaid *Peter* submitted himself and Companions being two 872.
Monks and one Lay-brother (*conversus*) to the Abbot of *Biland*.
Being fully possest of this House, *Roger* Abbot of *Biland* appointed 873.
John de Kinstan to be Abbot here, instituting him in these words, *I con-
firm thee Abbot, and I commit to thee the care of Souls and the Government of the
Abby of* Joreval, *with all its substance Persons and Possessions now had or to be
had, as well in Temporals as Spirituals, in like manner as* Serlo, *Abbot of*
Savigny *gave the same to me*. And then put into his hands the Rule of
St. *Benedict*, &c. *An.* 1150. Hereupon the said Abbot appointed to be of
his Convent, the aforesaid *Peter* and his two Companions, with nine
Monks of *Biland*, who removed from thence to *Jorvall*. After this the 874.
abovesaid Earl *Alan*, and his Son *Conan* Duke of *Britan* encreased
their Revenues, with the Gift of many other Lands. In the year 1156.
the said *Conan* translated these Monks from *Fors*, the place being poor and 875.
steril, to *East-Witton*, upon the River *Jor*, and this was by permission
and approbation of the Abbot of *Cisteaux* and the general Convent of
that Order. *Alanus* Earl of *Britan*, who was so great a Benefactor to this 877.
Monastery,

878.
879.   Monastery, was Brother and Heir to *Alanus Rufus*, who was the Son of *Eudo* Earl of *Britan*, who came into *England* with King *William* the Conqueror, and had given him by the said King all *Richmondshire*. *An.* 1268. *John* Duke of *Britan* and Earl of *Richmond*, confirm'd the Donations of his Ancestors. So also did King *Henry* the III. in the twelfth year of his Reign.

[Valued at 234 *l.* 18 *s.* 5 *d. per Annum.*]

881.   GREENFEILD, in **Lincolnshire**.

882.   Adulf de Aby gave Lands here and elsewhere for the Foundation and Endowment of a Nunnery in *Greenfeild*; which was confirm'd by *Hugh* Bishop of *Lincoln*, and *Eudo de Greinesby*, &c. *John* Son and Heir of *Adam de Welle* gave to this House 10 *l. per Annum* for the finding of two sufficient Chaplains to celebrate for him, and his Ancestors, and all the faithful in our Ladies Chappel in the Priory Church here for ever, to the finding of which *Margaret* then Prioress of this House did oblige her Successors by her Deed dated *Anno Dom.* 1348.

[Valued at 63 *l.* 4 *s.* 1 *d. per Annum*]

CUMB, in **Warwickshire**.

883.   Richard de Camvilla gave Lands to the Abbot and Monks of *Waverley*, for the founding of this Abby of *Cistercian* Monks. *Roger de Moubray* confirm'd the Estate so given, to the Monks of *Cumb*, quit of all secular service.

[Valued at 311 *l.* 15 *s.* 1 *d. per Annum.*]

STRATFORD-LANGTON, in **Essex**.

Founded *Anno.* 1135. for Monks by *William de Montefichet*, endow'd with all the Lordship for *Stradford* in *Westham*, &c. All which Gifts were confirm'd by King *Henry* the II.

[Valued at 511 *l.* 16 *s.* 3 *d. per Annum.*]

884.   FLEXLEY, in **Gloucestershire**.

The Abby here was founded and endow'd by *Roger* Earl of *Hereford*, their Lands were confirm'd by King *Henry* the II.

[Valued at 112 *l.* 13 *s.* 1 *d. per Annum.*]

BLANCLAND, in **Wales**.

This was founded by *John de Toryton*: The Lands given to these Monks were recited and confirm'd by King *John* in the sixteenth year of his Reign. *Vid. Vol.* 2. *p.* 918.

[Valued at 135 *l.* 3 *s.* 6 *d. per Annum.*]   HOLM-

HOLMCOLTRUM, in Cumberland. Founded An. 1150.

King *Henry* II seems to have been the Founder of this Abby, King *Richard* the I. in the first year of his Reign confirm'd their Lands, as did also K. *Henry* III. in the 39. year of his Reign. *John Gernoun* and *Margaret* his Wife, founded and endow'd a Chantry in this Abby Church for four Chaplains, Monks of this House, and two secular Chaplains. This *John* than held two parts of the Mannor of *Wyggeton*, by Cornage. As was found by Inquisition, 6 *E*. 3. *Vid. Vol.* 3. *p.* 34.

[Valued at 427 *l*. 19 *s*. 3 *d*. ob. q. per Annum]

TARENT, in Dorsetshire.

This Abby was founded for Nuns of the *Cistercian* Order, by *Richard* Bishop of *Durham*. *Joan* Queen of *Scots* gave to this House (cum corpore suo) with her Body, Lands in *Stanton* in *Cambridgeshire* to the value of 20 *l*. per Annum. All the Estate belonging to this Monastery was confirm'd by King *Henry* III. who was also himself a Benefactor.

[Valued at 215 *l*. 7 *s*. 9 *d*. per Annum]

TILTEY, alias Wudeham, in Essex.

Founded *Anno* 1152. This was first given by *Maurice* Son of *Jeffery de Teretia* to the Canons of the Church of St. *John* Baptist of *Wodeham*, and endow'd with several Lands, confirm'd by King *Henry* II. Afterwards King *Richard* the first confirm'd the same Estate to the Monks here settled of the *Cistercian* Order, in the tenth year of his Reign.

[Valued at 167 . 2 *s*. 6 *d*. per Annum.]

DEULACRES, in Cheshire.

Anno 1153. The Abby of *Pulton* in *Cheshire* was founded by *Robert Pincerna*, it was furnisht with Monks of the *Cistercian* Order from *Cumbermere*, and was therefore called a Daughter of that House. In the year 1214. the Convent was translated from *Pulton* to *Deulacres* by *Ralph* Earl of *Chester*. This *Ralph* afterwards coming from his Expedition in the *Holy Land*, was in a great Storm at Sea in the Night, confident of deliverance at Midnight, through the Suffrages of these Monks, then at their Nocturnal Devotions, accordingly the Storm did then begin to cease to the wonder of the Seamen. This *Ralph* and his Successors Earls of *Chester* gave and confirm'd divers Lands and Possessions to this Abby. *Vid. Vol.* 2. *pag.* 919.

CLUNOK-VAUR, in Wales.

The Original of this Monastery was by S. *Benow* of whom mention is made in the Life of St. *Winefrid*. The White Monks here were of a newer

newer Foundation. *Guithin,* Unkle to one of the Princes of *Northwales* gave the Village of *Clunok* to *Benow.* *Vide Vol.* 2. *pag.* 119.

893.   **STRATFLURE**, *in* **Cardiganshire.**

Founded and endowed with divers Lands by *Reese,* Prince of *Southwales.* The Estate of this House, (called also *Strata florida*) was confirm'd by King *Henry* II. and King *Edward* I.

[Valued at 118 *l.* 7 *s.* 3 *d. per Annum.*]

894.   **LEGBURN,** *in* **Lincolnshire.**

This Abby was founded for Nuns by *Robert de Lekeburn,* who was buried in the Chapter house of this Nunnery; at whose Interment, his Son and Heir *William,* declared publickly his confirmation of his Fathers Donations and Endowments, adding of his own gift the yearly Rent of
895.   two shillings in *Franckalmoign.* King *John* in the first year of his Reign confirm'd the Estate of this House.

[Valued at 38 *l.* 8 *s.* 4 *d. per Annum.*]

STRATMARGEL, *or* Strata-Marcella, *in* **Montgomeryshire.**

Founded *An.* 1170. by *Madock ap Griffin*; By his Deed dated *An.* 1222 he endowed it with divers Lands and Revenues.

[Valued at 64 *l.* 14 *s.* 2 *d. per Annum.*]

896.   **STANLAW,** *in* **Cheshire.** Founded An. 1172.

The first Founder of this House was *John* Constable of *Chester,* who en-
897.   dowed it with divers Lands and Liberties, his Deed bears date 1178. These Monks of *Stanlaw* were afterwards translated to the Church of *Whaley,* at which the Abbot and Convent of *Salley* in *Yorkshire* were very much grieved, alledging among other things that they were nigher to their Ab-
898.   by than the Constitutions of their Order do allow of, and that it was to their damage 27 *l.* 10 *s.* But the differences were composed in the year
899.   1305. by the Abbots of *Ryvalle* and *Belland.* The Church of *Whaley* was in being in the time when St. *Augustine* the Monk came into *England.* The Rectors of which Church were in after times called Deans and not Parsons, and were married men, who also had the ordinary Jurisdiction of the
900.   place committed to them by the Bishop. These Deans had an Estate of inheritance in the Church of *Whaly,* and the Chappels, which went from Father to Son, and the Cure of the Churches was supplied by certain Priests, whom the Deans provided and presented to the Bishop for his License. The Names of these Deans may be seen in the Book at large. But after the Council of *Lateran* (1215.) it was no longer permitted that this Church should go as an inheritance. Not long after this the Church of *Whaley* was given by *Henry de Lacy* Earl of *Lincoln,*
and

and Lord of *Blazbornshire*, to the Monks of *Stanlaw*, who enter'd upon this their new Seat in the year 1296. *Dom. George de Norbury* being then their Abbot; which Translation was ratified by the Bull of Pope *Nicholas* the IV. The Deed of the said *Henry*, whereby he gave this Church of *Whalley* with all its Rights, Liberties and Appurtenants, bears date in the year 1283. In the thirty fourth year of *Edward* the III. *Henry* Duke of *Lancaster*, Earl of *Derby*, *Lincoln*, and *Leicester*, gave divers Lands to the Abbot and Convent of *Whalley*, for the maintaining of a Recluse, or Anchorite, and his Successors, dwelling in a place within the Church-yard of the Parish-Church of *Whalley*, and for two Women their Servants, who shall be there continually praying for the said Duke his Ancestors and Heirs, *viz* to find them every Week throughout the year fifteen Loaves of the Convent Bread, each Loaf weighing fifty shillings sterling, and seven Loaves of the second sort, of the same weight; eight Gallons of the best Ale of the Convent, and three pence for their Companage; to deliver them yearly at the Feast of all Saints ten Stock-fish, and ten great Ling fish, one bushel of Oats for their Potage, one bushel of Salt, two Gallons of Oyl for their Lamps, one stone of Tallow for Candles, six Load of Turf, and one of Brushwood for Fuel, to keep their House in repair, and to find one of their Monks and a Clark to say Mass in the Chappel of the said Recluse, daily, *&c.*

The first Founder of this House, *John de Lacy*, Constable of *Chester* and Lord of *Halton* married *Alice* Sister of *William de Mandeville*, and died in the Holy Land. Of this Family was *Henry de Lacy* Founder of the Abby of *Kirkstall* (of whom before.)

901.
902.
903.
904.
905.

NUN-APLETON, in Yorkshire.

907.

THIS Priory of Nuns was founded by *Adeliza de Sancto-Quintino*, and *Robert* her Son and Heir, dedicated to God, St. *Mary*, and St. *John* the Apostle, and confirm'd by *Thomas* Archbishop of *Canterbury*. The several Donations made by the Founders and other Benefactors to this House were confirm'd by King *John*, in the sixth year of his Reign. Among the Injunctions prescribed to the Nuns of this House, *An.* 1489. These were some. That the Cloister Doors be shut up in *Winter* at Seven, and in *Summer* at Eight a Clock at night, and the Keys delivered to the Prioress. That the Prioress and all the Sisters lodge nightly in the Dorter, unless sick or diseased. That none of the Sisters use the Ale-house, nor the Water-side where course of Strangers daily resort. That none of the Sisters have their service of Meat and Drink to the Chamber, but keep the Frater and the Hall, unless sick. That no Sister bring in any Man, religious or secular, into their Chamber or any secret place day or night, *&c.* That the Prioress License no Sister to go Pilgrimage, or visit their Friends without great Cause, and then to have a Companion. That the Convent grant no Corodies or Liveries of Bread, or Ale, or other Victual, to any Person, without special License. That they take no Perhendinauncers or Sojourners, unless Children, or old Persons, *&c.*

908.
909.
910.

[Valued at 73 *l.* 9 *s.* 10 *d.* per *Annum.*]

GODEN-

CODENHAM Priory, in ······

Codenham was given to God, St. Mary, and St. John, by *Eustachius de Merch*, for Nuns of the Profession and Order of the Nuns of *Apeltun*.

BINEDON, in Dorsetshire.

Founded *An.* 1172. by *Roger de Novo-Burgo* and *Matilda* his Wife, endow'd with divers Lands by them and other Benefactors. All which was confirm'd to the Church of St. *Mary* of *Bynedone* and the Monks there, by King *Henry* the III. in the eighteenth year of his Reign. *Henry de Novo Burgo* granted power to the Abbot and Monks to choose whom they pleased for their Patron, who thereupon chose King *Henry* the III. and *Alianor* the Queen for their Patrons, which King accordingly took to him the Patronage, Advowson, and Protection of this Abby in the fifty sixth year of his Reign.

[Valued at 147 *l.* 7 *s.* 9 *d.* ob. q. *per Annum.*]

CROXDEN, in Staffordshire.

Bertram de Verdun built an Abby for Monks at *Chotes, Anno Dom.* 1176. *Anno* 1179. The Convent removed from thence to *Crokesden.*

Abbots of this House.

1. *Thomas*, ob. 1229.
2. *William de Choucomb.*
3. *William de Esseburn,* ob. 1237.
4. *John de Tilton.*
5. *Walter de London,* ob. 1268.
6. *William de Howton,* ob. 1278.
7. *Henry de Moysam.*
8. *John de Billesdon,* ob. 1293.
9. *Richard de Twiford,* ob. 1297.

A vacancy of above seven Months.

10. *William de Evera.*
11. *Richard de Esseby*, displaced, 1313.
12. *Thomas de Casterton.*

Richard de Esseby restored 1320.
13. *Richard de Schepesheved* 1335.

The Founder of this House *Bertram de Verdun* died in the Holy Land, and was buried at *Acon*, but most of his descendants were buried in the Church of this Abby. *Vid. Vol.* 3. *p.* 40.

[Valued at 90 *l.* 5 *s.* 11 *d.* per Annum.]

KELDEHOLM, in Yorkshire.

The Abby at *Keldeholm* was founded for Nuns by *William de Stutevill*, and endow'd by the same *William* and several others of that Family. Confirm'd by King *John* in the second year of his Reign.

[Valued at 29 *l.* 6 *s.* 1 *d.* per Annum.]

PONT-ROBERT, or Roberts-Bridge, in Suffex. 916.

Founded for Monks by *Robert de Sancto-Martino*, in the Reign of King *Henry* the II. *Anno Dom.* 1176. Their Estate was confirm'd by King *Edw.* the III. in the tenth year of his Reign. *Vid. Vol.* 2. *p.* 920.

[Valued at 248 *l.* 10 *s.* 6 *d. per Anunm.*]

WICKHAM, in Yorkshire.

THIS Nunnery was founded by *Paganus de Wicham*, whose Son *Theobald*, *Alan Buscell de Hoton*, and the Prior of *Bridlington*, were Benefactors. King *John* confirm'd their Estate in the 2d. year of his Reign. 917.

[Valued at 25 *l.* 17 *s.* 6 *d. per Annum.*]

ABERCONWAY, in Carmarthenshire. Founded An. 1185. 918.

THIS Abby of Monks was founded by *Lewelin* Son of *Gervasius*, Prince of *North Wales*, and by him endow'd not only with large Possessions in Lands, but with great Immunities and Privileges, as to be quit from maintaining for their Founder any Men, Horses, Dogs, or Hawks, to have the Election of their Abbot free to themselves, to have and enjoy Wreck of the Sea in all their Lands, to be Tole-free, &c. Whose Grant bears date *An.* 1198. King *Edward* the I. in the twelfth year of his Reign, translated this Abby from *Aberconway* to a place called *Maynan* which he had built to the honour of God, St. *Mary*, and all Saints, endowing it with Lands and Franchises. 920.

921.

[Valued at 162 *l.* 15 *s. per Annum.*]

NUN-COTUN, in Lincolnshire. 922.

INgeram de Muncels confirm'd the Gift of his Father *Alan de Muncells* of the Town of *Cotun*, and other Lands, to the Church of the blessed *Mary* of *Cotun* and the Nuns there. Pope *Alexander* granted them divers Priviledges, and *Hugh* Bishop of *Lincoln* settled the Constitutions of their House, ordering among other things, that the number of the Nuns should not exceed thirty, that no Nun after Profession should have property in any thing, that no Nun should be or speak with any Person, whether secular or religious, alone, without witness, &c. 923.

924.

[Valued at 46 *l.* 17 *s.* 7 *d. per Annum.*]

DUNKEWELL, in Devonshire. 925.

Founded *An.* 1201. By *William Briwer*. Their Lands were confirm'd to the Monks of this Abby, by King *Hen.* III. in the 11*th.* year of his Reign.

[Valued at 294 *l.* 18 *s.* 6 *d. per Annum.*]

BEAU-

BEAULEIU, in Hampshire.

926.

KING *John* being offended with the *Cistercian* Order in *England*, and the Abbots of that Order coming to him to reconcile themselves, he caused them to be trod under his Horses Feet, for which Action being terrified in a Dream, he built and endowed the Abby of *Beau-leiu* in *Newforest*, for thirty Monks of that Order, *An.* 1204.
Vid. Vol. 2. *p.* 921.

[Valued at 326 *l.* 13 *s.* 2 *d.* ob. q. *per Annum.*]

MENDHAM, in Buckinghamshire.

927.

THIS was a Cell to *Woburne*, founded by *Hugh de Bolebec*, and confirmed by King *John* in the second year of his Reign. The Convent of this Abby came hither from *Woburne* in the year 1204.

[Valued at 20 *l.* 6 *s.* 2 *d. per Annum.*]

GRACE-DIEU, in Wales.

THIS Abby was founded by *John* of *Monmouth An.* 1229. or according to others 1233. King *Edw.* 3. in the thirty fifth year of his Reign granted to this Abby the Hermitage of St. *Briavello* in the Forest of *Dene* for the finding and maintaining of a Chantery of two of their Monks, to celebrate there for the Souls of his Ancestors.

928.

HAYLES, in Gloucestershire.

ANno 1246. *Richard* Earl of *Cornwall* and King of the *Romans* founded this Abby of *Hayles* for twenty Monks who came from *Beau-lieu. An.* 1251. the Abby-Church was dedicated, the King, and Queen, and thirteen Bishops, being present at the Solemnity.

[Valued at 357 *l.* 7 *s.* 8 *d.* ob. *per Annum.*]

NEWENHAM, in Devonshire.

929.

930.

FOunded *An.* 1241. by *Reginald de Moun*, in his Mannor of *Axeminster*; with which and other Lands it was endowed. Confirmed by King *Edw.* 3. This *Reginald de Mohun* was the Son of *Reginald* Lord of *Dunsterre*, and *Alice* Daughter of *William Bruer*, by whom he inherited the Mannor of *Axeminster*. See in the Book at large the Progeny of the noble Family of *Mohuns*.

Abbots

Abbots of this House.

John Godard.	John de Northampton.	Ralph de Shapewike.	931.
Henry Spersholt.	William de Cornubia.	Robert de Puplisuirie.	932.
John de Ponte-Roberto.	Richard de Chichestre.	John de Cokyswill.	
Jeffrey de Blanchvil.	Richard de Piderton.	John de Geytingtone, ob. 1338.	
Hugh de Cokeswell.	William le Fria.	Walter de Hous.	

[Valued at 227 l. 7 s. 8 d. per Annum.]

GRACEDIEU, in Leicestershire. 933.

Founded by *Roesia de Verdun*, for Nuns. Endow'd by her with her Mannor of *Beleton*, &c.

LETLEY, in Hampshire.

KING *Henry* the III. was the Founder of this Abby of *Letley*, otherwise call'd *Locum Sancti Edwardi*, and endow'd it with Lands in the thirty fifth year of his Reign.

[Valued at 100 l. 12 s. 8 d. per Annum.]

REWLEY, in the Suburbs of Oxford. 934.

THIS was founded in the year 1281. for *Cistercian* Monks, by *Richard* Earl of *Cornwall*, and King of the *Romans*, who endow'd this Abby with divers Lands. They were found by Inquisition to be exempt from suit to the County and Hundred Courts. 935.

[Valued at 174 l. 3 s. ob. per Annum.]

DERNHALL, in Cheshire. 936.

KING *Edward* the I. founded and endow'd this Abby in performance of a Vow made in a great danger at Sea, his Deed of endowment bears date before he came to the Crown, in the four and fiftieth year of his Father's Reign. King *Henry* the III. granted his Letter of Request to all Religious Houses in *England* for the furnishing this House with Books. After King *Edward* came to the Crown in the seven and twentieth year of his Reign he translated these Monks to *Vale-Royal*, and granted them many great Immunities and Franchises.
Vid. 2. Vol. p. 921.

937.
938.

[The Abby of *Vale-Royal* was valued at 118 l. 7 s. 6 d. ob. per Annum.]

BOCLAND, in Devonshire.

939.

Founded by *Amicia* Countess of *Devon*, for *Cistercian* Monks; endowed by her and her Daughter *Isabella de Fortibus* Countess of *Albemarl* and *Devon*, with many Lands and Liberties. Confirm'd by King *Edward* the II. *Anno* 4.

940.

[Valued at 241 *l*. 17 *s*. 9 *d*. ob. per Annum.]

HILTON, in Staffordshire.

942.

Anno. 1223. *Henry de Audiddeley* founded and endow'd this Abby with many Lands and Liberties to hold in pure and perpetual Almes. King *Richard* the II. in the 19*th* year of his Reign, at the request of *Elizabeth* relict of Sir *Nicholas de Audley*, Licensed the Abbot and Convent of *Blanchland* in *Normandy*, to transfer to this House the Priory and Mannor of *Cameryngham*, which was thence forward united to this Abby.

943.

[Valued at 75 *l*. 14 *s*. per Annum.]

The Abby of Grace, near the Tower at London.

King *Edward* the III. founded this House in the Church-yard of the *Holy Trinity* near the Tower at *London*, and endow'd it with all the Messuages and Gardens lying on and about the *Tower Hill*, Anno Reg. 24. (1350.) Afterwards in the fiftieth year of his Reign he gave the Mannor of *Gravesend*, and other Mannors in *Kent* to be settled upon this House. All which was after done and confirm'd by King *Richard* the II. Anno Regn. 22.

944.

[Valued at 546 *l*. 10 *s*. per Annum.]

A CARTHVSIAN MONK

Of the Carthusians.

This Order was first founded, *Anno Dom.* 1086. By a certain learned man named *Bruno*, who professing Philosophy at *Paris* and hearing the dead Body of his Friend, who had the Esteem of a very good Man when living, cry out as they were about to bury him, *Justo dei judicio damnatus sum*, he and six Companions forsook the World; and betook themselves to a most austere Life in a Desert and Melancholy Place call'd *Cartusia*, in the Diocess of *Grenoble* in *France*. Their inward Habit is of Hair-Cloath; they never eat flesh; on *Fridays* fast with Bread and Water; never stir out of their Monasteries, except the Prior and Procurator; observe almost continual silence; and suffer no Women to enter into any part of their Houses, no, not their Churches. See more of their Rules in the *Monasticon* at large.

WITHAM, in Somersetshire.

KING *Henry* the II. founded this Monastery in the honour of the blessed *Mary*, St. *John Baptist*, and all Saints, for the Order of *Carthusians*, and endow'd it with divers Lands and Franchises. Imprecating on the Violator of that his pious Donation, the wrath of Almighty God, and his own Curse, unless the Party make Condign Satisfaction; but to all such as augment his Gift, or favour the Peace of the House, he wisht the Peace and Reward of the Eternal Father for ever.

HENTON, in Wiltshire.

ELa Countess of *Salisbury*, Widow of *William Longespee* Earl of *Salisbury*, founded this Monastery in her Park of *Henton*, for *Carthusians*, to the honour of God, the blessed *Mary*, St. *John Baptist*, and all Saints; and endow'd it with Lands and Liberties.

King *Henry* the III. in the four and twentieth year of his Reign granted and confirm'd to this House the same Liberties and free Customs which his Grandfather King *Henry* the II. had formerly granted to the *Carthusians* of *Witham*, with other Exemptions.

The Carthusians in the Suburbs of London.

KING *Edward* the III. in the forty fifth year of his Reign granted his License to Sir *Walter* Lord of *Manny*, to found this Monastery for

Q   *Carthusian*

Carthusian Monks in a certain place without the Bars of *West-Smithlfied*, called *Newe-cherche-hawe*, which House was to be called *la Salutation mere dieu*, and to endow the same with twenty Acres of Land there adjoyning.

Pope *Urban*, reciting that in the time of a great Pestilence Sir *Walter Manny* purchased this ground for a Church-yard to bury poor People in, and there intended to erect a Chappel and a Colledge of twelve Chaplains, by the License of Pope *Clement* the VI. but afterwards the said Sir *Walter* changing his intention, and erected here a Convent of *Carthusians*: the said Pope *Urban* granted his Bull of License for uniting to the said House of *Carthusians*, Ecclesiastical Benefices to the value of 200 *l. per Annum*.

BEAUVAL, or Bella-valle, in Nottinghamshire.

962. IN the year 1343. *Nicholas de Cantilupo* Lord of *Ilkeston*, by License of King *Edward* the III. founded this House in his Park of *Gryseleye*, in the County of *Nottingham*, for a Prior and twelve *Carthusian* Monks, to the glory of God, the blessed Virgin *Mary*, and all Saints, and endow'd it with Lands and Rents in *Greseleye* and *Seleston*.

963. This *Nicholas de Cantilupo* was lineally descended from *Robert de Muskam*, Seneschal or Steward to *Gilbert de Gaunt* that famous Souldier in the Army of *William* the Conqueror, from which *Gilbert* the said *Robert de Muskam* enjoy'd the Lordship of *Ilkeston*, conferr'd upon him in the Reign of King *Henry* the I.

Elizabeth Widow of *Brian Stapleton* Knt. and *William Ryther* Knt. and *Sibilla* his Wife, by License of King *Richard* the II. founded in this Church a Chantry, for the maintenance of two Chaplains, Monks of this House, to celebrate dayly for the Soul of *William de Aldeburgh*, &c.

St. ANNE, adjoyning to Coventry.

964. THIS was first founded in the year 1381. by *William* Lord *de la Zowche*, and first supplied with three Monks from the *Carthusians* at *London*, and with three others from *Bellevalle*. Besides the said Lord *Sowche* they had many other Benefactors, as *Richard Luff* Mayor of *Coventry*, *John Holmeton* of *Sleford*. *John Bokington* Bishop of *Lincoln*, *Thomas de Beauchamp* Earl of *Warwick*, &c. who erected several Parts of their Buildings. In the year 1385. King *Richard* the II. became the principal Founder, with his own hands laying the first Stone in the Foundation of their Church, protesting publickly to be the Founder and to finish the Buildings.

965. To this House were divers Churches appropriated and divers Lands given, among others the Mannor of *Ediweston* in the County of *Rutland*, by the Abbot and Convent of St. *George de Bauquerville*, in *Normandy*, with other Prior alians Lands, &c.

KINGSTON upon Hull, in Yorkshire.

966. *Michael de la Pole* Knt. Lord of *Wingfeild*, by his Deed dated at *Kingston* upon *Hull* 1378. Founded and endowed this House without the Walls of *Hull* for a Prior and twelve *Carthusians*, Monks, in lieu of *Minnoress* Nuns

Nuns of the Order of St. *Clare*, as his Father in his life time had once intended. The House was founded to the honour of God, and the glorious Virgin *Mary*, and of St. *Michael* the Archangel, and all Angels, and holy Spirits, St. *Thomas* the Martyr, late Archbishop of *Canterbury*, and of all other Saints of God. And by assent of the Prior of the Great *Carthusians* in *Savoy*, the chief House of the Order, *Walter de Kele* was by the Founder made the first Prior of this House.

Vid. 2. *Vol.* p. 930.

967.

MOUNT-GRACE, in Yorkshire.

968.

THomas de Holland Duke of *Surrey*, Earl of *Kent*, and Lord *Wake*, founded this House for *Carthusians* in his Mannor of *Bordelby*, near *Cleaveland* in *Yorkshire*, to the honour of God, the Virgin *Mary*, and St. *Nicholas*, willing the House to be called the House of *Mount-Grace* of *Ingelby*, and by assent of the Prior of the Grand *Carthusians*, made *Robert Tredewy* the first Prior of the same.

King *Henry* the VI. ratified and confirm'd this Foundation, in Parliament, in the nineteenth year of his Reign.

969.

EPWORTH, in the Isle of Axholme, in Lincolnshire.

KING *Richard* the II. in the twentieth year of his Reign granted his Licence of *Mortmain* to *Thomas* Earl of *Nottingham* Marshal of *England* to found a Convent for *Carthusian* Monks on his Land at *Epworth*, in the Isle of *Axholme*, in *Lincolnshire*, and to name it the Visitation of the Mother of God, to the honour of God, the Virgin *Mary*, St. *John* the Evangelist, and St. *Edward* the King and Confessor, and to endow the same with one hundred Acres of Land; Licensing also to the Abbot of St. *Nicholas* in *Angiers*, of the Order of St. *Benedict*, to grant over to this House their Priory of *Monks Kirkeby*, in *Warwickshire*, &c. to be appropriated to these *Carthusians* for ever, in pure and perpetual Alms.

970.

Pope *Boniface* the IX. in the eighth year of his Pontificate granted Indulgence to such who should visit this Church of the *Carthusians* on the second of *July* being the Feast of the Visitation of the blessed *Mary*, and contribute to the Buildings here.

971.

This was a plenary Indulgence, and of the same manner with that which was formerly granted to the Church of the Angels without the Walls of *Assisium* in *Italy*, of which you may read in the *Monasticon* at large, p. 971, 972, &c.

SHEEN Monastery, in Surrey.

973.

ANno Dom. 1414. King *Henry* the V. founded three Monasteries near his Royal Seat at *Schene*, one of *Carthusians*, one of *Celestin* Monks professing the Rule of St. *Bennet*, and one of *Brigettines* under the Rule of St. *Augustin*. The last was a Monastery of sixty Nuns, thirteen Priests, four Deacons, and eight Lay-Brothers; the Men and Women had two separate Convents, but one Church, in which the Nuns kept above in a kind of Gallery, and the men below.   Q 2   King

974. King *Henry* the V. by his Charter of Foundation dated in the third year of his Reign, appointed the House of *Carthusians*, which he founded at *Shene*, on the *North*-side of his Mannor there, to be call'd the House of Jesus of *Bethleem* at *Shene*; and to this House he gave the Lands of
975. several Priors aliens here in *England*, belonging to Abbies in *France*, granting in the said Charter that if any of the Lands so given should in time to come be evicted or recovered from the Prior and Monks of this House or their Successors, that then they should receive the like value yearly out of the Profits of the *Hanaper* in the *Chancery*, and out of the Customs arising in the Ports of *London*, St. *Botulphs*, *Southampton*, *Lenn*, and *Cicester*.
976. He gave also several other Benefactions, as the Fishery at *Shene*, four Pipes of *Gascon* Wine yearly at the Purification of the blessed *Mary* for ever, with divers great Liberties and Exemptions from all manner of Taxes and Impositions, granting to the said Prior, and Monks, and their Suc-
977. cessors Felons Goods, &c. and that they should have the return and execution of Writs in their Lands, with fines *pro Licencia Concordandi*, and all Amerciaments &c. Deodands, Treasure-trove, &c. Clerk of the Mercate, Wreck of the Sea, &c. Free Warren in all their Demesnes and Lands already given or to be given, tho' within the Bounds of a Forest, *Soc* and *Sac*, *Infangenthef*, and *Outfangenthef*, and view of *Frankpledge* of all their Tenants and Residents, with a Pillory and Tumbrel, and that they may erect Gallows on their Lands for the execution of Malefactors, whom they should apprehend on their Lands according to the said Liberty of *Infangenthef* and *Outfangenthef*, and that they should have a Market weekly every *Tuesday* at their Town of *Esthenreth* in *Berkshire*, and two Fairs yearly, with other such like great Priviledges and Immunities.

Additions,

Additions, relating to the Benedictine Order.

WINCHESTER Cathedral Church. Supra p. 38.

SOme Remarks of the Founder and Royal Benefactors to the Church of Winchester, Kings and Saints buried there, out of Leyland. Pope Innocent confirmed to this Church all their Possessions with the grant of divers Priviledges, as not to pay any Tithes for their Lands or Cattle in their own proper hands, to celebrate Divine Offices in the time of a general Interdict, with a low Voice, &c. King Edgar restored Monks in this Church confirming their Possessions and Liberties with grievous Curses to the Violators. King Edward the Elder conferr'd on them certain Lands to hold free from any secular service except what related towards the building of Forts and Bridges.

SHAFTESBURY, in Dorsetshire. Supra 217.

KING John in the seventh year of his Reign confirm'd to the Church of St Mary, and St. Edward at Shaftesbury, and to the Nuns there, their Lands and Liberties, among which was the whole hundred of the Mannor of Bradford, &c.

St. FRIDISWIDE, in Oxford. Supra 174.

THE Possessions of this House were enjoy'd by secular Canons for many years, till in the year 1122. (22 H. 1.) they were again restored to Regulars. Maud the Empress confirm'd to the Church of St. Frithesswithe and the Canons Regulars, divers Lands and Churches, and granted them a Fair. The like did King John in his first year.

St. WERBURG, at Chester. Supra 199.

ANno 1119. Richard Earl of Chester confirm'd the Possessions of this House given by many Benefactors, granting to the Abbot of this Monastery a Court of Pleas, and that the said Abbot should not be sued nor be forced to sue out of his own Court. Ralph de Meschines Earl of Chester, and his Son of the same name, were great Benefactors to the Abbot and Convent of St. Werburg; so also were Richard de Rullos and Robert his Brother.

WHITBY, in Yorkshire. Supra 75.

WIlliam de Percy having built and endow'd in a Grove or Wood at Dunesle, a Hermitage in honour of St. James the Apostle, he gave

gave it for ever into the Obedience and Subjection of the Church of St. *Peter* and St. *Hylda* of *Whitby*, so that they continually cellebrate the Divine Office there by some Priest of their House.

WULVERHAMTON, in Staffordshire.

991.
992.
IN this Town of *Hampton*, one *Wulfruna*, a religious Matron erected a Monastery to the honour of God, the ever blessed Virgin *Mary* (then term'd *Stella maris & Domina gentium*) and of all Saints, and endow'd the same with divers Lands, all which was ratified and establisht by *Sigerich* Archbishop of *Canterbury*, in the year 996. by the Consent of King *Ethelred*. The Estate of this House was afterwards confirm'd by King *Edward* the Confessor, King *William* the Conqueror, King *Henry* the II. and King *John*, who gave Timber out of his Woods towards the buildings in this Abby.

GLOUCESTER, in Gloucestershire. *Supra* 108.

993.
994.
995.
GLoucester became a Bishop's Seat in the year 189. soon after the Conversion of King *Lucius*. *Eldadym* in the year 489. and *Dubricius* in the year 522. were Bishops there. But the Seat was afterwards removed to *Menevia*, now call'd St. *Davids*. *Wolpherus* Son of *Penda* King of *Mercia*, according to *Malmesbury*, laid the first Foundations of the Monastery here, after whose death *Ethelred* his Brother and Successor carried on the Work, committing it to the care of *Ofric*, who for this purpose he made his *Prorex* or Lieutenant of this Province. This House was first a Nunnery and continued such under three Abbesses successively. Afterwards *Bernulphus* King of *Mercia*, placed here secular Canons, who, though Clerks and Preachers, were married-men, and differ'd not much in their Habit from secular Christians; thus it continued till in the year 1022. King *Canutus* displaced the Canons, and in their room put Regular Monks of St. *Benedicts* Order. This Monastery being afterwards burnt down, *Aldredus* Bishop of *Worcester* rebuilt it in the time of King *Edward* the Confessor, something distant from the place where it first stood, and more to the outside of the Town. It was twice destroy'd by fire since the Conquest, *viz.* in the years 1214. and 1223. in the Reigns of *Henry* the III. and *Edward* the I. The Buildings in and about this Church were increased and beautified by several Abbots of this Monastery, as *Thomas Seabrook*, *Richard Haulaces*; and *Parker*, who was the last Abbot here, and built the *South* Porch of this Church.

TAVISTOCK, in Devonshire *Supra* 219.

996.
998.
1001.
IN the time of King *Edgar*, Earl *Otdulphus* Son of *Ordgarus* begun this House in a place appointed by Revelation; finisht and confirm'd in the time of King *Ethelred*, An 981. Pope *Celestine* in the year 1193. granted to this Abby divers Priviledges and Exemptions. In the year 1304. The Prior of *Plympton*, of the Order of St. *Augustin*, did oblige himself and Successors to the Abbot of *Tavestock* and his Successors for the performance
of

of divers Services and Offices in his Deed mentioned. King *Henry* the VIII. in the fifth year of his Reign granted to *Richard Banham* then Abbot of *Tavistock* and his Successors to be Lords of Parliament; and to enjoy all Honours and Priviledges of such; and moreover in case they should at any time be absent from Parliament on the Affairs of their House he pardon'd such their absence, they paying for every whole Parliament that they shall be absent five Marks. 1003.

NORWICH. *Supra* 413.

*H*Erbert Bishop of *Norwich* translated the Monks hither from *Thetford*. This Bishop besides the Church at *Norwich*, caused to be built the Churches at *Elmham, Lyn,* and *Yarmouth*, and died *An.* 1119. 1004.

STOKE-CLARE. *Supra* 535.

*R*Ichard de Clare Earl of *Hertford* gave to this House the Hermitage of *Standune*, that Divine Service might be there celebrated for him and his. The Donations and Endowments given to this House were confirm'd by *Thomas* Archbishop of *Canterbury*; and by Pope *Alexander*, *Anno Dom.* 1174. 1005. 1010.

St. Mary de Pratis, at Northampton.

THIS was a Priory of Cluniac Nuns founded by *Simon de* St. *Liz*, Earl of *Northampton*, which Foundation, and all the Lands given thereunto as well by the said Earl *Simon* as others, was all at large recited and confirm'd by the Charter of King *Edward* the III. in the second year of his Reign. Which may be seen from *p.* 1011. to *p.* 1019. 1011.

[Valued at 119 *l*. 9 *s*. 7 *d*. q. per *Annum*.]

PILLA Priory, *in* Wales.

A Dam de Rupe founded here a Priory for *Benedictine* Monks of *Tiron*, which Priory he endow'd with divers Lands and Liberties. Dedicated to God, St. *Mary*, and St. *Budoco*. 1019.

HENINGHAM, *in* Essex.

*F*Ounded and endow'd for *Benedictine* Nuns, by *Abericus de Ver*, Earl of *Oxon*, and dedicated to God, St. *Mary*, St. *James*, and the holy *Cross*. *Hugh de Ver* Earl of *Oxford* founded without the Gates of the Castle of *Hegham*, an Hospital for poor and impotent People; which that it might not be to the prejudice of the Priory of the holy Cross at *Hegham*, nor to the Parish-Church there, was to be govern'd by certain Ordinances then made, among others, that the said Hospital should pay Tithes as well 1020. 1021.

great

great as small to the Parish Church, and that the Chaplains of the said Hospital before they are admitted, should swear fealty to the Prioress of that Priory.

[Valued at 29 l. 12 s. 10 d. per Annum.]

1022. LAPLEY, in Staffordshire, a Cell to St. Remigius, at Rhemes.

1023. Given by *Algarus* an Earl of *England*; the Appropriations belonging to this Priory were allow'd by *Walter* Bishop of *Coventry* and *Litchfeild*, Anno 1319. King *Edward* the I. in the twentieth year of his Reign, granted to the Abbot and Convent of St. *Remigius* at *Rhemes*, a Market in their Mannor of *Aston* in *Staffordshire* on the *Tuesday*, weekly, and a yearly Fair on the Eve and Day of St. *Peter Ad vincula*; with free Warren in their Demesnes of *Lapley*, *Merston*, and *Aston*.

TOTNES, in Devonshire.

Juhellus Son of *Alured* gave the Religious House here for a Cell to God and the holy Martyrs St. *Sergius* and St. *Bachus*, and to the Abbot of that Monastery at *Angiers* in *France*. That they should pray for the good Estate of King *William* the Conqueror while living, and after his death for his Soul, and for him the said *Juhellus* and all his Relations.

1024. BARNSTAPLE Priory of St. Mary Magdalen, *in the Diocess of Exeter*.

1025. THIS was founded for a Prior and six Monks; given by the said *Jubellus*, and confirm'd by King *William* the Conqueror to the Cluniac Monks of the Abby of St. *Martin de Campis* at *Paris*. The Church of St. *Peter* at *Barnstaple* was appropriated to this Priory by *William* Bishop of *Exeter*, by Deed dated, *An.* 1233. The same *William* Bishop of *Exeter* did also by his Deed recite and confirm the Lands and Priviledges given to this Priory by *Joel* Son of *Alured*, before named.

The Priory of St. James *without the Walls at* Exeter, *for a Prior and four Monks.* Supra 643.

1026. THIS Priory, with divers Lands and Priviledges, were given by *Baldewin de Riveriis* Earl of *Exeter*, to the foresaid Cluniac Monks of St. *Martins* Abby at *Paris*,

The Priory of St. Clare, *in* Wales.

FOR a Prior and three Monks. This was given with nine Houses at *Lundon*, by *William Giffard* Bishop of *Winchester*, to the foresaid Cluniac Monks of St. *Martins* Abby at *Paris*. Confirm'd by King *Hen.* the I.

SWINE-

SWINE Abby, in Yorkshire. *Supra p.* 834.

MAtilda Prioress of *Swine*, and the Convent of Nuns there, did covenant with Sir *Alexander Hilton*, Knight, who had given them nine Bovates of Land in *Swine*, that in case the said Sir *Alexander* should die in the year 1241. or in the second year after, that then three Bovates of the nine should return back to the Heirs of the said Sir *Alexander*; in case he die in the third year, then six of the said Bovates should return to the Heirs of the said Knight, but in case the said Sir *Alexander* should keep the said Nuns indempnified for the said three years, then the Nuns to give back the said Land with the Deed of Feoffment after the expiration of the term of six years, &c.

1027.

BYLAND, in Yorkshire. *Sup.* 775.

THE History of the Foundation of this Abby was writ at large by *Phillip* the third Abbot of this House; and is in short as follows, In the Reign of King *Henry* the I. *Anno Dom.* 1134. After the Foundation of the Abby of *Furnes*, whose Monks came from *Savigny* in *France*, an Abbot and Convent of twelve Monks went from the Abby of *Furnes*, to *Cald* in *Copland*, then newly erected, the Abbots name was *Geraldus*; here they remained for about four years, till in the year 1137. being plunder'd and their House almost wholly destroy'd, they were forced to return back to *Furnes*, but being refused entrance there, and distrest for want of a Habitation, they were partly through the recommendation of *Thurstan* Archbishop of *York*, and partly out of pitty to their Condition, relieved by *Gundrea* relict of *Nigellus de Albeney*, and *Roger de Molbray* her Son; which *Roger* settled them for a time at a place call'd *Hode*, a Hermitage belonging to one *Robert de Alneto* a Hermit; who upon their arrival resign'd the place to them, and became a Monk among them, this was in the year 1138. The said *Roger* gave these Monks for their maintenance the Tithe of all the Provision spent in his House, for the collecting of which they had a Lay-brother (*Conversus*) always remaining in his House, who collected the said Tithe, and sent it to the Monastery; but this being found, in time, inconvenient, was not long after chang'd into an Endowment of Land, *An.* 1140. After this Abbot, *Geraldus* seeing the Estate of his Monastery encrease, and fearing that the Abbot of *Furnes* would claim it, by reason that he and his Convent came from thence at first, and had therefore a kind of filial Relation, tho' they were since refused assistance from thence, when in distress, hereupon he made a Journey to *Savigny*, the Mother House of *Furnes*, and obtain'd from the Abbot there in a general Chapter of the whole Order (*An.* 1142.) to be discharged of all subjection to *Furnes*, and to be immediately subject to *Savigny*. This Abbot *Geraldus* dying in his return home, *Roger* then Master of the Novices, was unanimously chosen Abbot, and so confirm'd by the Archbishop of *York*, at the Presentation of *Roger Molbray* their Patron. After this the Abbot of *Furnes* placed another Abbot and Convent at *Cald*. *An.* 1143. *Roger de Molbray* gave to these Monks the Town and Church of *Bellalanda*, or *Biland*, with the Appurtenants, whether they afterward removed their Habitation. When Abbot *Roger* perceived the Inhabitants of *Scalton* (a Vill belonging to *Biland*) to suffer divers Inconveniencies in coming to the Mother Church

1028.

1029.

1030.

Church of *Biland* as well for Divine Service, as Sacraments, he obtain'd of *Henry Murdac* then Archbishop of *Tork*, Licenſe to build a Chappel at *Scalton* for the eaſe of the Inhabitants there, *An.* 1146. reſerving the burial of the dead to the Mother Church at *Biland*. The Licenſe thus obtain'd, the ſaid Abbot *Roger* and his Monks ſoon built a Church at *Scalton*, and furniſht it with Books, Veſtments, Font, and other neceſſaries, and cauſed one of the Bells of the Mother Church to be removed thither. This being finiſht, the ſaid *Roger* preſented a Clerk to the Archbiſhop, who was accordingly inſtituted to the Cure of the ſaid Chappel. After this, this Abby of *Biland* had many Donations; the ſaid *Roger de Molbray* giving ſo much, that the Abbot did at laſt refuſe to accept any more, laying he had ſufficient. *An.* 1147. It was decreed in the Council of *Rhemes* held under Pope *Eugenius* the III. that the Church of *Savigny* with thirteen Abbies, Daughters of that Church, ſhould be all ſubjected to the Church of *Clarevallis*, of the *Ciſtercian* Order. *An.* 1150. The Abbot of *Cald*, and the Abbot of *Furnes* ſeeing the Riches and Proſperity of this Houſe of *Biland*, began to ſet a Foot a Title and Pretence to a Juriſdiction over this Houſe, by reaſon of Paternity (or Maternity) againſt the Abbot of *Savigny*; which was ſo far proſecuted by the Abbot of *Furnes*, that at laſt the general Chapter of *Ciſtercians* did delegate the Cauſe to be heard and adjudged by the Abbot of *Ryevalle*, who determin'd it for the Abbot of *Savigny*. The foreſaid *Roger* Abbot of *Biland*, lived Abbot of the ſame fifty four years, and then by reaſon of his decrepid age, reſign'd, ſurviving near three years after. To him ſucceeded in this Office Abbot *Phillip*, who writ this Hiſtory, as he had heard it related from his ſaid Predeceſſor *Roger* and others, *An.* 1197.

1031.
1032.

1033.
1034.

1035. THE Alien Priories, ſuppreſt in the ſecond year of *Henry* the V. *An. Dom.* 1414. were in number one hundred and forty two, whoſe names ſee in the Book at large.

1037. The Religious Houſes ſuppreſt by Pope *Clement* the VII. and granted to Cardinal *Wolſey* by King *Henry* the VIII. in the ſeventeenth year of his Reign for the building of two Colledges, at *Oxford* and *Ipſwich*, were in number one and twenty; and afterwards ſix more by another Bull of the ſame Pope, which were granted alſo to the ſaid Cardinal for the ſame purpoſe, by King *Henry* the VIII. in the twentieth year of his Reign.

1037. i
uſq; ad
1046.

An exact Catalogue of the Religious Houſes was made in the twenty ſixth year of King *Henry* the VIII. with the Annual Values of almoſt all of them, as well in *Wales* as *England*. Which Catalogue was afterwards incerted into the Books of *Firſt Fruits* and *Tenths*.

Out of which Catalogue I have ſet down the Valuation of the Annual Rents of each Houſe, under the proper Head, in the foregoing Epitome, except ſome few not then valued.

1047. Having ſaid ſomething in the beginning, of the Inſtitution of the Monaſtical Life, I ſhall here add what Opinion Men had of the Subverſion of Monaſteries, even among Proteſtants.

The

The *Augustine* Confession, says, That Monasteries were heretofore Schools of sacred Learning, advantagious to the Church, and that Pastors and Bishops came from thence. *Calvin* in his Institutions, says, Monastick Colledges were then as Seminaries of the *Ecclesiastick* Order; and gives a very great Encomium of their manner of Life and Piety, Charity to the Poor, and Humanity, out of St. *Augustines* Epistles.

Hyperius says, That Monasteries at their Institution were no other than Convents of Good men, and Students; Schools where the Elder did teach the younger Religion, where they did spend their time in writing, and disputing, and instituting those who afterwards arrived to eminent places in the Church, as to be Bishops or Priests, &c. *William Perkins*, says, That the Monasteries of the Ancients were for the most part Publick Schools, that is, Communities of Teachers and Learners.

The Preamble of the Stat. 27 H.8.c.28. (omitted in the printed Act,) for the Suppression of certain Religious Houses, (*viz*. under the value of 200 *l*. per Annum.) hath these Words, *Forasmuch as manifest sin is dayly used, and commonly committed in such little and small Abbies and Priories*, &c. *where the Congregation of such religious Persons is under the number of twelve persons*, &c. *Considering also that divers and great solemn Monasteries of this Realm, wherein, thanks be to God, Religion is well kept and observed, be destitute of such full numbers of religious Persons as they might and may keep*, &c. Therefore the said lesser Monasteries were dissolved, and their Lands given to the King.

Sir *Edward Coke*, in his 4*th*. *Institut*. *p*. 44. says, In the Reign of *Henry* the VIII. the Members of both Houses of Parliament were informed, on the King's behalf, That no King or Kingdom was safe but where the King had ability to live of his own, and to defend his Kingdom upon any sudden Invasion or Insurrection, &c. It was therefore projected, that if the Parliament would give unto him all the Abbies, Priories, Nunneries, &c. that for ever in time then to come, he would take order that the same should not be converted to private use, but first that his *Exchequer* for the Purposes aforesaid should be enriched. 2*dly*. The Kingdom strengthened by a continual maintenance of forty thousand well trained Souldiers with skillful Captains and Commanders. 3*dly*. for the Benefit and Ease of the Subject, who should never afterwards in any time to come, be charged with Subsidies, Fifteenths, Loans, or other common Aides. 4*thly*, Least the honour of the Realm should receive any diminution (there being nine and twenty Lords of Parliament among the Abbots and Priors, who held of the King *per Baroniam*) the King would create a number of Nobles. The said Monasteries and their Possessions were given to the King, his Heirs and Successors. Now observe the Catastrophe; not long after the dissolution of the Monasteries, the said King demanded and had two Subsidies, and exacted divers Loans.

There were in the Reign of *Henry* the VIII. 645. Monasteries and Religious Houses, forty of which being granted to Cardinal *Wolsey* for the Endowment of his two Colledges: Soon after, as the Pope had given these to the Cardinal, the King with the Parliaments assent took the rest. *An*. 1536. those under 200 *l*. *per Annum*, were granted, amounting to 376, and soon after the Remainder, being in all 605 Monasteries. Besides them, were given 96 Colledges, 110 Hospitals, and 2374 Chantries and free Chappells. The Revenue of all which, is wisht to have been bestow'd for the Advancement of the Church, Relief of the Poor, &c. rather than

1048.

1049.

conferr'd

conferr'd with such a prodigal Dispensation on those who stood ready to devour *what was sanctified*. To this purpose one *Henry Brinklow* a Merchant of *London*, made a Complaint to the Parliament of the Abuse that follow'd in relation to Appropriations, which as he said were the best Benefices, and did amount to the third part of all the Parish Churches in *England*. Touching the Alms (*says he*) that they dealt, and the Hospitality that they kept, every man knoweth that many thousands were well received of them, and might have been better, if they had not so many Great mens Horses to feed, and had not been overcharged with such idle Gentlemen as were never out of the Abbies. But now that all the Abbies with their Lands and Impropriated Parsonages are in Temporal mens hands, where 20 *l* was given formerly to the poor yearly, in more than one hundred places in *England*, is not one meals meat given; where they had always one or other Vicar that either preached or hired some to preach, now there is no Vicar at all, but the Farmer is Vicar and Parson too.

1051. The Lord *Herbert* in his History of *Hen.* VIII. says, That the King was petition'd that some of the Houses, both for the Vertue of the Persons in them, and for the Benefit of the Country, (the Poor receiving thence great Relief, and the richer sort good Education for their Children) might be left for pious Uses; Bishop *Latimer* also moved that two or three might for those ends be left in every Shire. But *Cromwell* (by the King's permission) invaded all. However the King thought fit to have this Proceeding confirm'd by Act of Parliament. But the Christian World (says my Lord *Herbert*) was astonisht at these doings. Besides the Houses and Lands taken away, there was much mony made of the present Stock of Cattle and Corn, of the Timber, Lead, Bells, *&c.* and chiefly of the Plate and Church Ornaments, which is not valued, but may be conjectured by that one Monastery of St. *Edmunds Bury*, whence was taken five thousand Marks of Gold and Silver, besides divers Stones of great Value.

The End of the First Volum.

MONASTICON ANGLICANUM,
ABRIDGED.

VOL. II.

OF THE
Canons Regular
Of St. *AUGUSTIN*,

HOSPITALERS,
TEMPLARS,
GILBERTINES,
PRÆMONSTRATENSES, *and*
MATURINS, *or* TRINITARIANS.

PRACTICE
GEOMETRY

VOL. II

John Kerrigan

OF THE ORIGINAL OF CANONS.

OF the Author of this Institution there is great variety of Opinion. Some ascribe it to the Apostles, others to Pope *Urban* the I. about the year of Christ 230. Others to St *Augustine*; Others to Pope *Gelasius* the I. about the year 495. &c. Canons were first introduced in *England* by one *Berinus*, *An. Christi* 636. The Canonical Life being by little and little relaxt and fallen off, Canonical Clerks were in the Council of *Mentz*, *An.* 813. reduced back to their first manner of living, *viz.* to live in Common, to have but one Table, one Purse, and one Dormitory. About *An.* 1083. it was enjoyn'd that no Canon should dare to become an Abbot or Monk under the penalty of Excommunication. In process of time Canons becoming loose and disorderly, another sort of Canons began to be taken notice of, who observing a stricter Discipline, were call'd Canons Regular, and the others Canons Secular. The Canons Habit is a white Tunick with a Linnen Gown, under a black Cloak. St. *James* the Apostle and the first Bishop of *Jerusalem*, is said first to have assumed the Linnen Tunick, after the manner of the ancient Levitical Priests.

In the Proem.

This Order had formerly in *Europe* four thousand five hundred and fifty five Monasteries, In *Italy* seven hundred. Popes of this Order there have been thirty six, Cardinals three hundred, Holy men and such who have been reckon'd in the Catologue of Saints seven thousand five hundred.

For the Canons of this Order were made three Rules.

{ The first Rule which St. *Augustin* made for his Brethren, who promised to live together in Common, consists of nine Chapters; and treats of the Community of Goods, Self-denial, &c.

The second Rule of St. *Augustin* appoints the manner and time of Praying, Singing, Reading, Working, Living, and Conversing, and consists of Five Chapters.

The third Rule of St. *Augustin*, treats more largely of those things which appertain to the Community of living among Clerks, and consists of Forty Five Chapters.

A CANNON REGVLAR OF S. AVGVSTINE.

MONASTICON ANGLICANUM.

Vol. II.

Of the Order of St. AUGUSTIN.

DOVER, in Kent.

Julius Cæsar having Conquer'd Britain (now call'd England) forty seven years before the Birth of Christ, built a Tower at *Dover* where the Castle now stands. In the year of Grace 180, King *Lucius* then reigning in *Britain*, became a Christian under Pope *Elutherius*, and among other Pious Deeds built a Church in the Castle of *Dover*. *An*. 469, King *Arthur* repair'd the said Castle, and built the Hall there call'd *Arthur's*-hall. After this the *Saxons* came out of *Germany*, Conquer'd *Britany*, beat the *Britons* into *Wales*, who afterwards were call'd *Welchmen*, and the *Saxons Englishmen*, and being Pagans, demolisht Churches, and supprest Christianity throughout the Land. *An*. 586. Pope *Gregory* sent St. *Augustin* the Monk with others into *England*, who converted to Christ the King then reigning in *Kent*, named *Adelbert*, whose Son and Successor *Adelbold* placed twenty four Secular Canons in the said Castle to serve in his Chappel there. *An*. 686, *Withred* King of *Kent* built the Church of St. *Martin*, in the Town of *Dover*, and removed the said Canons thither, from the Castle; here they remain'd 400 years after. He built also three other Churches for the use of the Parishioners, which were however Chappels subordinate to St. *Martins*. But these Canons being very licentious by reason of their great Priviledges and Exemptions from the ordinary Jurisdiction. King *Henry* the I. in 1130. did give the said Church of St. *Martin* to the Archbishop of *Canterbury* and his Successors, and tho' *William Corboil* then Archbishop, built the *New Minster*, and design'd to have made it an Abby of Canons of St. *Augustin*, yet after his death *Theobald* Archbishop of *Canterbury*, in the Reign of *Henry* the II. put Monks of St. *Bennet* therein. The said King *Henry* the II. by his Charter subjecting the Government of this House to the Archbishop of *Canterbury* intirely, and that no other Order but that of St. *Bennet* should be herein. King *Edward* the III. in the thirtieth year of his Reign did unite and annex this House to the Priory of *Christ-Church* in *Canterbury* for ever, so that none for the future should be Prior here, but a Monk of *Canterbury*.

[Valued at the Suppression at 170 *l*. 14 *s*. 11 *d*. ob. *per Annum*.]

BODMYN, in Cornwall

5.

KING *Henry* the III. in the seven and fiftieth year of his Reign confirm'd to the Prior and Canons of *Bodmine*, the Mannor of *Newton*, in the County of *Devon*, formerly given them by King *Eadred*, with Exemption from suit to the County of *Devon* and Hundred of *Shefbury*, &c.

[Valued at 270 *l*. 0 *s*. 11 *d*. per Annum.]

St. GERMAINS, in Cornwall.

IT was found by Inquisition in the thirtieth of *Edw.* the III. That King *Canute* endow'd this Church, and that here was then a Bishops Seat for *Cornwall*, which was after united to *Cryditon*, and in the Reign of *Edward* the Confessor, removed from thence to *Exeter*; and that soon after, *Leofricus* then Bishop of *Exeter* did remove from hence the Secular Canons, and did found here a Priory of Canons Regular, and that hereupon the Bishops of *Exeter* for the time being became Patrons of this Priory, and enjoy'd the Profits of the Vacations of the said Priory when they happened.

[Valued at 243 *l*. 8 *s*. per Annum.]

PLIMTON, in Devonshire.

6.

HERE was formerly a Colledge consisting of a Dean and four Prebendaries, founded by some of the *Saxon* Kings, which Canons or Prebendaries were displaced by *Wil. Warwist* Bishop of *Exeter*, because they
7. would not leave their Concubines, and a Priory of Canons Regular erected here, which Priory was founded in the Mansion-house of the Rectory of the
8. said Church of *Plimpton*, and the said Foundation confirm'd by King *Hen.*
9. the I. who also granted and confirm'd to the Canons there, divers Lands, Liberties, and Immunities. Among other Benefactors to this Priory, King *Edgar* gave them divers Lands for the Maintenance of two Canons, *ad divina ibidem celebranda, & pro peregrinis & aliis hospitandis.*——After-
10. wards King *Edward* the I. granted to the said Canons, that for the future they might appoint and place in the Church of *Landoho*, where the said Revenue did arise, a Secular Vicar and Chaplain to celebrate there, and to perform the said Alms and Hospitality, *nomine dictorum Prioris & Canonicorum.*

[Valued at 912 *l*. 12 *s*. 8 *d*. ob. per Annum.]

WALTHAM, in Essex.

11.

THIS Monastery was built to the praise of our Lord Jesus Christ, and of the holy Cross, by Earl *Harold* (afterwards King) who endow'd the same with divers Lands and Goods. All which were confirm'd, with the Grant of great Liberties, by King *Edward* the Confessor, *An. Dom.* 1062. Which *Harold* being slain in Battle, by *William* the Conqueror,

queror, was buried in this Abby-Church. *An. Dom.* 1177. The Secular Canons here were removed and Canons Regular placed in their room, by King *Henry* the II. who confirm'd their Estate and Liberties, and ordain'd that in the said Abby, no Kinsman of the Abbot should be made Steward or other Officer, nor any Officer to hold his place by Inheritance, but removable at the Will of the Abbot and Canons. The like Confirmation was made by King *Richard*.

[Valued at 900 *l.* 4 *s.* 3 *d.* per Annum.]

PENTNEY, in Norfolk.

Founded to the honour of God, the glorious Virgin *Mary*, and the blessed *Mary Magdalen*, by *Robert de Vaux*, and by him endow'd with divers Lands and Churches. This *Robert* came into *England* with the Conqueror, from whom descended by an Heir General the Lords *Roos* who became thereupon Patrons of this Priory.

[Valued at 170 *l.* 4 *s.* 9 *d.* per Annum.]

WALSINGHAM, in Norfolk.

Galfridus de Favarches endowed a Chappel here, which his Mother had founded in honour of the perpetual Virgin *Mary*, with divers Revenues; confirm'd by *Robert Brucut*, and *Roger* Earl of *Clare*. The Chappel here was first begun in the Reign of *Edward* the Confessor, but the Canons introduced in the time of *William* the Conqueror. Here was a perpetual Chantry establisht for the Souls of *Thomas de Felton*, &c. in the Chappel of St. *Ann* in the Priory, consisting of four Chaplains. 8. *R.* 2.

[Valued at 391 *l.* 11 *s.* 7 *d.* per Annum.]

THREMHALE, in Essex.

Gilbert de Montefixo, or *Munfichet*, who was a *Roman* by birth, and Kinsman to the Conqueror, came into *England* in his Army, and having attained large Possessions here, gave Land in *Thremhale* for the building a Religious House with some small Possessions; and returning to *Italy*, the place of his Nativity, left issue *Richard de Munfichet* who gave to God and the Church of St. *James* the Apostle at *Thremhale*, divers Lands and Priviledges; from this *Richard* are descended by an Heir General the *Veres* Earls of *Oxford*, who became Benefactors to this House.

[Valued at 60 *l.* 18 *s.* 7 *d.* ob. per Annum.]

The Priory of Huntington.

Eustachius the Viscount, who also held the Barony of *Lovetot*, founded the Priory of St. *Mary* of *Huntingdon*, and endow'd it with divers *Henry* the I. In the Town of *Huntingdon* were h Churches, tho' at present there remains but four.

four. *David Bruce* Earl of *Huntingdon* was buried in this Priory. Pope *Eugenius* confirm'd to the Canons here all their Lands and Priviledges, *An. Dom.* 1147. and so did King *Henry* the III. in the seven and thirtieth year of his Reign.

[Valued at 187 *l*. 13 *s*. 8 *d. per Annum*.]

28. St. OSWALDS, *near* Gloucester.

Founded by *Ethelred* Earl of *Marches* and *Ethelfleda* his Wife before the Conquest, for Prebendaries, who translated hither the Body of St. *Oswald* from *Bardney*. But soon after the Conquest, this Colledge being impropriated to the See of *York*, that Archbishop changed the Prebendaries here to Canons Regular.

[Valued at 90 *l*. 10 *s*. 2 *d. ob. per Annum*.]

BARNEWELL, *near* Cambridge.

29. IN the time of *William* the Conqueror, lived one *Picot*, a *Norman*, a Person of great Note, who was Viscount or Sheriff in this County, he had also a Barony here. *Hugolin* his Wife being much devoted to St. *Giles*, made a Vow in her sickness to erect a Monastery to that Saint, which Vow her Husband confirm'd; this was erected near the Castle in *Cambridge*, and six Canons Regular placed therein under the Rule of one *Galfridus de Huntedon*. But *Picot* and his Wife dying before their intended Charity was fully compleated, and *Robert* their Son being after their death accused of Treasonable Practices for which he fled the Kingdom, King *Henry* the I. seized upon his Barony, and gave it to a *Paganus Peverelle*, who finding this House fallen to decay, undertook to restore it, and increase the Canons to the number of thirty. To this end he obtained of the King a peice of Ground lying without the Town of *Cambridge*, call'd *Barnewell*,

30. of sweet and delicate Situation: here he built a very fair Church, and removed the said Canons hither with great Solemnity from the place of their first Foundation in *Cambridge, Anno Dom.* 1112. after they had continued there just twenty years. From this *Paganus Peverell* the Patronage of this Priory descended by an Heir General to the *Peches. An. Dom.* 1284. *Gilbert Peche* gave the Patronage of this Monastery to King *Edward*, for ever. The abovesaid *Paganus Peverell* was Standard-bearer to *Robert* Son

32. of *William* the Conqueror in the holy Land. The Particulars of their Revenue was found by Inquisition. 3 *E*. 1. which see in the Book at large. The foresaid *Gilbert Peche*, by his Deed dated 1256. granted to the Canons of this House liberty to choose their own Prior, but that upon the death of the Prior, one or two of the Canons should come to him, if in *England*, and acquaint him therewith, and desire his leave (as Patron) to proceed to a new Election, that thereupon they should proceed, and

33. having made their Election, they should present the Person elected to him, and require his consent, that during the time of Vacation, he, his Heirs, or Successors, should not commit any Wast on the Goods of the said Monastery, nor have there more than one Servant with a Horse and a Boy.

[Valued at 256 *l*. 11 *s*. 1 *d. per Annum*.]

NOSTELL,

NOSTELL, in Yorkshire.

Robert de Laci founded the Church of St. Oswald at Nostell, and endow'd the same with divers Lands and Revenues, for Canons Regular, granting them free liberty to Elect their own Prior. King *Henry* the I. recited and confirm'd the several Grants of their Benefactors; the like did King *Henry* the II. to this Priory, by the name of the Church of the blessed *Oswald* the King and Martyr adjoyning to the Castle of *Pontefract*, in a place called *Nastle*. In the year 1231. the Prior and Convent here leased their Estate at *Canonthorp* to *William de Runeys*, Knt. for his Life, at the Rent of 13 s. 4 d. per Annum, the said *William* causing Divine Service to be celebrated at the Chappel there three days in every Week, viz. *Sunday*, *Wednesday*, and *Friday*, with other Covenants.

34.
36.
38.

[Valued at 492 l. 18 s. 2 d. per Annum.]

BREDON, in Leicestershire.

Robert Earl of *Nottingham* gave to the Church and Canons of St. *Oswald* of *Nostla*, the Church of St. *Mary*, and St. *Hardulf* of *Bredon* with divers Lands and Revenues to the same appertaining. Whereupon this House became a Cell to that of *Nostell* immediately before treated of; yet by subsequent agreement between the Prior and Convent of *Nostell*, and *Walter*, Advocate, or Patron of *Bredon*, the said Prior should upon a Vacancy at *Bredon*, choose two of the Canons there, or in case there should not be two fit Persons there then two of his own House, of which two the said *Walter* should choose one, and then the said Prior and *Walter* joyntly to present the party so chosen to the *Diocesan*, to be Prior of *Bredon*. Vid. Vol. 3. p. 41.

39.
41.

[Valued at 24 l. 10 s. 4 d. per Annum.]

Another Cell to *Nostell* was *Woodkirk* (or *Wodechurche*) in *Yorkshire*, endow'd for Canons by the Earls of *Warren*.

HYRST, in the Isle of Axholme, in Lincolnshire.

This was a Cell belonging to *Nostell*, endow'd with Lands by *Nigellus de Albani*, and *Roger de Moubray*.

42.

[Valued at 5 l. 10 s. 1 d. per Annum.]

SCOKIRK, in Yorkshire.

Was another Cell to the foresaid Priory of *Nostell*. To which *Gaufridus Fitz-Pagan* and others gave Lands and Tithes. *William de Archis* granted to the Canons here half the Tithe of his Bread made in his House for ever in pure and perpetual Alms.

43.

[Valued at 8 l. per Annum.]

COL.

COLCHESTER, in Essex.

44.

KING *Henry* the I. gave to the Church of St. *Julian*, and St. *Botolph* of *Colchester*, and to the Canons there the Tithes of all his Demesnes in *Hetfeld*, with divers Lands in and about *Colchester*; confirming to them other Lands which they had of the Gift of *Hugh Fitz-Stephen* to hold in Serjeancy by the finding of one Horse of the price of five shillings, and one Sack and one Prick, at the King's charges when he makes War against

45. the *Welch* for forty days. Pope *Paschall* the II. by his Bull dated A.D. 1116. granted to the Canons of this House, that as they were the first of this Order in *England*, so they should be the first in Dignity, and exempted

46. them from all Secular or Ecclesiastical Jurisdiction other than that only of the See of *Rome*, and finally that they should choose their own Superior, but present him when chosen to the Bishop of *London* to be Consecrated.

[Valued at 523 l. 17 s. per Annum.]

HAGHMON, in Shropshire.

47.

THIS was founded in the year 1100. (1. H. I.) by *William Fitz-Allen*. King *Edward* in the thirteenth year of his Reign confirmed to the Church of St. *John* the Evangelist of *Haghman*, and to the Canons there, all their Lands and Revenues given by several Benefactors, among whom were some of the *Welch* Princes. *Vide infra* 933.

[Valued at 259 l. 13 s. 7 d. per Annum.]

49. ## St. JAMES at Northampton.

Founded and endowed by *William Peverell*. Confirm'd by King *Henry* the II. With the grant of divers Liberties.

[Valued at 175 l. 8 s. 2 d. ob. per Annum.]

50. ## WIRKSOP, in Nottinghamshire.

Founded and endowed by *William de Lovetot*, 3 *Hen.* 1. and dedicated to God and St. *Cuthbert*: Which Estate was confirm'd and encreased by his Heirs. Pope *Alexander* the III. by his Bull dated An. Dom. 1161.

53. confirm'd the Estate of the Canons here, and granted them divers Priviledges, as to pay no Tithes for the Cattle and Lands in their own occupation; to present Priests from among their own Brethren to the Bishop to be instituted to the Parish Churches which they hold, who shall be answerable to the Bishop for the Cure of the People, and to the Priory for the Profit of the Livings; to have a Cæmitary free for the burial of such as desire to be buried with them, saving the Rights and Dues of the Parish-Churches from whence the dead are brought; and to celebrate the Divine Offices, privately, in the time of a general Interdict. Their

54. Lands and Liberties were also confirm'd by King *Hen.* II. *Vid. infra* 937.

[Valued at 239 l. 10 s. 5 d. per Annum.]

FELLEY,

FELLEY, in Nottinghamshire.

THIS was a Cell belonging to *Wyrksop* (alias *Radeford*) given to that House by *Radulphus de Annesley* and *Reinold* his Son, *An. Dom.* 1152. (2 *H.* 2.) In the year 1343 *William* Archbishop of *York* appropriated the Church of *Adingburgh* to this Priory of *Felley* for the encrease of four Canons more, there being but five before, so that for the future there should be nine, of which one to be Prior, reserving out of the Fruits and Profits of the said Church a sufficient subsistance for a perpetual Vicar, which Vicar was to be presented by the Prior and Canons of this Monastery.

[Valued at 40 *l.* 19 *s.* 1 *d. per Annum.*]

56.

57.

58.

LANTHONY, in Wales (after Translated to Gloucester.)

HERE was of old time a small Chappel of St. *David*, in a very solitary place, where a Knight called *William*, belonging to the Family of *Hugh de Lacy*, forsaking the World, led an Heremitical Life; whose eminent Fame for Holiness drew to him one *Ernisius* Chaplain to Queen *Maud*, Wife of King *Henry* the I. who became his associate in his Devotions and Austerity; this was *An. Dom.* 1103. under the Reign of King *Henry* the I. In the year 1108. they erected here a mean Church which was dedicated to St. *John Baptist*, by the Bishop of that * Diocess, and the Bishop of *Hereford*. Of these two Heremits *Hugh de Lacy* became a Protector and Benefactor. After some time, these two, through the Advice and Approbation of *Anselme* Archbishop of *Canterbury* were willing to encrease their number and to alter their poor House from a Heremits Cell to be a Monastery, and they chose from all the Religious Orders then in being, that of the Canons Regular. A certain number of Canons were thereupon assembled from the Monasteries of *Mereton*, the holy Trinity at *London*, and *Colchester*, and establisht here at *Lanthony*, over whom the foresaid *Ernisius* was made Prior; the number of Canons being about that time forty, or more. And many their Benefactors besides *Hugh de Lacy*, who conferr'd on them more Revenues than they were willing to receive. *Walter* the Constable, being the chief Officer in the King's Court, and one of the Greatest Men of the Kingdom, took on him a Religious Habit, and spent the remainder of his days in this House. On the death of *Ernisius*, *Robert de Retun* was chosen Prior, but he being afterwards made Bishop of *Hereford*, *Robert de Braci* was chosen to succeed him. After the death of *Henry* the I. the Canons of this House were much afflicted and disturb'd in their Possessions here, whereupon *Milo* Earl of *Hereford*, the Kings Constable (and Son of that *Walter* who became a Religious man among the Canons) gave them a piece of Ground without the Walls of *Gloucester* for a new Seat, here they built a new Church, which in the year 1136. was solemnly dedicated by the Bishops of *Worcester* and *Hereford*, in honour of the blessed *Mary*, yet still this House retain'd the name of *Lanthony*. After this *Robert de Braci* died and was buried in the new Monastery at *Gloucester*, to whom succeeded *William de Wycumb.* And now it was, that by Papal Authority the Church of St. *Mary* at *Gloucester* was confirm'd as

59.

60.

* *Landaff.*

61.

62.

63.

64.

a

a Cell to that of St. *John Baptist* at *Lanthony*. However the Canons being better pleased with their new Habitation, which was much braver and richer than their old Seat in *Wales*, chose to inhabit at *Gloucester*, removing and spoiling what they had at *Lanthony*. They became also very licentious in their way of living. During this *William* their Prior falling into Troubles and Vexation as well with the Canons of his own House, as *Roger* Earl of *Hereford* the Patron, was forced to resign his Office; to whom succeeded *Clement* the Sub-prior. This man reform'd the Abuses that were in the Monastery, especially as to the Church Service. From the aforenamed *Milo* Earl of *Hereford*, descended by an Heir General the Noble Family of *Bohuns* Earl of *Northampton*, *Hereford*, and *Essex*, who by reason thereof were Patrons of this Monastery. The first Founder, *Hugh de Lacy*, came into *England* with the Conqueror, but died without issue, and his Inheritance went to his two Sisters, from whom are descended divers Noble Families, of which Descents see the Book at large. King *John* in the first year of his Reign recited and confirm'd to the Canons of *Lanthony* the several Lands and Revenues given them by their Benefactors. The like did King *Edward* the II. in his eighteenth year. King *Edward* the IV. in the one and twentieth year of his Reign gave the Priory of *Lanthony* and all the Lands, &c. belonging to the same, to *Henry Deen*, then Prior of the Priory of the blessed *Mary* of *Lanthony* at *Gloucester*, and to the Canons there to be consolidated and united thereunto for ever, providing that the Prior and Canons at *Gloucester* shall for the future maintain at *Lanthony* one Prior dative and removeable at will, with four Canons to celebrate Masses and other Divine Offices there for ever, if not hindred by Rebels and Wars.

[Valued at 648 *l*. 19 *s*. 11 *d*. per Annum.]

CARLILE, in Cumberland.

KING *Henry* the I. gave the Churches of *New-Castle* upon *Tyne*, and *Newbourne*, to the Canons of St. *Mary* of *Carlile*. Besides that King, the King of *Scotland* and many others were Benefactors, all whose Gifts were confirm'd by King *Henry* the II. And others given by King *Edward* the I. and II.

[Valued at 418 *l*. 3 *s*. 4 *d*. per Annum.]

DUNMOW, in Essex.

THE Church here was built in honour of the blessed Virgin *Mary* by *Juga Baynard* Lady of little *Dunmow*, whose Son and Heir *Golfridus Baynard* by the assent of *Anselme* Archbishop of *Canterbury* placed Canons herein, *An. Dom.* 1106. The Estate here and that at *Castle Baynard*, in *London*, being forfeited by *William Baynard* (*An.* 1111.) was given by King *Henry* to *Robert* Grandson of *Gilbert* Earl of *Clare*, whose issue became Patrons of this House, till in the year 1216. *Robert Fitz-Walter* refusing to consent to King *John's* unlawful love to his Daughter *Matilda* the Fair, that King seized upon his Estate and Barony, and his Castle of *Baynard* at *London*; and *Matilda*, who was then here at *Dunmow*, not admitting

mitting the Kings Suit, was poison'd in a mess of Broth. These things occasioned the Barons Wars, which after a while, were again composed, and *Robert Fitz-Walter* restored to his Barony and the Kings Favour as formerly, *An.* 1268. *John* Prior of this Church was suspended, and the Conventual Church interdicted, because his tenth was unpaid the space of four days, but Appeal being made, the Suspension was denied, and disowned.

Priors of DUNMOW.

Briticus, ob. 1120.
Augustinus, ob. 1163:
Robertus, ob. 1179.
Radulphus, ob. 1208.
Durandus, ob. 1219.
Willielmus, ob. 1221.
Thomas, ob. 1238.
Johannes Pateford, ob. 1245.

Hugo de Steveinheth, ob. 1246.
Edmundus, ob. 1247.
Galfridus, ob. 1248.
Johannes de Codham, ob. 1270.
Hugo de Posslington Cessit, 1279.
Richardus de Wicham.
Stephanus de Noble, ob. 1312.
Robertus.

10 *August* 1502. The Bells in the Steeple at *Dunmow* were consecrated; the first in honour of St. *Michael*; the second in honour of St. *John Evangelist*; the third in honour of St. *John Baptist*; the fourth in honour of the Assumption of the blessed *Mary*; the fifth in honour of the Holy Trinity and all Saints.

Here was an ancient Custom continued till the dissolution of this Priory, that if any married man would come and take his Oath before the Prior and Convent, kneeling in the Church-yard upon two hard pointed Stones, *That he never repented of his marriage, nor had any brawls or contention with his Wife within a year and a day, nor ever made any nuptial Transgression in that time,* then he was to have delivered to him with great Solemnity, a Gammon or Flitch of Bacon. The Records of the House mention three People that have performed this, *Steven Samuel* of *Essex*, 7 *E.* 4. *Richard Wright* of *Norfolk,* 23 *H.* 6. and *Thomas le Fuller* of *Essex,* 2 *H.* 8.

[Valued at 150 *l.* 3 *s.* 4 *d. per Annum.*]

The Priory of the Holy Trinity, in London.

THIS Church was founded by *Richard Beumeys* Bishop of *London*; and as it seems, then called *Christ-Church,* who placed herein many Canons. *Maud* Wife of King *Steven*, *David* King of *Scots*, and many others gave Lands to this Priory. King *Henry* the I. gave to these Canons of the holy Trinity the *Soke* called *Cnihtengild*, and the Church of St. *Butulph,* with *Soc* and *Sac, Tol* and *Theam, &c.* King *Henry* the III. in the eleventh of his Reign recited and confirm'd the several Lands and Revenues given to this Priory, in which Deed he mentions Queen *Maud* Wife of King *Henry* the I. to be the Foundress of this House.

T TAUNTON,

TAUNTON, in Somersetshire.

83.

IT was found by Inquisition, *An.* 10. *E.* 2. that this Monastery was founded by *William Gifford* Bishop of *Winchester*, on a piece of Ground on the *North-side* of the Town of *Taunton*, without the *East-Gate*. Among other of their Benefactors, was *William de Monteacuto* Earl of *Salisbury*, who granted to the Canons here, the Mannor and Hundred of *Dulverton, cum pertin.* to hold in Fee-farm, at the yearly Rent of 10 *l.* Which demise is dated in the Chapter of the Priory of *Taunton*, 11. *E.* 3.

[Valued at 286 *l.* 8 *s.* 10 *d.* per Annum]

HASTINGS, in Sussex.

84.

THIS Priory was erected here, by one Sir *Walter Bricet* a Knight, and dedicated to the holy Trinity. But by reason of the Inundation of the Sea the Canons were not able to remain here, whereupon Sir *John Pelham* Knight, by Licence of King *Henry* the IV. founded for them another Church and Habitation at *Warbilton*, towards the Support of which the said King *Henry* the IV. in the fourteenth year of his Reign granted the Mannor of *Withiam*, then valued at 25 *l.* 5 *s.* 5 *d.* per Annum, for twenty years, which Estate was part of the Possessions of *Morteyn* an alien Priory, at that time seized into the King's hands by reason of his Wars with *France*.

[Valued at 51 *l.* 9 *s.* 5 *d.* ob. per Annum.]

St. MARY-OVERIE, in Southwark.

85.
86.

FOunded by *William Gifford* Bishop of *Winchester*, who here instituted Secular Canons, divers of the Family of the Earls of *Warren*, and of the *Moubrays* were Benefactors to his Priory. King *Steven* gave the Canons here (then Regulars) the tenth of his Farm of *Southwark*; *Cicely* Countess of *Hereford* gave them her Lands at *Ketebrok*, confirm'd by King *John*. *Vid. infra,* 940.

[Valued at 624 *l.* 6 *s.* 6 *d.* per Annum.]

BRISET, in Suffolk.

87.
88.

THIS Priory was founded in time of *Herbert* Bishop of *Norwich* by *Radulphus Fitz-Brian* and *Emme* his Wife, to God, St. *Mary,* and the holy Confessor St. *Leonard.* Which Founders endow'd it with divers Lands and Tithes, among which was the Tithes of *Smithfield* at *London*. From this *Radulph Fitz-Bryan* descended *Almaricus Peche,* who confirm'd all his Ancestors Donations to this House. *Walter* Bishop of *Norwich* granted to this *Almaric Peche* to have a Chantery in his Chappel at *Briset,* but that the Chaplain at his first admittance should make Oath in presence of the Prior or his Procurator (*inspectis sacrosanctis Evangeliis*) that he would pay over all the Oblations which he should receive in the said Chappel, to the Mother Church; and that he should not admit any Parishoner of the Mother Church to any Sacrament unless in imminent peril of death; and in sign of subjection to the Mother Church, that the said *Almaric* and all his Family should repair thither to the Great Mass on five days yearly, viz. *Christmass-day, Easter-day, Whitsunday,* the Assumption of the glorious Virgin, and St. *Leonards-day.*

CIRENCESTER, in Gloucestershire.   89.

KING *Henry* the I. founded this Priory, by the Consent and Authority of Pope Innocent; and by the Council and common Applause of the Archbishops and Bishops, Princes and Barons of the Kingdom, endowed it with divers Lands and Revenues, as well in the Town of *Cirencester* and County of *Gloucester,* as in *Wiltshire, Somersetshire, Dorsetshire, Oxfordshire,* and *Northamptonshire,* also with the Liberties of *Soc* and *Sac, Toll* and *Theam,* &c. Whose Royal Grant bears date A.D. 1133. King *John* was also a Benefactor to this House.   (N. 2.)

[Valued at 1051 *l.* 7 *s.* 1 *d.* per *Annum.*]

HEXHAM, or Haguftald in Northumberland.

THIS Town situate on the *South* Banks of *Tine,* was of old time magnificent and great, and made a Bishops Seat by the blessed *Wilfrid* in the year 674. and so it continued for above one hundred and forty four years under the Government of twelve Bishops successively, viz. 1. *Wilfridus,* 2. *Eata,* 3. *Tunbertus,* 4. *John,* 5. St. *Acca,* 6 *Fredbertus,* 7. St. *Alcmundus,* 8. *Tilbertus,* 9. *Ethelbertus,* 10. *Eadfredus,* 11. *Osbertus,* 12. *Tydferdus,* after which it ceased to be govern'd by a Bishop of its own. The Bishop of *Durham* exercising Ecclesiastical Jurisdiction here, till in the Reign of King *Henry* the I. it was given to the See of *York.* In the year 1113. *Thomas* then Archbishop of *York* placed here Canons Regular. *John de Normanville,* and *Robert de Insula* were Benefactors to the Canons here. It was found by Inquisition taken in the four and twentieth year of *E.* 1. That *Thomas* the second, Archbishop of *York,* did found and endow this Priory, the Lands by him given and by many other Benefactors, were all found and set forth in particular; which see in the Book at large, *p.* 93. 94, &c.   91. (N. 3.)   92.

[Valued at 122 *l.* 11 *s.* 1 *d.* per *Annum.*]

STODELY, in Warwickshire.   89. (O. 2.)

THese Canons were first establisht at *Wicton* by *Peter de Stodley,* and by him afterwards removed from thence to *Stodley,* and by him endow'd with Lands, confirm'd by King *Henry* the II. and King *Edward* the III. in the first year of his Reign. To this House *William de Cantilupo, William Comin,* and others were Benefactors.

[Valued at 117 *l.* 1 *s.* 1 *d.* ob. per *Annum.*]

LAUND, in Leicestershire.

90.
(O. 2.)

THE Priory here was founded by *Richard Baffet* and *Matildis Ridel* his Wife, for Canons Regular, and dedicated to St. *John Baptift*. It was endowed with the Town and Mannor of *Lodington* (within the Bounds of which it ftands) as alfo that of *Frifeby*, with the Tyths of feveral Churches, in the Neighbourhood, among others with the Church of *Warleg* and Chappel of *Belton*, and the Church of *Glaefton*, in *Rutland*. Confirm'd by King *Henry* the I. and King *Henry* the II.

91.

[Valued at 399 *l.* 3 *s.* 5 *d. per Annum.*]

THURGARTON, in Nottinghamshire.

92.

THE Priory of St. *Peter* at *Thurgarton* was founded and endow'd with divers Lands and Tithes by *Radulphus de Ayncourt*. Many were the Benefactors to this Houfe, among whom feveral of the Family of *Vilers*, all whofe Gifts were recited and confirm'd by King *Henry* the II. and by King *Edward* the III. in the feventeenth year of his Reign.

94.
95.

[Valued at 259 *l.* 9 *s.* 4 *d. per Annum.*]

DRAX, in Yorkshire.

96.

THIS Priory dedicated to St. *Nicholas*, was founded and endowed with divers Lands and Liberties by *William Paganell*. By Indenture dated *An*. 1383. The Prior and Convent of this Houfe did oblige themfelves, in confideration of twenty Marks received, to perform a yearly Obit on the day of the *Epiphany*, for the Soul of *Gilbert de Ounfravile* late Husband of *Maud* Countefs of *Northumberland*.

97.

[Valued at 104 *l.* 14 *s.* 9 *d. per Annum.*]

MARTON, in Yorkshire.

98.

Founded and endow'd by *Bertram de Bulemer*, and confirmed by his Grandfon *Henry de Nevill*. This Priory, as appears by the Charter of King *Henry* the II. was at firft given to Canons and Nuns, but the Nuns were afterwards tranflated to a place called *Molesbi*.

[Valued at 151 *l.* 5 *s.* 4 *d. per Annum.*]

BETHKELERT, in Wales.

100.

KING *Edward* the I. in the fourteenth year of his Reign confirm'd the Eftate and Lands given to this Houfe by *Lewelin* the Great, and others.

[Valued at 70 *l.* 3 *s.* 8 *d. per Annum.*]

BOLTON,

BOLTON, in Yorkshire.

*A*Nno 1120. *William Meschines*, and *Cecilia* his Wife Lady and Heiress of the honour of *Skipton*, founded and endow'd a Monastery of Canons at *Emmesey*, which House was dedicated in honour of the blessed Virgin and St. *Cuthbert* the Bishop. In the year 1151. these Canons were translated from hence to *Bolton*, which *Alice de Rumelli* gave them in exchange for other Lands of theirs. Which *Alice* being Heiress to their Founder, confirm'd all his Grants, and further granted them Free chace in her Chace of *Craven* Their Lands given by their several Benefactors were recited and confirm'd by King *Edward* the II. in the fifth year of his Reign. This Priory was in some sort subject to that of *Huntingdon* till discharged of that subjection in the time of Pope *Celestin* the III. The Prior and Convent here granted to *John de Insula* Lord of *Rougemount* to maintain a Chantery of six Chaplains in the Church of *Harewood*, &c.

[Valued at 212 *l*. 3 *s*. 4 *d*. per Annum.]

KIRKHAM, in Yorkshire.

*W*Alter *Espec* and *Adelina* his Wife by the consent of King *Henry* the I. founded the Priory of Canons of the Holy Trinity at *Kirkham*, and endow'd the same with divers Lands and Tithes; *inter alia*, with the Tithes of Venison, *& ferarum silvestrium*, which he and his posterity should take, and of all Foul taken in his Rivers. Likewise the said *Walter* granted them the tenth Penny, or Tith, of his Rents of his Lands in *Northumberland*. This *Walter Espec* was a man of a Giant-like stature, with a Voice like a Trumpet, of Noble Blood, but more noble in his Christian Piety; who having no Children of his own, tho' he had Nephews, gave the best of his Possessions to Christ, founding and endowing the Monastery of *Kirkham* for Canons Regular. In the year 1261. *William de Roos* Lord of *Hamlak*, among other things, granted to the Prior and Convent of *Kirkham* and their Successors, in lieu of the Tithes of his hunting, three good wild Beasts (*tres feras competentes*) also the Rent of 100 *s. per Annum* for other Tithes, for which consideration the said Canons did quit their claim of Free-chace in *Hamelak*.

[Valued at 269 *l*. 5 *s*. 9 *d*. per Annum.]

LAUNCESTON, in Cornwall.

*T*HIS Priory did stand on the *West South-West* part of the Suburb of the Town, and was erected by *William Warwist* Bishop of *Exeter*, for which he supprest a Collegiate Church of St. *Steven*, having Prebendaries, and gave the best part of their Lands to the Priory, and took the Residue himself. King *John*, and King *Henry* the III. confirm'd the Lands given them by several Benefactors.

[Valued at 354 *l*. 0 *s*. 11 *d*. per Annum.]

St.

St. DENNIS, near Southampton.

109.

THIS Priory was founded by King *Henry* the I. endowed with Revenues by King *Henry* the II. King *Seven*, King *Richard* the I. *Humphrey de Bohun*, &c.

[Valued at 80 *l.* 11 *s.* 6 *d.* per *Annum*]

110.

LEDES, in Kent.

112.

THIS Monastery was founded *An.* 1119. by *Robert de Crepito-Corde*; in French *Creveceur*, *Anglicè Creutor*, for Canons Regular. Dedicated to St. *Mary* and St. *Nicholas*. Divers of the Name and Family of *Creveceur* were Benefactors, granting to them divers Revenues and Liberties, and that the Canons here should have the Custody of their House and Goods in the time of Vacation, without any Impediment of them, the Patrons or their Heirs, and that upon the death of their Prior, they might freely proceed to the Election of another without leave-asking; however after Election, the new Prior must be presented to the Patron according to Custom. Confirm'd by King *Edward* the III. in the one and fortieth year of his Reign.

[Valued at 362 *l.* 7 *s.* 7 *d.* per *Annum.*]

113.

HASELBERGE, in Sommersetshire.

IN the Reign of King *Henry* the I. lived at *Haselburge* a certain Priest much famed for Sanctity and for the Spirit of Prophesie, called *Wulfricus*. In his time *William Fitz-Gualter* instituted Canons Regular here, and endow'd them with Possessions. But at his first undertaking this Foundation, *Wulfricus* told him, that *Those whom he designed to introduce here would not prosper in this place*. The said *Wulfric* died *An.* 1154.

114.

KENILWORTH, in Warwickshire.

115.
116.
117.
118.

Galfridus de Clinton, Chamberlain to King *Henry* the I. founded this Church for Canons Regular, in honour of St. *Mary*, to whom he gave all his Lands at *Kenilworth*, (except what he had retain'd to his Castle, and for making a Park) with many other Lands and Liberties, all which he enjoyn'd his Heir to observe and not to violate on pain of his Curse and God's Wrath. *Gaufridus* his Son confirm'd his Father's Gifts, and granted them Tithes of all manner of Provisions whatsoever that came to his Castle of *Killingworth*. *Henry* his Son made the like Confirmation, and granted still more. King *Henry* the I. recited and confirm'd all former Benefactions, and granted the Canons here great Liberties and Immunities. The like Confirmation was made by King *Henry* the II.

[Valued at 538 *l.* 19 *s.* per *Annum.*]

STONE,

A CANNON SECVLAR.

STONE, in Staffordshire.

Wulfer King of *Mercia*, was Son and Successor to *Penda*, a Pagan and Persecutor; he after his Father's death became a Christian and married *Ermenilda* a Christian Lady, Daughter of *Exbert* King of *Kent*, by whom he had two Sons *Wulfad*, and *Ruffin*; and a Daughter named *Werburg*: which two Sons being baptized by St. *Cedda* then a Hermit, and by him privately instructed and incouraged in Christianity, This did so offend their Father *Wulfer* who had apostatized from the Faith of Christ, that finding them at Prayers at St. *Cedd's* Cell, he killed them both with his own hands, their Martyrdom happened on the 9*th. Calend. August*. This sad News being known to the Queen, she caused their Bodies to be inclosed in a Stone Monument, and in process of time a Church to be erected in the place where they were martyr'd. *Wulfer* the King being horribly tormented in mind could find no ease till he repair'd to St. *Cedda*, who upon his repentance and contrition, absolved him and enjoyn'd him for Pennance, to suppress Idolatry throughout his Kingdom of *Mercia*, and establish the Christian Religion. This King hereupon built many Churches and Monasteries, among others *Peterborough* Abby; and in the place where the Martyrs suffered, was erected a Colledge for Canons then called *Stanes*, now *Stone*. In after-times one of this House went to *Rome* as a Procurator from the rest, and obtain'd from the Pope a Canonization for St. *Wulfad* and St. *Ruffin*. In the time of the *Normans* Conquest one *Robert* Lord of *Stafford*, (from whom the Barons of *Stafford* did descend) was chief Lord of this Place; here did Inhabit at that time two Nuns and a Priest, who were all slain by one *Enysan de Walton*, after which Murther, the abovesaid *Robert* by advice of *Geffry de Clinton*, did Establish here, Canons instead of Nuns. *Nicholas de Stafford* Son of *Robert*, gave this House as a Cell to *Kenilworth*. King *Henry* the II. confirmed all the Benefactions. The Church here was dedicated to St. *Wulfad*.

[Valued at 119 *l*. 14 *s*. 11 *d*. *per Annum*.]

BROKE, in Rutland, a Cell to Kenilworth.

*H*Ugh *de Ferrariis* granted to the Canons of *Kenilworth* the Land of *Broch*, with the Wood-ground and Essarts; and this was by the assent of *Walchelin* his Nephew, and *William* his Brother, all which was confirm'd to the said Canons by King *Henry* the II.

[Valued at 40 *l. per Annum*.]

LANERCOST, in Cumberland.

*T*HIS House dedicated to God and St. *Mary Magdalen*, was founded and endowed with large Revenues by *Robert de Vallibus* Son of *Hubert de Vallibus*, he granted to the Canons here, *inter alia*, Pasture and feeding in his Forest of *Walton*, for thirty Cows, and twenty Sows; with all the Bark of his Timber-Trees in the Woods of his Barony, with all

the

131.

all the dry Wood lying any where in his Forest for the support of their House. The Church here was dedicated by *Bernard* Bishop of *Carlile, An.* 1169. King *Richard* the I. confirm'd the several Lands, &c. given to the Canons of this Monastery. The abovesaid *Herbert de Vallibus* was

132.

the first Baron of *Gillesland*, which Barony went by a Daughter to the Name and Family of *Multon*, and in like manner from them to the Family of *Dacres*.

[Valued at 77 *l.* 7 *s.* 11 *d.* per *Annum.*]

DUNSTABLE, in Bedfordshire.

133.

Here was formerly a very Woody place just in the meeting of those two Royal Ways of *Watling*, and *Ickneld*, which made the Passage so unsafe and full of Thieves, that there was hardly any Travelling. King *Henry* the I. desirous to rectifie this, caused the Woods to be cut up, and a Royal Mansion to be built near the place which was called *Kingsbury*. He also caused Proclamation all over the Kingdom that who ever would come and inhabit in that place, should have Land for 12 *d.* an Acre per *Annum*, and enjoy the same Liberties and Freedoms as the City of *London* doth, or any other ancient Borough in the Kingdom, by this means People flock'd hither and built the Town, which from *Dunning* a noted Robber, who used to rob here, was named *Dunningstable*. Besides the Liberties abovementioned this Town had two Markets weekly, and a Fair at St. *Peter ad Vincula* for three days, and a Gallows for Felons. Within the Limits of this Borough that King erected a Church in honour of St. *Peter*, and built a Monastery for Canons Regular, to whom he gave the said Church, and all the Borough with its Markets, Fairs, and Liberties, retaining only in his own hands the Capital Mansion. All which, with the Grants of other Matters, were afterwards confirm'd to them by King *Hen.* the II. and King *Rich.* the I. King *John* did the like, and granted them also his House of *Kingsbury*, The said Canons had also a Court of Pleas there of their own. Some of the Tenants held *in Capite* of the Abbot, and some by Services to be done to the said Canons, but all were Freemen.

[Valued at 344 *l.* 13 *s.* 4 *d.* per *Annum.*]

134.

SUTHWIKE, in Hantshire.

This Monastery was founded and endowed with divers Lands by King *Henry* the I. who granted them all sorts of Liberties, and Freedom from Tributes, Taxes, and Exactions, and that they should not be impleaded for any matter or thing unless in the presence of him or his Heirs.

[Valued at 257 *l.* 4 *s.* 4 *d.* per *Annum.*]

MERTON, in Surrey.

Founded by King *Henry* the I. *An.* 1121. and by him endowed with the Town of *Merton* belonging to his Crown, and large Libertics.

[Valued at 957 *l.* 19 *s.* 5 *d. per Annum.*]

OSENEY, near Oxford.

Robert *de Oilley* (whose Uncle of the same name came into *England* with the Conquerour, and obtained from him the Baronies of *Oxford*, and St. *Waleries*) founded this Priory for black Canons among the Isles made by the River *Isis* near *Oxford.* It is said that his Wife *Edith* took occasion to incite her Husband to this Foundation, from the constant assembling and chattering of certain Magpies in that place whenever she walkt out thither for her recreation. The Church here dedicated to St. *Mary* was built, *An.* 1129. Which said *Robert* endowed the Canons here with divers Tenements in *Oxford*, and several Lands and Churches in the Neighbouring Towns. *Robert* one of the natural Sons of King *Henry* the I. having married a Daughter of the Founder, devoted himself to these Canons alive, or dead; and gave them 10 *l.* of Land in his Mannor of *Waneting.* The like did *Henry de Oily* his Brother-in-Law out of his Mannor of *Hocnorton.* The other Lands granted by divers Benefactors to these Canons see in the Book at large.

[Valued at 654 *l.* 10 *s.* 2 *d. per Annum.*]

RONTON, in Staffordshire.

This Priory was founded by *Robert* the Son of *Noel*, in a place then called St. *Mary des Essarz*, and was a Cell to *Haghmon* in *Shropshire.* Whose Foundation and Endowment was afterwards confirm'd by *Thomas* his Son, and by R. Archbishop of *Canterbury. Vid. inf.* 940.

[Valued at 90 *l.* 2 *s.* 11 *d.* ob. *per Annum.*]

PYNHAM, near Arundell in Sussex.

A*Deliza*, second Wife, and Widow of King *Henry* the I. (afterwards married to *William* Earl of *Arundel*) gave a parcel of Land then called *Pynham* adjoyning to *Arundell*, for the maintenance of two Chaplains. *William* Earl of *Arundell* gave the same Land and more, for the maintenance of Regular Canons, and building a Church to the honour of God and St. *Bartlemew*; he gave them also Common of Pasture in his Medow of *Arundell* for fourteen Cows, and two Bulls, &c. All which Gifts were confirm'd by *Ranulph* Bishop of *Chichester.*

LILLESHULL, in Shropshire.

THE Church here, dedicated to St. *Alcmund*, is said to have been first founded by *Adelfleda* a Queen of *Mercia*, but afterwards much amplified, and endow'd with ten Prebends, by King *Edgar*. Afterwards *Richard Beumeys* Dean of this Church, by assent of King *Steven*, and Authority of the Pope, gave this Church over to Canons Regular, coming from St. *Peter's* at *Dorchester*, which new Monastery was dedicated to St. *Mary* ever Virgin. Benefactors to this House were *Alan la Zouche*, the Lady *Hillaria de Trussebut*, &c. King *Henry* the III. confirm'd their Estate. *Vid. inf.* 941.

[Valued at 229 *l.* 3 *s.* *d.* per Annum.]

GISEBURNE, in Yorkshire.

Robert de Brus, by the Council of Pope *Calixtus* the II. and *Thurstin* Archbishop of *York*, founded this Priory to the honour of God and St. *Mary*, and endow'd it with divers Lands as well at *Gyseburn* as elsewhere, and with the Churches of *Skelton*, and *Herte*, &c. *Robert de Brus* was a noble *Norman* Knight, who came into *England* with the Conqueror, *An.* 1066. and obtain'd to himself the Castle of *Skelton*, the Lordships of *Danby*, *Kendal*, *Anendale*, *Herte* and *Hertnesse*, *Karlton*, and divers other Lands in the *North*. This *Robert* gave to his second Son, of his own name, *Anandal* in *Scotland*, and *Herte* and *Hertnesse* in *England*, and dying *An.* 1141. lies buried at *Gisburne* Priory of his own Foundation, to whose Estate succeeded *Adam de Bruse*, from whom descended *Peter de Bruse*, who dying without issue, *An.* 1273. his inheritance became divided among his four Sisters, *viz.* *Agnes*, married to the Lord *Walter Fauconberg*, who had for her purparty the Castle of *Skelton*, &c. *Lucia* married to the Lord *Marmaduke de Tweng*, who had with her *Danby*, &c. *Margaret* who married the Lord *Robert de Rose*, and with her went *Kendale*, and lastly *Laderina* married to the Lord *John de Bellew*, and had for her part *Charleton*, &c. From *Robert* the second Son of the first mention'd *Robert de Brus*, descended lineally *Robert de Brus* King of *Scotland*, who making War against King *Edward* the I. that King seiz'd upon his Lands of *Herte* and *Hertnesse*, as forfeited, and granted them to the Lord *Clifford*. These *Bruses* of the younger House gave divers Churches in *Scotland* to this Priory, confirm'd by *William* King of *Scotland*. *Vid. Vol.* 3. *p.* 46.

[Valued at 628 *l.* 3 *s.* 4 *d.* per Annum.]

SCARTHE, near Wharlton, in Yorkshire.

THIS House founded and endowed by *Steven de Manilio*, was given as a Cell to *Guisburne* by *Hugo de Rudby*, Chaplain to the said *Steven*, and by him appointed Trustee for this purpose.

NUT.

NUTLEY, in Buckinghamshire.

THIS Abby, otherwise called, *Sancta Maria de Parcho*, was founded and endowed by *Walter Gifford* Earl of *Buckingham*, and *Ermigardis* his Wife. Confirm'd by King *Henry* the II. and by King *John* with the Addition of great Liberties and Immunities, who also granted to *William Marescal* and his Heirs, the Gift of the Pastoral Staff of the Abby of *Nuteley*. To the Canons here was given the Church of all Saints at *Bradley* in the Diocess of *Sarum*; in which Parish was founded a Chappel for Leperous Women; which Chappel, before it could be dedicated by *Jocelin* then Bishop of *Sarum*, was publickly and solemnly declared by Oath not to be any ways prejudicial to the Mother Church in Tithes or Obventions, *&c.*

[Valued at 437 *l.* 6 *s.* 8 *d. per Annum.*]

BISSEMEDE, in Bedfordshire.

HUgh de *Bellocampo* founded, and endow'd this Priory with divers Lands and Commons, *&c.* He granted the Canons here besides other things, the Priviledge to have their Corn first ground at his Mills at *Hetune*, after that which should be found on. All which was confirm'd by *Roger de Bellocampo*. He granted also the Tithes of his Park of *Ettune*, (*tam de bosco quam de essartis*) as well of his Woods as arable Lands. Pope *Gregory* granted to this House divers Priviledges, as not to pay Tithes of their own Stock, to cellebrate privately in time of a general Interdict, *&c.* Here was formerly a Hermitage of great Veneration.

[Valued at 71 *l.* 13 *s.* 9 *d.* ob. *per Annum.*]

BRIDLINGTON, in Yorkshire.

WAlter de *Gant* establisht Canons in the Church of *St. Mary* of *Bridliuton*, and gave them all his Estate in that Town, and confirm'd to them all other Lands which his (*homines*) Tenants who held of him, had given them. *Gilbert de Gant*, his Son, Earl of *Lincoln*, confirm'd all that his Father gave, *&c.* The like did King *Henry* the II. *Gilbert de Gant* was born, baptized, and educated in this Priory, and therefore disposed his Body to be buried here. The Archdeacon of *Richmond* did use in time of his Visitation to come to a Church belonging to these Canons with a train of ninety seven Horse, one and twenty Dogs, and three Hawks, and in an hours time all their Provision was utterly consumed, till at last this great Oppression was prohibited by the Bull of Pope *Innocent* the III. *Ralph de Nevil* granted to these Canons to take Stone out of his Quarry of *Fivele*, with a way over his Ground, for the use of their Monastery, for ever.

[Valued at 547 *l.* 6 *s.* 11 *d. per Annum.*]

St. BARTLEMEW, in Smithfield, London.

RAherus founded the Church here in honour of St. *Bartholmew* for Canons of St. *Augustin*'s Rule, and himself became their Prior for the space of two and twenty years. This man had been formerly when young, a noted Drole or Jester, and by such means had become acceptable and familar to the great Ones at Court, and to the King himself. But being inspired with God's grace, he saw the Follies of that Course of Life; and finding his Conscience burden'd with many sins, he undertook a Journey to *Rome*; while he remain'd there he fell sick, and in his sickness made a Vow upon his return to Health, and his Country, to build there an Hospital for the Relief and Solace of Poor People. After this being restored to his Health, he began his journey homeward. On the Way St. *Bartholmew* appeared to him in a Nocturnal Vision or Dream, and directed him to build a Church in *Smithfield* at *London*, and name it to him. Being return'd to *London*, he obtain'd the King's License for this Foundation, without which it could not be effected, the Ground where the Building was appointed, being within the Kings Market-place. He began hereupon a double Work of Piety, the Hospital in performance of his Vow, and the Church according as directed, both not far distant; which last was founded, *An.* 1123. in the name of our Lord Jesus Christ, and memory of St. *Bartholmew* the Apostle. It is said that this very Foundation in this place, was foretold long before in a Vision, to King *Edward* the Confessor. Before *Raherus* began the Foundation of this Monastery, the Ground here was all overspread with Filth and Durt, and was the common place of Execution of Malefactors. The Priory being built and Canons assembled to inhabit it, *Raherus* became their Prior, who obtain'd for their maintenance sufficient from the Oblations of pious People, and from the King as large Liberties as any Church in *England* enjoy'd. King *Henry* the III. confirm'd all the Lands and Churches given them by divers Benefactors, namely, the place call'd *Smithfeld*, the Church of St. *Sepulcher de Ballie, London, cum pertinentiis suis infra Burgum & extra*, the Church of St. *Michael Bassingshagh*, &c. and that the Hospital of St. *Bartlemew* in *Smithfield* should be in the Disposition and Subjection of the said Prior and Canons.

[Valued at 653 *l.* 15 *s.* per *Annum*.]

WARTRE, in Yorkshire.

FOunded *An.* 1132. by *Galfridus Trusbut*, and by him endow'd with the Church of *Wartre*, and eleven Bovates of Land in the Field of that Town. Confirm'd by Pope *Innocent* the II.

Priors and Abbots of this House.

1. *Joseph*, Prior.
2. *Radulphus*, Prior.
3. *Richard*, Abbot.
4. *Yuo*, Abbot.
5. *Nicholas*, Prior.
6. *Richard*, Prior.
7. *Thomas*, Prior.
8. *Radulphus*.
9. *John Lestyngham*.
10. *John de Dunelmia*.
11. *Robert de Lunde*.
12. *John Queldreke*, in his time the Hospital

VOL. II. *of* St. AUGUSTIN. 149

Hospital of St. *Giles* of *Beverly* was annext to this House, *A.* 1278.
13. *John de Thorpe.*
14. *Richard de Welwyk.*
15. *Robert Balne.*
16. *William Feryby.*
17. *Henry Holme.*
18. *John Hemyngburgh.*
19. *William Tynyngton*, deposed by the Archbishop of *York.*
20. *Robert Takel.*
21. *Thomas Ruland.*
22. *William Wartre.*
23. *Robert Hedon.*
24. *William Tork.*
25. *William Spenser.*

173.

Several of the *Trussebuts* descendants of the Founder confirm'd the Possessions of these Canons; and so did *Robert de Ros* Lord of *Beuver, An.* 1279. being then Patron (*Advocatus*) of this Priory. Pope *Innocent* granted to these Canons of St. *James* of *Wartre* divers Priviledges, in the Case of non-payment of Tithes for their own Goods and Stock, in the Case of a general Interdict, &c.

174.
175.
176.

Valued at 221 *l.* 3 *s.* 10 *d. per Annum.*

TWYNEHAM, *in* Hantshire.

177.

IN the Reign of King *Edward* the Confessor, there were Secular Canons in *Christ-Church* at *Twyneham. Ranulph Flammard*, a great Favourite under King *William Rufus*, and afterwards Bishop of *Durham*, was Dean of this Church. In the Reign of King *Steven* Canons Regular were first introduced here. The aforesaid *Ranulphus*, or *Randulphus*, new built the Church of *Twynham*, which at that time bore the name of the Holy Trinity. *Richard de Redvers* endow'd it with Lands in the Isle of *Wight* and elsewhere. Which *Richard de Redvers* was by King *Henry* the I. made Earl of *Devon*, and had the Isle of *Wight*, and the Inheritance of this Town of *Twineham*, given to him. From whom descend the *Courtney's* Earls of *Devon. Baldwin de Redveriis* confirm'd the Estate given by his Father *Richard* to this Church, with the Grant of large Liberties; which *Baldwin* was the first who introduced Canons Regular into this Church, to whom his Son *Richard de Redveriis* junior, granted the free Election of their Prior, and confirm'd all their Possessions, *An.* 1161. *Vid. Vol.* 3. *p.* 45.

178.
179.
180.
181.

[Valued at 312 *l.* 7 *s. per Annum.*]

HERYNGHAM, *in* Sussex.

KING *Edward* the I. granted his License to *William Paynel* to grant certain Lands to the Prior and Canons of this House, for the finding of four Secular Chaplains to celebrate for his Soul, in their Church, *Statuto de terris ad manum mortuam non ponend. edito, non obstante.* Afterwards, upon the Petition of *Matilda* Neice, and heir of the said *William*, exhibited to King *Edward* the II. in Parliament, that King granted that instead of the four Secular Chaplains, the said Prior might for the future appoint four Regular Canons of his own House for that Office. King *Edward* the III. granted his License to appropriate the Hospital of St. *Anthony at Corkham* to this House.

182.

St.

St. OSITH at Chich, in Essex.

THE Priory of St. *Ositb* the Virgin and Martyr at *Chich*, was founded by *Richard de Belmeis* Bishop of *London*, who design'd to resign his Bishoprick and become a Canon Regular here himself, but was prevented by death. The second Prior of this House was *Ralph* afterwards Archbishop of *Canterbury*. King *Henry* the II. confirm'd all the Possessions given to this Priory by several Benefactors, with the grant of ample Liberties, free Waren and a Market at *Chiche*. King *John* granted the Patronage or Advowson of this Abby to *William* then Bishop of *London* and his Successors.

[Valued at 677 *l*. 1 *s*. 2 *d*. per Annum.]

IXWORTH, in Suffolk.

Gilbert Blundus who came into *England* with the Conqueror, founded this Priory of the blessed *Mary* of *Ixworth* near the Parish-Church of that Town.

[Valued at 280 *l*. 9 *s*. 5 *d*. per Annum.]

NORTON, in Cheshire.

THIS Priory of the blessed *Mary* of *Norton* was founded and endowed by *William* the Son of *Nigellus* Constable of *Chester*. *Roger* Constable of *Chester* confirm'd the Lands and Possessions given to these Canons in *Nottinghamshire*, *Leicestershire*, and *Oxfordshire*, who also granted them divers Priviledges, *inter alia*, to have two Deer, yearly, on the Feast of the Assumption, out of his Park of *Halton*. When *William Bastard*, to whom King *Edward* the Confessor had assigned the Inheritance of his Kingdom as his most worthy and nearest Kinsman, came into *England*, with him came *Hugh* to whom he gave the Earldom of *Chester*. With this *Hugh* came a Nobleman called *Nigellus*, to whom the said Earl gave the Barony of *Halton* and made him his Marshal, and Constable of *Chester*; and further conferr'd on him many and great Priviledges, such as shew'd a particular favour to him more than any other Baron of *Cheshire*. *William* Son of this *Nigellus* founded this Priory first at *Runcorn*, *An*. 1133. which was afterwards removed to *Norton*. From him descended *Roger* Constable of *Chester* abovementioned, to whom *Ranulf* Earl of *Chester*, for a particular Service done him in *Wales*, gave the Dominion of Shoo-makers and Stage-players, to hold to him and his Heirs for ever. This *Roger* died *A.* VIII. and lies buried in the Monastery of *Stanlowe*. Of this Line descended the *Lacies* Earls of *Lincoln*, and the Earls of *Lancaster*, *Leicester*, and *Derby*.

[Valued at 180 *l*. 7 *s*. 6 *d*. ob. per Annum.]

NEW-

NEWBURGH, in Yorkshire.

190.

Founded by *Roger de Molbray*, and endowed with divers Lands and Churches; who also confirm'd what the Freemen of his Fee had given, or should give to the Canons here. In the time of King *William* the Conqueror *Robert de Mowbray* was Earl of *Northumberland*, who taking part with other Great men, who rise against King *William Rufus* for having banish'd *Anselm* Archbishop of *Canterbury*, and destroy'd eighty Religious Houses to enlarge his Forrest, was taken by the King, beheaded, and his Estate seized; and afterwards given by King *Henry* the I. to *Negellus de Albeney*, whose Mother was a *Mowbray*; after which time the *Albanies* took on them the name of *Molbray*. Son of that *Nigellus* was the first abovemention'd *Roger de Molbray*, who founded this Priory, *An.* 1145. he founded also the Abby of *Bellaland*, and many other Religious Houses to the number of thirty five. From whom descended *Thomas Mowbray* who in the Reign of King *Rich.* II. was made Duke of *Norfolk*, Earl of *Nottingham*, Lord Marshal of *England*, &c. From whom descended two Co-heirs, the eldest of which *Ann*, was married to the Lord *Thomas Howard*, who in the second year of King *Edward* the IV. was created Duke of *Norfolk*.

192.

193.

194.

[Valued at 367 l. 8 s. 3 d. per Annum.]

HODE, in Yorkshire, a Cell to Newburgh.

195.

Hode was at first demised to the Canons of *Billalanda*, by *Robert de Alneto*, on condition that they should here found an Abby of their Canons. This was confirm'd by *Roger de Mowbray*. *Adam Fossard* gave *Hode* to the Canons of *Newburgh* with Lands lying about the same, which Canons did acknowledge the said *Adam* to be the Patron (*Advocatus*) of the said place, and of all belonging thereunto.

EGLESTON, in the Bishoprick of Durham.

196.

Philip Bishop of *Durham* confirm'd to God, *St. Mary*, and *St. John Baptist*, and to the Canons of *Egleston*, divers Lands which *Gilbert de Ley* held of him by the service of one Knights Fee, and had given them. *An.* 1273. the Abbot and Canons of this House covenanted with *John* Duke of *Britany*, and Earl of *Richmond*, to find six Chaplains Canons of this House, to say six Masses daily in the Castle of *Richmond*, for ever, the said Canons to be constantly resident in the said Castle, in consideration whereof the said Earl of *Richmond* granted to the Abbot and Convent of *Egleston* divers Lands and Possessions, and a place apart in his said Castle for the Habitation of the said six Chaplains, &c.

DORCHESTER, in Oxfordshire.

197.

Before the *Norman* Conquest here was a Bishops Seat; *Remigius* translated it to *Lincoln*. *Alexander* Bishop of *Lincoln* erected here an Abby of black Canons; the Body of which Church served for the Parish Church. After the Suppression the *East*-part of the Abby-Church was

was bought by a rich man of this Town for 140 *l*. and given to augment the Parish Church.

[Valued at 219 *l*. 12 *s*. per *Annum*.]

THORNTON, upon Humber, in Lincolnshire.

198.

Founded by *William Grose* Earl of *Albemarl*, Anno Dom. 1139. Canons Regular were introduced here from *Kyrkham*, under the Government of one *Richard* their Prior, who was afterwards made Abbot in the year 1148. by Pope *Eugenius* the III. Earl *William* the Founder died,

199. *An*. 1180. having endow'd this Abby with many Lands and Revenues. King *Richard* the I. confirm'd all the Possessions given to the Abby of St. *Mary* of *Thornton* and the Canons there, with the Grant of large Liberties and Immunities. Pope *Celestine* the III. granted them the Priviledge not to pay any Tithes of Cattle, &c. for their own use.

Abbots of this House were

1. *Richard*.
2. *Philip*, 1152.
3. *Thomas*, 1175.
4. *John Benton*, 1184.
5. *Jordan de Villa*, 1203.
6. *Richard de Villa*, 1223.
7. *Jeffrey Holme*, 1233.
8. *Robert*, 1245.
9. *William Lyncoln*, 1257.
10. *Walter Hotoft*, 1273.
11. *Thomas de Ponte*, 1290.

201. The Advowson of this Abby, together with all the Lands, and Possessions of the Earl of *Albemarl*, did escheat to King *Edward* the I. Which being thus in the Crown, King *Edward* the III. in the sixth year of his Reign granted, by advice of the Prelates and Barons in Parliament, that the said Advowson should remain ever annext to the Crown; and that the said Abbot should not be oblig'd to attorn to any, in case any grant of the said Advowson should be made.

[Valued at 594 *l*. 17 *s*. 10 *d*. per *Annum*.]

BRUMMORE, in Wiltshire.

Baldwin *de Riveris* and *Hugh* his Unkle, were the Founders of this Monastery for Canons Regular, King *Henry* the II. confirm'd the Lands given them, and granted them feeding for one hundred Cattle, and one hundred Hogs in *Newforest*, and dead Wood for their fuel as much as necessary.

HAREWOLD, in Bedfordshire.

202.

This was a Priory of Nuns of St. *Augustin*, founded by *Sampson de Forte*, *Malcolm* King of *Scotland*, as Earl of *Huntington* confirm'd certain Lands to this Church of St. *Peter* of *Harewold*, and to the Prior,

203. and Canons; and Sisters there serving God. The like did King *William* of *Scotland*. King *Henry* the IV. of *England* gave to the Prioress and Nuns of *Harewold*, one Messuage in *Chakirstone* of the yearly value of 2 *s*. with the Advowson of that Church.   BRIN-

BRINKEBURNE, in Northumberland

FOUNDED by *William Bertram*, *Hawys* his Wife, and *Roger* his Son, for Canons. Their Poffeffions were confirm'd by *William* Earl of *Northumberland*, *Henry* Earl of *Northumberland* Son to the King of *Scotland*, and by King *Henry*. III.
[Valued at 68 *l*. 19 *s*. 1 *d*.]

204.

LEYE, in the Ile of Gersey, Dioceffe of Exon.

THIS was at firft a Priory of Canons, but afterwards in the Reign of King *Edward*. I. it was changed to a *Nunnery* of *Canoneffes*; it was dedicated to St. *Mary* and St. *John Evangelift*.

205.

BRIWETON, in Somersetshire.

William *de Moyne* Earl of *Somerfet* gave divers Lands, *&c.* to the Canons Regular of this Houfe, which was before the Conqueft an Abby of Monks founded by *Algarus* Earl of *Cornwal*, but the faid *Moyne*, or *Mohun*, placed Canons here fince the Conqueft. *Sauvaricus* Bifhop of *Bath* and *Glauftonbury* confirm'd to God and the Bleffed *Mary* of *Briweton*, and the Canons Regular there, the Lands, *&c.* given by their Benefactors.
[Valued at 439 *l*. 6 *s*. 8 *d*.]

206.

BRADENSTOKE, in Wiltshire.

FOunded and endowed by *Patricius* Earl of *Saliibury* and *Walter* his Father. *William* Bifhop of *Sarum* appropriated divers Churches to the proper ufe of thefe Canons, *falvis Vicariis ordinandis & taxandis.* King *Henry*. III. confirm'd all their Poffeffions.
[Valued at 212 *l*. 19 *s*. 3 *d*. *per Annum*.]

208.
209.

NOCTON in Lincolnshire.

THE Priory of *Nocton Park* was founded by *Robert de Areci*, Lord of *Nocton*. It was dedicated to St. *Mary Magdelen*. The Heir general of *Norman de Arcy* defcended from the Founder, married to *John de Lymbury*. The Poffeffions given by feveral Benefactors were recited and confirm'd by King *Henry*. III. in the 55th. year of his Reign.
[Valued at 44 *l*. 3 *s*. 8 *d*. *per Annum*.]

211.
212.

WIGMORE in, Herefordshire.

OLiver *de Merlymond* cheif Senefchal of all the Lands of *Hugh de Mortimer*, in the time of King *Steven*, built the Church of *Schobbedon*, which Town his faid Lord *Hugh de Mortimer* had given him in Confideration of his

313.

his Service. This *Oliver* being kindly entertain'd at St. *Victors* Abby at *Paris* in his return from a Pilgrimage, he was so highly pleased with their good life and Regular devotion, that he afterwards obtain'd from that Abby two of their Canons to come over and Institute a House of Religion at his new built Church of *Schobbedon*, to which he annext divers Lands and profits. But after this a great dissention arising between the said *Hugh de Mortimer* and *Oliver de Merlymond*, in so much that the said *Oliver* departed from his Service and went to *Miles* Earl of *Hereford*, *Mortimer* seized upon all his Estates, and took from the Canons all the Goods which *Oliver* had given them, whereby the said Canons were reduced to such extreamity that they were about to leave their House. But this difference, being at last composed by the mediation of the Bishop of *Hereford*, *Mortimer* not only restored them their Lands, &c. of which he had deprived them, but gave them more, among other Benefactions, the Church of *Wigmore*, and advanced their Prior to the title of an Abbot. But soon after he took from them again the Town of *Schobbedon*, and it was once more restored by mediation. After this these Canons removed their habitation to a place call'd *Eye*, and from thence to *Wigmore*. After this they removed once more into the Field of *Beodune*, where they built from the ground a Monastery and Church, which Church was dedicated to St. *James* by *Robert Foljoth* then Bishop of *Hereford*, the aforesaid Sir *Hugh de Mortimer*, conferring thereon at the Dedication great Benefactions both in Lands, and Plate for the Altar. Which Sir *Hugh* died a Chanon of this House, being very antient. Whose Son and heir Sir *Roger de Mortimer* behaved himself so unkindly to the Canons of this House, that the Abbot and most of the Convent were forced, for some time to retire to *Schobbedon*, but the difference was made up by the Interposition of King *Henry*. *Isabell de Ferrers* Widow of the said Sir *Roger*, built a House of Religion at *Lechelade* after her Husbands decease, and endow'd it with Lands for the good of his Soul. The said Sir *Roger* tho' unkind at first, yet before his death confirm'd all that his Father had given to these Canons, with other Lands given by himself.

Among those 260 most famous and valiant Knights that King *William* the Conqueror brought into *England* with him in his Army, was *Ralph de Mortuomari* one of the chief; which *Ralph* obtain'd to himself the Lordship of *Wigmore*, and other Possessions in the Marches of *Wales*.

This *Ralph* built the Castle of *Wigmore*, and left issue *Hugh* and *William*, *Hugh* became the Founder of the Abby of *Wigmore*, as has been said, and endow'd it largely *An.* 1179. and dyed in this Monastery *An.* 1185. Grandson of this *Hugh* was *Ralph de Mortuomari*, who being sent over into *Normandy* by King *John* in order to defend that Country against the King of *France*, who had invaded and Seized all *Normandy* (because King *John* refused tho several times summon'd, to do homage for the same) was, by the said King of *France* taken Prisoner. During whose absence from these Parts the *Welch* invaded this Monastery of *Wigmore*, plundered the Canons of all their movables, and burnt all the Buildings except the Church. Son of which *Ralph* was *Roger*, who married *Matilda* daughter of *William de Breuse* Lord of *Bregnoc*, and was so faithful an adherent to King *Henry* III. against his rebellious Barons, that he was the chief means of defeating that formidable Commotion, and establishing the King in his Throne. Grandson of this *Roger*, was *Roger Mortimer* who was created the first Earl of *March*, *An.* 1. *Edward*. III. Which Earl

Earl *Roger* was great grandfather of *Edmund Mortimer* who married *Philippa* only daughter and heir of *Leonel* Duke of *Clarence*, second Son of King *Edward*. III. Which *Edmund* having buried his said Wife went over into *Ireland* the Kings Lieutenant, and *An.* 1381. departed this life in that Kingdome, being but twenty nine years of age. His body was brought over, and buried in this Abby Church of *Wigmore*, with his Countess, and most of his Ancestors. Which *Edmund* and *Philippa* had issue two Sons *Roger*, and *Edmund*, and two Daughters *Elizabeth* and *Philippa*. *Roger Mortimer* was slain in *Ireland*. *An.* 1398. But left Issue by his Wife *Alianora* daughter and coheir of *Thomas Holland* Earl of *Kent*, two Sons *Edmund* and *Roger*, and two daughters *Anne* and *Alianore*. *Anne* was marriedto *Richard de Condsborough* Earl of *Cambridge*. The two Sons, and the other daughter died all without issue.

[Valued at 267 *l.* 2 *s.* 10 *d.* ob *per Annum.*]

THORNHOLME, in Lincolnshire.

IT was found upon Inquisition at the Assizes at *Lincoln*, 4 *John*, that King *Steven* founded this Priory and placed Canons in it. That *Henry*. II. gave the Mannour of *Aplebi*, in which the Priory is scituated, to *William de Lungespe* his Brother, who after gave the Manour to *John Malekerbe*.

DERLEY, in Darbyshire.

Hugh the Priest, intitled *Dean of Derby*, gave to *Albinus*, and his Canons of St. *Helens* near *Derby*, the Land which he held at Little *Derby*, for the erecting of a Church and Habitation for him and the said Canons, with divers Lands of his Patrimony. Which Estate the said *Albin* and his Successors, Abbots of this House, quietly enjoyed all the time of the life of the said *Hugh*, and of *Henry* his Son, which Son he begat in lawful marriage before he received holy Orders, and of two daughters and heiresses of the said *Henry*, who dying in the Reign of King *Henry*. III. that King supposing the said two daughters to dye without heirs, claim'd the *Advowson* of this Abby as an *Escheat Vid. Vol.* 3. *p.* 57.

[Valued at 258 *l.* 14 *s.* 5 *d.* per *Annum.*]

St. AUGUSTINS at Bristol, in Gloucestershire.

ROBERT *Fitz Harding* a *Burgesse* of *Bristol*, to whom King *Henry* II. gave the *Barony* of *Berkly*, built this Abby, and gave to the Canons Regular of this House, the Church of *Berkly*, with divers others. Whose Estate was confirm'd to them by King *Henry*. II. while he was yet Duke of *Normandy* and Earl of *Anjou*: also by *John* Earl of *Morton*, &c.

[Valued at 670 *l.* 13 *s.* 11 *d.* ob *per Annum.*]

COKES.

COKESFORD near Rudham, in Norfolk.

234.

John de Querceto (or Cheney) gave to God, and St. Mary, and the Canons of Rudham divers Lands, Churches, and Mills, & Duos homines scilicet G. & V. & terram illorum, two of his Tenants with the Land which they held of him. Harvey Beleth gave them the Mannor of Rudham for the maintenance of an Hospital, by him founded at Boycodeswade.

235.

[Valued at 121 l. 18 s. 10 d. ob. per Annum.]

BRUNNE, in Lincolnshire. (Bourn.)

Founded by Balwin Son of Gissebert, who endow'd it with divers Lands, Churches, and Tithes of sundry kinds, An. 1138. The Wakes were principal Benefactors to this House, and became Patrons of the same, being Lords of the Mannor of Bourn, and descended from the Founder, and as Patrons had the Custody of the Abby in time of Vacation, &c. which was allowed by King Edward the II. who for that purpose granted his mandate to Matthew Broun Escheator for the Counties of Lincoln, Northampton, and Roteland, in the seventeenth year of his Reign, notwithstanding that some of the Possessions of this Abby were held of the King in Capite.

236.

237.

NEWENHAM, in Bedfordshire.

238.

Before the Conquest, the Church of St. Paul in Bedford was a Colledge of Prebendaries or Secular Canons, till one of the Canons killing a Butcher, they were forced to remove their Habitation to a place call'd Newenham, a Mile distant from Bedford, and there they became Regular Canons. Roisia Wife of Paganus de Bellocampo, to whom King William the Conqueror gave the Barony of Bedford, and Simon her Son, were the founders of their House at Newenham. Which Simon endow'd them with divers Lands and Possessions, among others the Church of St. Paul at Bedford with all its Possessions, and the Tithes of the Mill of the Castle of Bedford, &c. These Canons had also large Liberties granted them on the River, for fishing, and for keeping Swans as many as they pleased; feeding for thirty Hogs yearly quit of Paunage in the Wood of Kerdington, free Pasture for twelve Oxen, in all the Grounds of the Patron where his own Oxen fed, with Liberty to elect their own Prior, saving to the Patron the Custody of the outward Gate of the Monastery in time of Vacation, &c. All whose Lands and Liberties were confirm'd to them in 15 R. 2. by Thomas Earl Mareschal, and Earl of Nottingham, Lord Moubray and Segrave, then Patron of this Priory.

239.

240.

241.
242.
243.

[Valued at 293 l. 5 s. 11 d. per Annum.]

St. RADEGUNDIS at Bradsole, in Kent. 244.

KING *Henry* the III. confirm'd the several Lands and Revenues given to this House by sundry Benefactors, among whom *Henry de Wengham* Dean of St. *Martins* in *London*. *Vid. Vol.* 3. *p.* 69.

[Valued at 98 *l*. 9 *s*. 2 *d*. ob. *per Annum*.]

KIME, in Lincolnshire. 245.

THE first founder of this Priory was Sir *Philip de Kyme* Knt. the Canons of this House held Lands in *Thorpe*, and *Billingey*.

[Valued at 101 *l*. 0 *s*. 4 *d*. *per Annum*.]

BUTLEY, in Suffolk.

Founded by *Ranulph de Glanvilla*, and by him endowed with divers Churches and Lands, in the year 1171. This *Ranulph de Glanvill* was heretofore Chief Justice of *England*, and left only three Daughters, among whom he parted his Land before he made his Voyage to the Holy Land, to the eldest who married one *William de Aubervil*, he gave the intire Mannor of *Benhall* and the Advowson of the Monastery of the blessed *Mary* of *Buttele*, and to the other Sisters other parts of his Estate. *Vid. Vol.* 3. *p* 110. 246.

[Valued at 318 *l*. 17 *s*. 2 *d*. *per Annum*.]

NEWSTED near Guildford, in Surrey. 247.

Founded by *Rualdus de Calua* and *Beatrix* his Wife with the assent of *William Malbanc* their Heir, in honour of the blessed Virgin *Mary*, and St. *Thomas* the Martyr, in a place call'd *Aldeburi* in the Mannor of *Sandes*, for Canons Regular; whose Estate was confirm'd by King *Henry* the III. and King *Edward* the II.

BERLIZ, in Somersetshire. 249.

THE several Lands, Churches, and Tithes given to the Prior and Canons of this House, dedicated to St. *Nicholas*, by *Matilda de Say* and others, were confirm'd by King *Henry* the III. *An. Regni* 40. and by *Edw.* the III. *An.* 13. 250.

WOMBRIGGE, in Shropshire. 252.

Founded by *William Fitz-Alan*. Dedicated to God, St. *Mary*, and St. *Leonard*. Many were the Benefactors to this House, among whom the Lords of *Cherinton* gave divers Lands and Revenues in that Town, 255.

Town, &c. All the Possessions of these Canons, with divers Liberties to them granted by their severeal Benefactors were recited and confirm'd by King *Edward* the II. *An. Reg.* 12.

[Valued at 65 *l*. 7 *s*. 4 *d. per Annum*.]

257.   CALDEWELL, *in* Bedfordshire.

*S*Imon *Basket* an Alderman of *Bedford* was the first founder of this House, but the Advowson came afterwards to the Lords *Latymer*. *Robert* Son of *William de Houton* gave Lands to the Order of Fryers of the Holy Cross at *Caldewell*, confirm'd by King *Hen* the III. *An. Reg.* 57.

[Valued at 109 *l*. 8 *s*. 5 *d. per Annum*.]

258.   TONEBRIGGE, *in* Kent.

*F*Ounded by *Richard de Clare* Earl of *Hertford*, for Canons Regular, and by him endow'd with certain Rents, the feeding of one hundred and twenty Hogs yearly in his Forrest of *Tonebrigge* freely, and to have yearly one Buck at the Feast of St. *Mary Magdalen*.

ANGLESEYE, *in* Cambridgeshire.

259.   *E*Lizabeth *de Burgo* Sister and one of the Heirs of *Gilbert de Clare* Earl of *Gloucester* and *Hertford*, Patroness of this Priory, granted the Monks here liberty to choose their Prior, *An.* 1333. The same *Elizabeth* granted a Rent of 20 *l. per Annum* to the Prior and Convent of this House, in consideration of which they obliged themselves to find two Chantry Priests, Seculars, to celebrate at the Altar of the holy Cross in their Church for ever, for the said *Elizabeth* her Ancestors and Heirs, and to allow to the said two Priests their Lodging and Diet, and to each 20 *s. per Annum*, or else twelve Marks yearly, which they shall think most convenient; which Grant bears date 6. *E.* 3.

[Valued at 24 *l*. 19 *s. per Annum*.]

260.   TRENTHAM, *in* Staffordshire.

*R*Alph Earl of *Chester* was the Founder, or rather Restorer, of this House; granting to the Canons here a yearly Rent of 100 *s. per Annum*. Confirm'd by King *Henry* the II. with the grant of large Liberties and Immunities.

[Valued at 106 *l*. 3 *s*. 10 *d. per Annum*.]

WORM-

WORMLEY, in Herefordshire. 261.

Steven *de Ebroicis* gave to this Church, dedicated to God, and St. *Leonard*, and to the Canons here, certain Mills, Lands, and Tithes in *Lenhale*, for the maintenance of three Chaplains. Confirm'd by *Gilbert de Lacy* in consideration of 100 s. by the said Canons to him paid. And by *William* Son of the said *Steven*, *An.* 1240. *Vid. Vol.* 3. *p.* 48. 263.

[Valued at 83 *l.* 10 *s.* 2 *d. per Annum.*]

ROYSTON, in Cambridgeshire. 264.

Founded and endow'd by *Eustach de Merc.*. King *Richard* the I. confirm'd to this Monastery by the Name of the Monastery of St. *Thomas* the Martyr *apud Crucem Rhosiæ*, and to the Canons here, all their Possessions given by several Benefactors, and further granted a yearly Fair during all *Whitsun-week*, and a Market every *Wednesday*, with the same Liberties as were enjoy'd by the Canons at *Dunstable*, with very large Immunities in his Grant specified, dated in the first year of his Reign.

ERDBURY, in Warwickshire. 265.

Ralph de Sadle was a principal Benefactor to the Canons of this House. *An.* 1232. *Alexander* then Bishop of *Coventry* and *Litchfeild*, order'd the following Settlement between the Prior of *Erdbury*, and the Vicar of *Dercet*, and their Successors, *viz.* that the Vicar should have all the Altarage of the said Church, and Tith-Corn of eight yards Land in *Radewey*, and of two yard Land in *Derced* in the Demeans of the said Prior, with a House, *&c.* That the Vicar of the said Church should be a Priest and not of any lesser Order, and shall have an Associate constantly, and a Deacon, who together with him shall officiate in the said Church, the Vicar to bear all usual Charges except the Repairs of the Chancel, for which the Prior and he are to joyn proportionably. This Monastery being decay'd in its Revenues, King *Henry* the VI. *An.* 23. granted the Prior and Convent License to obtain and receive Lands and Tenements to the value of one hundred Marks without fine to the King. 266.

[Valued at 94 *l.* 6 *s.* 1 *d. per Annum.*]

POGHELE, in Barkshire.

Founded by *Ralph de Chadelewurth*, dedicated to God and St. *Margaret*, endow'd with divers Lands and Revenues by the said *Ralph* and others, all which was recited and confirm'd by King *Henry* the III.

ROU-

ROUCESTRE, in Staffordshire.

267.

Richard Bacun founded and endowed this House for Canons Regular, with large Possessions and Liberties: All which were confirm'd to the said Canons by *Ranulph* Earl of *Chester*, to hold in pure and perpetual Alms. Confirm'd also by King *Henry* the III. in the thirtieth year of his Reign.

268.
270.

[Valued at 100 *l.* 2 *s.* 10 *d.* ob. per *Annum.*]

CUMBWELL, in Kent.

Founded by *Robert de Turneham*, dedicated to God, and St. *Mary Magdalen*, endow'd with divers Lands and Possessions, all which were confirm'd by *Steven de Turnham*, Son of the said *Robert*, and by King *Henry* the III. *An. Reg.* 11.

[Valued at 80 *l.* 17 *s.* 5 *d.* per *Annum.*]

WOSPRING, in Somersetshire.

271.

The several Lands, Rents, &c. given to this Church, dedicated to God, St. *Mary*, and St. *Thomas* the Martyr, by *William de Courteney* and others, were recited and confirm'd to the Prior and Canons here, by King *Edw.* the II. *An. Reg.* 18. *Vid. Vol.* 3. *p.* 47.

[Valued at 87 *l.* 2 *s.* 11 *d.* ob. per *Annum.*]

MARLEBURGH, in Wiltshire.

272.

King *Richard* the II. *An. Reg.* 22. granted his Pardon to the Prior and Convent of St. *Margaret* near *Marlbergh* (which House was founded by his Progenitors) for having accepted divers Lands of *John Lovel* Chevaler, without License first obtain'd; and further ratified and confirm'd the Possession of those Lands to the said Convent.

IVICHURCH, in Wiltshire.

273.

King *Henry* the III. granted to the Prior and Canons of this House certain Lands and Priviledge in his Forrest of *Clarendon*; King *Edw.* the III. granted more, also Pasture for forty Oxen and Cows in his Meadow of *Clarendon*, and 100 *s.* of Rent out of his Mannor of *Clarendon*. King *Hen.* the II. founded this Monastery for four Canons.

274.

[Valued at 122 *l.* 18 *s.* 6 *d.* ob. per *Annum.*]

BUCK-

BUCKENHAM, in Norfolk.

Founded by *William* Earl of *Chichester* in honour of God, St. *Mary*, and St. *James*, and by him endowed with Churches, Lands, and Tithes. Confirm'd by King *Edw.* the II. *An. Reg.* 11.

[Valued at 108 *l.* 10 *s.* 2 *d.* per *Annum.*]

COLDE-NORTON, in Oxfordshire. 275.

KING *Hen* III. *An. Reg.* 13. confirm'd to the Prior and Canons of this House, dedicated to St. *John* the *Evangelist*, their several Lands and Possessions given by *Reginald* Earl of *Bolon*, and *Ida* his Wife, and divers other Benefactors. *Vid. Vol.* 3. *p* 55.

OSULVESTON, (Ouston) in Leicestershire. 276.

Founded by *Robert Grimbold* in honour of our Lord Jesus Christ, St. *Mary*, St. *Andrew* the Apostle, and all Saints, for Canons; to whom he gave the Church and Town of *Osolveftone*, &c. in pure and perpetual Alms. *Robert* Bishop of *Lincoln* confirm'd the several Churches granted to this Monastery, and further, granted to these Canons to be for ever free and quit from the Payment of Sinodals, and all other Episcopal Customs except *Peter-pence*, denouncing a Curse to such as shall infringe or violate his Grant. *Robert Grimbold* was a Judge under King *Henry* the II. whose Seal 278. did represent a Figure setting in Judgment, holding in one hand a pointed Sword, signifying Justice, and in the other a Sword with the point abated or broken off, representing Mercy. Among other Benefactors to this House was *William de Ros* Lord of *Beaver*, &c.

[Valued at 161 *l.* 14 *s.* 2 *d.* per *Annum.*]

THORKESEY, in Lincolnshire.

KING *Henry* the III. *An. Reg.* 21. granted to the Prior and Canons of this House the Scite of their Monastery in *Fraukalmoine*, and four hundred and ninety eight Acres of Land, and fifty Tofts in *Torkesey* to hold at the yearly Rent of 10 *l.* for ever. Beside which the Prioress and Convent of *Fossa* near *Torkesey* held one hundred and twenty Acres of Land and Meadow, and seven Tofts in *Torkesey* at the yearly Rent of 46 *s.*

Valued at 13 *l.* 1 *s.* 4 *d.* per *Annum.*

CHAUCUMBE, in Northamptonshire. 279.

Founded and endow'd by *Hugo de Chaucumb*. *Amabilia de Segrave* Lady of *Chaucumbe*, and others of the *Segraves* were Benefactors; all whose Gifts were recited and confirm'd by King *Edward* the III. *An. Reg.* 2.

[Valued at 83 *l.* 18 *s.* 9 *d.* ob. per *Annum.*]   Y   REPIN.

REPINDON, in Darbyshire.

280.

Founded *An.* 1172. (18 H. 2.) by *Matilda* Widow of *Ranulph* Earl of *Chester*, and dedicated to the holy Trinity. King *Hen.* the III. *An. Reg.* 57. confirm'd to the Canons of the holy Trinity of *Repondene*, and of *St. Giles* of *Calc*, all the Lands and Possessions given them by the said *Matilda* and others; the like did King *Edw.* the II. *An. Reg.* 18.

282.

[Valued at 118 l. 8 s. 6 d. per Annum.]

KAERMERDIN, in Wales.

King *Henry* the II. gave and confirm'd to the Church of *St. John* the *Evangelist* at *Kayrmerdin*, and the Canons there, the old City of *Kayrmerdyn* with its appurtenances, with the Church of *St. Peter* there, and the Chappel in the Castle.

[Valued at 164 l. 4 d. per Annum.]

WIKES, in Essex.

283.

King *Henry* the II. gave to God and the Nuns of *St. Mary* at *Wikes*, the Church of *Wikes*, with certain Land and seven Villains in that Town. He also granted them two Grayhounds, and four other Dogs (*Bracatos*) for taking Hares in his Forrest of *Essex*; with divers other Liberties and Immunities.

BISSETER, in Oxfordshire.

284.

Gilbert *Basset* gave to the Canons of this House large Possessions, so did *William Lungespeye*, among other things Pasture for fifty Cattle at *Erdintone*, to feed among his own Cattle there; another Benefactor was *Philip Basset* Brother of *Fulc Basset* Bishop of *London*. All whose Gifts were recited and confirm'd by King *Edw.* the II. *An. Reg.* 9.

[Valued at 147 l. 2 s. 10 d. per Annum.]

HERTLAND, in Devonshire.

285.

Founded by *Ganfridus* Son of *Oliver de Dynam*; and the Canons Secular, changed to Canons Regular of St. *Augustin* by the Authority of *Bartholomew* Bishop of *Exeter*. All whose Possessions King *Richard* the I. in the first year of his Reign, confirm'd with the Grant of great Immunities, and Liberties; namely to have a Court to hold plea of all things, but Life and Member, arising in their own Lands and Estate, *&c.*

286.

[Valued at 306 l. 3 s. 2 d. per Annum.]

HELAGHE,

HELAGHE, in Yorkshire. 287.

Founded by *Bertramus Haget*, in a place where formerly was a Hermitage in some sort belonging to the Prior and Convent of *Marton*, who by their Deed, under their Convent Seal, did disclaim, resign, and quit all title to the same, *An.* 1203. The Lord *Jordan de Sancta Maria* marrying *Alice* an Heir General of the foresaid *Bertram*, became a second Founder of this Priory, who confirm'd their Estate, and so did *Alice* his Widow after his decease.   288.

Priors of Helaghe-Park.

1218. William de Hamelecis.	1435. Richard Areton, translated to Gisburn.	289.
1233. Elias.		
1257. John Nocus.	1437. Thomas Botson, translated to Bolton.	
1260. Hamo de Eboraco.		
1264. Henry de Quetelay.	1440. Thomas Collingham.	
1281. Adam de Blide.	1460. Christopher Losthous, under an ill Character, for the Book says, *juratus est bona hujus domus*.	
1300. William de Grimstone.		
1320. Robert de Sposford.		
1333. Steven Levington.	1471. William Berwick.	
1357. Richard.	1475. William Brammam, Vicar of Helagh.	290.
1358. Thomas de Tarum.		
1378. Steven Clarell, 45 years.	1480. William Ellington.	
1423. John Birkyn.	1499. Peter Kendayl.	
1429. Thomas Tork.		

William de Percey Lord of *Kildale* gave to the Canons of St. *John* the *Evangelist* of *Helagh-Park*, the Chappel of St. *Hilda* at *Kildale* with divers 291. Lands, for which the said Canons were to find two of their own House, or two Secular Priests, to celebrate the Divine Offices in the said Chappel for ever.

[Valued at 72 *l.* 10 *s.* 7 *d.* per Annum.]

CANONS-ASHBY, in Northamptonshire.

The *Pynkeneyes* Lords of *Wedone* were great Benefactors to the Canons here, giving them divers Lands in *Wedone* and *Weston*, with Common for 100 Sheep, 8 Oxen, 5 Cows, and 5 Mares in the Pasture of *Wapham*, and feeding for Sixscore Hogs in the Woods there.   292.

[Valued at 119 *l.* 4 *d.* per Annum.]

HAVERFORD, in Wales. 293.

Robert de *Haverford* gave to the Canons here divers Churches and Tithes in his *Barony* of *Haverford*, all which were confirm'd to them by King *Edward*. III. *An. Reg.* 5.

[Valued at 133 *l.* 11 *s.* 1 *d.* per Annum.]

WOD-

294. WODHAM, in **Essex**.

This place being formerly a Hermitage of St. *John Baptist*, *Maurice de Tiretta* founded here a Priory of Canons, and gave them divers Lands, confirm'd by King *Henry* II.

295. IPSWICH, in **Suffolk**.

King *John* in the fifth year of his Reign confirm'd to the Canons of the Church of the holy *Trinity* at *Gypewic*, the several Lands, Churches, and Possession, given them by many Benefactors, among the rest a Fair to last for three days at the Feast of the holy Cross in *September*.

296. FINSHEVED, in **Northamptonshire**.

297. Founded and endow'd with divers Lands and Possessions by *Richard Engaine*, Lord of *Blatherwick*, in the Reign of King *John*. After the year 1367 the Male Line of the said Founder failing, his estate became divided among three Sisters, married to the Families of *Goldinton*, *Pabenham*, and *Bernake*. *John Engayne* gave divers Lands in *Blatherwick*

298. and *Laxton*, to the Canons of the blessed *Mary* of *Finnisheved* for the maintenance of two Chaplains in the Chappel at *Finnisheved*, and two other Chaplains in the Chappel of *Blatherwick*.

[Valued at 56 l. 10 s. 11 d. ob. *per Annum*.]

KEINSHAM, in **Gloucestershire**.

299. Founded by *William* Earl of *Gloucester*, at the desire of *Robert* his Son, then dying. Dedicated to God, the blessed *Mary*, and the Apostles St. *Peter* and St. *Paul*. *Gilbert de Clare* Earl of *Gloucester* and *Hertford* confirm'd the several Lands, Possessions and Liberties, given to the Canons of this House, and so did also King *Edward* II. *An. Reg.* 11.

KIRTMELE, in **Lancashire**.

300.
301. *William Marescallus* founded and endow'd this Priory for Canons, providing that it should always remain a Priory independent of any other House, yet it should never be made an Abby, and upon the death of the Prior, two Canons to be chosen and presented to him or his heirs, of which he or his heirs to elect one to be made Prior. Confirm'd by King *Edward* II. *An. Reg.* 17.

LESNES, in **Kent**.

302. Founded by *Richard Lucy* Prefect of *England*, *An.* 1178. In the year 1179, the same *Richard* quitting his Office of Chief Justice, became
himself

himself a Canon Regular of this House, and soon after died and was here buried. The Lands and Possessions given to these Canons by their founder, and others, were confirm'd to them by King *John*, and King *Edward*. II.

BURSCOUGH, in Lancashire. 303.

Founded and endow'd with large Possessions by *Robert* Lord of *Lathom*. King *Edward* I. granted to these Canons to have a mercate every *Thursday*, and a Fair for five days at the Feast of the *Decollation* of St. *John Baptist* yearly, at their Mannour of *Ormeskirk*. *Walter* Lord of *Scaresbrek* and many others were Benefactors, all whose gifts were recited and confirm'd by King *Edward*. II. *An. Reg.* 17.

[Valued at 80 *l*. 7 *s*. 6 *d*. *per Annum*.]

304.
305.

STEVERDALE, in Somersetshire. 306.

Richard Lovel Chivaler, gave certain Lands of the value of 40 *s*. to the Prior and Convent here for the finding of one Chaplain to celebrate daily for the Souls of the said *Richard* and his Ancestors, in the Church of this Priory. This House was founded by the Ancestors of *Richard de Sancto maure*; and united to the Monastery of *Taunton*, 24. *Henry*. VIII.

307.

DODFORD, in Worcestershire.

Founded and endow'd by King *Henry* I. But in process of time the Revenues of this House being so decay'd that there remain'd here but one Canon, it was united to the Abby of *Hales Owen*, *An*. 4. *Edward* IV.

308.

The Abby de PRATIS, near Leicester.

Founded *An*. 1143. by *Robert* Earl of *Melent* and *Leicester*, and largely endow'd by him and others with Churches, Lands, Rents, Tithes, and Liberties, in and about *Leicester* and elsewhere with the grant of two Bucks yearly, one at the Feast of the Assumption, and one at the Feast of the Nativity of the Virgin *Mary*, &c. *Margaret de Quincy* granted to the Canons here divers Possessions, among other things House-bote and hay-bote, and timber for repairs, out of her Forrest of *Charnwood*, as often as occasion requires; also one Buck yearly out of the said Forrest. *Roger de Quincy* granted them among other things the right Shoulder of every Deer taken in his Park of *Acle*, and free pasture for all their Cattle throughout the Forrest of *Leicester*. Their Possessions were confirm'd by King *Steven*, and King *Henry*. II. *Robert* Earl of *Mellent* came into *England* with the Conqueror who gave him the Earldom of *Leicester*, which City being destroy'd with the Castle there, he re-edified the Church of St. *Mary*, in the said Castle, and placed in it twelve Secular Canons and a *Dean*, appropriating thereunto all the Churches in *Leicester* (except *St. Margarets* which is a Prebend of *Lincoln*) with divers Lands. *Robert* his Son and Heir having founded the Abby *de Pratis* transferred all the Possessions and

309.
310.

311.
312.

and Prebends of the Church of St. *Mary* to his new built Abby. This last mentioned *Robert* (commonly call'd *Boſſu*) took the Habit of a Canon Regular in this Abby, and died here, *An.* 1167. He also founded an Abby of Monks at *Geroudon*, and a Nunnery at *Eaton*, in which his Countefs *Amicia* became a Nun. After some time the Male Line of this *Robert* failing, the Eſtate became divided between two Siſters Co-heirs, *Amicia* married to *Simon de Montefort*, and *Margaret* married to *Sayer de Quincy*. Theſe Canons had alſo a Grant of one Load of Wood, daily, out of the Forreſt of *Leiceſter, ad focum domus infirmariæ Canonicorum,* for Fewel to ſerve in the Infirmary.

315.

[Valued at 951 *l.* 14 *s.* 5 *d.* ob. *per Annum.*]

316.

GRIMESBY, *in* Lincolnſhire.

KING *Henry* the I. founded and endowed this Priory, granting to the Canons here among other things, the tenth Penny of all his Farmes in *Leiſeby*, and *Grymesby*, and the Tith of all Fiſh in his Port of *Honflet*, in pure and perpetual Alms, with large Liberties and Immunities. All which were confirm'd by King *Henry* the II.

[Valued at 9 *l.* 14 *s.* 7 *d. per Annum.*]

St. THOMAS *the Martyr near* Stafford.

317.

FOunded by *Richard Peche* (Biſhop of *Coventry* and *Litchfield,* 1162.) who in his later days became a Canon Regular in this Houſe, in which Habit he died and was buried; his Epiſcopal Habit being taken away by his Coſin *G. Peche* a Monk of *Coventry*. *Robert de Ferrars* Earl of *Derby* gave to this Priory certain Lands together with his Body, after his deceaſe, to be buried here.

[Valued at 141 *l.* 13 *s.* 2 *d. per Annum.*]

NEW-STEAD, *in the Forreſt of* Sherwood, *in* Nottinghamſhire.

318.

FOunded by King *Henry* the II. for Canons Regular, to whom he gave the Town and Church of *Paplewic* and other Lands, with large Liberties. Alſo two great Waſtes called *Kygell*, and *Ravenſhede*. King *John* while Earl of *Morton* gave other Lands, all which he confirm'd after he was King, *An.* 6.

[Valued at 167 *l.* 16 *s.* 11 *d.* ob. *per Annum.*]

319.

HICKLING, *in* Norfolk.

FOunded and endow'd by *Theobaldus de Valeines*. Confirm'd by King *John, An. Reg.* 5.

[Valued at 100 *l.* 18 *s.* 7 *d.* ob. *per Annum.*]

STONE-

STONELEY, *near* Kimbolton, *in* Huntingtonshire.

THIS was a Priory of seven Canons, founded by *William Mandeville* Earl of *Essex*. To this House the Rectory of *Kymolton* was appropriated. The *Bigrames* were Benefactors and lay here buried.

[Valued at 46 *l*. 0 *s*. 5 *d*. ob. *per Annum*]

MODBERLEY, *in* Cheshire.

Founded by *Patricius de Modberley* for Canons Regular, and by him endow'd with several Lands and Commons of Pasture. He also granted the Canons free power, upon the decease of their Prior, to elect another according to their own pleasure.

320.

SPINEY, *in* Cambridgeshire.

First founded by *Beatrice Malebisse* one of the Co-heirs of the Lordship of *Wikes*, within the said Lordship, for three Canons Regular. Afterwards *Maria de Basingburne*, encreased the number to four, two of which were to come daily and officiate in the Church of *Wykes*. She also gave a Messuage and other Lands for the Prior and Canons to maintain therein seven Poor men, allowing to each daily a Loaf of a Farthing, and among all a measure of Ale of a Penny, to each three Ells of Linnen Cloath at two pence *per* Ell, and every two years a Woollen Garment price two shillings and six pence, &c. Also to make three distributions of Alms *per Annum* to three thousand poor People. But these Charges being found to extend to much more then the Revenue of the Lands by her given, *Richard Aithilwald* and *Matilda* his Wife, Cousin and Heir of the Foundresses, did *An.* 6. *H.* 5. release the coming of the two Canons to the Church of *Wykes*, and changed the three distributions abovesaid, to the giving thirteen shillings and four pence yearly in Alms to the Poor of *Wykes*, &c. King *Henry* the VI. *An* 27. granted his Licence to the Prior and Convent of this House to give their Convent and all their Revenues to the Prior and Convent of *Ely*.

321.

322.

MOTESFONT, *in* Hantshire.

Founded by *William Briwer* who endowed this Priory with divers Lands, and gave his Mannor of *Merton* for the maintenance of four poor men in Diet and Aparel, &c. Divers others were great Benefactors, among whom *Peter de Rivallis* Brother of the Founder then commonly call'd *The Holy Man in the Wall*: *Alienora* Wife of King *Edward* the I. gave divers Possessions for an Anniversary, and for daily Alms to seven poor Widows, &c. Confirm'd by *Margery de la Ferte* or *Feritate* Daughter of *William Briwer*, and Co-heir after the death of *William* her Brother; *William* Son of *Reginald de Brus* married *Grace* eldest Daughter and Co-heir of

324.

325.

325. of this *William Brewere*, from whom descended four Daughters, married to the Earl of *Hereford, Cantelow, Fitzherbert,* and *Mortemer.* The Estate of these Canons was confirm'd by King *John*, *An.* 6.

[Valued at 124 *l.* 3 *s.* 5 *d.* ob. *per Annum.*]

326. **FRITHELSTOKE,** *in* 𝔇𝔢𝔟𝔬𝔫𝔰𝔥𝔦𝔯𝔢.

IT was found by Inquisition 15 *John.* That *Robert* Son of *Robert de Bello Campo* founded and endow'd the Priory of Canons here dedicated to God, the blessed *Mary* and St. *George*; saving to the Patrons the liberty of appointing one to guard the Gate of the said Priory in time of Vacation, and take care that the Goods of the same be not wasted, the said Guardian to have nothing but his sustenence, and upon confirmation of a new Prior to retire.

[Valued at 127 *l.* 2 *s.* 4 *d. per Annum.*]

WROXTON, *in* 𝔒𝔵𝔣𝔬𝔯𝔡𝔰𝔥𝔦𝔯𝔢.

Founded by Master *Michael Belet* in the time of *Hugh* Bishop of *Lincoln,* and by him endowed with his Mannors of *Wroxton,* where it was founded, and *Thorpe* near *Rowell* in *Northamptonshire.* Confirm'd by King *Hen.* the III. with Liberties of *Sac* and *Soc, &c.*

[Valued at 78 *l.* 13 *s.* 4 *d. per Annum.*]

327. **DE PRATO,** *between* North-Creyke *and* Burnham, *in* 𝔑𝔬𝔯𝔣𝔬𝔩𝔨.

ANno 1206. *Robert de Nerford* founded a Church here, which *Robert* was principal Warden of *Dover Castle* under *Hubert de Burgo* then Chief Justice of *England.* He also built a Chappel to the honour of St. *Bartholomew* with an Hospital for thirteen poor men, and four Chaplains

328. and a Master. After the death of the said Founder, the said Master and his Brethren took the Habit of Canons Regular, and from that time were called Prior and Canons. The Chappel and new erected Priory was dedicated, *An.* 1221. *Alice* Widow of the said *Robert* made several Orders for the Government of the said Hospital, among others that the Brethren

329. who should be admitted into the said Hospital should at their entry promise Chastity, and Obedience to the Master, that none should have property, and that a Light should burn night and day in the Church. After that the said *Alice* confirm'd with *Warranty* all the Lands and Possessions given to this House, to the Canons for the same. She at last convey'd the Advowson and Patronage of this Priory to King *Hen.* the III. who made it an Abby, and confirm'd all their Possessions, *An. Reg.* 15.

ACORN-

ACORNBURY, in Herefordshire.

THE Lady *Margery de Lacy* founded this Priory for Nuns, and endow'd it with the Forrest of *Acornbury*, as was found by Inquisition, *An.* 49. *H.* 3. which King in the fiftieth year of his Reign confirm'd their Estate. *Catherine de Lacy* Daughter of the Foundress gave certain Lands to these Nuns for the finding of a Chaplain to celebrate daily in their Church for the Souls of her Ancestors, and in case the said service should not be duly performed, then the Bishop of *Hereford* to compel the Prioress and Nuns to the performance. *Margaret* Widow of *Walter de Clifford* gave her Heart to these Nuns, to be buried in their Church, and with her Heart, fifteen Marks sterling, in Alms; this was by Deed dated, 1260. *John de Breuse* gave to the Nuns of *Cornebery* the Rents of ten (*Burgagia*) Borough-houses in *Tettebiri*, which Gift was confirm'd by *William* his Son, 18 *E.* 1.

[Valued at 67 *l.* 13 *s.* 2 *d.* ob. per *Annum.*]

BILSINGTON, in Kent.

Founded *An.* 1258. by *John Mansel* Provost of *Beverley*, who endow'd it with certain Lands in *Bilsington*, and granted that upon the death of the Prior, the Superior and Convent should have the Custody of their own House and all their Possessions, and might proceed to the Election of a new Prior without License first obtain'd from any one. Some of the Lands of this Priory being overflow'd by the Sea, King *Edw.* the III. granted the Canons License to drain, and include the same with Walls according to the Law of the Marish. This was after a writ of *ad quod dampnum* first sued out and return'd.

[Valued at 81 *l.* 1 *s.* 6 *d.* per *Annum.*]

BRADLEY, in Leicestershire.

Founded by *Robert Bundy*, it had but two Canons. Of later time, the Lord *Scrope* had the Patronage.

[Valued at 20 *l.* 3 *s.* 4 *d.* per *Annum.*]

MICHELHAM, in Sussex.

Founded by *Gilbert de Aquila* in honour of the Holy Trinity, for Canons, and endowed with divers Lands, free Pastures, and Priviledges in his Wood Grounds in *Sussex*. All which with other Lands given by many other Benefactors were recited and confirm'd by King *Edward* the II. *An. Reg.* 14.

[Valued at 160 *l.* 12 *s.* 6 *d.* per *Annum.*]

RATLINGCOPE, in Shropshire.

LEwelin Prince of *North-Wales* granted his Letters of Protection to the Canons of this House, to exempt them and theirs, from all Rapine and Depredation or any other molestation by the bordering *Welch*, and this was on the account of one *Walter Corbet* a Canon of this House, his Kinsman.

RAVENSTON, in Lincolnshire.

PEter *Chaceport* Keeper of the Kings Wardrobe, having bought certain Lands here with the Advowson of the Church, *Hugh* his Son and Heir surrender'd them into the hands of King *Henry* the III. who with them founded and endow'd a Priory of Canons, granting them to have the custody of their own House in time of vacation, and not to be charg'd with any Sustentation or Pension to any Clerk, Servant, &c. or keeping any of the Kings Horses.

GLANNAUCH, in Wales.

FOunded and endow'd by *Lewellin* Prince of *North-Wales, An.* 1221. After him several other *Welch* Princes confirm'd the Estate and Possessions of the Canons of the Isle of *Glannauch*. So also did King *Edw.* the I. *An. Reg.* 23.

CHETWODE, in Buckinghamshire.

FOunded by *Robert Grostefte* Bishop of *Lincoln*. Here was formerly a Hermitage and Chappel of the holy Martyrs St. *Steven* and St. *Laurence*, founded by Sir *Robert de Chetwode* Knt. It was vulgarly called a Hermitage, not that it was the Habitation of a Hermit, but because it was situated in a solitary Place. This Priory was given with all its Possessions to the Abby of *Notteley*, 1 E. 4.

LACOCK, in Wiltshire.

FOunded by *Ela* Widow of *William Longaspata*, for Nuns, among whom she her self took the Habit, *An.* 1236. and after became Abbess of this House. This *William Longespee* was Son of King *Henry* the II. and Earl of *Rosmar* and *Salisbury* in Right of *Ela* his Wife, descended from *Walter de Ewrous*, to whom King *William* gave the said Earldom of *Salisbury*. The said Countess *Ela* founded two Monasteries in one day, *viz.* 16. Cal. Maii, Anno. Dom. 1232. Namely *Henton* for Carthusians, and this of *Lacock* for Canonesses. The said *Ela* became Abbess here, *An.* 1240. resign'd *An.* 1257. died 1261. aged 74.

[Valued at 168 l. 9 s. 2 d. per Annum.]

SEL-

SELEBURNE, in Hantſhire.

Founded by *Peter de Rupibus* Biſhop of *Wincheſter*, and by him endow'd with divers Lands and Churches, ſaving to the Vicars of the ſaid Churches a Sufficient ſuſtentation, the Preſentation to the ſaid Vicarages to belong to the Prior and Canons,

---

KIRKBY Beler, in Leiceſterſhire.

Anno 13 *Edward* I. *Roger Beler* of *Kirkeby* founded a Houſe of one *Cuſtos* and 12 Chaplains to Celebrate in the Chappel of St. *Peter* at *Kirkby*, and gave them the Advowſon of the ſaid Church, and the Mannour of *Buckminſter*. *Vid inf.* 246.

[Valued at 142 *l.* 10 *s.* 3 *d.* per Annum.]

ASHERUGGE, in Buckinghamſhire.

Edmund Son of *Richard* King of the Romans and Earl of *Cornwal*, founded here a Houſe for a Rector of *Good men* Brothers of the Church, in honour of the precious bloud of Jeſus Chriſt; here were to be 20 Brethren, of which 13 at leaſt to be Prieſts. For the maintenance of theſe he gave divers Lands, Poſſeſſions, Liberties, and Priviledges, among other things to be free and quit of all Tolls, &c. and to be quit of Scutage as oft as it ſhould happen; alſo to have the Cuſtody of their own Houſe on the death of their Rector, and Liberty to choſe another without preſenting him to the Patron. *Vid. infra.*

[Valued at 416 *l.* 16 *s.* 4 *d.* per Annum.]

KIRKBY Belar.

An. 1326. *Roger Beler* was ſlain in *Leiceſter*. After whoſe death, his Widow with the aſſent of his Son and heir tranſlated the Chantry of Secular-Prieſts by him founded at *Kirkly* to the uſe of Canons Regular, of whom the firſt Prior came from the Abby of *Oluſtone* (*Ouſton*).

The iſſue of *Roger Belar* the firſt Founder failing, the Biſhop of *Lincoln*, became Patron.

More of ASHRUG.

The Lord *Edmund* Earl of *Cornwal*, who founded this Houſe of Religious Men call'd *Bonos homines*, or *Bonhomes*, was buryed in the Church here, wherein was carefully preſerved a ſmall parcel of our Lords Bloud, with the heart of *Thomas de Cantilupo* Biſhop of *Hereford* the holy Confeſſor, and other Reliques.

RIGATE, in Surrey

347. Seems to be founded by some of the *Warens* Earls of *Surrey*, *John de Waren* Earl of *Surrey* released to the Canons of this House a Rent of 19 *s*. 4 *d*. one plow-share, four horse-shooes and nails, which the said Canons used to pay yearly to his Ancestors for certain Tenements in *Reygate*, he also granted to these Canons 46 *s*. 11 *d*. *per Annum*. for the Celebrateing one Masse daily in his Castle of *Reygate*, for ever.

[Valued at 68 *l*. 16 *s*. 8 *d*.. *per Annum*.]

HALTEMPRISE, in Yorkshire.

348.
349. This Monastery was first founded and endow'd at *Cottingham* by *Thomas Wake*, Lord of *Lydel*, with License of King *Edw*. II. Pope *John* XXII. granted to the said *Thomas Wake* Liberty to translate the said Monastery from thence to *Altemprise*. The said *Thomas Wake* granted to the Canons, Regular of this House several Mannours and Lands with Great Liberties of Leets, &c. and Commons of Pasture, &c. in pure and perpetual Alms, with general Warranty, *John de Meaux* of *Bewyke* by his Deed dated *An*. 1361 (31 *Edward* III.) gave to the Prior and Convent of this House his Mannour of *Willardby*, &c. conditionally for six Canons to celebrate for the Souls of him and his Ancestors, &c. Matins Masse, Vespers and Complin, &c. and in the case of *non* performance of the Conditions his heirs to re-enter.

[Valued at 100 *l*. 0 *s*. 3 *d*. ob. *per Annum*.]

BADLESMERE, in Kent.

351. King *Edward* II. *An*. 13. granted his License to *Bartholmew de Badlesmere* to found and endow a House of Canons Regular in his Mannour of *Badlesmere*, with a *Non obstante* to the Statute of Mortmain.

MAXSTOKE, in Warwickshire.

352.
353. Founded by *William Clinton* Earl of *Huntington*, in honour of the holy Trinity, the Blessed *Virgin*, St. *Michael*, and all the Saints, for Canons Regular, *viz*. One Prior elective, and a Convent of twelve Canons. In whose deed of Foundation, dated *An*. 1336, he appointed several Ordinances relating to their habit, the Election of the Prior, none to meddle with the Custody of the House in time of the Vacation but who the Superior and Convent shall appoint, Of the quality of such as are to be received for Canons, Of the Number of Canons to be encreased, as the Revenue increases, The Prior and Convent not to sell or grant any Corrodies or Pensions unlesse compelled by inevitable necessity, Of the Accompt, Of the founders Anniversary, Of the number of Masses, That at the end of every Office of our Lady the Priest who Officiate shall say the Angelic Salutation, in manner following, *Ave Maria gracia plena Dominus tecum, Benedicta tu in Mulieribus & benedictus fructus ventris tui Jhesus,*
Amen.

Amen. *Et benedicta sit venerabilis mater tua* Anna, *exqua tua Caro virginea & immaculata processit*. Amen. With some other Orders; all which were confirm'd by *Roger* Bishop of *Coventry* and *Litchfield, An.* 1337. King *Edw.* the III. granted his License to these Canons to exchange their Mannor of *Shustoke*, for certain Lands in *Maxstoke*.

[Valued at 87 *l.* 12 *s.* 3 *d.* ob. *per Annum*.]

BISHAM, in Barkshire.

Founded by *William de Monteacuto* Earl of *Sarum* and Lord of *Man*, and *Dynbeghe*, who by his Deed dated *An.* 1338. endow'd the Canons here with divers Lands, Churches, and Rents, and granted that upon the death of the Prior, neither he nor his Heirs should intermeddle with Custody of the House, or any of their Possessions. King *Henry* the V. *An.* 8. gave License to *Matilda* Widow of *John de Monteacuto* Earl of *Sarum*, to remove the Bones of her said Husband buried in the Abby of *Cirencester*, to this Priory of *Bustlesham* and bury them here.

[Valued at 285 *l.* 11 *s.* ob: *per Annum*.]

FLANESFORD, in Herefordshire.

Founded by *Richard Talebot*, in honour of God, St. *Mary* the Virgin, and St. *John Baptist*, for Canons Regular, and by him endow'd with divers Lands and Possessions, which Lands being held of the King *in Capite*, King *Edw.* the III. *An.* 20. granted his License for so doing.

[Valued at 14 *l.* 8 *s.* 9 *d. per Annum.*]

EDINDON, in Wiltshire.

William *de Edindon* Bishop of *Winchester* being born in this Town, founded in the Parish-Church of *Edindon* a perpetual Chantry for Secular Chaplains, and endow'd the same with sufficient Revenues, but being afterwards minded to turn the same to a Priory of Brethren of St. *Augustines* Order called *Boni homines* (or *Bonhomes*) he laid the Foundation of a Monastery, *An.* 1352. which was dedicated in honour of St. *James* the Apostle, St. *Catherine*, and all Saints, by *Robert* Bishop of *Sarum*; *An.* 1361. *William de Edyndon* the Founder died, *An.* 1366.

[Valued at 442 *l.* 9 *s.* 7 *d.* ob. *per Annum*.]

DERTFORD, in Kent.

Founded by King *Edward* the III. for Nuns of St. *Augustines* Order, living under the Care of the Friers of the Order of Preachers, and and by him endow'd with Lands and Revennes in *Kent*, and elsewhere; they enjoy'd also divers Houses and Rents in *London*, all which was confirm'd to them to hold in *Frankalmoine*, by the Grant of the said King, dated in the six and fortieth year of his Reign. King *Richard* II. *An.*

An. 8. granted to the Prioress and Convent of this House (*Monasterium Sororum Prædicatissarum de Derford*) the Mannor of *Massingham* in *Norfolk* with its Fairs, Markets, and Liberties, &c. for the finding of one Chaplain to celebrate in the Chappel of the Infirmary of this House, and for the Relief and Sustentation of the Sisters and Brethren in the said Infirmary.

[Valued at 380 *l.* 9 *s.* ob. *per Annum.*]

360.

SYON, in Middlesex.

361.

Founded by King *Henry* the V. *An. Reg.* 2. To the honour of the holy Trinity, the glorious Virgin *Mary*, the Apostles and Disciples of God, and all Saints, especially St. *Briget*, for sixty Nuns of which number one to be Abbess, of the Order of St. *Augustin*, and for five and twenty Religious Men, of which number thirteen to be Priests, four Deacons, and eight Laymen, all to be under the Government of the Confessor. To live separately, *viz.* The Nuns in a part of the House by themselves, and the Confessor and Brothers in a part distinct, chastely both in mind and body, according to the Regular Institute of St. *Bridget.* This Religious House was founded in his Mannor of *Istelworth* in the Parish of *Twykenham*, near the *Thames*, and called by the name of *the Monastery of St.* Saviour, *and St.* Briget *of* Syon, *of the Order of St.* Augustin: by which name or Title the said Abbess and Nuns were enabled to purchase Lands, to sue, and be sued. *Matilda Newton* was appointed the first Abbess, and *William Alnewyk* the first Confessor. The said King *Henry* the V. endow'd this House with the Rent of one thousand Marks to be paid yearly out of the *Exchequer*, till he or his Heirs should settle Lands of that value.

[Valued at 1731 *l.* 8 *s.* 4 *d.* ob. *per Annum.*]

362.

Some other Houses are reckon'd of this Order, of which there remains little or nothing of note but only their Names, which are *Flixton*, in *Suffolk*; *Hempton*, in *Norfolk*; *Wodebrigge*, in *Suffolk*; *Leyes*, in *Essex*; *Vlvescrofte*, in *Leicestershire*; St. *John Baptist* at *Exeter*; *Canonleghe*, in *Devonshire*; *Shelbrede*, in *Sussex*; *Torpington*, in *Sussex*; *Merkeby*, in *Lincoln*; *Westwde*, *Kent*; St. *John*, *Northampton*.

Hospitals

Hospitals for the Infirme,

Of St. Augustins Order.

It was Decreed in the Council of *Lateran*, *An. Dom.* 1179. That where a Number of Leperous People are gather'd together in Community they shall be permitted to enjoy to themselves a Church, Church-yard, and Priest of their own. But they must take care that this be no ways injurious or prejudicial to the Rights of Parish-Churches. Yet shall not the Leprous or Lazer-houses be compelled to pay Tithes of the increase of their own proper Cattle.

St. LEONARD's *Hospital, in* York.

Anno Dom. 800. King *Egbert* in a Parliament at *Winchester*, chang'd the name of his Kingdom of *Britain*, into that of *England*. A. 924. *Athestan* succeeding his Father King *Edward* the elder in this Kingdom, he substituted *Howel*, King of *Wales*, and *Constantin*, King of *Scotland*, saying, *it was more glorious to make a King than to be one.* Which *Constantin* (more *Scottorum perjurium non timens* (they are the Authors words) soon after rebell'd against him, and wasted the *Northern* parts about *Northumberland*. Hereupon King *Athelstan* rais'd an Army and in his Journey towards *Scotland* made his Supplications to God for Victory, at *Beverlay, York,* and *Durham*; after which he overcame *Constantin*; and imploring Almighty God to shew some token whereby the present and future Ages might know that the *Scots* ought to be subject to the Kings of *England*, he strook his Sword into a Rock of Stone near *Dunbar* Castle, and made therein a gash of an Ell deep, which remains (says my Author) to this day. This King returning out of *Scotland* Victorious, did divers works of Charity, in particular, he gave to the Clergy or Ministers of the Church of St. *Peter* at *York*, call'd *Colidei*, for the better Relief of the Poor, and Maintenance of Hospitallity, certain Revenues, and a piece of Ground for erection of an Hospital; which Hospital when built was call'd the Hospital of St. *Peter*, until the Reign of King *Steven*, who built there a Church in honour of St. *Leonard*, after which it was called the Hospital of St. *Leonard*. King *William Rufus*, King *Henry* the I. King *Hen.* the II. and others were Benefactors to this Hospital. *Walter de Langton* Master of this Hospital in the 22 *E.* 1. made certain Orders for Government of the Brothers and Sisters in the same, containing an exact direction how the Chaplains were to spend the day both in the Church and out of it, in their Religious Offices, &c. That the Lay-Brothers should not go beyond the Door of the Nave of the Church unless in processions, that the Sisters have a convenient place appointed for them in the Church, that neither

neither any of them, nor the Lay-Brothers, go out of the Bounds of the Hospital without leave, &c.

[Valued at 362 l. 11 s. 1 d. ob. per Annum.]

CARMANS Spittle, in Yorkshire.

372. FOunded by one *Aceborne* in the time of King *Athelstan*, for one Alderman and fourteen Brothers and Sisters, in the Town of *Flixton*. Designed for the Relief of Travellers that they might not be exposed to Wolves and other wild Beasts of the Woods; the said Founder endowing it with divers Possessions in *Flixton*, with common of Pasture for twenty four Cows and one Bull, &c. The Vicar of the Church of *Folketon*, in which Parish this Hospital was situate, was used yearly on the Feast of St. *Andrew* the Apostle, to cellebrate a Solemn Mass in the Chappel of this Hospital; the Assistants at which Mass enjoy'd several Indulgences. King *Henry* the VI. *An.* 25. confirm'd the Possessions and Liberties of
373. this Hospital naming it for the future *Carmans Spitell*.

St. GREGORY's Hospital, in Canterbury.

FOunded by *Lanfranc* Archbishop of *Canterbury* without the North-Gate of the City. For infirm Men, and Women to live a part in separate Divisions of the House. The said *Lanfranc* built near this Hospital a Church in honour of St. *Gregory* the Pope, placing Canons therein
374. who were to take care of the Souls of the said Poor, and were to receive their Provision daily from the Hospital, these Canons were endow'd with fair Revenues, which in the year 1384. were taxt or estimated in the whole at 133 l. 15 s. These Canons were at first Secular, as established, by
375. *Lanfranc*, but afterwards they were changed into Regulars by *William* Archbishop of *Canterbury*.

[Valued at 121 l. 15 s. 1 d. per Annum.]

BRACKLEY, in Northamptonshire.

RObert Earl of *Mellent*, who came into *England* with the Conqueror, founded this Hospital, where his Heart was kept intire, preserved with Salt. *An.* 6 *Hen.* 5. *Matilda* Widow of *John* Lord *Lovel* granted her Mannor of *Bagworth* and *Thornton* in *Leicestershire* to certain Trustees and their Heirs, for them to grant to *Thomas Coltone*, and several others then Members of this Hospital, Pensions for Life; and by another Deed dated 8 *H.* 5. declared her Intention and Will to be to change this Hospital into a Priory of Friers, Preachers, consisting of twelve and a Prior, the Kings License being first obtain'd; after which the said Trustees to re-enfeoff her or her Heirs with the said Mannor, or convey it to them back again. *Vid. Vol.* 3. *p.* 83.

St. JULIANS near St. Albans, in Hertfordshire.

THE Church and House of St. *Julian* near *Eyewode* was founded for *Lazares*; by *Gaufridus* Abbot of St. *Albans* with the advice and consent of his Convent, and endow'd with divers Tithes and parcells of Tithes in St. *Albans*, *Bradewey*, and elsewhere. Confirm'd by King *Henry* the II. For the Government of these *Brethren* several Orders were made, as that their Habit should be a Tunick, and Supertunick of plain Russit, that they should be single, or if married to separate from their Wives, both parties being willing; that no Woman should enter into the House except the common Laundress, or a Mother, or Sister, to visit their Relation when sick with Licence of the *Custos*, that every Brother at his admitance should make Oath to obey the Abbot of St. *Albans* and his Archdeacon, &c.

RIPPON, in Yorkshire.

FOund by Inquisition, that it was founded by *Thurstan* Archbishop of *York*, for the Relief of Poor and Leprous People. Endow'd with Revenues given at first to certain Sisters who lived here, wherewith to find a Chaplain to celebrate in the said Hospital, and to relieve all such Leperous People, who, being born in *Ripshire*, should repair to this House, where they were to receive one Garment called *Bak*, and two pair of Shooes *per Annum*, and every day to each man one Loaf, half a Flagon of Ale; &c. Which said Sisters being dead, the Archbishop that then was gave the Hospital to the Possession and Government of a Master and certain Chaplains, but in time Leperous People decaying, in the 15 E. 3. there were neither Brothers nor Sisters in this Hospital, otherwise it remain'd as it ought. *Vid. Vol.* 3. *p.* 89.

St. GILES, in the Suburbs of London.

QUeen *Maud* Wife of King *Henry* the I. built on the *West-side* of *London* a House for the Relief of Leperous People, with an Oratory, and call'd it the Hospital of St. *Giles*. It was endowed with several Revenues by the said Queen and others, all which were confirmed by her Grandson King *Henry* the II. *Vid. inf. p.* 400.

St. MARY of Bethelem without Bishopsgate, in the Suburbs of London.

SImon *Fitz-Mary* Citizen of *London*, having an extraordinary affection to the memory of the Incarnation and Nativity of our Saviour which was wrought in *Bethelem*, gave all his Lands in the Parish of St. *Butolph* without *Bishopsgate*, to a Church of St. *Mary* of *Bethelem* by him there erected, and for the instituting of a Priory of a Prior, Canons, Brethren and Sisters, to live according to the Rule and Order of the Church of

St. Mary at *Bethelem,* all which were to wear the Sign of a Star on their outward Garment; this Priory was also for the reception of the Bishop of *Bethelem,* or any of the Canons or others belonging to that Church when they should come into *England,* to which Bishop as a sign of Subjection, this Priory was to pay a Mark yearly at the Feast of *Easter* in nature of a Rent. The Deed of Foundation and Endowment of this House by the said *Simon Fitz Mary* bears date, *An.* 1247.

383.

St. MARY's *Hospital without* Bishopsgate, *at* London.

Founded by *Walter Brun* Citizen of *London,* and *Roisia* his Wife, on a parcel of Land given for that purpose by *Walter Fitz Aldred* Alderman, and endowed with divers parcells of Land and Rents of Tenements in several Parishes in and about *London.*

385.

A Composition was made between *John Witing* Rector of the Church of St. *Butolph* without *Bishopsgate,* and *Godefrey* then Prior, and the Canons, and Brethren of this Hospital, about Parochial Rights; containing, that the said Prior should pay to the said Rector, in lieu of Tithes and Offerings for the territory and space of Ground belonging to his Priory, 10 *s.* yearly, at four quarterly Payments; in all other their Lands without the said Bounds Tithes to be paid; the said Prior and Canons to admit no Parishoner of the said Church to make oblation, or pay any Right that is due to the Parish Church, nor to be buried with them, unless the Parish Church be first satisfied, and for the Performance hereof the said Prior made Oath before the Bishop of *London,* and so were all his Successors to do. The first Stone of this Hospital was laid by *Walter* Archdeacon of *London, An.* 1197.

[Valued at 478 *l.* 6 *s.* 6 *d.* per *Annum.*]

386.

St. BARTLEMEWS *Hospital in the Suburbs of* London.

King *Henry* the I. granted and confirm'd to the Prior and Canons of St. *Bartholomews* and to the Poor of the Hospital belonging to that Church, very great Liberties, (*Et liberam esse sicut coronam meam*) whose Charter bears date *An.* 1133. (33 *H.* 1.) This Hospital was founded for

387.

the receit of all poor infirm People, till such time as they should be cured of their Infirmities, and for the lying in of poor Women, and maintenance of their Children (in case the Mothers should die in Childbed in the Hospital) till the said Children be seven years old. On this Account King *Edward* the III. freed the Master, Brethren, and Sisters, of this House, from being taxt to the Publick Taxes of that time.

[Valued at 305 *l.* 6 *s.* 7 *d.* per *Annum.*]

388.

St. INNOCENTS *near* Lincoln.

Founded by King *Henry* the I. for ten Lepers and a Warden, with two Chaplains and a Clerk, and endowed with several Rents, &c. as appeared by Inquisition in the Reign of King *Edward* the III. at which
time

time there was here, nine Brethren and Sisters, and but one of those a Leper, and he taken in not of Charity, but for 100 s. paid for his entrance; here were also seven Women taken in for money, contrary to the first Institution. King *Henry* the VI. *An.* 35. granted this Hospital and all the Revenues thereunto belonging, after the death of the then Warden, to *William Sutton* Master of the Order of *Burton*, St. *Lazarus*, Warden of the Hospital of St. *Giles* of *Lepers* without *London*, and to the Brethren of the said Order and their Successors, for the finding and maintenance of three Lepers of the Kings Houshold Servants, if any such shall be, &c.

389.

ILLEFORD, in Essex.

390.

This *Hospital* was Founded by the Abbess and Convent of *Barking* for thirteen Leperous Brethren, two Chaplains, and a Clerk. For whose Regular Government *Ralph de Baldock* Bishop of *London* made Certain Orders, *viz.* That the Lepers were to be chosen out of the *Demeasns* of the Abby of *Barking* if any such there, That the Abbess present to one place, and the Master and Brothers to the next alternately, That no married Leper shall be admitted unless the Wife is minded to vow Chastity, That every Brother shall constantly frequent the Divine Offices at the Church unless hinder'd by Sickness, &c. That no Woman be admitted to enter the said *Hospital*, unless the Abbess, near Relations to visit when Sick, or the Common Laundress, and that at open day, That no Leper shall go abroad without special License, That the Abbess shall appoint the Master of the said *Hospital*, That every Leper shall at his reception make Oath to live chastly, to be obedient to the Abbess and Convent of *Barking*, to have nothing in propriety, &c. Which Orders bear date *An. Dom.* 1346.

391.

392.

[Valued at 16 *l.* 13 *s.* 3 *d.* per *Annum.*]

St. PETERS in the City of York.

King *Henry*. I. gave and confirm'd to the *Hospital* of St. *Peter* at *York* divers Lands by him, and *Eustachius Fitz-John*, and others, granted together with divers Liberties, as *Sac & Soc, Tol & Them*, &c. and as a more especial Mark of his favour to this House took to himself the name of a Brother and Warden of the same (*Frater enim & Custos ejusdem Domus Dei sum*) The Like did King *Henry* III. and King *John*. Their Possessions were also confirm'd by King *Henry* II. and King *Edward* I. Other Benefactors were *William de Fortibus*, Earl of *Albemarl*, Several of the *Percys*, and *Moubrays*, &c.

393.

394.
395.

St. MARY MAGDALEN at Colchester, in Essex.

396.

Founded by *Eudo Seneschal* of King *Henry* I. by that Kings Command. King *Richard* I. granted to the Lepers of this *Hospital* a fair two days yearly, *viz.* on the *Vigil* and day of St. *Mary Magdalen*.

St. JOHN, and St. Leonard, at Alesbury, in Buckinghamshire.

Founded and endow'd by *Robert Ilkale*, *Robert atte Hide*, &c. for the maintenance of Leperous and other poor People of *Aylesbury*; Confirm'd by King *Henry* I. and King *Henry* II. These were two *Hospitals*. That of St. *John* valued at 33 s. 4 d. per *Annum*, and that of St. *Leonard* at 20 s. per *Annum*. But it was found by Inquisition, 34 *Edward*. III. that for eleven years before, they were both decay'd, and their Possessions come to the hands of Laymen.

397.

BURTON Lazers, in Leicestershire.

Founded for Leperous people by *Roger de Moubray*, and dedicated to God, St. *Mary*, and St. *Lazerus* of *Jerusalem*, and by him endow'd with divers Lands in *Burton*. *Nigellus de Moubray* granted to this House the Tith of all the Meat and Drink of his Family wherever he should inhabit, and charged his Heirs diligently to perform the same. *William de Burdet* gave to *Burton* St. *Lazarus*, and the infirm Brethren of *Jerusalem*, the Hospital of *Tilton*, and the Church of *Louseby*, &c. Sir *John Digby* Knight, and *Thurbert de Rochebi*, &c. were also Benefactors. Confirm'd by King *Henry* II. and King *John*. King *Edward* III. granted to the Master and Brethren of St. *Lazarus* of *Jerusalem* in *England*, Founded for Lepers, and Souldiers that fight against the Enemies of the Cross, to be free and quit of all Tenths, Tallages, and other Aids and Contributions granted or to be granted to the King and his Heirs.

398.
399.

[Valued at 265 l. 10 s. 2 d. ob. per *Annum*.]

400.

St. GILES, without London. Sup. p. 381.

King *Edward* the III. *An.* 27. at the Request of the Master of the Order of *Burton* St. *Lazarus* in *England*, and in consideration of the Release of a yearly Rent of forty Marks formerly granted out of the *Exchequer*, to the said Master and Brethren of that Order, granted to the said Brethren and their Successors the Custody of the Hospital of St. *Giles* without *London*.

YARUM, in Yorkshire.

401.
402.

Founded by *Alan de Wilton*, who gave to this Hospital divers Lands in *Hooton* to hold at the yearly Rent of two Marks, also other Lands in *Mydilton*, for the maintenance of three Chaplains in the said Hospital, and thirteen poor people. The same *Alan* did afterwards grant this Hospital and all its Appurtenances in pure and perpetual Alms, to the Canons of *Helagh-Park*. The like grant was made to the said Canons by *Peter de Brus*, which *Peter de Brus* gave divers Lands to the Brethren of this Hospital, with free grinding in all his Mills, and free Pasture for all their proper Cattle, in his Land.

St.

St. JAMES near Westminster.

THE Master of the Hospital of St. *James* near *Westminster* being summon'd in a *Quo Waranto*, 22 *E*. 1. appear'd and pleaded, that King *Henry* the III. granted to the Leperous Women of St. *James* without *London*, near *Westminster*, their Lands then given, or to be given, to be held with *Soc*, and *Sak*, *Thol* and *Them*; and that King *Edward* the I. granted them a Fair yearly on the Vigil, day, and Morrow of St. *James*, and for four days following, *& profert*. &c. *Ideo prædictus Magister, quoad hoc sine die*, &c.

TANREGGE, in Surrey.

ODo *Dammartin* gave to God and the Hospital of St. *James* in his Village of *Tanregge*, and to three Priests there serving God, certain Lands, *&c.* for the maintenance of Infirm and poor People, and Travellers, he also gave them his Relicks, two Silver Cups for the making a Chalice, with all the Vestments, Books and other Furniture of his own Chappel.

[Valued at 78 *l*. 8 *s*. 10 *d*. ob. *per Annum*.]

St. JOHN BAPTIST at Stamford, in Lincolnshire.

THIS Hospital dedicated to St. *John Baptist* and St. *Thomas* the Martyr, consisting of a Master and Brethren, was founded by one *Syward*; among other Benefactors were *Richard de Humez* and *Bertran de Verdun* who gave part of a Meadow lying near the Bridge towards the *North*, wherein to build a Church and make a Cœmitery. Confirm'd by King *Richard I*. and by Pope *Alexander*. It was situated at the end of *Stamford-Bridge*, on the *South-side*; for the Reception of Travellers and poor People.

SAUTINGEFELD, near Wytsande.

KING *Henry* the II. confirm'd divers Lands to this Hospital and to the Brethren here serving God.

SCARDEBURGH, in Yorkshire.

THE Hospitals of St. *Nicholas*, and St. *Thomas* the Martyr, were erected by certain Burgesses of *Scardeburgh*, and were both under the Inspection of the Bayliffs and Burgesses of that Town, *&c*. as was found by Inquisition, *An*. 26 *Edw*. the I.

St. GILES, without Shrewsbury.

KING *Henry* the II. granted to the Poor of this House a Rent of 30 *s.* out of his Farm of *Shropshire*. King Henry the III. granted them out of every Sack of Corn coming to *Shrewsbury* Market, a handful of both hands, and out of every Sack of Wheat a handful of one hand, also a Horse-load of dead Wood daily in his Wood call'd *Linewood*, for their firing.

ROMENALE, in Kent.

FIRST founded by *Adam de Cherrings* in honour of the blessed Martyrs St. *Steven*, and St. *Thomas* Archbishop of *Canterbury*, and by him endow'd with Lands, Rents, and Possessions for the maintenance of certain Lepers, and one Chaplain. But in process of time this Hospital becoming decay'd and neglected, by reason, chiefly, that no Lepers could be found to inhabit here for many years, *John Franceys* Patron of this Hospital, *An.* 37. *Edward* the III. in order to revive and restore the same, made divers Orders, *viz.* That in lieu of the Lepers that used to be here, there should for the future be two Priests to celebrate for the Founders and Benefactors, one of which to be Custos or Master, to be instituted and inducted by the Archbishop of *Canterbury*, and to be Resident, which two Priests shall celebrate daily in the Chappel of this Hospital, Matins, and the Canonical hours; that upon the death of the Custos, the Patron to present another to the Archbishop of *Canterbury* to be admitted Custos, within the space of two Months, or in default of the Patron, the Jurates of the Town of *Romenale*, or the major part of them, *&c.*

St. BARTHOLMEWS without Oxford.

THE following Orders were made in the Parliament at *Lincoln*, *An.* 9. *Edward* the II. That there should be six infirm Brothers of this Hospital, and two sound Brothers to labour about the Affairs of the House, each of which eight, to receive 9 *d.* a Week, that there should be a Priest to be the Master of the said Hospital to say Mass daily, and to administer the Sacraments to the Infirm, his Salary six Marks *per Annum.* Queen *Margaret* Widow of *Edward* the I. was during her Life Patroness and Visitor, and after her death the King or his Chancellor. The said King *Edward* the II. *An.* 14. granted his License, the former Ordination *non obstante*, for the Master and Brothers of this Hospital to admit *John Sertbe* into the next void Place, the said *John* having given eighteen Marks, to the Repairs of the Chappel, then ruinous.

MAIDEN-

MAIDEN-BRADLEY, in Wiltshire.

Manserus Byset, a Baron, did first institute this House for Leperous Women, and appointed there certain Secular Priests, who he named *Curators of the Women.* Hubert Bishop of *Salisbury* translated those Priests into Canons Regular. The Church of *Kiderminster* was appropriated to this House, by *Roger* Bishop of *Worcester*, after the death of *Robert* then Parson. This *Manserus*, or *Manasserus Byset* was Dapifer, or Sewer, to King *Henry* II. King *Henry* III. confirm'd the several Lands and Possessions given to the Leperous Sisters of *Maiden-Bradlegh*, and to the Prior and Brethren there.

[Valued at 180 *l.* 10 *s.* 4 *d. per Annum.*]

St. THOMAS of Acon, in London.

King *Edw.* III. *A.* 14. confirm'd to the Master and Brethren of this Hospital divers Lands, Tenements, and Rents in *London*, and elsewhere. as *Westhame, Stratford, Bromley,* and *Stepney*, &c. *Jeffrey Fitz-Peter* Earl of *Essex* granted to the Brethren of this Hospital of St. *Thomas* the Martyr of *Acon,* the Custody of the Hospital of St. *John Evangelist* at *Berchamstede.*

Anno 23. *Henry* the VI. *John Neel* then Master, and his Brethren of this House, exhibited their Petition in Parliament, setting forth, that *Thomas* Son of *Theobald de Helles,* and *Agnes* his Wife, Sister of St. *Thomas* the Martyr Archbishop of *Canterbury,* gave to the Master and Brethren of this House then being, all the Land with the Appurtenances sometimes belonging to *Gilbert Beckit* Father of the said St. *Thomas,* in which Land the said Martyr was born, to make there a Church in Worship of God, the blessed Virgin, and the said Martyr, which Lands lye in the Parish of St. *Mary* of *Colchirche* in *London,* that the Endowment of the said Hospital was enlarg'd by King *Henry* the III. *An.* 52. in which house have always been, ever since, a Master and Brethren professing the Rule of St. *Austin,* and Priests and Clerks to the number of twelve or more, that of old time this House hath been dispoiled, and great part of their Evidences lost and destroyed, they pray therefore that his Majesty by the assent of the Lords Spiritual and Temporal, and by the Authority of this present Parliament would ordain, stablish and approve, that the Master and Brethren of the House or Hospital of St. *Thomas* the Martyr of *Acres* in the City of *London,* may by that name plead and be impleaded, purchase Lands, have a Common Seal, and choose their own Master, presenting him to the Ordinary, and that they may not be charged with any Corrody or Pension, and that their present Lands and Possessions may be confirm'd to them; all which was granted as desired, by the King, with the advice and assent of the Lords Spiritual and Temporal, and Commons in that Parliament, and by Authority of the same.

[Valued at 277 *l.* 3 *s.* 4 *d. per Annum.*]

St. JOHN BAPTIST *at* Lynn, *in* Norfolk.

Founded by *Ulfketel* Son of the Nun of *Sceringes*, and by him endow'd with a parcel of Land in *Linn*, to hold in pure and perpetual Alms. The Mayor and Burgesses of *Linn* did use to present and establish the Master and Warden of this Hospital, till the time of *John* of *Ely* Bishop of *Norwich*.

[Valued at 7 *l*. 6 *s*. 11 *d*. *per Annum*.]

414.

St. MARY MAGDALENS *at* Lenne.

Thomas *de Cant*. and *Robert Winchelsey* Archbishops of *Canterbury*, in their Visitations, and *Peter* the Chaplain, the Founder, made several Orders for the Government of this Hospital; as, that any Brother being a detractor or vexatious to the rest to be punish't by the Prior and Brethren, and if incorrigible to be expell'd; founded with a Church and Cœmitary for twelve Brothers and Sisters, some sound, and some infirm, with a Chaplain; to dwell in the House, the infirm not to come into the Chancel, Cellar, Kitchin, or Curtelage, nor to intermeddle with the Offices of the House, to have a Common Seal, &c. All the Brothers and Sisters to have equal Portions in the Revenues with the Prior, if any of the Infirm withdraws himself for one month, his Salary for a year to be forfeited, if for a year, he to be expell'd; a general Chapter to be held yearly the next day after the Feast of St. *Mary Magdalen*, &c. Which Orders were 415. ratified and confirm'd by *William de Turbus* Bishop of *Norwich, Anno Dom.* 1174.

KYNEWALDGRAVES, *in* Yorkshire.

Roger Archbishop of *York*, and other Archbishops of that See were Benefactors to the poor Sisters of this Hospital dedicated to St. *Mary Magdalen*, all confirm'd by *Thomas* Archbishop of *York, An.* 1301. Which with many other Possessions by others given were all recited and confirm'd by King *Edward* the III. *An.* 1.

417.

St. MARGARETS, *at* Huntingdon.

Seems to be founded by *Malcolm* King of *Scotland*, who gave to the Infirm of this Hospital, Lands, and Rents, so did *Isabel de Brus*, Daughter of Earl *David*; *Robert de Brus*, Son of the said *Isabel*, Lord of *Anandale* gave them divers Tenements in *Cunyngtone*, with view of *Frankpledge* to be held there twice *per Annum*, viz. after *Easter*, and after *Michaelmass*, with small Courts to be held there at their Will as oft as expedient. The like Grant by *Bernard de Bruys*; all which was confirm'd to the Master and Brethren of this House by King *Edw*. III. *An.* 12.

HORNE-

HORNECHIRCHE, in Essex.

THE Master and Confraters of the Hospital of *Hornchurch* were removable at the Will of the Master of the Hospital of St. *Bernard de Monte* in *Savoy*, to which Hospital this was only a Cell, having no Common Seal of their own, nor power to sue or be sued.

HERBALDOUNE, in Kent.

FOunded by King *Henry* II. who assigned to the Lepers of this Hospital a Rent of twenty marks *per Annum* out of his Revenue of *Canterbury*, till such time as he assigns them other Provisions in Churches or Rents elsewhere.

[Valued at 109 *l*. 7 *s*. 2 *d*. per *Annum*.]

St. SEPULCHERS at Hedon in Yorkshire.

A *Lan* Son of *Oubernus* gave a parcel of Land to God and the Lepers of St. *Sepulchres* at *Hedon*; *Alexander de Thuriestal* and many others were Benefactors to this *Hospital*, all whose Gifts were recited and confirm'd by King *Edw*. the II. *An. Reg.* 19.

HAVERING, in Essex.

KING *Henry* the II. gave the Church of *Havering* to the poor Brethren of the Church of St. *Bernard de Monte Jovis*. Confirm'd to them with other Lands by King *Richard* the I. and King *Henry* the III. *An*. 37.

ELLESHAM, in Lincolnshire.

THIS Hospital, begun by *Beatrix*, and finisht and confirm'd by *Walter de Amundevil*, was by him conferr'd upon Canons Regular, to whom he gave divers Lands and Churches, for the maintenance of Hospitality and Sustentation of poor People. Confirm'd to the Canons by *John* Son of *William de Dyve*, *An. Dom.* 1277. The abovesaid *Walter de Amundevile* became a Canon here, and was here buried. The Hospitallers of *Jerusalem* having by fraud obtain'd this House from the then Patron, were by Letter from Pope *Alexander*, made to relinquish their Pretensions.

[Valued at 70 *l*. 0 *s*. 8 *d*. per *Annum*.]

St. MARY's at Dover, in Kent.

Founded by *Hubert de Burgo* Earl of *Kent*. King *Henry* III. *An.* 11. granted to the Brothers and Sisters of this Hospital the Tith of all profits arising from the Passage of the Port of *Dover*, to hold to them and their Successors in *Frankalmoign*. The same King, *An.* 13. granted them a yearly Rent of 10 *l.* at the feast of St. *Michael* to be paid out of the profits of his Port of *Dover*, beside the tith above mention'd. *Vid. Vol.* 3. *p.* 86.

424.

CONYNGESHED, in Lancashire.

425.

William de *Lancaster* gave to God and St. *Mary* and to the Brethren of this Hospital, all *Conyngsheved*, and divers other Lands, Possessions, and Commons of Pasture, &c. He also gave the Canons of this House the Advowson of the House of Lepers of St. *Leonard* at *Kirkeby* in *Kendale*, &c. Divers other Benefactors gave Many Lands and parcels, all

427. which were recited and confirm'd by King *Edward* II. *An.* 12. *Magnus* King of *Man* and the *Iles*, by his deed dated *An. Dom.* 1256. granted to the Prior and Convent of this House that their Ships and Goods should be free from toll, and all other demands and Customs, throughout all his Dominions.

St. JOHN Baptist, at Coventry.

428.

Laurence Prior of *Coventry*, and the Convent there granted the Scite of this House, and the apurtenances, in perpetual Alms for the Receit of Poor and infirm people. And this was at the petition of *Edmund* Archdeacon of *Coventry*. Confirm'd by *Richard* Archbishop of *Canterbury*, and by Bull of Pope *Honorius* III. dated, *An.* 1221. King *Henry* III. *An.* 45. granted to the Brethren and Sisters of this Hospital liberty and protection by themselves or Messengers to ask, gather, and receive Almes abroad, for Releif of their House, for the space of seven years. *An. Dom.* 1425, *Richard Crosby* being then Prior of the Cathedral and Regular Church of the Blessed *Mary* of *Coventry*, and *Thomas Everdon* Master or Custos of this Hospital, Several Orders were made for the Government of this House,

429. containing, That the Prior and Convent aforesaid shall be accounted Founders of this Hospital, and *Edmund* formerly Archdeacon of *Coventry* Principal Benefactor, that the Master of the Hospital be Subject to the Prior, who is to have the placing, Creation, and reception of the said Master and all the Brethren and Sisters, that the said Prior and his Successors may Visit in the said Hospital once a year, attended with eight persons on-

430. ly, the Master to make Oath of Fidelity to the Prior at his admission, the Brothers and Sisters a Promise in Writing sign'd and Seal'd, The Master to be in Priests Orders, the Habit of the Master and Brothers to be of Dark Colour sign'd with a black Crosse, and on their Mantles also a black Crosse; without which habit they ought not to appear abroad, The Master to hold Chapter every *Fryday*, or however once a week, The Divine Offices to be devoutly celebrated in the said Hospital at the usual hours *Secundum usum sarum*, The Lay Brothers and Sisters that are illerate to say

instead

A CANNON HOSPITALLER OF S.t IOHN BAPTIST
AT COVENTRY

instead of *Matins* thirty *Paters*, and as many *Aves*, with the Creed, and for every of the other hours seven, But those Brothers that have learning sufficient, to say the Office of the Blessed *Virgin*; The Sisters to be always intent and Solicitous about the Care and Service of the Infirm in the said *Hospital*, The Common Seal to be kept under three Keys, one to remain with the Master, the other two with the Senior Brother and Sister, That the Master shall pay predial Tithes to the Prior, but not of Cattle nor Wood, That the said *Hospital* shall have a free *Sepulture* for those who choose to be buried with them, &c.

[Valued at 83 l. 3 s. 3 d. per Annum.]

BRUGWALTER in Somersetshire.

Founded by *William Briewerr*, for thirteen poor People, beside Religious men, and Travailers. Several Churches being of the Advowson of the Master and Brethren of this *Hospital* of St. *John Baptist* at *Brudgwalter*, were appropriated hereunto by the Bishop of *Bath* and *Wells* and the Bishop of *Exeter*, *An.* 1284. The Patronage of this *Hospital* coming to the hands of the Lord *de la Zouche* in Custody of King *Henry* VI. by reason of his Nonage, that King granted his Licence to the President and Brethren of this House to elect a New Master, on the death of the former.

[Valued at 120 l. 19 s. 1 d. ob. per Annum.]

BRUGENORTH, in Shropshire.

It was found by Inquisition, 14 *Edward* IV. that *Radulf le Strange* Founded and endow'd this *Hospital* in honour of the blessed *Trinity*, the *Virgin*, and St. *John Baptist*; From which *Ralf le Strange* did lineally descend *John Talbot*, created first Earl *Salisbury* of that name. And it was then further found that the name of Custos of this *Hospital* was in Process of time changed to that of Prior.

[Valued at 4 l. per Annum.]

St. JOHN'S in the City of Wells.

First Founded by *Hugh* Bishop of *Lincoln*. *Joselin* Bishop of *Bath*, and Sir *Edmund Lyons* were Benefactors. These were so bountiful to this *Hospital*, that at first this House had two hundred marks of annual Rents.

[Valued at 40 l. 0 s. 2 d. ob per Annum]

STRODE, in Kent.

Founded by *Gilbert* Bishop of *Rochester*, for the Receit of Poor, weak and infirm People, as well known, as Strangers, and Travellers, and for their releif with Bed, Meat, and Drink, till they either die or depart in health; The Master or Governour of which House by the name and title of *Iconomus*, he appointed to be a Regular, and to have with him at least two Priests to celebrate daily two Masses. The said Bishop endow'd this Hospital with divers Churches and Tithes, &c. All which Revenues were confirm'd by the Prior and Convent of *Rochester*, *Hubert* Archbishop of *Canterbury*, and King *Richard* the first. Whose Several Deeds were all Recited and confirm'd by King *Edward* III. *An.* 6. by *Inspeximus*. The same King *Edward* III. *An.* 16. granted his License to *Mary* of St. *Paul* Countess of *Pembroke* to grant her Mannour of *Strode* to any House of Religious Men or Women, already built, or to be built by her, with a *Non obstante* to the Statute of *Mortmain*.

[Valued at 52 *l.* 9 *s.* 10 *d.* ob. per Annum.]

SHIREBURNE, in the Bishoprick of Durham.

Founded and endow'd with Lands and Churches by *Hugh de Puteaco* (or *Pudsey*) who placed there Leperous People collected all over his Diocess, endowing it with Lands and Churches.

SUTTON, in Yorkshire.

Jeffrey Fitz-Peter Earl of *Essex* gave certain Lands here to *William de Wrotham* Archdeacon of *Tanton*, for the erection of an *Hospital* in honour of the holy and individual Trinity, and the blessed Virgin, and of all Celestial Virtues, and all Saints, and for the maintenance of thirteen poor People and three Chaplains.

MERLEBERGE, in Wiltshire.

To this Hospital dedicated to St. *John Baptist*, and to the Brothers and Sisters here, King *John*, *An.* 16. confirm'd divers Lands given by *Henry de Kenet*, *Levenot* Son of *Levenot*, and others.

[Valued at 6 *l.* 18 *s.* 4 *d.* per Annum.]

St. LAURENCE near Bristol, in Somersetshire.

King *John*, *An. Reg.* 9. and King *Henry* the III. *An.* 32. confirmed divers Lands to the Masters and Brethren of this Hospital of Lepers of St. *Laurence* in the Suburbs of *Bristol*.

BOCKLAND, in Somersetshire.

Loretta Countess of *Leicester*, Widow of Earl *Robert*, gave divers Lands to God and the blessed *Mary*, and St. *John Baptist*, and to the blessed Poor of the Hospital-house of *Jerusalem*, for the Sustentation of the Sisters of *Bocklaund*, and for the finding of a Chaplain to celebrate daily in the Church at *Bokland*.

St.

St. THOMAS, in Southwark.

Founded by *Peter de Rupibus*, and endowed with a Rent of 343 *l.* *Gilbert de Clare* Earl of *Gloucester* and *Hertford*, *An.* 7. *E.* 1. exchanged with the Master and Brethren of the Hospital of St. *Thomas* the Martyr in *Southwark*, the Church of *Blechyngelegh* for certain Lands in *Surrey*; which Church King *Edward* the II. gave them License to impropriate to their Hospital, and to hold it to them and their Successors, so impropriated.

[Valued at 266 *l.* 17 *s.* 11 *d.* per *Annum*.]

DOMUS DEI, in Southampton.

Gervase *de Hamton*, *Margaret de Redvariis*, and many others gave divers Lands, &c. to this Hospital, all whose Gifts were recited and confirm'd by King *Edward* the III. *An. Reg.* 6. The same King, *An.* 17. gave the Custody of this Hospital, then being of his Patronage, to the *Prepositus* and Scholars of *Queens-hall* in *Oxford*, and to their Successors for ever, which Hall was then newly founded and endow'd with Possessions by Queen *Philippa* Wife of that King. He also granted to the Custos, Scholars, Brothers and Sisters of this Hospital, to be freed for themselves and Lands from all Taxes and Tallages, &c. for ever. King *Edward* the IV. *An.* 1. granted to the Custos, Chaplain, and Brethren of this Hospital, and their Successors, the Alien Priory of *Shirburne* in the County of *Southampton*, with all its Lands, &c. *Richard* Duke of *York* the Father, and *Richard* Earl of *Cambridge* the Grandfather of that King, are in the said Grant alledged to be buried in this Hospital.

SANDONE, in Surrey.

To the Master and Brethren of this Hospital dedicated to the Holy Ghost, *William de Perci* Son and Heir of *Henry de Perci* gave and confirm'd divers Lands and Rents for the Maintenance of six Chaplains. The Heart of which *William* being buried here, the Prior and Brethren of this House oblig'd themselves to find a Lamp and Wax-Candle to burn for him in the Church of *Standone* at the time of Mass, for ever, *An.* 14. *Henry* 6. That King granted his License to the Cardinal Bishop of *Winchester* to annex and unite for ever this Hospital, being founded by his Predecessors, to that of St. *Thomas* in *Southwark*.

ROUNCEVAL, by Charing-Cross in the Suburbs of London.

It was found by Inquisition 7 *R.* 2. that *William Marechall* Earl of *Pembroke* gave to the Prior and Convent of the Hospital of the blessed *Mary* of *Rouncyvall* and his Successors for ever, one Messuage and certain Lands and Tenements in *Charing*, where the Chappel and Hospital are situated. Confirm'd by King *Henry*.

St.

St. JOHN's *Hospital* at Oxford.

414.

KING *Henry* the III. in the seventeenth year of his Reign, erected a noble Inn, or Hospital, not far from the *East gate*, in *Oxford*, for the Reception and Relief of the Necessities of the Infirm and Travellers, himself laying the first Stone. The same King gave the Master and Brethren of this Hospital his Mill at *Edendon*, and the *Jews* Garden in the Suburbs of *Oxford* without the said *East-gate*, and granted that as often as he came to *Oxford* they should receive of him Alms for one hundred poor People on the first day of his coming to Town. He also granted to this Hospital of St. *John Baptist* at *Oxford* a parcel of his Wood of *Shottoure*, with the Pasture adjoyning, &c.

NEWSTEDE *near* Stamford, *in* Lincolnshire.

445.

446.

447.

William *de Albiniaco* the III. gave to this Hospital, founded in honour of the blessed *Mary* ever Virgin, at the Bridge of *Wass* between *Stamford* and *Offington*, and to the Brethren there, divers Lands, &c. With the Tith of all the Bread, Flesh, and Fish, spent in his Family, and free Pasture for one hundred sheep, &c. The Master of the said Hospital to be a Priest and a Canon Regular of some House, and to have with him some other Canons living according to the Rule of St. *Augustin*, and seven poor and infirm men to be maintain'd in the Hospital. The same *William*, the Founder of this House, by another Deed appointed the number of the Brothers here to be as follows, two Priests, one Deacon, one Clerk, and thirteen infirm People. *William Albiniaco* the IV. confirm'd what his Father had given, and granted that upon death of the Prior, the Canons here might freely choose another and present him to the Patron, and in the mean time, the Canons to have the Custody of the House, and Liberties of the same. All which things were confirm'd by King *Edward* the III. *An. Reg.* 11.

[Valued at 37 *l.* 6 *s*; *per Annum.*]

St. JOHN BAPTIST, *at* Nottingham.

448.

ANno Dom. 1241. *Walter de Gray* Archbishop of *York* made the following Order and Rule for the Brothers and Sisters of this Hospital. That the Master or Custos provide two Chaplains or more to celebrate there for ever, that all the Brethren rise together to Matines, which are to be so early that they may be finisht by or before day-break, from the Feast of St. *Michael* to *Easter*; which done then shall follow *Prime* and *Terce*, then Mass, and after Mass, *Sext* and *None*; the Brothers shall mind their business in the House, and if not hindred with necessary Occasions, they shall hear *Vespers* and *Complin*; that they shall be all obedient to the Custos, and none shall have any thing in property for seven days under pain of Excommunication; they shall be all cloathed and fed in common, eat no flesh but three days in the Week, *Sunday*, *Tuesday*, and *Thursday*; lie in one Dormitory; they shall be chast and sober; their Habit of Russet and Black, &c.

Here

Here was in this Town of *Nottingham*, another Hospital, founded by *John Plumtre*, by License of King *Richard* the II. *An. Reg.* 16. for two Chaplains, one of which to be Master or Custos, and for thirteen old and poor Widows (*senio confractis & paupertate depressis*) which said *John* endow'd the same with ten Messuages and two Tofts in *Nottingham*; and ordained that the Community of the Town of *Nottingham*, and the Prior of *Lenton* should present to the Chantry in the Chappel of this Hospital, and that the two Chantry Priests should receive for their stipends 100 s. to each yearly. Whose Orders bear date *An. Dom.* 1400.

St. JOHN BAPTIST at Ludlow, in Shropshire. 449.

Founded by *Peter Undergod*, near the Bridge at *Ludlow*, and by him endow'd with divers Lands, &c. for the maintenance of certain Religious Brethren, and for the Sustenance of poor and infirm People. He also granted to the Brothers, that after his deccase, they might freely choose one of themselves to be their Master or Custos : and so as often as occasion should be, and the Master and Brothers to admit the Poor, &c. which Lands, &c. so given as abovesaid were confirm'd by *Walter de Lacy* the Chief Lord of the Fee, and by King *Henry* the III. *An.* 5.

[Valued at 17 *l*. 3 *s*. 3 *d*. per Annum.]

The House of Converts, in the Suburbs of London. 450.

Founded by King *Henry* the III. in a place then called *Newstrete*, and by him endow'd with seven hundred Marks for the Maintenance of Converts, and for the building their Church, &c. to be paid yearly out of the *Exchequer*, one Moiety at *Easter* and the other at *Michaelmas*, till other Provision shall be made, in Lands or Rents. And by another Charter dated 33 *H.* 3. that King gave to this House by him founded for Convert *Jews*, between the old and new Temple at *London*, certain Escheated Lands to hold to the Master and Brethren of the said House converted and to be converted from Judaism to the Catholick Faith.

LECHELADE, in Gloucestershire. 451.

Founded by *Richard* Earl of *Cornwal* Brother of King *Henry* III. and *Senchia* his Wife. Confirm'd by King *Henry* III. Which King *An.* 54. granted to the Brethren of this Hospital, dedicated to St. *John Baptist*, the Hermitage of *Lovebury* in the Forrest of *Whichewode*, they providing one Chaplain to celebrate daily in the said Hermitage. King *Edward* the IV. *An.* 12. granted the Patronage or Advowson of this Hospital to his Mother *Cecily* Dutchess of *York*, with Licence to change it into a Chantry of three perpetual Chaplains to celebrate the Divine Offices daily at the Altar of our Lady in the Church of *Lechlade*, which three Chaplains to be a Body incorporate, able to purchase Lands &c. and to have a Common Seal. By the same Deed he granted License to *John Twynyho* to found another Chantry at the Altar of St. 452.

LEDBURY, in Herefordshire.

453. Founded by *Hugh Foliot* Bishop of *Hereford* for the Reception of poor People and Travellers, and dedicated in honour of God and St. *Katherine* the Virgin; he endow'd it with several Churches, and Tenements, &c. all which with other Lands given by others, King *Edw.* the III. *An. 2.* confirm'd.

[Valued at 22 *l.* 5 *s.* per Annum.]

St. LEONARDS, at Leicester.

454. *Robert* the III. call'd for distinction *Blancmains*, Earl of *Leicester*, had issue, among others, *William* a Leper, who founded this Hospital.

LANGRIGH, in ....

Richard de Singelton, and *Walter Nutun* of *Ribelcester* gave to the Master and Brethren of this Hospital, dedicated to God and St. *Saviour*, Divers Lands in *Ribelcester* and elsewhere.

BILLESWIKE near Bristol, in Gloucestershire.

455. Founded by *Robert de Gurnay*, and by him endow'd with the Mannor of *Poulet*, &c. for the Maintenance of a Master and three Chaplains, and for the refection of one hundred poor People daily, for ever, each of the said Poor to have a quantity of Bread of the weight of 45 *s.* with a sufficient quantity of Potage made of Oat-meal: the Bread to be made of an equal mixture of Bean-flower and Barly *(de frumento fabarum, & ordeo.)*

[Valued at 112 *l.* 9 *s.* 9 *d.* per Annum.]

GLANFORDBRIGGE, in Yorkshire.

456. Founded by the Ancestors of Sir *Ralph Paynel* Knt. but the Abbot and Convent of *Seleby* had the power of placing one of their Brotherhood, in this Hospital, to have the Custody of the same, yet so that he should not convert the Goods of the Hospital to any other use but only to the Sustentation of the Poor and Needy.

St. BARTLEMEW's, in Gloucester.

IT was found by Inquisition 30 E. 3. That in the time of Hen. the II. one Nicholas Walred, a Chaplain, undertook the building of the West-Bridge here, to whom many Workmen reforting, one William Myparty a Burgess of Gloucester, erected a certain Habitation for the said Nicholas and the other Workmen, in which House for a long time after the said Nicholas and William did dwell together, with the Workmen and divers infirm People of both Sexes, having always a Priest for their Governor all living on Alms, till King Henry the III. An. 13. gave them the Church of St. Nicholas in this City, with other Lands, from which time the said House became an Hospital bearing the name of St. Bartlemew, the same King granted them Liberty also to choose a Prior, which accordingly they did. This Hospital consisted of a Master, and three Brothers, beside the Poor.

[Valued at 44 l. 7 s. 2 d. ob. per Annum.]

GRETHAM, in the Bishoprick of Durham. 457.

Founded by Robert Bishop of Durham in honour of God, St. Mary, and St. Cuthbert, for a Master and Brethren, and for the Sustentation of the poor and needy People that should resort thither; who also endow'd it with the Mannor of Gretham, &c. He granted also that the Master and Brethren of this House should be free from all Tolls, Aids, and Tallages; and to all their Benefactors, being contrite and confess'd, he releas'd forty days Penance. Whose Deed, confirm'd by Hugh Prior of Durham and the Convent there, bears date An. Dom. 1262.

[Valued at 97 l. 6 s. 3 d. ob. per Annum.]

ESTBRIGGE, in Canterbury. 458.

THIS Hospital founded in honour of St. Nicholas, St. Catherine, and St. Thomas the Martyr, was compounded of several, united into one; the poor and infirm Brethren of which, William Cokyn Citizen of Canterbury made his Heirs of all his Lands, Possessions, and Chattles, which with divers other Gifts from other Men, King Edward the II. An. 7. recited and confirm'd to the Master and Brethren here, and their Successors.

[Valued at 23 l. 18 s. 9 d. ob. per Annum.]

BOLTON, in Northumberland.

Founded and endow'd by Robert de Roos for three Brothers and Chaplains, and thirteen Leperous Men, and certain Lay Brothers. Constituting the Abbot of Rivall, and the Prior of Kyrkham joyntly to be the principal Wardens or Governors of this Hospital to whose Power, he committed the placing the Master, or displacing him if occasion be.

459.

Cc BASING-

BASINGSTOKE, in Southamptonshire.

Founded by King *Henry* the III. *ad sustentatiom ministrorum Altaris Christi*, For the support of those who serve at God's Altar.

460.
St. KATHERINES *near the Tower, at* London.

Founded by Queen *Alianore* Widow of King *Henry* II. For a Master and Brethren, and by her largely endow'd with Lands, Rents, and Tenements in *East-Smithfield, Kent,* and *Hertfordshire.* Reserving to her self and the succeeding Queens of *England* full Power to place the Master or Custos of the Hospital, for ever. Ordaining that out of the Revenues of this House should be maintain'd three Priests together with the said Master, to celebrate daily in the said Hospital; that on the 16th. of *November* on which day King *Henry* the II. died, a half-penny a peice should be distributed in Alms to one thousand poor People, and on every day in the year 12 *d.* to twenty four poor People, that upon the death of any Brother or Sister, another to be substituted by her, or the succeeding Queens of *England,* who are after her death, to be the Patronesses and Conservators of this House. Whose Deed of Foundation and Settlement, bears date *An. Dom.* 1273.

[Valued at 315 *l.* 14 *s.* 2 *d. per Annum.*]

461.
St. JOHN BAPTIST, *in* Exeter.

Founded by *Gilbert* and *John,* Merchants of *Exeter,* here were five Priests, nine Boys, and twelve poor People.

St. PAUL *at* Norwich.

Founded by *Edward* (or *Eborard*) the II. Bishop of *Norwich.* *Vid. Vol.* 3. *p.* 43.

St. GILES *at* Norwich.

Founded by *Walter Suffeld,* alias *Calthorpe,* Bishop of *Norwich,* for a Master, three Priests, and twelve poor Women.

[Valued at 90 *h* 12 *s. per Annum.*]

WELLE, *in* ....

Founded by *Ralph Neville* for three Chaplains, and certain poor and infirm People, and by him endow'd with divers Lands which he held of the honour of *Richmond,* for which he had the License of King *Edward* the III. *An.* 16. *Vid. Vol.* 3. *p.* 89.

PONTFRACT, in Yorkshire.

Founded by *William le Tabourere*, for one Chaplain and eight poor People, and endow'd by him and others, with the License of King *Edward* the III. granted *An.* 8.

ELSING-SPITTEL, in London.

William Elsyng Citizen of *London* founded here a Colledge consisting of one Warden and four Secular Priests; and an Hospital of poor People in the Parishes of St. *Alphege*, and St. *Mary Aldermanbury*, on which Colledge and Hospital he bestow'd certain Tenements and Rents in the said Parishes and elsewhere in *London*; and gave the Patronage of the same to the Dean and Chapter of St. *Paul's*, who united to this House, and appropriated the Church of *Aldermanbury*, &c. The said Dean and Chapter to place the Warden and two of the Priests, and the said *William Elsyng*, the other two; the Custos to be in Priestly orders, and unbeneficed elsewhere; so also the four Priests. Other Rules and Orders were made for the Government of this House, as that the Custos or Warden shall at his admittance be sworn to the due Administration of his Office ; that the Warden and Priests shall daily say Mattins, Masses, and the Hours, Vespers and Complin in the Chappel of the Hospital, and visit the infirm People there; that within three days after the Nativity of the blessed Virgin yearly the four Priests and Warden be new cloathed, in like manner, the four Priests Apparel not exceeding 30 s. for each, and the Warden in a Garment of the same colour not exceeding 40 s. and that the Priests be allowed more for Linnen and Shooes, &c. 20 s. per *Annum* to each, and the Warden 40 s. to be paid yearly, eight days after *Easter* ; that ninety eight blind and poor People of both Sexes be received and lodged in this Hospital, and Poor, Blind, or paralitick Priests, if any such offer themselves, to be received before any others, &c. Which orders were seal'd by the said *William Elsyng*, *An. Dom.* 1331. (5 *E.* 3.) in the presence of *John de Polteney* then Mayor of *London*, the two Sheriffs, and several Aldermen, &c. Not long after this, *viz.* An. 1340. *Ralph* Bishop of *London* changed the Warden and Secular Priests of this Hospital of St. *Mary* within *Cripplegate*, into a Prior and Canons Regular of St. *Augustin*, under the Patronage of the Dean and Chapter of *Paul's*, still; all other things concerning the said Hospital relating to the poor, &c. to remain as before ; and this Commutation was upon the Petition of the Founder *William Elsyng*.

[Valued at 193 *l.* 15 *s.* 5 *d.* per *Annum*]

BERKING-CHIRCHE, near the Tower at London.

King *Edward* the III. *An.* 44. granted his License to *Robert Denton* Chaplain, to found an Hospital in his House or Messuage within the Parish of *Berking*-Church, *London*, for the Habitation of poor Priests and other poor men and Women, who fall into Frensies and lose their Memory ; he also Licensed him to give and assign the same House and another Messuage in the Parish of St. *Laurence Pounténey* (both which Messuages were held of him in Burgage) to certain Chaplains, &c. for the celebrating the Divine Offices, &c. But the intended Foundation here not taking effect, King *Rich.* the II. *An.* 2. at the Petition of the said *Robert*, granted him License to assign the Premisses, &c. to the Hospital of St. *Katherine* near the Tower.

468.

St. MARY's *in* Leicester.

Founded by *Henry* Duke of *Lancaster* near the Castle in *Leicester*, *An. Dom.* 1330. And by him endow'd with divers Lands, &c. Here was also of his Erection a Collegiate Church, in which he was buried *An.* 1361. The whole was to maintain a Dean and twelve Canons, and as many Vicars, one hundred poor People and ten able Women to serve them. *Vid. Vol.* 3. *part.* 2. *p.* 139.

[Valued at 23 *l.* 12 *s.* 11 *d. per Annum.*]

HEHTE, *in* Kent.

King *Edward* the III. *An.* 16. granted his License to *Hamon* Bishop of *Rochester* for the founding of this Hospital for thirteen poor People, with a *non obstante* to the Statute of *Mortmain*.

469.

HOLBECHE, *in* Lincolnshire.

Founded with License of King *Edward* the III. by *John de Kirktone* for a Warden being a Chaplain, and fifteen poor People. Dedicated in honour of all Saints, and by the said *John* endowed with divers Lands, held of the Abbot and Convent of *Croyland*.

St. NICHOLAS *near* York.

470.

This Hospital being of the Advowson or Patronage of the Kings of *England*, was *An.* 1303. Visited by *William de Grenefeud* at that time Lord Chancellor, at which time he made certain Orders for the Government of this House, *viz.* that all the Brothers and Sisters of this Hospital should at their Admittance profess due Obedience to the Master and Warden, and inviolably observe perpetual Chastity, That both Brothers and Sisters should be present at Matins, Mass, and the other hours, unless hinder'd by Sickness, &c. and that they should say during the time of Divine Service, the Lord's Prayer and Angelick Salutation, with due devotion, iterating the same as often as the Lord shall inspire them; That the Brothers and Sisters should not live under the same Roof, &c. That whatever they have for their several uses shall after their death come to the House; That they shall have a Common Seal; that they shall not demise, or bind any of their Possessions, unknown to the Chancellor of *England* or his Successors; That for the future none shall be Master or Custos of this House but such only as will undertake the Government in his own person;

If any transgress against their due obedience the Master or Custos shall for the first Offence punish the Offenders by with-holding their Commons for some days, as the offence requires, which punishment shall for the second offence be doubled, for the third the party shall be expell'd &c.

[Valued at 29 *l*. 1 *s*. 4 *d*. *per Annum*.]

BOWES, *in the Ile of* Gerneseye.

Founded with License of King *Edward* III. *An.* 35. by *Peter* of St. *Peters* in *Gernsey*, in the Parish of *Saintpierport* in that *Iland*, for a Master or Custos, Brethren, and Sisters; and by him endow'd with twenty yardland, and the delivery of fourscore quarters of wheat yearly, arising out of certain Land in the said Parish; which Land was held *in Capite* of the King, by a Service call'd *Chaumpert*, *viz*. the payment of the eleventh Sheaf arising on the said Lands yearly.

WOLVERHAMPTON, *in* Staffordshire.

Founded, with License of King *Richard* II. *An.* 16. by *Clement Lusone*, and *William Waterfall*, for one Chaplain and six poor people.

The Holy Trinity *in* New Sarum.

King *Richard* II. *An.* 17. granted his License to *John Chaundeler* to make an Hospital in honour of the holy Trinity of two mesuages in a Street call'd *Newestreet* in New *Sarum*, for the Releif of poor weak and Infirm people, whereof the Mayor of the said City for the time being to be Master, and to rule and govern the same, and to endow the same with a certain Rent of 13 *s*. 4 *d*. King *Henry* IV. *An.* 1. granted License to the then Master to purchase Lands of 20 *l*. value *per Annum*.

KNOLS Alms-house *at* Pontfract, *in* Yorkshire.

Founded by Sir *Robert Knolls* Knight Citizen of *London*, and *Constance* his Wife, in honour of the Holy Trinity, and blessed Virgin *Mary*, for certain Chaplains whereof one to be Master, two Clerks, and thirteen Poor people, such especially as by misfortune come to want, and two Servants to help the said Poor. The Master to have twenty marks for his sustenance, the two Clerks each ten marks, and the thirteen Poor amongst them 34 *l*. 4 *s*. 3 *d*. ob, *per Annum*. *viz*. 1 *d*. ob, a day to each. Which Deed of the said *Roberts* Foundation bears date *An. Dom.* 1385.

[Valued at 182 *l*. 14 *s*. 4 *d*. *per Annum*.]

OKE.

OKEHAM, in Rutland.

474.

King *Richard* II. *An.* 22. granted his License to *William Dalby* of *Extone* to found this Hospital for two Chaplains, of which one to be Custos, and thirteen poor Men, and to endow the same with one Messuage and two acres of Land at *Okeham*, and to grant the Patronage of the same to the Prior and Convent of St. *Anne* of the Order of Carthusians at *Coventry*, with a further License to the said Prior and Convent to give a yearly Rent of 40 *l*. to be issuing out of some of their Possessions where ever they pleased to assign, to the Custos of the said Hospital and the said Poor men for their maintenance, for ever.

[Valued at 12 *l*. 12 *s*. 11 *d*. per *Annum*.]

DONYNGTON, in Barkshire.

King *Richard* II. *An.* 16. gave License to *Richard Abberbury* to found an Hospital in his Mannor of *Donyngton*, which he held of the King, as of his honour of *Walingford*, for certain poor people, of which one to be chief, by the name and Title of *The Minister of God of the poor House of Donyngton*, and to endow the same with divers Lands.

[Valued at 19 *l*. 3 *s*. 10 *d*. per *Annum*.]

THORNTONS Hospital in *New Castle* upon *Tine*, in Northumberland.

475.

Founded by *Roger Thornton* in honour of St. *Catherine* for one Chaplain, who is Custos, nine poor men, and four Poor Women, to be continually resident, for which foundation King *Henry* IV. *An.* 13. granted his License, and that they might have a Common Seal. Endow'd by the said *Roger* with yearly Rents of 10 *l*.

EWELME, in Oxfordshire.

476.

King *Henry* VI. *An.* 15. granted his License to his Cousin *William de la Pole* Earl of *Suffolk*, and *Alice* his Wife to found an Alms House in this Town, for two Chaplains and thirteen poor men, and that they should be a Body Corporate, and that he might endow the same with one hundred Marks *per Annum*. This Hospital was Founded *An. Dom.* 1448. and call'd *Gods House*. The two Priests were, one to instruct the Poor in Religious Dutyes; the other to be a Schoolmaster and teach the poor; both to have for *Salery* 10 *l*. the Minister 16 *d*. a week, the other twelve poor men, 13 *d*. a week.

[Valued at 20 *l*. per *Annum*.]

SHIRE-

A KNIGHT TEMPLAR

SHIREBURNE, in Dorsetshire.

Founded, with License of King *Henry* the VI. *An.* 15. by *Robert Nevyle* Bishop of *Sarum*, *Humfrey Stafford*, Knt. *Margaret Goghe*, *John Fauntleroy*, and *John Baret*, to the honour of God, St. *John Baptist*, and St. *John Evangelist*, for twenty Brethren, twelve poor and impotent men, and four poor and impotent Women, and for a perpetual Chaplain; and that the Brothers of this House might elect one among themselves to be their Master from year to year, and upon the death of any of their number the rest might elect others to succeed in their room, &c.

BOCKING, in Essex.

KING *Henry* the IV. granted his License to *John Doreward* to erect a perpetual Chantry of one Chaplain in the Parish-Church of *Stanewey* in *Essex*, and to endow the same with a Mansion lying near the Church-yard there, and with 7 *l.* of yearly Rent. Which Licensed Foundation not being effected in the Life of the said *John*, King *Henry* the VI. did afterward grant License to *John Doreward* Esq; his Son, to found a certain House at *Bocking* to be called *Maison Dieu*, for seven poor People, one of which to be call'd *Præpositus Villæ de Bokking*, and to have the Government of the said poor, &c. and to endow the same, and a Chantry by him founded in the Parish Church of *Bokking*, with Lands and Rents.

TODINGTON, in Bedfordshire.

KING *Henry* the VI. *An.* 21. granted his License that *John Broughton* or his Feoffees might erect an Hospital in honour of St. *John Baptist* in *Todyngdone*, for one Chaplain, and three poor Men, to be a perpetual Community and Body Corporate. Also that he might give to the Prioress and Nuns of St. *Margaret* at *Dertford* an Annual Rent of 8 *l.* and that the said Nuns might assign the said Rent, and also another Rent of 5 *l. per Annum* to be issuing out of their own Lands to this Hospital, which House of *Dertford* was of the said Kings Patronage being founded by his Progenitors.

RICHMOND, in Yorkshire.

HERE being of old time a poor Hospital dedicated to St. *Nicholas* in which was only one Chaplain, of the Kings Patronage by reason of the honour of *Richmond*, and that Hospital being fallen to extream decay, *William Ayscogh* one of the Justices of the *Common-Pleas*, repair'd it, and added another Chantry Chaplain, in consideration whereof, and that he was become as a second Founder, King *Henry* the VI. *An.* 26. granted him the Patronage.

[Valued at 10 *l. per Annum.*]

DERT:

DERTFORD, in Kent.

480. KING Henry the VI. *An.* 31. gave License to *John Bamburgh, William Rothele, Roger Joxet,* and *Thomas Boost,* and to the Survivors of them to found an Alms-House in honour of the holy Trinity (to which the Parish Church there is dedicated) for the perpetual Vicar of that Church, and the Gardians of the Goods, and Chattles of the said Church, and for five poor decrepid Men; and that the said Vicar, and Gardians, and their Successors should be *Master* of the said House, and a Body Corporate, and have a Common Seal. With License to give and assign Lands and Rents to the said Hospital of the value of 20 *l. per Annum.*

The Alms-house within the Precinct of St. Crosses at Winchester, in Hampshire.

481. FOunded by *Henry,* Cardinal, and Bishop of *Winchester,* half Brother of King *Henry* IV. who by License of King *Henry* the VI. *An.* 21. granted to the Master and Brethren of the Hospital of the Holy Cross near *Winchester,* divers Mannors, and Lands, &c. to the yearly value of 500 *l.* Within which this Alms-house was erected for two Chaplains, five and thirty poor Men, and three Women, to be govern'd by the Master of that Hospital; but the Cardinal dying before this Foundation was perfectly compleated, King *Henry* the VI. *An.* 33. did incorporate

482. them under a Rector of their own, by the name of *The New Alms-house of Noble Poverty, establisht near* Winchester *by* Henry *Cardinal of* England, *and Bishop of* Winchester, *Son of* John *late Duke of* Lancaster *of noble Memory;* with grant of a Common Seal, and Power to purchase, &c.

[Valued at 84 *l.* 4 *s.* 2 *d. per Annum.*]

STOKFASTON (Stockerson) *in* Leicestershire.

FOunded with License of King *Edward* the IV. *An.* 5. by *John de Boyville* Esq; near the Town Church, for one Chaplain, and three poor men, who were a Body Corporate, and might retain Lands to the value of 10 *l. per Annum.*

---

483. ## HEITSBURY, *in* Wiltshire.

FOunded with License of King *Edward* the IV. *An.* 11. by *Margaret* Widow of *Robert* Lord *Hungerford, John Cheyne* of *Pynne* Esq; and *John Mervyn* Esq; for one Chaplain, twelve poor Men, and one poor Woman, of whom the Chaplain to be Custos or Warden. Which Hospital was made a Body Corporate, &c. and endow'd with divers Lands, and

484. had a grant of twenty Load of Wood for firing, out of the Wood of *Southleghe* in *Wiltshire.*

The

The Savoy, *in the Suburbs of* London.

KING *Henry* the VIII. *An.* 2. granted the place, or peice of Ground, called the *Savoy*, parcel of the Dutchy of *Lancaster*, and lying in the Parishes of St. *Clements Danes* without the Bars of the *New Temple* at *London*, and St. *Mary* of the *Stronde* in the County of *Middlesex*, to *Richard* Bishop of *Winchester*, *Richard* Bishop of *London*, *Thomas* Bishop of *Durham*, *Edmund* Bishop of *Sarum*, *William* Bishop of *Lincoln*, *John* Bishop of *Rochester*, *Thomas* Earl of *Arundel*, *Thomas* Earl of *Surrey*, *Charles* Lord *Herbert*, Sir *John Fyneux* Chief Justice of the *Kings Bench*, Sir *Robert Rede* Chief Justice of the Common Pleas, *John Young* Master of the *Roles*, Sir *John Lovell*, and *John Cutte*, Executors of King *Henry* the VII. for the founding and establishing of an Hospital. And by another Deed dated *An.* 4. he granted License to the said Executors to found such Hospital for five Secular Chaplains, one of which to be Master, to pray for the good Estate of him and *Catherine* his Consort; and for the Souls of King *Henry* the VII. and *Elizabeth* his Consort, and of *Arthur* Prince of *Wales*. Which Hospital was to be called *The Hospital of* Henry *the* VII. late King *of* England, *at the* Savoy ; to be a Body Corporate, to have a Common Seal, and yearly Revenues, to the value of five hundred Marks *per Annum*, for maintenance of the said Chaplains, and for performance of such other Works of Mercy and Piety as by the said Executors shall be appointed and exprest. With a *Non obstante* to the Statute of Mortmain.

585.

[Valued at 529 *l.* 5 *s.* 7 *d.* ob. *per Annum.*]

Of the Knights, Hospitallers of St. John of Jerusalem.

489.
490.
491.
492.
493.
494.
495.
496.
497.
498.

THE Patron of this Order of Knights was St. *John Baptist*, from whom they took their Denomination. The Hospital of St. *John Baptist* and the Poor at *Jerusalem*, is said to be first built in the time of *Julius Cæsar* Emperor of *Rome*, and *Antiochus* Prince of *Antioch*, with certain Treasure which one *Melchiar*, a Priest in the *Temple*, had taken out of the Sepulcher of *David*; here the Poor and Infirm were kindly received and entertain'd from all parts of the World. The same Author delivers that when our Saviour Christ became incarnate and conversed on Earth, when he came to *Jerusalem*, he resorted frequently to this House, and that it was in this House that he appear'd to his Apostles after his Passion and Resurrection, the Doors being all shut. After his Ascension, St. *Steven* and others of his Disciples served the poor in this Hospital-house according to our Lord's Precept. When the Christians were expell'd from *Jerusalem*, and the City was possest by the *Saracens*, one *Conradus*, or *Gerardus*, a devout Servant of God, lived here and served the Poor in like manner, who at such time as *Jerusalem* was besieg'd by *Godfrey* of *Bullen*, and the Christian Pilgrims, and a great Famine being in the Christian Camp, was accustomed to go upon the Walls and throw over Loaves, which he carried secretly about him for that purpose, as if he were eager in throwing Stones against the Besiegers. This *Gerard* was the first Master of this Hospital, which after the City was taken by the Christians was very much favour'd, and its Revenues augmented by the Kings of *Jerusalem*, &c. After the death of this *Gerard*, Frier *Raymund de Puy* became Master, who establisht a Rule for the Hospitallers, confirm'd by Pope *Innocent* the II. and Pope *Boniface*. This Rule consists of nine and twenty Articles, among which it is ordain'd that every Brother or Frier, at his admission to the Service of the Poor here, is to profess these three things, Chastity, Obedience, and to live without Property, that when the Friers go abroad they shall not go alone, but two or three together, that if any be publickly guilty of Fornication, he shall be publickly whipt, and then expell'd the Society. The Infirm at their first Reception into the Hospital, shall be confest, and communicate, and then carried to bed, and there served and attended as Lords and Masters of the House, That all the Brothers shall wear a Cross on their upper Garments as a Badge of their Faith, &c.

Others give another account of the Original of the Hospitallers, affirming that after the *Turks* of *Arabia* had over-run *Syria* and *Egypt* about the year 612. certain *Italian* Merchants of the City of *Malfe*, trading into these parts, and being favour'd by the Turks on the account of their Trade, they obtain'd from the *Calife* of *Egypt* a peice of Ground lying before the Temple of the Sepulcher, for their Habitation; here those Merchants built a Monastery and Church in honour of the blessed Virgin, placing therein an Abbot and Monks: After that they built another little Church

Church in honour of St. *Mary Magdalen*, for the Reception of Women Pilgrims, and placed therein certain Nuns, and lastly considering the danger of those who came in Pilgrimage to the holy places, who were often robbed by the Turks, they built an Hospital or *Domus Dei* for the Reception of Men, whether Well or Sick, who arrived here in Pilgrimage; and another Church for them, dedicated to St. *John Elemon, Patriarch* of *Alexandria*. These three Houses subsisted only by Alms, collected for them, yearly, by the said Merchants of *Malfy*, till the Christians conquer'd *Jerusalem* and expelled the *Saracens* : At which time lived in the Abby of Monks, the before-mention'd *Girald* to whom the Abbot committed the Reception and Relief of the Poor and Pilgrims in the foresaid *Domus Dei* or Hospital ; and after such reduction of the City, the said Hospital flourisht daily more and more, procuring to it self great Revenues, and to be discharged from its subjection not only to the Abbot, but Patriarch also. These and the like mighty Priviledges granted them by the Court of *Rome*, were the occasion of great Troubles and Disorders between the Hospitallers and the Patriarch of *Jerusalem*. These Hospitallers on their admission were to make Oath upon the *Missal*, as follows, *Tou promise and vow to God, our Lady, and my Lord St.* John Baptist, *to live and die under the obedience of such Superior, whoever he be, as God shall give you, you vow farther and promise to live chastly until death, and also without property ; we also make another promise, which no Religious Men besides us, make, for we promise to be Servants and Slaves of the Infirm our Masters*. After the making this Vow, he who admits him says, *And we promise you Bread and Water, and humble Cloathing, for nothing more you can require, and we make you a Partaker of all the good Works done in our Order*, &c.

499.

500.

A List of such who have been Masters.

501.
502.
503.

1. *Girardus*.
2. *Raymundus de Podio*.
3. *Augier de Ballen*.
4. *Arnaudns de Comps*.
5. *Gilbertus Assailli*.
6. *Castus*.
7. *Jobertus*.
8. *Gaufridus de Dinsono*.
9. *Hermengandus Daps*, in his time the Christians lost *Jerusalem*.
10. *Rogerius de Molins*.
11. *Garnerius de Neapoli*, he had been Prior of St. *John's* at *London*. Vid. p. 550.
12. *Alfonsus de Portugalia*, resigned.
13. *Gaufridus Rat*.
14. *Garinus de Monteacuto*.
15. *Bertrandus de Gexi*.
16. *Garinus*.
17. *Bertrandus de Cons*.
18. *Petrus de Villa Brida*.
19. *Willielmus Castello Novo*.
20. *Hugo Ryvell*.
21. *Nicholaus de Lorgne*.
22. *Odde*.
23. *Guillelmus de Villareto*.
24. *Fulco de Vilareto*, in his time the Knights Hospitallers took the Island of *Rhodes*, and removed the Convent from *Cyprus*. He was deposed.
25. *Mauricius de Paygnaco*.
26. *Elionnus de Villa Nova*.
27. *Deodatus de Gosono*.
28. *Petrus Cornelian*.

505. *The Hospital of St.* John *of* Jerusalem, *in the Suburbs of* London.

Founded by *Jordan Briset*, a Baron, about the year 1100. on ten Acres of Land which he had in exchange from the Nuns of *Clerkenwell*, which Nunnery he had founded not long before. The Church of this Hospital was dedicated in honour of St. *John Baptist* by *Heraclius* Patriarch of *Jerusalem, An. Dmo.* 1185.

506. The foresaid *Jordan* endow'd this House with fourteen Acres of Land adjoyning upon the *Clerks Well*. Robert de *Fun* gave to the Brethren of this House the Hermitage of *Tevelie*, with a Condition that the said Brothers should admit him into their Order, at such time as he pleased, whether in Health or Sickness. Many o-

507. thers were Benefactors, among the rest *Robert de Vere* Earl of *Oxford* gave to the Prior and Brothers of the Hospital of St. *John* of *Jerusalem* in *Eng-*

508. *land* two Knights Fees, *William* Earl of *Ferrars, Hugh de Bellocampo*, *Gil-*

510. *bert de Montefichet*, &c. gave divers other Lands, and Churches, &c. re-

511. cited and confirm'd by King *John, An.* 1. These Knights of St. *John* claimed a Priviledge to bury the Bodies of such who had given Alms to their Fraternity, however they came to their death, whereupon it happen'd, *An.* 4 *E.* 1. that certain Fellons having been executed, some of the Servants of these Knights went to the *Gallows* and took 'em down to bury, one of which Fellons, *Adam le Messer* by name, being laid in the Grave came to life again, and fled to the Neighbouring Church for Sanctuary, where he remain'd till he abjured the Realm. Pope *Clemens* having in the Council of *Vienna* suppress the Order of Knights Templers, and given all their Lands and Possessions, moveable and immoveable to these Knights

512. Hospitallers of St. *John* of *Jerusalem*, King *Edw.* the II. *An.* 7. granted his Letters of *Mandamus* all over *England*, for putting the same in execution, in this Kingdom. The like Grant was made by Act of Parliament, *An.* 17.

513. *E.*2. However *Hugh Spencer* the younger by force seized and held from them

514. their Mannor of the *New Temple, London*, which upon his Attainder came to the hands of King *Edward* the III. who in the twelfth year of his Reign, did, give, grant, and sell, in consideration of 100 *l*. part of the said Mannor of the *New Temple* then valued at 7 *l*. 5 *s*. 2 *d*. together with the Church, *Cœmitary*, and *Cloyster*, &c. to the Prior of St. *John*'s and his Successors.

Vid. Vol. 3. *p.* 108.

Of the Knights Templers in England.

517. ANno Dom. 1118. Certain Religious Knights, of whom the principal were *Hugh de Paganis*, and *Godfrey de S. Audomaro*, engaged themselves to the Service of Christ, before the Patriarch of *Jerusalem*, and undertook to live after the Mannor of Canons Regular. King *Baldwin* granted them a Habitation in part of his Palace adjoyning to the Temple, and he and others gave them other Gifts whereon to subsist. Their chief profession was to guard the Roads from Theives for the safety of Pilgrims. Their Habit was white with a red Cross. Their number did in a little time so increase, that they had in their Convent above three hundred Knights, besides others, and as their number so their Possessions

518. did swell to a vast and invidious value. *An. Dom.* 1240. the Church belonging

longing to these Knights at the Place call'd the *New Temple* in *London* was dedicated on Ascention day, the King and a great Concourse of Peers and great Persons being present, *An. Dom.* 1147. *Conrad* Emperor of *Germany*, and *Lewis* King of *France*, with great forces of French, English, Normans, and Britains, made an expedition against the *Pagans* in the Holy Land, but returned with Little or no success at that time; These Knights Templers having been very Treacherous to the Christians at the Seige of *Damascus*, which City had been taken by King *Lewis* but for them. *An. Dom.* 1307. (1 *Edward* 2.) These Knights were Imprison'd throughout all Christendome, for certain Enormities and Superstitions crept into their Order, and all their Estates real and personal Seized.

519.

Of the *New Temple* at London.

King *Henry* III. by a solemn and formal Deed of Grant dated the nineteenth year of his Reign, gave his Body to be buried, when it shall please God to take him out of this Life, at the *New Temple* in *London* The like did Queen *Alianor*. The said King *Henry* III. granted to the Master and Brothers of this House (*Magistro & Fratribus militiæ Templi Salomonis Jerusalem*) and to their Successors 8 *l.* yearly out of the Exchequer for the Maintenance of three Chaplains in the *New Temple* at *London*. King *Henry* the II. gave the said Knights the whole Water Course of *Fleet* with a place near Castle *Bainard* for the making a Mill, with a Messuage upon the *Fleet* near the Bridge. He also granted the Church of St. *Clements Danes* with all it appurtenances. Pope *Innocent* granted that none who should fly into the Houses of these Knights Templers for safety or Protection, should be disturb'd, nor their Goods taken, under Pain of Excommunication. One of these Priviledged Places belonging to these Knights was *Parish=Gardyn*, otherwise call'd *Wideflete*, in *Suthwark* (*vide pag.* 543) Concerning which divers Statutes and Orders were made by *John* Duke of *Bedford*, Farmer of that place, *An.* 1320. Some of which were, That every person flying thither for safety should be examined for what Cause he flyes, whether for another mans Debt, or Felony, or Trespass; and then his name and the Cause to be registred, That he shall be sworn to be of good behaviour in the said Priviledged place, while he remains there, &c. If his flight be for Fellony he shall be kept under a Guard of six men of the Society, If any person strike another he shall pay to the Lord 6 *s.* 8 *d.* if he draw bloud, 13 *s.* 4 *d.* If any one commit fellony after his reception he shall lose his Priviledged and be committed to the Prison of the Kings Bench. If any person take in a Whore or be convict of Fornication or Adultery within the Priviledged places, he shall forfeit to the Lord 6 *s.* 8 *d.* and lose his Priviledge. *Bernard de Ballolio* gave to these Knights 15 *l. per Annum.* of his Lands in *England*, arising at *Hichen* in *Hartfordshire*. This guift was made at *Paris*, in the Presence of the Apostolick Lord *Eugenius*, the King of *France*, Several Arch-Bishops and one hundred and thirty Knights of this Order. Confirm'd afterwards by King *Steven*. *An. Dom.* 1185, an Inquisition was made by *Frier Galfrid* Son of *Steven*, of all the Lands, Churches, Mills, Rents of Assize, &c. belonging to this Order in *England*; which Perticulars take up fifteen pages, and being as I conceive, of no use in this Abridgment, I shall not take any further notice of them, but refer the Curious to the Book at large. *An. Dom.* 1434. Frier *John Stillingfleet* compiled a Book of the names,

521.

522.

523.

524.
526.

541. of all the Several Founders or Benefactors of the Hospital of St. *John* of *Jerusalem* in *England*, and of all the Lands, Churches, Preceptories Mannors, Houses, Rents, &c. given as well to the said Hospital, as to the Knights Templers in *England*. He begins with the Lord *Jordan Briset* who in the Reign of King *Hen.* I. Founded the House and Hospital of St. *John* at
542. *Clerkenwell*, and since him reckons up some hundreds of other Benefactors, with the Lands, &c. by them given, among whom, I shall observe, *Wil. Maundeville* Earl of *Essex* gave to the Brothers of this Hospital five Bucks to be received yearly between the Feasts of St. *John Baptist*, and St. *Michael*, and five Does between St. *Michael* and *Lent*, for ever out of his Park of *Enfelde*. *William Longeford* Knt. *William Coterell* and others gave divers Tenements in the Parish of St. *Dunstans West*, with divers Rents in *Fleet-street*, the
543. Pasture call'd *Fiketzfeld*, the Mills of *Wideflete*, with the Garden called *Parish-Garden*, with many other Lands, Tenements, and Pastures in *Southwark*, *Lambethe*, and *Newington*, &c. The Lady *Joan Gray* Widow of Sir *Robert Gray* Knt. gave them the Mannor of *Hampton* near *Kingston* with all the Appurtenances, *An.* 1212. with other Lands elsewhere. Sir *Thomas*
544. *de Saunford* Knt. gave them the Mannor of *Saunford* in *Oxfordshire*. *Roger de Moubray* gave to the Templers many Lands, among the rest, he gave
545. them the Preceptory of *Balsalle*, in *Warwickshire*. *Maud* Countess of *Clare*,
546. Widow of *William*, and Mother of *Richard* Earl of *Clare*, gave divers
547. Lands. *Hubert de Ria*, gave the Templers divers Revenues *in the same year* that Thomas *Archbishop of* Canterbury *out of anger and ill will departed from the King at* Northampton; So runs the Date of the Deed. *Robert de Everyngham* gave the Templers the Mannor of *Ronstone*,&c. and *Gilbert de Gressy* gave them, there, two Quarentenes or Furlongs of Heath (*bruerae*) and Pasture for five hundred Sheep, this Preceptory was call'd *Temple*
548. *Bruer*. *Simon de Montefort* Earl of *Leicester* gave the Templers large Pos-
550. sessions near *Leicester*. *William de Erlegh* had given *Rucklande* to be a Monastery of Canons, but they having misbehaved themselves and forfeited their Estate there, King *Henry* the II. about the year 1180. gave their House and Estate thereto belonging, to the Prior of St. *John* of *Jerusalem*, for the Habitation of certain Sisters of that Order, conditioning that this should be the only House in *England* for such Sisters. *Robert de Ros* and
551. abundance of the greatest Lords of this Kingdom were Benefactors to these Knights. But above all they held themselves so far obliged to *Roger de Moubray*, that the Templers granted to the said *Roger* and his Heirs, that if at any time they should happen to find any Brother of the said Order put to publick Penance for any Fault or Offence against his Rule, yet the said *Roger* or his Heirs should have power to release him from his said Penance, without any contradiction. And the Hospitallers granted *An.* 1330. to *John* Lord *Moubray* and his Heirs for ever, that in case he or they come at any time in devotion to any of their Convents beyond the Seas, to be as honourably received and served as any under the Degree of
552. their King. King *Steven*, King *Henry* the II. King *John*, and King *Henry* the III. were great Benefactors to the Templers, the last of which granted them free Warren, Fairs and Markets, in many of their Mannors and
553. Towns. King *Richard* the I. had a special love for the Knights Hospitallers by reason he had received from the Master and Brothers of the Hospital many benefits for himself and followers, when in the holy Land. King *Richard* the I. granted to the Templers, and also to the Hospitallers, Markets and Fairs in divers of their Towns. King *Edward* the II. granted

all

all the Estate of the Templers to the Knights Hospitallers of *St. John*, by Act of Parliament in the seventeenth year of his Reign. King *Edw.* the III. King *Richard* the II. and King *Henry* the IV. were also very kind to these Knights of *St. John*, the last mention'd granted to these Knights to receive from his Wood of *Pederton* three Load (six Horses to a Load) of underwood weekly, *viz.* of *Thorne, Allez, Maple*, and *Hazel*, for the use and profit of the Prioress and Sisters of *Buckland*, and their Successors for ever.

Jeffrey de Say granted to the Knights Templers (*fratribus militiæ Templi Salomonis*) his Mannor of *West-Grenewiche*, &c. A fine was past 19 *H.* 3. between *Robert de Stanford* Master of the Warfare of the Temple in *England*, Plantiff, and *John de Curtenay* and *Emme* his Wife Deforciants (*impedientes*) of certain Lands in *East-Hyrst*. King *John* confirm'd to the Knights Templers the Island of *Lundy* lying in the Mouth of the *Severn*, first granted by his Father King *Henry* the II. In short, the foresaid King *Henry* the III. granted and confirm'd to the Templers in the eleventh year of his Reign, all Royal Liberties in all their Lands, exempting them and their men from Tolls, Taxes, &c. with all the Immunity that the Royal Power can grant (*cum omnibus Libertatibus & liberis consuetudinibus, quas regia potestas liberiores alicui domui Religionis conferre potest.*)

555.
557.
558.

In the Pontificate of Pope *Clement*, the Knights Templers being accused of hainous Crimes, he issued out his Commission to certain Cardinals to examine the Matter in *France*, before whom the Master and Preceptors of this Order for that Kingdom appeared, and being sworn, confest themselves guilty of the Crimes whereof they were accused, and shewing great signs of Repentance, were absolved. After which the same Pope sent out his Bull into *England* to commissionate the Archbishop of *Canterbury* and divers other Bishops to make the like enquiry in this Kingdom. *An. Dom.* 1309. The Articles exhibited against these Knights were principally these; That at their Reception into the Order they are caused by those who receive them, to deny Christ crucified, and sometimes God; That they affirm and teach that Christ is not true God; That they hope not to have Salvation through him; That they spit, and piss against the Cross and Image of Christ thereon, and tread it under foot; that they used to assemble together for that purpose on *Good Friday* it self; That they do not believe the Sacrament of the Altar, nor any other Sacraments of the Church; that they injoyn the Priests of their Order not to say the words of Consecration in the Canon of the Mass; That they affirm and believe that the Great Master of their Order can absolve them from their Sins, so their Visitor, and Preceptors, tho' Laymen; That they use several obscene and wicked actions at their admission (*deosculabantur in ano seu spina dorsi, aliquando in virgâ virili*); That they mutually commit the Sin of *Sodomy* with one another, and affirm it to be no Crime but lawful; that they adore Idols, especially in their great Chapters and Assemblies, as their God and Saviour; that such Admissions are therefore private, none suffer'd to be present but those of the same Order; that they are sworn not to reveal the manner of their Reception under pain of Death or Imprisonment; and that these things are reported by publick fame, common opinion, and also confest for the most part by many of their own Order in full Consistory before the Pope and Cardinals. The abovesaid Inquisitors sate upon these Matters in the Bishop of *London's* Hall in *Octob.* 1309. before whom divers Knights of this Order appearing, two of which being severally examin'd, discover'd the manner of their Reception into the

559.
560.

561.

562.

563.

564. the said Order, but not any thing appear'd to be criminal, absolutely denying that any are received in any other manner. The like Inquisitors sate at *York*, and tho' both at *London* and *York* they were accused of many things, yet nothing appear'd for which the Order deserved in Justice to be suppressed (*nihil inventum est quod de jure videretur statum illorum anullare*.) However they were all in one day seized on throughout *England*, and imprison'd. And in the Council of *Vienna, An. Dom.* 1312. the whole Order of the Templers was condemn'd and perpetually annull'd; with an Inhibition that none for the future should take that Order, Profession or Habit, under pain of the greater Excommunication. After which the Knights Hospitallers of St. *John* obtain'd most part of their Possessions: At this time *William* Archbishop of *York*, moved with Charity to consider the helpless condition of the Templers in his Diocess, placed them in several Monasteries in that County, and order'd them maintenance during Life. *Vid. inf.* 943. and *Vid. Vol.* 3. *p.* 62. 108.

[Valued at 2385 *l.* 12 *s.* 8 *d. per Annum.*]

565.
567.
568.
569.
570.

Thomas *Wolsey* Cardinal Priest of St. *Cicily*, and Archbishop of *York*, by Virtue of a Commission from Pope *Leo* X. *An. Dom* 1519. Composed certain Ordinances and Decrees for the better Government of the Canons Regular of St. *Augustin* in *England*: Consisting of these several Heads. Of the Union, and General Chapter of all the Canons Regular in *England*, to be once every three years. Of their admittance into the Order, and form of Profession. Of their Obedience, Poverty, Clausure, Habit and Tonsure; Of the Canonical Hours and Offices in the Church, and the manner of their Divine Service in their lesser Houses. Of their Dormitory, and Refectory. The Duty of Abbots and Priors; of Recreations, of the Accounts of the Houses, of forreign Affairs, of teaching Latin and sending their Students to the University of *Oxford*, and of the number of Canons in their Houses or Monasteries.

These Statutes to be publisht and observed in every House or Monastery of Canons Regular in *England*, by their several Abbots, &c.

A NVN OF Y^e ORDER OF St GILBERT.
Vol. 2 P. 669

A CANNON REGVLAR OF S.ᵗ SEPVLCHRE

Of the Canons of the Holy Sepulcher.

The Priory of the Holy Sepulcher *in the Suburbs of* **Warwick**. 573.

ANno Dom. 1109. Black Canons were first brought into *England*, and settled first at *Colchester*, then at *London*, &c. *Henry* Earl of *Warwick* erected the Priory of the Holy Sepulcher at *Warwick*. About that time the Christians had newly taken the Holy Land, and had instituted Canons in the Church of the Sepulcher at *Jerusalem*, which Canons wore the same Habit with other Canons Regular, without any distinction besides a double Cross of red in the Breast of their upper Garment. This House in *Warwick* was the first and Superiour of this Order in all *England*, *Wales, Scotland,* and *Ireland,* till the loss of *Jerusalem*, after which this Order decay'd almost to nothing, their Profits and Priviledges being transferr'd to the *Trinitarians.* *Simon* Bishop of *Worcester* dedicated their Altar, and Cimitery at *Warwick*, with express provision that the Parish-Churches of *All-Saints*, and St. *Maries*, should not suffer any diminution or detriment in their Tithes, Buryings, Oblations, Confessions, visiting the Sick, or any other accustomed Benefits to the said Churches belonging; and that these Canons should pay to the Parish or Mother Church of *All Saints*, an acknowledgment of 30 d. yearly at the Feast of all Saints.

[Valued at 41 *l.* 10 *s.* 2 *d. per Annum.*]

THETFORD, *in* **Norfolk**. 574.

BUilt and endow'd with Lands and Revenues by the old Earls of *Warren*, for Canons of the Holy Sepulcher. Who enjoy'd here large Liberties. *Hamelin* Earl of *Warren* base Brother of King *Henry* the II. granted to these Canons among other things, three Fairs, *viz.* One on the Invention of the Holy Cross in *May*, another on the Feast of the Holy Sepulcher, and the third on the Feast of the Exaltation of the Cross, &c. All which Grants of his Ancestors were confirm'd by *John* Earl of *Warren, An. Dom.* 1315. (8 *E.* 2.) 575.

[Valued at 39 *l.* 6 *s.* 8 *d. per Annum.*]

scended the noble Family of *Vesey*, whose Heirs General were married to *Muscamp*, and *Bolbek*.

[Valued at 189 *l.* 15 *s.* per *Annum*.]

BLIBURG, *in* Suffolk.   593.

KING *Richard* the I. recited and confirm'd to these Canons the several Lands and Rents given them by many Benefactors. The Founder and Patron of this Priory, was the Abbot of St. *Osiths*. 594.

[Valued at 48 *l.* 8 *s.* 10 *d.* per *Annum*.]

HEPPE, *in* Westmerland.

THIS Priory was first founded in honour of St. *Mary Magdalen* at *Preston*, by *Thomas* Son of *Gospatric*, and by him endow'd with divers Lands; among other things he gave the Canons here as much Wood as they would take out of his Woods, and to grind at his Mill toll-free. The said *Thomas* gave them also Pasture in and about *Swindale*, for sixty Cows, twenty Mares, five hundred Sheep, &c. With other Possessions in the Territory of the Town of *Heppe* where this Convent was new erected. Confirm'd by *Robert de Veteriponte*. 595.

[Valued at 154 *l.* 17 *s.* 7 *d.* ob. per *Annum*.]

TUPHOLME, *in* Lincolnshire.   596.

KING *Henry* the III. *An.* 20. Confirmed to the Abbot and Canons of St. *Mary* of *Tupholm*, the several Lands and Possessions given them by *Gilbert de Nevill*, and *Alan de Nevill* his Brother, and divers other Benefactors. The first Founder was *Robert de Nova Villa*, or *Nevill*, who held Lands of the King *in Capite* from the time of the Conquest, wherewith he endow'd this House. 597.

[Valued at 100 *l.* 14 *s.* 10 *d.* per *Annum*.]

WELLEBEC, *in* Nottinghamshire.

JOceus le Flemangh* came into *England* in the Conquerours Army and obtain'd from that King divers Lands in *Cukeney*, &c. In this Town lived on *Gamelbere*, an old Tenant *in Capite* before the Conquest, who held of the King two Carucates of Land, by the Service of shooing the Kings Palfrey on all four feet, with the Kings Nails (*de cluario Domini Regis*) as oft as the King should lie at his Mannour of *Maunsfeld*, and if he should lame (*si includet*) the Palfrey, then he should give the King another Palfrey of four marks price, this *Gamelbere* dying without issue the said Estate came by Escheat to King *Henry* I. who gave it [to] *Richard* Son of the said *Joceus*, and his heirs to hold by the same Service. This *Rickard* had issue by *Hawise* a Kinswoman of the Earl of *Ferrars [Thom]as*; who became the Founder of this Abby, where a Church of St [Jam]es 598.

599. was then erected, he also endow'd the same with Lands and Revenues augmented and confirm'd by his Descendents *Simon Fitz-Simon* and *Isabel* his Wife, *Walter de Faucumberge* and *Agnes* his Wife &c. *An. Dom.*
600. 1329. *Henry de Faucumberge* past the Mannour of, and all his Estate in *Cukeney*, with the Advowson of this Abby, to *John de Hothom* Bishop of *Ely*, who four days after conveyed all the premisses, except the Advowson
601. of the Abby, to the Abbot and Convent of St. *James* at *Welbeck*; and by another Deed dated 25 days after in the same year *John de Nottingham* then Abbot of this Abby, obliged himself and Successors to find eight Canons of his Abby for the daily celebration of the Divine Offices for the Souls in the said Deed mention'd and to celebrate the Anniversary of the said Bishop in like manner as of their first and principal Founder, &c. And to this also he and all the Canons of this House obliged themselves by Oath
602. before a publick Notary, &c. *Richard Basset* Knight gave to this Abby the Town of *Duckmanton*, which being held of the Barony of *Henry de Stutevill*, was by him confirm'd saving to him the Service of one Knights Fee. The other Lands, &c. belonging to this Abby in *Cukeney* and elsewhere, were all confirm'd by King *Henry* II.

[Valued at 249 *l.* 6 *s.* 3 *d.* per *Annum.*]

603. CROXTON, *in* Leicestershire.

William *Parcarius* Son of *Ingeram Parcarius* gave two parts of the Park of *Croxton* to this Priory; *Hugh* Brother of the said *William* confirm'd the said Gift, and gave other Lands, &c. towards the Building of the Church. Also he gave his whole Demeasne of *Croxton* to these Canons to hold in fee farm at the Rent of four marks *per Annum*.
604. *Margery de Sancto Albino* gave them the other third part of *Croxton* Park. *William* Earl of *Bolon*, and *John* Earl of *Morton*, Confirm'd their Estate at *Croxton*, and gave other Lands. The abovementioned *Ingeram Parcarius* was also call'd *Ingeram le Porter*, and came into *England* at the Con-
605. quest. King *Edward* I. *An.* 1. confirm'd to the Abbot and Canons of the Church of St. *John* the *Evangelist* and Apostle, at *Croxton*, otherwise call'd the Church of St. *John de Valle* all their Lands, and granted them free Chace at *Croxton*. *Vid. Vol.* 3. *p.* 73.

[Valued at 385 *l.* 10 *d.* ob. per *Annum.*]

606. LEYSTONE, *in* Suffolk.

Founded in the time of King *Henry* II. by *Radulphus de Glanville*, and by him endow'd with the Mannour of *Leystone*. The Advowson of this Abby coming to the Crown by the forfeiture of *Michael de la Pole* Earl of *Suffolk*, King *Richard* II. *An.* 12. confirm'd to the Abbot and Convent of this House their Estate, and granted them free Election of their Abbot, that in time of Vacation neither he nor his heirs nor any of his or their Officers would seize the Temporalities, nor intermeddle in the same, nor should any Abbot and Convent of this House be ever compell'd to grant any Corody or Pension to any Person. *Vid. Vol.* 3. *p.* 74.

[Valued at 181 *l.* 17 *s.* 1 *d.* per *Annum.*]

BEAUCHIEF, in Derbyshire. 907.

Robert Fitz-Ranulf Lord of *Alferton, Norton,* and *Marnham,* was one of those four Knights, who martyr'd the Blessed *Thomas* Arch-Bishop of *Canterbury,* in expiation of which Act he founded this Monastery of *Bello Capite,* or *Beauchef*; dedicated to St. *Thomas* the Martyr. *Thomas de Cadurcis* (or *Chaworth*) descended by an Heir General from the said *Robert,* gave divers Lands to this House, and confirm'd all the Gifts of his Ancestors. King *Edward* II. *An.* 9. recited and confirm'd the Lands, &c. given to the Abbot and Canons of this House, by their several Benefactors.

608.
609.
610.

[Valued at 126 l. 3 s. 4 d. *per Annum.*]

BLANCLAND, in Northumberland. 611.

Founded for twelve Canons of the Order of Premonstratenses by *Walter de Bolcbek,* and by him endow'd with divers Lands &c.

[Valued at 40 l. 9 d. *per Annum.*]

NEWBO, in Lincolnshire. 612.

Founded and endow'd with Lands and Churches by *Richard Malebisse.* Confirm'd by King *Henry* III. *An.* 9. Among other things the foresaid *Richard* gave the Canons of this House certain Lands in *Estwisell* held of *John de Lascy* Earl of *Lincoln* by Ward, Releif, and Scutage, &c. all which Services the said Earl afterwards released and quit claim'd to these Canons in pure and perpetual almes.

[Valued at 71 l. 8 s. 1 d. ob. *per Annum.*]

LAVINDENE, in Buckinghamshire. 613.

Founded by *John Bidun* and by him endow'd with divers Lands and Churches. *Ranulph* Earl of *Chester,* and *Ralf de Bray,* with divers others, were Benefactors, all whose gifts were confirm'd to the Canons of the Church of St. *John Baptist* at *Lavindene* by King *Henry* III. *An.* 11.

[Valued at 79 l. 13 s. 8 d. *per Annum*]

WENDLYNG, in Norfolk.

Founded and endow'd with Lands, &c. by *William de Wendlyng,* in free and perpetual Almes. Confirm'd by King *Edward* III. *An.* 6. And by *Robert de Stutevill, An.* 1273. (1. *Edward* I.)

[Valued at 55 l. 18 s. 4 d. *per Annum.*]

HAG.

(626.) **HAGNEBY**, *in* Lincolnſhire.

Founded in honour of St. *Thomas* the Martyr, Archbiſhop of *Canterbury*, by the Lady *Agnes de Orreby*, Wife of *Herbert de Orreby*, *An*. 22. *Henry* the II. *Richard* Biſhop of *Lincoln* (52 *H*. 3.) and *Philip de Kyme* (4 *E*. 1.) with divers others were Benefactors.

[Valued at 87 *l*. 11 *s*. 4 *d*. per *Annum*.]

STANLY *Park, commonly call'd* Dale, *in* Darbyſhire.

627. It is said that a certain Baker living in the Pariſh of St. *Mary* at *Derby*, a man very Religious and a great Alms-giver, was admoniſht in a Viſion to leave all that he had, and betake himſelf to a ſolitary Life in a Place call'd *Depedale*, which accordingly he did. This was a Deſert and Moorish place *Eaſt* from *Derby*, near *Stauley*. *Radulfus* Son of *Geremundus*, Lord of the place, accidentally diſcovering this Hermit in his poor Habitation, as he was hunting, and commiſerating his Condition, granted him the Soil where his Hermitage ſtood and alſo the Tith of his Mill of
628. *Burg*, for his maintenance. The Daughter of this *Radulfus* was married to *Serlo de Grendon* Lord of *Badeley*, to whom his Aunt and Godmother, call'd *The Gome of the Dale*, (*Gome* in old *Engliſh* ſignified a Godmother) gave *Depedale*. Theſe two aſſembled hither certain Canons from a Religious Houſe at *Kalke*, to whom they gave this Place, where they built a
629. ſumptious Church and Monaſtery, which obtain'd from *Rome* ample Priviledges. But theſe Canons becoming very relax in their Divine Offices, and more given to hunting, and the Pleaſures of the Forreſt, than to the Church and Prayer, for which being in danger to be removed, they by way of Prevention reſigned all they had here into the hands of their Patron, and return'd to the place from whence they came, except *Humfrey* their Prior who retired to a place call'd the *Magdalen*, and became a Hermit. But this Houſe became not hereby deſolate, but afterwards riſe to a greater degree of honour, (*Ludit in adverſis divina potentia rebus*) for after this there came hither ſix Canons of the Order of *Præmonſtratenſes* from *Tupholme*, invited by the Patron. But theſe alſo misbehaved themſelves, and were recall'd to *Tupholme*. Hereupon *William de Grendhon*, then Patron, procured five other Canons of the ſame Order from *Welbeck*.
630. Theſe alſo after ſome time return'd back, diſcouraged by exceſſive Poverty. At laſt *William* Son of the foreſaid *Radulf*, with his Daughter *Maud* married to *Jeffrey Sawcemere*, but childleſs, and the foreſaid *William de Grendon*, the Patron, his Siſters Son, joyn'd together in making a Fair and ſufficient Endowment of Lands to this Houſe, procuring nine Canons from *Newhouſe*, to whom they gave the Town and Park of *Stanley*, the
631. Dominion of *Depedale*, with other Lands in *Okebroke*, &c. All which with their other Poſſeſſions given by other Benefactors, were confirm'd to the Abbot and Canons of *Stanlegh* Park by King *Henry* the III. *Au*. 19.

Vid. Vol. 3. *p.* 72.

[Valued at 144 *l*. 12 *s*. per *Annum*.]

LANG-

LANGDONE, in Kent, a Cell to Leyſtone. (622.)

Founded by *William de Auberville*, and by him endow'd with the Town of *Langedone* and divers other Lands; confirm'd by *Simon de Albrinciis* his chief Lord, and *Nicholas de Cryoll* deſcended of the foreſaid *William* the Founder.

623.

WEST-DERHAM, in Norfolk. 624.

Founded by *Hubert* Dean of *York*, for the good of his own Soul, and the Souls of his Father and Mother, and of *Ranulph de Glanville* and *Bertra* his Wife who brought him up. He became afterwards Archbiſhop of *Canterbury*, and endow'd this Abby with many Lands, all which was confirm'd by King *John*, *An.* 1. who alſo granted to the Canons of this Houſe very great Liberties, and Immunities; as to be quit from all Tolls throughout the Kingdom, both for themſelves and their men, &c.

625.

[Valued at 228 *l.* ob. *per Annum.*]

BILEGH, alias Maldone, in Eſſex. 626.

The Canons of *Perendune* removed to *Maldon*, *An. Dom.* 1180. *Robert Mantell* was their Founder. King *Richard* the I. *An.* 1. confirm'd all their Lands and Revenues, with the grant of Liberties.

[Valued at 157 *l.* 16 *s.* 11 *d. per Annum.*]

SULBY, in Northamptonſhire. 627.

This Abby of St. *Mary de Welleford* afterwards call'd the Abby of *Suleby* was founded by *William de Wideville*. King *Richard* the I. granted theſe Canons divers Immunities. *Robert de Pavily* Knt. granted them his Mannor of *Suleby* to hold of the Abbot and Convent of *Weſtminſter*, being Lords of the Fee, at the yearly Rent of 102 *s.* and of him the ſaid *Robert* by the Payment of one pound of *Cummin*, (*Cimini*) or 2 *d.* at *Eaſter* yearly, for all Services and Demands. Divers other Benefactors gave other Lands in *Northamptonſhire* and elſewhere, among whom were *John de Lacy* Conſtable of *Cheſter*, *Ralph Baſſet*, &c. All confirm'd and recited by King *Edward* the II. *An.* 9.

629.

[Valued at 258 *l.* 8 *s.* 5 *d. per Annum.*]

COKERSAND, in Lancaſhire. 631.

Founded by *Theobald Walter*, Brother of *Hubert* Archbiſhop of *Canterbury*, for Canons of the *Premonſtratenſes*, to whom he gave in pure and perpetual Alms the *Hay* (or incloſed ground) call'd *Pyling* for the erecting of this Abby. Confirm'd by King *John*, *An.* 2. All which, with

632. with other Lands granted by *William de Lancaster, John de Lascy* Earl of
633. *Lincoln*, and Constable of *Chester*, and by *Jeffrey* Son of the Lord *John*, and others, were recited and confirm'd by King *Richard* the II. *An* 7. A Con-
634. test happening between the Prior of *Lancaster*, and the Abbot of *Cokersand*, about Tithes and other Rights of the Church, it was agreed and settled by Papal Authority, *An.* 1216. that the Prior should have two parts of the Corn Tithes in *Lancaster* and *Pulton*, and this Abbot one third part; also
635. that the Abbot of *Cokersand* shall not admit any of the Parishioners of the Prior of *Lancaster* to Sepulture at his Convent, without the Priors Li-
636. cense, &c. The Abbot and Convent of *Leicester* (*de pratis*) granted to the Canons of *Cokersand* the Scite of the Hospital of *Cokersand*, for the making of an Abby, which change from an Hospital to a Monastery, of *Premon-stratenses*, was made *An.* 1190.

BEGEHAM, in Sussex.

637. THIS Abby was first founded at *Hotteham*, by *Ralph de Dena*, and by him endow'd with Lands, &c. Translated from thence to *Bege-ham*, otherwise call'd *Benlin*, by *Ela de Saukvile* Daughter of the first Founder, whose Son *Jeffrey de Saukvile* confirm'd the Estate of these Ca-nons. Confirm'd also by *Gilbert de Aquila, Robert de Turnham, Walkelin*
638. *Maminot*, and *Richard* Earl of *Clare* and *Hereford* were also Benefactors,
639. all whose Gifts were confirm'd by King *John*. King *Henry* the III. *An.* 35.
640. granted to these Canons a weekly Market on the *Thursday*, at their Man-
642. nor of *Rokeland*, and a Fair there for three days at *Midsomer*. Which with their other Possessions, was confirm'd by King *Edward* the II. *An.* 6.
Vid. Vol. 3. *p.* 77.

BARLINGS, in Lincolnshire.

643. FOunded by *Ralph de Haye* with the Consent of *Richard Haye* his Bro-ther, confirm'd by King *Henry* the II. and King *John*, *An.* 16. The
644. *Bardolfs*, and *Longspes* were Benefactors.
645.

BRODHOLME, in Nottinghamshire.

646. KING *Edward* the II. *An.* 12. recited and confirm'd the several Lands and Possessions given to the Brothers and Sisters of *Brodholme*, by divers Benefactors; among whom, *Ralph de Albaniaco, Walter de Clif-
647. ford* and *Agnes* his *Wife*, &c.

[Valued at 16 *l.* 5 *s.* 2 *d.* per *Annum.*]

COVER-

COVERHAM, in Yorkshire.

THIS Monastery was first founded at *Swayneby*, An. Dom. 1190 by *Helewisia* Daughter and Heir of *Ranulf de Glanvilla* a Baron, and Capital Justice of *England*, in the time of King *Henry* the II. and *Richard* the I. It was afterwards translated from *Swayneby* to *Coverham* near *Midleham*, by *Ralph Fitz-Robert* descended from the said *Helewisia*. The Lands, &c. given to this House by the Foundress and her Son *Walleran Fitz-Robert*, and *Ralph Fitz-Robert*, *Edric Neusum*, and others, were all confirm'd by King *Edward* the III. *An*. 22. Of this Family did descend two Sisters Co-heirs, *Mary* Lady of *Midlham*, married to *Ralph de Nevile*, and *Joan* married to *Robert de Faterstall*.

[Valued at 160 *l*. 18 *s*. 3 *d*. per Annum.]

St. AGATHA near Richmund, in Yorkshire.

FOunded by one *Roaldus* the Constable (possibly of *Richmond* Castle) *Roger de Moubray*, *Alan Bygot* and others were Benefactors, whose Grants were recited and confirm'd by King *Edw*. III. *An*. 3. *Richard le Scrope* of *Bolton*, by License of King *Rich*. II. granted to the Abbot and Convent of this House a yearly Rent of 150 *l*. for the Maintenance of ten Canons, over and above the common number then in the Monastery, and of two Secular Chaplains to celebrate for the said *Richard* and his Heirs, &c. and for the Maintenance of twenty two poor men in the said Abby. This *Richard le Scrope* had been the Kings Chancellour, and gave also to this Abby the Mannor of *Brompton* upon *Swale*, then valued at 10 *l*. 3 *s*. 4 *d*. per Annum.

[Valued at 111 *l*. 17 *s*. 11 *d*. per Annum.]

TORRE, in Devonshire.

THIS Church and Abby of St. *Saviours* of *Torre* was founded by *William Briwer*, and by him endow'd with many Lands and with the Church of *Torre*, &c. to hold in free, pure, and perpetual Alms. King *John* confirm'd to these Canons all their Possessions, with the Grant of large Franchises, and Immunities from Scutage, and all Gelds, and Tolls &c. for themselves and their men. From this *William Briwere* the Founder descended *Reginald de Mohun*, who in the thirty six of King *Henry* the III. had a grant from this Abbot and Convent of Liberty to erect a Chappel in his Court at *Thorre* for himself and proper Family, but not to baptize there, nor admit any of the Parishioners to any Ecclesiastical Rights, the said Abbot and Convent to receive one Moiety of all Oblations or Obventions arising in the said Chappel, &c.

[Valued at 396 *l*. 11 *d*. per Annum.]

HALES.

HALES-OWEN, in Shropshire.

655.

THE Mannor and Advowson of the Church of *Hales* was given by King *John*, *An.* 16. to *Peter de Rupibus* Bishop of *Winchester*, for the erecting of a Religious House, which was accordingly founded here by that Bishop, and by him endowed with this Estate. Confirm'd by King *Henry* the III. *Roger* Bishop of *Coventry* and *Litchfield*, *An.* 1248, appropriated the Church of *Waleshale* to this Abby, after the death of *Vin-*

656. *cent* then Rector of the said Church, saving out of the same a Vicaridge of thirteen Marks to be assigned to a Vicar, with all Obventions, &c. *An. Dom.* 1270. *Godfrey* Bishop of *Worcester* made a Settlement between the Abbot of *Hales*, and the Perpetual Vicar of the Parish Church there, the said Vicar to have and receive from the Abbot ten Marks yearly, a House with Out-Houses, Orchard, Garden, and the Vesture of the Church-yard: The Canons to find another Priest to be under the Vicar (*Presbiterm secundarium*) and to bear all ordinary and extraordinary Charges.

657. *John de Hamptone*, *Joan Botetourt*, and *John* her Son, gave divers Manners,
658. and Advowsons, to this Abby, conditioning for Chantrys. *Wolstan* Bishop of *Worcester* appropriated to this Abby the Church of *Clent* and Chappel of *Rouley*, reserving to the perpetual Vicar who hath the Cure of Souls there, a Revenue of 10 *l.* viz. a Messuage and Curtelage on the *South side* of the Church-yard, with Tith of Calves, Lambs, &c. and all small Tithes (except of the Monasteries proper Lands) Mortuaries; the Herbage and Trees of the Church-yard, and all the Altarage.

[Valued at 280 *l.* 13 *s.* 2 *d.* ob. per Annum.]

LANGLEY, in Norfolk.

659.

Founded by *Robert Fitz-Roger*, and endow'd with Lands, &c. All which were confirm'd to these Canons by King *John*, *An.* 1. with the grant of large Liberties, and Immunities from all Tolls and Taxes.

Valued at 104 *l.* 16 *s.* 5 *d.* ob. per Annum.

TITCHFIELD, in Hampshire.

660.

KING *Henry* the III. *An.* 16. granted his Mannor of *Tichefeud* to *Peter de Rupibus* Bishop of *Winchester*, to found an Abby of *Premonstratenses*, and further granted to the said Abby very great Liberties in the said Mannor and their other Lands, with very great Immunities, and to be free and discharged from Tolls, &c. and from

661. suit to any Forrest Courts, and from the expeditating or lawing of Dogs, and this not only for themselves, but all their Men dwelling on their Lands. Other Benefactors to this Abby were *Eua de*
662. *Clinton*, *Reginald de Albamara*, *Baldwin de Ripariis* Lord of the Isle,
663. *Gilbert le Mansel*, *Peter de Sukemund*, who gave certain Land in *Ingepenne* to hold of the Chief Lord of the Fee by the Service of half

half a Knights Fee, and of himself and his Heirs by one pair of Spurs, or 3 *d.* at the Feast of St. *Michael*, &c. All whose Gifts were confirm'd to this House by King *Edward* the II. *An.* 11. An Inventory of the Goods of this Monastery was taken, *Anno Dom.* 1420. before *John Powle* Abbot of *Hales-Owen*, Visitor of this Place, and it was then found that they had no Monies in their Treasury, but were 43 *l.* 4 *s.* in Debt; and the House ingaged in 62 *l.* 6. *d.* In the Sacristy, one Silver-Cup gilt for keeping the Sacrament, two great Chalices gilt, and twelve lesser ones, a great Silver Vessel full of Relicks, a great Silver Cross gilt with the Images of *Mary* and *John*, two Candlesticks Silver and gilt, &c. In the Treasury many pieces of Plate, some of great size, &c. In divers Mannors belonging to this Church four and thirty Horses, ten Mares, four Foals, one hundred and fifty four Oxen, seven Bulls, nine and fifty Cows, &c. three hundred eighty and one Muttons, one hundred Lambs, &c. seventeen Boars, twenty four Sows, thirty three Hogs, one hundred and twenty six lesser Swine, and eighty nine Pigs.

664.
665.
666.

[Valued at the Suppression at 249 *l.* 16 *s.* 1 *d.* *per Annum.*]

Of the Order of St. Gilbert of Sempringham.

669. The Life of this St. *Gilbert* is writ very largely, out of which I shall here observe only the most Remarkable Passages, as breifly as may be. He was born at *Sempringham* in *Lincolnshire* his Fathers name was *Jocelinus*, of *Norman* Extraction, but having large Possessions in this County. In his youth he was sent into *France* for the Improvement of
670. his Learning. At his return to the place of his Nativity, he instructed the Country Children, Boys and Girls, in the Rudiments of Learning and the Methods of a Religious Life. And the Churches of *Sempringham* and *Tirington* being void, his Father Presented him Parson of the
671. same. After this he became a Domestick Clerk in the Family of *Alex-*
672. *ander* Bishop of *Lincoln*, by whom he was made Priest. All this while he was of such Exemplary Piety that he became of great note for Sanctity of
673. life. Worldly Honours and Riches he despised, and refused to be an Archdeacon in the Church of *Lincoln*, which was offered him with considera-
674. ble Advantages. This was in the Reign of King *Henry* I. At which time he begun his Order after this Manner; Seven young Virgins, who voluntarily left the World, shut themselves up in a solitary Habitation adjoyning to the North wall of the Church of St. *Andrew* at *Sempringham*, and submitted to his Government and direction in Spirituals. Their Apartment had but one Door kept Lockt, Their Diet and Releif they received in at a Win-
675. dow. For the Assistance of these he appointed certain Lay Sisters, and for the outward Service of the House certain Lay Brothers. From this Be-
676. ginning this Order encreased to many Monasteries, built, endow'd, and
677. encouraged by the great Men of this Kingdom. Pope *Eugenius* gave him the headship or Government of this Order. To assist him in his Office of Superspection be Collected Clerks who might take part of the Care of the Government of his Nunneries off of him, and this was the Original of the Canons of this Order. These Canons were to live in a
678. Separate habitation, and never to have any access to that of the Nuns, unless for the administration of some Sacrament, and that before many Witnesses, but the same Church to serve for both. Yet had they two Rules; the Nuns that of St. *Benedict*, the Canons that of St. *Augustin*, with some
681. pecial Orders. St. *Gilbert* tho' Cheif of this Order yet lived with as much hardship in fasting, Watching, and all other Austerities as the meanest of
682. them all. He abstain'd wholly from flesh, unless in Sickness, and from
684. Fish also in Lent and Advent. In the Reign of King *Henry* II. he fell into great Troubles by reason of his siding with *Thomas* Archbishop of *Canterbury* and his releiving him with monies when he fled into *France*,
685. but at length he was freed from them, and set at Liberty. After this he
686. had new Afflictions from the malicious Scandals of some lay Brothers of his own Order, but his patience brought him out of these Troubles also, and his Innocency and merit was certified by almost all the Bishops of
687. *England*, and by King *Henry* II. himself. In his old Age he was depriv-
ed

ved of his fight, but the vigor of his mind remain'd as perfect as ever, with all the vertuous faculties of his Soul not in the least decay'd. Observing still the same, or greater austerities in the Course and Discipline of living. The day he spent in, either hearing somthing read, or in Prayer, or spiritual Discourses; he heard nothing with patience but what related to God and a good life, and himself spoke little, and that only what was holy and useful. He lived to be above one hundred years of age, and dyed *An. Dom.* 1189. and was buried at *Sempringham*, four days after his death, in the Presence of all the Priors and Prioresses of this Order, several other Abbots and Noble persons, and people of all qualities above two thousand. Many Miracles are said to be wrought through his intercession, after this. An enquiry into the truth of which Reports was made at *Sempringham, An.* 1201. before certain Commissioners appointed by *Hubert* Archbishop of *Canterbury*, and again after that, by Papal Authority. The Consequence of which was the Canonization of St. *Gilbert* and the Inserting his name into the Catalogue of Saints, *An. Dom.* 1202. in the Papacy of Innocent III.

688.
690.
691.
693.
694.
696.

The Institutions made by the blessed *Gilbert* and his Successors for the Government of this Order of *Sempringham*, are very large and consist of Divers general Chapters, or Heads, and those divided into many Subdivisions. I shall take Notice only of the Principal Titles, And refer to the Book at large for particulars.

The first Treats of the Rise and beginning of the Order, and of the Election of the Master, &c. 669.
Of the Principal Examiners or Searchers (*Scrutatoribus*) their Constitution, and Authority, &c. 705.
Of the four Procurators in each House of this Order, &c. 711.
Of the Canons and Novices, and their Age, and of the Lay Canons, &c. 717.
Of the Brothers, their Institution, Apparel, and Duties, &c. 739.
Of the Nuns, and such matters as relate to them and their Houses. 755.
Of the Lay Sisters, their Apparel and manner of Life. 771.
Of the Sick and Infirm Nuns and Sisters, how to be treated. 775.
Of the Office of the Dead, and Funeral Matters, &c. 779.
Of some Rules relating equally to the Nuns and Sisters. 783.
Of the Unity and friendship between all the Houses of this Order. 785.
Of the Grand Chapter of the Order to be held yearly. In the end of this last Chapter; the Founder of the Order Provides that in the Several Houses of the Men the Number shall not exceed 394 in all; and in those of the Women the number of Nuns and Sisters together shall not exceed 960. 787. 788.

This order was first Instituted in *England* in the Reign of King *Steven, An. Dom.* 1148. by Master *John Gilbert* of *Semplingham*; *William* Bishop of *Norwich* writ a very high Commendation of this *Gilbert*, and of all the Religious of his Order, by way Testimonial, to Pope *Alexander* III. 789. 790.

The

The Priory of Sempringham, in Lincolnshire.

791.
792.
Founded by *Gilbert de Gaunt*, and by him and others endow'd with divers Lands in *Lincolnshire*. *John Dalderby* Bishop of *Lincoln* by his Deed dated at *Buchden*, *An. Dom.* 1303. granted License to the Schollers of the Convent of *Sempringham*, Studying Divinity or Philosophy, in St. *Peter's* Parish in *Stamford*, to have a Chaplain to celebrate in their private Chappel there, saving the Rights of the Parish-Church of St. *Peter* there. *Robert Lutterel*, Rector of *Irnham*, gave for the maintenance of the said Schollers so studdying at *Stamford* as aforesaid, the House where they inhabited, with divers Lands and Tenements in *Keten*, *Cotismore*, and *Casterton*, in *Rutland*.

Vid. Vol. 3. p. 107.

[Valued at 317 *l.* 4 *s.* 1 *d. per Annum.*]

HAVERHOLME, in Lincolnshire.

Founded by *Alexander* Bishop of *Lincoln*, and by him endowed with the Isle then called *Hasreholm*. *An. Dom.* 1139.

[Valued at 70 *l.* 15 *s.* 10 *d.* ob. *per Annum.*]

CHIKESAND, in Bedfordshire.

793.
794.
*P*Aganus *de Bellocampo* and *Rohaisa* his Wife gave many Lands to this House. King *Edward* the II. in the tenth year of his Reign granted his License to *John Blundel* to give the Mannor of *Chikesonde* with its appurtenances to the Prior and Convent of this House.

[Valued at 212 *l.* 3 *s.* 5 *d.* ob. *per Annum.*]

BOLINGTON, in Lincolnshire.

795.
Founded by *Simon Fitz-William* in his Park of *Bolyngton*, and by him endowed with part of his said Park, and divers other Lands in pure and perpetual Alms. *William de Kima* confirm'd to the Prior and Convent of both Sexes at *Bolyngton*; all their Lands and Revenues, *A. D.* 1256. *Robert Putrel* of *Cotes* being received into the Fraternity of this House, gave them at the same time the Church of *Houtun* and Advowson of the same. The *Crevequers*, or *Creukers*, Barons of *Redburn*, were Benefactors to this Priory, giving divers Lands in pure and perpetual Alms.

[Valued at 158 *l.* 7 *s.* 11 *d. per Annum.*]

A CANNON REGVLAR OF St GILBERT

WATTON, in Yorkshire.

Founded by *Euſtachius* Son of *John* and *Agnes* his Wife, for Nuns, and thirteen Canons to ſerve and provide for them, according to the Inſtitution of the Order of *Sempringham*. To whom he gave the Town of *Watton*, &c. Confirm'd by *William Foſſard* Lord of the Fee, and by *Henry* Archbiſhop of *York*. Confirm'd alſo by *Roger de Laſci* Conſtable of *Cheſter* deſcended from the ſaid *Euſtachius*. King *John* alſo gave them Lands in the firſt year of his Reign. *Euſtachius* the Founder married for his firſt Wife a Daughter and Heir of *Ivo de Veſcy*, from which match deſcended ſeveral of the *Veſcys*; and for his ſecond Wife *Agnes* Daughter of *William* Conſtable of *Cheſter*.

[Valued at 360 *l*. 16 *s*. 10 *d*. ob. per Annum.]

ALVINGHAM, in Lincolnshire.

Peter *de Melſa* and *Beatrix* his Wife gave to the Church of St. *Mary* of *Alvingham*, and to the Nuns and Brethren there, divers Lands and Revenues in *Alvingham* and elſewhere, confirm'd by *John* their Son, *An. Dom.* 1232. *Henry* Biſhop of *Lincoln* certified to the Treaſurer and Barons of the Exchequer, *An. Dom.* 1401, the names of all the Churches that were appropriated to the Order of *Gilbertines*. Pope *Innocent* the III. confirm'd the Lands and Poſſeſſions of this Order, &c.

[Valued at 128 *l*. 14 *s*. 2 *d*. per Annum.]

St. ANDREWS, in the Suburbs of York.

Founded at *Fiſhergate* at *York*, by *Hugh Murdac*, and by him endow'd with Lands, Tenements, and Rents in and about *York*. A. D. 1202, an exchange of certain Revenues was made by mutual conſent between *Simon* then Dean, and the Chapter of St. *Peter's* at *York*; and *Roger* then Prior of this Houſe, and *Hugh Murdac*.

[Valued at 47 *l*. 14 *s*. 3 *d*. ob. per Annum.]

STIKESWOULD, in Lincolnshire.

It was found by Inquiſition taken at *Stanford* 3 *E*. 1. That the Maſter and Nuns of *Stikeſwald* held divers Lands at *Huntington*, of the Gift of ſeveral Benefactors.

[Valued at 114 *l*. 5 *s*. 2 *d*. ob. per Annum.]

ORMESBY, in Lincolnshire.

Founded and endowed with Lands by *Gilbert* Son of *Robert de Ormesby*.

SIX

810. SIXILL, in Lincolnshire.

Founded by one —— de Grelle Ancestor of *Thomas de la Warre*. *Agnes de Percy* and others were Benefactors.

[Valued at 135 *l.* 9 *d.* per Annum.]

811. MARESEY, in Lincolnshire.

Founded and endowed by *Isabell de Chauncy* Widow of Sir *Philip de Chauncy*.

[Valued at 130 *l.* 13 *s.* ob. per Annum.]

Newsted at ANCOLM, in Lincolnshire.

813. Founded and endow'd, with the grant of very great Liberties and Immunities, by King *Henry* the II. Confirm'd by King *Edward* the II. An *suo*. 13. Divers Lands and Revenues were given to the Nuns of the Order of *Semplingham*, by *Peter* Son of *Henry de Bilingey*, whose Cousin and Heiress became the Wife of *William Mason*.

[Valued at 38 *l.* 13 *s.* 5 *d.* per Annum.]

814. KATTELEY, in Lincolnshire.

Peter Son of *Peter de Belyngey* confirm'd to the Nuns of *Catlei* and their Brethren Clerks and Laics, divers Lands in *Bilingey* and *Walcot*, given by his Ancestors.

St. CATHERINES, in the Suburbs of Lincoln

Founded by *Robert* the second, Bishop of *Lincoln*, with the assent of his Chapter, and endowed with the Prebend of *Canewich*, and with the Church of *Newerc*, and divers Lands and Revenues at *Newerc*, &c. Confirm'd by King *Henry* the II.

[Valued at 202 *l.* 5 *s.* ob. per Annum.]

815. HEYNINGS, in Lincolnshire.

Founded by *Reynerus de Evermu*, and by him, and *Odo de Sanctâ Cruce*, endowed with Lands. Confirm'd by King *Henry* the III. An. *suo* 52.

[Valued at 49 *l.* 5 *s.* 2 *d.* per Annum.]

HOL-

HOLLAND BRIGG, in Lincolnshire.

Founded by one *Godwin* a Rich man of *Lincoln*; and named the Priory of St. *Saviour*.

MALTON, in Yorkshire.

816.

Founded for Canons of this Order of *Semplingham*, by *Eustachius* Son of *John*. Which said *Eustachius*, and *William de Vesci* his Son, conferr'd on these Canons many Lands and Churches, so did the *Flamvills*, &c. from the *Vescies* descended *Gilbert de Aton*, who became Patron of this Priory, and died, *An. Dom.* 1307. The Lands of this Priory were confirm'd to these Canons by King *John*. *An. Dom.* 1200. *William Laceles*, &nt. granted to these Canons two Bovates of Land in old *Malton*, in lieu of certain Tithes by them granted to the Church of *Soureby*.

817.
818.
819.

820.

[Valued at 197 *l.* 19 *s.* 2 *d. per Annum*.]

SHOULDHAM, in Norfolk.

Founded by *Galfridus* Son of *Peter*, Earl of *Essex*, for Nuns and their Brethren, Clerks and Laicks, and by him endow'd with the Mannor of *Shouldham*, and many other Lands and Churches. After which Foundation he removed the Body of his Wife *Beatrix de Saÿ*, who died in Child-birth and had been buried at *Chikesand*, to this Priory.

821.

[Valued at 138 *l.* 18 *s.* 1 *d. per Annum*.]

ELLERTON, in Yorkshire.

Founded by *William* Son of *Peter*, who gave all his Inheritance in *Ellerton* for the making a Priory of Canons of the Order of *Sempingam*, and for the Habitation, and Maintenance of thirteen poor Men. *An. Dom.* 1387. *German de Hay* then Patron of this Priory, obtain'd a grant from the Prior and Convent of this House by Indenture, that whereas the said *German* had then but the presentation of one poor man of the thirteen that were to be maintain'd in this Priory, for the future the said *German* his Heirs and Assigns Lords of the Mannor of *Aghton*, shall present nine of the thirteen, with the Penalty of 10 *l.* for every refusal to admit any poor man so presented. *Vid. Vol.* 3. *p.* 103.

822.
823.

824.

[Valued at 62 *l.* 8 *s.* 10 *d. per Annum*.]

825. **OVETON** in Hertnes, *in the Bishoprick of* Durham.

FOunded and endow'd with divers Lands in *Oveton* and elsewhere by *Alan de Wiltone.* For Canons of the Order of *Semplingham.* Confirm'd by King *John, An. suo,* 5.

[Valued at 11 *l.* 2 *s.* 8 *d. per Annum.*]

826. **WELLS,** *in* Lincolnshire.

FOunded by *Jeffrey de Hauvill,* for Canons. To whom he gave all his Lands and Tenements, &c. in *Wells,* saving to him and his Heirs Pasture of sixty Cattle to feed with the Cattle of the Canons, saving also the Annual Rent of 5 *s.* to be paid to him and his Heirs. Confirm'd by King *John, An. Reg.* 5.

[Valued at 95 *l.* 6 *s.* 1 *d. per Annum.*]

827. **PULTON,** *in* Wiltshire.

FOunded in the Reign of King *Edward* the III. by Sir *Thomas de Sancto Mauro,* Knt. and by him endow'd with the Mannor of *Polton* then valued at 10 *l. per Annum,* the Mannor of *Chelesworth* then valued at 5 *l. per Annum,* with other Lands, King *Edward* the III. *An. suo* 28. granted to the Canons here very large Liberties and Immunities.

Of the Order of the Holy Trinity, *for the Redemption of Captives.*

The RULES *of the Monks of the* Holy Trinity *were approved by Pope* Innocent III. *and were,* 830.

THat they should live in Chastity and without property, That all their Revenue, or what comes to their hands lawfully shall be divided into three parts; with two parts of which they shall supply their own Necessaries, the third part shall be laid by for the Redemption of Christian Captives, taken by Pagans, either by purchasing their freedom for a Sum of Mony, or by purchasing Pagan Captives in order to exchange them for Christians.

That all Churches of this Order shall be intituled of the holy Trinity, and be of plain work.

That the Brethren cohabit together, three Clerks, and three Laymen, besides their cheif, who shall be call'd their *Minister.*

Their Garments to be of woollen Cloath, and white. They may wear Cloaks and Breeches, but must put them off when they lie down. They shall lie in Woollen, and not on feather Beds in their own Houses, unless in time of Sickness.

They may not ride on Horses, but on Asses they may.

They may drink Wine, provided it be with Temperance.

From the *Ides of September* to *Easter* they shall fast on the *Monday, Wednesday, Friday,* and *Saturday* (unless some solemn festival happen) so also in *Lent* and other accustomed times of the Church.

Flesh they may eat if given them from abroad, or of their proper feeding, but that only on *Sundays* from *Easter* to *Advent*, and from *Christmas* to *Septuagessima*; and on *Christmasday, Epiphany, Ascention,* the Assumption, and Purification of the Blessed *Mary*, and Feast of *all Saints*. They shall buy nothing for their own Dyet, but Bread, Beans, Pease, Herbs, Oyle, Eggs, Milk, Cheese, and Fruit; but no Flesh, nor Fish, nor Wine, unless for the necessities of the Sick, and on Jorneys, *&c.*

In Towns where they have Houses of their own they shall not eat, nor drink out of the same, unless Water, tho' invited; nor lye out of their own Houses. The Infirm shall lye and eat by themselves: Strangers especially Religious men, that come to their Houses shall be kindly entertain'd according to the ability of the House. No Brother either Clerk or Lay but shall labour in some Office or other. They shall observe silence in the Church, Refectory, and Dortour, unless upon necessary Occasions, A Chapter shall be held every *Sunday* if possible, in which they shall consider of the affairs of the House, and then also an

Exhortation shall be made in a plain manner to all the Brethren and others of the House, instructing them in their duty of what they are to beleive and practice. If any Brother give Scandal, or strike another he shall be punisht at the will of the *Minister*, more or less. A General Chapter shall be held once a year, and that in the *Octaves of Pentecost*. The *Minister* shall be Elected by the Common Council of the Brethren, not for the dignity of his Birth but the Merits of his person. The *Minister* is either greater or Lesser; The Greater may hear the Confessions of all the Congregations of his Order; the Lesser only of his own House. If any desire to enter into this Order he shall first undergo a years Probation, or more if there be occasion, and none shall be received under the age of twenty years.

None shall swear an Oath unless upon great Necessity by License of the *Minister*, or by command of the Bishops, and for an honest and just cause.

THELESFORD, in Warwickshire.

831.

This House, dedicated to God, St. *John Baptist*, and St. *Radegund* the Virgin, was founded by *William* Son of *Walter de Cherlecote*, for the Releif of the Poor, and for the Receit of Travellers, or Pilgrims and Religious Men there serving God; he endow'd it with several Revenues in *Cherlecote*. Other Benefactors were *Fulk* Son of *William de Lucy*; *William de Narford* Lord of *Bereford*, who among other things granted to the *Minister* and Friers of this House free Fishing in his Water of *Avon*, on all days but *Sundays*, with other great Liberties and Priviledges; and *William de Bello Campo* Earl of *Warwick*. All whose gifts and Grants King *Edward* III. in the third year of his Reign, confirmed to *Thomas de Offinton* at that time *Minister*, and the Friers of this House, and their Successors, to hold free and quit of all Secular demands and Exactions, whose Deed bears date at *Kenylworth*.

832.

833.

[Valued at 23 *l*. 10 *s*. per *Annum*.]

MOTTIDEN, in Kent.

This House of Friers of the holy Cross, was first founded by Sir *Robert de Rokesley* Knight; the Modern Patron was the Earl of *Northumberland*.

[Valued at 50 *l*. 13 *s*. ob. per *Annum*.]

INGHAM, in Norfolk.

William *Staferton* was the first Founder of this Priory, of later time *Francis Calthorp* became Patron.

[Valued at 61 *l*. 9 *s*. 7 *d*. ob. per *Annum*.]

KNARE-

A TRINITARIAN

Vol. 2. P. 871

KNARESBOROUGH, in Yorkshire.

King *John* gave certain Lands in *Swiniefco*, to Frier *Robert* a Hermit in this place, which his Son King *Henry* III. confirm'd to *Frier Ivo*, by the title of Hermit of the holy Cross of *Knaresburg*, in the twelfth year of his Reign.

Richard King of the *Romans* and Earl of *Cornwall*, Brother to King *Henry* III. gave to God and to the Brothers of the Holy Trinity of Captives at *Knaresburgh* the Chappel of St. *Robert* at *Knaresburgh*, and all the Land which King *John*, his Father gave to the said Saint *Robert* in his life time, with other Lands, and Commons of Pasture for twenty Cows, and three hundred Sheep, and Paunage for forty Hogs, &c. Whose Deed bears date at *London, An. Dom.* 1257. All which was afterward confirm'd by King *Edward* I. and King *Edward* II.

834.

[Valued at 35 *l*. 10 *s*. 11 *d*. per Annum.]

Additions to the First Volum of the Monasticon Anglicanum.

837.

Pag. 18. GLASTONBURY.

842.

Divers other Grants of Lands, Revenues, Liberties, &c. were made to this Monastery by several Kings and Bishops in the times of the *Saxons*, &c. King *Etheldred, An.* 987; granted to the Abbot and Monks here certain Lands to hold and possess, *quamdiu fides in Anglorum catholicâ premanserit plebe.* So long as the Catholick Faith shall remain among the People of *England*; or, while the People, there, shall remain Catholicks.

844.

Pag. 31. ROCHESTER.

In the year 1197. *Hubert* Archbishop of *Canterbury*, exchanged the Mannor and Church of *Darent* to the Monks of St. *Andrew* at *Rochester*, for the Mannor and Church of *Lammedhe* (*Lambeth*) with all the Appurtenances thereto belonging, as well in the said Mannor as in *Suwerc* (*Southwark.*) And this was by the assent of King *Richard* the I. and *Gilbert* then Bishop of *Rochester*.

845.

Pag. 49. DURHAM.

846.

KING *William* the Conqueror commanded the men of *Carlile*, and those Parts, that they should receive Christianity of the Bishop of *Durham* and his Archdeacon. *Nigellus de Albeney* a great Favourite to King *Henry* the I. spoil'd the Monastery of *Durham* of two Mannors, but being afterwards very sick and weak, repented and restored them. *Hugh* Bishop of *Durham* was highly favour'd by King *Richard* the I. who made him Earl of *Northumberland*, and committed the Government of the Realm to his care during his absence in his Voyage to the *Holy Land*, but afterwards falling into the King's displeasure he was devested of the Earldom of *Northumberland* before his death, which happen'd in the year 1194. *Anthony Beek* elected Bishop of *Durham* in the year 1283. was a man of so great Authority, that he usually had in his retinue one hundred and forty Knights. He had a grant of the Isle of *Man* for life; he was a great Builder; he died, *An:* 1310. and was the first Bishop that was buried in the Church of *Durham*.

Pag.

Pag. 62. WESTMINSTER.

IN the year 1556. Cardinal *Pole*, then Archbishop of *Canterbury* and *Legat de Latere*, upon the Petition of the Dean and Chapter of St. *Peter's* at *Westminster*, granted them License to give and surrender all and singular their Goods, moveable and immoveable, Actions, and Rights, whatsoever, to their Church, or to them in right of their Church, belonging, to King *Philip* and Queen *Mary*, that with the same they might endow the Abbot and Convent of the said Church in perpetual Alms, and restore it to the condition of a Monastery as formerly. Which License was dated at his Mannor of *Croydon*, 17th. *Kal. October*, in the second year of the Pontificate of Pope *Paul* the IV. (which was 3, 4. *P.* and *M.*)

Pag. 143. BARDNEY.

THE Monastery of St. *Peter* and St. *Oswald* at *Bardney* was re-edified and made an Abby by *Gilbert de Gant*, whose Off-spring confirm'd and augmented the Lands and Endowments of the same. From the said *Gilbert de Gaunt*, who came into *England* with the Conqueror, descended the Earls of *Lincoln* of that name. *Hugh* Bishop of *Lincoln* recited and confirm'd the several Donations made to this Monastery.

Pag. 152. EVESHAM.

THE first and principal Founder of this Monastery was King *Ethelred* Son of *Penda* King of *Mercia*. Which King *Ethelred* after he had reigned thirty years, relinquisht his Kingdom, and became a Monk at *Bardney*. Of later years several of the name of *Bushell* were Benefactors to this House.

Pag. 169. CROWLAND.

Angtoft was given to this House, *An.* 819. And the Mannor and Church of *Baston, An.* 825. the first by *Fregistus*, the other by *Algarus*, two Knights.

Pag. 176. DEREHAM.

Saint *Wythburga* the Virgin was Daughter of *Anna* (King of the *East-Angels*) and devoted to a Monastick Life. She caused this Monastery to be built at *Derham*, in which she lived a Nun; this House was at first so poor, that upon her earnest Prayer, the Nuns here were supported by a kind of miracle, two Does or Hinds, being used to come daily to be milked at a certain place for a long time, till the Chief man or Bayly of the Town envying, hunted them away with Hounds, but suffer'd God's Judgment for his malice and broke his neck in hunting. St. *Wythburg* died and

and was buried in the Church-yard at *Derham*; and five and fifty years after her Body was found uncorrupted, and tranflated thence into the Church, *An.* 798. But in the year 974. it was tranflated from *Durham*, to *Ely*.

Pag. 191. WINCHCUMBE.

855. *ANno* 1175. Pope *Alexander* the III. recited and confirm'd the Lands and Poffeffions of this Houfe, and by the fame Bull granted the Abbot and Monks here divers Priviledges, *viz.* that they might prefent Priefts of their own Election to the Bifhop to be inftituted in the Churches belonging to their Monaftery, which Priefts were to anfwer to the Bifhop for the Cure, and to the Monaftery for the Temporalties of the place; that no one fhould exact Tithes of them for their Lands or Cattle, in their own hands or Occupation; that they might have free Sepulture for thofe who defired to be buried with them, faving the Rights and Dues of the Parifh Churches: that they might cellebrate Divine Offices in time of a general Interdict, with a low Voice, and Doors fhut, &c. That Chrifme and holy Oyl, Confecration of their Church, Ordination of their Monks and Clerks to Sacred Orders, fhould be received from none but their Diocefan Bifhop, if he be Catholick and in the Communion of the Apoftolick See, and if he will do his Office freely and willingly, otherwife

856. they might repair for thefe matters to any other Bifhop. *An.* 1404. *Richard* Bifhop of *Worcefter* confirm'd the Appropriation of their Churches. *An.* 5. *R.* 1. *Robert* the IV. was chofen Abbot of this Houfe; he ordain'd, that on every Morrow of All Souls (*Novemb.* 3.) yearly, one hundred poor People fhould be relieved, here, with Bread, Drink, and Meat. 30 *H.* 3. *John Tamworth* was chofen Abbot on the death of *Henry*. 9 *E.* 2. *Richard Tdeburi* was chofen Abbot on the death of

857. *Thomas*. 4 *E.* 3. *Robert de Ippewell* then Abbot did freely and of his own accord, *Abdicate* the faid Office, and *Walter Winfort* was chofen to fucceed him.

Pag. 191. WILTON.

Wulftan Earl of *Ellendin* was the firft Founder of the Chantry at *Wilton* (which is the fame with *Ellendin*.) King *Egbert* founded the Priory, at the requeft of *Elburga* his Sifter and Widow of the forefaid Earl *Wulftan*, *An.* 773. In which fhe became a Nun with twelve others. But the firft Founder of the Abby or Monaftery of St. *Edith* in *Wilton* was King *Alrud*, who gave all his Mannor and Liberties at *Wilton* to the

858. Nuns, in perpetual Alms. King *Athelftan* was a great Benefactor,
859. *An.* 933, and 937. So was King *Edgar*, *An.* 968, &c.

Pag. 193: AMBRESBURY.

THE Nuns here, being about thirty in number, were for their notorious scandal and naughty Life, removed from hence, and placed in other Monasteries, and other Nuns brought from *Font Ebrald* in *France* and eſtabliſht here; to whom King *Henry* the II. upon their firſt eſtabliſhment, gave divers Lands; all which, with other Revenues given by other Benefactors were confirm'd to the ſaid Nuns of *Font Ebrald* by King *John*, in the ſecond year of his Reign.

Pag. 242: RAMSEY.

IN the year 1100. ſeveral Great men of this Kingdom raiſed a War againſt King *Henry* the I. who were forced to fly into *Normandy*; *Guiſcard de Lymoſin*, Lord *Molyns* appeared there on the King's behalf, and proſecuted the War againſt them, for which ſervice he was highly favoured by the King who brought him with him over into *England*, and gave him Caſtles, Lands, and Honours. This *Norman* Lord built that part of *Ramſey* Monaſtery which was call'd *Norman's* iſle. And from him deſcend the Lords *Molins*. *Roger* a younger Son of this Family was *Caſtellan* of *Nottingham*, and call'd himſelf *Roger de Leumeſin* (anglicè *Waterhouſe*.)

Pag. 253. CHATERIDGE.

THIS Nunnery and Church were all burnt down by a caſual fire in the time of *Robert Orford* (who was Biſhop of *Ely, An.* 1302.) whereupon the ſaid Biſhop wrote to the Biſhop of *London* ſetting forth the diſtreſt Condition of the Abbeſs and Nuns here, in order to have them excuſed from the Payment of Tenths in conſideration of their great Loſs.

Pag. 276. BURTON.

NIgellus Abbot of *Burton* with the Conſent of the Chapter there, gave to one *Orme* their Land at *Acoure*, under condition that he pay yearly twenty pieces of old Coyn, each worth 16 *d*. (xx. *oras*) and thereupon the ſaid *Orme* became the Abbot's man, and ſwore fealty, and that when dead his Body ſhould be brought (*cum totâ pecuniâ ſuâ*) to be buried at *Burton* Abby; after which his Son was to appear in their Chapter-houſe, to pay his Relief, to take ſuch Oath, to make ſuch Payments, and to hold as his Father had done. By other Deeds this Tenure was ſpecified to be by the Payment of two Marks yearly at *Martlemaſs*, to go with the Abbot to *London* when he goes thither on the Affairs of this Houſe, at the Abbot's Charge, and come to his Court, if ſummon'd, to judge Felons.

871.

Pag. 310. SPALDING.

THIS Monastery was given in the time of *William* the Conqueror to the Abby of St. *Nicholas* at *Angiers*, by one *Ivo Talboys*, and became a Cell to that Abby. But it being found highly inconvenient to the good of this House that the Prior and other principal Officers here should come from beyond Sea, and be removeable at the pleasure of the Abbot of *Angiers*, they carrying away with them what they could get from this place; after many contests it was agreed that the Prior of this House should be instituted by the Diocesan, and be immoveable; and that the Abbot of St. *Nicholas* at *Angiers* should not have to do with any of the Temporalities of this House, but only receive an annual Rent of 40 *l*. and the Board and Maintenance of four Monks.

872.

Pag. 352. MERKYATE.

ANno 1145. *Radulph*, Dean of St. *Paul's* in *London*, and the Chapter of that Church, granted to *Christina*, and the Nuns of the Monastery of the holy Trinity of the Wood near *Merkyate*, the Ground where the said Monastery is situated, reserving a yearly Payment of 3 *s*. as a Ground Rent, and Fealty. *Alexander* Bishop of *Lincoln* consecrated the Nuns Church here in the abovesaid year 1145.

873.

Pag. 356. TUTBURY.

WIlliam Earl of *Ferrars* granted to the Monks of St. *Mary* of *Tutbury*, the Tithes of all his Forrest of *Duffeld*, viz. of Paunage, of hunting of Honey, and of Money (*i. e.* Rents.) *William* Prior, and the Convent, of

874. *Tutbury*, granted to *William Fitz-Herbert* and to his Heirs, *Norbury* in Fee, at the yearly Rent of 100 *s*. and if he be summon'd, to assist or be present at the Pleas and Affairs of the Church of *Tutbury*, with Relief, and other

875. Services to the said Prior and Convent. Afterwards by Deed dated 30 *H.* 6. *Nicholas Fitz=Herbert*, Esq; and *Ralph Fitz-Herbert* his Son and Heir apparent, set forth that whereas they had demised to *Thomas Gedney* Prior of *Tutbury* certain Lands at *Osmondstone* in *Com. Derby*, for four years; in consideration that the Prior and Convent had by their Deed under seal releas'd to the said *Nicholas* and his Heirs all their Right and Claim of a Rent of 5 *l*. per Annum, and other Services issuing out of the Mannor of *Norbury* in the said County, they the said *Nicholas* and *Ralph* did release to the said Prior, and Convent, and their Successors for ever all their Right and Claim to and in the Lands demised as abovesaid, with Warranty.

876.

Pag. 367. MALVERN.

THE Priory of Great *Malvern* was before the Conquest a Hermitage founded by one *Urso d'Abytot*; afterwards a certain Abbot of *Westminster*, with the Assent of the said *Urso*, did place here a Prior and Monks, and gave them three Mannors; others gave other Lands, all which were confirm'd by King *Henry* the I. *Pag.*

Pag. 370. *St.* NEOTS.

TEdbald de Eschalers gave Lands to the Monks here, whose Deed 877. concludes —— *Et quoniam ego Sigillum non habui, petitione meâ Dominus meus Stephanus hanc donationem meam sub Sigillo suo confirmavit.* Other Benefactors to this House were *Roger de Clare* Earl of *Hertford*, *William de Albiney Brito*, and *Peter de Montefort*, which last by his Deed dated at *Preston*, *An.* 1245. gave and confirm'd to the Monks here divers Lands in *Wenge* (*Com. Rut.*) with the Advowson of the Church there.

Pag. 439. COLNE.

SEveral Countesses of *Oxford* were Benefactors to the Monks here. *Roger Bigot* Earl of *Norfolk* gave them the Church of *Dovercourt* and 878. Chappel of *Herewich*.

Pag. 479. BLAKEBERGH. 879.

TO the Nuns of this House divers of the Family of *Scales* were great Benefactors. *Emma de Bellofago* Widow, gave to the Nuns of 880. *Blakebergh* four hundred Eels out of her Fishery at *Wilton, per Annum*, at the beginning of *Lent*, in pure and perpetual Alms.

Pag. 489. STANFORD.

TO the Nuns of *St. Michaels* in *Stanford* were given by several Benefactors, the Church of *St. Clement's* in *Stanford*, the Church of *All-Saints* in *Stamford*, the Church of *St. Andrew* in *Stamford* then (1170) held by *Peter* the Dean, who was to enjoy it during his Life. Also the 881. Church of *St. Martin* at *Stamford*, of which last mention'd Church it was certified by *Oliver* Bishop of *Lincoln*, *An.* 1289. that the Vicarage of the said Church did consist in the whole Altarage of the same, the Vicar paying yearly to the said Nuns two Marks, that the Nuns should be at the Charge of supplying the Chappel of *Burgele* in the said Parish, that the Vicar should pay the Sinodals only, but the Nuns the Archdeacons Procurations, and all other Charges. They had also given them the Church of *Corby* and Chappel of *Upton*. *William* Earl of *Waren* granted them a Rent 882. of 40 *s. per Annum*, for their Kitchin.

Pag. 496. DENNY. 883.

RObert the Chamberlain Earl of *Richmond*, gave divers Lands to the Monks here, exhorting and commanding his Children to do more for the advantage of this Church, and cursing any one of his Heirs who shall take away any thing that he hath given. These Monks were first founded

founded in an Isle call'd *Elmeney*, but for the inconveniences of that Scituation, translated to a higher Ground, in the Isle of *Denney*, by *Albericus Picot*.

Pag. 528. GODSTOW.

884.
885.

Among other Benefactors to this House were *Osbert Fitz-Hugh*, who gave a Salt-pit in *Wiche*. So did *Walter de Clifford* for the health of his Soul, and of *Margaret* his Wife, and *Rosamund* his Daughter, whose Bodies were buried in this Nunnery; dedicated to St. *Mary* and St. *John Baptist*.

Pag. 529. COLCHESTER.

886.

Hugh Abbot and the Convent of Monks of St. *John Baptist* of *Colchester*, granted and quit-claim'd the Church of *Hecham* to the Nuns of *Lillechircke* in *Kent*, in exchange for *Duniland*; this exchange was confirm'd by King *Steven*, and also by *Walter* Bishop of *Rochester*, who with the consent of *Amphelisa* then Prioress of *Lilchurch* establisht a Settlement for the Vicar of the said Church. Pope *Alexander* granted an Indulgence of forty days to all those who should contribute to the new building of the Church of St. *Mary* of *Hegham* (the same with *Lilchurch*.)

Pag. 534. KYNGTON.

887.
888.
889.

Among other Benefactors, *Roger de Mortuomari* gave to the Nuns of St. *Mary* of *Kyngton*, in pure and perpetual Alms, the whole Tith of his House, of Bread, and Ale, (*de pane & allece*). *Roger de Villiers* gave them the second Tithes (*secundas decimas*) of the Corn of all his Demeines, and the Tithes of his meat or flesh Provision, not bought in, (*decimas Carnis meæ non emptæ.*) *Robert Burnell* Bishop of *Bath* and *Wells* gave them the Advowson of the Church of *Kyngton*, belonging to that See.

Pag. 544. HOLAND.

THE Colledge here dedicated to St. *Thomas* the Martyr, was at first founded for Secular Canons, but in the year 1318: it was by the Patron Sir *Robert de Holland* Knt. translated into a Priory of *Benedictine* Monks: Upon the death of whose Prior the Monks were to choose three; out of whom he was to elect one to be by him presented to the *Diocesan* to be Prior.

COLCHESTER, in Essex.

890.

ON the South side of *Colchester* is a small hill, on the North side of which was of old time the habitation of one *Siricus* a Priest, and a Church composed of Boards and dedicated to St. *John the Evangelist*, wherein in the night time was often seen wonderful light, and musick heard praising God, no body being then in the place. This Church being famed for this and the like miraculous adventures, and being also of a delicious Scituation, *Eudo* the Kings *Major Domo*, or Steward; to whom King *William Rufus* had given the Custody of the City of *Colchester*, erected here a Monastery of which he lay'd the first Stone, *An. Dom.* 1097. Which being finisht some Monks were brought hither from *Rochester*.

891.

But they not being endow'd here, according to their own mind, return'd to *Rochester*. After this *Eudo* received other thirteen Monks from the Abbot of *York*; these began upon a New Foundation, which prosper'd so well that in a short time, one of the thirteen was chosen Abbot, and Consecrated by *Maurice* Bishop of *London*, About the year 1104. Their number increased to above twenty, who all lived very regularly. The founder *Eudo* dyed in *Normandy*, and deviled his Body to be buried in the Abby

892.

of his foundation at *Colchester*, which was accordingly done, the Monks meeting it a Mile from the Monastery, *An.* 1120. This *Eudo* endow'd this Monastery with several Mannours, Tithes, and Churches, among

893.

others with the Church of St. *Mary* in the *Westcheping*, Call'd the *Newchereh*, and his Stone House near the same, also the Church of St. *Steven Walebroch*, in *London*. King *Henry* II. released the Tax of *Danegeld*, &c. in the Lands of these Monks.

SNAPES in Essex. *A Cell to* Colchester.

894.

WIlliam Martell, being Seised of the Mannour of *Snapes* enjoy'd Wreck of the Sea from *Thorp* to *Hereford Nesse*, and gave this Mannour to the Abby of *Colchester* for the founding of a Priory here, which Priory was founded accordingly and made a Cell to that Abby, *An.* 1155. This Priory paid half a mark yearly to *Colchester* as a Pension of acknowledgment. Twice a year the Abbot of *Colchester* was to Visit here, with twelve Horses, and abide here four days.

St. HELENS in Bishopsgatestreet, London.

ALardus Dean of St. *Pauls London*, and the Chapter of that Church, granted License to *William* Son of *William* the Goldsmith, Patron of the Church of St. *Helen*, to constitute Nuns in the said Church, and erect a College there, endowing them with the Advowson of the said Church; The Prioress to be, upon election, presented to the *Dean* and

895.

Chapter of *Pauls*, and to swear fealty to them, and to pay them a Pension of half a mark yearly at *Easter*, &c. In the year 1439. *Raynold Kentwode* Dean of *Pauls* made other Constitutions for the Government of this Nunnery; some of which were, *That Divine Service be by them duly perform'd night and day*; *That no secular person be locked within the Bounds of the Cloy-*

ster

896. ...ster, nor come within it after the Complin Bell, except Women Servants, and maid Children; that none of the Sisters receive Letters from, or speak with any secular Person without License of the Prioress, and some other Nun to be present; That they grant no Corody or Pension without License of the said Dean and Chapter, that no Dancing or Reveling be used in the House except at Christmass, and then among themselves and in the absence of Secular persons; That there be a Door made to the Nuns Quire that no Strangers may look on them, nor they on the Strangers when They be at Divine service; That no Nun have any Key to the Postern Door that goes out of the Cloyster into the Churchyard, but the Prioress, &c. These Orders were to be Read publickly in their Chappel four times a year, and kept and observed under the pain of Excomunication.

[Valued at 314 l. 2 s. 6 d. per Annum.]

CATESBY, in Northamptonshire.

897. King *Henry* III. in the fifty seventh year of his Raign, recited and confirm'd to the Nuns of *Kateby*, the Church of the blessed *Mary* of *Kateby* with the Chappel of *Helidene*, with the Church and divers Lands in great *Esseby*, and several other Revenues given them by divers Benefactors. Confirm'd also by the Bull of Pope *Gregory* the VIII.

[Valued at 132 l. 1 s. 11 d. per Annum.]

St. MARY, de Pratis, adjoyning to Derby.

898. King *Henry* II. granted and confirm'd to the Nuns of St. *Mary de Pratis* near *Darby* among other things, twenty seven acres of Land in his Forrest of the *Peak*, with large Commons in the said Forrest; King *Henry* III. granted them 100 s. per Annum. to be received from the Baylies of the Town of *Nottingham* out of the Farm of the said Town.

[Valued at 18 l. 6 s. 2 d. per Annum.]

GRIMSBY, in Lincolnshire.

The Church, and all the Monastery of Nuns here, being of the Kings Foundation and Patronage, together with all their goods and Movables and all their Writings and Evidences concerning their Lands and Estate in *Lincolnshire* and *Yorkshire*, being burnt and consumed by a casual fire, King *Henry* IV. in the seventh year of his Reign, confirm'd to this Prioress and Convent all their Grants, &c. made as well by his Progenitors as others.

NEWTON, in Yorkshire.

King *Edward* II. in the fifteen year of his Reign granted his Licence To his well beloved Cousin *Thomas Wake* to give one Messuage with the appurtenances in the Town of *Newtone* for the erection of a Religious House

House of what order he pleased, and to endow it with Lands in *Neuton* and *Cottingham*, &c. *Vid. Vol.* 3. *p.* 88.

BROMHALE 899.

Henry *de Lacy* Earl of *Lincoln* and *Margaret* his Wife, did release and quit claim to the Nuns of *Bromhale* one hundred acres of Land in their Waft of *Afferige* with the Appurtenances.

Pag. 551. LEUESHAM, in Kent. 890.

King *Alured*, and his Son King *Edward* the Elder, gave, and King *Edward* the Confessor confirm'd, to the Abby of St. *Peters* at *Gant*, the Mannour of *Luesham*, with all its appurtenences, *viz.* Greenwic, Wullewic, Modingham, and *Cumbe*, with other Lands and great Liberties and Franchises, as large as the King himself had in the said Lands, &c. Dated *An. Dom.* 1044.

Pag. 551. St. MICHAELS MOUNT, in Cornwal. (901.)

Richard King of the Romans, *Edmund* Earl of *Cornwal*, and *Conan* 902. Duke of *Britany*, were Benefactors to this House. Pope *Adrian* in the year 1155. confirm'd to the Abbot and Monks of this House, by the 903. name of the Monastery of St. *Michael de periculo maris*, all their Lands and Revenues, lying most in *Normandy*, and also in *England*.

Pag. 558. BERGAVENNY. 904.

Henry *de Bellocampo* confirm'd to the Monks of *Bergavenny* all those Possessions which his Ancestors, *Hamelinus de Balon*, and others, Lords of *Bergavenny*, had given them, and further gave and confirm'd to the said Monks divers other Revenues.

Pag. 595. GOLDCLIVE.

Robert *de Candos* founded the Priory at *Goldclive* in *Wales*, being then Lord of *Karlyon*; The Patronage of which House came afterwards to *William* Earl of *Gloucester*, and after that to *Richard* Duke of *Tork*.
905.

CARESBROKE in the Ile of Wight.

William *Fitz Osbern* was *Mareshal* to *William* the I. and Conquer'd the *Ile* of *Wight* at such time as the other Conquer'd *England*; King *William* made him Earl of *Hereford*. The Estate of this *William* descended to *Baldwin* Earl of *Exeter* who granted all the Churches and Tithes

Tithes of this *Hand* to the Abby of St. *Mary* of *Lira*. King *Henry* II. recited and confirm'd the several Possessions given to those Monks as well in *France*, as *England*, and *Wales*.

Pag. 614. WENDLOCK.

907.

William *de Boterell* and *Isabella de Say* his Wife, gave the Church of St. *George* of *Clune* to the Monks of St. *Milburge* at *Wendloke*.

Pag. 614. DUDLEY.

908.

The Church and Monastery of St. *James* at *Dudley* was founded and endow'd by *Gervaise Paganel*, or *Painel*, who granted that in whatsoever Pastures his own Cattle fed, there also the Cattel of the Monks of *Dudley*, might freely feed, except in his Parks; with tithe of his Bread, hunting, and fishing, while he remains at *Dudley*. An. 1290, *Roger* Bishop of *Coventry* and *Litchfield* granted a Remission of forty days penance to those who being truly contrite and confest, should say the Lords Prayer and Salutation of the Blessed Virgin, for the Soul of *Roger de Somery* buried in the Conventual Church of *Dudley*, and for the Souls of all the Faithful deceas'd.

Pag. 619. LEWIS.

To this House did belong divers Lands, Churches and Tithes in *Devonshire*, *Sussex*, *Surrey*, *Kent*, and *Norfolk*, the several Names of which, and of the Benefactors who gave them may be seen in the Book at large.

Pag. 636. BROMHOLME.

909.

King *Edward* II. granted to the Monks here the Mannour of *Blaketon* to hold in fee farm at the yearly Rent of twenty pound, which Mannour did formerly belong to *Edmund* Earl of *Kent*.

Pag. 668. MONTEACUTE.

This Monastery was founded by *William* Earl of *Moriton*, near the Castle of *Monteacute* for Monks of *Cluny*; and to it he gave the *Burgh*, and Castle of *Montacute*, and the Chappel in the Castle, together with many other Mannours, Lands, Churches, Tiths, Fairs and Hundreds.

Pag.

VOL. II. *Additions to the First Volum.* 241

Pag. 687. TICKFORD.

GErvasius Paganell gave and confirm'd to the Monks of the Church of the blessed Mary at Newport, divers Lands and Revenues given them by his Ancestors, and by other men which held of his Fee, An. 1187. These Monks of Newport (the same with Tickford) were here as a Cell to St. Martins call'd Majus Monasterium, or Marmonstier, in France.

Pag. 704. WAVERLEY.

POpe Eugenius the III. by his Bull dated at Paris, An. 1147. granted to the Monks of this House and their Successors, inter alia, that no Tithes should be by any exacted of them for their Lands or Cattel in their own hands or occupation.

Pag. 768. CUMBERMERE.

BAldwin and Hubert successive Archbishops of Canterbury confirm'd to these Monks and their Successors several Churches and Chappels to them given, among the rest, that of Namptwitche.

Pag. 782. BILDWAS.

FOunded by Roger Bishop of Coventry. Hugh Bishop of Coventry gave these Monks an Inn in Litchfield for their Reception when they came thither. William Fitz-Alan gave them the Town of Little Bildewas, with other Lands. Henry Abbot of this House granted to Hamon de Benthale, in consideration that his Mother was burden'd with many Children, and at her instance, a certain Allowance and stipen'd in this Monastery for Term of his Life, which afterwards, 11 E. 2. in consideration of a Sum of Money in hand paid to him, by John then Abbot, the said Hamon did Release and Quit-claim. An. 1287, Henry de Lacy Earl of Lincoln and Constable of Chester confirm'd an exchange made between the Monks of this House, and those of Crokesden, viz. of Caldon-Grange in Com. Stafford (being of his Fee) for certain Lands in Edwyneye in Com. Salop.

Pag. 802. NEWMINSTER.

THE first and principal Founder of this Abby was the Lord Ralph de Merley, from whom descended two Sisters who became Co-heirs to the Barony of Merley; Mary, married to William Baron of Graystok, and Isabella, married to the Lord Robert de Somervill; all whose descendants were great Benefactors to this House, so also were the Bertrams Barons de Mitford, with divers others. Ralph Baron of Graystok who died, An. 1483. was also Baron of Wemme. George Dacre Lord of Gillesland and Graystok died young and untimely, by the accidental fall of a Wooden Vaulting-Horse, An. 1569. he being then in Wardship with the Duke of Norfolk.

Pag. 866. DORE.

ROger de *Clifford* gave his Body to God and the blessed *Mary*, and the Monks of *Dore*, to be buried in the Church of *Dore*, and with his body he gave them certain Land, *nomine Dotis*.

Pag. 885. BLANCLAND

PAganus de *Cadurcis* Son and Heir of the Lady *Hawifia de London*, gave to the *Cistercian* Monks of *Albaland* nineteen Acres of arable Land, that every Priest of the said House should daily in the Canon of the Mass make special commemoration for the Souls of such and such of his Family, *pro vivis inter Vivos, & pro defunctis inter mortuos.* Whose Deed bears date *An.* 1270.

919.

Pag. 892. DEULACRES.

ROger de *Menilwarin* gave to the Monks of this House, for the Health of the Soul of *Ranulph* Earl of *Chester* and *Lincoln*, his Mothers Brother, in pure and perpetual Alms, free Common in his Wood of *Pevere*, House-bote and Hay-bote, with Paunage for fifty Hogs.

Pag. 893. CLUNOCK-VAUR.

FOunded and endow'd by one *Gwithno.* King *Cadwalader*, and divers *Welch* Lords gave large Possessions to this Abby, dedicated to God and St. *Beyno*.

920.

Pag. 916. ROBERTSBRIG.

ALice Countess of *Eu*, Daughter of *William* Earl of *Arundell* and of Queen *Alizia*, gave Lands to this Abby in pure and perpetual Alms, *ad hospitalitatem sustentandam*, for the maintenance of Hospitality. Which Lands were confirm'd to them by *William* the third Earl of *Sussex* her Brothers Son, and by *John de Augo* her Son.

921.

Pag. 926. BEAULIEU.

KING *John* gave out of his Treasury one hundred Mark for the building this Abby in *Newforest*, and directed his Letters to all Abbots of the *Cistercian* Order, to be helpful to the re-edifying of the same out of their several Stocks.

Pag.

Pag. 936. VALE-ROYAL.

PRince *Edward* Son of King *Henry* the III. being in great danger of drowning at Sea, as he return'd from the Holy Land, vow'd in case he and his came safe to Land, to erect a new Monastery in honour of God's blessed Mother *Mary*, in some proper place in *England*, and endow the same with sufficient maintenance for one hundred *Cistercian* Monks. Which Monastery being afterwards built and by him named *Vale Royal*, a Convent was translated thither from the Abby of *Dore*. In the year 1277, the said *Edward* being then King of *England*, laid the first Stone of a new Building in the place design'd for the great Altar, and after his example, all the prime Nobility of the Land did the like in honour of our Lord Christ, the Virgin *Mary*, and the Holy Confessors St. *Nicholas*, and *Nichasius*. Their first Habitation was but small, yet there they remain'd for the time of four Abbots, till in the year 1330. the Convent was translated to a new Monastery, on the Feast of the Assumption of the Blessed Virgin. The place where this Monastery was situated was before call'd *Munechene wro*, in Latin *Monachorum silua*, *Munchene* in old *English* signifying a Monk or Nun, and *Wro* a Wood. 'Tis said that many years before this Monastery was founded, in that place, Shepherds and Country People did usually on the Solemn Feasts of the Virgin, about Midnight hear Cœlestial Musick, and see such wonderful brightness as seem'd to turn the night into day. The Royal Founder brought with him from the Holy Land a piece of our Saviour's Cross, which he gave to this Monastery. Queen *Elianor* his Wife was a bountiful Benefactress, so that not only at all Masses here, but at all Canonical hours the Monks of this House did use a special Collect for this King and Queen, and at Grace aftermeat, the President did use to say, *Animæ Regis Edwardi, Reginæ Alianoræ, & omnium fidelium defunctorum per misericordiam dei requiescant in pace*, to which they all answer'd, *Amen*. At the Solemn Consecration, and Benediction of this House by the Patriarch of *Jerusalem*, *Anthony Beck* Bishop of *Durham*, with several other Bishops, a Sentence of the greater Excommunication was solemnly denounced against any one who should enter into this Monastery any other ways than by the Gates of the same. The first Abbot of *Vale-Royal* was *John Chaumpneys*, 2. *Walter de Hereford*, 3. *John de Oo*, or *Hoo*, this man was so highly favour'd by the King, that he often bid him ask what he would and he would grant it, who thereupon desired the King to give him leave to resign his Office, which tho' the King was by no means willing to grant, yet at last he obtain'd after much importunity. He was a very meek and compassionate man; always considering and bearing in mind this Distich, ———

Peccantes dampnare cave, nam labimur omnes;
Aut sumus, aut fuimus, aut possumus esse quod hic est.

The fourth Abbot was *Richard de Ewesham*, a holy Man, reported to have done Miracles. Great Sums of Mony were allow'd by the King for the Building of the new Work of this Abby, and in the Parliament at *Acton-Burnel* (11 E.1.) the Abbot of *Vale-Royal* was ordered to receive yearly for the carrying on the said Work one thousand pound, partly out of the *Wardrobe* and partly out of the Profits of the County of *Chester*. It appear'd by by the Accounts of the Kings Treasurer that he paid for the new Work of the *Vale-Royal*, in all, thirty two thousand pounds sterling.

MARHAM, in Norfolk.

Isabella *de Albany* Countess of *Arundel*, Daughter of *William* Earl of *Warren*, and Widow of *Hugh* Earl of *Arundel*, founded and endow'd this House for *Cistercian* Nuns. This Nunnery was incorporated *An.* 1252.

Pag. 966. KINGSTON *upon* Hull.

930.

KING *Edward* the III. in the one and fiftieth year of his Reign, reciting that he had granted License to *William de la Pole Sen.* to found and endow an Hospital of Chaplains and poor People at *Kingston* upon *Hull*, and that the said *William* was afterwards minded to change the said Hospital into a Nunnery, granted his License to *Michael de la Pole* Son and Heir of the said *William*, to establish there instead of the said Nuns, thirteen *Carthusian* Monks, thirteen poor Men, and thirteen poor Women, and to endow them with twenty Acres, and 20 *l.* Rent held of the King, and with other Revenues not held of the King to the value of two hundred Marks *per Annum*.

931.

The Abby *de* Loco Dei.

William *Longspee* Earl of *Salisbury*, by his Will dated, *An.* 1255. gave to the building and establishing of this House for *Carthusians*, besides Land, and Church Utinsils, one thousand Ewes, three hundred Muttons, forty nine Oxen, and twenty Bulls, &c.

Additions to the Second Volum.

Pag. 49. HAGHMON.

KING *Henry* the II. at the defire of *Alured* Abbot of *Haghmon*, granted the Cuftody of that Abby, in times of Vacation, to *William Fitz-Alan* and his Heirs. *An.* 3. *H.* 5. *Ralph* then Abbot of this Houfe and his Convent, at the inftance of *Thomas* Earl of *Arundel* and *Surrey*, granted to *Robert Lee* one Corrody for his Life, he being with the faid Abbot as his Squire with a Boy and two Horfes, to have Meat and Drink for himfelf, Boy, and Horfes, as others of the Abbots Squires for the times paft ufed to have, during fuch time as the faid *Robert* fhall pleafe to abide in the faid Monaftery, fo alfo for Apparel. In the Reign of *Henry* the VI. *Thomas Holden* Efq; granted to the Prior of the holy *Trinity* at *London* and his Succeffors, in behalf of the whole Order of Canons Regular, one Meffuage and Garden, in the Parifh of St. *Peter*, and St. *Michael*, near the North Gate in *Oxford* for a Colledge for thofe of that Order to ftudy in. *Richard* Bifhop of *Coventry* granted to this Monaftery of *Haghmon* that the *Sacriftan* under the Abbot, might baptize as well *Jews*, as Children, in the Monaftery, and might ufe parochial Rights within the fame. *Nicholas* Abbot of this Houfe, in the year 1332. allotted certain Revenues for the maintenance of the Kitchin, and for twenty Hogs yearly for the Bacon of the Houfe, &c. *Richard Burnell* Abbot, in the year 1459. made certain Ordinances relating to the Offices of the Prior and Sub-prior, whereby he fettled their Precedencies. &c. Pope *Alexander* the III. granted to the Canons of this Houfe divers Priviledges; as not to pay Tithes of the Lands and Cattel of their own Poffeffion; to have a free Buryal-place, (*libera Sepultura*); to prefent Clerks to the Perochial Churches which they hold, who fhall account to the Houfe for the Profits; to celebrate the Divine Offices privately in the time of a general Interdict; to pay no Tithes of their Mills and Meadows, unlefs the ufage hath been otherwife, &c. Pope *Boneface* IX. granted Indulgences to thofe who fhould vifit this Church on certain days yearly, being truly penitent and confeft.

Pag. 56. WYRKSOPE

THIS Houfe was founded on the 3d. of *March*, in the third year of King *Henry*, third Son of *William* the Conqueror, by Sir *William Lovetot* who lies buried in this Church near the High Altar, from whom defcended by Heirs General the Lords *Furnival*, and the *Talbots* Earls of *Shrewsbury*.

Pag. 86. St. MARY-OVERIE, in Southwark

940. Richard Bishop of *Winchester* confirm'd to the Canons of St. *Mary* of *Suwerch*, the several Churches and Possessions given them by their Benefactors.

Pag. 143. RANTON

Hubert Archbishop of *Canterbury* confirm'd the Grants of *Robert Noel*, and *Thomas Noel* his Son, to the Canons of this House. By Composition between the Abbot of *Haghmon*, and the Prior of *Ronton*, it was agreed, that the Prior and Canons of *Ronton* should be call'd to the Election of the Abbot of *Haghmon* when it should happen; that the Abbot of *H*. should visit at *Ronton* once a year, or oftener if occasion be; that the Prior of *Ronton* may admit a Canon or Brother into his House at R. without the consent of the Abbot of *H*. first askt, so long as he makes his profession to the Abbot of *H*. and lastly that upon the Election of a Prior of *Ranton*, the Canons of *R*. shall elect one of the Canons of *Haghmon*, and one of their own House out of which two the Abbot of *H*. shall make choice of one to be the Prior at *R*. The Priory 941. of *Ronton* paid to the Abby of *Haghmon* a yearly Pension of 100 s. Vid. Vol. 3. P. 53.

Pag. 144. LILLESHULL.

This Church dedicated to St. *Alcmund* was in old time of high Veneration. *Ædelfleda*, Queen of *Mercia* is said to have founded it, but it was much enrich'd by King *Edgar*, who descended of the same Lineage with the said *Alcmund*. *Gilbert de Cumedore* indeavouring to defraud 942. these Canons of one of their Prebends, he was excommunicated, till at last he was prevaild with to restore the Prebend, and to do penance, receiving from every Canon of this Church a Publick Discipline and Correction. In the time of *Roger* Bishop of *Coventry*, and Pope *Eugenius*, the Secular Canons, or Prebendaries, were changed to Regular Canons, 943. *An. Dom.* 1405. the Canons of this House obtain'd of the Popes Nuntio in *England*, the Appropriation of the Parish-Church of *Hulme*; their Petition setting forth that they could make no advantage of their Rents and Possessions by reason of the Wars with *Wales*; and by reason of their situation on the High-way call'd *Watlingstreet*, they were impoverisht by the continual conflux of Guests and Travellers, who eat up their Provision, &c.

Pag.

Pag. 564. KNIGHTS TEMPLERS.

ANno Dom. 1319. *Walter* Archbishop of *Canterbury*, having received the Popes Bull directed to all Archbishops, and Bishops, setting forth that since the Suppression of this Order divers of the Knights had lived like Lay men, and married Wives contrary to their Vow, which was not discharg'd by the Council of *Vienna* at such time when it suppreſt the Order, he commanded therefore that the Brethren of that Order should be admonished that within the space of three Months they should enter themselves into some Religious House, there to live in God's service during their Lives, under pain of losing the Stipends which had been assign'd them at the Suppression of their Houses; in pursuance of this Bull the said *Walter* Archbishop of *Canterbury* directed his Letters to the Prior of *Christ-Church, London,* for the Reception of *Roger Stowe* a Priest of the Templers, into that Priory, which was accordingly perform'd. In the following year the same Pope sent his Bull to the said Archbishop of *Canterbury* whereby he order'd Excommunication against all those who should withhold any Lands, Houses, Churches, Revenues, or Goods moveable or immoveable formerly belonging to the Templers, from the Master and Brethren of the Order of St. *John* of *Jerusalem*, on whom the said Poſseſsions had been conferr'd, and united for ever, by Pope *Clement* the V. in the Council of *Vienna*.

944.

945.

Addi-

French *Monasteries*.

947.

948.

Robert Abbot of *Molesme* in *Burgundy* was the first Institutor of the *Cistercians* (a Reform of the Benedictines) to whom *Odo* Son of *Henry* Duke of *Burgundy* gave the place call'd *Cistertius* which gave name to the Order. This order encreased so fast that from the year 1098. to the year 1152. almost 500. Abbies were erected for them. Much about the same time that this Order of Cistercians began in the Diocess of *Chalons* in *Burgundy*, the Carthusians began their order in the Diocess of *Grenoble* : They observe their offices both by night and day according to the Rules of St. *Benedict*.

St. GEORGE *of* Bauquerville, *in* Normandy.

951.

952.

R*alf de Tancerville* gave divers Lands to this Abby, both in *Normandy* and *England*, confirm'd to them by *William* his Son, Chamberlain to King *Henry* II. among whose Lands in *England*, was *Edyweston* lying within the Bounds of the Forrest of *Rutland*; which Lands, King *Henry* II. granted License to these Monks to convert into tillage, and conferr'd divers Liberties on them.

BEC, *in* Normandy.

953.

954.

First founded in a Place call'd *Burneville*, by *Gilbert* Earl of *Brionne*, a great Souldier, and Nephew of *Richard* the first, Duke of *Normandy*, who at the age of forty years became a Monk here, Priest, and then Abbot of this Monastery. The habitation of these Monks was afterwards removed into a vally near a River call'd *Bec*. King *Henry* II. confirm'd their Lands and Possessions, several of which lay in *England*, at *Athelstone* in *Warwickshire*. *Islip* in *Oxfordshire* with divers others places in other Countries.

BELBEC, *in* Normandy.

955.

The Lands and Possessions of this House were confirm'd by King *John*, and after him by King *Henry* V. who also confirm'd to the Abbot and Convent of this House the grant formerly made to them by *Blanch* Queen of *France* of forty pound *Parisian* mony, *per Annum*, for the maintenance of one Mass there daily, and supporting some other Charges, for ever.

St.

St. STEVENS at Caen, in Normandy. 956.

Founded by King *William* (the Conqueror) King of *England*, and Prince of *Normandy* and *Main*, and by him largely endow'd with Lands both in *Normandy* and *England*. Several others of the Nobility of *Normandy* were Benefactors to this House, all whose gifts were confirm'd by King *Henry* I.

957.

The HOLY TRINITY, at Caen in Normandy. 958.

King *William* II. and King *Henry* I. gave to the Nuns of this Abby divers Lands and Liberties in *England*. Confirm'd by King *Edward* II. in his seventeenth year.

St. VIGOR at Cerify, in Normandy.

Founded in a Place then call'd *Ciriciac*, *An. Dom.* 1032. by *Robert* Earl of the *Normans*, who also endow'd this Abby with Possessions adjoyning round about it. *William* Duke of the *Normans*, Son of the Said *Robert*, gave many other Lands; The Like did others of Principal quality. Confirm'd by King *Henry* I. *An. Dom.* 1120.

959.
960.
961.

CORMEL, in Normandy. 962.

Pope *Alexander* III. by his Bull dated 1163. confirm'd the Possessions of this House, granting them a free Sepulture of their own, to pay no Tithes of their proper Cattle, to celebrate privately in time of a general Interdict, &c. King *Henry* II. confirm'd divers Lands given them in *England*.

963.

St. DENNIS, near Paris. 964.

An. Dom. 792. *Bertoaldus*, a Duke among the English Saxons, being afflicted with a Distemper which the Phisitians could not cure, travail'd into *France* to the Abby of St. *Dennis*, and there found, through the mercy of God, a perfect Recovery. Hereupon he gave to that Abby his Town of *Ridrefeld* in *Sussex*, with other profits; Confirm'd to these Monks by King *Offa*, then Reigning. King *Edward* the Confessor gave them other Lands in *Oxfordshire*, *An. Dom.* 1059. *William* Earl of *Ferrers* granted them yearly one wax Candle or Torch, price thirteen pence, one fat Buck, and one fat Boar, to be sent them by proper Messengers on the Feast of St. *Dennis*, in perpetual Almes, whose Deed of grant bears date *An. Dom.* 1189.

965.

St. EBRULF at Utica, in Normandy.

966.
967.
To this Abby, built by St. *Ebrulf* a Confessor, in a Desert and Solitary place, King *William* the Conqueror gave Lands in several Counties of *England, An. Dom.* 1081. Also *Robert* Earl of *Leicester*, and *Robert* his Son were Benefactors.

L'ESSAY, in Normandy.

968.
969.
970.
King *Henry* II. and after him King *Henry* V. confirm'd to this Abby (lying in the Town of St. *Oportune*) their Lands as well in *England*, as *Normandy*, given by divers Benefactors, among whom *Robert de Haia, Roger Foliot*, &c.

FISCAMPE, in Normandy.

971.
972.
William, Patron of the *Normans*, and King of the *English*, confirm'd to this Abby all its Possessions in *England* and *Normandy* with the grant of Liberties, in like manner as his Predecessor *Richard* Earl of the *Normans* had given them.

St. FLORENCE at Saumers in Anjou.

973.
King *Henry* II. confirm'd to the Monks of this Abby their Possessions, among others their Cell of *Sele* in *Suffolk*.

FONTANE, in Normandy.

974.
Founded by *Ralf Taxo*, and by him endow'd with large Lands and Possessions, with the good will of *William* Prince of the *Normans* (*qui Regnum Angliæ armis subjugavit, & strenuè gubernavit*) which King *William* the Conqueror confirm'd to the Monks of this Abby four Churches with all their Tithes and Customes in *England*, among which *Toucester* in *Northamptonshire*.

FONT-EBRALD, in Normandy.

975.
King *Henry* II. granted to the Nuns of this Abby the Mannour of *Lesson* in *Bedfordshire*, with other Lands amounting to 60 *l.* per *An.* with the Confirmation of a yearly Alms out of the Exchequer of 24 *l.* per *Annum*, granted by his Grandfather King *Henry* I. King *Henry* III. confirm'd to these Nuns all their Lands, &c. in *England*.

FULC-

FULCARDIMONT. 976.

A Lice Countess of *Eu* (*Augum*) confirm'd to the Monks of this Abby the several Lands given them in *England* by *John* Earl of *Eu*, her Grandfather.

JUMIEGES, in Normandy. 977.

KING *Henry* the II. confirm'd the Lands given to these Monks by *William* Son of *Rollo*, *Robert* Archbishop of *Rhoan*, King *William*, &c.

GOISLAFONTAN. 979.

Founded and endow'd for Nuns by *Hugo de Gornaio*, and others.

GRANDIMONT, in Normandy.

KING *Henry* the V. *An 'suo* 8. confirm'd to the Prior and Convent of this place all the Lands granted by his Progenitors Kings of *France* and *England*. *Robert* Earl of *Mellent* was the Founder, and many the Benefactors. King *Henry* the II. granted them an annual Rent of 200 *l.* in free Alms, confirm'd by King *John*.

980.
981.

GRESTAIN, in Normandy. 982.

KING *Richard* the I. confirm'd to the Monks of this House, their Lands given by King *William* the Conqueror and others. The like did King *Edward* the II.

983.

LIRA, in Normandy. 985.

KING *Henry* the II. confirm'd to the Monks their Lands and Cells in *England*. The Earls of *Leicester* were great Benefactors to this House, so were divers others of prime quality in *England*.

986.
987.
988.

LONLEY, in le Maine. 989.

Founded in the *Chatellery* of *Danfront*, and Diocess of *Mans*, by *William de Belesmo*, and endowed with Revenues in and about *Dumfront* in *Normandy*.

990.

Kk 2   St.

991.
* Marmon-
stier.

St. MARTIN of the * Major-Monastery, in Tourain.

KING Henry the II. granted to the Monks of this place divers Lands and Tithes in England.

St. JOHN's in Poictou.

KING John confirm'd to the Monks here the Church of St. Nicholas.

MONTISBURG, in Normandy.

992.

THE Estate of these Monks in England, given by Richard de Rivers and others, was confirm'd by King Hen. II. and King Edw. 3.

NOA, in Normandy.

Founded by Maud the Empress, Daughter of King Henry the I. for Monks.

993.

St. MARTINS, in the Suburbs of Paris.

STeven Earl of Albamarl, and Havisia his Wife Daughter of Ralph de Mortuomari, were Benefactors to the Monks here.

St. REMIGIUS, in the City of Reims.

KING Edward the III. An. suo 6. confirm'd to the Monks of this Abby divers Lands in England.

994.

DE PRATO, at Rhoan.

Founded by King Henry the I. and by him and Maud the Empress endow'd with Lands both in Normandy and England.

995.

St. AMAND, at Rhoan.

996.

THE Abby of Nuns here was founded by Goscelinus the Viscount and Emmelina his Wife. Endowed by them and several others, among the rest King William the Conqueror, and Queen Maud.

SVIAG-

SAVIGNY, in Normandy. 997.

King *Edward* III. confirm'd to the Monks of this Abby their Lands in *England*, among which their Cell of *Benyngton* in *Lincolnshire*.

St. MARTINS, at Alcey in Normandy. 999.

Founded and endow'd by *Steven* Earl of *Albamarl* and his Ancestors without the Walls of the Castle of *Albemarl*.

St. NICHOLAS at Angiers. 1000.

First founded by *Fulk* Earl of *Anjou*, An. Dom. 1020. whose Son *Jeffrey* married *Maud* the Empress, daughter of King *Henry* I. She granted to the Monks of this Abby, divers Lands and Churches in *England*, as *Spalding* in *Lincolnshire*, &c. See more in *Spalding*, Vol. 1. p. 306.

St. SAVIOURS, at Constantine. 1001.

Their Possessions in *England* were confirm'd to these Monks by King *Henry* II. with the grant of great Liberties and Priviledges in his Forrests.

St. MARTINS of Troarne. 1002.

The Possessions of these Monks were confirm'd by *Henry* Duke of *Normandy*, and *Aquitain*, and Earl of *Anjou*.

St. VICTORS at Calete, in Normandy.

King *Henry* II. Confirm'd the Estate of the Monks of this place, which they had both here and beyond Seas, with the grant of Liberties &c.

St. WALERIC, in Picardy. 1003.

King *Henry* II. Confirm'd to the Monks here *Takley* in *Essex*. &c. with divers Liberties and great Immunities.

St. WANDRAGISILUS, in the Dioc. of Roan. 1004.

Founded and endow'd at *Fontanell* by *Richard* II, Duke or Prince of the *Normans*, An. Dom. 1024.

XAN-

XANTON, *in* Aquitain.

1006. King *John* confirm'd the Liberties granted to the Nuns of this Abby.

CLUNY, *in the* Dutchy *of* Burgundy.

Roger Earl of *Salop* and *Adelina* his Wife gave the Manner of *Chelton* to this Abby.

AULNAY.

1007. AN *Dom.* 1199. *William de Similleio,* and his Ancestors founded and endow'd this Abby, in the Diocess of *Bajeux*; for Cistercians. They demised certain Tithes in *Oxfordshire* for the Rent of 40*s. per Annum*, *An.* 1304.

de BONOPORTU.

Founded for Cistertian Monks by *Richard* I. King of *England*, and endow'd among other things, with one hundred marks yearly issuing out of his Rents in the Town of *Dieppe*.

1008. *St.* MARY *de* Voto, *at* Cherburg, *in* Normandy.

Founded and endow'd by King *Henry* II. and his Mother *Maud* the Empress, Confirm'd by King *Richard* I. and King *Henry* III. for Cistertians.

1010. *St.* MARTIN, *and St.* Barbara, *in* Normandy.

King *Henry* II. confirm'd the Lands given to the Canons of this Abby both in *Normandy* and *England*.

BELENCUMBRIS.

1012. William *de Waren* and *Isabel* his Wife gave divers Lands and Rents to this Priory of *All Saints, An. Dom.* 1135.

St. WLUAR, *at* Bologne *in* Picardy.

King *Henry* I. at the Solicitation of *Ida* Countess of *Bologne*, gave and confirm'd to the Canons of this Priory, *Notfield* in *Surrey*.

FOU-

FOUGERES, in Britany.

CONAN Duke of *Britan* gave the Canons of this Place the Church of *Cestrehunt*, in the Diocess of *London*. *Ranulph* Earl of *Chester* writ to the Bishop of *London* on behalf of these Canons, and because he had not his own Seal by him at that time he sent his Letters under the Seal of the Lady his Mother, yet the said Letters conclude *Teste meipso apud Martillum*.

The Hospital of St Mary Magdalen, *at* Bologn.

1013.

KIng *Henry* I. confirm'd to this Hospital 20 *l. per Annum.* arising out of *Kent*.

The Hospital of Lepers *of* Kenilli, *near* Roan.

KIng *Henry* II. founded this Hospital for Leperous Women, and gave it 200 *l. per Annum.* King *Richard* I. gave them 40 *l. per Annum.* But this was *Anjou* pounds.

The Hospital of Vernon, *in* Normandy.

1014.

FOunded and largely endow'd by St. *Lewis* King of *France*, *An. Dom.* 1260.

The Hospital of the HolyGhost, *at* Rome.

FOund by Inquisition 20 *Edward* III. that King *John* gave the Church of *Wrytele* in *Essex* for the maintenance of the Poor in this Hospital call'd the English Hospital at *Rome*.

BLANCLAND, *in* Normandy.

1015.

FOunded for Canons, and endow'd with Lands in *England* by *Richard de Hay* and his Wife.

De BELLO PORTU, *in* Normandy.

1016.

AN. *Dom.* 1202. *Alen* Son of Earl *Henry* gave divers Lands in *England* to the Canons Regular of this Abby, *Premonstratenses.*

Dominican Nuns, near Roan.

Founded by St. *Lewis* King of *France*, beyond the Bridge at *Roan*, and by him endowed with 500 l. *Turnois, per Annum*, and divers Liberties, *An. Dom.* 1269.

1017.

The Cathedral Church at Roan.

Divers Lands in *England* were formerly given to the Canons of this Church and their Succeſſors, by King *Henry*, Earl *Otho*, and more especially by King *John, viz*. The Mannor of *Clere* in *Hampshire*, *Oteri* in *Devonshire*, *Kilburn* in *Torkshire*, &c.

Irish Monasteries.

1019.

St. ANDREWS, in the Territory of Ardes, (Ardee.)

Founded by *John de Curceio*. At first a Cell to the Abby of *Lonley* in *Normandy*, and by them granted to the Archbishop of *Armach*.

1020.

The Nuns, at Corke.

Found by Inquisition 29 *E*. 1. that it was not to the Kings damage for *William Barry* and others, to settle certain Lands there mention'd on *Agnes de Hareford* and other Nuns and their Succeſſors in the House of St. *John Baptist* in St. *John's-street* in *Cork*.

St. PATRICKS at Downe.

Founded *An. Dom.* 1183. for Monks and a Prior from St. *Werburgs* at *Chester*, but without any Subjection to the Church of *Chester*. The Bishop of *Down* was Custos and Abbot of this Monastery, in like manner as the Bishops were in the Churches of *Winchester* and *Coventry*. *John de Curci* the Founder of this Monastery endow'd it with divers Revenues, and Tithes, among other things of all his hunting.

1021.

1022.

The Nuns, at GRANE, in the County of Kildare.

Pope *Innocent* the III. *An. Dom.* 1207. confirm'd the Lands given to this House by *Walter de Rideleford* and others; the like confirmation was made by King *John* in the ninth year of his Reign.

KILCUMYN.

Founded by *Philip de Wigornia*, Constable of *Ireland*, and furnished with Monks from *Glastonbury*.

1023.

NEDDRUM, *a Cell to St.* Bege, *in* Yorkshire.

Anno Dom. 1177. (23 *H.* 2.) the Lord *John de Curci* subdued *Ulster*. *An.* 1178. he gave *Neddrum* to the Monks of St. *Bege*, with great Priviledges. Divers Benefactors gave Lands to this Priory, all which was confirm'd, *An. Dom.* 1202. by *John* Cardinal of St. *Steven* in *Mont-Cælius*, Apostolick Legat.

1024.

OCYMILD.

Founded by *William de Burgo*, and given to *Richard* a Monk of *Glastonbury*.

1025.

ARKEL, *a Cell to* Furnes, *in* Lancashire.

Founded by *Theobald Walteri*, Butler of *Ireland*, and by him given to the Monks of the *Cistercian* Order at *Furnes*, with divers Liberties.

BELLO BECCO, *another Cell to* Furnes.

Founded and endow'd by *Walter de Lascy* for *Cistercian* Monks, who afterwards by License of King *Edward* the III. transferr'd their Estate here to the Abbot and Convent of *Furneys*.

1026.

DUNBROTHY, *in the County of* Wexford.

Harvey de Monte Marisco, the Kings Marshal of *Ireland*, gave this place with divers other Lands for a Cell to the Abby of *Bildwas* in *England*, *William Marshal* Earl of *Pembroke* was a great Benefactor to this House, whose Gifts were confirm'd by King *Edward* the III. among which things they had a grant of Pasture for eighty Cows, and one thousand five hundred Sheep yearly.

1027.

1028.

JEREPONT.

Founded by *Damwald* King of *Ossery*, and endow'd by him with *Baleochellam* in which the Monastery was founded, and other Lands; all confirm'd by *John* Lord of *Ireland* and Earl of *Morton*.

KYLLECONIL.

1029. Founded by *Donald O Bryan*. Confirm'd by King *Henry* the III. *An. suo,* 4.

MELLIFONT.

1030. KING *John* confirm'd to the Monks of the Church of St. *Mary* at *Drogheda* divers Land which they enjoy'd before the coming of the *French* into *Ireland*. The like confirmations were made by King *Henry* the III. and King *Edward* the III.

NEWRY, in the County of Down.

1031. Founded and endowed for *Cistercian* Monks by *Mauritius mag Lochlain* King of all *Ireland*, by the unanimous consent of the Great men and Petty Kings of *Ulster*.

ROSGLAS.

Founded and endow'd by *Dermitius O Demesy*, King of *Osalia*.

St. SAVIOURS.

1032. Founded by *William Marischal* Earl of *Pembroke*, confirm'd by King *Henry* the III. with the grant of great Liberties. To this Abby was 1033. afterwards united the Abby of *Kilkenny*.

TYNTERNE.

Founded according to the last Will of *William Marischal* Earl of *Pembroke*, and ratified by King *John*.

DE VALLE SALUTIS.

Founded by *Dermitius* an *Irish* King, and by him and his Subjects endow'd with divers Lands. Confirm'd by King *John*.

WONEY, in the County of Limerick.

1034. Founded *An. Dom.* 1205. and endowed with Lands and Liberties by *Theobald Walteri*, Butler of *Ireland*.

St:

St. CROSSE in the County of Tiperary. 1035.

Founded and endowed by *Donald* King of *Lumney* (*Lumnicensis.*)

BALLINTOBBER, in the County of Maio. Canons Regular. 1037.

Founded by *Catholus O Conogher* King of *Connaught, An. Dom.* 1216.

CONNAL, a Cell to Lanthony, in England.

Founded *An.* 1202. by *Maylerus* Son of *Henry*, for Canons Regular Confirm'd by King *John.*

The Hospital of St. Mary's near Drogheda. 1038.

Founded and endowed by *Ursus de Swemele*, for the maintenance of poor and infirm People, and such as are in Want; The Custos of which Hospital to be chosen by the Good men (*Proborum hominum*) of *Drogheda.*

ALL-SAINTS, in the East-part of Dublin. 1039.

Founded and endowed for Canons by *Dermont* King of *Leimster*, confirm'd by King *Henry* the II.

St. THOMAS the Martyr, in Dublin.

Founded and endowed by *William* Son of *Audelinus*, Sewer to King *Henry* the II. by Authority of that King, and for him.

FERNE, in the County of Wexford. 1040.

Founded and endowed by *Dernatius* King of *Leimster, An.* 1158. He also granted them free choice of their own Abbots, according to the Rule of St. *Augustine.*

KENLIS, and Inistiock, in the County of Kilkenny.

Jeffrey Son of *Robert* came into *Ireland* with *William* Earl *Marischal*, and obtain'd the Barony of *Kenlis* in *Ossorey*, at which place he afterwards built a Monastery for Canons Regular, which he brought over from *Bodmin* in *Cornwall.* One of whom was *Hugh de Rous*, who after that became the 1041.

first

first *English* Bishop of *Ossery*. About *An.* 1206. *Thomas* Son of *Anthony* founded a Priory at *Iristiock*, which became as a Cell to *Kenlis*. *Hugh de Lacy* and *Walter de Lacy* were Benefactors.

1042.   The Hospital of St. John Evangelist at **Kilkenny**.

Founded and endowed *An.* 1220. by *William Mareschal* Earl of *Pembroke*.

1043.   KILVAYNARD, *a Priory of* Augustin *Nuns*.

Pope *Celestin* the III. *An.* 1195. confirmed their Lands and Possessions with the grant of divers Liberties.

1044.   St. JOHN BAPTIST *at* Nenath, *in the County of* **Tiperary**.

Founded about the year 1200. by *Theobald Walter* Butler of *Ireland*, and by him endow'd with Lands for the Maintenance of Canons, and thirteen poor and infirm People.

1045.   FERMOY.

Founded and endowed for Canons Regular of St. *Augustin*, by *Alexander* Son of *Hugh*. Confirm'd by King *Edward* the I. *An. suo*, 18.

1046.   TOBERGLORIE, *in the County of* **Down**.

Founded and endowed by *John de Curcey*, and by him given as a Cell to the Prior and Canons of St. *Mary* at *Carlile*.

TRISTERNAGH, *in the County of* **Meath**.

Founded and endowed about the year 1200. by *Jeffrey de Constantine*, for Canons Regular.

1048.   *The Cathedral Church of the* Trinity, *at* **Dublin**.

SItricus King of *Dublin* gave the Ground where this Church now stands to *Donatus* the first Bishop of *Dublin*, for the erecting of a Church to the Holy Trinity, with Revenues. Which *Donatus* in his time built the *Nave* and side Isles. Many years after, *Laurence* the second Archbishop of *Dublin*, and *Richard Strigul*, and the Earl Marshal, *&c.* added the Quire, Bells, and two Chappels. After *Laurence*; *Henry*, and *Luke*, two other Archbishops, carried on the Building, and after them, *John de S. Paul* finisht all. King *John* was a Benefactor to this Church, while Earl of

1049.   *Morton*, and after he was King.

Scotch

Scotch Monasteries.

COLDINGHAM, *a Cell to* Durham. 1051.

Saint *Ebba* Sister of *Oswy* King of *Northumberland*, was the first Institutor of a Religious Life in this Place, here she had a Monastery consisting of both Sexes, under her Government. King *Edward* the III. in the first year of his Reign, granted his Letters of Protection to this Priory.

LINDORS. 1052.

Founded by *David* Earl of *Huntington*, Brother of the King of *Scotland*, and by him endowed with divers Churches.

ABERBROTHE. 1053.

Founded by *William* King of *Scotland* in honour of God and St. *Thomas* the Archbishop and Martyr, and by him endowed with Lands and Liberties.

DRYBRUGHE. 1054.

Founded and endowed by *David* King of *Scotland*, for Canons; with the grant of divers Liberties and Immunities.

DUMFERMLINGE.

Founded by *Malcolm* King of *Scotland* (*in monte Infirmorum*) and by him and others endowed with large Possessions. Confirm'd by King *David* the first, youngest Son of King *Malcolm* and *Margaret* his Wife. 1055.

BELMERINACH, *in* Fife. 1056.

Founded and endowed by *Alexander* King of *Scotland*, in honour of God, St. *Mary*, and the holy King *Edward*, for *Cistercian* Monks:

Of

Of the Cistercian Monasteries in 𝔖𝔠𝔬𝔱𝔩𝔞𝔫𝔡.

1057.

SAint *David* Son of *Malcolm* and *Margaret* founded Six of this Order. *Henry* Prince of *Scotland* Son of the said *David* founded *Hadington*. St. *Malcolm* Son of the said *Henry* founded three. *William* King of *Scotland* founded one. Others of the Nobility founded many others, *viz. Patrick Dunbar* Earl of *March*, and *Agatha* his Wife founded *Coldstream* in the Marshes. The Earl of *Fife* founded *Northberwick* where a peice of our Lord's Cross was preserved with great Veneration. *John* Lord of *Kirconell* founded *Sacrum-Boscum*, commonly call'd *Holywood*; of this House, it is said, was the famous *John de Sacro-bosco*, who writ of the Sphere and other Astronomical matters, &c.

The End of the Second Volum.

MONASTICON ANGLICANUM,
ABRIDGED.

VOL. III.

OF THE
CATHEDRAL and COLLEGIATE } CHURCHES.

MONASTICON ANGLICANUM,

ABRIDGED.

VOL III.

OF THE

Cathedral and Collegiate Churches.

MONASTICON ANGLICANUM,

Abridg'd.

Vol. III. and laſt.

Additions to the Firſt Volum.

Pag. 31. ROCHESTER.

Gundulphus Biſhop of *Rocheſter*, by authority, will, and command of King *William*, and by the advice, help, and aſſent of *Lanfranc* Archbiſhop of *Canterbury*, did inſtitute ſixty Monks in the Room of five Clerks (all that then were) in the Church of St. *Andrew* the Apoſtle; and transferr'd the poſſeſſions formerly given by divers Benefactors to that Church, to the maintenance of thoſe Monks, with other endowments of his own guift, for the maintenance of them, Strangers that ſhould come there, and poor people, and for Serjeants to ſerve them. He alſo made Proviſion for a Feſtival on St. *Andrews* day, for himſelf and Succeſſors, if they ſhould be preſent at the Celebration of the ſame. Whoſe Charter bears date the twentieth day of *September* 1089.

Boniface Archbiſhop of *Canterbury*, recited the Grant of *Anſelm* his Predeceſſor by which he granted and confirm'd divers Lands given to this Church by Biſhop *Gundulf* and others, in *Kent, Surrey, Suffolk, Buckinghamſhire,* and *Glouceſterſhire*, dated at *London* in a Council of Biſhops A. D. 1101, And the ſaid *Anſelm's* Confirmation of Archbiſhop *Lanfranc's* Grant to the ſaid Church, dated 1087. and confirm'd all the ſaid recited Grants by his Deed of Confirmation dated 1254.

King *Henry* II. confirm'd all their Lands and Poſſeſſions, with large Priviledges and immunities ſuch as the Church of *Canterbury* enjoys, whoſe Charter bears date at *Nottingham*.

An. Dom. 1197. An Exchange was made by conſent of King *Richard* I. between *Hubert* Archbiſhop of *Canterbury* and the Prior and Convent of *Rocheſter*, the ſaid Prior and Convent granting to the ſaid Archbiſhop and Succeſſors their Mannour of *Lambeth* with the Church there, and the Liberties and appurtenances thereunto belonging as well in *Southwark* as in the Soke of *London*, except a Mill which the Monks have upon the *Thames* over againſt the *Tower* of *London*, &c. And the ſaid Archbiſhop gave in Exchange to the ſaid Monks the Mannour of *Darent,* &c. with mutual Warranty on both ſides, and a reſtriction that it ſhall not be lawful for the ſaid Archbiſhop or his Succeſſors ever to alienate the ſaid Mannour of *Lambeth* from the Archbiſhoprick, or for the ſaid Monks to alienate the Mannour of *Darent*, &c.

Pag. 1.

2.

3.

4.

5.

Pag. 413. NORWICH.

6.

7.

John Archbishop of *Canterbury* at the requeſt of the Prior and Convent of the Cathedral Church of *Norwich*, exemplified the Charter of *Herbert* Biſhop of *Norwich*, by which he gave to the Monks, whom he had eſtabliſht in the ſaid Cathedral Church, divers Lands, Tithes, and other Revenues; and of *Anſelm* Archbiſhop of *Canterbury*, *Primate of the Greater Britain and Ireland, and Vicar of Pope Paſcal*, by which he confirm'd the Eſtabliſhment of the Monks which the ſaid *Herbert* had made in the ſaid Church of the Holy Trinity at *Norwich*, which Church King *William*, and King *Henry* his Brother and Succeſſor had conſtituted to be the head and Mother of all the Churches of *Norfolk* and *Suffolk*. The foreſaid Deed of Exemplification bears date at *Lambeth*, *An. Dom.* 1281.

Radulphus Fitz Godric gave to this Church the Mannour of *Newton* confirm'd to the Monks by King *Henry* I.

Pag. 120. GLOCESTER.

8.

AN. Dom. 1138. King *Steven* in the third year of his Reign confirm'd to the Church St. *Peter* of *Glouceſter*, all the Lands, Churches, Tithes, and other donations given by Divers Benefactors.

9.

Pag. 395. St. MARYS at YORK.

Ivo de Taleboyſe, from whom deſcended the Noble families of the *Roſſes* Lords of. *Werke, Faucumberge, Twenge*, and *Beleus*, &c. gave to the Church of St. *Mary* in *York* and to the Abbot and Monks there, divers Lands and Churches. This *Ivo de Tailbois* held of the King in *Capite* the Barony of *Hephall*, which Barony was held by his Anceſtors in *Thenagio*, paying to the King 50 s. yearly, but King *William* the Conqueror changed the Tenure into the Service of one Knights Fee.

Pag. 258. WHERWELL.

10.

Pope *Gregory* the IXth. recited and confirm'd to the Abbeſs and Nuns of *Wherwell* all their Lands, Tithes and Churches, that they then had, or for the future ſhould obtain, and exempted them from Tithes, for their own Cattel, with priviledge to receive and retain in their Monaſtery ſuch ſecular Women as are free and at their own diſpoſal, to celebrate Divine Service privately in the time of general Interdict, to have a free Sepulture, and a free Election of their Abbeſs &c. Whoſe Bull bears date, *An. Dom.* 1228.

11.

Pag. 327. WALLINGFORD.

Nigellus de Alboney and *Alan Fitz-Amfrid* gave divers Lands to the Monks of St. *Albans* in the Church of the Holy Trinity of *Wallingford*, Con-

Confirm'd to them by *Joceline* Bishop of *Salisbury*, and after him by *Robert* Bishop of *Salisbury*, and by the *Dean* and Chapter of that Church, *An. Do.* 1243.

Pag. 525. WILBERFOSS.

GEorge Duke of *Clarence* and Lord of *Richmond*, as Patroon the Nunnery of *Wilberfoss*, exemplified and confirm'd to *Elizabeth* then Prioress, and to the Nuns there, the several Deeds of Endowments and Grants made to them by *Jordanus Fitz Gilbert, William de Percy*, &c. Whose Deed of Confirmation bears date at *Staunford* 10th. of *August*, 4 *Edward* IV.

Pag. 487. STODELEY.

THis Nunnery was first founded by *Thomas de Sancto Walerico*, but his Estate, and consequently the Patronage of this House, coming to the Crown, King *Richard* II. in the first year of his Reign, on the death of *Margery* the last Prioress, confirm'd the Election of *Elizabeth Fremantell* then Subprioress into the Office of Prioress, and signified the same to the Bishop of *Lincoln*.

Pag. 482. SANFORD, alias LITTLEMORE.

ROger de *Thoeni*, Roger de *Sanford*, and *Thomas Buscel* (whose Deed bears date 1254 (8. *Henry* III.) gave Lands to the Church of *St. Nicholas* and Priory of Nuns here. *Robert* Abbot of *Abington* and *Benjamin* Rector of the Church of St. *Nicholas* granted and confirm'd to them certain Tithes. *Roger de Quency* Earl of *Winton*, and Constable of *Scotland* released to them their Suit to his Court. Pope *Innocent* IV. in the second year of his *Pontificate* Released ten days of enjoyn'd Pennance to all such of the Dioceses of *Lincoln*, *Ely*, and *Salisbury*, who being penitent and confest, should contribute and assist to the reedifying of the Church of this Priory.

Pag. 597. GROSMUNT, in Yorkshire.

JOan Wife of *Robert de Torneham*, and daughter of *William Fossart*, gave divers Lands, Profits, and Priviledges in *Yorkshire*, to the Prior and Monks of *Grandmont* in *France*, confirm'd by her said Husband *Robert de Torneham*, who also gave other Lands of his own.

Pag. 505. CRESWELL in Herefordshire.

THis was another Cell of the Monks of *Grandemont*, to which *Walter de Lacy* gave Lands in pure and perpetual Alms, with warranty. *Peter* Bishop of *Hereford* having bought Lands of the Prior of *Creswell*, for 550. marks granted by his Deed dated 1256, that in case he or his Succescessors should happen to be impleaded for the said Lands, the said Prior nor this Successors should not be obliged to defend and Warrant the same beyond the Sum of 550 marks.

18.

Pag. 542. MISSENDEN.

Joan de Pedinton widow of *Guy de Ryhal*, with *Thomas* Son and heir of the said *Guy*, confirm'd to the Canons of *Missendin*, the Hermitage of *Muswell*, which *Ralf* the Hermit built and inhabited by permission of the foresaid *Guy*, with a Chappel built in honour of the Holy Cross. Confirm'd also by *Albricus* Earl of *Damarun*, and *Simon de Gerardmulin*.

19.

The Priory of EWENNY, a Cell of the Abby of Gloucester.

THe *Turbervilles* gave to the Church of St. *Michael* and the Monks there, divers Lands and Possessions, with Liberty of fishing in the River of *Ewenny* as far as their Lands extend, and to retain a moiety of the fish so caught, the other moiety to be the *Turbervilles*.

The Priory of Blithe, in Nottinghamshire.

20.

POpe *Honorius* confirm'd the Possessions of this House to the Monks here, and exempted them from paying of Tithes of their Cattel. It was founded by *William de Cresey*.

William Gifford Archbishop of *York*, *An. Dom.* 1277. made certain orders for their Government, *viz.* That Almes and Hospitality should be used as of old time, That all and singular do humbly and devoutly obey the Prior as their head, &c. *Vid. Vol.* 1. *p.* 553.

21.

BUSTLESHAM Abby, in Barkshire.

KIng *Henry* VIII. by Patent dated in the 29*th.* year of his Reign, recites that out of the sincere and intire devotion which he bears to God and the Blessed Virgin *Mary*, and to the Increase of the Divine Worship, &c. He does erect, found, and establish to indure for all future times, a Monastery or Conventual House of one Abbot and thirteen Monks of the order of St. *Benedict*, in the place of the late disolved Priory or Monastery of *Bisham* alias *Bustlesham* in *Barkshire*, which on the fifth day of *July* in the 28*th* year of his Reign was surrender'd to him by *William* Bishop of St. *Davids* then Prior of that Priory and the Convent there, and this he did for the good estate of himself while living, and for the good of his Soul after death, and for the good of the Soul of his most dear Wife *Jane* late Queen of *England* deceased, and for the Souls of his Children, and Progenitors. And gave all the Lands, Houses, Church, Bells, and all utensils then in his hands and formerly belonging to the late disolved Monastery, to *John Cordrey*, whom he made Abbot of this new Monastery and to the Monks of the same. Which *John Cordrey* was lately Abbot of the Monanastery of St. *Peter* at *Chertsey* in *Surrey*. He did also incorporate this new Monastery by the name of the Abbot and Convent of the new Monastery of the Holy Trinity of King *Henry* VIII. at *Buslesham*, with power to purchase Lands, and by that name to sue and be sued, &c. and for the Abbot and his Successors to use an Episcopal Miter. He also endow'd the said New Monastery with all the Lands and Revenues belonging to the late Monastery here, and also to that of *Chertsey*, in divers Counties of *England* and *Wales*, and in the City of *London*, also with the dissolved Priories of *Cardigan* in *Southwales*, and *Bethelkellard* in *Carnarvanshire*, with all the Lands and Revenues of the same, and with divers Rents issuing out of the Lands and Revenues of several other Monasteries, then in Lease for twenty one years, and the Reversion of the said Lands, &c. With view of Frank pledge and all other Franchises and Liberties which have been formerly enjoy'd in the several Lands &c. To hold by the Service of one Knights fee, and the yearly Rent of 72 *l.* and 17 *d.* in the name of a Tenth, to be paid into the Court of augmentations at *Michaelmas*. This new Monastery to be exempt from the ordinary Jurisdiction, and to be visited only by the King his heirs and Successors; and the present Abbot *John Cordrey* to be exculed from the payment of first Fruits and Tenths given by Statute, made in the twenty sixth year of this King, provided notwithstanding that his Successors shall pay first Fruits, which are valued at 661 *l.* 14 *s.* 9 *d.* ob. But no tenths, which amount to 66 *l.* 3 *s.* 5 *d.* ob. q. *non obstante* the said Stat. or any other Law. Which Patent bears *teste* at *Westminster* 18th *December* in the foresaid twenty ninth year of *Henry* VIII.

22.
23.
24.
25.
26.
27.
28.

29.

30.

Pag. 648. LENTON.

King *Steven* granted the Church of the Holy Trinity at *Lenton*, which *William Peverell* and others had endow'd, to the order of Cluniac Monks to be enjoy'd with all its possessions, inviolably.

The Priory of HORKESLEY.

Robert Fitz Godibold gave divers Lands, Churches, and Tithes to the Cluniac Monks of *Tefford*, with intention that the Convent of that House should transmit some of their Monks to the Church of St. *Peter* at *Horchesley* there to reside in the Service of God and St. *Peter*. Their Possessions so given was confirm'd to them by *Gilbert* Bishop of *London*, and *Hubert* Archbishop of *Canterbury*.

31.

32.

Pag. 867. SIBETON.

With King *William* the Conqueror, who came into *England* in the year 1066. came *Walter de Cadamo*, who after the Conquest held the Barony of *Horsford*, He had issue *Robert* who built the Church of St. *Peter* at *Sibton*, who had issue *John* call'd the Vicount, and *William*. *John* being very infirm in his health vow'd to erect an Abby of *Cistercian* Monks;

Monks; but himself dying, left his vow to be perform'd by *William* his Brother and heir, who enjoy'd after his death his Barony and Vicounty. This *William* founded the Monastery of St. *Mary* at *Sibton* in the Reign of King *Steven*, *An. Dom.* 1149. And endow'd the same with Lands and

33. Revenues. He had issue *Margaret* married to *Hugh de Cresfy* who confirm'd her Fathers Guift.

An. 28. *Henry* VIII, *William* then Abbot of *Sibton* Com. *Suffolk*, and the Convent there, of their free will and unanimous Consent, gave, granted, and confirm'd to *Thomas* Duke of *Norfolk*, *Anthony Rouse* Esquire, and *Nicholas Hare*, Gent. their heirs and assigns to the use of the said Duke his heirs and assigns for ever, all the said Monastery, and Estate thereunto belonging, and Constituted *Thomas Heydon*, and *Robert Whinwery* their lawful Attorneys to deliver Seizin accordingly. This was under their

34. Convent Seal, and Sign'd by the Abbot, and seven Monks of the House

---

Pag. 887. HOLMCOLTRAM.

DAvid King of *Scotland* confirm'd the Donations of his Son *Henry*, to this Abby; the like did afterwards *Malcolm* King of *Scotland* Son of the said *Henry*.

John King of *England* in the 16. year of his Reign, granted to the Monks here the Hermitage of St. *Hilda* in the Forrest of *Englewode*, with all the

35. Land which *Roger Croky* late Hermit held, and a Vaccary there for forty Cows, *&c.* *John* Bishop of *Carlile* licensed the Monks of *Holmcoltram* to build a Church or Chappel in their territory of *Arlosk* for their Tenants and the Inhabitants of those parts, which Church or Chappel he did appropriate and annex to the said Monastery, and exempt the same from the Visitation of the Ordinary; The said Church to be served by a secular Priest of their election, but to be presented to the said Bishop or his Successors, and by them admitted to the said Cure. The said Priest so admitted to receive for his support 4 *l.* to be pay'd him yearly out of the profits of the said Church, and a House and Curtilage to be assigned him. The said Priest to pay to the Bishop in the name of a *Cathedratic*, half a mark, and to the Archdeacon when he Visits 40 *d.* for procurations. Which Deed of Appropriation bears date at *Linstock*, *An.* 1304. *Hugh Morville*, *Cecily*

37. Countess of *Albemarl*, *Lambert de Multon*, and others, were Benefactors to these Monks. *William* Earl of *Albemarl* gave them a Forge and Iron Mine at *Egremond*; *Robert* King of *Scots* (whose Father lies buried in

38. their Church at *Holmcoltram*) gave them a yearly farm of 10 *l.* Pope *Lucius* III. confirm'd to them their Lands and Revenues, and granted

39. them divers Liberties, as to be free from the payment of Tithes for their Cattel, and Fishing, *&c.* Whose Bull bears date *An.* 1185.

Pag. 914. CROKESDEN.

40. THe Abby of the *Vally of St. Mary* of *Crokesdene* was founded by *Bertram de Verdon*, and by him endow'd with divers Revenues in *Crokesdene*, *Stanfort*, *Castretone*, *&c.* and a Salt work in *Midlewich*.

Additions

Additions to the Second Volum.

Pag. 461. NORWICH.

John Bishop of *Norwich* exemplified the Deeds belonging to the Hospital of St. *Paul* in *Norwich*, viz. the Charter of the Convent of the Holy Trinity of *Norwich*, (who founded and endow'd the said Hospital to the support of poor people, for the Soul of Bishop *Herbert*,&c.) of *Adam de Bellofago*, *Morellus de Morley*, some Bishops of *Norwich* his Predicessors, and King *Henry* I. who were all Benefactors. Which Deed of Exemplification bears date in the year 1301.

Pag. 181. TWINEHAM.

IN the Reign of King *Steven*, An. Dom. 1150, *Henry* Bishop of *Winchester*, and *Hillary* then Dean of *Christ Church*, at the Petition of Earl *Baldwin*, introduced Canons Regular into the said Church, in place of the Canons secular that then were there, the secular Canons to enjoy their Prebends while they lived; But all the Lands and Revenues belonging and possest by the said Church in the time of the Deans to be for the future to the only use of the Prior and Canons Regular.

Pag. 152. GISBURNE.

WAlderus Son of Earl *Cospatric* gave the Town of *Apleton* to the Church of St. *Bridget*, commonly call'd *Brydekirk*, in the County of *Cumberland*. The Lady *Alice de Rumeley* gave this Church of *Brydekirk*, with *Apleton*, and all other Lands thereunto belonging to the Canons of *Gisburne*.

Pag. 272. WORSPRING.

WIlliam de Curtenai founded a Convent for Canons Regular of St. *Augustin*, at the Chappel of St. *Thomas* the *Martyr* in *Worspring*, and notifying so much to *John* then Bishop of *Bath*, desired that by his authority the Church of *Worle*, at that time vacant, might be appropriated to the said Convent.

Pag. 263. WORMLEY.

John de Baskerville gave to God and the Church of St. *Leonard* of *Pyonia*, and to the Prior and Canons there, in *Frankalmoine*, all his Land of *Stanley* which

which he held of the Mannour of *Wormley*; and *Nicholas de Wormley* Lord of the said Mannour, reciting the said Grant, confirm'd the same to the said Prior and Canons, and also released and quit claimed to them, one pair of spurs or sixpence of yearly Rent, by which the foresaid *John* held that Land.

49. *Robert de Staunton*, *Gilbert Talebot*, *Robert Boter*, and others,
50. were Benefactors to the said Canons, confirm'd by *Roger de Montuomari*
51. Lord of *Winfretone An. Dom.* 1304. *Gerard de Eylesford* gave them the
52. Advowson of the Church of *Psona Regis*, or *Kings Penne*; *Peter* Bishop of *Hereford* appropriated the Church of *Wormesley*, of which these Canons were Patrons to this Convent, for the said Canons to enjoy the Fruits thereof to their proper use, but so as not to defraud the said Church of due Service. Whose Deed bears date, *An.* 1262. Here was a Chantry
53. founded by the Lady *Basilia de Bourhull*.

Pag. 941. RANTON.

54. *R*Obert Fitz-Noel, or Son of *Noel*, founded and endow'd the Priory of *Ranton*, for Canons under the Rule and obedience of the Church of *Haman* (*Hamanensis Ecclesiæ*) Whose Donation was confirm'd by *Thomas Noel* his Son. *Noel* who came into *England* with King *William* the Conqueror, had issue *Robert*, and he *Thomas*. *Thomas* had issue *Alice* and *Joan*, his Co-heirs. *Alice* was married to *William de Harecourt*, and had in partition the Mannour of *Elinhale*, from whom descended Sir *Robert Harecourt* Knight, who married *Anne* the daughter of *Thomas Lymerik*.

Pag. 276. COLD NORTON, in Oxfordshire.

55. *W*Illiam Fitz-Alan founded this Priory for Canons in his Mannour House at *Coldnorton*, to God, St. *Mary*, St. *John*, and St. *Giles*,
56. and endow'd it with divers Lands. *Reginald* Earl of *Bolon*, and *Ida* his Wife confirm'd the Donations of their Ancestors, *An.* 1201. *Ralf* Earl of *Stafford*, gave to this Priory his Mannour of *Rowlandright* in *Oxfordshire*, for the maintenance of two Canons to celebrate for his Soul, &c. for ever, whose Charter indented bears date at his Mannour of *Tysho* in *Warwickshire*. 44 *Edward* III. *Hugh Croft* Esquire released and convey'd over to King *Henry* VII. all his right, title, and Claim, to the said Priory, and Patronage of the same, and all the Lands and Revenues thereunto belonging, formerly enjoy'd by *John Wotton* late Prior of the said Priory, whose Deed bears date 21. *Feb.* 22. *Henry* VII.
57. It was found by Inquisition taken at *Dorchester* in *Oxfordshire* 24. of *Apr.* 22 *Henry* VII. before *William Young* Escheater of that County, that *John Wotton* late Prior of this Priory, was seized of the said Priory, the Mannour of *Coldnorton*, and divers Lands, &c. in the said Inquisition exprest, in right of the said Priory, and being so seized dyed on the eve of *Palm Sunday* in the 11 year of that King without having any Convent of Canons, or any profest Canon in the said Priory at that time, and that the succession of the

the said Priory did thereupon wholly finish, dissolve, extinguish and determine, by which means the said Priory, and all the Estate, thereunto belonging did Escheat to the King whose Ancestors were Founders and Patrons of the same, and that the Revenue of the said Priory is of the value of 50 l. per Annum, over and above all Reprises.

Pag. 232. DERLEY.

AN. 1271. Robert Sauncheverel past a fine before *John de Reygate*, the Kings Justiciary, of the Church of *Bolton*, to the Abbot of *Derley*; saving the Presentation of a fit Chaplain to the same by the said *Robert*, and that such Chaplain shall receive the small Tithes of *Bolton*, for serving the Cure.

Robert Fitz-Steven the Kings Chamberalin, Henry de Luy, Hubert Fitz-Ralf, William Peverel of *Nottingham*, Robert Earl of *Ferrars*, &c. were Benefactors. Walter Bishop of *Coventry* confirm'd the Lands given to the Canons of this House, gave them the Care of the Nunnery of Virgins, which the Abbot of *Darby* erected at a mile distance, and exempted the said Abbot and his Successors from paying Tithes of their proper fields, and granted that the said Abbot and his Successors shall be Dean of all their Churches in *Derbyshire*, especially of all the Churches in *Derby*.

58.
59.
60.
61.

Pag. 41. BREDON.

William de Ferrariis Earl of *Derby* gave to the Canons Regular of *Bredon*, divers Churches, Lands, and Commons of Pasture in the *Peke* and elsewhere.

62.

Pa. 564. TEMPLERS.

Thomas de Santford gave all his Land of *Santford*, &c to the Knights of the Temple, in pure and perpetual Alms, for the releif of the holy Land, and for the maintenance of one Chaplain to celebrate Mass for ever, at the House of the Templers at *Bustlisham*. King *Steven* and Queen Matilda his Wife, and William Marescal Earl of *Pembroke* were Benefactors William de Vernon granted Lands at *Eremne* for the founding of an Hospital, to William Maskerel, which foundation was confirm'd by *Baldwin* Archbishop of *Canterbury*, and Godfrey Bishop of *Winchester*, and was afterwards granted by the said Maskerel to the Knights of the Temple of *Salomon*.

63.

64.

STANLEY Priory, in Gloucestershire.

Theobald Archbishop of *Canterbury*, Primate of the English, and Apostolick Legate, confirm'd the Lands and Revenues given by Several Benefactors to the Church of St. *Leonard* and Canons of *Stanley*.

65.

SHELFORD Priory, in Nottinghamshire.

IT was found in a *Plea* of Affize taken before *Hugh Bigod* Jufticiary of *England*, *An.* 42. *Henry* III. Between *William Bardolf*, and *Adam Everingham*, who both pretended to the Patronage of this Priory, that *Ralf Haunfelyn* Anceftor of the faid *William Bardolf* was the founder of the faid Priory, and that *William Bardolf* was the true Patron of the fame, who thereupon had Judgment againft the faid *Adam*, and the faid *Adam in mifericordia*. And the Archbifhop of *York* was commanded to admit a fit Perfon to be Prior there at the Prefentation of the faid *William*.

[Valued at 116 *l.* per *Annum*.]

SANDELFORD Priory, in Barkshire.

STeven Archbifhop of *Canterbury*, Primate of all *England*, and Cardinal of the holy Roman Church, confirm'd to the Canons of *Sandelford* divers Lands and Rents granted to thofe Canons by *Jeffrey* Earl of *Le Perche* (*Pertici*) in *France*.

ASSERUGG, in Buckinghamshire

EDmund Earl of *Cornwal*, Son and heir of *Richard* King of the Romans, gave and confirm'd to the Rector of the *Good men* Brothers of the Church founded in honour of the precious blood of *Jefus Chrift* at *Efferugg*, the Mannour of *Efferugg* and other Lands, *&c.* for the fupport of twenty Brothers, Clerks, of which 13 at the leaft to be Priefts; and with thofe Lands he granted divers Liberties, and Franchifes extream large, and that neither he nor his heirs fhould meddle nor interpofe in the concerns of the Houfe at fuch times as it fhall happen to be void of a Rector, *&c.*

[Valued at 416 *l.* 16 *s.* 4 *d.* per *Annum*.]

Pag. 245. BRADSOLE.

KIng *John* confirm'd to God and the Church of St. *Radegund* at *Bradfole*, and the Canons there of the Order of Premonftratenfes, divers Lands given by his Brother King *Richard* I. and others; With other Lands of his own guift. He alfo granted them the Church of St. *Peter* of *Rivery* and his Houfe there, for the building a new Monaftery for their ufe, and to tranflate the old Abby thither. There was formerly in this neighbourhood a fmall Houfe of Religion call'd *Blakewofe*, which was fubject to a Monaftery of this order call'd *Lavendene*, but the Canons of that place being poor and diftant, it occafion'd fcandal, whereupon the Canons of *Blakewofe* were difcharged of their obedience to the Abbot of *Lavendene* and Subjected to the Abbot of St. *Raudegund*. *Hugo de Burgh*, Jufticiary of *England*, and *Hamon de Crevequer* were Benefactors to this Abby.

Pag. 622. STANLEY.

Hubert Fitz-Ralf, and *Serlo de Grendon*, confirm'd to the Canons of Stanley Park, the Estate formerly given by *William de Grendon*. *Maud de Salicosa Mara*, daughter of *William Fitz-Ralf* late Steward of *Normandy*, was also a Benefactress to this House.

The Abbots of Stanley Park.

1. *Walter de Senteney*, ruled 31. years.
2. *William*, Ruled here 2. years.
3. *John Grauncorth*, govern'd 19. years.
4. *Hugh de Lincoln*, govern'd 14 years.
5. *Simon* 5. years.
6. *Laurence*, 16. years.
7. *Richard de Normanton*, ruled the first time 8. years.
8. *John de Lincoln*, 6. years.
9. *Richard de Normanton*, the second time, Ruled 1. year.
10. *John Horsley*, 26. years.
11. *Joh Wodhouse*, 15. weeks.
12. *William Horsley*, 21. years.
13. *Roger de Kyrkton*, 3. years.
14. *William de Boney*, 42. years.
15. *Henry Monsasche*, 39. years.
16. *John Spondone*, 33. years.
17. *John Stanley*. 22. years.
18. *Richard de Nottingham*, 19. years.

Pag. 605. CROXTON.

A *Vicia de Romely* Lady of *Bescaudeby* was married to *William Paynel* who came into *England* with *William* the Conqueror, and of whose guift he had divers Towns in *Yorkshire*, *Lincolnshire*, and *Leicestershire*, which *William* and *Avice*, had issue a daughter named *Alice* (or *Avice*) whom King *H*. II. gave in Marriage to *Robert de Gant*, who had issue by her another *Alice* (or *Avice*) whom the same King *Henry* gave in Marriage to *Robert Fitz-Harding* of *Bristol*, who had issue *Maurice*, who dying without issue, his Mothers Inheritance came to *Andrew Lutterel*, as next of the Bloud of the *Paynells*.

Pag. 607. LEYSTONE.

Ranulfus de Glanville founded the Abby of St. *Mary* at *Leestune* and endow'd it with the Mannour of *Leestune*, which he had of the guift of King *Henry* II. and with certain Churches, which he had formerly given to the Canons of *Buttele*, and now by them resign'd to the Canons of this place. King *Richard* I. confirm'd the Estate so given to these Canons of *Leystone* with a Grant of divers Franchises, confirm'd also by *Richard* Archbishop of *Canterbury*, and by *Roger Bygot* Earl of *Norfolk*. Pope *Lucius* granted these Canons divers Priviledges as not to pay Tithes of their proper Goods and Cattel, to celebrate privately in time of a General Interdict, with absolute freedom in the Election of their Abbot, with Liberty of Burial for any (not Excommunicate) who desire to be buried with them, saving the Rights of those Churches from whence the Bodies come, &c.

Pag. 643. BEGEHAM.

William de *Burgelle* granted certain Marish Lands to the Canons of *Oiteham* (afterwards translated to *Begeham*) saving to the Lord of the Soil, the Service of half a pound of Pepper, to be paid yearly on the Vigil of *Christmass* for all Custom and exaction.

---

78.   DURFORD *Abby, in* Sussex.

Founded and endow'd with Lands, &c. by *Henry Hosatus* Lord of *Herting* in the County of *Sussex*; confirmed by King *Henry* the II. who also
79. granted them a Fair for three days yearly at *Herting*, viz. on the Nativity of St. *John Baptist*, and two days next before. Confirm'd also by
80. *Hillary*, and *Seffrid* Bishops of *Chichester*, and by *William de Percy*, &c.

[Valued at 98 l. 4 s. 5 d. per Annum.]

---

81.   STIXWOLD *Abby, in* Lincolnshire.

KING *Henry* VIII. in the 29th. year of his Reign, out of the sincere Devotion which he had to the Virgin *Mary*, and for the increase of Virtue, and the Divine Worship, &c. founded a new Monastery of Nuns of the Order of *Præmonstratenses*, in the place Scite and Precinct of the Old Monastery of *Stixwold* in *Com. Lincoln*, lately suppreft by Authority of Parliament, to consist of a Prioress and Nuns, there to officiate in the Divine Offices for the good Estate of him and of his most dear Confort *Jane* Queen of *England* while they lived, and after their deaths for their Souls, and the Souls of their Children and Progenitors. And made and constituted *Mary Missenden* Prioress of the said new Monastery; and incor-
82. porated the said Prioress and Nuns by the name of the Prioress and Convent of the *New Monastery of King* Henry *the VIII. of Stixwold*, with capacity to receive Lands by that name, to sue and be sued, and to have a Common-Seal. He further gave and settled on them, all the Lands, and Estate real and personal belonging to the old Monastery of *Stixwold*, in as full and ample manner as *Helena Key* late Prioress of the said Monastery enjoy'd the same on the 4th. of *Feb*. in the seven and twentieth year of his Reign, or any time before, at which time it came to his hands by reason of an Act of Parliament then past for the dissolving of certain Monasteries. Which said Revenue was then rated at the clear yearly value of 152 l. 10 s. 7 d. and was granted to the said new Monastery, to hold *in Capite* by the twentieth part of a Knights Fee, and by the yearly Rent of 15 l. 5 s. 1 d. to be paid into the Court of *Augmentations* at *Mi-*
83. *chaelmas*, and *Lady-day*; the Statute of *Mortmain*, or any other Statute *non obstante*. Whose Grant bears date on the 9th. of *July* in the said nine and twentieth year, and is witnessed by *Thomas* Archbishop of *Canterbury*: and divers others, among whom Sir *Thomas Crumwell* Knt. Lord *Crumwell* Keeper of the Privy-Seal, &c.

Vid. 1. *Vol.* 486.

Pag. 376. BRACKLEY.

Robert Earl of *Leicester* gave to *Salomon* the Clerk and his Successors one Acre of Land in *Brahole* (*Brackley*) in the love of God, and honour of St. *John* the Apostle and Evangelist, to build a House thereon for the Receipt and Entertainment of poor People. This was confirm'd afterwards by *Robert* his Son and Heir, which Father and Son endow'd the said Hospital with divers Lands to hold in *Frankalmoine*. *Hugh* Bishop of *Lincoln* confirm'd the Foundation of this Hospital, with all the Lands and Liberties given and conferr'd upon it. The like did King *Henry* III. in the twelfth year of his Reign.

84.

85.

Pag. 423. DOVER.

86.

King *Henry* the III. in the twelfth year of his Reign, confirm'd to the Hospital of St. *Mary* at *Dover*, divers Lands and Rents given by *Simon de Wardune*; he also confirm'd the Mannor of *Rivere* to the said Hospital at the Petition of *Hubert de Burgo* who founded the same for the sustentation of poor People and Travellers who should come thether. He also ordained that upon the death or removal of the Master, the Brothers of the said Hospital shall freely choose another, and present him to the King or his Chief Justice, who shall without difficulty give assent; and then he shall be presented to the Archbishop of *Canterbury* to be by him instituted. He also granted to the said Hospital the tenth part of the Profits of the Passage in the Port of *Dover*, besides 10 *l*. and 50 *s*. which by two Deeds he had formerly granted them. With other Revenues elsewhere.

87.

Pag. 899. NEWTON.

88.

Thomas Archbishop of *York* made a Decree between *Edmund Litchfield*, who pretended to the Office of Custos or Master of the Hospital of St. *Mary Magdalen* at *Newton* in *Holdernesse*, and *Edmund Percy* then in Possession of the said Hospital, containing that the said *Percy* (whose title the Bishop confirms) and his Successors shall pay to the said *Litchfield* during his Life a yearly Pension of 100 *s*. on the day of the Annunciation of the Blessed Virgin, in the Collegiate Church of St. *Thomas* of *Acon* in *London*, under pain of incuring the Sentence of Excommunication, if upon request he does not within thirty days perform this Decree, and besides it shall and may be lawful for the said *Litchfield* on the Possessions of the said Hospital to enter and distrain, and the distress to detain till his said Annuity and the Arrearages and his Expences be fully satisfied. This Decree was made by consent and approbation of both Parties, and bears date in the Archbishops Inn at *Westminster* (now *Whitehall*) *An. Dom.* 1485. Approved, ratified, and confirm'd by the Dean and Chapter of *York*, and by the Master, Brothers, and Sisters of the said Hospital, in the same year.

89.

Pag. 381. RIPPON.

IT was found by Inquisition taken at *Rippon*, 10 E. 2. that in the Hospital of St. *Mary Magdalen* there, according to the Foundation, there ought to be two Chaplains daily celebrating; that Strangers, poor Clerks, or other indigent People, coming to the said Hospital in their travells, ought to be lodged there one night, and entertain'd with Victuals, and Bed, and in the Morning depart; and that on St. *Mary Magdalen's* day yearly ought to be distributed in Alms to every poor Body that comes, one Loaf of the value of a half-penny, the quarter of Wheat being prized at 5 s. But they find that the then Costos of this Hospital had perverted the Founders Charity in several particulars.

Pag. 461. WELLE.

90.

Ralph de Neville, Knt. Lord of *Midleham*, by Indenture dated *A.* 1342. Founded the Hospital at *Welle* in the Archdeaconry of *Rickmond*, for the Augmentation of Divine Worship, and for the sustentation of poor and miserable People, and other Works of Piety, and endow'd the same with Lands and Revenues, and establisht therein one Master, two Priests, and four and twenty poor and infirm People. And appointed that the Master and two Priests should constantly observe and keep the Canonical hours, and celebrate three Masses daily.

KYPIER *Hospital, in the County* Palatine *of* Durham.

FOunded by. *Ranulphus* Bishop of *Durham*, *An.* 1112. to the honour of God and St. *Giles*, for the Relief of the Clergy there serving, and for the sustentation of poor People, who also endowed it with divers Lands and Revenues; confirm'd and augmented by *Hugh* Bishop of *Durham*, and other Benefactors. The said Bishop *Hugh* granted to this Hospital Common of Pasture in his Forrest with certain Priviledges, *viz.* that the feet of their Dogs should not be cut or clipt, but that the Shepherds might lead them in slips (*ligatos*) for the safety of their Cattle from wild Beasts and Wolves. *An.* 1297. A Composition was made between the Prior and Convent of *Durham*, and the Hospital of. St. *Giles*, whereby the said Prior and Convent did quit-claim to the Brothers of that Hospital their Tithes of Corn at *Clifton*, which till that time they had used to pay to the Church of St. *Oswald*, in recompence whereof the Brothers of the said Hospital were to pay yearly upon the Altar of St. *Oswald* on the day of that Saint, one *Bisantium* or 2 s. &c. The Men of *Bedelyngtonshire* being obliged by their Lords the Bishops of *Durham*, to give to the Hospital of St. *Giles* without *Durham*, one Thrave of Corn out of every Plowland which they held, they granted under their Seals, in lieu thereof 9 s. in mony, to be paid to the said Hospital at the Feast of St. *Michael*, with a *Nomine penæ.*

91.
92.
93.
94.

[Valued at 167 l. 2 s. 11 d. *per Annum.*]

STOKE

STOKE Hospital, near Newarke, in Nottinghamshire.

John Chaufon, Master of the Hospital of St. Leonard's-at Stoke, and others, Confraters of the fame, fettled, by their Deed dated in the year 1332. forty Acres of Land, and thirty fhillings of Rent, which they had obtain'd of Friends, for the profit of the faid Hofpital, and provided that the Mafter of the fame fhould caufe fixty Maffes to be celebrated yearly for ever, for the faid Benefactors, &c. To this every Mafter is to be fworn at his admiffion. This Deed was ratified and confirm'd the fame year by *William* Archbifhop of *York*.

95.

St. GILES Hofpital, near Maldon, in Essex.

IT was found by Inquifition taken before *Helming Leget*, Efcheator in the County of *Effex*, that the Kings of *England* were Founders of this Hofpital, for the fupport of Leprous Burgeffes of *Maldon*; that they had the Forfeitures of all Bread, Ale, Flefh, and Fifh, that was not good and wholefome in the faid Town; and that when the Mafter of that Hofpital fhould ceafe to take the fame for the fupport as aforefaid, then the faid Hofpital fhould come and revert to the King as forfeited; that *Robert Manfeild*, Clerk, late Provoft of *Beverley*, being made Cuftos of this Hofpital, for above three years paft has maintained neither Chaplain nor any Leprous Perfon in the fame, and that the faid Hofpital was therefore feized into the King's hands. But King *Henry* the IV. being advifed by his Juftices and Serjeants at Law that this was no fufficient caufe of feizure, directed his writ to the faid Efcheator to amove his hand, &c. and meddle no further.

96.

GINGES Hofpital, in Essex.

Michael de Capra, and *Rofe* his Wife, and *William* his Son and Heir, gave to God and the Church of *St. Mary* and *St. Leonard* in their Wood of *Ginges*, and to *Toby* Prior of the faid Place and the Brothers of the fame, one Hide of Land, Paunage for forty Hogs, and divers other advantages.

BURCESTRE Hofpital, in Oxfordshire.

KING *Edward* the III. in the nine and twentieth year of his Reign, licenfed *Nicholas Jordan* Hermit, Cuftos of the Chappel of St. John Baptift of *Burceftre*, to found an Hofpital at *Burceftre* to the honour of God, the glorious Virgin Mary and St. *John Baptift*.

[Valued at 147 l. 2 s. 10 d. per Annum.]

CALC Priory, in Derbyshire.

.97

Matilda Countefs of *Chefter* gave to the Canons of this place, an Eftate at *Rependone* near *Trent*, conditionally that they fhould
make

98.   ARUNDELL *Hospital, in* Suffex.

KING *Richard* the II. *An.* 18. Licensed *Richard* Earl of *Arundel* to give four Messuages and two Tofts to the Master and Chaplains of the holy *Trinity* at *Arundell*, for the founding of an Hospital call'd *Meysondewe* in honour of the holy *Trinity*, &c.

[Valued at 42 *l.* 3 *s.* 8 *d. per Annum.*]

         FOSS-GATE *Hospital, at* York.

99. JOhn Archbishop of *York*, Primate of *England*, and Legate of the Apostolick See, ordain'd and establisht in the *Foss-gate-street* at *York* an Hospital in honour of our Lord Jesus Christ, and the blessed Virgin *Mary*, That there be one Chaplain to have the Government of the same, and to be named Master or Custos, the right of presenting to the Office of Custos to belong to Mr. *John de Roucliff* and his Heirs, in their default to the Mayor of *York* for the time being; in his default to the Official of *York* Court, and in his default that the Archbishop or Dean and Chapter may, for that time confer the place without presentation, the Custos on his admission to be sworn to a just and true Administration, &c. That there be constantly resident in the said Hospital thirteen poor and weak Persons, and two poor Clerks teaching Schools, to be chosen by the Custos, every of which to receive from the Custos weekly 4 *d.* of Silver, the Custos to have ten Marks of yearly Revenue, which is judged sufficient for his support, that it shall not be lawful for him to convert to his own use more than that Sum of the Goods of the said Hospital, &c. Which Orders are dated at *Thorpe* near *York*, *An.* Dom. 1373.

[Valued at 6 *l.* 13 *s.* 4 *d. per Annum.*]

         WHITINGTON'S *Hospital, at* London.

100. JOhn *Coventry*, *John Carpenter*, and *William Grove*, Execuors, of *Richard Whitington* late Citizen and Mercer of *London*, and several times Mayor of that City, according to the desire and appointment of the said *Richard*, founded in the Church of St. *Michael Royal* at *London*, where the said *Richard* and *Alice* his Consort lye buried, a Colledge of certain Priests and Clerks to celebrate daily for the said *Richard* and *Alice*; also an Almshouse for 13 poor People in the Parish of St. *Michael* aforesaid and adjoyning to the Church, And establisht divers Orders by Licence of King *Henry* VI. and *Henry* Archbishop of *Canterbury*, &c. touching the same; as, that there shall be always inhabiting in the said Hospital 13 poor People of one or both Sexes, of which one to be Cheif, and called *Tutor*, the first of which Office they placed themselves, by name *Robert Chesterton*, to whom they gave the said Hospital with all the Appurtenances for a perpetual habitation for him and the poor People and their Successors, by the name of the

101. *House of God*, or the *Almshouse*, or the *Hospital* of *Richard Whityngton*;
                                                                    that

that the Mayor of *London*, and his Successors, shall be Supervisers, and the Wardens and Communalty of Mercers, Conservators of the said House; that the Tutor and poor People have Lodgings or Cells apart and several; that within 20 days after the Death of a Tutor the Wardens of the Mercers shall elect or depute another fit person to succeed in the said Office, and upon their neglect for 20 days, the Power of so doing shall for that time, be in the Mayor of *London*; that as the poor People dye, the Master of the foresaid Colledge shall place one in the first Vacancy, and the Wardens of the Mercers in the Six next Vacancies, then again the Master in the next one, and then the Wardens for the six next, &c. yet it shall not be lawful for the said Wardens to put one that is of the Livery of their own Company, or any other Company of the said City, into the said places, yet poor Citizens of *London*, and especially the poor of the Mercers, who are not, nor have been of the Livery, (*qui de liberatâ minimè fuerint*) and whom the Company are not bound to maintain, and poor Clerks and inferiour Officers of the Colledge aforesaid, are to be preferr'd to the said places before others; that the Tutor and poor People be daily present at Mattins, Masses, Vespers, and Complin, in the Colledge or Church abovemention'd, and at the prayers to be there made for the Souls of *Richard Whitington* and *Alice* their Founders, Sr. *William Whitington* Knight, the Lord *Ivo Fitz Waryn*, and the Lady *Maud* his Wife, Parents of the said *Richard* and *Alice*, King *Richard* II. and *Thomas* late Duke of *Gloucester*, &c. That they shall say for the said Souls as often as they can conveniently, three, or at least two Psalters, *i. e.* fifty *Aves*, and fifteen *Paters*, and three Creeds; that they should all go daily to the Tomb of the said *Richard* and *Alice*, and there say the Psalm *de Profundis*, after which the Tutor to say aloud in English *God have mercy on our Founders Souls, and all Christen*, and the rest answer, *Amen*; that the Tutor shall not be absent from the said House above ten nights in a year, nor any poor Man, above one whole day without License, or great necessity; That they have a Common Chest, and a Common Seal, the Chest to have three different Keys, &c. That the Tutor have and receive every week for his Pension 16 *d.* and every poor person 4 *d.* that no Leprous, or mad Man be admitted into the House, &c. if any Estate falls to any poor Man of the clear yearly value of five marks, that he be removed, and another poor Person put in his place, but if it be under five marks *per Annum*, let him give half to the Common Chest and keep the other half; Vicious persons after the third fault to be expell'd the Hospital as incorrigible; That these Orders and Statutes be read, and intelligibly expounded, before the Tutor and poor People once every quarter of a year; With power reserved to the said Executors while they or any of them live, to add, correct, or alter any of these Orders. Dated 21. *December An. Dom.* 1424. (3. *H.* 6.)

101.

102.

103.

104.

RUTHYN *Hospital in* Denbighshire.

Queen *Elizabeth*, at the Petition of *Gabriel Goodman* Doctor of Divinity, and Dean of the Collegiate Church of *Westminster*, erected, created, founded, and establisht, an Hospital in *Ruthyn* in the County of *Denbigh*, to be call'd *Christ's Hospital* in *Ruthin*, to consist of one Preacher and twelve poor People for ever; and ordain'd, that there should be one President, and one Warden of the same, and nominated the then Bishop of

105.

Bangor

106. *Bangor* and his Succeſſors, for the time being, to be Preſident, and *Eubolus Theloall* Maſter in Arts, to be the firſt Warden of the ſaid Hoſpital, and all the Poſſeſſions, Lands and Goods thereunto belonging; that the ſaid Preſident and Warden be a Body corporate for ever, by the name of the Preſident and Warden of *Chriſt's Hoſpital* in *Ruthin*, by the ſaid name to purchaſe and receive Lands, &c. as well of the ſaid *Gabriel Goodman*, as any other perſon, for the ſupport and maintenance of the ſaid Hoſpital; that they have a Common Seal; that they may ſue and be ſued by the ſaid name in all Courts; with power to the ſaid *Gabriel Goodman* during his Life to elect, nominate, and appoint the Wardens and poor People of the ſaid Hoſpital as often as there ſhall be occaſion, and to make and appoint Statutes and Orders for Government of the ſame; with licenſe to the ſaid Preſident, and Warden, and their Succeſſors to purchaſe Lands not exceeding the clear yearly value of 100 l. &c. the Statute of *Mortmain* or any other Stat. *non obſtante*. Letters Patents to be paſt of all this under the Great Seal of *England* without any manner of Fine or Fee to be paid &c.

107. DROHEDA *Hoſpital, in* Ireland.

Founded by *Urſus de Swemele*, without the *Weſt*-Gate of *Droheda*, for the relief of poor and helpleſs People, and by him endow'd with all the Lands and Rents that he had in *Ireland*, and gave the Election of the Cuſtos (after his death) to the Honeſt men, or Free-men (*probos homines*) of *Drohida*.

Pag. 792. SEMPRINGHAM.

THE Maſter and Canons of *Sempringham* declared by their Deed, that they and theirs in the place call'd *Mirmaude*, the Gift of *Ralph de Hauvill*, are ſubject to the Juriſdiction of the Biſhop of *Ely* as their Dioceſan, notwithſtanding their Priviledges.

108. *Pag.* 825. ELLERTON.

Gilbert the II. Maſter of the Order of *Sempringham*, and *John* Prior and the Convent of *Ellerton*, obliged themſelves to the maintenance of thirteen poor People in the Hoſpital of the Church of *Ellerton*, founded by *William Fitz-Peter*.

Pag. 514. St. John *of* Jeruſalem, *in the Suburbs of* London.

109. KING *Philip* and Queen *Mary* by their Letters Patents, and Cardinal *Pole* Legate *a Latere*, reſtored and eſtabliſht the Hoſpital of St. *John* of *Jeruſalem* in *England*, to its Priſtine Eſtate, and the Priory and Hoſpital of St. *John* of *Clerkenwell* lately diſſolved, and conſtituted Sir *Thomas Treſham* Knt. Prior of the ſame, *Richard Shelley*, *Peter Felices*, *Cuthbert Laithen*, *Edward Brown*, *Thomas Thornell*, *Henry Gerard*, *George Aylmer*, *James Shelley*, and *Oliver Starkey*, Commendators or Preceptors of the ſaid
Hoſpital

Hospital, whom the said King and Queen incorporated by the name of Prior and Confraters of the Hospital of St. *John* of *Jerusalem* in *England*, to have perpetual Succession, and by that name to sue and be sued, to purchase and take Lands, &c. and to have a Common Seal; and gave them all that Capital House and Scite of the said Hospital of St. *John* of *Jerusalem*, scituate and being near *Clerkenwell*, in *Middlesex*, with the Church and all Houses and Buildings, Gardens and Orchards, &c. thereunto belonging, also all that Wood and Wood-ground call'd *Grete St. John's Wood*, lying near *Maribone-Park* in *Middlesex*, and all other Lands and Tenements whatsoever that were in the Possession of the Prior and Confraters of the said Hospital at the time of the Dissolution of the same, and all Goods and Furniture belonging to the said House, &c. Which Letters Pattents bear date at *Grenewiche*, *April* the 2d. in the fourth and fifth year of their Reign.

Pag. 247. BUTLEY.

110.

KING *Henry* the VII. in the four and twentieth year of his Reign granted to *Robert Brommer* Prior of the Monastery of *Butley*, and the Convent of the same, the Priory of the blessed *Mary* of *Snape* in *Suffolk*, with all Lands and Revenues thereunto belonging, or which *Thomas Neylond* late Prior of the said Priory enjoy'd in right of the same, to hold in pure and perpetual Alms without Account or any Rent, and to be annext to the said Priory of *Butley*.

NEWINTON-LONGVILLE, an alian Priory in Buckinghamshire.

111.

THIS was a Cell to the Abby of St. *Faith* at *Longville* in *Normandy*, to which *Walter Gifford* Earl of *Buckingham*, gave and confirm'd divers Lands and Revenues, with great Priviledges in his Forrest of *Waddon*, free and discharged of all Exactions, &c.

CATHEDRAL CHURCHES
Of Canons Secular.

115.   **CHICHISTER** *Cathedral, in* 𝔖𝔲𝔰𝔰𝔢𝔵.

A*Nno Dom.* 673. *Ceadwalla* King of the *South-Saxons*, at the Request of Bishop *Wilfrid*, gave divers Lands for the Building and Endowment of a Monastery at *Selesey*. *Brnny* Duke of *Suffex*, *Northelmus* King
116. of *Suffex, An.* 692. *Numa* King of *Suffex, An.* 714. *Oslac* Duke of *Suf-*
117. *sex, An.* 780. were Benefactors to this Religious House of *Selesey*. Abbot
118. *Pleghaard* having transferr'd certain Revenues in *Deaton* to the Episcopal Church at *Selesey*, which Revenues he had of the Gift of King *Offa*, they were fixt and establisht to the said Church, in a Synod held at *Clobe-*
119. *ham, An.* 825. King *Athelstan* gave Lands to the said Church, *An.* 930. the like did King *Edmund*, King *Eadwyn*, King *Ethelred*, and *Ethelbert*. King
120. *William* gave Lands and Liberties to the Church of *Chichister* (the See being
121. then translated thither) the like did King *Henry* the I. and King *Steven*,
122. which last gave and confirm'd to the Church of the holy *Trinity* at
123. *Chichester*, and to *Hillary* Bishop of the same, divers Lands and Franchises, some of which Lands the said Bishop and his Successors were to hold by being Chaplains to *Maud* his Queen and her Successors. *William*
124. Earl of *Chichister* gave to this Church among other things, the fourth part of the City; King *John* confirm'd to this Church all the Lands, *&c.* and Liberties which they then had or should have; The like did King *Henry*
125. the III. to *Ralph* the II. Bishop of *Chichester*, his Chancellor. The Prior
126. and Convent of St. *Bartholmew's* at *London* granted to the Bishops of this See, certain Houses in the Parish of *St. Sepulchers*, without *Newgate*, to hold by the yearly Rent of one pound of *Frankincense*, or six-pence, at
127. the Feast of St. *Michael*. *Ranulphus* Bishop of *Chichister*, (who writes himself the humble Minister of the Church of *Chichister*) caused to be provided for the Manrriors of that Bishoprick, a stock or store of Cattel, *viz.* two hundred and fifty two Oxen, one hundred Crows, ten Bulls, three thousand one hundred and fifty Seep (*Bidentia*) one hundred and twenty she Goats, and six he Goats, and ten Plow-horses, which Stock he ordered to be continued by all his Successors under censure of Excommunication, and to be *Anathema Maranatha*; Confirm'd and ratified by King *Henry* the III. *John* Earl of *Eu*, restored to this Church, by Deed dated *An.* 1248. the Mannor of *Bixle*, which his Grandfather and Father had unjustly taken, and a long time detain'd from it.

---

128.   *St.* **PETERS** *Cathedral, at* 𝔜𝔬𝔯𝔨.

O*N Easter-day, An.* 627. *Edwyn* King of the *Northumbers* was baptized by *Paulinus* at *York*, in a small Church built on purpose, of Wood. This Church dedicated to St. *Peter*, was made the Archiepiscopal Seat of the said *Paulinus*, who had converted all that Province to the Christian Faith;

Faith. Afterwards in the year 1067. *Thomas* a Canon of *Bayeux*, being made Archbishop, built the Church of Stone, after a larger manner. *An* 958. King *Eadway* gave *Suthwell* to *Oscytell* Archbishop of *Tork*. King *Athelstan*, King *Canute* the Dane, King *Edward* the Confessor, were Benefactors to this Church. King *William Rufus*, who stiles himself *Son of King William*, who succeeded King Edward *by hereditary Right*, gave to *Thomas* Archbishop of *Tork* and his Successors the Abby of St. *German* of *Seleby*, and the Church of St. *Ofwald* at *Gloucester*, in lieu of the Jurisdiction which the said Archbishop claim'd over *Lincoln*, and *Linfey*, which the said Archbishop thereupon quitted, for ever. The said King confirmed all the Liberties of this Church, as did also Pope *Honorius*, who exempted this Archbishop from Subjection to that of *Canterbury*. Pope *Alexander* granted to *Thomas* Archbishop of *Tork* the *Pallium*, to be by him worn on Solemn Occasions. King *Hen.* I. and II. and *Maud* the Empress, granted Lands, Churches, and Liberties, to the Canons of this Cathedral. *Roger* Archbishop of *Tork*, built anew the Quire and Vaults under it at St. *Peter's*, and the Archiepiscopal Pallace thereunto adjoyning; he also built the Chappel of the holy Sepulcher adjoyning to the Gate of the said Pallace, and dedicated it in honour of the Virgin *Mary* and the holy Angels, endowed it with eleven Churches, and settled therein thirteen Ministers, *viz.* four Priests, four Deacons, four Sub-deacons, and one Sacristan to be chief, each Priest to have ten Marks *per Annum*, each Deacon 100 *s.* and each Sub-deacon six Marks, the rest to the Sacristan; *Sewallus* who was consecrated Archbishop of *Tork* in the year 1256. perceiving the Revenue of the said eleven Churches to be very much increased, caused Vicars to be establisht in the said Churches, presentable by the foresaid Sacristan; and made Orders for the Government of the said Ministers or Canons of the Chappel aforesaid; The names of which eleven Churches are these, *Thorp-Arches, Colingham, Berdeseye, Otteleye, Calverley, Hoton-Paynel, Sutton, Everton, Hayton, Clareburgh,* and *Retford,* the Vicars of all which he caused to be endow'd, some with the whole Altarage, others with part, &c. King *Henry* the VI. in the three and thirtieth year of his Reign granted his License to *William* then Archbishop of *Tork* and others to purchase a House to be a Colledge, wherein the Chantry Priests of the Cathedral Church might inhabit together, which said Priests be incorporated, with License to purchase Lands to the value of ten Marks *per Annum*. The like Letters Pattents were granted by King *Edward*. IV. in his first year, for erecting a Colledge of the said Chantry Priests, (*Persones in Kyrk of Tork*) with Licence to the said Colledge to purchase Lands, &c. to the value of 100 *l.* per Annum. Pope *Innocent* confirm'd the Lands, &c. of this Church, and the use of the *Pall* to the Archbishop. Pope *Paschalis*, and *Calixtus*, exempted this Archbishop from Subjection to *Canterbury*.

William King of *Scotland* certified to Pope *Alexander* that the Church of *Scotland* was of old times subject to the Church of *Tork*, and desired that by his Authority it may be made so again. Pope *Honorius* writ to the King of *Norway* to restore to *Ralf* Bishop of the *Orcades* consecrated by, and Subject to the Jurisdiction of the Archbishop of *Tork*, the Possessions belonging to the said Bishoprick. *Olaus* King of the Isles writ to the Archbishop of *Tork* at the recommendation of the Abbot of *Furnes*, to obtain from him the Consecration of a Bishop to propagate the Christian Religion in the Isles. Pope *Calixtus* writ to the Bishop of *Glascow*, commanding him to submit himself to the Jurisdiction of the Archbishop of *Tork*

York within thirtty days after the receit of his Letters. Pope *Honorius* writ to the Bishop elect of *Galloway* (*Candida casa*) to repair to the Archbishop of *York* as his proper Metropolitan, for Consecration, *&c.*

146. Pope *Paschal* writ to all the Bishops of *Scotland* to submit to *York* as their
147. Metropolitan; the like did *Calixtus* and *Innocent*, which last writ to the Archbishop of *Canterbury*, his Legate, to denounce the Bishop of *Glascow* excommunicate unless he submits himself to the Archbishop of *York* within three Months, after admonition. Pope *Honorius* writ to the Archbishop of *Canterbury* and all the Bishops of *England*, and to King *Henry*, that the Archbishop of *York* may, according to antient Custome, be permitted to have his Cross born before him, in all parts of *England*, and to Crown the King, in such manner as has been used. The Bishop
148. of *Galloway* made a formal Act of Subjection and Canonical Obedience to this Archbishop, in like manner as did *Durham*, and *Carlile*.

149. Roger *de Mowbray*, *Peter de Ros*, *William Paynell*, the Lord *William de Percy*,
150. who gave the Church of *Topcliffe*, to the Fabrick of this Church, (in
151. return for which the Dean and Chapter promised to find a fit Chaplain for ever to celebrate in the Chappel of the Blessed *Mary* at *Topcliffe*,
152. and to allow him 100 s. yearly) *Jeffry Fitz-Peter* Earl of *Essex*, the Abbot and Convent of *Albemarl*, who gave *Preston*, and other Churches
153. in *Holderness An.* 1228. *Nicholas de Stutville* who gave *Michael de Ha-*
154. *melscia* his Native or Villain, and all his progeny; *Henry Fitz Thomas*, and others, were Benefactors to this Church. An Inquisition was taken *An. Dom.* 1275. (4. *Edward* I.) in which all the Lands and Liberties
155. of the Church of *St. Peter*, in the City and Suburbs of *York*, were set forth and exprest, some of which the Jury then found to have belong'd
156. to that Church time out of memory. *Walter Gray* Archbishop of *York* granted to the Chapter of *York* by Deed dated, *An.* 1241. All his Mansion
157. House, and all his Lands, *&c.* in *Thorp St. Andrew*, or Bishops *Thorp*, with Provision that the said Chapter reconvey the Premisses to his Successors to hold by the Rent of 20 marks *per An.* at the feast of St. *Martin*,
158. which twenty marks to be distributed to poor People on the day of his Anniversary, *&c.* The said *Walter* in the 33 year of his consecration caused certain Vicarages to be endow'd in the Churches of *Tickhill* &c. which Churches were appropriated to the Prior and Convent of St. *Oswald* of *Nostel*; in particular to the support of the Vicar of *Tickhill*, and one associate Priest, a Deacon, and Subdeacon there, he appointed the whole Altarage, in which name he specifies all Oblations, Tithes and profits of the Church of *Tickhill*, except Tithes of Corn, pulse, and hay, and the Lands belonging to the said Church, saving a Competent Mansion to be assign'd to the Vicar, which Tithes of Garbs, and Hay, and the said Lands, shall remain to the said Convent of *Nostell*, &c. *Herbert* the Chamberlain,
159. Brother of King *Steven*, and *Steven* and *Reginald* his Sons were Benefactors
160. to this Church of St. *Peter*. King *Henry* II. granted to Archbishop *Walter*, and his Successors Free Warren, in their Mannours of *Shirburn*,
161. and *Cawood*. *Aufridus de Chanci*, *Paganus de Vilers*, *John* Constable of
162. *Chester*, *Robert de Vavasour*, and others, were also Benefactors. *Thomas*
163. Archbishop of *York*, before mention'd, dyed at *York* on the *Octaves* of St. *Martin*, *An. Dom.* 1100, in great Reputation; as appears by his Epitaph enter'd in the Register of that Church.
164. There were certain Customes and Orders used of old time in this Church, as, that upon the Archbishops first coming to this City after his
Con-

Confecration, he was to be received in folemn Proceffion, fo alfo when he returns at any time from beyond Sea, &c. That the Bifhop of *Durham* was to prefent him with a rich Cope after his Confecration; that every Prebendary fhould in his life-time give a Cope value 10 *l.* or after his death twenty Marks, and at his death his Palfrey; that the Dean is to be inftall'd by the Precentor, &c. That the Dean is bound to feed forty poor People daily, that he is the greateft in the Church, next The Archbifhop, and in the Chapter the greateft of all, *An. Dom.* 1200. the then Dean and Canons did order and ordain, that four Perfons fhould be conftantly refident, *viz.* the Dean, the Chantor, the Chancellor, and the Treafurer, the Archdeacons to refide for three months in a year, other Canons for half a year, the common Profits to be divided among thofe only who are refident, that no Vicar fhall be admitted for favour, but only fuch as are worthy and proper for the Service of the Church, that none be promoted but by the Dean and Chapter, and that no Vicar or inferior Minifter be admitted into the Quire unlefs he have a good Voice. King *Henry* the VIII. made and eftablifht new Statutes by Letters Patents, in the time of *Edward* Archbifhop of *York*, whereby reciting that they had in this Church an evil Cuftom, long ufed, that every Canon Prebendary was bound to fpend in feafting the firft year of his Refidency one thoufand Marks, or elfe he could not partake of the Emoluments of the Place, he abolifhes the faid Cuftom, and all Statutes relating thereunto, and Orders that the Statutes relating to the great Refidency be obferved, and that they have their Diftributions and Emoluments on the account of Refidency duly paid from the day of their firft entry on the fame; if there be none refiding then all the common Profits of the Church to go wholly to the Treafury of St. *Peter*, That all Canons then being in the City of *York*, as well not refident as refident, be called to affift at all Chapters, that to the Cheft wherein the Common-Seal is kept, be three different Locks and Keys, one to be kept by the Dean, the other two by the two Senior Refidents, or if there be not at that time two Refidentiaries then by the Precentor, and Chancellor, &c. that all Cuftom incouraging Pomp and Prodigality be abolifht, that a divifion of the Profits be made at the Feaft of St. *Martin* according to the Days, Weeks, or Months of the Refidentiaries refiding; which Canons in the time of their Refidency are to be prefent at Vefpers, Mattins, and high Mafs, at leaft, without juft excufe, under pain of lofing that days diftribution when abfent, &c. Every Canon Refidentiary to live at a Houfe within the Clofe of the Cathedral, and to have in Benefices at leaft 100 *l. per Annum*, That the Vicars Choral fhall when every Canon begins his greater Refidence, receive 5 *l.* and afterwards 6 *l.* 13 *s.* 4 *d. per Annum*. That every Canon having a Prebend worth 8 *l. per Annum*, fhall yearly at the Feaft of St. *Martin* contribute and pay into the hands of the Chancellor of this Church 6 *s.* 8 *d.* for the providing of Preachers in the faid Church, which Preachers are to be provided on the Rogation-days, Sundays, and other days at difcretion; this not to excufe the Dean, and Chancellor, or any others to preach themfelves as they are obliged by Statute or Cuftom, &c. Which Letters Pattens bear date 3 *June* 33 *H.* 8.

165.

166.

167.

168.

169.

To this Cathedral Church did belong abundance of Jewels, Veffels of Gold and Silver, and other Ornaments, rich Veftments and Books, *viz.* ten Miters of great value, among which one fmall Miter with Stones for the Bifhop of the Boys, or Children (pro *Epifcopo puerorum*) one Silver and

170. and gilt Pastoral Staff, many Pastoral Rings, among which one for *the Bishop of the Boys*; Chalices, Vials, Pots, Basons, Candlesticks, Thuribules,
171. Holy Water-Pots, Crosses of Silver, one of which weighed eight pound
172. six ounces, Images of Silver and Gold, Relicks in Cases extreamly rich,
173. great Bouls of Silver, a Unicorns-Horn, a Table of Silver and gilt with the
174. Image of the blessed Virgin enamiled thereon, weighing nine pounds eight ounces and a half; several Gospellaries, and Epistollaries, richly adorn'd
175. with Silver, Gold, and precious Stones; Jewells affixt to Shrines and
176. Tombs, of almost inestimable value; Altar Cloaths, and hangings very
177. rich, Copes of Tissue, Damask, and Velvet, white, red, blew, green, pur-
178. ple, and black, with other Vestments of the same Colours. Besides this
179. there was a great Treasure in the Common Chest, in Gold Chains, collors
180. of *S S. &c.* with Sums of old Gold, and Silver deposited in the years 1517, 1518, 1519, and 1520.

HEREFORD *Cathedral*.

181. Milefrid King of the *Mercians* built and endowed this Church, and constituted a Bishop here; this he did as a kind of expiation for the death of *Ethelbert* (King of the *East-Angels*, murdered by *Offa* King of *Mercia*, and) reputed a Saint and Martyr. King *Edward* the Confessor granted Liberties to the Priests of this Church. In the time of the said King *Edward*, *Walter* then Bishop of this Church had one hundred *Masuras* wanting two (each *Masura* contains about four Oxgangs of Land) *Robert* Bishop here (who succeeded the other) found forty Hides of Land belonging to this See, but all wasted. The Canons of *Hereford* held many Mannors and Lands, &c. in right of their Church at the time of the Conquest, as appears by *Domesday-Book*, a true Copy whereof expressing the particulars in the several Hundreds where they lay, is transcribed and printed *P.182, 183, 184. the whole in the said Bishoprick amounting to 300
185. Hides of Land. *Ralph* Bishop of *Hereford* granted to the Dean and Chap-
186. ter of that Church, all his Land of *Hamme*, then valued at 15 *l* per *Annum*, which he had lately purchased of *Simon de Clifford*, to hold by the service of one Knights Fee and a half, and the said Dean and Chapter granted to him to celebrate the Divine Offices on the day of his *Obit*, yearly. The Mannor of *Hamme*, in which the said Land lay, was given to the Prior and Convent of *Crassewell*, by *Walter de Lasey*, and by the Prior and Convent of *Crassewell* sold and convey'd to *Peter de Aquablanca* Bishop of *Here-*
187. *ford* and his Heirs, for the Sum of five hundred Marks; which *Peter* gave the said Mannor and several other good Gifts to the Church of *Hereford*. King *William* the Conqueror restored to this Church divers Mannors unjustly taken from it by Earl *Herald*. *Ralph Murdac* confirmed to the Church of St. *Mary* and St. *Ethelbert*, and to the Canons of the same, the Church of *Putley*, given them by *William D'evereus* his Predecessor.

LANDAFF Cathedral.

188.

Anno Dom. 156. *Lucius* King of the *Britains*, having applied himself to Pope *Elutherius*, He and the Chief of his Kingdom were baptized into the Christian Religion ; the sincere Doctrines of which they preserved uncorrupted till the *Pelagian* Heresie arose ; to reform and confute which, St. *Germanus*, and *Lupus*, being sent for out of *France*, they before they went back consecrated Bishops in several parts of this Isle, in particular they consecrated *Dubritius* a holy and great Doctor, an Archbishop ; and appointed for him an Episcopal Seat, which was by the grant of King *Mouric*, founded at a place called *Podum Lartani* in honour of St. *Peter*, and by that King endow'd with all between *Taf*, and *Elei*. and by Apostolick Authority with great Ecclesiastical Priviledges. This *Dubricius* founded divers Churches, and settled Bishops in the Right side of Britain (per dextralem Britanniam) in particular he consecrated *Daniel* Bishop in the City of *Bangor*. *Guorduc* offered up (immolavit) his Virgin Daughter *Dulon* to *Dubricius* Archbishop of *Landaff*, whom he consecrated a Nun, for ever ; her Father gave with her divers Lands. *An. Dom.* 612. St. *Dubricius* Bishop of *Landaff* departed this life, and in the year 1120. was with great Solemnity translated from the Isle of *Enli*. to his Church of *Landaff*, at which time and action, some miraculous Events are said to happen. *Urban* Bishop of *Landaff* complained to Pope *Calixtus* that whereas this Church was at its first erection, the Mistress of all the Churches of *Wales*, and had once four and twenty Canons, of which there remained at that time but two, and the Revenues almost desolate, by the Invasion of Laymen and Monks, and also of his own Brothers, the Bishop of *Hereford*, and the Bishop of St. *Davids*, he therefore prays the said Pope to succour him and his Church.

189.

190.
191.

192.

Idon a *British* King was a great Benefactor to this Church, in the time of St. *Teliau*, Successor to the foresaid *Dubricius*. Also King *Margetud*, and King *Aircol*, and one *Tutuc*, gave to the same Archbishop *Teliau*, divers Lands and Possessions, as an expiatory penance for certain Murders. King *Mouric* before mentioned was the Son of King *Teudiric*, who having settled his Kingdom in Peace, resigned the Government to his Son, and himself became a Hermit ; but his Kingdom being afterwards invaded by the *Saxons*, and his Son in great danger of losing it, he was admonisht by an Angel that he should leave his Retirement and head the Army, that they would fly at his sight, and that he shou'd, however, receive a wound and die in peace after three days ; all which happened as foretold, and he dying in an Isle call'd in Welch *Echni*, his said Son built there an Oratory and Cimitery, and gave all the Territory about it to the Church of *Landaff*, this was in the time of *Oudoceus* the third Bishop of this See. The said *Mouric* having by treachery killed *Cynvetu*, after he had sworn to a firm peace with him, before the Relicks of the Saints, was Excommunicated, for redemption of which, and as part of his pennance, he gave to this Church four Towns with their Liberties. King *Morcant*, and *Augustus* King of *Brecknoc*, and King *Judhail*, were Benefactors ; so was *Gurvodius* upon his having obtained a great Victory over the *Saxons*. In the time of Bishop *Gurvan*, *Teudor* and *Elgist* Kings of *Brecknock*, swore a firm and mutual Peace with each other, before the Relicks of the Saints, after which King *Teudor* took occasion to Kill *Elgist* ; for which Homicide and Perjury being excom-

193.

194.

195.

196.

197.
198.

P p   mu-

	municate, and upon his Absolution being Enjoyn'd for Penance, Almes, Prayer, and Fasting, he gave in Almes to this Church of *Landaff* divers Lands and Revenues. *Briteon hail* Son of *Devon* sacrificed (*immolavit*)
199.	to God, and St. *Dubricius*, six Churches with all their Liberties and Profits, in one day. King *Clotri* and King *Judgvalaun*, having sworn a
200.	firm Peace before the holy Gospells and Reliques upon the Altar, in Presence of Bishop *Berthguin* and the Clergy, after which *Clotri* killing *Judgvalaun*, he was for his homicide and perjury, excommunicated with all his Progeny and Kingdom, by the said Bishop and Clergy in a full Synod. Afterwards being absolved and enjoyn'd Penance, as part of the same he gave divers Lands to this Church of *Landaff*. *Guidnerth* having
201.	slain his Brother, was for his homicide and Fratricide, excommunicated by Bishop *Oudoccus* in a full Synod, and after three years, having perform'd an enjoyn'd Pennance into *Cornwal* (the Brittons and those of *Cornwal* being of the same language and Nation tho' divided in territory) he was upon his great sorrow and tears absolved, after which he gave divers Lands to
202.	this Church. *Gurcan* who succeeded *Guinan*, having lived incestuously with his Mother in Law, was therefore in full Synod excommunicated by Bishop *Erthguin*, and after upon his reformation being absolved, gave
203.	divers Lands to this Church. King *Clitauc* Son of *Clitguin*, was a Prince who governed his Kingdom in Peace and exact Justice, and became afterwards a Martyr on this account: A young Virgin of quality was in love with him so far as to declare she would never marry unless to *Clitauc*, whereupon a Nobleman of the Court, whose Sute she had refused, for the Kings sake, in revenge murder'd the innocent King in hunting. After whose Murder the Bishop of *Landaff* caused to be built, and consecrated, a Church to his memory, in the place where he was buried near the
204.	River *Myngui*, &c. Which with divers Lands given to the same, was afterwards granted to the Bishops of *Landaff*, by King *Judhail* Son of *Morcant*. A Noble man of the same name, *Judhail* Son of *Edelvirth*, going with his Wife on a Sunday to hear divine Service at St. *Clitauc's*, was so far prevail'd upon by the Devils instigation and his own lust, as to lie with his Wife in a Meadow on the Bank of *Mingui*, and having perform'd the Act, and about to withdraw, he found himself not able to disjoyn, but was forced to remain in that Posture inseperable from his Wife, whereupon he call'd out to his Attendants, and order'd them to repair to the Monument of the Martyr *Clitauc*, and there offer in his name that Meadow which he had unjustly taken from that Church, this being done, with promise of amendment of Life, he was again separated from that vexatious Conjunction. *Convur* bought certain Lands
205.	of King *Fernvail*, Son of *Judhail*, for an excellent horse of the price of 12 Cows, a Dog that had kill'd Birds, with a Hawk (*cum Ancipitre*) of the Price of 3 Cows, and another Horse of the Price of 3 Cows, which Lands so purchased he gave to the Bishops of this Church of *Landaff*.
206.	*Fernuhail, Convelin*, King *Ris* Son of *Judhail*, and abundance of other Kings
207.	and great Men in *Wales*, were Benefactors to this Church. King *Hovel* being excommunicated by the Bishop and Synod at *Landaff* for killing *Galcun*, after a peace sworn, upon his Absolution gave divers Lands to this Church; the like did *Ili* Son of *Conblus*, who was excommunicated for killing *Camauc* after a Peace sworn between them. *Agvod* Son of *Jovaf* having an angry Contest betwixt his family and the Bishops, came up to the Church Door, and threw stones into the Church, and then fled, under an *Anathema*;

thema; for which he afterwards beg'd pardon and gave divers Lands to *Corenbiro* then Bishop and his Successors. King *Nongui* gave Lands for violating the Liberties of this Church and committing Sacriledge. *An. Dom.* 955. *Pater* being then Bishop of this Church, six men of the Family of *Nongui*, broke into a Church in this Diocess, and there kill'd a Deacon before the Altar, who had fled thither for Sanctuary, for which they were delivered up to the Bishop, and remain'd imprison'd six months in Chains, and they were further sentenced by a Synod that they should forfeit all their Lands and Substance to the Church which they had prophaned. *Asser* Son of *Marchvid*, having kill'd *Gulacguin* by treachery, gave to this Church the Town of *Segan*, &c. *Brochmail* Son of *Mouric*, gave to this Church certain Lands which he had before given to his Daughter whom he made a Nun, but she being seduced from her Vow by *Etgar* Son of *Levi* had a Son, incestuously. *Teudur* King of *Brecknock*, King *Grifud*, &c. were also Benefactors.

209.
210.
211.

An. Dom. 982. *Gucaun* Bishop of *Landaff* was consecrated by the Metropolitan *Dunstan* Archbishop of *Canterbury*, and had his Pastoral Staff given him by *Edgar* the Supream King of the *English*. At the same time, lived *Edgar* King of all *Britain*, *Huwel da*, and *Morgan ben*, which two last were subject to King *Edgar*.

212.
213.

Etguin King of *Guenti* having a great contest with *Bledri* Bishop of *Landoff*, it went so far that the Bishop himself was wounded, whereupon he summon'd and assembled all the Clergy from *Taratir* in *Gui*, to *Tigui*, who in full Synod Anathematized the King, with his whole Family, and put his Country under interdict; but the King seeking absolution, obtain'd it, and thereupon gave divers Lands to this Church. *Mouric* Son of *Hivil*, after he had solemnly sworn to a Peace and Friendship with *Etguin* a Neighbouring King, before *Joseph* Bishop of *Landaff*, seized upon the said *Etguin*, cast him in Prison, and put out his eyes, which occasion'd his death, for which being curst in a Synod, he afterwards obtain'd absolution, and gave several Towns to this Church. King *Mouric*, and *Caratanc* one of his Lords, being under censure for violating the Sanctuary of this Church, obtain'd remission and gave divers Lands. The like happened in the Cases of *Catguallaun*, *Ringuallaun*, *Gistinus*, and others, who being guilty of like Crimes, made the like Compensations.

214.
215.

When King *William* conquer'd *England*, *Hergualdus* was Bishop of *Landaff*, *Catguacaun* Son of *Mouric* King of *Glatmorcant*, *Caratoc*, and *Riderch* Kings of other parts of *Wales*, all which Kings served King *William*, and died in his time.

216.

LITCHFELD *Cathedral*.

THIS was formerly call'd the *Mercian* Church, and first founded in the year 657. upon the Conversion of this Province to the Christian Religion, it was then made a Cathedral, and *Duina* the first Bishop of the *Mercians* or *middle English*, who govern'd here but two years and died. To him succeeded *Cellach*, a *Scot*. After him *Trumhere*, and after him *Jarman*, both *Englishmen*, but ordain'd Bishops in *Scotland*. To these succeeded St. *Cedda*, *An. Dom.* 667. who had been before that Bishop of *York*. After whose death succeeded *Winfrid* and after him *Sexwolf* who founded the Abby of *Peterborough*, after whose death the Province of *Mercia*

217.

cia was divided into two Dioceſſes (*Parœchias*) *Litchfield* and *Leiceſter*, tho' after a while they were both united again under *Hedda* Biſhop of *Litchfield*, who died, *An.* 721. In the time of *Ethelred* King of *Mercia*, the Biſhoprick of *Litchfield* was divided into five Dioceſſes, viz. *Hereford*, *Worceſter*, *Litchfield*, *Leiceſter*, and *Lindiſey*. After this diviſion *Litchfield* had five ſucceſſive Biſhops till the time of *Adulphus* who was made Archbiſhop of *Litchfield* by Pope *Hadrian*, *An.* 764. and a Juriſdiction given him over all *Mercia* and the *Eaſt-Angles*, but after him there was no more Archbiſhops. From his time to the *Norman* Conqueſt were fifteen Biſhops of *Litchfield*, ſoon after which the Epiſcopal Seat was tranſlated from *Litchfield* to *Cheſter*. *An.* 1075. The ſecond Biſhop of *Cheſter* was *Robert de Lymeſi*, who *An.* 1095. removed his Seat again, from *Cheſter* to the rich Monaſtery at *Coventry*, not long before built, and magnificently endow'd by Earl *Leofrick* and *Godeva* his Wife. To him ſucceeded *Robert Peche*, *Roger de Clinton*, *Walter Durdent*, *Richard Peche*, and *Gerard de Puella*, all of them ſucceſſively Biſhops of *Coventry*, and moſt buried there. The following Biſhops were called Biſhops of *Coventry* and *Litchfield*, whoſe names are *Hugo de Novant*, who in the year 1190. diſplaced the Monks from the Monaſtery at *Coventry* and introduced Secular Canons in their ſtead (but the Monks were reſtored again after ſeven years) *Jeffrey de Muſchampe*, *An.* 1199. *William de Cornhill*, *An.* 1215. *Alexander de Savenſby*, *An.* 1224. in whoſe time Pope *Honorious* ordered that one time the Election of the Biſhop ſhould be made in the Church of *Coventry* by the Convent of Monks there and the Chapter of *Litchfield*, and the next time in the Church of *Litchfield* by the ſaid Convent and Chapter. *Hugo de Pateſhull*, *An.* 1240. *Roger de Weſcham*, *An.* 1245. *Roger de Meyland*, *An.* 1256. *Walter de Langton*, *An* 1296. he was a great Benefactor to the Church of *Litchfield*. *Roger de Norburgh*, *An.* 1322.

Penda King of the *Mercians*, a Man phanatical and impious (*fanaticus & impius*) after he had reign'd thirty years was overcome by *Oſwy* King of the *Northumbers*, *An.* 656. Which *Oſwy* becoming King of *Mercia*, was the occaſion of the Converſion of that Province to the Chriſtian Faith, and founded the *Mercian* Church, now call'd *Litchfield*, and died, *An.* 670. In the City of *Litchfield* were two Monaſteries, one in the *Eaſt*-part where St. *Cedda* uſed to make his Prayers, and preach to the People, which place is ſince called *Stow*, the other was in the *Weſt*-part, and dedicated to the bleſſed Virgin *Mary*; here the Biſhop made his Seat, his Habitation contained ſix and thirty foot in length, and twenty eight in breadth; the Deans Apartment adjoyn'd to that of the Biſhop, and contained half the Dimenſions, the Manſions of the Canons contain'd each half the Dimenſions of the Deans. *Roger de Clinton* the third Biſhop of *Coventry* was the firſt Erector of a Colledge of Canons at *Litchfield*, there being before that time only five Prieſts in that Church ſerving at five Altars. Theſe Canons of *Litchfield* did ſometimes refuſe to admit the Biſhop when choſen and enthronizated at *Coventry*, the Prior of which place had of right the firſt Voice in his Election. The Prior of *Coventry* and his Convent pretended to have the ſole and free choice of the Biſhop, but King *John* after a long conteſt with them, over-aw'd them at *Nottingham* to choſe *William de Gray* his Chancellor their Biſhop, and not only ſo, but to joyn with the Canons of *Litchfield* in the Election. But that Election being ſet aſide as forced, the Prior and Monks only, choſe *William de Cornhull*, Archdeacon of *Huntington*; all this was done in the time of a general Interdict. The

Cathedral Churches.

The Episcopal Seat was tranflated from *Litchfield* to *Chefter* in the time of *William* the Conqueror, and from *Chefter* to *Coventry* in the Reign of King *Henry* the I. *Boniface* Archbifhop of *Canterbury* recited and confirm'd the Grant of *Roger* Bifhop of *Coventry* and *Litchfield*, whereby, with the Confent of the Prior and Convent of *Coventry* he granted and confirm'd to the Dean, and Chapter, and Church of *Litchfield*, divers Lands and Rents, and alotted the fame to fuch and fuch Offices and Duties, and ratified the Conftitutions of *Hugh* his Predeceffor, and granted and eftablifht by his Pontifical Authority, that the Churches of *Coventry* and *Litchfield* fhould have equal Power in the Election of the Bifhop. Which Confirmation by the Archbifhop of *Canterbury* bears date, *An. Dom.* 1259. King *Richard* the I. granted divers Lands and Franchifes to this Church, confirm'd by Pope *Honorius*. *John* Archbifhop of *Canterbury* made and provided feveral good Orders and Conftitutions to be obferved by the Dean and Chapter of this Church, in relation to the reparing the Parifh Churches and Chappels to them belonging, for the Augmentation of the Vicars and other Clergymens Profits therein, and for providing Books and Ornaments for the fame, alfo that they be moderate in receiving their Mortuaries and Tithes, he having heard great complaints of their rigorous exactions that way, *&c.* Dated, *An. Dom.* 1280. King *John*, while Earl of *Moreton*, was a Benefactor to this Church whofe grant was confirm'd by his Son King *Henry* the III. *An.* 50. *Roger* call'd the *Amnener* gave and confirm'd to *Roger de Mulent* Bifhop of *Coventry* and *Litchfield*, a parcel of Land and Buildings lying in the Parifh of St. *Mary le Stronde* without *London* towards *Weftminfter*, between the High-way that leads from *London* to *Weftminfter* and the *Thames*, to hold to the faid *Roger* and his Succeffors, by the yearly Rent of 3 *s.* payable at *Eafter*, for the purchafe of which the faid Bifhop gave twenty Marks of Silver. Pope *Eugenius* confirm'd the Lands and Poffeffions given to this Church, and eftablifht the Epifcopal Seat at *Coventry*, *An.* 1151. *William* Bifhop of *Coventry* gave and confirm'd to the Canons of *Litchfield* the Church of *Hope*, and Chappel of *Tidefwell* for their common Provifion in Bread and Beer. King *Steven* granted to the Church of St. *Cedd* at *Litchfield*, and *Walter* Bifhop of *Coventry* and his Succeffors for ever, a Mint for the Coyning of Mony at *Litchfield*. King *Edward* the I. granted to *Roger Meuland* Bifhop of *Coventry* and *Litchfield*, and his Succeffors, the Forreft or free Chafe of *Canok* in *Staffordfhire*, with the ufual Liberties, to hold in *Frankalmoine*, &c.

An. Dom. 1397. *Thomas de Stretton* Dean of *Litchfield* and the Chapter of that Church, depofited two hundred Marks in a Cheft called the Cheft of Grace, to be kept under four feveral Locks and Keys, to be opened and ufed, when the *Steward* has not fufficient of the ufual Income to fupply the Commons of the Canons Refidentiary and Vicars, for fo much only as fhall be wanting, the fame to be paid again by the Steward to the Common Cheft before he paffes his Accounts, &c. All which was confirm'd and ratified by *Richard* Bifhop of *Coventry* and *Litchfield*. Anno *Dom.* 1411, *John* Bifhop of *Coventry* and *Litchfield*, granted and demifed to the Chantry Priefts in the Church of *Litchfield* a common Lodging or Habitation within the Clofe at *Litchfield*, to have and to hold to them and their Succeffors for the term of ninety eight years at the Rent of 12 *d.* per *Annum* payable to the Bifhop and his Succeffors. There were formerly in this Church feventeen Chantries founded by feveral Perfons.

Jeffrey

240. Jeffrey Bishop of *Coventry* and *Litchfield*, *James Denton* Dean, and the Chapter of the said Church, made a Collection of all Statutes and Orders that had been made in the times of former Bishops, altering some, and adding others as there was occasion, and having out of that Collection compiled a body of Statutes, presented it to Cardinal *Wolsey* Archbishop of *York* and Legat *de Latere*, to be confirm'd by his Legantine Authority; In which Statutes are contain'd directions for saying the Divine Offices and the several Canonical hours; The Offices and Duties of the four
241. Principal Persons in the Church of *Litchfeild*, viz. The Dean, Precentor,
242. Treasurer, and Chancellor, also of the Sacristan, and after what manner the several Bells are to be toll'd or Rung at the several hours and Offices.
243. Also of the Archdeacons, and Succentor; That the Dean is the Head of the Chapter, that when he enters or passes by, all the Clergy ought to stand up &c. The Office and duty of the Vicars, and secular Clerks
244. commonly call'd *Clerk Vicars*; The manner of installing the Canons, all
245. whose stalls and proper Seats are set out in a Scheme; That all Clerks
246. entring into the Quire, bow first to the Altar, then to the Bishop, or in his Absence to the Dean, with directions when to stand up, and kneel,
247. &c. and what habits and collours are to be used upon such and such days; That the Dean be continually Resident, that he Celebrates Mass on all
248. double Feasts, that he preach on *Ash Wednesday* and *Advent Sunday*, &c. That every Canon have a Vicar continually serving in the Church; That
249. one or two of the Canons be Chosen at *Michaelmas* yearly, to receive and distribute the Common Goods of the Church, and to account for the
250. same; The manner of calling and holding the Chapters; That on the Festivals of St. *Cedde*, and the assumption of the Virgin *Mary*, the Dean feast all the Quire, the Canons to be singly invited eight days before the
251. time; That from *Trinity Sunday* to *Christmas* Mattins be immediately said after Complin, and the several Masses at such and such hours, &c. That
252. Mattins and Vespers, and all the hours be perform'd according to the *Salis-*
253. *bury* use; That in case any difference shall happen among the Canons it shall be composed among themselves, if it may be, if not, by the Dean and Chapter within two Months, if not by them, then by the Bishop within two Months more, if that cannot be, the party injured may be at
254. Liberty to seek redress in Law elsewhere as he sees convenient; That the Statutes of this Church be writ fair in a Book of Parchment, and that to be
255. chain'd in such place where the Canons, but not others, have access to it. That no Minister of this Church lie a night in the Town, without reasonable Cause to be approved by the Dean and Chapter; that no Vicar or Quirister receive or admit any Woman into his Garden, unless in com-
256. pany of other honest Women, &c. All which Statutes and Ordinances with many more, filling twenty one Folio's and a half, were declared and establisht by the foresaid Dean and Chapter, and confirm'd by the Bishop in the year 1526. The Bishop of *Litchfield* is sworn to defend the Rights and Liberties of this Chuerh to his ability, to observe the Statures and approved antient Customes of the same, and not to alienate the Episcopal Possessions. The Dean is sworn to make continual Residency as is accustomed, to be faithful to the Church, not to reveal the secrets of the Chapter, to observe and defend the Statutes, and approved and antient Customes, to behave himself with humility and Patience, and to excite all those who are Subject to his Government to do the like. Every Canon is sworn to be obedient to the Dean and Chapter in Canonical Com-
mands,

mands, to defend the Rights and Liberties of this Church, to observe the Statutes and antient and approved Customes, to be faithful to the Church and not to reveal the Secrets of the Chapter. Every Vicar is sworn to be obedient to the Dean and Chapter, to be faithful, to perform the Day and Night Service according to his reasonable ability. The Sergeant is sworn to be true to the Church of *Litchfeild*, to keep Council, truly to do his Office of Sergeantship, and when he is sent on Errands to give a true Report, &c.

LINCOLN *Cathedral*.

Paulinus Archbishop of *York*, who converted a great part of the North among the rest converted to the Christian Religion the Prefect of the City of *Lincoln* call'd *Bletta*, and caused a Church to be erected, and therein consecrated *Honorius* Archbishop of *Canterbury*.

An. 1092, Bishop *Remigius* removed his Episcopal Seat from *Dorchester* by Licence of King *William* the Conqueror to *Lincoln*, and began to build there a sumptuous Church, on the Hill near the Castle, but *Thomas* then Archbishop of *York* pretending that *Lincoln* and all the Province of *Lindsey* was within his Diocess, gave some obstruction for a while. But it was afterwards finisht by King *William* II, who caused it to be dedicated by two Cardinal Legates, in the presence of eight Archbishops and sixteen Bishops, and secular Canons to be establisht therein. This King *William Rufus* Confirm'd all the Lands and Revenues which his Father had given to this Church, and was himself a great Benefactor, he quieted the Dispute between the Archbishop of *York* and the Bishop of *Lincoln*, about Jurisdiction, giving *Thomas* Archbishop of *York* such satisfaction to quit his Claim for ever, as has been already mention'd, *pag.* 131. King *Henry* I. gave to this Church among other Lands the Mannour of *Bicheleswade* with great Liberties, also a Fair to be held at their Castle of *Newark*, on St. *Mary Magdalens* day and four days before; he also granted to *Robert* Bishop of *Lincoln* Liberty to make a Passage through his Castle Wall, he also granted to the said Bishop and the Canons of this Church his Vineyard at *Lincoln* and all that belongs to it. He also granted them several Churches, as *Hempingham*, *Derby*, *Wercheford*, to be Prebends, with all the Churches of *Lincoln* within and without the Borough, and Freewarren in all their Lands in *Lincolnshire* and *Nottinghamshire*. King *Henry* II. granted and confirm'd to *Robert* Bishop of *Lincoln* and his Successors the Houses that were the Knights Templers in the Parish of St. *Andrew Holburn*, at *London*, which the said Bishop had purchased of those Knights for one hundred marks, and the yearly Rent of three pieces of Gold (*tres aureos*). The same King gave to this Church and Bishop all the ground from the *Bale* Westward to the City Wall Eastward, at *Lincoln*, to build on; he also confirm'd the Donations of their other Benefactors, he also composed a difference between the Bishop of *Lincoln*, and *Robert* Abbot of St. *Albans* about the Jurisdiction over fifteen Churches to the said Abby belonging. Pope *Honorius An.* 1125. confirm'd the Revenues given to this Church; the like did Pope *Innocent*, who also granted that no Bishop should be imposed on this Church of *Lincoln* without the free election of the Clergy and People, *An.* 1138. King *Henry* III, in the fortieth year of his Reign upon the Petition of the Dean and Canons of *Lincoln* for his Licence

258.

260.

261.
262.
263.
264.
265.
266.
267.

268.

269.
270.

to

to remove some part of the City Wall, that so they might enlarge their Church Eastward, issued out a Writ of *Qued damnum*, in order to the same.

271.   The names of the Deans of *Lincoln*.

Ralf Ramerus.
Simon Bloet, An. Dom. 1100.
Adelmus, 1162.
Hamo.
Jeffry Killing.
Rober de Rolveston, 1198.
William de Tornaco, 1227.
Roger de Wescham, 1237. after Bishop of *Coventry* and *Litchfield*.
Henry de Lenington, 1243. after Bishop of *Lincoln*.
Richard de Gravesend, 1254 after Bishop of *Lincoln*.
Robert de Mariscis, 1260.
William de Lenington, 1262.
Richard de Mepham, 1273.
John de Maydenclon 1275.
Olive Sutton, 1276. after Bishop of *Lincoln*.
Nicholas de Hecham, 1280.
Philip de Willughby, 1289.
Gotzesinus de Kyrington, 1305.
Raymundas, a Cardinal, 1307.
Roger de Martival, 1310. after Bishop of *Sarum*.
Henry de Mansfeild, 1315.
Anthony Beak, 1328. after Bishop of *Norwich*.
John de Nottingham, 1340.
William de Norwich, 1343. after Bishop of *Norwich*.

John de Offord, 1345.
Simon Bresley, 1348.
John de Stretley, 1364.
John de Shepy, 1388.
John Mackworth, 1412.
Robert Fleming, 1451.
George Fitzhugh, 1483.
Jeffry Simion, 1505.
Thomas Wulcy, 1509. afterwards Bishop of *Lincoln*, and *York*, and Cardinal.
John Constable, 1514.
George Heneage, 1528.
John Tayler, 1539. after Bishop of *Lincoln*.
Mathew Parlur, (or Parker,) 1552. after Arch-Bishop of *Canterbury*.
Francis Mallet, 1554.
John Whitgift, 1571. after Bishop of *Worcester*, and Archbishop of *Canterbury*.
William Wicham, 1577. after Bishop of *Lincoln* and *Winchester*.
Ralf Griffin, 1585.
John Rainold, 1598.
William Cole, 1599.
Laurence Staunton, 1601,
Roger Parlur, 1613.
Anthony Topham, 1629.
Michael Honywood, 1660.

272. Anno 1536. (28. *Henry* VIII.) An Inventory was made of all the Jewels, Vestments, and other Ornaments belonging to the Revestry of this Church, consisting in Chalices, in number six, one of which was all Gold enricht with Pearls and divers precious stones in the soot, weighing thirty two Ounces, Several rich *Feretrums*, one of Silver and gilt for the Sacrament, weighing 341. ounces, several rich Philatories, Ampuls,
273. and Tabernacles with Relicks in them, Rich Images Silver and gilt, Di-
274. vers Rich Chests for Relicks, Pixes, Crosses and Crucifixes some of Gold some of Christial, and some of Silver and gilt, one of which weighed
275. 128 Ounces besides the Baes, &c. Divers Rich Candlesticks, among which one Pair of extraordinary size and Workmanship was all Gold, and weigh'd 450 Ounces, the gift of *John* Duke of *Lancaster* Son of
276. King *Edw.* III. Five Pair of Censors Silver and gilt, Several rich Basons Sil-
277. ver and gilt, &c. Pastoral Staves, Texts of the Gospells with Rich Covers,
Chrism-

Chrismatories and Ampuls for Oyl Silver and gilt, eight Myters, Chesables and Copes of Cloath of Gold, Sattin, Velvet, imbroidered, red, white, some of Damask, some set with Pearls, of purple and blew, some of which had the Donors names imbroidered thereon, with *Orate pro anima*, &c. of green, of black, rich Moises of Silver and gilt, Garlands of Silver and gilt, set about with precious Stones and Pearls, rich Altarcloaths of Cloth of Gold and images imbroidered, &c. King *Henry* VIII. directed his Letter dated the 6th of *June* in his two and thirtieth year, to Dr. *George Heneage* then Archdeacon of *Taunton*, and others, to take down a Shrine, and the superstitious Jewels, Plate, Copes, &c. in this Cathedral Church of *Lincoln*, and to see the same safely and surely to be convey'd to his Jewel-house in the *Tower*. Which Commission was executed on the 11th of *June* 1540. And by force thereof there was taken out of the said Cathedral in Gold two thousand six hundred and twenty one ounces, in silver four thousand two hundred and eighty five ounces, besides a great number of Pearls, Diamonds, Saphires, Rubies, Turky, Carbuncles, &c. The Bishop of *Lincoln* had a Miter wonderfully thick set with precious Stones. Here were then two Shrines, one of St. *Hugh* all of Gold, the other of St *John* of *Dalderby* all of Silver.

278.
279.
280.
281.
282.
283.
284.
285.
286.
287.

In the seventh year of King *Edward* the VI. another Inventory was taken of what then remain'd in this Church, which contain'd only three Chalices, one Pix, one Ampul, and that was all the Plate, the rest of the Treasure was in Copes of red, green, blew, black and white, some old and decayed, with divers Chesables, Tunicles, and Albes, &c. Altar-Cloaths of Diaper *meetly good*, and five other Cloths of Diaper *sore worne*.

288.
289.
290.
291.
292.

In the fourth and fifth *Ph. Ma. An. Dom.* 1557. another Inventory was made, and there was then in this Church seven Chalices Silver and gilt, one of which weighed four and thirty ounces, four Pixes, with some few Phials, Crosses, Censers, Ampulls, but most poor, with divers Chesables, and Copes, red, purple, white, blew, green and black, and divers Altar-Clothes, some of Cloath of Gold, and of Damask imbroidered with Gold, &c.

294.
295.
297.

St. PAUL's *Cathedral*, in **London**.

298.

ANno Dom. 185. *Lucius* King of the greater *Britain*, now call'd *England*, obtain'd from Pope *Eleutherius*, two Doctors to be sent hither to instruct the King and Kingdom in the Christian Faith; then were the Temples of Idols dedicated to the Service of the true God, and three Metropolitan Seats placed in the three chief Cities, *viz. London*, to which all the *Southern* part of *England* was subject; *York*, under whose jurisdiction was all the *North* of *Humber*, and *Scotland*; and *Cehster*, whose Jurisdiction extended over *Wales*. *London* continued the chief Episcopal Seat and Primacy, till the coming of St. *Augustin*, who in the year 604. transferr'd the Metropolitan Dignity to *Canterbury*; and made *Mellitus* Bishop of *London*. To which *Mellitus*, King *Ethelbert* gave the Land then called *Tillingham*, for the Support and Maintenance of his Monastery of St. *Paul*. Pope *Agatho* granted to *Erkenwald* Bishop of the Monastery of St. *Paul* in *London*, that the Election of the Bishop should belong solely to the

299.

the Congregation of that Monastery. Which *Erkenwald* was a Scholler to Bishop *Mellitus*, and built two Monasteries, one for himself at *Chertsey* in *Suffex*, the other for his Sister *Edleburga* at *Barking* in *Effex*. He was a man of most exemplary Piety, and after the death of Bishop *Cedde*, became Bishop of *London*. He died at *Barking*; after whose death his Body was much contested for, by the Nuns of *Barking*, the Monks of *Chertsey*, and the Citizens of *London*, but the latter prevailed, and he was buried at *London*, with the Reputation of a Saint. King *Athelstan* renew'd and restored the Liberties of the Monastery of St. *Paul* the Doctor of the *Gentiles*, in *London*. King *Edgar* granted to the same, divers Lands and Immunities, in the year 867. Other Benefactors to this Church were King *Ethelred*, *Cnute* King of *Denmark* and *England*, King *Edward* the Confessor, King *William* the Conqueror, who confirm'd all their Lands and Liberties to be as free as he desired his own Soul to be in the day of Judgment; he also granted and confirm'd the four and twenty Hides of Land adjoyning to the City of *London*, which King *Ethelbert* gave to this Church when he founded it. It appears by Domesday-Book that at the time of the Conquest, the Church of St. *Paul's* held Lands in the Counties of *Middlesex*, *Effex* in divers Hundreds there, *Hertford*, and *Surrey*. *An.* 1070 A Provincial Council was assembled in the Church of St. *Paul* at *London* under *Lanfranc* Archbishop of *Canterbury*, where among other things it was decreed that none should marry in his own Kindred till the seventh Degree; That none should buy or sell holy Orders, or an Ecclesiastical Office with cure of Souls, which crime St. *Peter* first condemn'd in *Simon Magus*; and that no Bishop or any of the Clergy should judge in loss of Life or Limb. In those times it was proved, and declared, that the Church of *York* ought to be subject to that of *Canterbury*. The foresaid King *William* granted to *Maurice* Bishop of *London* the Castle of *Storiford* and other Lands with *Soc* and *Sac*.

In the year 1295. A Visitation was made in the Treasury of this Church, by *Ralph de Baudak*, then Dean, and an Inventory taken containing divers rich and curious Morses, some all of Gold, Silver Candlesticks, Silver Censers, rich Crosses of Silver, and Silver and gilt, twelve rich Chalices, some of which were all Gold, whereof one weighed five and thirty ounces 10 *d.* weight, divers rich Feretrums, divers rich Miters adorned with Pearls and precious Stones, Sandals of Silk imbroider'd, Pastoral Staves, abundance of Copes, imbroider'd with Images, and enricht with Gold and Silver, Amicts some of Cloath of Gold, divers Vestments, Tunicks and Dalmaticks, &c. Church Books as Psalters, Antiphonaries, Homelies, Martyrolgies, Processionals, Missals, Manuals, Graduals, &c. Epistolaries, and Gospellaries, &c. Also a Chronicle composed by *Ralph de Diceto*, &c. *Baudekins*, and other sorts of Cloaths; there was also an Inventory taken of such things as belong'd to the Chappel of the Charnel-house in St. *Paul's Church yard*; in the Chappel of St. *Radegund*; at our Ladies Altar in the Nave of the Church; at the Altar of St. *Steven*, at that of St. *Thomas* the Martyr, of St. *Silvester*, of St. *Cedde*, of the Apostles, of St. *James*, of St. *John Baptist*, of the blessed Virgin in the new Work, of St. *Michael*, of St. *John* the Evangelist, of St. *Catherine*, of St. *Andrew*, of St. *Laurence* over-against the Sacristy: and in the year 1298. a like Inventory was taken of all the Plate, Vestments, and Books belonging to the Church of St. *Faith* in the Vaults under St. *Pauls*. *Ralph de Diceto* once Dean of St. *Paul's* gave to this

Church

Church divers Relicks, beside which there were divers others, among the rest the Cheek-bone of St. *Ethelbert* the Confessor, Founder of this Church, and an Arm of St. *Mellitus*, &c.

The Bishop of *London* is, at his first coming to St. *Paul's* Cathedral, and at his coming from beyond Seas, to be received by the Dean and Choire at the *West*-Door, in solemn Procession and ringing of Bells, at other times with ringing of Bells only. He ought to administer in Person on *Christmas, Easter, Ascention*, and *Whitsundays*, and on the Feasts of St. *Paul* and St. *Erkenwald*, *Ashwenesday*, and *Corpus Christi*: He is to dispose of all the Thirty Prebends and Dignities of this Church, when void, except the Deanery, but they are to be admitted into Possession and inducted by the Dean and Chapter. The Principal Persons in this Church next the Bishop, are the Dean, the Archdeacons of *London*, *Essex*, *Middlesex*, and *Colchester*, the Treasurer, Precentor, and Chancellor. The Dean is chosen by the Chapter, and then presented to, and confirm'd by the Bishop, and by him also, or his Deputy, install'd; his Office is to reside, to govern over all the Canons, Priests, and other Ministers of this Church, to assemble a Chapter every *Saturday*; he is to invest the Canons, the rest of the Canons Residentiary being present; and ought to visit within the Jurisdiction of the Dean and Chapter every third year. The Sub-dean is chosen from among the petty Canons, his Office is to govern the Quire in the absence of the Dean. Two others of the petty Canons are to be chosen who are call'd Cardinals of the Quire, their Office is to observe the defaults of all that belong to the Quire, and to present the same, &c. The Treasurer's Office is to keep the Plate, Vestments, Relicks, &c. of the Church, under him is the Sacristan, who is his Coadjutor; under the Sacristan are three Virgers, who ought to serve in Person all three daily; their Office is to open and shut the Church-Doors; to ring the Bells at accustomed hours; to see that no one be cover'd; to keep out of the Church infamous Persons, especially publick Whores, Porters carrying burdens through the Church, importunate Beggars; to be single and not married, &c. The Office of the Chantor is to take care of the Song and Singers, to begin the Antiphons, &c. His Deputy is call'd the Succentor; the Chancellor is the Scribe of the Church and Chapter, he has the custody of the Seal, he Presides over the reading part, as the Chantor does over the singing part of the Choire, and he appoints the Master of the *Grammar*-School, as the Chantor does of the Song-School; and the Chancellor hath under him a Subscribe or Register. The Almoner of this Church ought to educate eight Boys of honest Parentage, and cause them to be instructed in Song and Learning, so as to be useful to God's Service in the Choire. Under the Dean are thirty Canons in the Church of St. *Paul* instituted by Pope *Lucius* the III. these were of old time Regulars according to the Rule of St. *Augustin*, and all constantly resided, but in process of time they became Seculars, and neglected their Residence, to reform which several Orders were provided by several Bishops and Deans, out of which Dean *Collet* collected the Sum, *viz.* that every Canon at the time of his Instalation shall swear on the Evangelists to be obedient to the Dean and Chapter, to be faithful to the Church of St. *Paul*, to defend her Rights and Liberties, to observe her laudable Customs, &c. Every Canon shall diligently observe the Canonical Hours, and humbly and devoutly perform the Divine Office, &c. A Canon Residentiary is so call'd from his duty

duty to be continually residing, which he ought solemnly to promise in the Chapter before all the Brethren; if after such promise he resides in any other Church, he shall lose the profit and advantage of this. To re-side in the Church of *Pauls* is to be present at the Canonical hours, on great Feasts at every Office, on other days at some one; the Vicars of this Church were formerly thirty in number, every Canon had his Vicar, but in Dean

344. *Collets* time there were but six, some of which were married, they ought to officiate constantly in the Quire day and night, they ought not to be Proctors or Attorneys, &c. The Petty, or Minor Canons, were to be Priests, who daily attended the Service of the Quire, and said Masses at the high Altar instead of the Canons, &c. Here were also divers other Priests who had Chantries and celebrated at particular Altars; but these used to assist in the Quire, especially on the greater Feasts, at Mattins,

345. Prime, Mass, and Vespers; and they could not be otherways Beneficed, &c. King *Richard* II. in the two and twentieth year of his Reign, directed his Letters to the Bishop of *London*, and Dean and Residentaries

346. (or *Stagiaries*) of this Church, commanding that the Residency in this Church be for the future observed according to the form and manner of the Church of *Salisbury*. The Thirty Canons belonging to this Church, had each his several Prebend, and peculiar Seat in the Quire, and to each belonged certain Psalms to be by him said daily for the living and

347. dead Benefactors to this Church, which Psalms were writ over his Stall.

An. Dom. 1518, *John Collet* Dean of St. *Paul's* exhibited certain matters to the Cardinal of *York*, Legate *a Latere*, for the Reformation of the State of the Residentaries, consisting of several Heads, relating to the Dean

348. and his authority, the four Residentaries, and their Behaviour in the
349. Quire, &c. Of the Chapters. That the Residentaries live near the Church,
350. and that they admit no Women into their Houses, of the distributions
351. among the Residentaries, and that the Dean have a double Proportion in
352. all things without fraud; of divers other Officers belonging to this Church,
353. relating to the Temporalties, as the Receiver General, Chamberlain, Steward of the Courts, Auditor of Accounts, &c. *Thomas* Archbishop of
354. *York* and Chancellour of *England* decreed by consent of the Dean and Chapter, that the number of Residentaries should not exceed four with their Dean, at one time. The State of the Lands of this Church, amounted

355. to the Sum of 1196 *l*. 11 *s*. 2 *d*. q. *per An*. besides Casualties, as Fines, &c.
356. Out of which Sum went yearly in Charges and payments 791 *l*. 3 *s*. 9 *d*. So that there remain'd 405 *l*. 7 *s*. 3 *d* q. and out of that they Set off for Reparations 200 *l*, and for Casualties 26 *l*. 14 *s*. 4 *d*. Remaineth 178 *l*. 15 *s*. 11 *d*. q.

357. The Names of the Thirty Prebendaries of St. *Paul's* are; *Totehal, Wesden, Holburn, Wildeland, Sneating, Kentistown, Ruculnesland, Wilesdon, Wenlakesbyri, Kadington, Portepole, Cudington, Cheswicke, Twiford, Brandeswood, St. Pancrace, Ealdeland, Herlestone, Chaumberlengeswood, Ealdstreet, Oxgate, Consumpta, Brunnesbury, Neweton, Hoxton, Rugemere, Iseldon, Mapelsbyri, More, Halywell*.

To the Patronage of the Dean and Chapter of St. *Paul's*, belong twenty one Churches in the City of *London*.

In the seventh of *Edward* VI, an Inventory of the Plate and Ornaments &c. of this Church was delivered into the Kings Commissioners at *Guildhall*, out of which at the request of the Dean and Chapter, they left only

358. three Chalices, two pair of Basins, a Silver Pot, a Canopy for the King
when

when he cometh to *Paul's*, two Palls for Funerals, twenty four old Cushions, &c. as things of necessary use.

In the year 1430. (9. *Henry* VI.) *John Carpentor*, Citizen and Clerk of the Communalty of *London*, Executor of *Richard Whytington*, late Citizen and Mercer, and often Mayor of the said City, founded a perpetual Chantry of one Chaplain to celebrate daily in the Chappel of the Blessed *Mary* formerly built over the Charnel House in St. *Paul's* Church-yard, by *Roger Beyvene* and other Citizens of *London*, and endow'd the same with eight Marks of yearly Rent, &c. *An. Dom.* 1458. An Inventory or Catalogue, Indented, was made by *William Say* Dean and the Chapter of St. *Paul's* of all the Books given by *Walter Shirington* a Canon Residentiary of this Church, and placed in a new Library by him erected over the Cloyster about the Church-yard call'd *Pardon Chirchehawe*. Which Library consisted of many Volums, among which, *Chronica Radulphi de Diceto*; *Postilla Radulphi de Diceto super Ecclesiasticum,& librum Sapientiæ*; The Works of St. *Augustin*; and of St. *Thomas*; *Visio Sancti Edwardi Confessoris*; *Una Magna Biblia*; *Tractatus Magistri Roberti Grostest in gallico, de lapsu & reparatione generis humani*; *Tractatus de decimis per Dominum Stephanum quondam Archiepiscopum Cantuar.* &c. There were also divers other Books remaining in the Treasury, *An.* 1486. relating chiefly to the Church Service, among which *Vetus Missale secundum usum St. Pauli*; *Unum Ordinale secundum primariam ordinationem, & antiquam, Ecclesiæ S. Pauli Londoniensis*, &c.

359.
360.
361.
362.
363.
364.
365.

The Names of the Bishops of *London*.

Mellitus consecrated by *Augustin* Archbishop of *Canterbury*, *An.* 605.
Ceddus, 621.
Wyne.
Erkenwald, 680.
Walter.
Ingnald.
Eguf.
Wychet.
Filbrith.
Edgar.
Kenwald.
Ebald.
Herbert.
Osmund.
Ethenod.
Celbert.
Cerulph
Stributulph.
Etstan.
Wulfius.
Edelward.
Elstan.
Wlstan.
Elsun, 1000.
Alwyn, 1044.

Elphword.
Robert, 1050.
William, 1051.
Hugh de Aurevalle.
Mauricius, 1077.
Richard, 1108.
Gilbert.
Robert de Sigillo, 1139.
Richard Beumies, 1151.
Gilbert Foliot, 1163.
Richard, 1190.
William, 1199.
Eustachius de Faukenbergh, 1221.
Roger le Veir, 1229.
Fulc Basset, 1244.
Henry de Wengham, 1259.
Richard Taleboth, 1262.
Henry de Sandwic, 1262.
John de Chishull, 1274.
Richard de Gravesend, 1290.
Ralph de Baldok, 1306.
Gilbert de Seagrave, 1313.
Richard de Newport, 1317.
Steven de Gravesend, 1319.
Richard de Binteworth, 1338.
Ralph de Stratford, 1339.

366.

Michael

Michael Northburgh.   Cuthbert Tunstal, 1522.
Simon de Sudbury, 1362.   John Stokesly, 1530.
Robert Braybroke, 1381.   Edmund Boner, 1540.
Roger Walden, 1404.   Nicholas Ridley, 1549.
Nicholas Bubwith, 1406.   Edmund Grindal, 1559.
Richard Clifford, 1407.   Edwin Sandes, 1570.
John Kemp, 1422.   John Elmer, 1576.
William Gray, 1426.   Richard Fletcher, 1594:
Robert Fitz-Hugh, 1431.   Richard Bancroft, 1597.
Robert Gilbert.   Richard Vaughan, 1604.
Thomas Kemp, 1449.   Thomas Ravis, 1607.
Richard Hill, 1489.   George Abbot, 1609.
Thomas Savage, 1496.   John King, 1611.
William Warham, 1503.   George Mountaine, 1621.
William Barnes, 1505.   William Laud, 1628.
Richard Fitz-James, 1506.   William Juckson, 1635.

The Names of the Deans of St. *Pauls* since the Conquest.

Ulstan.   Richard de Neuport.
William.   Vitalis Basco.
Elfwin.   John de Everton, 1328.
Luired.   Gilbert de Bruera, 1339.
Ralph, 1150:   Richard de Kilmington.
Alard de Burnham.   Thomas Trillek.
Robert de Watford.   John de Apelby.
Hugh de Marinis.   Thomas Evere.
Ralph de Diceto, 1183.   Thomas Stowe.
Martin de Pateshull.   Thomas More.
Walter de Langford.   Reginald Kentwode.
Jeffrey de Lucy, 1237.   Thomas Lyseus, 1441.
William de S. Mariæ Ecclesia, 1237.   Laurance Bothe, 1456.
Henry de Cornhill, 1245.   William Say, 1457.
Walter de Salern.   Roger Ratclyff, 1468.
Robert de Barthone.   Thomas Wynterburne, 1471.
Peter de Neuport.   William Worsley.
Richard Taleboth.   Robert Shirburne.
Jeffrey de Feringes, 1263.   John Collet.
John de Chishulle.   Richard Pace.
Hervicus de Borham, 1276.   Richard Sampson.
Thomas de Ingelesthorpe, 1279. after   John Incent.
     Bishop of Rochester.   William May.
Roger de la Leye, 1287.   John Fecknam.
William de Montfort, 1292.   Henry Cole.
Ralph de Baldok, 1297.   Alexander Nowell.
Arnald de Cantilupo, 1308. after a   John Overall.
     Cardinal.   Valentine Cary.
John de Sandale.

367.   The *Dance of Death* (formerly painted about the Cloyster of St. *Pauls*) was writ in *French* by one *Machabree*, and translated into old *English* Verse by *Dan John* of *Lydgate*, Monk of *Bury*. In this Dance Death leads
368.   all sorts of People, and first takes out, and speaks to the Pope, then the
     Emperor,

Emperor, then the Cardinal, the King, Patriarch, Conſtable, Archbiſhop, 369.
Baron, Princeſs, Biſhop, Eſquire, Abbot, Abbeſs, Bayly, Aſtronomer, 370.
Burgeſs, Canon Secular, Marchant, Chartreux, Sergeant, Monk, Uſurer, 371.
Phyſician, the amorous Eſquire, the Gentlewoman, the Man of Law, 372.
Mr. *John Rikil*, the Parſon, Juror, Minſtral, Laborer, Frier Minor, the 373.
young Child, the young Clerk, the Hermite, to all which Death makes
a ſhort addreſs and they as ſhort an anſwer, with the Author's Moral Re- 374.
flection.

The Cathedral Church of 𝖘𝖆𝖑𝖎𝖘𝖇𝖚𝖗𝖞. 375.

OSmund Biſhop of *Salisbury*, who ſucceeded on the death of Biſhop
Herman in the year 1076, built the new Church at *Salisbury*, and
compoſed the Book of the Eccleſiaſtical Office call'd *Conſuetudinarium*,
which was uſed, in a manner, throughout all *England*, *Wales*, and *Ireland*.
Biſhop *Oſmund*'s Deed of Foundation and Endowment of this Church
bears date, *An. Dom.* 1091. (4 *William* 2.) King *Henry* the I. King 376.
Henry the II. and King *John* were Benefactors to this Church of St. *Mary* of
Sarum. King *Henry* the III. in the eleventh year of his Reign confirm'd
the tranſlation of this Church from the Caſtle to a lower Scituation, and
made *New Sareſbirie* a free City, and granted to it all the Liberties which
the City of *Winchester* enjoys, and granted to the Biſhops here a yearly 377.
Fair at *New Saresbury* from the Vigil of the Aſſumption to the morrow
after the Octaves of the ſaid Feaſt, and every Week a Mercate on the
Tueſday, &c.

Collegiate

COLLEGIATE CHURCHES

Of Canons Secular.

A Second Part of the Third Volum.

BEVERLEY, in Yorkshire.

[Provosts of Beverley. Vol. 1. p. 171.

1. *Thomas*, Nephew of *Thomas* Archbishop of *York*.
2. *Thurstinus*, afterwards Archbishop of *York*.
3. *Thomas Normannus*.
4. *Robertus*.
5. *Thomas Beket*.
6. *Robertus*.
7. *Galfridus, Temp. H.* 2.
8. *Simon*.
9. *Fulco Basset*.
10. *Johannes Cheshub*.
11. *Gulielmus Eborisensis, Temp. H.* 3.
12. *Johannes Maunsel*.
13. *Alanus*.
14. *Morganus*.
15. *Petrus de Chester*.
16. *Haymo de Charto*.
17. *Robert de Alburwik*.
18. *Walterus*.
19. *Gulielmus de Melton*.
20. *Nicholaus Hugate*.
21. *Gulielmus de la Mar. Temp. E.* 3.
22. *Richard de Ravensar*.
23. *Adam Limbergh*.
24. *Johannes Thoresby*.
25. *Johannes Manfeld*.
26. *Gulielmus Kinwolmarsh*.
27. *Robertus Nevile, Temp. H.* 6.
28. *Robertus Rolleston*.
29. *John Gerningham*.
30. *Laurence Bouthe*, afterwards Bishop of *Durham*.
31. *John Bouth*, afterwards Bishop of *Exeter*.
32. *Henry Webber*.
33. *Petrus Tastar*.
34. *William Potman*.
35. *Hugh Trotter*.
36. ....
37. *Thomas Dalby*.
38. *Thomas Winter*.]

3.

IN the year 1664. certain Relicks were found in a Leaden Chest in this Church, with an Inscription which spoke them to be the Bones of St. *John* of *Beverley* therein deposited in the year 1197.

King *Adelstan* in his march against *Constantine* King of *Scotland*, visited the blessed *John* at *Beverley*, and promised, in case he obtain'd Victory, to augment the Revenues of this Church, which he did in his return. Being in *Scotland*, he besought God that at the Prayer of St. *John* of *Beverley*, he would shew some sign whereby the *Scots* may be known to be of right subject to *England*, hereupon the King struck a Stone with his Sword, near the Castle of *Dunbar*, and made therein a gash of an Ell long. King *Richard* the II. in the twelfth year of his Reign, confirm'd to this Church, certain Revenues given by King *Athelstan*, in the

Vid. Vol. 2. p. 367.

East

East-riding of *Yorkshire*; the like had been done before by King *Henry* the II. *Thomas* Archbishop of *York*, by advice and consent of the Chapter of this Church, made divers Statutes and Orders for Government of the same; namely, that there be always nine Canons, a Precentor, a Chancellor, and a Sacristan, nine Vicars, *&c.* belonging to this Church; in the number of which Canons, the Archbishop himself is included for one, and hath the chief and first Stall in the Choire; that the Provostship (which Office is only temporary) when void, if not supplied in forty days, shall be collated by the Archbishop and his Successors, *&c.* That all beside the Canons be obliged to continual Residence; That the Provost for the time being pay to each of the nine Canons the Sum of 10 *l.* per *Annum*, by quarterly Payments; to the Precentor 10 *l.* to the Chancellor, and Sacristan, as formerly, to the Clerks and Virgers 6 *s.* 8 *d.* each, and to the Parsons 6 *l.* 13 *s.* 4 *d.* each, and further to each of the nine Canons and three Officers above mentioned, two and forty quarters of Oats yearly; to each Vicar 8 *l. per Annum*, &c. That the Provost makes due and punctual Payment of the Sums due to the Ministers of this Church at the proper times or within fifteen days after, under pain of five Marks to the Fabrick of the Church of *York*, and as much to this, *&c.* Which Statutes bear date in the year 1391.

5.
6.
7.
8.
9.
10.

SUTHWELL, in Nottinghamshire.

AT the time of *Domesday* Survey, *Thomas* then Archbishop of *York*, and the Canons of this Church, held Lands in *Torgartone Wapentac*, valued at 40 *l.* 15 *s.* and in *Binghamhou Wapentac* other Lands, amounting in value to 150 *s. Turstan* Archbishop of *York* gave one Prebend to this Church, and the tenth of all the Increase of his Lordship of *Southwell*. Pope *Alexander* the III. granted to the Canons of *St. Mary* of *Southwell* Power to excommunicate any of their Parishioners, who should be injurious to them; and that as well the Clerks as Laity of the County of *Nottingham* do repair to this Church in Procession, at *Whitsuntide*, yearly, according to ancient Custom, *&c.* Whose Bull bears date, *An. Dom.* 1171. King *Henry* the I. confirm'd the Liberties of this Church, and the Lands given them by Archbishop *Turstan*. *John* Archbishop of *York*, and *Robert Malluvell*, were Benefactors to this Church. *Alexander* Archbishop of *York* and Legate, at the Petition of *Richard de Chesterfeild* Canon of the Collegiate Church of *Suthwelle*, in the year 1379. granted his License for the building of a new House for the Habitation of the Vicars in the Church yard, their old House being too remote; which House was afterwards set out and appointed by the Parishioners to be erected in the *East* part of the said Church yard. King *Henry* the VI. in the seventeenth year of his Reign granted to this Church the Alien Priory of *Ravendale* in *Lincolnshire*, then valued at 14 *l. per Annum*. Which with other Lands, was also granted to this Church, by King *Edward* the IV. in the first year of his Reign.

This Collegiate Church being founded anew by King *Henry* VIII. Queen *Elizabeth* in the twenty seventh year of her Reign confirm'd and establisht certain Statutes and Orders for Government of the same, consisting of twenty six Chapters, in which it is provided that Divine Service be

11.
12.
13.
14.
15.
16.
17.

perform'd here as in the Metropolitan Church of *York*, thrice every day, and Sermons by the Canons or Prebendaries every Sunday and Holyday;

18. that there be at least six Vicars Choral, six singing Men, and six Boys;
19. That the Canons shall duly reside, and that the Debts of the Colledge be paid; that the Receiver account yearly on the 3d. or 4th. of *November*;
20. That there be a Sacristan, Virger, Bell-ringer, and Porter, a Master, and
21. Rector of the Choire, a Master of the *Grammar-School*; That to make a a Chapter there must be present three Canons at the least; that there be
22. a Warden or Clerk of the Fabrick, who is to take care of the Repairs of the Church; that the Seal be kept under three Keys remaining with three
23. several Prebendaries; that there be Divinity Lectures thrice, or at least twice. a week, and Catechising on Sundays in the Afternoon: That the
24. Chapter constitute under them a Vicar general, for the Exercise of their
25. Ecclesiastical Jurisdiction, and a Register; Every Canon before his Installment to take an Oath whereby he renounces the Papistical Worship, and engages to embrace the Doctrine established by the regal authority, &c. and to observe the Statutes of this Church; The Vicars and under Officers to be sworn to the same purpose.

[Valued at 16 *l.* 5 *s.* 2 *d.* per Annum.]

St. MARTINS LE GRAND, in London.

26. KIng *William* the Conqueror (*consanguinitatis hæreditate Anglorum Basileus*) confirm'd the Lands and Estate given to this Colledge by *Ingelricus*, and *Girardus* his Brother, the Founders, and further gave to the same all the More-Land without *Criplegate*, &c. And freed this Church
27. and the Canons here from all disturbance and exaction of any Bishop, Archdeacon, or their Ministers, and from all Regal Services. And granted them *Soc* and *Sac*, *Tol* and *theam*, with all those antient Liberties, &c. in the fullest manner that any Church in *England* hath. Whose Charter bears date in the year 1068. the Second year of his Reign. Confirm'd by *John* and *Peter* Cardinals of *Rome*, and Legates of Pope *Alexander*.

St. MARY'S at Warwick.

28. HEnry Consul, or Earl, of *Warwick*, gave divers Lands to this Church, confirm'd and augmented by Earl *Roger*, his Son. The same *Roger* granted to the Canons of this Church of *St. Mary* to have a Dean and
29. Chapter, in like manner as the Canons of *London*, *Lincoln* *Salisbury*, and *York*. He also in the year 1123, translated the Colledge which was in the Castle of *Warwick* to the Church of *St. Mary* and *All Saints*, and by and with the Episcopal authority of *Simon* Bishop of *Worcester*, the Canons and Clerks were transferr'd thither. The same *Simon* consecrated an Alter
30. at St. *Sepulchers*, and a Burial Place there for the Canons only, the same
31. being call'd the Priory of the Holy *Sepulcher*. To this Collegiate Church the aforemention'd *Roger* Earl of *Warwick* gave several Churches, among others; the Church of the Holy *Sepulcher* at *Warwick*, and the Parish Church of *Greetham* in *Rutland*; Which Churches being alienated from this Colledge; the said Church of St. *Sepulchers* being made a Priory of Canons Regular, and *Greetham* appropriated to the same, those two were not in a Possibility to be restored, but the other Churches which had

been

been alienated, seven in number, were restored and reunited to the Collegiate Church of St. Mary at Warwick, by Decree of *William* Bishop of *Worcester*; and all the Parishoners of the several Churches in *Warwick* order'd to repair to the said Church of St. *Mary* for Sacraments and Sacramentals, and not to bury elswhere than in the Church-yard of the same. The said *William* Bishop of *Worcester* decree'd that the Dean, who is bound by this Place to reside, receive 40 *l.* every residing Canon, twenty marks every other Prebend who does not reside but 40 *s.* only, and every Vicar ten marks, *per Annum.*

[Valued at 247 *l.* 13 *s.* ob. *per Annum.*]

WALLINGFORD, in Barkshire.

IN the tenth year of *Edward* I. *Edmund* Son of *Richard* King of the *Almains*, and Earl of *Cornwall*, gave to the Chappel of St. *Nicholas* in his Castle of *Wallingford* 40 *l.* of yearly Rent, for the maintenance of six Chaplains, six Clerks, and four Acolyts or Taber-bearers. To the Dean and Chaplains of this Colledge, *Edward* the Black Prince, King *Richard* II. and King *Henry* VI. gave other Revenues in augmentation of their Endowment.

[Valued at 147 *l.* 8 *s.* ob. q. *per Annum.*]

LANCADANC, in the Diocess of St. Davids.

AN. Dom. 1283, *Thomas* Bishop of St. *Davids*, with the Assent of King *Edward*, and the Chapter of St. *Davids*, made the Church of *Langadanc* Collegiate, and endow'd the same with Revenues for the maintenance of twenty one Canons under the Government of a Precentor, of which Canons seven to be Priests, seven Deacons, and seven Subdeacons, each Canon to have his Vicar, *&c.*

LANGECESTRE, in the County Palatine of Durham.

AN. Dom. 1283, *Anthony* Bishop of *Durham* made the Church of *Langecestre*, lying in his Diocess, and being of his Patronage, a Collegiate Church for one Dean and seven Prebendaries, the Dean to be continually resident and to have the Cure of Souls, and to find two Chaplains to assist him therein, and to cause three Chappels of ease to be served with competent Ministers, that the seven Prebendaries have their several Vicars, that every of them be *Hebdomodarius* in his turn, to order, correct, and govern the Choire. He also endow'd the Church with divers Revenues, *&c.* All which was by consent of this Chapter of *Durham*, and confirm'd by King *Edward* I.

AUKLAND, in the Bishoprick of Durham.

40. TO this Collegiate Church of St. *Andrew* of *Aukland*, the foresaid *Anthony* Bishop *Durham* had been a Benefactor, and made divers Orders for Government of the same in the year 1292. as that the Vicar of the Church be a Dean, that the Canons have all Vicars daily to officiate, the five first Canons, Priest Vicars, the four next, Deacon-Vicars,
41. the others, Subdeacons; that the Divine Offices be sung according to the use of *York*, or *Salisbury*, &c. To which Orders *Thomas* Bishop of *Durham*,
42. in the year 1428, made some alterations and additions, namely, that every Prebendary of this Collegiate Church do personally reside, and be present at the daily Offices, or provide a sufficient Vicar to do it for him, that the Priest-Vicars have ten marks *per An.* the Deacon-vicars seven marks
43. *per An.* &c. That Mattins be not said at Midnight, but in the Morning, for the conveniency of the Parishoners, &c.

CESTRE, in the County Palatine of Durham.

44. THE beforemention'd *Anthony* Bishop of *Durham*, in the yeas 1286.
45. perceiving the Parish of this place to be large, and the Revenues of this Church to be sufficient to maintain many Ministers, made it Collegiate; to consist of one Dean and seven Prebends, that the Dean have the cure of Souls in the Parish and be continually resident, &c. with other Orders, as he before made in the case of *Langecestre* abovemen-
46. tion'd, *mutatis mutandis*. That the tenth part of the Portion of every non-Resident, be given to the Residents, and in case there be no Residents, then to the use of the Church, or of the Poor. All which was confirm'd by King *Edward* I.

St. ELISABETH's, near Winchester.

John de Pontisaria Bishop of *Winchester*, founded this Chappel of St. *Elizabeth* daughter of the King of *Hungary*, before the Gate of his Castle of *Wolvesay*, and therein establisht seven Chaplains, of which one to be Provost, and six Clerks; three of which to be Deacons, and three Subdeacons. The Provost, Chaplains, and Clerks, to be placed and supply'd, upon all avoidences, by the Bishop of *Winchester* for the time being, or his Lieutenant, the Chaplains and Clerks to have their Board from the
47. Provost; all to live and Dyet together in the same House, every Chaplain to have a little Clerk to serve him in the Church and in his Chamber, and not to be allow'd any other Servant, that constantly at day break they rise and repair to the Chappel, there say first the Mattins of the Blessed Virgin with a low voice, and then sing the Mattins of the day, &c. that in all the Divine Offices they observe the *Salisbury* use; that no Wo-
48. man shall enter into any part of the House except the Chappel and the Hall; the Provost and every Chaplain and Clerk to be sworn, at their admission; to the observance of these Orders, and to personal Residence. Which Deed of Foundation bears date in the year 1301, (30. *Edward* I.) *Simon de Farham*, and divers others were Benefactors to this Chappel, and gave

gave divers Mannors, Lands, and Rents to the same. All confirm'd by King *Edward* I. and II.   49.

[Valued at 112 *l.* 17 *s.* ¼ *d.* ob. *per Annum.*]

KIRKBY Super Wretheck, *in* Leicestershire.

ROger Be!er founded a Chantry of one Custos and twelve Chaplains, in the Chappel of St. *Peter* adjoyning to his Mannour of *Kirkeby*, and endow'd the same with the Advowson of the Church of *Kirkeby*, the Mannour of *Bokeminster*, and other Lands and Rents, with Warrantry; and gave the power of presenting to the Custos or Wardens place, to the Dean and Chapter of *Lincoln* &c. Whose Deed of Foundation bears date in the year 1319 (13. *Edward* II.)   50.
51.

WENGHAM, *in* Kent.

POpe *Gregory* X. licenced *John* Archbishop of *Canterbury* to establish a Provost and a Colledge of ten secular Canons, in the Parish Church of *Wengham*, instead of a Rector, the said Provost to have the Parochial cure of Souls; which Colledge being accordingly founded by the said *John*, he appointed that six of the said Canons should be Priests, two Deacons and two Subdeacons, and set out their several Prebends, and how the Common distributions should be made, &c, Whose Deed of Foundation bears date, *An. Dom.* 1286. and was confirm'd by King *Edward* I.   52.
53.
54.
55.

MEREWELL.

FOunded by *Henry de Blois* Bishop of *Winchester* for four Priests, and by him endow'd with 13 *l.* per An. of Rent. *Peter de Rupibus* Bishop of *Winchester* made certain Orders for the Government of the said four Chaplains or Priests, as that they keep one Deacon to serve them in the Church and at home, that they choose yearly one of them to be their Prior, that what ever Chaplain be guilty of Incontinency or other foul crimes, he also shall be expell'd, and further granted them, besides their first endowment, fifty quarter of Corn, for their Common use, and four Load of Hay. Whose Deed bears date, *An. Dom.* 1226.   56.

GLASENEY, *in* Cornwall.

PEter Bishop of *Exeter*, in the year 1288., made a further Provision for the Vicars of this Church, first founded by his Predecessor *Walter*, for thirteen Canons, and as many Vicars.   57.

[Valued at 205 *l.* 10 *s.* 6 *d.* per Annum.]

The Collegiate Church of Ruthin in Denbighshire.

58.
59.

John Gray Lord of the Cantred of *Deffencloyt* in the Diocess of *Bangor*, instituted a Colledge in the Chappel of St. *Peter* at *Ruthin*, for at least seven Priests to celebrate there daily the Divine Offices, one of whom to serve in the Chappel of the Castle, and endow'd the same with two hundred and fifty acres of Land, with Tithes, and large Commons of Pasture, and Paunage in his Woods for sixty Hogs, &c. to hold in pure free, and perpetual Almes, with Warranty. Whose Deed of Foundation bears Date, *An.* 1310.

OTERY, in Devonshire.

60.

The Dean and Chapter of *Roan*, in the year 1335 (9. *Edward* III.) granted, with Licence of the Apostolick See, and the King of *England*, their Mannour of *Otery* St. *Mary*, in the County of *Devon*, &c. to *John de Grandisson* Bishop of *Exeter*, and instead of Warranty they delivered up to the said Bishop all their Deeds and Writings concerning the same. King *Edward* III. in the eleventh year of his Reign granted his Licence to the said Bishop of *Exeter* to erect a Monastery or Collegiate Church to consist of a certain number of secular Canons at *Otery* St. *Mary*, either in the Parish Church there or in some other place, and to endow the same with the Mannour of *Otery*, and to appropriate the Tithes of the said Town to the same. Which Colledge was accordingly founded and endow'd by the said Bishop, *An.* 1337.

[Valued at 303 *l.* 2 *s.* 9 *d. per Annum.*]

The Collegiate Church or Chappel of St. Steven, within the Royal Palace at Westminster.

61.
62.
63.
64.

The Chappel of St. *Steven* in the Pallace at *Westminster* was nobly finisht by King *Edward* III, tho' begun by his Progenitors, which King founded therein a Dean and twelve Canons, with as many Vicars, and other Ministers accordingly, and gave them by his Patent, dated in the two and twentieth year of his Reign, his great House in *Lombardstret*, *London*, with some advowsons, obliging himself and Royal Heirs to make it up to them a Revenue of 500 *l. per An.* In the two and thirtieth year of his Reign he gave them a Tower in *Bokelesbury* in *London*, call'd *Sewtes Tour*, with the Appurtenances. In the three and fortieth year of his Reign he gave them another House in *London* call'd the *Reole*, with the appurtenances, then valued at 20 *l. per An.* In further augmentation of the said Foundation, he granted them all the ground from the said Chappel Northward to the receipt of the Exchequer, between *Westminster Hall* and the *Thames*, for making a Cloyster and other necessary Buildings, with free Entrance day and Night at the Gate adjoyning to the Kings Bridge, also a Chamber within the said Gate formerly belonging to his Clerk of the Kitchin, with the Houses formerly used for Stables of War-horses and other Horses, &c. with a Free Passage to the said Chappel by day light thro' the great Hall, and exempted the said Dean and Canons and all

their

their Lands from the Payment of any Aydes, or Taxes whatsoever. King 65.
Richard II. compleated the full endowment of this Colledge, by settling on 66.
it divers Mannours and Lands in *Kent*, &c. according to the direction and
desire of his Grandfather in his Testament.

[Valued at 1085 *l*. 10 *s*. 5 *d*. *per Annum*.]

The Royal Collegiate Chappel in the Castle at Windsor. 67.

A Chappel for eight Canons secular having been begun in the Castle of
Windsor, King *Edward* III. who was baptized there, finisht and
compleated the same, in honour of Almighty God, his glorious Virgin
Mother, St. *George* the Martyr, and St. *Edward* the Confessor, and establisht therein a Custos or President to the former eight Canons, and an 68.
addition of fifteen Canons more, and four and twenty poor Knights, with
other Ministers of the said Chappel, and endow'd the same, in the two
and twentieth year of his Reign with divers Churches, and promised for
himself and Heirs, to encrease the Revenue to the Sum of 1000 *l. per An.*

Pope *Clement* the VI. granted power to the Archbishop of *Canterbury*, and
the Bishop of *Winchester*, to establish the said Canons and Knights by A-
postolick authority, and exempted the said Chappel and Colledge and all 69.
the members thereunto belonging from the Jurisdiction of the Archbishop
or any other Bishop or Ecclesiastical Judg, and that the Custos of the same
shall have perpetual Jurisdiction over the Members of the said Colledge,
paying to the Apostolick Chamber one Mark Sterling on the feast of St.
George, yearly. The foresaid King *Edward* III. granted to this Colledge 70.
divers Churches, and Revenues among other things, a Rent of one hundred marks *per An.* payable by the Bailiffs of the Town of *Northampton*
out of the Kings Farm of the said Town. King *Henry* IV. granted to the 71.
Custos and Canons here a void peice of Ground within this Castle near the
great Hall, call'd *Wodehawe*, for Building Houses for the Vicars and Choristers. King *Edward* IV. granted and confirm'd to them the Alien Priory of *Okeburn* with all the Lands and Churches thereunto belonging,
which had been formerly granted to *John* Duke of *Bedford* by King *Henry* IV. late *de facto & non de jure*, King of *England*, and afterwards by
the said *John* Duke of *Bedford* given to this Collegiate Chappel, (the said
Duke being desirous wholly to abdicate such spiritual Profits, and restore
them to their pristine Nature) which gift was afterwards ratified and confirm'd by *Henry* V. *de facto & non de jure*, King of *England*, *non obstante* 72.
the Statute of *Mortmain* and now by the said King *Edward* IV. in the first
year of his Reign ; Which King gave them also the Alien Priory of *Up-* 73.
havenne with all Rights thereunto belonging, and divers other Lands and 74.
Revenues, also the Alien Priory of *Monkenlane* in the County of *Hereford*,
he also gave them the Custody and Advowson of the Hospital or Free
Chappel of St. *Anthony* in *London*, and to enjoy the same with all the
Estate thereunto belonging to their own proper use when it shall become
void by death, resignation or otherways. He also gave them the Alien 75.
Priories of *Brimesfeld* and *Charleton*, and divers other Lands in the seventeenth year of his Reign. The said King *Edward* IV. in the nineteenth year 76.
year of his Reign (reciting the first Foundation of this Collegiate Chappel
by King *Edward* III, and that *Henry* VI. *de facto & non de jure* King of
England, in his Parliament held at *Westminster* in the eighth year of his
pre-

77. *pretended Reign*, had paſt an Act whereby he will'd and declar'd that this Colledge ſhould bear the name of the Cuſtos or Dean, and Canons of the free Chappel of St. *George* within his Caſtle of *Wyndeſore*) did for the future incorporate them by the name of the Dean and Cannons of the Free Chappel of St. *George* within the Caſtle of *Wyndeſore*, by that name to purchaſe, ſue, and be ſued, &c. And granted Licenſe to *John* Duke of *Suffolk* and *Elizabeth* his Wife to confer the Manour of *Leighton-Buzzard* and other Revenues on the ſame, and alſo his general Licence to all other Perſons of this Kingdom of *England*, to grant Lands, Rents, or Advowſons, to the Dean and Canons of this Chappel to the yearly value of 500 *l* the Statute of *Mortmain*, or any other Statute or Law notwithſtanding.

78.

79. In the eighth year of King *Richard* II. *Walter Almaly* being then Cuſtos
80. an Inventory or Regiſter was made of all the Books, Veſtments, Relicks, Chalices, &c. belonging to this Chappel Royal, in which is particular mention of divers Miſſales, and other Church Books, ſeveral Volumes of
81. the Decretals, and Canon Law, &c. Veſtments of different Colours,
82. Qualites, and Richneſs, Copes, Coffers, Croſſes, Tabernacles, Images,
83. and Relicks, adorn'd with Jewels and precious Stones, of extraordinary
84. great value, Morſes of Silver and gilt, eight Chalices, of which one of Gold and ſet with precious Stones, Candleſticks, Cenſors, Croſſes, and Baſons of Silver gilt, &c. Miters ſet with precious Stones, a Paſtoral Staff,
85. &c. A Silver Bell to ring before the Body of Chriſt in the Viſitation of
86. the Sick. Beſides divers Jewels and Relicks in the Treaſury, Three
87. Crowns of Silver and gilt ſet with precious Stones one for the Bleſſed *Mary*, another for her Son, and the third for St. *Edward*.

RIPPON *Collegiate Church*.

88. A*Nno* 1331. *William* Archbiſhop of *York* finding in his Viſitation at this Church, the ſame almoſt deſtitute of Canons Reſidentiary, ordered, with conſent of all Parties concern'd, that ſuch Canons as are willing to reſide and do actually reſide, ſhall have the Profits in his Deed ſpecified, that the Vicars ſhall be paid their Stipends out of the common Profits, that every Cannon Reſidentiary ſhall reſide twelve weeks in the year, and that they be preſent at the Canonical hours in this Church, in like manner as in his Collegiate Churches of *Suthwell*, and *Beverley*. King *Henry* the V. in the ſecond year of his Reign, granted that the ſix Vicars belonging to this Church (for whom *Henry* Archbiſhop of *York* propoſed to build a Habitation within the Cloſe of the Church, where they might eat and ſleep together) might chooſe among themſelves a Superior by the name of Procurator, and that the ſaid Procurator and Vicars, and
89. their Succeſſors, might have a Common Seal, be capable to purchaſe and receive Lands, and by that name to ſue and be ſued, &c.

[Valued at 35 *l*. 3 *s*. 8 *d*. *per Annum*.]

SIBETHORP, *in Yorkſhire*.

THomas de *Sibethorp* Parſon of the Church of *Bekingham*, by Licenſe of King *Edward* the III. (*An. Reg* 10.) gave ſixteen Meſſuages

one

one Toft, three Bovates; one hundred and seventy Acres of Land, fifty Acres of Meadow, and 30 s. of Rent in *Sibethorp*, &c. to *John Cofin* Cuftos of the Chappel of the Bleſſed *Mary* of *Sibethorp*, for the maintenance of him and other Chaplains in the ſaid Chappel, and Succeſſors, and for the finding of thirty Wax-lights in the ſame, and a Lamp to burn before the Crucifix.

TUXFORD, in Nottinghamſhire. 90.

KING *Edward* the III. granted his Licenſe to *John de Lungvilers* to found a Colledge of five Chaplains, of which one to be Cuſtos, in the Parſonage houſe of the Church of *Tuxford*, and to give the Advowſon of that Church (which was held *in Capite* of the King) to the maintenance of the ſaid five Chaplains there celebrating; But the ſaid *John* not purſuing his Foundation in that manner, the ſaid King, on his Petition, granted him a new Licenſe in the one and thirtieth Year of his Reign, to give the ſaid Advowſon to the Prior and Canons of *Newſted* in *Shirewode*, for their finding five Chaplains, *viz*. three in the Church of *Tuxford*, and two in the Church of the Convent of *Newſted*, to celebrate for his Soul, &c.

SUDBURY, in Suffolk. 91.

KING *Edward* the III. in the nine and fortieth year of his Reign, granted his Licenſe to *Simon* of *Sudbury* Biſhop of *London*, and *John* his Brother, to give and aſſign a Meſſuage call'd *Lamberds-hill*, and three Shops in the Pariſh of St. *Mary Magdalen* Old *Fiſh-ſtreet*, *London*, to the Prioreſs and Convent of *Nun-Eaton*, in exchange for the Advowſon of the Church of St. *George* of *Sudbury*; with Power to the ſaid Biſhop and his Brother to found in the ſaid Church a Colledge to conſiſt of certain Chaplains, of which one to be Cuſtos or Warden. King *Richard* the II. in the third and ſeventh years of his Reign, granted to this *Simon*, then Archbiſhop of *Canterbury*, and *John de Chertſey*, Licenſe to endow the ſame with certain Mannors and Lands.

[Valued at 122 *l*. 18 *s*. 3 *d*. *per Annum*.]

ASTELEY, in Warwickſhire. 92.

SIR *Thomas de Aſteley*, Knt. founded and endowed a Chantry in St. *Mary*'s Chappel in the Church of *Aſteley*, for one Warden and three other Prieſts, and afterwards ſupplicated *Roger* Biſhop of *Coventry* and *Litchfield*, that it might be made a Colledge to conſiſt of a Dean and two Secular Canons, Prieſts; and it was accordingly ſo made by the ſaid Biſhop; and ſeveral Orders eſtabliſht, *viz*. that the Dean be ſworn to a Perſonal Reſidence in the ſame, that he have for his Habitation the Rectory-houſe of *Aſteley*, that he diſtribute to the poor 10 *s*. yearly; that the Dean find and preſent to the Dioceſan a perpetual Vicar to officiate in the ſaid Church, and that he pay him the Sum of five Marks *per Annum*, quarterly; that he find alſo a Pariſh Chaplain, and a fitting Clark; 93.

94. that he celebrate in Person on the greater Feasts, and provide Lights, &c. that he pay the Procurations and Sinodals of the said Church of *Astely*, and bear all other Charges, except Books and Vestments; that every Canon find a Vicar, presentable, to whom he is to pay five Marks yearly, and one other Priest also, unless he be willing to reside himself, and celebrate Mass

95. dayly in Person; that the Dean and Chapter have a common Seal, under the the Custody of the Dean and three Vicars, &c. Which Orders were ratifyed under the several Seals of the said Bishop, and *Thomas* the Founder, *An. Dom.* 1343.

[Valued at 39 *l.* 10 *s.* 6 *d.* per *Annum.*]

96. COTHERSTOKE, in 𝔑𝔬𝔯𝔱𝔥𝔞𝔪𝔭𝔱𝔬𝔫𝔰𝔥𝔦𝔯𝔢.

King *Edward* III. in the twelfth year of his Reign, granted his Licence to *John Giffard*, Clerk, to give and assign the Mannour of *Cotkerstoke* and divers other Revenues, to a Præposit and twelve Chaplains, secular or Religious, for the maintenance of them and two Clerks daily celebrating in the said Church, to hold in free, pure, and perpetual Almes, discharged and quit of all secular exactions.

97. HEMMINGBURGH, in 𝔜𝔬𝔯𝔨𝔰𝔥𝔦𝔯𝔢.

King *Edward* III. granted his Licence to the Prior and Convent of *Durham* to appropriate the Church of *Hemmingburgh*, of which they had the Advowson, to their own proper use for ever, under condition that they find a Monk or secular Chaplain to celebrate daily in the Church of *Durham* in a place there call'd the *Galeley*, for the Soul of King *Edward* I. and his Ancestors, and two other Monks or secular Chaplains to celebrate daily, one at the Altar of St. *Cuthbert* there, and one in this Church of *Hemmingburgh*, with a certain number of Waxlights, and that they observe the Anniversary of K. *Edw.* III. in the Quire of their Church, yearly, and on that day distribute to one thousand poor People 1 *d.* a peice. But this never taking effect by reason they could not obtain the Popes Licence and Confirmation for the said appropriation, King *Henry* VI. in the fifth year

98. of his Reign, granted his Licence to the said Prior and Convent of *Durham*, to erect in this Church of *Hemmingburgh* a Colledge to consist of one Præposit, three Prebendary-Canons, six Vicars, and six Clerks, with other Ministers to celebrate, and observe the Anniversary abovemention'd, the said King in the Charter of Licence incorporating the said Colledge, by the name of the Præposit or Custos, Prebendaries, Vicars, and Clerks of the Collegiate Church or Colledge of the Blessed *Mary* of *Hemmingburgh*.

[Valued at 36 *l.* 0 *s.* 7 *d.* per *Annum.*]

BRUSEYARD, in 𝔖𝔲𝔣𝔣𝔬𝔩𝔨.

Founded by *Matilda de Lancaster*, late Countess of *Ulster*, but at that time a Nun in the Collegiate Church of Nuns of *Campess*, for five Chaplains; for whose Government *William* Bishop of *Norwich* made in the

the year 1354. the following Ord.rs, viz. that the said five Priests sleep all in the same Dormitory, and eat together in the same Refectory; that one of the five be Custos or Master, that their habit be all alike and agreeable to the Canons, that they observe the *Salisbury* use in the Divine Offices; That they choose one of them for Treasurer, whose Office is to take care of all matters relating to the Chappel;. That the Custos be chosen by majority of voices, and in case he be not chosen in four months time, then the Election to be in the Bishop, that turn; that the Custos being elected is to obtain the Prioress of *Campesses* Letters of Presentation to the Bishop, who is thereupon to confirm him in the Office; that there be a Chest with three different Keys in which the Common-Seal and Accounts are to be kept, &c.

99.

100.

ABERGWILLY, in the Diocess of St. Davids.

Henry Bishop of St. *Davids*, in the year 1331: with the consent of the Chapter of this Collegiate Church o *Abergwilly*, made and created three Dignities in the same, viz. the Precentor Chancellor, and Treasurer, and appointed certain Prebends to belong particularly to the said Offices, &c.

101.

[Valued at 42 l. per Annum.]

ARUNDELL, in Sussex.

King *Richard* II. in the third year of his Reign granted his Licence to *Richard* Earl of *Arundell* and *Surrey* to found a Chantry or Colledge in the Parish Church of St. *Nicholas* at *Arundell*, without the Walls of the Castle there; which was at that time a Priory of Monks of the Order of St. *Benedict* sometimes belonging and Subject to the Abby of *Sees* in *France*, and which seldom or never had in it more then one Prior, and three or (at most) four Monks, with Licence to the said Prior and Monks to grant and alienate their Priory and all their Lands, &c. to the same belonging, to the said Earl, and he to confer the same on thirteen secular Chaplains, of which one to be cheif and call'd Master, therein, to be establisht, &c.

102.

103.

[Valued at 168 l. 7 d. ob. per Annum.]

St. MICHAELS in Crooked Lane, London.

104.

There having been several particular Chantries in this Church, founded and endow'd with divers Rents by several Citizens of *London*, which were by course of time Impoverisht, *William de Walworth* Citizen and Merchant of *London*, supplicated King *Richard* II. that with the Rents belonging to the said Chantries and other Revenues of his own augmentation, he might found there a Colledge of one Master and nine Chaplains, to celebrate for ever, for that King, the said *William*, *Margeret* his Wife, and *John Lovekyn* his late Master, &c. Which King did in the fourth year of his Reign, grant his Licence to the said *William* out of the special Affection which he had for his Person, and in consideration of the

105

the laudible Service which he had often done him, to found the Colledge accordingly.

106.

St. MARY'S, near Winchester.

King *Richard* II. in the sixth year of his Reign granted his Licence to *William Wykeham* Bishop of *Winchester* to found a Colledge, House or Hall, near *Winchester*, for the honour and glory of God, and the glorious Virgin *Mary* his Mother, and therein to establish a Custos or Warden, and seventy poor Scholars, Students in Grammar. *Infra.* 133.

[Valued at 628 *l.* 13 *s.* 6 *d.* per *Annum.*]

PONTFRACT, in Yorkshire.

107.

King *Richard* II. in the eighth year of his Reign, granted his Licence to *Robert Knolls* Chevalier, and *Constance* his Wife, to found a Colledge or Chantry, in *Pontfract* of seven Chaplains, whereof one to be Custos, and for thirteen poor People, two Clerks, and one or two Servants to attend the poor.

[Valued at 182 *l.* 14 *s.* 7 *d.* per *Annum.*]

BUNBURY, in Cheshire.

King *Richard* II. in the tenth year of his Reign, granted his Licence to *Hugh de Calveley* Chivalier to found a Chantrey or Colledge of one Master and six other Chaplains in the Church of *Bunbury*, with Liberty to the said *Hugh* to endow the same, and the said Mr. and Canons to have a Common-Seal.

108.

IRTLYNGBURGH, in Northamptonshire.

King *Edward* III. granted Licence to the Abbot and Convent of *Peterburgh*, and *John Pyel*, to erect a Colledge of six Canons secular, of which one to be Dean, and four Clerks, in the Parish Church of *St. Peter* of *Irtlyngburgh*, the Right of Presenting to the said Canons places to be in the Abbot and Convent of *Peterborough*, and the said *John*, by Turns; But the said *John* dying before this Foundation was perfected, King *Richard* II. in the eleventh year of his Reign, for twenty marks paid by *Joan* his widow and Executrix, granted his Licence to compleat the same.

109.

[Valued at 64 *l.* 12 *s.* 10 *d.* ob. per *Annum.*]

CLOVELEY, in Devonshire.

King *Richard* II. in the eleventh year of his Reign, Licenced *William Cary* to convert the Parish Church of *Cloveley*, the Advowson whereof did belong to the said *William*, into a Collegiate Church, for seven

ven Chaplains, of which one to be Custos or Warden, to found a Colledge and Buildings for their Habitation, in the Rectory, and to appropriate the said Advowson to them.

RUSHWORTH, in Norfolk.

KING *Richard* the II. in the thirteenth year of his Reign granted his Licence to several Persons to confer the Mannor of *Rushworth*, &c. on the Master or Custos of the Colledge of St. *John* the Evangelist of *Rushworth* and the Brethren of the same. *An.* 1360. *Thomas* Bishop of *Norwich* made several Statutes and Ordinances for the Government of this Colledge, late founded by the Lord *Edmund de Gonevill*, viz. That there be in the said Colledge, five Chaplains of which one to be Master or Custos, that as the Revenues increase the number be increased, and every new Fellow to have at least ten Marks, that they all sleep in one House and eat together, that the Master have the Cure of the Parishioners of the Town of *Rushworth*, with direction for their saying of their Masses and Offices, and that they be all continually resident, &c.

[Valued at 85 *l.* 15 *s.* ob. per *Annum*.]

110.

111.

112.

The Collegiate Church of St. David's, in Pembrokshire.

JOhn Duke of *Lancaster*, and the Lady *Blanch* his Wife, and *Adam* Bishop of St. *David's* considering that Priests were procured out of *England* with great difficulty and charges to officiate in the ancient Metropolitan Church of St. *David's*, they therefore founded a Chappel or Chantry of one Master and seven Priests, in the manner of a Colledge, on the *North* side of the said Cathedral Church, and built there divers Buildings and a Cloyster for their Habitation, and endow'd the same with the Appropriating to it divers Churches, *An. Dom.* 1365. Which Bishop made divers Statutes and Orders for Government of the same, viz. that the said Master and Priests should live together in a Collegiate way; that they should perform the Divine Offices in their Chappel according to the *Salisbury* use, &c. That the said Master and Chaplains shall assist on all Sundays and double Feasts, at High-mass and Vespers, in the Cathedral Church among the Vicars there; that neither the Master nor any of the Priests of the said Chantry go abroad alone, but with a Companion; That the Master receive yearly twenty Marks, and each Chaplain ten Marks; That the said Priests be daily apparell'd in long Garments (*vel Gownis, non Cotis curtis*) unless they ride, or go abroad; that the said Master and every Priest may hold another Benefice with cure within the Diocess of St. *David's*, but is not bound to reside there; That there be always two Choristers remaining in the House under the care of the Præcentor, who is to instruct them in Grammar learning, and singing, &c. Which Orders bear date, *An. Dom.* 1382.

[Valued at 106 *l.* 3 *s.* 6 *d.* per *Annum*.]

113.

114.

115.

116.

117.

BRAD-

BRADGARE, in the Diocess of Canterbury.

118.

KING *Richard* the II. in the sixteenth year of his Reign, granted his Licenfe to *Robert de Bradgare* Clerk, and others, to found a Colledge of one Chaplain, and two Clerks Schollers, to celebrate in the Parifh-Church of *Bradgare*, and to endow the faid Colledge with three Meffuages, two hundred Acres of Land, one hundred and fifty Acres of Pafture, fixty Acres of Wood, thirteen fhillings and four pence of Rent, and the Rent of eight Hens, and half a pound of Pepper. *An. Dom.* 1398. the faid *Robert* made divers Orders for the Government of this Colledge, *viz.* that the faid Chaplain and his Succeffors fhall continually refide in the Colledge except only the fpace of one month, containing thirty two days; that the faid Chaplain and his Succeffors fhall maintain at their own Charge one Servant to ferve them daily at Mafs, and in other Offices; that the Chaplain fhall not procure to himfelf any other Benefice or Office whereby his perfonal Refidence here may be hinder'd; that the Chaplain and Clerks be Natives of the Diocefs of *Canterbury*, and of the Confanguinity or affinity of the faid *Robert*; that no Chaplain be admitted unlefs he can read, conftrue, and fing well, nor any Clerk unlefs

116.
130.

he can read well, and fing indifferently; that the two Clerks Schollers remain Fellows of the Colledge till their Age of twenty five years and no longer; that the faid Chaplain and Schollers and their Succeffors fhall have a Common Lawyer in conftant Fee, one of the Council of the Archbifhop of *Canterbury* for the time being, to whom they fhall pay 6 s. 8 d. per Annum, &c.

PLECY, in Effex.

131.

KING *Richard* the II. in the feventeenth year of his Reign granted his Licenfe to his dear Uncle *Thomas* Duke of *Gloceſter* to found and eſtabliſh in the Pariſh Church of *Plecy* a Colledge of nine Chaplains one of which to be Maſter and Cuſtos, and of two Clerks, and two Choriſters, *non obſtante*, &c. And to endow the fame with divers Lands, &c.

[Valued at 139 l. 3 s. 10 d. per Annum.]

MAYDENSTONE, in Kent.

132.

KING *Richard* the II. in the nineteenth year of his Reign granted his Licenſe to *William de Courtney* Archbifhop of *Canterbury*, and Legate, his dear Kinfman, to convert the Pariſh-Church of the bleſſed *Mary* of *Maidenſtone* into a Colledge of one Maſter or Cuſtos, and as many Fellows, Chaplains, and other Miniſters as he fhould think expedient, and to endow the fame with Lands and Churches, in particular with the Hofpital of St. *Peter* and St. *Paul* of *Maidenſtone*, with all the Lands thereunto belonging, &c.

[Valued at 159 l. 7 s. 10 d. per Annum.]

KING *Richard* the II. in the nineteenth year of his Reign granted further to *William de Wykeham* Bishop of *Winchester*, whereas by his Licenfe he had founded a Colledge of one Cuftos, and feventy Schollars learning Grammar, commonly call'd *Saynt Mary Colegge of Wyncheftre*, and endowed the fame with Poffeffions for the Maintenance of the faid Cuftos and Schollars, and ten perpetual Chaplains, three other Chaplains, and three Clerks, he now alfo freed and acquitted the faid Colledge and all their Tenents for ever, from all Toll, Geld, Scutage, &c. and from all Taxes and Exactions whatfoever, and that the faid Colledge fhall never be obliged to grant any Penfions, Corrodies, or any maintenance to any one, at the demand or command of the King or his Heirs. And King *Edward* the IV. in the firft year of his Reign, ratified and confirm'd to this Colledge the alien Priory of *Andever* in the County of *Southampton*, and all Lands, &c. to the fame belonging, to hold in free, pure, and perpetual Alms, notwithftanding the Statute of *Mortmain*, or that the faid Priory was of the Foundation of the Kings Progenitors, or that the Lands were given by them for the fupport of Chantries, Hofpitality, or other works of Piety, there, or that exprefs mention is not made of the true value of the fame in this prefent grant, or any other Statute, Act, Law, or Reftriction to the contrary whatfoever.

133.

134.

135.

136.

BOLTON, in Yorkshire.

KING *Richard* the II. in the twentieth year of his Reign, granted his Licenfe to *Richard le Scrope* Chivalier, to found a Chantry of fix Chaplains, of which one to be Cuftos, in his Caftle of *Bolton*, and to endow the fame with a yearly Rent of 43 *l.* 6 *s.* 8 *d.* Alfo to give to the Abbot and Convent of St. *Agatha* in *Yorkfhire*, the yearly Rent of 106 *l.* 13 *s.* 4 *d.* for the fupport of fix Chanons-Chaplains to celebrate for him in the faid Abby, and for the finding and maintenance of two and twenty poor men in the faid Abby for ever to pray for him, &c.

137.

WENSLAW, in Yorkshire.

KING *Richard* the II. in the twenty fecond year of his Reign licenfed the before-mentioned *Richard le Scrope de Bolton*, to erect the Parifh Church of the Holy Trinity at *Wenflaw*, being of his Patronage, into a Colledge, to confift of one Mafter or Cuftos, and as many Fellow-Chaplains and other Minifters as he fhould think fit, and to endow the fame with Lands and Revenues to the value of 150 *l.* which yearly Sum he had formerly granted to the Abbot and Convent of St. *Agatha* in *Yorkfhire*, for the finding of ten Canons above their own number, and two Secular Chaplains, with two and twenty poor men, but they had releafed his Grant.

138.

139.
St. MARY's at Leicester.

KING *Henry* IV. in the first year of his Reign, reciting, that *Henry* Duke of *Lancaster* his Grandfather, had begun the Foundation of a Collegiate-Church at *Leicester*; in honour of the Annunciation of the blessed *Mary*, and certain Buildings for the Habitation of Canons, and Clerks, and infirm People there dwelling, and that *John* Duke of *Lancaster*, his Father, did desire to compleat the same, he approving their pious Intentions, assigned *John de Byngham*, and others, to provide Masons, Carpenters, and other Workmen to the number of four and twenty, and to provide Timber and Stone for carrying on and finishing the Work, commanding all Mayors, Bayliffs, &c. to be aiding and assisting.

Infra p. 140.

LEDBURY, in Herefordshire.

140.
KING *Henry* the IV. in the second year of his Reign, licensed *John* Bishop of *Hereford* to found a Colledge in the Parish Church of *Ledbury* for nine Chaplains, of which one to be Master or Custos, and they to have a Common Seal, be capable of purchasing and receiving Lands, of suing and being sued, &c.

141.
IN the eighteenth year of King *Henry* the VI. *Henry* Cardinal of *England* Bishop of *Winchester*, *Henry* Archbishop of *Canterbury*, and Sir *Walter Hungerford* Knt. Feoffees of *Henry* late King of *England*, of certain Lands in the Dutchy of *Lancaster*, granted and settled upon the Dean and Canons of the Collegiate Church of the blessed *Mary* at *Leicester*, a Rent Charge of one hundred Marks *per Annum* arising out of divers Towns in *Darbyshire*, and payable at *Michaelmas* and *Easter*.

[Valued at 595 *l.* 7 *s.* 4 *d. per Annum.*]

NORTH-YEVEL, in Bedfordshire.

142.
King *Henry* IV. in the sixth year of his Reign, granted his License to *Gerard Braybrok* Chivalier, and others to purchase of *John Wateryng* Clerk, and others, the Advowson of the Parish Church of *North-Tevell*, and to erect and change the same into a Colledge to consist of one Master or Custos, and as many Fellow-Chaplains, and other Ministers, as they shall think expedient and to endow the same by appropriating thereunto the said Church of *North-Tevell*, and that the said Master and Chaplains, may out of the said Appropriation grant a pension of five marks yearly, to a Chaplain celebrating for the Dead in the Chappel of the Mannour of *Quye* in the County of *Cambridge*.

[Valued at 61 *l.* 5 *s.* 8 *d.* ob. *per Annum.*]

AT-

ATTILBURGH, in Norfolk.

King *Henry* IV, in the 7*th.* year of his Reign, for 100. Marks granted his Licence to *Henry Packenham* Senior, and *Simon* Parson of the Church of *Scultone* to found a Chantry in the Parish Church of *Attilburgh* in honour of the Exaltation of the Holy Cross, to consist of five Chaplains, one of which to be Custos or Master; and to endow the same, among other things, with the Church of great *Elyngham* to be appropriated to the said Colledg, provided that a Vicar of the said Church be sufficiently endow'd, and a competent Sum of mony be appointed by the Ordinary of the Place to be distributed to the Poor of the said Parish, according to the Statute, 15 *R.* 2. *c.* 6.

[Valued at 21 *l.* 16 *s.* 3 *d.* per *Annum.*]

STAYNEDROPE, in the County Palatin of Durham.

Thomas Bishop of *Durham*, in the third year of his Pontificate, granted his Licence to *Ralf de Nevill* Earl of *Westmerland*, to found a Colledge of one Master or Custos, and certain other Chaplains continually to reside, and for certain poor Gentlemen, and other poor People in the Town of *Staynedrope* in his Liberty of *Durham*; and to endow the same with the Advowson of the Church of *Staynedrope*, which was held of him *in Capite*; with Licence to the said Master or Custos, and Chaplains to receive the same, the Statute of *Mortmain non obstante*, and by the same Grant incorporated the said Colledge, making the said Master and Chaplains, &c. capable of purchasing and receiving Lands, to sue and be sued, and Granted them a Common-Seal. Dated at *Durham* in the third year of his Pontificate.

[Valued at 126 *l.* 5 *s.* 10 *d.* per *Annum.*]

143.

TONGE, in Shropshire.

King *Henry* IV. in the twelfth year of his Reign, for the Sum of 40 *l.* paid into the Hanaper, granted his Licence to *Isabel* Widow of *Fulk de Penbrugge* Chivaler, and others, to purchase of the Abbot and Convent of the Abby of *Salop*, the Advowson of the Church of St. *Bartholomew* at *Tonge*, and to erect and change the same into a Colledge of five Chaplains, of which one to be Custos, and to endow the same with Lands and Churches, for the Maintenance of the said Custos and Chaplains, and thirteen poor People, more or less, whom he incorporated, &c. Settling the Patronage of the said Colledge on *Richard de Penbrugge* in special tail, with divers remainders over. King *Henry* V. in the third year of his Reign, setting forth that by an Act made in the Parliament late held at *Leicester*, all the alien Priories were given to him and his Heirs, granted to the Custos and Chaplains of this Colledge the Priory of *Lappeley*, and all the Revenues thereunto appurtaining, being heretofore part of the Possessions of the Abby of St. *Remigius* at *Reymys* in *Champeyne*, Provided that the Vicarage of the Church of *Lappeley* be sufficiently endow'd, and a competent Sum allow'd to the Poor of the Parish, according to the Statute. The foresaid *Isabel* and others who were Founders of this Colledge, made divers orders for Government of the same; among others, that none of the Chaplains be capable of holding any other Ecclesiastical Benefice, except only the Custos, who may; that there be two Clerks

144.

145.

146.

148. Clerks, of the firſt Tonſure, to aſſiſt in the Divine Offices; that there be thirteen poor People; that the Maſter or Cuſtos be choſen out of the number of the Chaplains, by the reſt; if they do not chooſe in fifteen days, then he is to be appointed, for that turn, by the Patron, if he neglects for four Months, then by the Biſhop of the Dioceſs, and if he neglects for one Month, then by the Chapter of *Litchfield*, if they neg-
149. lect for fifteen days, then by the Archbiſhop of *Canterbury*; The Cuſtos on his admiſſion to be ſworn to a faithful Adminiſtration of his Office, and to obſerve the Statutes, every Chaplain to be ſworn to be obedient to
150. the Cuſtos, &c. That the Cuſtos be Confeſſor to the other Chaplains and that every of them be obliged to confeſs to him at leaſt once a
151. year; That the Sub-Cuſtos govern in the abſence of the Cuſtos, and take care of the Affairs of the Chappel; that the Cuſtos ſhall not be Non-reſident above two months in a year, nor any Chaplain above one;
152. that the Cuſtos ſhall appoint one of the Chaplains to have the Cure of the Pariſh, who ſhall be call'd the Parochial Chaplain, and another of the Chaplains to teach the Clerks and Miniſters of the Colledge, and alſo the poor Children of the Town, and other Neighbouring Towns, in Reading, Singing, and Grammar, for which he ſhall receive half a Mark *per Annum*; That Mattines ſhall begin ſoon after day, and that it be celebrated according to the *Salisbury* uſe, with directions for the ſeveral
153. Maſſes; that after Veſpers and Complin they ſhall ſay the Antiphon, *Salve Regina*, or ſome other Antiphon of the bleſſed *Mary*, according to the time;
154. That every Brother ſhall forbear as much as he can to bring in any
155. Stranger, but rarely or never any Woman, &c, that no Prieſt or Clerk ſhall uſe Hunting, or Hawking, or keeping a hunting Dog in the Colledge; That the Maſters Sallary ſhall be ten Marks *per Annum*, Every Chaplains four Marks *per Annum*, The Parochial Chaplain, and the Steward to have half a mark each, more than their Sallary yearly, and each of the poor Men one Mark *per Annum*, beſides their Habitation; That the
156. Colledge ſhall have a Seal, with this Circumſcription *Sigillum commune S. Bartholomæi Apoſtoli de Tonge*, which Seal to be kept in a Cheſt under two different Locks, and in the ſame Cheſt the Charters, Indentures, and Muniments of the Colledge; that the Cuſtos and Prieſts ſhall not grant any
157. Corrodies or Penſions; That if any of the Brethren become guilty of ſuch a Crime as renders him irregular as homicide, &c. he ſhall no longer adminiſter in his order, but ſhall be expell'd; if it be ſuch a Crime, as after penance he may continue to miniſter in his Order, as Adultery, falſe Witneſs, Sacriledge, Theft, &c. he may after penance, be tollerated in his Office and Order, making Oath that for the future he will never be guilty of the like Crime again; if he be guilty of a leſſer Crime, as ſimple Fornication, Diſobedience, Drunkenneſs or the like, being twice admoniſht by the Cuſtos, upon the third offence he ſhall be expell'd the Houſe as incorrigible, &c. Which Statutes and Orders bear date *Anno*
158. *Dom.* 1410. (12 H. 4.) And were confirm'd by *John* Biſhop of *Coventry* and *Litchfield*, *An. Dom.* 1411.

[Valued at 22 *l.* 8 *s*; 1 *d. per Annum.*]

FODRING-

FODRINGHEY, in Northamptonshire.

KING *Henry* the IV. in the thirteenth year of his Reign, together with *Edward* Duke of *York*, founded a Colledge of one Master, twelve Chaplains, eight Clerks, and thirteen Choristers, upon six Acres of Land in the Lordship of the said *Edward* Duke of *York* at *Fodringhey*, and the said King incorporated them by the name of the Master and Colledge of the blessed *Mary* and *All Saints* of *Fodringhey*, &c. and granted to them the Profits of the Alien Priories of *Newent*, and *Anebury*, during his Wars with *France*, &c. And exempted and discharged this Colledge from all Tolls and Taxes of what nature soever, as well for their Goods as Lands, given by the said King or any other Benefactors, and granted them *Frankpledge*, Felons Goods, &c. with abundance of Royal Liberties and Franchises. King *Henry* the V. in the third year of his Reign, granted to his beloved Cousin *Edward* Duke of *York* liberty to enfeoff *Henry* Bishop of *Winchester*, *Thomas* Bishop of *Durham*, Sir *Walter Hungerford*, Knt. *Roger Flore* of *Okham*, and others, with his Castle, Mannor, and Town of *Fodringhay*, and several other Mannors and Lordships which he held of that King *in Capite*, for the carrying on and compleating the Buildings and Charges of this Colledge. *William Horwod* of *Fodringhay* Indented with *William Wolston* Esquire, and *Thomas Peckham* Clerk, Commissioners for the Duke of *York*, to make up a new Body of the Church joyning to the Quire of the Colledge of *Fodringhey*, of the same heighth and breadth with the said Quire, to be fourscore foot in length, &c. A Porch on the *South* side twelve foot in length, another Porch on the *South* side adjoyning to the Cloyster; and in the *West* end of the said Body a Steeple fourscore foot in higth from the Ground-Table Stone, twenty foot square within the Walls, and the Walls six foot thick, the Duke to find Carriage and Stuff, for which well and duly to be made, the said *Horwode* to have 300 *l.* Sterling; which Indenture bears date 13 *H.* 6.

159.
160.
161.
162.
163.
164.

[Valued at 19 *l.* 11 *s.* 10 *d.* ob. per Annum.]

STOKE-CLARE, in Suffolk.

THIS being formerly a Priory of *Benedictines*, was by *Edmund* Earl of *March*, by whose Ancestors it was founded, changed into a Collegiate Church of a Dean and Secular Canons, which change was ratified by the Papal Authority of *John* the XXIII. and *Martin* V.

Thomas Barneslay Dean of the Collegiate Church of *Stoke juxta Clare*, by the Authority and Command of *Edmund Mortimer* Earl of *March* and *Ulster*, and Lord of *Wigmore* and *Clare*, first Founder and Patron of the said Colledge, made several Statutes and Ordinances for Government of the same, viz. That there be always one Dean and six Secular Canons, that every Canon reside full two and thirty weeks in the year, or otherwise he shall receive but 40 *s.* for his Prebend that year in which he has not so resided; that neither the Dean nor any Canon lie in Bed in the Morning longer than six a Clock, or half an hour past; that there be in the said Colledge eight Vicars sworn to continual Residence, and two greater Clerks, also five Chorists or honest Boys to sing and serve in the

165.
166.
167.

Quire; that the Chorists have five Marks *per Annum* each; that there be two inferiour Clerks who are to take care of the Vestry, and ringing the Bells, that they ring to Mattins at five and go at six, to high Mass at eleven, and that they ring to Vespers so that they may be ended about five in the Afternoon; That no Canon who cannot spend 40 *l. per*

168. *Annum*, and no Vicar nor Clerk shall use hunting, nor any of them keep any Hounds in the Colledge, except the Dean, who may keep four; that no Canon or Clerk shall wear any Arms in the said Colledge, under the penalty of forfeiting the said Arms for the first offence, and of twenty shillings for the second; that none of the Canons, Vicars, or Clerks shall be married, or suspected of having any scandalous communication

169. with Women; That if any one be convicted of Heresie, or Sodomy, or Magick he shall be expell'd; that no Canon, Vicar, or Clerk, shall go abroad alone, but with a Companion; That they shall all duly and honestly pay their Debts to their Creditors; That there be a Porter of the said Colledge, who shall shut the Gate at *Coverfeu* time, and admit

170. none after that time; That one of the Vicars be appointed by the Dean to be Precentor, for the Government of the Quire in singing, and Ceremonies, &c. who is to receive on that account 20 *s. per Annum*, That the Colledge have a Common Seal, to be kept with their Evidences and Jewells, in a common Chest under three different Keys, one of which to be kept by the Dean, the other two by the two Senior Canons; That there be no precedency among the Vicars at the Table, but that they sit

171. as they come; but in the Choire according to Seniority; That all the Vicars eat together in the Common Hall, and that at Meal time some part of the Bible be always read to them; That every Vicar have liberty eight weeks in the year, and every Clerk six, to visit their friends and recreate themselves; that nothing shall be sealed with the Common Seal unless it be first Registred in a Book to be kept for that purpose; That every Dean within a year after his instalment give to the Colledge one Cope of the value of 5 *l.* and make a Feast for the Canons, &c. or

172. pay for it 40 *s.* That upon vacancy of the Deanery, the Patron of the Colledge present to the Bishop, a Graduate in some University, at least Master in Arts, or Batchelour in Law, to be instituted Dean; which

173. Statutes and Orders bear date in the year 1422.

[Valued at 324 *l.* 4 *s.* 1 *d.* ob. *per Annum.*]

NORTH-CADBURY, in Somersetshire.

174. KING *Henry* the V. in the fourth year of his Reign, granted his Licenfe to *Elizabeth* Widow of *William Botreaux* the elder, Chivalier, to found this Colledge for seven Chaplains of which one to the chief, to have the Cure of Souls there, and to be call'd Rector of the Colledge of St. *Michael* of *North-Cadbury*, and for four Clerks, with Licence to the said *Elizabeth*, and *William Botreaux* the yonger, to appropriate the Church of *North-Cadbury* thereunto, and endow the same with divers Lands, &c.

MAN-

MANCHESTER, in Lancashire.

King *Henry* V. in the ninth year of his Reign, granted his Licence in consideration of two hundred marks paid in the Hanaper, to *Thomas* Bishop of *Durham*, and other Feoffees of *Thomas la Warre* Clerk, to erect the Church of *Manchester* into a Collegiate Church, and to establish therein a Master or Custos with as many fellow Chaplains, and other Ministers, as they should think fit, whom he incorporated, &c.

HIGHAM-FERRERS, in Northamptonshire.

IN the 10 *Henry* V. that King granted his Licence to *Henry Chichley* Arch-bishop of *Canterbury* to found a Colledge at *Higham-Ferrers*, the Place of his Nativity, for eight Chaplains of which one to be Master, and four Clerks, one of which Chaplains or Clerks to teach Grammar, and another Song, and for six Choristers, whom the said King incorporated by the Name of the Master and Colledge of the Blessed Virgn *Mary*, St. *Thomas* of *Canterbury*, and St. *Edward* the Confessor, of *Higham-Ferrers*, and granted Licence to endow the same with Lands, &c.

[Valued at 156 l. 2 s. 7 d. per Annum.]

175.
176.

St. MICHAEL Pater noster Chirche, or Whitington Colledge, in London.

HEnry Archbishop of *Canterbury*, in the year 1424. granted his Licence, to *John Coventre*, *John Carpenter*, and *William Grove*, Executors of *Richard Whitington* late Citizen and Mercer, and several times Mayor, of *London*, to erect a Colledge, pursuant to the Will of the said *Richard* in the Parish Church of St. *Michael* call'd *Pater noster Chirche* in the *Riol*, in *London*, for five or six Chaplains and other Clerks and Ministers, and an Almes-House of thirteen poor People, and to make orders for the Government of the same. And accordingly the said Executors did found such a Colledge in honour of the Holy Ghost, the Blessed Virgin *Mary*, St. *Michael*, and All Saints, and made divers Orders touching the said Foundation; as that there shall be five Chaplains not elsewhere beneficed, one of which to be Master, two Clerks besides the Parish Clerk, and four Choristers, appointing the first Chaplains to be *William Brooke*, *John Whyte*, *Nicholas Gaytone*, *Richard Olyue*, and *Gregory King*; and that *William Brooke*, at that time Rector of the said Church of St. *Michael*, be the Master of the Colledge; that on all Sundays, when Sermons are Preacht at St. *Paul's* Cathedral, the Masses in this Church be finisht in such time, that the Parishoners of this Parish, and Mr. and Chaplains of the Colledge, may go to *Paul's* and be present at the Sermon, unless there be a Sermon in this Church also on the same day; That in the Canon of their Masses special mention be made of the Souls of the said *Richard Whityngton*, and *Alice* his Wife, and of Sr. *William Whityngton* Knt, and the Lady *Joan* his Wife Parents of the said *Richard*, &c. That two Solemn *Obits* be yearly celebrated for the said *Richard* and *Alice*, one on the three and twentieth or four and twentieth of *March*, the other on the thirtieth or one and thir-

177.
178.
179.
180.
181.

thirtieth of *July*, and that then the Master receive 20 *d*. every Chaplain 12 *d*, every Clerk 6 *d*, and every Chorister 3 *d*. That the said Master, Chaplains, Clerks, and Choristers, inhabit altogether in a Messuage built for that purpose at the East end of the said Church of St. *Michael*; That the Master receive yearly, over and above the Profits of the Parish as Rector, the Sum of ten marks, every Chaplain eleven marks, the first Clerk eight marks, the second 100 *s*. and every Chorister five marks, beside their habitations; that they keep Commons together in the Hall of the Colledge, and that there be always at their Meal time, something read out of the Holy Scriptures, Sermons or Homilies of the Saints, *&c.* That there be a Common Chest for keeping the Seal and Evidences, *&c.* under three different Keys, one to be kept by the Master, the other two by two other of the Chaplains, and that no one presume to keep all three, or any two of the said Keys; and that all overplus Revenue and Income, more then defrays the usual charges of the Colledge, be laid up and carefully preserved in the said Chest, for the Common Benefit of the House; That the Master be not absent or non resident above sixty days in a year, nor any of the Chaplains above twenty; That the Master and Chaplains, at the time of of their admission be sworn to observe the Statutes; that the Mayor of *London* for the time being be Overseer, and the Wardens of the Company of Mercers, Conservators and Patrons of the Colledge, *&c.* Which Orders bear date the seventeenth and eighteenth of *December* 1424. (3 *Henry* VI.) *vide inf.* p. 189.

[Valued at 20 *l.* 1 *s*. 8 *d*. per *Annum*.]

185.   BATTLE-FEILD, *in* Shropshire.

King *Henry* IV, in the eleventh year of his Reign, granted to *Roger Tve* Rector of the Chappel of St. *John* Baptist of *Adbrigton Husee* two acres of Ground in that Lordship adjoyning to *Shrewsbury*, in a Place call'd *Bateleyfeld*, being the Place where he fought with, and overcame, *Henry Percy*, and the Rebells with him, for the Building thereon a Chappel in honour of St. *Mary Magdalen*, for the Master and five Chaplains, of which Chappel and five Chaplains he appointed the said *Roger*, and his Successors Rector of the said Chappel of St. *John* Baptist, to be Masters or Wardens; and *Richard Husee* Lord of *Adbrigton* and his Heirs to be Patrons of the same; incorporating the said Foundation, and freeing them from Tenths, Subsidies, and all Taxes; with the Grant of a Fair to be held there yearly on the Feast of St. *Mary Magdalen*. Which *Roger Tve* by his Will dated 30. *Octob. An.* 1444. (24 *Henry* VI.) gave to this Colledge three Chalices Silver and gilt, one *Paxbrede*, Silver gilt, two Phiols Silver, three Bells in the Steple, three Crosses gilt, with several Vestments and Books for Church Service, and divers houshold goods, *&c.* and encreased the Stipends of every of the five Chaplains from eight marks to ten marks per *Annum*, Conditionally that they pray in a more especial manner for the Souls of King *Henry* IV. and King *Henry* V. Founders of this Colledge, *Richard Husee* first Patron of the same, *&c.* and for the Souls of all the Faithful slain in the fight of *Bataylfeld*, and there buried; All the Residue of his goods and Chattels he gave to the Fabrick, and Work, of the said Colledge, and to the relief leif of the Poor in the Hospital of the same. He also appointed a new Seal to be made for the Colledge with this Circumscription, *S. Commune Domini Rogeri Ive primi Magistri, & Successorum suorum Collegii beatæ Mariæ Magdalenæ juxta Salop.*

[Valued at 54 *l*. 1 *s*. 10 *d. per Annum.*]

THE beforemention'd *John Coventre*, *John Carpenter*, and *William Grove*, Executors of *Richard Whytington*, by their Deed dated 13 *Feb.* 3 *Henry* VI. granted a yearly Rent of 63 *l*. sterling, to the Colledge by them Founded as before mention'd, and alter'd and added some few things to the Statutes and Orders relating to the said Colledge.

189.

THELE, in Hertfordshire.

King *Henry* VI. in the ninth year of his Reign, at the request of *William* Bishop of *London*, Patron and Ordinary of this Colledge, which had been founded and endow'd for the maintenance of one Custos and four Chaplains, who by ill management had lost, and wasted most of their Estate, granted his Licence to *John Howeden* Clerk then Custos of this Colledge to transfer divers Lands and Impropriations in *Essex* and *Hertfordshire* yet remaining, to *Henry Hoddesden* Prior of the Hospital of *Elsing-Spitell* in *London*, and to the Convent there, they finding two Canons Regular to celebrate in this Colledge, and three other Canons Regular to celebrate in the said Hospital, for the Souls of the Founders of this Colledge.

190.

191.

WYE, in the County of Kent.

King *Henry* VI. in the tenth year of his Reign, granted his Licence to *John* Archbishop of *York*, who had had the Custody of both the Privy Seal, and great Seal, to found a Colledge at *Wye* in the Diocess of *Canterbury*, the place of his Nativity, for one Master or Provost, and such number of Priests or Chaplains, and Ecclesiastical Ministers, as he shall see fit, to be call'd the Colledge of St. *George* and St. *Martin*, whom he incorporated, and granted to the said Archbishop Power to endow the same with Lands, and appropriate Churches, and to appropriate the Vicarage of the Parish Church of *Wye* thereunto, any Law or Statute to the contrary *non obstante*. The said King also granted to this Bishop divers Lands, &c. formerly belonging to *Katherine* late Abbess of *Guynes* in the County of *Artoys* valued at 14 *l. per Annum.* to be conferr'd on this Colledge; with divers other Revenues.

192.

193.

[Valued at 93 *l*. 2 *s*. ob. *per Annum.*]

TATE-

TATESHALE, in Lincolnshire.

194.

KING *Henry* the VI. in the seventeenth year of his Reign, licenced *Ralph Cromwell*, Knt. and others to convert the Parish Church of *Tateshale*, into a Collegiate Church, or Colledge of seven Chaplains (of which one to be Master or Custos) six Clerks, and six Choristers, and to erect an Alms-house thereunto adjoyning for thirteen poor People of both Sexes, and incorporated the same by the name of the Master or Custos, and Chaplains of the Colledge and Alms-house of the Holy Trinity of *Tateshale*, with licence to the said Colledge, &c. to purchase, receive, and hold Lands, &c. to the value of 200 l. *per Annum* over and beside the Profits of the Advowson and yearly value of the Church of *Tateshale*, &c.

[Valued at 348 l. 5 s. 11 d. ob. q. *per Annum*.]

ETON by Windsor, in Barkshire.

195.

196.

FOunded by King *Henry* the VI. in the nineteenth year of his Reign; for the carrying on of which work he appointed *Robert Kent*, *William Lynde*, and *William Waryn*, to be his Procurators and Agents. It did, in the first Institution, consist of one Provost, or Præposit, ten Priests, four Clerks, and six Boys Choristers, five and twenty poor and indigent Grammar Schollars, and five and twenty poor and decrepid men, also one Master to teach Grammar learning to the foresaid poor Schollars and others coming from any parts of *England*, freely and without any manner of exaction; of this Foundation he made *Henry Sevor* Clerk, the first Provost, and incorporated them by the name of the Provost and Royal Colledge of the Blessed *Mary* of *Eton* near *Wydesor*; he also gave

197.

them the Advowson of the Parish-Church of *Eton*, to be made Collegiate, and intirely united to their own proper use, without endowing a Vicar, or appointing a competent Sum to be yearly distributed to the Poor of the Parish out of the same, the Statute *non obstante*, with Licence to purchase Lands to the value of one thousand Marks *per Annum*, the Statute of *Mortmain non obstante*, and discharged them from the Payment of *Corrodies*, or any Pensions, or Annuities whatsoever. The said King

198.
199.
200.

granted to this Colledge divers Rents rising out of several Alien Priories, with the Reversions of the said Estates, and all Liberties and Franchises to those Alien Priories belonging, in as full and ample manner as they were ever used by the former Possessors, with warranty, &c.

NEWPORT, in Shropshire.

KING *Henry* the VI. in the twentieth year of his Reign Licensed *Thomas Draper* to purchase and receive from the Abbot and Convent of St. *Peter's* at *Shrewsbury*, the Parish Church of *Newport*, and therein to found and erect a Colledge of one Custos, a Priest, and four Chaplains, whom by the name of the Custos and Chaplains of *Seint-Marie-College of Newport*, he incorporated, with License to endow the same with Lands, &c. of the value of 10 *l.* per *Annum* and appropriated the said Parish Church to the same, provided that the Custos for the time being takes the cure of Souls, and ministers all and singular the Sacraments to the Parishoners, &c.

St. MARY's at Stafford.

King *Henry* the VI. in the four and twentieth year of his Reign, granted the Patronage and Advowson of the Deanery of his free Chappel at *Stafford*, to *Humphrey* Duke of *Buckingham*; and Licensed him to give one hundred marks of Land, &c. to the Dean and Canons of the said free Chappel.

[Valued at 35 *l.* 13 *s.* 10 *d.* per *Annum.*]

WESTBURY, in Gloucestershire.

King *Edward* the IV. in the fourth year of his Reign, gave to *Henry Sampson* Clerk, Dean of this Colledge, and the Chapter of the same and their Successors, the Mannor of *Aylmystere*, to hold in pure and perpetual Alms, with view of *Frankpledge*, &c.

[Valued at 232 *l.* 14 *s.* per *Annum.*]

BARNARD-CASTELL, in the County Palatine of Durham.

King *Edward* the IV. in the seventeenth year of his Reign, granted his License to his most dear Brother *Richard* Duke of *Gloucester* to erect a Colledge at *Barnard-Castle*, in the Castle there, of one Dean, and twelve Chaplains, ten Clerks, six Chorists, and one other Clerk, whom he incorporated by the name of the Dean and Chaplains of the Colledge of *Richard* Duke of *Gloucester* of *Baynard Castell*, and that the said Dean and Chaplains may purchase Lands, &c. to the yearly value of four hundred marks, over and above all reprises.

204.   MIDDELHAM, in Yorkshire.

IN the same year, the said King *Edward* the IV. licensed his said Brother *Richard* Duke of *Gloucester* to erect another Colledge at *Middelham* of a Dean, six Chaplains, four Clerks, six Choristers, and one other Clerk, to celebrate Divine Service in the Parish Church there, whom he incorporated by the name of the Dean and Chaplains of the Colledge of *Richard* Duke of *Gloucester* of *Middelham* in the County of *York*, and that they may purchase Lands, &c. to the value of two hundred Marks *per Annum* over and above all Reprises, &c.

ROTHERAM, in Yorkshire.

King *Edward* the IV. in the twentieth year of his Reign, granted his Licence to *Thomas Rotheram* Bishop of *Lincoln* to erect a Chantry
205. of one Chaplain to celebrate daily at the Altar newly built by the said Bishop within the Parish Church of *Rotheram*, in honour of our Lord *Jhesu Christ*. Two years after that the same King Licensed the said *Thomas*, then Archbishop of *York*, to found a Colledge in *Rotheram* to consist of one Provost, a Preacher of the Word of God, and of two Fellows, one of which to be a Teacher of Grammar, and the other a Teacher of Song, with such other Fellows as the Revenues shall admit of, for the Preaching of the word of God in the Parish of *Rotheram*, and elsewhere in the Diocess of *York*, and for the free teaching of Grammar, and Song, to any Schollers who are desirous to learn, and come to the said Colledge
206. from any parts of *England*; and incorporated the same by the name of the Provost and Fellows of the Colledge of *Jesus* at *Rotheram*, with License to the said *Thomas* to give the Soil whereon the said Colledge shall be built to the same, and other Lands and Possessions, &c. to the value of one hundred Marks *per Annum*, and to appropriate the Church of *Laxton* in the
207. County of *Nottingham*, thereunto.

[Valued at 58 *l*. 5 *s*. 9 *d*. ob. per Annum.]

The Kings free Chappels have been of old time, and ought to be exempt from the ordinary Jurisdiction, and all Payment of Procurations, or any other impositions or exactions whatsoever.

POpe *Paul* the IV. confirm'd to Sir *William Peter*, Knt. and a Coun-
cellor of State, divers Mannors and Lands, &c. formerly belonging
to several Monasteries, and by him purchased and obtain'd from King
Henry the VIII. and others, and absolved him from all Excommunications,
and other Ecclesiastical Censures or Penalties that he might incur
for holding the same, and decreed that he might for the future without
any scruple of Conscience continue the Possession of the same;
with command to the Bishop of *London*, &c. not to permit him to
be vext or disturb'd in relation to his foresaid Lands, &c. under
pain of the severest Censures of the Church. Whose Bull bears
date at St. *Peter's* in *Rome*, *An. Dom.* 1555. (2 3 *Ph. & Ma.*)

208.

209.

F I N I S.

A CATALOGUE

OF

The Religious Houses, &c. as they were Scituated within the several Counties in England.

BARKSHIRE.

Abingten, Wallingford, Hellenflow, Hurley, Reading, Sandford, Poghele, Bisham, Donyngton, Windsor, Eaton.

BEDFORDSHIRE.

Beaulein, Margate, Wardon, Woburn, Dunftable, Biffemede, Harewold, Newenham, Caldewell, Todington, Chikefand, North-Tevel.

BUCKINGHAMSHIRE.

Ankerwik, Snellefhall, Ivingbo, Burnham, Miffenden, Tikeford, Bittlefden, Mendham, Nutley, Chetwode, Afherug, Alesbury, Lavingdene, Newinton-Longville.

CAMBRIDGESHIRE.

Ely, Thorney, Chateriz, Romburgh, St. Radegunds, Denny, Waterbecham, Swanefey, Barnewell, Anglefeye, Royfton, Spiney.

CHESHIRE.

St. Werburghs, Birkened, Chefter Nunery, Cumbermere, Deulaeres, Stanlaw, Dernhall, Norton, Modberley, Bunbury.

CORNWALL.

St. Petrocus, St. Germains, Sylley Ifle, St. Michaels Mount, Tywardreit, Budmin, Launcefton, Glafenaye.

CUMBERLAND.

Armethwayt, St. Bees, Wetherhall, Seaton, Calder, Holmcultrum, Carlile, Lanercoft.

DARBYSRHIE.

Darby, Derley, Repindon, Beaucheif, Dale, St. Mary de Pratis, Calc.

DEVONSHIRE.

Taveftock, Exeter, St. Micholas at Exeter, St. Catherines Exeter, Modbury, Ottery, Stoke Curcy, St. James, Barneftaple, Ford, Buckfaft, Dunkewell, Newenham, Bocland, Totnes, Barnftaple, Plimton, Hertland, Fritbelftoke, Torre, Cloveley.

DORSETSHIRE.

Sherburn, Winburne, Midleton, Shaftesbury, Horton, Cerns, Abbotsbury, Shirburn, Lodres, Frampton, Tarent, Binedon.

DURHAM.

Durham, Wyrmouth, Finchale, Egleston, Shireburne, Gretham, Oueton, Kypier, Langeceftre, Aukland, Chefter, Staynedrope, Barnard-Caftle.

ESSEX.

Berking, Colne, Walden, Merfey, Horfeleyh, Prittlewell, Stannefgate, Cogeflsall, Stratford-Langton, Tilfey, Heningham, Thrembale, Colchefter, Waltham, Dunmow, St. Ofiths, Wykes, Wodham, Illeford, Hornechirche, Havering, Bocking, Maldone, Snapes, Plecy.

GLOUCESTERSHIRE.

Gloucefter, Tukesbury, Winchcumb, Derehurft, Kingfwood, Flexley, Hayles, St. Ofwalds, Ciremefter, Briftol, Keinfham, Lechelade, Billefwike, Stanley, Ginges, Weftbury.

HANT

A Catalogue of the Religious Houses, &c.

HANTSHIRE.
Winchester, Hide, Rumsey, Warwell, Winteney, Andever, Apledercomb in the Isle of Wight, Shireburn, Quarre in the Isle of Wight, Beaulein, Letley, Suthwike, Twineham, Motesfont, Seleburn, Southampton, Basingstoke, St. Crosses, Titchfield, Caresbroke Isle of Wight.

HEREFORDSHIRE.
Hereford, Ewyas, Leominster, Lingebrook, Cresswell, Monkenlen, Cliffords, Dore, Wigmore, Wormley, Acornbury, Flanesford, Ledbury.

HERTFORDSHIRE
St. Albans, Hatfeild, Peverell, Hertford, St. Mary de Prato, Sopewell, Flamsted, Chesthunt, Rowney, St. Julians.

HUNTINGTONSHIRE.
Ramsey, St. Ives, St. Neots, Huntington, Saltre, Stoneley by Kimbolton.

KENT.
Canterbury, Rochester, St. Mildred, Folkstone, Liming, Raculfa, Shepey, Malling, Daviniton, Levisham, Patrickiburn, Horton, Feversham, Bexley, Dover, Ledes, St. Radegundis, Tonebrigge, Cumbwell, Lesnes, Bilsington, Badlesmere, Dertford, St. Gregories at Canterbury, Romenale, Herbaldown, Strode, Hethe, Langdone, Mottidon, Wengham, Wye, Bradgare, Maydenstone.

LANCASHIRE.
Penwortham, Lytbom, Holand, Lancaster, Furnes, Kirimele, Burscough, Conyngeshed, Cokersand, Manchester.

LEICESTER.
Langley, Hinkley, Geroudon, Grace-dieu, Bredon, Laund, Ouston, de Pratis, Bradley, Kerkby-Beler, Burton, Leicester, Stockerson, Croxton, Kerby super, Wrethek.

LINCOLNSHIRE.
Bardeney, Croyland, Spalding, Belvoir, Santoft and Henes, Frestone, Stikeswould, Stanford, Foss, Steinfeild, Covenham, Burwell, Willesford, Minting, Long-Benington, Hagh, Swinesbead, Louthpark, Kirksted, Revesby, Valledei, Greenfield, Legburne, Nun-Cotun, Epworth, Hyrst, Thornton, Nocton, Thornholme, Bourn, Kyme, Thorkesey, Grimesby, Ravenston, St. Innocents, Lincoln, Ellesham, Newstede, Holbeche, Newhus, Tupholm, Newbo, Hagneby, Barlings, Sempringham, Haverholme, Bolington, Alvingham, Ormesby, Sixill, Maresey, Ancolm, Katteley, St. Catherines, Heynings, Holland-Brig, Wells, Tateshale.

LONDON.
Minoresses, Abby of Grace, Carthusians, Trinity Priory, St. Bartlemew, St. Giles, St. Mary Bethelem, St. Mary Spittle, St. Bartholmews Hospital, St. Thomas of Acon, Rouncival, Converts, St. Katherines, Elsing-Spittle, Berking-Chirch, Savoy, St. Johns, St. Hellens, Whitingtons Colledge and Hospital, St. Pauls, Crooked-lane.

MIDDLESEX:
Westminster, Kilburn, Clerkenwell, Halywell, Syon, St. James, St. Stevens Chappel at Westminster.

NORFOLK.
Dereham, Wymundham, Binham, Norwich, Horsham, Carhow, Blackebxrgh, Waburn, Wells, Toft, West-Acre, Castle-Acre, Mendham, Bromholm, Reinham, Slevesholm, Thetford, Sibeton, Pentney, Walsingham, Cokesford, Buckenham, Hickling, de Prato, Linne, Wendlyng, Langley, Shouldham, Ingham, Russworth, Attilburgh.

NORTHAMPTONSHIRE.
Peterborough, Peykirk, Wyrthorp, Sewardsley, Lusseild, Weden-Pinkney, Northampton, Daventrey, Pipwell, St. Mary de Pratis, Chaucombe, Canons Ashby, Brackley, Sulby, Catesby, Cotherstoke, Irtlyngburgh, Fodringhey, Higham-Ferrers.

NOTTINGHAMSHIRE.
Wallingwells, Blith, Lenton, Rufford, Beau valle; Wirksop, Felley, Thurgarton, Newstead, Nottingham, Wellebeck, Brodholm, Shelford, Stoke, Suthwelle, Tuxford.

NORTHUMBERLAND.
Tinemouth, Hallistane, Lambley, Hexam, Brinkeburne, Bolton, New-Castle, Alneweke, Blanland.

OXFORDSHIRE.
Oxford, Eynesham, Stodely, Godstow, Glosterhall, Coges, Tame, Brure, Rewley, Oseney, Dorchester, Cold-Norton, Bisseter, Wroxton, Ewelme, Burcestre.

RUTLAND.
Broke, Okeham.

SHROP-

A Catalogue of the Religious Houses, &c.

SHROPSHIRE.
Shrewsbury, Bromfield, Chirbury, Abberbury, Wenlock, Bildwas, Haghmon, Littleshull, Wombrigge, Ratlingcope, St. Giles, Brugenorth, Ludlow, Hales-Owen, Tonge, Battlefield, Newport.

SOMERSETSHIRE.
Glastonbury, Bath, Wells, Atheling, Dunster, Bristol, Clive, Montacute, Witham, Taunton, Haselberge, Briweton, Berliz, Wospring, Stenerdale, Brugwalter, St. Laurence, North Cadbury.

STAFFORSHIRE.
Burton, Tutbury, Canewell, Farwell, Blithbury, Sandweil, Dudley, Croxden, Hilton, Wulverhampton, Lapley, Stone, Ronton, Trentham, Rowcestre, St. Thomas, Wolverhampton, Litchfield, Stafford.

SUFFOLK.
Hulme, St. Edmundsbury, Eye, Sudbury, Radingfield, Edwardston, Campess, Kersey, Stoke-Clare, Blackeham, Briset, Ixworth, Butley, Ipswich, Bliburg, Leyston, Begeham, Bruseyard.

SUSSEX.
Selsey, Battel-Abby, Sele, Boxgrave, Levenestre, Lewes, Roberts-bridge, Hastings, Binham, Heryngham, Michelham, Durford, Arundel, Chichester.

SURRY.
Chertsey, Bermundsey, Waverley, Sheen, St. Mary-Overy, Merton, Newsted, Rigate, Tanregge, Southwarke, Sandone.

WARWICKSHIRE.
Polesworth, Coventry, Aucot, Wroxhall, Pinley, Bretford, Aleester, Henwood, Nun-eaton, Wotton-waven, Kirkby, Stonely, Mereval, Cumb, Stodely, Kenilworth, Erdbury, Maxstoke, Warwick, Thelesford, Asteleye.

WESTMERLAND.
Heppe.

WILTSHIRE.
Malmsbury, Wilton, Ambresbury, Kington, Okeburn, Farley, Stanleigh, Henton, Brummore, Bradenstroke, Marleburgh, Ivichurch, Merleberge Salisbury, Heitsbury, Pulton, Leycock, Edindon, Maiden-Bradley.

WORCESTERSHIRE.
Worcester, Evesham, Pershore, Malverne, Westwood, Bordesley, Dodford.

YORKSHIRE.
Lestingham, Whitby, Beverley, Rippon, Selby York, St. Marys, St. Martins at Richmond, Midlesburg, Flakenes, Grendale, Nunkelliug, Monkton, Marrigg, Kirkley, Little-Marais, Nunburnham, Arden, Rossedale, St. Clements, Wilbersoss, Tykehead, Holy Trinity, York, Hedlay, Birstall, Gromond, Alverton, Pontefract, Monk-Breton, Arthington, Rieval, Fountains, Biland, Meaux, New-Minster, Sinningthwait, Esseholt, Hampole, Swine, Rupe, Hoton, Basedale, Salley, Kirkstall, Jerval, Nun-Apleton, Keldeholm, Wickham, Kingston, Mountgrace, Swine, Byland, Nostell, Woodkirk, Scokirk, Drax, Marton, Bolton, Kirkham, Gisburne, Scarthe, Bridlington, Wartre, Newburgh, Hode, Helaghe, Haltemprise, St. Leonards York, Carmans Spittle, Yarum, Scardeburgh, Kynewaldgraves, Hedon, Sutton, Glanfordbrigge, St. Nicholas, Richmond, Coverham, St. Agatha near Richmund, Watton, St. Andrews York, Malton, Ellerton, Knaresborough, Newton, Sivetborpe, Hemmyngburgh, Wenslaw, Middelham, Rotherham, Fossgate in York.

In WALES.
Brecknock, Cadwelli, Tallach, Margan, Abergavenny, Lankywan, Goldclive, Monmouth, Nethe, Basingwerk, Tintern, Cumbire, Blancland, Clunoc-vaur, Stratflure, Stratmargell or Strata-Marcella, Abercomway, Grace-dieu, Pilla, St. Clare, Lanthony, Bethkelert, Kaermerdin, Haverford, Glannauch, Ewenny, Raithyn, Landaffe, Lancadant, Abergwylly, St. Davids.

A
General Table
Of all the
RELIGIOUS HOUSES
Treated of in all the Three VOLUMS.

Note, That the Pages here named relate to the Book at large, and are to be sought for in the Margin of this Abridgment. *Note* also, That the Third Volum consists of Two Parts, and Two Numbers.

A.	Vol. 1.	Vol. 2.	Vol. 3.		Vol. 1.	Vol. 2.	Vol. 3.
				Ashby-Canons,		291	
				Asherugge.		344	1. 67
Aberbury.	605			Astley.			2. 92
Abbotsbury.	276			Atheling.	202		
Aberconway.	918			Attilburgh.			2. 142
Abergevenny.	557			Aucot.	367		
Abergvilly.			2. 100	Aukland.			2. 39
Abington.	97			**B.**			
Acornbury.		330					
St. Albans.	176	376		**B**adlesmere.		351	
Alcester.	470			Bardney.	142		
Alesbury.		396		Burlings.		643	
Alien Priories.	547			Barnard Castle,			2. 203
	1035			Barnstable.	684		
Alnewick.		591		Barnstaple.	1024		
Aluerton.	599			Barnwell.		28	
Aluingham.		802		St. Bartholomew, London.		166	
Ambresbury.	191			Basedale.	840		
Ancolm.		812		Basingstoke.		459	
Andever.	552			Basingwerk.	720		
St. Andrews, York,		808		Bath.	184		
St. Andrews, Northamp.	679			Battail Abby.	310		
Anglesey.		258		Battle-feild.			2. 185
Ankerwike.	482			Beaucheif.		607	
Apledercom.	571			Beauval.	962		
Arden.	500			Beaulieu.	925		
Armethwayt.	324			St. Bees.	395		
Arthington.	690			Begeham.		636	1. 77
Arundel.			1. 98	Beleien.	325		
			2. 101				

Bel-

A TABLE.

	Vol. 1	Vol. 2	Vol. 3		Vol. 1	Vol. 2	Vol. 3
Belvoir.	327			Bromfeild.	464		
Berliz.		249		Bromhale.		899	
Berking.	79			Brook.		130	
Bermonſey.	639			Brudgnorth.		433	
Bethkelert.		100		Bruere.	855		
Beverly	169	2.	1	Brugwalter.		432	
Biland.	775			Bruges.			2. 207
Billeſwike.		455		Brummore.		201	
Bilwas.	779			Bruſyard.			2. 98
Bilſington.		333		Buckenham.		274	
Binedon.	911			Buckfaſt.	792		
Binham.	343			Bunbury.			2. 107
Birſtal.	587			Bungey.	513		
Birkney.	484			Burcejier.			1. 96
Biſhem.		355		Bawnham.	534	327	
Biſſemede.		157		Burton.	265		
Biſſeter.		283		Burton-Lazers.		397	
Biclefdon.	783			Burſcough.		303	
Blackburgh.	478			Burwell.	579		
Blakenham.	573			Bury St. Edmunds.	284		
Blaukland.	884	611		Buſleſham.			1. 21
Bliburgh.		593		Butley.		246	1. 110
Blith	553		1. 19	Bylegh.		626	
Blithbury.	468						
Bocking.		477		C.			
Bockland.		438					
Bocland.	939			Cadwelli.	424		
Bodwin.		5		Calder.	774		
Bolington.		794		Caldwell.		257	
Bolton.		459	2: 137	Calke.			1. 97
		100		Campſey.	490		
Bordeſley.	803			Canterbury.		373	
Bourn.		235		Canterbury Cathedral	18		
Bows.		471		—— St Auguſtines.	23		
Boxgrave.	592			Canwell.	439		
Boxley.	827			Cariſbrook, Iſle of Wight.		905	
Brackley.		375	1. 83	Carlile.		73	
Bradley.		334		Carmans Spittle.		372	
Bradenſtoke.		206		Carthuſians.	949		
Bradſole.		244	1. 69	Caſtle acre.	624		
Bradgare.			2. 117	Cateſby.		896	
Brecknock.	319			Cathow.	426		
Bredon.			39	1. 62 Cern.	253		
Breford.	464			Chaterige.	251		
Bridlington.		161		Chaucumb.		279	
Brinkburn.		203		Cherbury.	500		
Briſet.		86		Cheſter.	507		2. 44
Briſtol.	513	438			199		
		232		Chertſey.	75		
Briweton.		205		Cheſhunt.	512		
Brodholm.		646		Chetwode.		339	

A 3   Chich

	Vol. 1.	Vol. 2.	Vol. 3		Vol. 1.	Vol. 2.	Vol. 3
Chich.		182		Derham west.		624	
Chichester.			1. 115	Derehurst.	547		
Chickesand.		793		Derly.		230	1. 57
Cirencester.		89		Dernhall.	936		
Cistercians.	695			Dertford.		357	
St. Clare.	1026					479	
St. Clements, York.	510			Deulacres.	890		
Clerkenwel.	428			Dodford.		307	
Clifford.	623			St. Dogmells,	444		
Clive.	530			Donyngton.		474	
Clouely.			2. 109	Dorchester.		197	
Cluniac's.	611			Dore.	862		
Clunac-Vaur.	892			Dover.		1	
Codenham.	910					423	
Coges.	573			Dovore.			1. 86
Cogeshall.	821			Drax.		96	
Cokesford		234		Droghedah.			1. 107
Cokersand.		631		Dudley.	614		
Colchester.		44		Dunkewell.	925		
		396		Dunmow.		75	
		889		Dunstable.		132	
Coldnortou.		275	1. 55	Dunster.	477		
Coln.	436			Durford.			1. 78
Combermere.	764			Durham.	38		
Cotherstoke.			2. 96				
Covenham.	555			**E.**			
Coverham.		648					
Coventry.	302	427		Dington.		357	
Coventry, Carthusians.	963			St. Edmunds Bury.	284		
Creswell.	504		1. 17	Edwardston.	468		
Crokesden.			1. 40	Egliston.		196	
Crokeston.			1. 73	Ellesham.		421	
Croxden.	912			Ellerton.		821	1. 108
Croxton.		603		Elsing Spittle, London.		462	
Croyland.	163			Ely.	87		
Cumb.	882			Epworth.	969		
Cumbwell.		270		Erdbury.		265	
Cumhile.	825			Esseholt.	828		
				Estbrigg.		458	
D.				Eton.			2. 195
				Evesham.	144		
			1. 72	Ewelme.		475	
Dale. Darby.	505	897		Ewenny.			1. 19
Daventry.	672			Ewyas.	413		
St. Davids.			2. 112	Exeter.	220	461	
Davington.	501				643		
St. Dennis, France.		108		Exeter, St. Nicholas.	352		
Denny.	492			Eye.	356		
Deping.	469			Eynesham.	258		
Derby.		897					
Derham.	176						

Farewel

A TABLE.

F.	Vol. 1	Vol. 2	Vol. 3
Farewell.	441		
Farley.	620		
Felly.		56	
Feversham.	687		
Finchale.	512		
Finsheved.		296	
Flanesford.		356	
Flamsted.	503		
Flexley.	884		
Fodringay.			2. 158
Falkston.	85		
	560		
Ford.	785		
Fosse.	502		
Fountains.	733		
Frampton.	571		
Freeston.	443		
Frithelstoke.		326	
Furnes.	704		

G.			
Garoudon.	768		
St. Germains,	213		
St. Germains, Cornwal.		5	
Ginges.			1. 96
Giseburn.		147	1. 46
Glannaugh.		338	
Glasseney.			2. 56
Glastonbury.	1		
Glocester.	108	28	1. 7
		456	2. 207
Glocesterhall.	540		
Godstow.	525		
Goldclive,	590		
Grace abby, Lond.	943		
Grace Dieu.	927		
	933		
Greenfeild.	881		
Grendale.	427		
Gretham.		457	
Grimesby.		898	
		316	
Gromond.		597	
Grossmunt.			1. 15

H.			
Hagh.	602		
Haghmon.		46	

	Vol. 1	Vol. 2	Vol. 3
Hagneby.		526	
Hakenes.	414		
Hales Owen.		655	
Haleston.	476		
Haliwell.	53		
Haltempriſe.			347
Hampole.	830		
Harewold.		102	
Hasleberge.		113	
Hastings.		84	
Hatfeild-Peverel.	330		
Haverholm.		792	
Haveford.		293	
Havering.		420	
Hayles.	928		
Heden.		418	
Hedley.	565		
Heitbury.		483	
Helaghe.		287	
Helenstow.	359		
Hemmyngburgh.			2. 97
Henningham.	1020		
Henton.	960		
Henwood.	479		
Heppe.		594	
Herbaldown.		418	
Hereford.	406		1. 180
Hertfold.	331		
Hertland.		285	
Heryngham.		181	
Heth.		468	
Hexham.		90	
Heynings.		815	
Hide.	208		
Hicling.		319	
Higham-ferrers.			2. 175
Hilton.	942		
Hinkley.	603		
Hode.		195	
Holbreche.		469	
Holland.	544		
Holland Brig.		815	
Holmcoltrum.	885		
Horkesley.			1. 30
Horsham.	414		
Horseley.	604		
Hornchurch.		418	
Horton.	220		
	621		
Hospitallers, Knights.		489	
Hoton.	840		
Hulme			

A TABLE.

	Vol. 1.	Vol. 2.	Vol. 3.		Vol. 1.	Vol. 2	Vol. 2.
Hulme.	282			Landaffe.			1. 182
Huntington.	530	517		Lanercoſt.		130	
Hurley.	363			Langley.	481	659	
Hyrſt.			42	Langdone.		622	
				Langceſter.			2. 38
I.				Langrigh.		454	
				Lankywan.	580		
ST. James, Briſtol.	513			Lanthony.		58	
St. James, Weſtminſt.		402		Lapley.	1022		
Jerval.	869			Lavindene.		613	
Illsford.		390		Launceſton.		107	
Ingham.		833		Laund.		90	
Ipſwich.		295		Lechlade.		451	
Irtlingburgh.			2. 198	Ledbury.		453	2. 139
St. Ives.	255			Ledes.		110	
Ivichurch.		273		Legburn.	894		
Ivingho.	490			Leiceſter.		308	2. 139
Ixworth.		184				454	
						468	
K.				Lenton.	645		1. 648
				Leominſter.	420		
KAermerden.		282		Leſtingham.	62		
St. Katherines, Exeter.	503			Leſtune.			1. 74
Katteley.		814		Lesnes.		301	
Keinſham.		298		Letley.	933		
Keldeholm.	914			Leveneſtrey.	606		
Kenelworth.		114		Leviſham.	550		
Kertmele.		300		Lewis.	615		
Kerſey.	532			Leye.		204	
Kilburn.	361			Leyſtone.		606	
Kime.		245		Lilleeherch.	528		
Kimolton, or Kimbolton.		319		Lilleſhull.		144	
Kinſwood.	811			Liming.	85		
Kingſton, Hull.	966			Lincoln.		288	
Kinton.	534			Lincoln, St. Catherines.		814	
Kirby Beler.		344	2. 49	Lincoln Cathedral.			1. 257
Kirkby.	562			Lirgebrook.	471		
Kirkham.		105		Lithom.	499		
Kirkley.	487			little marais.	496		
Kirkſtall.	854			Little more.			1. 13
Kirkſted.	806			Litchfeild Cathedral.			1. 216
Knareſborough.		833		loco Dei.		931	
Kynewalgraves.		515		Lodres.	570		
Kypier.			1. 90	London			
				Minoreſſes	542		
L.				Carthuſians.	961		
				Trinity		80	
LAcock.		341		St. Bartholomew.		166	
Lambley.	506			St. Hellens.		894	
Landcadane.			2. 36	St. Giles.		381	
Lancaſter.	566			Bethelem.		382	
							St. Maries

A TABLE.

	Vol. 1	Vol. 2	Vol. 3		Vol. 1	Vol. 2	Vol. 3
St. Marys without Bishops-Gate.		583		Mersey.	552		
				Merton.		135	
St. Bartholomews Hosp.		386		St. Michaels Mount.	551		
St. Giles.		400		Michel.	197		
St. Thomas of Acon.		41		Micheham.			
Converts (Jews.)		450		Midaeburg.	413	334	
St. Katherines.		460		Middleton.	193		
Elsing-spittle.		46		Middeham.			2. 204
Berking Church.		467		Minting.	592		
The Savoy Hosp.		484		Mirmaunde.			1. 107
St. John of Jerusalem		505		Missenden.	541		1. 18
Cathedral S. Paul.			1. 298	Medberley.		320	
Whittingtons Hospital			1. 99	Modbury.	507		
St. John of Jerusalem			1. 108	Monkton.	476		
St. Martins.			2. 26	Monkbreton.	660		
Crooked Lane Coll.			2. 104	Moukenlen.	597		
Elsing Spittle.			2. 190	Monmouth.	60		
Whittington Coll.			2. 189	Montacute.	668		
Long Bennington.	597			Motesfont.		323	
Louth Park.	805			Mottinden.		833	
Ludlow.		449		Mauntgrace.	963		
Luffeild.	520						
Lyn.		413		N.			
				St. Neots.	368		
M.				Nethe	719		
				Newbo.		612	
Maiden Bradley.		408		Newburgh.		190	
Maidston.			2. 132	Newcastle.		474	
Malling.	352			Newenham.	929	238	
Malmesbury.	49			Newhuse.		589	
Malton.		816		Newinion,			1. 111
Maluern	365			Newminster.	800		
Manchester,			2. 174	New Monasteries of H. 8.			1. 21
Margan.	477			foundation.			81
Marham.		929		Newport.			2. 201
Marleburgh.		272		Newsted, Giltford.		247	
Marrig.	484			Newsted, Sherwood.		37	
Marsey.		811		Newsted, Stamford.		444	
Marton.		98		Mewton.		898	1. 88
St. Mary de Pratis.	1011			Noclon.		211	
St. Mary Overy.		84		Northampton, St. Andr.	679		
St. Marys in Dublin.	782			Northampton, St. Mary.	1011		
Maxtoke.		351		Northampton, St. James.		49	
May in Scotland.	422			North Cadbury.			2. 173
Meaux.	792			North Creyke.		325	
Mendham.	926			Norton.		185	5
	631			Norwich.	407	461	1.
Mereval.	830						1. 43
Merewell.			2. 55	Nostel.		33	
Mergate.	350			Nottingham.		447	
Merlebergh.		437				448	

A Table.

	Vol. 1	Vol. 2	Vol. 3
Nunapleton.	907		
Nunburnham.	498		
Nun-Cotun.	922		
Nun Eaton.	518		
Nunkelling.	474		
Nutley.		154	

O.

	Vol. 1	Vol. 2	Vol. 3
Okeburn.	581		
Okeham.		473	
Ormesby.		809	
Oseney.		136	
St. Osiths, Chiche.		182	
St. Oswalds, Gloucester.		28	
Oterey.	549		2. 59
	569		
Overton.		825	
Ouston.		276	
Oxford.	173	407	
	540	443	

P.

	Vol. 1	Vol. 2	Vol. 3
Patricksburn.	576		
Pembroke.	510		
Penecriz.			2. 207
Pentney.		19	
Penwortham.	360		
Pershore.	203		
Peterborough.	63		
St. Petrocus.	213		
Peykirk.	305		
Pilla.	1019		
Pipwell.	815		
Plecy.			2. 120
Plimpton.		6	
Poghele.		266	
Pollesworth.	197		
Pontefract.	648	461	2. 106
Pontrobert.	916		
De Prato, St. Albans.	347		
Prittlewell.	619		
Præmonstratenses.		579	
Pulton.		826	
Pynham.		143	
Pynley.	442		

Q.

	Vol. 1	Vol. 2	Vol. 3
Quarre.	760		

R.

	Vol. 1	Vol. 2	Vol. 3
R Aculf.	86		
St. Radegunds.	480		
Radingfeild.	417		
Ramsey.	231		
Ratlingcope.		336	
Ravenston.		337	
Reading.	417		
Reinham.	636		
Rependon.		280	
Revesby.	822		
Rewley.	934		
Richmond.	401	479	
		649	
Rieval.	727		
Rindelgras.	422		
Rippon.	172	380	1. 89
			2. 87
Roche.	835		
Rochester.	27		1. 1
Romburg.	404		
Romenale.		405	
Ronton.		143	1. 53
Rossendale.	507		
Rotheram.			2. 204
Roucestre.		267	
Rounceval.		443	
Rowney.	516		
Royston.		164	
Rudham.		234	
Rufford.	848		
Rumsey.	219		
Rushworth.			2. 110
Ruthyn.			1. 105
			2. 57
Rygate.		346	

S.

	Vol. 1	Vol. 2	Vol. 3
Salesbury.			
Salley.	841		1. 375
Salop.			2. 207
Saltree.	850		
Sandone.		441	
Sandwell.	475		

Sand.

A TABLE.

	Vol. 1.	Vol. 2.	Vol. 3.		Vol. 1.	Vol. 2.	Vol. 3.
Sanford.	481		1. 13	Stoke-Clare.	535		2. 164
			1. 66	Stoke Cursy.	577		
Santoft and *Henes*.	403			Stokefaston.		482	
Sarum.		472		Stone.		119	
The *Savoy*.		484		Stoneley.	820	319	
Sautingfeld.		404		Stratmargel, or Strata Marcella.	895		
Scarthe.		143					
Scokirk.		43		Stratfleure, or Strata florida.	893		
Scotch Monasteries.		1051					
Selburn.		343		Stratford.	443		
Selby.	371			Stratford-langton.	883		
Sele.	581			Strode.		434	
Selsey.	153			Stykeswold.	486	809	1. 81
Sempringham.		791		Sudbury.	367		
Seton.	482			Surhwell.			2. 10
Sewardsley.	496			Suthwike.		134	
Shaftesbury.	313			Sutton.		437	
Shelford.			1. 65	Swanesey.	572		
Shene.	473			Swine.	834		
Shepey.	152			Swineshead.	773		
Shireburn.	62	423		Syon.		360	
	423	476		**T.**			
	577						
Shouldham.		820		Tallach.	465		
Shrewsbury.	375			Tame.	802		
Sibeton.	866		1. 32	Tanregge.		403	
Silly Isle.	516			Tarent.	887		
Sinningthwait.	827			Tateshale.			2. 194
Sixill.		810		Taveslok.	217		
Sleveholm.	638			Taunton.		83	
Snapes.		894		Temple Knights.		517	1. 62
Snelshall.	483			Thanet, St. Mildreds.	83		
Sopewell.	347			Thele.			2. 190
Southampton.		108		Thelesford.		831	
		439		Therford.	664	574	
Southwark.		439		Thorkesley.		278	
Spiney.		320		Thorney.	242		
Stafford.		316		Thornton.		198	
Stamford.		403		Thornholm.		230	
		444		Thremhale.		23	
Stanesgate.	623			Thurgarton.		92	
Standford.	488			Tikeford.	685		
Stanfield.	506			Tiltrey.	889		
Stanlaw.	896			Tinemouth.	333		
Stanleigh.	867			Tintern.	721		
Stanley-Park.		626	1. 64	Titchfeild.		660	
Stayndrope.			2. 142	Toddington.		478	
Sternshall.	71			Toft.	593		
Stivendale.		306		Tonbridge.		258	
Stodeley.	486	89		Tong-Castle.			2. 143
Stoke.			1. 94	Torre.	652		
							Toten-

A Table.

	Vol. 1	Vol. 2	Vol. 3		Vol. 1	Vol. 2	Vol. 3
Totenhall.			2. 207	Whalley.	896		
Totnes.	1023			Wherwell.			1. 9
Trentham		260		Whitby.	71		
Trinitarians.		830		Wigmore.		213	
Tukesbury.	153			Wikes.		282	
Tupholme.		596		Wikham.	916		
Tutbury.	354			Wilesford.	584		
Tuxford.			2. 90	Wilberfosse.	524		1. 12
Twyneham.		177	1. 54	Wilton.	191		
Tykhead.	529			Wimundham.	337		
Tywardreit.	586			Winchester.	31	480	2. 46
					212		2. 106
V.				Winburne.	163		
				Winchcomb.	187		
Vale-Royal.	936			Windsor.			2. 67
Vaudey.	831			Winteney.	483		
				St. Wirburghs, Chester.	199		
W.				Wirksop.		50	
Waburn.	490			Witham.	959		
Walden.	445			Woburn.	829		
Wallingford.	326		1. 11	Wodham.		294	
			2. 34	Wolverhampton.	988	472	2. 207
Wallingwell.	502			Wombrigge.		252	
Walsingham.		20		Worcester.	120		
Waltham.		11		Wormley.		261	1. 48
Wardon.	784			Wospring		271	1. 47
Wartre		172		Wolton waven.	558		
Warwell.	256			Wroxhall.	433		
Warwick.		573	2. 27	Wroxton.		316	
Watton.		798		Wulverhampton, vid. Wolverhampton.			
Water-Becham.	543			Wudeham.	889		
Waverley.	703			Wye.			2. 191
Weden-Pinkney.	584			Wymburn minster.			2. 207
Welbeck.		597		Wyremouth and Gerwy.	96		
Welle.		461	1. 89	Wyrthorp.	489		
Wells.	186	826					
		434		**Y**			
Wells, Norfolk.	574						
Wengham.			2. 52	Yarrow.	96		
Wendling.		613		Yarum.		409	
Wenlock.	613			Yres.	718		
Wenslaw.			2. 137	York.		367	1. 125
Westbury.			2. 202			392	
Westacre.	619					469	
Westminster.	55	402					
Westminster, St. Stevens Chappel.			2. 61	York, St. Marys.	381		
				York, Trinity.	563		
Westwood.	574			York, St. Andrews.		808	
Wethehall.	397						

FINIS.

www.ingramcontent.com/pod-product-compliance
Lightning Source LLC
Chambersburg PA
CBHW030357230426
43664CB00007BB/626